Families in the New Millennium

Anne-Marie Ambert
York University

Allyn and Bacon
Boston • London • Toronto • Sydney • Tokyo • Singapore

Series Editor: Jeff Lasser
Editor in Chief, Social Sciences: Karen Hanson
Editorial Assistant: Susan Hutchinson
Marketing Manager: Jude Hall
Editorial-Production Administrator: Annette Joseph
Editorial-Production Coordinator: Holly Crawford
Editorial-Production Service: Lynda Griffiths, TKM Productions
Text Designer: Carol Somberg, Omegatype Typography, Inc.
Photo Researcher: Katharine Cook
Composition Buyer: Linda Cox
Electronic Composition and Art: Omegatype Typography, Inc.
Manufacturing Buyer: Suzanne Lareau
Cover Administrator: Linda Knowles

A Pearson Education Company
160 Gould Street
Needham Heights, MA 02494

Internet: www.abacon.com

Between the time Website information is gathered and then published, it is not unusual for some sites to have closed. Also, the transcription of URLs can result in unintended typographical errors. The publisher would appreciate notification where these occur so that they may be corrected in subsequent editions. Thank you.

Library of Congress Cataloging-in-Publication Data
Ambert, Anne-Marie.
Families in the new millennium / Anne-Marie Ambert.
p. cm.
Includes bibliographical references and index.
ISBN 0-321-05048-7
1. Family–Research–United States. 2. Family life–Research–United States.
3. Sociology–Methodology. I. Title.
HQ535 .A577 2000
306.85′07′2–dc21
00-038975

Printed in the United States of America
10 9 8 7 6 5 4 3 2 1 RRDV 05 04 03 02 01 00

Photo credits appear on page 564, which constitutes a continuation of the copyright page.

To
Jean-Paul

Brief Contents

PART 1 FOUNDATIONS OF FAMILY STUDY 1

1 Theoretical and Methodological Perspectives in Family Studies 2
2 Historical Perspectives and Contemporary Issues Concerning Family Life 28
3 Family Diversity and Adaptation: Immigration and Minority-Group Status 54
4 Partner Selection, Sexual Relations, and Reproduction 88
5 Patterns of Family Formation: Single Motherhood, Cohabitation, or Marriage? 120

PART 2 SOCIAL AND CULTURAL FAMILY CONTEXTS 153

6 Effects of the Economy and Economic Inequalities on Families 154
7 Impacts of Neighborhoods and Environments on Family Life 182
8 Roles of Education and Religion in Family Life 208

PART 3 FAMILY RELATIONSHIPS 239

9 Family Developmental Stages 240
10 Spousal and Partner Relationships 272
11 The Parent/Child Relationship and Parenting 302
12 Sibling Relationships and Situations 332

PART 4 FAMILY PROBLEMS AND SOLUTIONS 363

13 Divorce and Remarriage 364
14 Family Violence, Abuse, and Child Neglect 398
15 Family Dynamics and Emotional, Behavioral, and Delinquency Problems 432
16 Family Futures and Social Policies 460

Contents

Preface xxiii

PART 1 FOUNDATIONS OF FAMILY STUDY 1

1 Theoretical and Methodological Perspectives in Family Studies 2

HOW CAN FAMILIES BE DEFINED? 5

The Nuclear Family 5

The Extended Family 5

Types of Marriage 7

Relevance of Definitions 7

WHY IS A MULTIDISCIPLINARY APPROACH HELPFUL? 8

WHAT THEORETICAL PERSPECTIVES INFORM FAMILY STUDIES? 10

Structural Functionalism 10

Symbolic Interactionism 11

Interactional-Transactional Perspectives 12

Social Exchange and Rational Theories 13

Developmental (Life Course) Perspectives 14

Social Constructionism 14

Behavior Genetics 15

WHY IS FEMINISM A PARTICULARLY IMPORTANT PERSPECTIVE? 16

The Analysis of Gender Stratification and Gender Roles 17

Feminist Analyses of the Family 17

WHAT ARE THE MAIN THEMES IN THE TEXT? 18

WHAT METHODS ARE USED IN FAMILY RESEARCH? 19
Qualitative and Quantitative Methods 21
A Qualitative Method Example: Students' Autobiographies 22
CONCLUSIONS: UNITY IN DIVERSITY 23
Summary 24
Key Concepts and Themes 25
Study and Review Questions 25
Suggested Readings 26
Suggested Weblinks 27

2 Historical Perspectives and Contemporary Issues Concerning Family Life 28

COMPARATIVE PERSPECTIVES ON FAMILIES 31
AMERICAN FAMILIES OF THE PAST 31
Multiple Historical Roots 32
The Colonial Period 32
Families Become More Diverse and Stratified 33
Industrialization and New Social Definitions 34
The Twentieth Century 35
ARE CHILDREN BECOMING DEFAMILIALIZED? 36
THE AUDIOVISUAL MEDIA AND FAMILY LIFE 38
Television Restructures Family Life 38
The Family on Television: A Historical Overview 39
Effects of Family-Related Programs on Children 41
The Evolution of Sexual Contents and Effects on Adolescents 42
Children and Television Violence 43
The New Cultural Revolution: The Internet 44
FAMILY CHANGE OR DECLINE? THE DEBATE 45
Has the Family Lost Its Functions? 46
Are Traditional Family Values Necessarily under Attack? 48
CONCLUSIONS: THE PACE OF CHANGE 50
Summary 50
Key Concepts and Themes 52
Study and Review Questions 52
Suggested Readings 53
Suggested Weblinks 53

3 Family Diversity and Adaptation: Immigration and Minority-Group Status 54

IMMIGRANT FAMILIES 56
Immigrant Families' Diversity 57
Immigrant Families' Adjustment: The Environmental Constraints 59
Immigrant Generations 59
Intergenerational Conflict 60
Intergenerational Continuity 61

NATIVE-AMERICAN FAMILIES 62
Native Families: Diversity and Adaptation 63
Sources of Poverty among Native Families 64
Native Intermarriage and Family Types 65

AFRICAN-AMERICAN FAMILIES 66
Single Motherhood and Marriage: A Historical Perspective 66
Impacts of Prejudice, Discrimination, and Segregation 68
Middle-Class Families 70

LATINO-AMERICAN FAMILIES 73
Mexican-American Families 74
Puerto Rican Families 76
Cuban-American Families 78

ASIAN-AMERICAN FAMILIES 79
Chinese-American Families 79
Korean-American Families 82

CONCLUSIONS: MINORITY FAMILIES PAY A HEAVY PRICE 83
Summary 83
Key Concepts and Themes 85
Study and Review Questions 85
Suggested Readings 85
Suggested Weblinks 86

4 Partner Selection, Sexual Relations, and Reproduction 88

DATING 91
Heterosexual Dating 91
Same-Sex Dating 92

DATE AND PARTNER SELECTION 93
Heterosexual Mate Selection 94
Same-Sex Partner Selection 95
Same-Sex Marriage 96
Arranged Marriages 96

SEXUAL RELATIONS 98
Early Sexuality 98
Marital and Cohabitational Sexual Relations 100
Extracouple Sexual Relations 103

FAMILY PLANNING, FERTILITY, AND ABORTION 104
Family Planning 104
Fertility Rates 105
Abortion 106

NEW REPRODUCTIVE TECHNOLOGIES 108
Types of Reproductive Alternatives 109
Surrogate Mothers 110
Multiple Births 111

SINGLEHOOD AND MARRIED CHILDLESSNESS BY CHOICE 112
Types of Singles 113
Factors Facilitating Singlehood 113
Advantages and Disadvantages of Single Life 114
Childless Marriage by Choice 115

CONCLUSIONS: THE CHANGING PROFILE OF REPRODUCTION 115
Summary 116
Key Concepts and Themes 117
Study and Review Questions 117
Suggested Readings 118
Suggested Weblinks 118

5 Patterns of Family Formation: Single Motherhood, Cohabitation, or Marriage? 120

SINGLE MOTHERHOOD 122
Trends in Unmarried Motherhood 123
Trends in Single-Parent Families 124
The Economic Perspective on Unmarried Mothering 125

SINGLE ADOLESCENT MOTHERHOOD 127
What Is Known about Teen Mothers? 127
The Adolescent's Life Course 128
Who Are the Babies' Fathers? 129
What Are the Effects of Single Adolescent Parenting on Children? 130
COHABITATION 131
What Is Known about Cohabitation? 131
Cohabitation and Children 132
SAME-SEX-PARENT FAMILY FORMATION 133
An Overview of Same-Sex-Parent Families 133
Consequences for Children 134
ARE THERE ADVANTAGES TO MARRIAGE? 136
Is Marriage Good for Adults? 136
Is Marriage Good for Children? 138
Is Marriage Good for Society? 139
ADOPTION AND FOSTER FAMILIES 140
How Do Adopted Children Develop? 140
What Is Involved in Stepchild Adoption? 142
What Are the Issues in Transracial Adoption? 143
What Is Open Adoption? 144
Reunions with Birth Parents: Functions and Consequences 144
Foster Families: A Strained System 146
CONCLUSIONS: FAMILY FORMATION ALTERNATIVES IN CONTEXT 148
Summary 149
Key Concepts and Themes 150
Study and Review Questions 151
Suggested Readings 151
Suggested Weblinks 152

PART 2 SOCIAL AND CULTURAL FAMILY CONTEXTS 153

6 Effects of the Economy and Economic Inequalities on Families 154

OVERVIEW OF ECONOMIC CHANGES 156

EFFECTS OF ECONOMIC CHANGES ON FAMILIES 158
General Effects of Economic Changes on Family Life 158
Effects of Economic Changes on Family Structure 160
The Dual-Income Family 161
Is Maternal Employment Detrimental to Children? 162
Parental Employment and Children 163
CAUSES OF FAMILY POVERTY 165
What Are the Structural Causes of Poverty? 165
What Are the Sociopersonal Causes of Poverty? 169
Is Welfare an Incentive to Single Mothering? 171
CONSEQUENCES OF FAMILY POVERTY 172
For Mothers 173
For Fathers 174
For Children 176
CONCLUSIONS: THE COSTS OF POVERTY 178
Summary 178
Key Concepts and Themes 180
Study and Review Questions 180
Suggested Readings 180
Suggested Weblinks 181

7 Impacts of Neighborhoods and Environments on Family Life 182

TYPES OF URBAN AND SUBURBAN AREAS AND FAMILY LIFE 184
Diversity of Urban and Suburban Areas 185
Families' Class Differences and Neighborhood Location 186
INNER-CITY NEIGHBORHOODS 187
What Is a High-Poverty Neighborhood? 187
How Did Inner-City Poverty Come About? 188
The Addition of Social Problems 189
Risk Factors of High-Poverty Areas for Children 190
Well-Functioning Families in High-Risk Areas 193
HOMELESS FAMILIES 194
What Are the Causes of Homelessness? 194
What Are the Effects of Homelessness on Mothers and Children? 195

RURAL AREAS AND FAMILY LIFE 197
Characteristics of Farm Families 198
Farm Families' Adaptation to Economic Crises 199
Kinship and Gender Roles 199
FAMILIES' HOUSING CONDITIONS 200
The "Mansionization" of Suburban Housing 201
Family Privacy 202
Overcrowding 202
RESIDENTIAL MOBILITY 203
CONCLUSIONS: THE MEANING OF NEIGHBORHOOD AS CONTEXT 204
Summary 205
Key Concepts and Themes 206
Study and Review Questions 206
Suggested Readings 207
Suggested Weblinks 207

8 Roles of Education and Religion in Family Life 208

THE EDUCATIONAL SYSTEM: AN OVERVIEW 210
CHILD CARE: QUALITY AND CHILD OUTCOMES 211
Extent and Quality of Child Care 211
The Effects of Child Care on Children 212
The Effects of Child Care on Parents 214
Early Childhood Education for Children in Low-Income Families 214
FAMILIAL FACTORS RELATED TO CHILDREN'S SCHOOL SUCCESS 216
Parental Involvement 216
Families' Social Class and Children's Achievement 219
Family-School Compatibility 219
POOR FAMILIES AND POOR SCHOOLS 221
Description of Poor Schools 221
Consequences for Children and Families 222
PRIVATE EDUCATION 223
Private Schools 224
Home Schooling 225

Are Objections to Home Schooling Valid? 225

RELIGION AND FAMILY LIFE 226

How Is Religiosity Measured? 226

Demographic Factors Related to Religiosity 227

Parents' and Children's Religiosity: The Socialization Aspect 229

Religiosity and Parenting Practices: Conservative Protestants 231

IS RELIGIOSITY FUNCTIONAL FOR THE FAMILY? 231

Religiosity Correlates with Well-Being 232

Religiosity Relates to Marital Stability 232

Religiosity Supports the Parental Role 233

Limitations of Religion for Nontraditional Families 234

CONCLUSIONS: THE BALANCING ACT OF FAMILY FUNCTIONS 234

Summary 235

Key Concepts and Themes 236

Study and Review Questions 237

Suggested Readings 237

Suggested Weblinks 238

PART 3 FAMILY RELATIONSHIPS 239

9 Family Developmental Stages 240

THE GENDERED SOCIAL CONSTRUCTION OF PARENTHOOD 243

Motherhood 243

Fatherhood 245

THE PREBIRTH STAGE 246

THE INFANT'S ARRIVAL 248

Among Married Couples 248

In Other Family Structures 249

Delayed Parenthood 252

Generational Compressions and Successions 254

SUBSEQUENT STAGES 255

The Early Years 255

Pets as New Family Members 257

The Adolescent Years 258
The Empty Nest: Or Is It? 259
THE GRANDPARENT STAGE 260
Grandparenting as a Role 260
Grandparents Who Provide Child Care 261
Grandparents Who Raise Grandchildren 262
Grandparenting after Divorce 264
Stepgrandparenting 265
THE DEATH OF ADULTS' PARENTS 266
CONCLUSIONS: FAMILY DEVELOPMENT IN CONTEXT 267
Summary 268
Key Concepts and Themes 269
Study and Review Questions 269
Suggested Readings 270
Suggested Weblinks 270

10 Spousal and Partner Relationships 272

TYPES OF MARRIAGES AND HOW THEY CHANGE 275
The Conflict-Habituated Relationship 275
The Devitalized Relationship 275
The Passive-Congenial Relationship 276
The Vital Relationship 276
The Total Relationship 277
Marriages Change 277
DIVISION OF LABOR AND INEQUALITY 278
A Classification of the Domestic Division of Labor 279
The Effect of Marital Quality: Overview of Recent Changes 281
Division of Labor in Remarriages with Stepchildren 284
The Silent Division of Labor: Emotional Work 285
ASPECTS OF SPOUSAL RELATIONSHIPS 286
Marital Happiness, Satisfaction, and Success 287
Marital Quality through the Decades 288
Partner Conflict and Marital Problems 288
The Conjugal Relationship in Later Life 290

The Next Time Around: Remarriage 292
SAME-SEX-PARTNER RELATIONSHIP 293
THE EFFECT OF THE PARENTAL RELATIONSHIP ON CHILDREN 294
The Effect of Parental Conflict 294
How to Explain the Effect of Marital Quality on Children 295
CONCLUSIONS: DEFINITIONS OF MARITAL QUALITY ARE CULTURE SPECIFIC 298
Summary 299
Key Concepts and Themes 300
Study and Review Questions 300
Suggested Readings 301
Suggested Weblinks 301

11 The Parent/Child Relationship and Parenting 302

THE BEGINNING OF THE PARENT/CHILD RELATIONSHIP 304
PARENTS' SOCIALIZATION PRACTICES 305
Authoritative Parenting 306
Authoritarian and No-Nonsense Parenting 306
Permissive and Uninvolved Parenting 307
Additional Parenting Styles 308
DETERMINANTS OF PARENTING SOCIALIZATION PRACTICES 309
Contextual and Cultural Determinants 310
Parents' Personalities and Beliefs 312
Parental Adaptation to Children 312
THE PARENT/ADOLESCENT RELATIONSHIP 313
The Social Construction of Adolescence 313
How Do Parents and Adolescents Get Along? 314
Parental Influence 316
THE ROLE OF PEERS IN THE PARENT/ADOLESCENT RELATIONSHIP 318
Peer Groups and Parental Isolation 318
Peer Spillover Effect 319
THE RELATIONSHIP BETWEEN PARENTS AND ADULT CHILDREN 320
When the Child Is a Young Adult 320

When the Child Is 30 to 40 Years Old 322
Senior Parents Help Their Adult Children 323
Adult Children Help Their Elderly Parents 325
CONCLUSIONS: THE MACRO AND MICRO ASPECTS IN THE PARENT/CHILD RELATIONSHIP 327
Summary 328
Key Concepts and Themes 329
Study and Review Questions 330
Suggested Readings 330
Suggested Weblinks 331

12 Sibling Relationships and Situations 332

THE SIBLING RELATIONSHIP BEGINS 334
The Only Child Becomes the Older Child 335
Consequences of Children's Spacing 336
Consequences of Family Size 336
CHILD AND ADOLESCENT SIBLING RELATIONSHIPS 337
Older and Younger Siblings 338
Gender and Class in the Sibling Relationship 338
Linkages to the Parent/Child Relationship 339
Sibling Influence 340
Supportive Sibling Relationships 342
DIFFERENTIAL PARENTAL TREATMENT 344
Birth Order and Development Stage as Factors 344
Gender as a Factor 346
Developmental Impact of Differential Treatment 346
ADULT AND STEPSIBLING RELATIONSHIPS 348
Adult Sibling Relationships 349
Stepsibling Relationships 350
HOW CAN SIBLINGS BE SO DIFFERENT? 351
What Are the Sources of Sibling Differences? 351
Children's Different Perceptions of Familial Environment 352
Families That Provide a More Powerful Shared Environment 353

SIBLING SIMILARITIES AND DIFFERENCES: TWIN STUDIES 354
Twins as Natural Experiments 354
Is Parental Influence Really So Unimportant? 357
CONCLUSIONS: THE NATURE AND NURTURE OF PARENTAL INFLUENCE 358
Summary 359
Key Concepts and Themes 360
Study and Review Questions 361
Suggested Readings 361
Suggested Weblinks 362

PART 4 FAMILY PROBLEMS AND SOLUTIONS 363

13 Divorce and Remarriage 364

DIVORCE RATES 367
What Are the Overall Trends in Divorce Rates? 367
How Are Divorce Rates Measured? 369
WHAT ARE THE FACTORS ASSOCIATED WITH DIVORCE? 370
Sociocultural Factors 370
Demographic Factors 371
What Reasons Do People Give for Divorcing? 372
How Do Marriages Break Down? 374
THE AFTERMATH OF DIVORCE FOR ADULTS 375
What Factors Are Associated with Adjustment? 376
What Is a Successful Divorce? 377
Changes in Ex-Spouses' Social Networks after Divorce 377
Custodial Fathers and Mothers 379
SERIAL DIVORCES 380
How Frequent Are Serial Divorces? 380
Who Are the Persons Who Divorce Serially? 381
WHAT ARE THE EFFECTS OF DIVORCE ON CHILDREN? 382
How Does Divorce Affect Children? 383
Theories Explaining How Divorce Affects Children 384

WIDOWHOOD AND BEREAVEMENT 387
Stages of Bereavement 387
Consequences of a Parent's Death for Children 388
REMARRIAGE 389
The Aftermath of Remarriage for Spouses 390
What Are the Effects of Remarriage on Children? 392
CONCLUSIONS: THE FAMILIAL AND SOCIAL MEANINGS OF DIVORCE 393
Summary 394
Key Concepts and Themes 396
Study and Review Questions 396
Suggested Readings 396
Suggested Weblinks 397

14 Family Violence, Abuse, and Child Neglect 398

DATING AND PARTNER ABUSE 400
Dating and Courtship Violence 400
Verbal and Psychological Abuse of Partners 402
Spousal and Partner Physical Abuse 404
Same-Sex-Partner Violence 406
The Effect of Spousal Violence on Children 407
CHILD ABUSE AND NEGLECT BY PARENTS 409
Child Abuse by Parents 409
Child Neglect by Parents 414
Is Child Abuse by Parents Increasing? 416
CHILD SEXUAL ABUSE BY ADULTS 417
Who Are and Where Are the Abusers? 417
Consequences of Sexual Abuse for the Child 418
SIBLING ABUSE 420
Sibling Violence 420
Sibling Sexual Abuse 421
PEER ABUSE 422
How Common Is Peer Abuse? 422
Consequences and Context of Peer Abuse 423

Peer Sexual Harassment and Abuse 424

ABUSE OF PARENTS BY CHILDREN 425

Physical Abuse of Parents by Children and Adolescents 425

Abuse of Elderly Parents by Adult Children 426

CONCLUSIONS: THE LARGER CONTEXT OF FAMILY VIOLENCE 428

Summary 428

Key Concepts and Themes 430

Study and Review Questions 430

Suggested Readings 431

Suggested Weblinks 431

15 Family Dynamics and Emotional, Behavioral, and Delinquency Problems 432

PARENTS WHO SUFFER FROM DEPRESSION 435

What Are the Causes of Depression? 435

Consequences of Parental Depression for Children 436

The Research Focus on Depressed Mothers 436

A Critique of Maternal Causality 437

ALCOHOLISM IN THE FAMILY 439

What Are the Causes of Alcoholism? 439

Consequences of Parental Alcoholism for Children 440

CHILDREN WITH BEHAVIORAL PROBLEMS 442

What Are the Causes of Behavioral Problems? 442

Gendered Family Dynamics: Mothers and Difficult Children 445

DELINQUENCY: FAMILY DYNAMICS 446

The Life Course Perspective on Delinquency 447

What Are the Causes of Delinquency? 448

Delinquency and Family Dynamics 449

HOW RELATIVES AND EXPERTS AFFECT FAMILY DYNAMICS 451

Relatives and Friends 452

Professional Authority over Parents 453

Professionals' Social Constructions 454

The Blaming and Marginalization of Parents 455

CONCLUSIONS: FAMILY VULNERABILITY 455
Summary 456
Key Concepts and Themes 457
Study and Review Questions 458
Suggested Readings 458
Suggested Weblinks 459

16 Family Futures and Social Policies 460

SALIENT THEMES REVISITED 462
Social Inequalities 463
Diversity of Families 463
A Surplus of Family Functions 464
The Functional Community 464
The Cultural Context 465
Interactional and Genetic Themes 465
Gender Stratification and Roles 466
WHAT DOES THE FUTURE HOLD? 466
Age Distribution and Fertility 466
Cohabitation 467
Divorce 467
Nonmarital Family Formation 468
Same-Sex Parenting 469
Interracial Unions 469
The Longer Time Frame 469
SOCIAL POLICIES PERTAINING TO FAMILIES 470
Reducing Poverty 471
Encouraging and Strengthening Marriage 474
Planning for Divorce 476
Supporting the Parental Role 477
CONCLUSIONS: THE FAMILY IN CONTEXT 479
Family Research and Historical Context 479
Family Functions and Their Environmental Context 480
Summary 480
Key Concepts and Themes 481

Study and Review Questions 481
Suggested Readings 482
Suggested Weblinks 482

GLOSSARY 483
BIBLIOGRAPHY 486
NAME INDEX 541
SUBJECT INDEX 554

Preface

The field of family studies has recently benefited from an injection of innovative research from other areas of sociology as well as other disciplines. *Families in the New Millennium* is the first family textbook to integrate this new body of knowledge, which also includes additional theoretical perspectives, in such a comprehensive manner. It follows that this book is different from most others in terms of some of its contents, as explained below. As well, some aspects of its format and organization are distinct.

CONTENTS

Families in the New Millennium includes all of the relevant information traditionally found in family textbooks, but it also contains several chapters and many sections that are quite unusual. This is particularly evident in Part 2, where we look at how the economy, neighborhoods, as well as educational and religious institutions affect families. The contents of these chapters reflect the fact that the best scholarly journals in sociology, family studies, and child development now regularly publish articles in these domains. This is probably the only family sociology textbook on the market that focuses on these areas combined, including the role that religion plays in marriage and child socialization. The media as a sociocultural context for family life is also discussed more fully than is usually the case.

What are the consequences on family dynamics when one member suffers from a severe emotional problem, or a behavioral disorder, or delinquency? Such a question is explored in Chapter 15, which is likely a precedent in textbooks on the sociology of the family. Furthermore, an entire chapter is devoted to siblings: their relationship, how they grow up to be different, and how they relate to their parents. The book also includes reasonably substantial sections on adoption, foster families, reproductive technologies, the impact of children's peers on the family, peer abuse, same-sex-parent families, ex-spouses' relationships after divorce, and the role of pets in family dynamics.

In the same vein, I have introduced a wide range of theoretical frameworks. In addition to the better-known theories, such as structural functionalism, others, including social constructionism, are much in evidence. For instance, interactional-transactional theories are used in the many chapters in which socialization, parent/child relationships, and family problems are discussed. Not only do we look at the socialization of children by parents but we also examine how children affect their parents' ability to raise them within specific environments—in other words, how parents, children, and their environment interact. Furthermore, I have borrowed from the field of behavior genetics in order to acquaint students with new concepts, ideas, and explanations that are now regularly encountered in the area of family research: the interaction between nature and nurture. Students can examine behavior genetics within a critical sociological framework alongside interactional-transactional theories and even symbolic interactionism.

Therefore, although a sociological perspective informs this text, the results and theories from several other fields of inquiry are placed within its analytical framework. Moreover, the interplay between the macro- and microsociological levels of analysis is evident in all chapters. The interdisciplinary nature of the contents makes this book suitable for classes in both sociology and family studies.

Certain themes and theories that predominate in some areas of sociology and other disciplines pertaining to the family are emphasized. These themes—for instance, those of social inequalities, gender roles, and the functional community—link the various contents together within an integrative framework. The themes give this text its particular theoretical flavor; some are at the source of one of the emphases of the book: social policies pertaining to families.

It is equally important to point out that *Families in the New Millennium* focuses on the nuclear family, broadly defined, rather than on the couple; it is centered on the intergenerational axis rather than on adult "intimate" relationships in general. Although four chapters discuss couple formation and couple relationships nearly exclusively, most of the contents of the remainder of the text look at the nuclear family as a unit constituted by parents and children or one parent and children. In other words, this is a book on the family, on intergenerational relationships within various contexts, as well as on social policies that could enhance family life and child socialization.

FORMAT

The text of this book includes a great deal of qualitative sociology in the form of quotes, case studies, and summaries from my fieldwork. This qualitative material serves several functions. It provides lively, illustrative material supporting the statistical information presented. In other instances, it helps explain statistical results. In some chapters, the material constitutes the only information that is available in the literature on some topics. The latter is the case when we discuss the effect of delinquency on parents, serial divorces, and ex-spouses' as well as new spouses' social networks after divorce and remarriage. Unlike other textbooks, where qualitative material tends to be presented separately in boxed inserts as anecdotes, here it is an integral part of the contents.

I present a great deal of factual information, both quantitative and qualitative. However, I have chosen to include far fewer statistical tables, graphs, and especially boxed inserts than is usual in most texts. How facts are obtained and research is carried out are important issues to me as an instructor. As a result, I have included at least one Family Research insert in each chapter; these inserts illustrate various research methods pertaining to the contents. This feature will allow students to get a better idea of the range of methods that are used in family research, both qualitative and quantitative. In other words, the Family Research features say, "Here is how various researchers do it, and how they get their information on family life."

ORGANIZATION

Families in the New Millennium is divided in four parts. Part 1, Foundations of Family Study, introduces definitions, perspectives, and issues pertaining to the family. This includes a brief historical overview, a discussion of current concerns about "family decline," the ethnoracial diversity of family life in the United States, as well as the diversity of structural bases for couple and family formation. Part 2, Social and Cultural Family Contexts, focuses on the settings and conditions that affect family life and structure. These include the economy, neighborhoods, schools, and religion. Part 3, Family Relationships, introduces the developmental stages of family life before moving on to successive chapters on the spousal, parent/child, and sibling relationships. Part 4, Family Problems and Solutions, begins with a chapter on divorce, widowhood, and remarriage. It then examines violence, abuse, and neglect within the family; this is followed by a chapter on the dynamics and interactions that take place in families with a problematic parent or child. The last chapter reexamines the themes that have linked the contents, and then focuses on family change and social policies designed to prevent or ameliorate problems faced by families.

PEDAGOGY

Each chapter begins with a detailed outline. Throughout the text, many concepts and themes are bolded or italicized in order to help students memorize key concepts and ideas as well as note emphases. Concepts that might need additional explanation are further defined in the Glossary at the end of the book. This Glossary contains fewer but lengthier definitions to serve as a reference for students who have never taken a sociology course before. Each chapter has a clearly identified but brief conclusion that serves an integrative function. As is the usual convention, chapters end with a summary, a list of key concepts and themes, study and review questions, suggested readings, as well as suggested weblinks.

The Instructor's Manual contains a test bank that is also available under computerized format from Allyn and Bacon. Above all, the Instructor's Manual is characterized by innovative features replacing the usual outlines and summaries (which are found in the textbook itself). Instead, each chapter in the Instructor's Manual opens with an introduction especially designed for instructors on the contents of the matching chapter in the text. This is followed by additional material that can be used in class lectures to complement what is in the text or to form the basis of new lectures. Beginning with Chapter 2, a section entitled Chapter Linkages will be particularly useful to instructors who favor an integrative approach. These three pedagogic features have been added to help instructors with some of the new perspectives and research presented in the text. Instructors who are generally burdened with class preparation, tests, and grading will find this Instructor's Manual very useful.

ACKNOWLEDGMENTS

The following reviewers have provided detailed comments on various chapters. These comments have served as a basis for major structural and contents improvements. I wish to thank Emily Stier Adler, Rhode Island College; Peter Adler, University of Denver; Mary Blair-Loy, Washington State University; Clifford L. Broman, Michigan State University; Susan A. Farrell, Kingsborough Community College; Tina Fitzgerald, University of Utah; Lee K. Frank, Community College of Allegheny County South Campus; Sandra French, Indiana University Southeast; Norval D. Glenn, University of Texas at Austin; Nancy Greenwood, Indiana University at Kokomo; Lutz Kaelber, Lyndon State College; Miho Kawai, Syracuse University; Joachim S. Kibirige, Missouri State College; Diane Levy, University of North Carolina at Wilmington; Lynn Magdol, State University of New York at Buffalo; Sandra Rezac, University of Nebraska at Lincoln; Jon A. Schlenker, University of Maine at Augusta; William L. Smith, Georgia Southern University; and Mary Lou Wylie, James Madison University.

I also acknowledge the advice of Mary Ellen Lepionka, Developmental Editor at Allyn and Bacon; Annette Joseph, Production Administrator; and Lynda Griffiths of TKM Productions. Furthermore, the continued interest of four Sociology Editors, at both Addison Wesley Longman and Allyn and Bacon, while the companies were merging, is recognized: in chronological order, Alan McClare, Priscilla McGeehon, Sarah Kelbaugh, and especially Jeff Lasser.

My ability to be productive has been greatly enhanced by the moral support I have received from two people who have been key elements in my life in the past 20 years. First, Jean-Paul—I would need several paragraphs to do justice to his support. The second acknowledgment is more unusual in the sense that few people think of their mothers-in-law in this respect. But who would not enjoy being for her mother-in-law the daughter she always dreamt of having? To Astrid, my warmest thanks. Mothers are too often vilified—and I write about this in the text. It is therefore fitting that I am grateful for having had two mothers: one for childhood and one for adulthood.

I wish also to acknowledge my daughter Stephanie's help. She has word-processed the many drafts, has put some order in the reference section, and has helped with the indexes at the end of the road. She is a student and has worked on my various books, both authored and edited, since age 12. My books all pertain to children and the family, so they form the basis of a "family business" in more ways than one.

Once more, I have received some help from a long-time friend: Martine Aumont contributed the biographical sketch of her grandmother, which serves as the opener for Chapter 2. I am especially indebted to the hundreds of couples as well as parents who have given so generously of their time and their hospitality for my various research projects. Quotes and case studies from these families have greatly enriched this text, as has the material gathered from my students who wrote semi-structured autobiographies in my classes. Many of my research ideas and theoretical revisions throughout my career have been influenced by this parental and student contribution to my knowledge of real life as lived by others in their families. I must also say that the knowledge gathered through the autobiographies came in handy when my children were growing up: By then, my students had unwittingly taught me all the "tricks of the trade"—at times to my children's sheepish consternation!

Anne-Marie Ambert

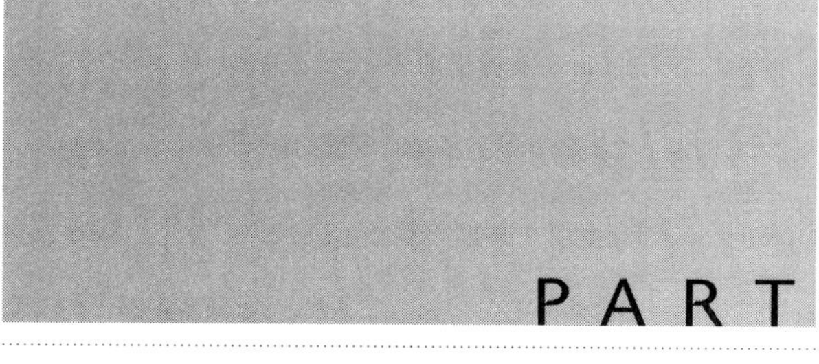

PART 1

Foundations of Family Study

This book focuses on two interrelated levels of family studies. First, it looks at the internal dynamics of families, such as how they are formed and the ways they adapt, as well as the relationships that take place within them, such as between partners, parents, and siblings. The parent/child relationship and the socialization of the child/adolescent occupy salient places in this analysis. At the second level, this book examines the contexts that shape family dynamics, influence the quality of relationships, and affect socialization processes.

I am particularly interested in the problems that families encounter in terms of dynamics, relationships, individual life courses, and socialization outcomes given that their environments are often less than supportive. Consequently, families' contexts are discussed with an eye to social policies that could prevent or remedy the difficulties faced by families, parents, as well as children and adolescents.

Chapter 1 defines the various types of families and situates their study within a sociological perspective that is complemented by a multidisciplinary analysis. The main theories that inform family research are introduced and linked to the themes that run throughout the text. Methodological research considerations are also discussed.

Chapter 2 places American families within their historical context, including more recent technological developments such as television and the Internet. The chapter also examines family change and discusses some of the concerns regarding the "decline" of the family.

Chapter 3 discusses how families are affected by and adapt to their ethnic/racial status or diversity.

Chapter 4 emphasizes couple formation, sexual relations, and reproduction. The latter topic includes matters of fertility, family planning, abortion, as well as reproductive technologies and surrogate motherhood.

Chapter 5 completes the foundation of family study. It examines family formation patterns, including single motherhood, cohabitation, marriage, and same-sex parenting. The topics of adoption and foster families are also discussed as alternative modes of family formation.

CHAPTER 1

Theoretical and Methodological Perspectives in Family Studies

OUTLINE

How Can Families Be Defined?
The Nuclear Family
The Extended Family
Types of Marriage
Relevance of Definitions

Why Is a Multidisciplinary Approach Helpful?

What Theoretical Perspectives Inform Family Studies?
Structural Functionalism
Symbolic Interactionism
Interactional-Transactional Perspectives
Social Exchange and Rational Theories
Social Exchange Theory
Rational Theory
Developmental (Life Course) Perspectives
Social Constructionism
Behavior Genetics

Why Is Feminism a Particularly Important Perspective?
The Analysis of Gender Stratification and Gender Roles
Feminist Analyses of the Family

What Are the Main Themes in the Text?

What Methods Are Used in Family Research?
Qualitative and Quantitative Methods
A Qualitative Method Example: Students' Autobiographies

Conclusions: Unity in Diversity

Summary
Key Concepts and Themes
Study and Review Questions
Suggested Readings
Suggested Weblinks

My publisher suggested that I begin this chapter by answering a personal question: What in my own family life has led to my becoming interested in family studies? Simply put—and this may at first appear to be a strange answer coming from a sociologist—I think it was largely in my genes, because I clearly recall being fascinated by family matters as young as age 6. There was no objective reason for this interest, for my family life was then uneventful.

Then, at age 7, I inherited four European siblings ranging in age from 15 to 21. At the time, I was merely concerned by the mixed blessing that such a drastic family restructuring brings to the life of a child and also that of her 30-year-old mother. I was too little to understand how dislocated these fun-loving young people's lives had been. Their mother had died when they were small; my father had left them in the care of two of his sisters and had moved to Canada in search of adventure. When World War II arrived, their house was occupied by the Germans, and so they had to relocate to the south of France. Finally, two years after the war was over, the four children moved to Canada.

Besides a large age gap, there were then and remain to this day striking differences between my father's two sets of children. For example, only one in the older group became a professional, whereas all of us younger ones did. We "little ones" had several advantages: We had stable lives and a very energetic mother, we benefitted from stimulating older siblings, and we were well spaced—all four years apart. True, we all shared one absent-minded, intellectual father with a gift for writing that ran in his family. A strange "coincidence" developed: We children, so very different from one another in terms of personality and educational level, share one characteristic—all of us are good writers; five took up writing as a job under one form or another and three published books. I am sure that, somehow, this peculiar aspect of my family profile is responsible for my awareness of the combined impact of environmental and genetic forces on family dynamics. We children were probably born with this "gift," but we would not have been able to develop it had our parents and the tradition on our father's side of the family not encouraged us in this direction.

Overall, however, and I will return to this point in the last chapter, I would say that what has most influenced my adult perspectives on the family has been the fieldwork I have done for my research: learning about the lives of the hundreds of children, adolescents, parents, and couples I have interviewed and observed throughout the years. Furthermore, as the reader will see at the end of this chapter, many of my students have written about their families in autobiographies. These lives, put together, have shown me that often the questions that were asked in family research, especially about the parent/child relationship, were not the right ones. The theories were too limited and did not always fit the facts I was discovering. This is what has led me to search for and consider a wider range of theoretical perspectives, as will become obvious in this chapter.

Notice that the title of this book contains the word *families* rather than *the family;* indeed, several types of families exist under one rubric. Despite this diversity, the family can be analyzed as an institution. In fact, the family is the most basic institution of any society, because it is within its folds that citizens are born, sheltered, and begin their socialization. **Socialization** is the process whereby a child learns how to think and behave according to the ways of the society and the group in which he or she is born. It is through the process of socialization that a society transmits its culture, with some modifications, to the next generation. It is also through socialization that a society perpetuates its gender structure as well as the roles, masculine and feminine, that flow from it.

Why is the family called an institution? An **institution** is a recognized area of social life that is organized along a system of widely accepted norms that regulate behaviors. The elements of organization and norms contribute to the predictability of life: People know what to expect. Over time, each society evolves a set of norms or rules that dictate the behaviors of family members toward each other and toward other institutions. Other key institutions in a society are the religious, educational, economic, as well as political contexts. We will study these institutions as they pertain to the family in subsequent chapters, particularly in Part 2 and Chapter 16.

When a society is small and there is a great deal of consensus on values, norms, and behaviors, an institution such as the family benefits from this stability. Life scripts do not change much over the generations and the level of continuity is high. But in American society, which is a large one constituted by people from many different backgrounds, there is less consensus about family norms and behaviors as well as less stability. Change has become a part of the institution of the family, and, as we see in the next chapter, this situation leaves many people uncomfortable about the future of the family and raises concerns about family values in their minds.

HOW CAN FAMILIES BE DEFINED?

In addition to being an institution, a family is an **intergenerational** group of individuals related to each other by blood, adoption, or marriage/cohabitation. The minimum requirement to meet this definition at the nuclear level (see Table 1.1) is the combination of two generations in one household.

The Nuclear Family

A parent and his or her children as well as two parents with their children form the most elementary type of family—often referred to as the *nuclear family*. When a person or a couple has a child, whether by birth or adoption, a nuclear family of *procreation* is formed. What is important is not whether the offspring are biological or adopted but that a new generation is added. Under this definition, a grandmother who raises her grandson also constitutes a nuclear family and so does a single man who is fostering a boy, provided they live in the same household. A husband and wife, a cohabiting couple, and a same-sex couple fall under the category of *couples*. They constitute a nuclear family only upon the arrival of their first child. These couples are, however, members of their own families of *origin* or orientation. That is, they "belong to" or originate from their parents.

The Extended Family

Other relatives constitute the *extended* family or *kinship* group: grandparents, aunts, uncles, cousins, as well as in-laws. There is much fluidity between the nuclear and the extended families. It is not an either-or category (see lower part of Table 1.1). Most people belong to an extended family as well as to a nuclear family. However, only a minority of individuals actually share a household with members of their extended

TABLE 1.1 Typology of Unions and Families

Type	Description
Unions	
Legal marriage	Socially/legally/religiously sanctioned union, which is generally heterosexual but could also be of same-sex partners
Cohabitation (common-law)	Union that is not legally sanctioned but is consensual; it can involve same-sex or opposite-sex partners
Monogamy	A legal marriage or cohabitation involving only two partners
Serial monogamy (serial polygamy)	Sequence of spouses or partners over time as in the sequence of marriage, divorce, and remarriage; spouses succeed each other
Polygamy	Multiple partners or spouses at the same time
Polygyny	One man married to more than one woman at the same time
Polyandry	One woman married to more than one man at the same time
Families	
***Nuclear** family*	At least one parent and one child living together
Conjugal	Husband, wife, and child(ren) Cohabitants with child Same-sex parents with child
Single parent	One parent and his or her child living together
Grandparent/grandchild	One grandparent or two grandparents and grandchild living together
Reconstituted	Remarried spouses or cohabiting spouses when at least one had a child from a former union
***Extended** family*	All the members of a family, including child, parents, grandparents, and other ascendants, plus uncles, aunts, and cousins (by blood, adoption, or marriage)
One household	At least one parent and his or her child living with another relative, generally a grandparent or aunt; two sisters, brothers, or aunt and niece living together
Multiple households	All the members of a family, including child, parents, grandparents, and other ascendants, plus uncles, aunts, and cousins (by blood, marriage, or adoption) living in separate dwellings and interacting on a regular basis

family, although quite a few people live near relatives. Therefore, the level of exchange taking place between the nuclear family and the extended family varies by coresidence, by proximity of neighborhood, and even because of emotional reasons. In American society, most relationships between members of an extended kin system are optional. For example, if two brothers and their wives or children do not get along, they are not forced to see each other, particularly if they live at a distance.

Of course, the extended family is still fairly institutionalized in Western society, at least at the normative level, so that it "looks" better if all the members appear to get along. Furthermore, as we will see in Chapter 3, most minority-group families are far more kinship oriented than are white families. Among the former, the extended family is more institutionalized: They entertain higher values of reciprocity and have more exact rules of behaviors concerning their extended kin.

In some ethnic groups—Mexican Americans and Puerto Ricans, for instance—friends are assimilated into the family as they become godparents to children. This is a system of *compradazgo.* When a father's friend is a frequent visitor to the house, he may be called an uncle *(tio)* and a mother's friend becomes an aunt *(tia),* thus creating what some researchers call **fictive kinship** bonds. For many individuals who belong to a large extended family group living in close proximity, there is often less of a necessity to make friends outside the family, as all interactional needs are met within this system. This situation is further explained by a student belonging to a "white ethnic" family:

> *"We've always lived near my grandparents and several uncles and aunts on both sides of the family so I grew up with a very secure feeling of belongingness. There was always someone to play with or talk to and we never had to kill ourselves making friends at school because we had so many cousins."*

Types of Marriage

The only type of marriage that is legally accepted in the United States today is that between a man and a woman—that is, two persons of the opposite sex. Polygamy in the form of *polygyny* (a man with two or more wives) became illegal in 1878. However, an unknown number of polygamous Mormon families still exist today in the United States, although they are not recognized by the mainstream Church of Jesus Christ of Latter Day Saints. Polygyny is widespread in Africa and Asia, particularly in Muslim countries, and is generally found among the well-to-do. *Polyandry* (a woman with two or more husbands) is less frequently encountered across the world and tends to be localized in smaller societies. It often occurs within the context of one woman being married to husbands who are brothers.

Relevance of Definitions

The typology of families presented here does not include unrelated single people living together, even though they constitute a *household* unit or share an address. Such persons are members of their family of origin but do not constitute a nuclear family. Although this definition is restrictive in terms of what constitutes a family (not a couple, not roommates sharing a house), it is quite inclusive as to the number and sex of parents present. In contrast, traditional definitions of the nuclear family do not include unmarried mothers or same-sex-parent families.

This definitional distinction is important, not only in terms of accuracy but also because it carries family policy implications (Hula, 1991). For instance, one often reads that children are born more and more "outside of the family." Such a statement is accurate when a traditional definition is applied, but is inaccurate as soon as one accepts a mother and her child as a type of nuclear family. Furthermore, in terms of policy, if a same-sex couple and their children, for instance, are not accepted as a family, they will not benefit from tax exemptions meant to help low-income families.

WHY IS A MULTIDISCIPLINARY APPROACH HELPFUL?

The topic of the family is a complex one and recourse to several disciplines is essential in order to obtain a more complete and refined perspective. Although a sociological perspective informs this text, the results and theories from several other fields of inquiry are placed within its analytical framework. That is, the results from other disciplines are integrated within a sociological framework. At the same time, however, theoretical perspectives from other disciplines help complement and even balance the sociological knowledge of the family.

Sociology itself tends to be divided between two poles (macrosociology and microsociology). We will first learn what these concepts mean and then see why they are linked rather than separate levels of analyses. **Macrosociology** studies large-scale phenomena and developments in a society, such as its social structure and organization. Macrosociology deals with economic forces, social class, gender and racial stratification, as well as cultural contexts, such as religion and value systems. It places the family within its broader historical and sociocultural context and examines how global forces combine to shape both family structure and, at a more intimate or micro level, family dynamics.

Microsociology focuses on the interactions between individuals within smaller contexts, such as a family or a group of friends. Microsociology examines relationships between family members as well as the impact of these relationships for human development, both for children and their parents. Perhaps there is too much concern in sociology in maintaining these two levels of analysis separately. The reality is, that when dealing with families, there is a constant *interaction* between macrosociology and microsociology. One begins to see that they are not opposite poles after all. The interplay between the two levels will be reflected within the chapters of this book.

Table 1.2 presents the various disciplines that constitute this text, more or less in order of importance in the contribution they make to the understanding of families within a sociological perspective. Some of these disciplines operate more at the macrosociological level, such as demography and economics. Others integrate themselves more within a micro context, particularly psychology, child development, and biology. Still others straddle both dimensions of sociology—for instance, anthropology, history, social work, and criminology, and even some aspects of demography and anthropology. Thus, a multidisciplinary approach helps link together *all* levels of sociological inquiry. What is important to retain is that no one single field of study

TABLE 1.2 **Disciplines That Contribute to a Better Understanding of Families within the Framework of Sociology**

Disciplines	What They Help Us Understand about the Family
Sociology	Global sociocultural context that shapes families Community organizations that impact on family diversity and life Evolution of family structure and functions Family as a dynamic system Roles (fathers, mothers, children, breadwinners) Interactions within the family
Psychology	Interpersonal relations; feelings and emotions Family members' psychological processes and characteristics, such as temperament Child, adolescent, and adult development
Economics	How economic reorganization affects family life Impact of poverty on family structure The family as a unit of consumption Economic diversity among families
Demography	Trends in cohabitation, marriage, births, deaths, divorce, remarriage, residential patterns, intermarriage, immigration
Child (human) development	Human development from birth to death The contribution of the family to human development
History	Changes in family life, definitions, and roles over time
Biology and genetics	How genes and the environment (nature *and* nurture) interact to produce human characteristics Biological factors that affect family life New reproductive methods and contraception
Anthropology	Families in other cultural contexts
Social work	Problems encountered by families Social policies to help families and promote family life
Criminology and juvenile delinquency	Illegal behaviors of family members, their origins, and their consequences

can adequately cover the complex topic of the family—neither can a single level of sociological analysis. A multidisciplinary approach is essential and several levels of analysis are necessary.

WHAT THEORETICAL PERSPECTIVES INFORM FAMILY STUDIES?

In this section, the main theoretical perspectives that are encountered in the sociological study of the family are examined. To these are added three others that, although psychological in origin, are sociologically oriented and inform several discussions in this book. They are part of the multidisciplinary approach of the text. Each theory that follows explains certain aspects of family life, but no theory explains family life in its entirety. Often, two or three theories combined provide a more thorough explanation of reality; some theories are complementary. As well, two theories considered together can present competing perspectives—that is, two entirely different ways of explaining reality. Researchers may then test which theory is correct by verifying which is most faithfully supported by facts.

Structural Functionalism

Structural functionalism analyzes a society's organization, its structure, and the linkages between its various systems. Within this perspective, the family is an important unit that fulfills key **functions** for society, such as reproduction and child socialization. In turn, a society's social structure provides the overall cultural and organizational contexts that influence family life. The analogy is organic: An organism (the society) is a system with many subsystems that collaborate or function together to optimize its success. The various systems fulfill functions or do things for each other.

The sociologist responsible for the propagation of structural functionalism was Talcott Parsons (1951). Structural functionalism was, to some extent, a conservative theory with assumptions of consensus or equilibrium. It left little room to address and redress inequalities in the social structure, because these inequalities were perceived to be fulfilling necessary functions for the entire social system. Thus, structural functionalism was not sufficiently flexible to analyze family developments. The changing role of women, for instance, could not be adequately examined because, under this perspective, the "liberation" of mothers threatened the family's equilibrium. Nevertheless, if one rereads Parsons and Bales's *Family, Socialization and Interaction Process* (1955), much of their analysis of the family as a system is still relevant today. Particularly important is the view that, as agents of socialization, parents must "interpenetrate" other systems in order to be successful in their role (p. 35), a perspective that is linked to the discussion of family functions in the next chapter.

Structural perspectives have since emerged to explain social inequalities based on the organization of society. This **social structural** orientation is evident in this text when inequalities between families are discussed, particularly in Chapter 3 and in Part 2. Families' living conditions are analyzed through political, economic, and even cultural arrangements of society rather than through individuals' deficits or merits. This interpretation does not defend the status quo; rather, it suggests the necessity for change at the global level.

Structural functionalist terminology has persisted and has been utilized in family research without its original, consensual focus. The concept of **dysfunction**, now widely used both in sociology and in psychology, refers to situations, characteristics, or behaviors that prevent the various parts of the system from working well together. At the individual level, a dysfunctional characteristic, such as hyperactivity, is one that prevents a child from doing well at school or from integrating himself or herself within the peer group. A dysfunctional family is one that is so disorganized or debilitated by conflict, incompetence, and various deficiencies that it is unable to care for its members and socialize its children. However, as we will see later in this text, a majority of "dysfunctional" families have become dysfunctional or are so labeled, because they have been socially marginalized by poverty or discrimination.

Symbolic Interactionism

Symbolic interactionism is a popular theory in family research. It "focuses on the connection between symbols (i.e., shared meanings) and interactions (i.e., verbal and nonverbal actions) and communications" (LaRossa and Reitzes, 1993:135). The **self** and **self-concept** occupy a singular position in symbolic interactionism, as do societal contexts whose meanings and structures are perceived by individuals while interacting with one another. People develop their self-concepts through other people's views of them. Basically, an individual acquires his or her self-definition through interaction with **significant others**—that is, people who play an important role in that individual's life, such as parents. Parents, teachers, peers, and even sports figures and movie stars may become **reference groups** for children as they grow up. This means that children look up to these individuals and groups and use them as role models or as points of reference to guide their own behaviors, develop their sense of self, and interpret social contexts.

Both symbolic interactionist and interactional perspectives view the child as a social actor who coproduces his or her development. A mother can teach her child to read, for instance, only with the child's cooperation and active participation.

The best-known symbolic interactionists were George Herbert Mead (1956) and Herbert Blumer (1969). Erving Goffman probably became the most popular symbolic interactionist upon the publication of his *The Presentation of Self in Everyday Life* (1959), perhaps in great part because he focused on dramaturgy (using theater or drama terms such as *roles, actors, frontstage, backstage*, and *setting*).

Symbolic interactionism views socialization as a process whereby children participate in the formation of their identities (LaRossa and Reitzes, 1993:149). The more recent perspective on the **child as a social actor** has been inspired by symbolic interactionism (Corsaro, 1997). As will be discussed, interactional theories, which constitute an extension of symbolic interactionism, are growing in importance in the study of child development. In this text, symbolic interactionism is utilized mainly in Chapters 10 through 15, where relationships and crises are examined, generally in conjunction with interactional theories and behavior genetics, a combination of perspectives that constitutes a precedent in a sociology textbook.

Interactional-Transactional Perspectives

The interactional-transactional framework posits that an individual creates his or her own environment, at the interpersonal level, at the same time that he or she is being shaped by this environment (Maccoby and Jacklin, 1983). This theory is particularly useful in the study of the parent/child relationship: It corrects the biases or flaws inherent to earlier socialization and child development perspectives whereby children were seen as the passive recipients of their parents' actions. Instead, the child is studied as an active social actor with individual characteristics, as are parents. *Interactions* between parents and children *feedback* on each other. Similarly, the socialization process involves the interaction between children's personalities and parental teachings (Ambert, 1997a). The child becomes **coproducer** of his or her own development (Lerner, 1982). Although this dynamic was recognized as early as 1968 by Bell, it has been largely ignored in terms of research.

The interactional causality model is multidimensional and bidirectional. It flows *both* from parents and children interacting with and reacting to each other and responding to the environment that impacts on them (Magnusson, 1995). Thus, the interactional perspective is also *transactional* in the sense that it involves a multiplicity of causality; in other words, it involves transactions between a child, his or her parent, and their environment within a feedback model. Interactional-transactional perspectives are very sensitive to the diversity of a family's environment, including culture and ethnicity (Sameroff, Seifer, and Bartko, 1997). This theory applies equally well to other interactions within the family, such as between spouses or between siblings. Several chapters are informed by the interactional-transactional perspective, particularly Chapters 10 through 15.

Interactional theories are often developed within an **ecological framework** whereby the various levels of a child's or a family's environment influence development and interactions (Lerner, 1995). In other words, whereas children are coproducers in their development, both parents' and children's actions are enhanced, limited, and constrained by the larger environment in which they are situated (Bronfenbrenner, 1979, 1989). This is also a tenet of transactional theories and is a guiding principle in this textbook. Within sociology, these perspectives are located at the intersection of the macro- and microsociological levels.

Social Exchange and Rational Theories

Both social exchange and rational theories are the product of the sociocultural environment of the twentieth century and they were influenced by the discipline of economics. Resources occupy a key role in both these perspectives.

Social Exchange Theory

The basic assumption behind social exchange theory is that people interact so as to *maximize* their own *benefits* or rewards and to *minimize* their *costs*. Exchange takes place daily, although people's motives may not be quite as rational as assumed in the theory. Distributive justice occurs when the parties in an exchange receive "rewards" that are perceived to be equivalent. Exchange theory has been particularly useful in explaining gender relations, the household division of labor, and why people enter into, remain in, or leave relationships (see Chapters 4 and 10, for instance).

In the market metaphor of exchange theory, **resources** and **power** occupy a central position. As explained by Sabatelli and Shehan (1993:386), "Each spouse's resources and each spouse's dependence on the relationship must be taken into account, for example, when attempting to study marital power." The spouse who has alternatives outside a marriage weighs the advantages of these alternatives against those secured in the current marriage (Levinger, 1976). This market or economic orientation to human relations presents some difficulties for researchers whose values may be more altruistic and collectivist. The early proponents of exchange theory were sociologists George Homans (1961) and Peter Blau (1964) as well as psychologists John Thibaut and Harold Kelly (1959).

Rational Theory

An extension of the market metaphor expressed in exchange theory is reflected in rational theory, which is currently used in the study of certain domains of family life. James Coleman (1990a) has been at the origin of this theoretical interest in family research. In this book, the concepts of social and human capitals are used extensively to explain the socialization outcomes of children of various social classes, for instance (Coleman, 1988, 1990b). These concepts are particularly evident in Chapter 8.

Human capital refers to abilities, skills, education, and positive human characteristics inherited or acquired by a person. **Social capital** is a resource that resides in relationships, particularly family and community relations, that benefits child socialization and the acquisition of human capital. Social capital is especially evident when parents cooperate, agree, and share authority. This allows their children to learn norms more effectively. The same results occur when the parental role is supported by a community. In both cases, *social closure* exists; that is, children are not subjected to conflicting norms. Furthermore, Coleman and Hoffer (1987) have been the proponents of the **functional community:** parents' linkages to other parents and to a community with a particular prosocial set of values. An effective or functional community enhances parents' social capital and contributes to the monitoring of all children. It allows for social closure and constitutes an element of *collective socialization.*

Developmental (Life Course) Perspectives

Paul Glick (1947) and Evelyn Duvall (1957) were the first to propose a developmental sequencing to family life. This is the aspect of family **life stages** that largely informs Chapter 9 and structures Chapter 11 on the parent/child relationship. Families have a *life course* or trajectory but do not all follow the same sequencing of events. Developmental theories are both micro- and macrosociological: Families are viewed as long-lived groups with a history of internal interactions as well as transactions with the rest of society.

One key contribution of the developmental perspective has been to present a more **longitudinal** or long-term framework for research on families (Aldous, 1996). Longitudinal studies follow individuals or families over time as opposed to interviewing them just once. Furthermore, the developmental perspective examines the careers of families within their particular socioeconomic context, and takes into consideration the dynamics between the various trajectories and life stages of its members (Elder, 1998). Developmental theories recognize that individual life courses at times do not mesh well with those of other family members, such as when an adolescent has a baby and this transition forces her own young mother to become a grandmother at a time when she is still raising small children (see Chapter 9).

This theory has been particularly useful in the study of intergenerational phenomena and relations in the context of different historical periods (Elder, 1991; Hareven, 1987). The concept of *role* recurs in this perspective as each individual's role evolves when additional members arrive, as children age and enter the economic system or depart to form their own family units, and as grandchildren are born.

Dynamic concepts include **transition** or passage from one stage to the next as well as individual transitions within a particular family stage, such as when an older child moves out but all other children who are younger remain at home. **Timing** is a key concept that is also encountered in the sociology of adult development (Clausen, 1986). Today, normative timing includes a 26-year-old woman who marries and has her first child two years later. Less normative is the 17-year-old who has a baby. The first woman is "on time," whereas the second is "off time" (that is, too young according to the norms of society). Similarly, a 50-year-old woman who gives birth is considered to be off time. Transitions may also include changes in family structure, such as the occurrence of divorce.

Social Constructionism

Social constructionism has its roots in the classical sociology of knowledge, from Karl Mannheim's *Ideology and Utopia* (1936) through the better known Berger and Luckmann's *The Social Construction of Reality* (1966). The theory argues that various phenomena that are taken for granted and seem natural are actually culturally defined or socially constructed. A case in point is childhood which, as described in Chapter 2, has been redefined throughout the centuries according to prevailing socioeconomic changes (Ariès, 1962). In a now classical article, William Kessen (1979) explained how children are socially constructed by psychologists. He described the U.S. child and psychology as two cultural "inventions," or social constructs. A **social construct** is a socially accepted definition of a situation. It is a cultural creation or interpretation.

Another example is that of motherhood when it is described as "instinctive" and "natural." These two adjectives are synonymous with destiny and presuppose a lack of change in the way motherhood is practiced. Therefore, these terms are used to ensure the stability of gender roles (men as breadwinners and women as stay-at-home mothers) and the perpetuation of *patriarchy* (masculine dominance in the major spheres of social life). This social construction of motherhood is not valid because, in actuality, motherhood includes practices and roles that differ from society to society and from century to century.

Family life is socially redefined according to the socioeconomic needs of a society at any point in time (Ferree, Lorber, and Hess, 1999). This social construction of family life generally comes from those who are in power (males) as well as experts who produce the knowledge that is valued by a society at a particular time in its history. Such valued knowledge can be religious, medical, psychological, or even legal expertise—all of which has evolved from a masculine power base. It is not surprising, then, that social constructionism is related to feminism (D. Smith, 1987). Both emphasize culture as an explanation for the definition of gender roles as well as masculinity and femininity.

Behavior Genetics

The framework of behavior genetics, which was casually introduced in my autobiographical opener, is not well known by sociologists. It should not be confused with sociobiology, which has much to do with explaining human behaviors and social institutions on the basis of evolution. Nor should it be equated with approaches that foster the notion of inequalities based on presumed genetic inferiority versus superiority between racial groups, for instance. Rather, the field of behavior genetics studies *within*-family phenomena to explain how **nature and nurture** (or genetics and environment) *combine* and *interact* to produce personalities, parent/child interactions, the home environment, how parents raise their children, and why children grow up to be who they become (Plomin et al., 1998).

Parents influence their children, not only through their behaviors and attitudes, but also through the genes they transmit to the children and the indirect effect of their own genes on the family environment. Parents' genes are expressed through their personalities, their socialization practices, and the lifestyle choices they make for their families, all of which are even more influenced by the environment (Turkheimer, 1998). A parent's environment includes his or her economic and cultural situations and relationship with the other parent; it also includes his or her children, their personalities, and their behaviors, which in turn affect the parent and his or her socialization practices. In other words, in a family, each person is part of the others' environment. Behavior genetics, then, is closely related to the multicausality model of interactional and transactional theories.

Because of their different personalities, siblings in the same family do not experience their **shared environment** in exactly the same way (see Chapter 12). The shared environment consists of family events and circumstances of which everyone partakes, such as family outings, dinners, parental teachings, and even divorce. Therefore, depending on their own temperament, birth order, and spacing, siblings experience the shared environment differently. (There is a link with symbolic interactionism here in terms of the development of different meanings attached to experiences.) If one adds to this other experiences that children in the same family do not necessarily share—such as illnesses, classrooms, and peers (the **nonshared environment**)—it is not surprising that siblings grow up to be different to some extent (Plomin and McClearn, 1993).

The closer the genetic link between two persons, the more similar their personalities and personality-driven behaviors. Thus, identical twins raised together resemble each other more than fraternal twins. Furthermore, the closer the cultural link between two persons, the more similar their behaviors become. Therefore, identical twins raised together resemble each other behaviorally more than identical twins raised separately (Kendler, 1996). Genes and the environment constitute the two engines that guide human development—*not* the environment alone and not genes alone. As such, behavior genetics represents an important perspective for sociologists because nearly all the research on families has ignored the fact that human beings are biochemical entities that affect and are affected by their environment. Behavior genetics *complements* sociological perspectives.

WHY IS FEMINISM A PARTICULARLY IMPORTANT PERSPECTIVE?

Feminism is an interdisciplinary set of perspectives united by a common analysis of the patriarchal organization of society. This social structure privileges male attributes (Thorne, 1992; Zinn, 1990) and male morality (Gilligan, 1993), and leads to unequal gender roles in all social settings, beginning with the family. Feminist scholars, however, vary in the extent to which they emphasize some of these elements over others (Hess and Ferree, 1987). Feminist theories also contribute to the examination of social inequalities and diversities in general (Allen and Baber, 1992); as such, they are useful in other realms of analysis, such as race (Nakano Glenn, 1999; Roschelle, 1999).

Feminist theories are woman centered and aim at documenting and explaining the feminine experience (Osmond and Thorne, 1993). They amalgamate both the macro- and microsociological levels of analysis and they range from liberal feminism to radical and socialist feminism (Madoo-Lengermann and Niebrugge-Brantley, 1992). Above all, feminist scholars have highlighted the fact that women's and men's experiences of life are largely different and unequal—a theme that has a multitude of ramifications for family life.

The Analysis of Gender Stratification and Gender Roles

Gender roles represent the social definition of what, in a society, is constructed as appropriately masculine or feminine in terms of behavior. **Gender roles** are norms or rules that define how males and females should think and behave. They have the result of making men and women accept their proper place in society according to the dictates of the overarching structural arrangement by gender (Lorber, 1994). The transmission of gender roles occurs at the interrelated macro- and microsociological levels.

At the macrolevel, gender roles are supported by the masculine, patriarchal organization or **stratification system** of the society that provides more resources, authority, opportunities, and autonomy to men than to women (Ferree and Hall, 1996). In other words, men in general have more *power* and, at the micro level, this affects the way they think and behave—differentiated gender roles. Girls and boys are socialized to occupy different roles in society, to think and feel differently, beginning with a preference for separate toys and activities. This process of socialization is so subtle that it is taken for granted as normal or as a result of nature, thus unavoidable. Consequently, on average, boys and girls grow up along divergent developmental paths and experience relationships as well as family life differently, even as adults (Bernard, 1972). This fact is particularly relevant in the study of the family (Coltrane, 1997). Feminist theories have influenced researchers who study men as well as the development of boys (Messner, 1997). For instance, there is a great deal of concern over the problems created and encountered by boys in U.S. society as a result of their masculine socialization emphasizing toughness, emotional distance, and even bravado (Garbarino, 1999).

Feminist Analyses of the Family

Families cannot be understood outside of the forces in society that are dominated—at the political and economic levels—by a masculine as well as a racial structure (Collins, 1990). The resulting division of labor by gender, both within society at large and within households, is a fundamental focus of feminist analyses. Thus, feminism emphasizes the fallacy of the family as an entirely private world that is untouched by society's inequities. In this respect, there is a kinship to structuralism as used in this text. Feminists see the division of individuals' lives between the public and the private spheres as analytically flawed (Ferree, 1990). Not only is the private domain affected by the public (culture, economy, polity), but the private becomes a political issue. For instance, the notion that family relations, including wife battery, are purely a personal matter has been challenged by feminists and successfully placed on the social policy and legal agendas.

Feminism also analyzes motherhood as a social construct rather than as a purely natural product. Therefore, many aspects of feminist theories are related to social constructionism and have enlarged as well as informed this theoretical perspective (D. Smith, 1974). Marriage is seen as an institution that generally contributes to feminine inequality and perpetuates it in private life, including the bedroom. The gendered nature of marriage is particularly evident in the division of labor between husbands and wives concerning household work and child care, one of the topics in Chapter 10.

WHAT ARE THE MAIN THEMES IN THE TEXT?

Within the theoretical perspectives just described, this book emphasizes several themes. These are topics as well as explanatory models that link the contents of chapters and provide the distinct conceptual framework and flavor of this text. Social class or socioeconomic status (SES), gender, and race or ethnicity, which are key demographic variables in sociological analyses in general, are woven into this multiple thematic framework.

The first theme of **social inequalities** is the dominant perspective of Part 2 and other chapters, particularly Chapter 3. This theme is informed by structural and ecological theories as well as social capital or rational theory. Based on their economic situation and their ethnicity, families have an unequal access to the key resources of their society. Further inequalities cut across economics and ethnicity, as men and women also have a differential access to societal resources and opportunities. This is reflected at the micro level in an unequal division of labor at home (see Chapter 10) and a differential impact of children on women (see Chapter 14).

A second theme is related but not limited to the first one: **family diversity**—that is, diversity in structure, culture, and inequalities. Therefore, inequalities and diversity are the two overarching themes guiding Parts 1 and 2. My concerns about *social policies* pertaining to families flow from these two themes as well as from family functions (discussed next). Social policies are intended to prevent and remedy familial difficulties created by social inequality (i.e., poverty) as well as diversity (i.e., one- versus two-parent families).

The third theme, which will be initially examined in the next chapter, focuses on **family functions;** it is related to structural functional theories. The text will document that not only has the family not lost its functions, as is commonly believed, but it has actually acquired new ones. As Parsons and colleagues (1955) would put it, the family has become more specialized in the functions it fulfills for its members and for society as a whole. Above all, the book will document how individual families are too often ill equipped to fulfill their functions, in part because of a lack of social investment in families—an important social policy critique that recurs and is expanded on in the final chapter.

A fourth theme running through the text is that of the **functional community,** particularly the role it plays or can play in child socialization and the successful integration of families in society. This theme, which is inspired by rational theories, emphasizes how functional communities constitute social capital that supports families. In turn, this social capital allows children to develop their own human capital: positive qualities, socially acceptable behavior, and school completion and achievement, among others.

A fifth theme revolves around the **cultural context** and includes a recourse to *social constructionism.* The social construction of reality, within the broader cultural context, is often used to show how it impacts on family dynamics. A good example of this is the social construction of adoption and how it can affect children's development (see Chapter 5). As well, the cultural context involves the audiovisual media and its impacts on family interaction and child socialization. This theme of *media influence* first appears in the next chapter but is mentioned in several other sections of the text. Not only have the media restructured family time but they also offer social constructs of reality that affect adults' and children's mentality.

The sixth theme in this book is especially important for Parts 3 and 4 and it has a double theoretical focus. First, it emphasizes the **interactional** aspect of family relations as opposed to the traditional models that, for instance, tend to explain children's problems strictly through their parents' negative socialization approach. The interactional theory, as we have seen earlier, implicates feedback between the environment, the parents' characteristics and behaviors, and the children's characteristics. Second, this theme points to the complementary importance of paying attention to family members' **genetic inheritance** and its own interaction with the environment in creating personalities and family relationships.

Finally, the seventh theme of **structural gender inequalities** and consequent **gender roles** originates from feminist theories as well as social constructionism. Boys and girls as well as men and women experience family life differently because of their unequal situation in the stratification system and because of their respective socialization trajectories. The theme of gender roles forms the cornerstone of several specific discussions throughout the text.

WHAT METHODS ARE USED IN FAMILY RESEARCH?

Let's briefly return to the matter of theory. A **theory** is a set of interrelated propositions that explains a particular phenomenon. A good theory can be tested against facts with a set of hypotheses. A **hypothesis** is a testable proposition or sentence. For instance, exchange theory can give rise to the following hypothesis: Employed wives are less happy with their marriages when they perceive inequity in the household division of labor. In methods language, marital happiness is the *dependent variable*—it depends on the wives' perceptions of inequity. Inequity then becomes the *independent variable*, the one that will make marital happiness change. The independent variable (perceived inequity) is the presumed cause of the dependent variable (marital happiness).

Theories inform the questions that researchers ask about the family and provide explanatory models. **Methods** are the means or tools utilized to answer researchers' questions or obtain information. The methods utilized in family research are those of sociology, psychology, and demography in general. They are summarized in five categories in Table 1.3. This table will be useful throughout the following chapters where all these methods are mentioned or are described in conjunction with various results

TABLE 1.3 Methods in Family Research

Method	Description
Surveys	Questionnaires given in groups (such as a classroom) Questionnaires distributed to homes (includes the U.S. Census) Face-to-face interviews in homes or elsewhere Phone interviews
Observations	Observation in naturalistic settings (at homes, public places, village center, streets) Participant observation where the researcher plays a role in the life of the respondents Laboratory observations (particularly of mother/child interactions) and one-way mirror; events are recorded as they occur
Experiments	"Natural" experiments: the study of families before and after a social event or a natural phenomenon occurs (introduction of the Internet in the home, for instance; earthquakes) Laboratory experiments (observations, questionnaires, interviews) before and after a variable is introduced or while the dynamics of an interaction are ongoing
Evaluative research	May involve any of the above methods in order to study the impact of social policy initiatives and clinical interventions
Content and secondary analyses	Content analysis of public documents, media programs, newspapers, books Content analysis of archives and personal documents such as diaries for historical research Content analysis of diaries and autobiographies Secondary analyses of surveys, census, and other statistical sources (*secondary* refers to the fact that the researchers who do the analyses were not the ones who had designed the original study or data gathering)

found by researchers on a wide variety of topics. Furthermore, a special Family Research insert on methods of particular interest appears in Chapters 2 through 15.

The matter of methods is a serious one with great consequences: The utilization of inappropriate methods simply creates useless and even misleading or false results. In turn, false or misleading results could inspire people to adopt dysfunctional behaviors. An example resides in widely exaggerated reports of extramarital affairs (see Chapter 4), when the reality is that husbands and wives who remain together are overwhelmingly faithful. Such reports could lead to marital insecurity or could even inspire husbands or wives to "join the (imaginary) club." False results could also lead legislators to enact family policy that might have negative consequences. One such example is illustrated in Chapter 6, where we will see that welfare availability has not been a main cause in the increase of children born to single mothers. The belief to the contrary, based on poor and inherently flawed research, has recently led to a severe curtailment of help to poor families, with potentially damaging consequences for children in the future.

Qualitative and Quantitative Methods

Methods are generally separated into two large categories: quantitative and qualitative. *Quantitative methods* are based on numbers, percentages, and averages; they are expressed in statistical tests. In contrast, *qualitative methods* are not based on numbers. Rather, in order to describe and explain various family phenomena in depth and to arrive at conclusions, qualitative researchers report what family members say, write, and do in the form of extracts, quotes, case studies, and summaries (Denzin and Lincoln, 1994). The reader will find many examples of such reports throughout the text, particularly in terms of quotes from students' autobiographies, excerpts from conversations with parents during interviews, and various case studies from my fieldwork. Many researchers use the information that they have gathered qualitatively and summarize it numerically. For instance, they may present averages and percentages to provide an overall view of the themes and situations that have emerged in their qualitative material. This is particularly useful when large samples are involved and can lead to more sophisticated statistical analyses.

A distinction has to be made between qualitative data and "anecdotal" material. Qualitative research follows rigorous methods of information gathering. In contrast, anecdotes are gathered casually. For instance, every individual has stories to tell about his or her life that may hold great emotional and personal meanings for that person. But these have limited *sociological* value because they reveal no information about general trends and do not explain where each anecdote is situated along a continuum of life experiences on a given topic. In other words, one life incident does not form a sociological perspective.

In this text, the quotes presented throughout are part of rigorously designed studies seeking to obtain a wide range of family experiences so as to offer larger perspectives that lead to conclusions. An example of anecdotes, in contrast, can be found on p. 309 of Chapter 11, where I report conversations overheard accidentally. But, because they are guided by a researcher's theoretical framework—in this case the interactional perspective—these anecdotes can constitute *exploratory data.* These are insights gathered informally that are then used to design state-of-the-art qualitative or quantitative studies later on, particularly with the goal of testing hypotheses.

Qualitative and quantitative research methods are *equally scientific* and complement each other (Ambert et al., 1995); they are found within all five categories summarized in Table 1.3. In other words, both sets of methods can be used in surveys, observations, experiments, evaluative research, and content analysis. The latter includes historical documents (Schvaneveldt, Pickett, and Young, 1993). Both groups of methods can also be utilized to test hypotheses based on most theories described earlier. However, sociologists who favor symbolic interactionism and feminism often prefer qualitative methods, whereas structural researchers, demographers, and behavior geneticists generally have recourse to quantifications.

Family sociologists should be concerned with choosing a research approach that can best describe the human reality they wish to study within its social context, whether it is a qualitative or quantitative approach. Methods should be selected depending on what is being investigated. For example, if one wants to study public opinion about extramarital sexuality, then clearly a large sample is required and statistical analysis is needed. At the same time, however, one might want to inject more human texture and depth into the statistics by including qualitative information. This can be achieved by intensive interviewing of a small subsample of the larger one to allow the interviewees to talk at some length about the issues raised, their experience, and feelings. As well, certain aspects of spousal interaction may be difficult to approach with methods based on statistics derived from surveys, and may be more fruitfully grasped by qualitatively informed approaches, such as observations in a naturalistic setting or lengthy conversations.

A Qualitative Method Example: Students' Autobiographies

One key source of qualitative material for this book is the research I have done from my students' autobiographies. This type of research falls under the rubrics of surveys and content analysis in Table 1.3. Throughout the years, undergraduate students in some of the sociology classes I have taught have written autobiographies that were semi-structured (i.e., in response to a set of **open-ended questions**). Open-ended questions allow respondents to say anything they want; they are the opposite of multiple-choice questions. This project was first initiated in the academic year 1972–73 when a format was tested on several hundred students. By the year 1974–75, the students' responses had confirmed that the questionnaire was nonsuggestive (I was not putting words into their mouths), easily understood, and yielded answers that could be analyzed into themes. From 17 questions in the 1974 schedule, there were 31 by 1990, and a few more have since been added and some deleted as this book goes to print. Over 1,400 autobiographies have been collected.

The core of the autobiographies resides in the following questions: "When you look back on your early childhood (0–5 years), what is it that you like best to remember about it? (What made you the most happy?)" In a second question: "And what is it that you remember being most painful to you? (What above all else made you unhappy?)" These two questions are repeated for the 6–10, 11–14, 15–18, and current age brackets. Initially, I worried that students might resent an intrusion into their recent personal lives, so I stopped this inquiry after the 11–14 age bracket. This ethical concern was superfluous, however, as students were actually quite happy about the entire exercise. Consequently, in future years, I added questions to cover later ages.

A great proportion of the autobiographical pages are devoted to these core questions as students utilize them to narrate the main themes of the story of their lives. Other questions whose answers are used in this textbook result in descriptions of students' neighborhoods and their relationships with parents, siblings, and peers within each age bracket. Students are also asked about their values as well as that of their parents and peers and about their personality. At the end, they are requested to project themselves into the future and predict where they think they will be in 10 years.

No specific question is asked about age, race, ethnicity, religion, or marital status, as these could help identify individual students. Nevertheless, most students provide this information somewhere in their narratives. The autobiographies (as well as all other papers and tests) are submitted *anonymously.* Students are instructed to write their college identification numbers on the cover pages only. After reading an autobiography, I tear off the cover sheet and turn it over to a teaching assistant who then enters the grade on the class list. When no teaching assistant is available, students collectively help out in this task. Over the years, only one or two students annually chose not to write the autobiography and elected to write another research paper instead.

A formal 1990 evaluation of this assignment indicated that students not only trusted the anonymity of the procedure but also felt that they generally had benefited from the experience (Ambert, 1994a). Many students elect to write well beyond the call of duty (12 single-spaced pages); most autobiographies are in the range of 20 to 30 single-spaced pages, with many running between 40 and 60 pages. Students have always known from the very beginning that they were working for a research project and they were keenly interested in seeing "their" work published. I have often been queried as to when the results would "finally" appear.

The students have been reliable or truthful in writing their autobiography—a factor of great importance to a researcher. How do I "test" for truthfulness? First, I total up a few answers every other year or so and compare the results to statistics and research available for the population of students and parents. The students' profile on these questions matches that of available statistics. Second, the data provided by students on parents' marital happiness and relationship with peers replicate other research evidence. Finally, answers to several different but related questions produce a congruent profile, with the same themes recurring within a particular autobiography, thus assuring authenticity (Brown and Sime, 1981). Furthermore, students' answers indicate that they have tried very hard to project themselves back into the particular age brackets. A frequent remark is, "Of course, when I think about this now, I laugh, but it was really a terrible problem for me at that age."

CONCLUSIONS: UNITY IN DIVERSITY

Families are tremendously diverse but they are united under the rubric of the family as an institution. The theories used to study and explain the family are numerous but they form a totality that allows one to see the family in all its entirety—to study families in the plural and yet find important similarities among them. Furthermore, the various theories discussed in this chapter have illustrated the point made earlier: The family is an ideal phenomenon for a linkage, rather than a polarization, between the macro and micro levels of sociological analysis. Thus, some of the chapters that follow have a macrosociological framework, specifically Chapters 6, 7, and 8, on the economy, neighborhoods, and educational and religious institutions. Yet, within these larger contextual frameworks, family interaction and dynamics (micro level) are discussed in terms of how they are affected by these larger forces.

On the other side of the coin, some chapters have a microsociological framework. Cases in point are the "relationship" chapters in Part 3 and much of the "problems" chapters in Part 4. Yet, these relationships and problems are situated within their larger context and, in part, are explained in terms of macrosociology. Similarly, the themes that form the basis of this text, although diverse, are unified because, when placed together, they present a holistic view on family life. This view can then be translated into social policies pertaining to supporting the family as an institution and consequently supporting individual families.

SUMMARY

1. The family is defined as an institution and an intergenerational group of individuals related by blood or adoption. The nuclear family is generally enclosed in an extended network of kinship. The study of the family is interdisciplinary and amalgamates the macrosociological and microsociological levels of analysis.
2. The main theoretical perspectives informing family research are as follows: (a) Structural functionalism emphasizes global forces in society that affect family life, with a focus on the functions fulfilled by social systems and their subsystems. (b) Symbolic interactionism focuses on shared meanings, self-concept, reference groups, and interactions. (c) The interactional-transactional perspective explains how family members create their environment at the interpersonal level while also being shaped by this environment. It considers bidirectional feedback between parents and children; the latter are coproducers of their development. This perspective fits well within the ecological framework of environmental influences. (d) Resources occupy a central position in social exchange and rational theories. Social exchange theories see people interacting so as to maximize their own benefits and minimize their costs. Rational theory also focuses on resources in the guise of social and human capitals in the area of child socialization. The concept of the functional community is also important. (e) Developmental or life course perspectives emphasize the longitudinal approach, transitions, timing, as well as the personal and historical contexts in which family stages evolve. (f) Social constructionism argues that social phenomena that are taken for granted and seem natural are actually culturally defined or socially constructed. (g) Behavior genetics studies within-family phenomena to explain how genes and environment combine and interact to produce personalities and the home environment, and affect parent/child relations as well as child socialization.
3. Feminism is a particularly important theoretical perspective in family studies because the intimate world of the family is guided by gender roles that are supported by the patriarchal organization of society at large. Important aspects of feminism include the transmission of gender roles, the social construction of motherhood, and the study of the family from a female perspective.
4. This text emphasizes seven themes that recur throughout the chapters: social inequalities, family diversity, family functions, the functional community, the cultural context and social constructionism, interactional and behavior genetics perspectives, and gender roles.

5. Qualitative and quantitative research methods in family research are equally scientific and complement each other. Qualitative methods are distinguished from mere anecdotes. Qualitative researchers do in-depth interviewing or observation. Quantitative methods use statistics. The description of students' autobiographies used in this text is presented as an example of a qualitative study.
6. The chapter concludes by emphasizing the unity that exists amidst the diversity of levels of analysis and theoretical as well thematic approaches to the study of the family.

KEY CONCEPTS AND THEMES

Child as coproducer of own development, p. 12
Child as social actor, p. 12
Collective socialization, p. 14
Dysfunctions, pp. 10–11
Ecological framework, p. 12
Extended family, p. 5
Family diversity, p. 18
Fictive kinship, p. 7
Functional community, pp. 14, 18
Functions, pp. 10, 18
Gender roles, pp. 17, 19
Gender stratification, p. 17
Genetic inheritance, p. 19
Human capital, p. 13
Hypothesis, p. 19
Institution, p. 5
Interactions, p. 12
Intergenerational, p. 19
Life course, p. 14
Life stages, p. 14
Longitudinal, p. 14
Macrosociology, p. 8
Methods, p. 19
Microsociology, p. 8
Nature and nurture, p. 15
Nonshared environment, p. 16
Nuclear family, p. 5
Open-ended questions, p. 22
Polygamy, p. 7
Power, p. 13
Qualitative methods, p. 21
Quantitative methods, p. 21
Reference groups, p. 11
Resources, p. 13
Self-concept, p. 11
Shared environment, p. 16
Significant others, p. 11
Social capital, p. 13
Social closure, p. 13
Social construct, p. 15
Social definition of childhood, p. 15
Social inequalities, p. 18
Social policies, p. 18
Social structural, p. 10
Socialization, p. 4
Student autobiographies, p. 22
Theory, p. 19
Timing, p. 14
Transitions, p. 14

STUDY AND REVIEW QUESTIONS

1. What is important in the definition of the family?
2. Explain the linkages between macrosociology and microsociology in terms of the family.
3. Define the concepts of functions and dysfunctions. Provide an example of each.
4. Describe symbolic interactionism.
5. Give two important characteristics of the interactional-transactional perspective.
6. What are two very useful concepts derived from rational theory in the study of the parent-child relationship?
7. Give an example of the usefulness of social constructionism.
8. Why is behavior genetics an important addition to the sociology of the family?
9. What are important concepts of feminist theories that pertain to the family?
10. What are the main themes of this book? Link each one to a theoretical perspective.
11. How do qualititative and quantititative methods differ and complement each other?

SUGGESTED READINGS

Boss, P. G., Doherty, W. J., LaRossa, R., Schumm, W. R., and Steinmetz, S. K. (Eds.). 1993. *Sourcebook of family theories and methods: A contextual approach.* New York: Plenum Press. This large text presents an overview of family theories and methods. The authors detail the historical development of each theory and methodology, as well as its assumptions and its major concepts, and present sections on research examples and other applications.

Cochran, M., Larner, M., Riley, D., Gunnarsson, L., and Henderson, C. R., Jr. 1990. *Extending families: The social network of parents and their children.* Cambridge: Cambridge University Press. This is probably the only comprehensive collection of articles on family networks. It includes sections relating networks to race, class, work, time, and human development.

Denzin, N., and Lincoln, Y. (Eds.). 1994. *Handbook of qualitative research.* Thousand Oaks, CA: Sage. This collection of articles presents the various approaches, methodologies, and methods of qualitative research.

Gilgun, J. F., Daly, K., and Handel, G. (Eds.). 1992. *Qualitative methods in family research.* Newbury Park, CA: Sage. This collection of articles presents an accessible introduction to qualitative methods in the domain of family life. Various family settings serve as contexts and topics.

Klein, D. M., and White, J. M. 1996. *Family theories: An introduction.* Thousand Oaks, CA: Sage. The authors focus on five theoretical perspectives in family research: exchange, symbolic interactionism, family development, systems theories, and the ecological perspective.

Moen, P., Elder, G. H., Jr., and Lüscher, K. (Eds.). 1995. *Examining lives in context.* Washington, DC: American Psychological Association. This book was put together in honor of Urie Bronfenbrenner's ecological or contextual approach to family life. The articles present analyses of various aspects of family life and the parent/child interaction from the ecological perspective. Some of the articles also include the interactional perspective.

Neuman, W. L. 2000. *Social research methods: Qualitative and quantitative approaches* (4th ed.). Boston: Allyn and Bacon. This introductory text covers a wide range of research methods.

Roschelle, A. R. 1997. *No more kin: Exploring race, class, and gender in family networks.* Thousand Oaks, CA: Sage. This is a theoretical and research book comparing exchange of services among kin and friends among non-Hispanic whites, blacks, Mexican Americans, and Puerto Ricans.

Rowe, D. C. 1994. *The limits of family influence: Genes, experience, and behavior.* New York: Guilford Press. The author presents a review of the literature as well as a great deal of research results using behavior genetics theory as baseline.

Thorne, B., with Yalom, M. (Eds.). 1992. *Rethinking the family: Some feminist questions* (rev. ed.). Boston: Northeastern University Press. The various authors present a feminist analysis of several aspects of family life, including motherhood. The senior author's introduction is particularly relevant to general, feminist theories.

SUGGESTED WEBLINKS

For general information and additional links on the theories and theorists described in this chapter, click to *Sociology Internet Pathfinder* at the *Yahoo* search engine at **<http://www.yahoo.com/social_science/sociology/>.**

For examples of quantitative and qualitative sociological research methods in action, sample articles and abstracts published in electronic journals, consult *Sociological Methodology,* published by the American Sociological Association **<http://depts.washington.edu/socmeth2/>**, and *Qualitative Report*, an online journal **<http://www.nova.edu/ssss/QR/index.html>.**

CHAPTER 2

Historical Perspectives and Contemporary Issues Concerning Family Life

OUTLINE

Comparative Perspectives on Families

American Families of the Past
Multiple Historical Roots
The Colonial Period
Families Become More Diverse and Stratified
Industrialization and New Social Definitions
The Twentieth Century

Are Children Becoming Defamilialized?

The Audiovisual Media and Family Life
Television Restructures Family Life
The Family on Television: A Historical Overview
Effects of Family-Related Programs on Children
The Evolution of Sexual Contents and Effects on Adolescents
Children and Television Violence
The New Cultural Revolution: The Internet

Family Change or Decline? The Debate
Has the Family Lost Its Functions?
The Family's Functions: More Gains than Losses
Can All Families Equally Fulfill Their Functions?
Are Traditional Family Values Necessarily under Attack?
Concerns over Same-Sex-Parent Families
Should It Be a Different Debate?

Conclusions: The Pace of Change

Summary
Key Concepts and Themes
Study and Review Questions
Suggested Readings
Suggested Weblinks

Victoria Leeds, named after Queen Victoria, was born in a large mansion in the countryside south of Manchester, England, in 1870. For many years, before she died in 1960, she entertained her granddaughter, one of my best friends, with the intimate details of her life when she was growing up. Victoria was the youngest of four surviving children. Her father was a rich industrialist. The family was of the nuclear type but over 12 household servants lodged on the upper floor. Behind the house were small cottages where a similar number of staff lived who took care of kennels, stables, and grounds. Victoria and her older sister had a governess as well as tutors. Her brothers had tutors first but then went on to boarding schools. The brothers and sisters lived separate existences. Once or twice a week, a carriage brought other little girls and their mothers to visit. The girls played parlor and outdoors games, went riding, gave concerts, and mounted plays or puppet shows.

Victoria saw her father only two or three times a week, which were always formal occasions: The children were dressed in their best attire, the girls curtseyed, the boys shook their father's hand, and then they all had dinner together. The father asked them about their lessons and their riding, and then entertained them with stories about the rest of the world, particularly the British Empire. The mother was close to her children, partook of many of their activities, and always went to their rooms to kiss them goodnight.

The nannies bathed the small children in a tub placed near a roaring fireplace on cold days. For the sake of modesty, the children were clad in their undergarments while being washed. As they aged, powder, sachets, and perfumes were added to their personal grooming as awareness of the impropriety of certain body odors among the well-to-do classes was growing. Victoria's mother had strict orders for the servants to bathe once a week, which they would not have done otherwise, for they were afraid that washing would "sicken" them. Victoria recalled that she could recognize people in the dark by their smell.

Victoria had her first menstrual period at 15, a normal age at that time. It was something a young lady was supposed to hide, but all the servants knew about it because of the rags that were worn, then washed or burned. Above all, she recalls how she learned about sex when she was age 14. Late on a long June day, she strolled to the stables to visit her favorite horse. She heard "squeals" and "interesting human movements" and approached silently. She peeked into a stall to see one of the grooms and one of the housemaids in the throes of sexual intercourse: "I had absolutely no idea what was going on but it seemed interesting and it certainly involved physical contact with the opposite sex way beyond what I knew was permissible. But my curiosity was piqued and I began observing the two on a regular basis. Over the course of the summer, what with one question to my sister, another to a cook, another to a parlormaid, I had it all pieced together."

When she was 20, Victoria's parents chose a well-to-do young Frenchman she favored as her husband; the two families had become acquainted during their yearly vacations in France. It was 1890. Apart from cultural differences, her new domestic life closely resembled that of her parents because of social class similarities. But the structure of daily tasks had already begun to change as technological innovations penetrated affluent homes with indoor plumbing and electricity, followed by the telephone, phonograph, cars, and radio. Looking back on her long life, Victoria, then a very old grandmother, felt that these innovations had brought with them new habits, attitudes, tasks, and knowledge that radically changed family life and how children eventually grew up.

COMPARATIVE PERSPECTIVES ON FAMILIES

Victoria Leeds's early life, although characterized by a privileged class position, overlaps in many respects with that of U.S. families of the nineteenth century. Similarities are particularly striking in the domains of gender roles, intimate details of family life, personal grooming, and parental roles. This case study illustrates the importance of analyzing family life within the context of the time period in which it takes place—one of the main goals of this chapter. The historical study of the family uses a comparative approach based on *time*.

But families also differ widely across the world, and the study of these variations represents the comparative perspective based on place and *culture*. For instance, a Saudi Arabian family today is characterized by masculine dominance, male bonding, segregation of the sexes, feminine "invisibility" in public domains, male polygamy among the well-to-do, paternal responsibility but not care of children, and a dress code that is recognized throughout the world. Family life is guided by Muslim precepts and restricted by the geographic necessities of the environment: the desert, the heat, and, until recently, the scarcity of water.

At the opposite extreme are Tahitians, who, like the Saudis, also live in a world wedded to its physical environment: the Pacific Ocean and the mountains. Tahitians' beliefs are a mixture of Christianity and Polynesian ancestral religions. Their educational, legal, and political institutions have been forged by France, under whose rule they live. Tahitians dress sparsely, the sexes mix freely, sexuality is more open, homosexuality and transvestism are not hidden, mother-headed families commonly occur, and much of family life takes place outdoors. The culture contains a complex mixture of masculine and feminine values. Although certain tasks, such as fishing, tend to be carried out by men, there is no great rigidity in the general division of gender roles.

I have chosen these two radically different societies as brief examples to illustrate how culture and physical environment influence family structure and dynamics—all the while keeping in mind that both Saudi Arabia and Tahiti are not completely homogeneous. These countries contain class and local differences and, in the case of Tahitians, differences based on levels of assimilation and island of residence. Nevertheless, both of these societies are poles apart, especially the Saudi, from the way Americans live their family life. In the various chapters of this text, there will be frequent mentions of differences between the United States and other countries, particularly other Western countries, in terms of family life. This comparative approach with other Western nations is particularly useful when discussing social policies, because these countries share a similar economic organization but different political values.

AMERICAN FAMILIES OF THE PAST

Although many of the subsequent chapters present historical overviews of specific aspects of the family, this section provides the broad strokes, or the general outlines, of the history of U.S. families. These families' historical roots are found in several different civilizations.

Multiple Historical Roots

Chronologically, the first set of civilizations belonged to the Natives: They were quite diverse by the time the first colonists arrived. In the South, some Native nations had already been in contact with Spaniards, and in the Northeast, other Native nations had been trading and even intermarried with the French. Much later on, in 1867, Alaskan Natives were included after having been under Russian rule; to this day, many still carry Russian surnames. The second set of historical roots lies in Protestant Europe, particularly England, of the seventeenth century. These British Europeans became the dominant group in American society.

A wide spectrum of African societies, whose members were brought to the U.S. shores in chains, formed the third influence on American family life. The Latinos, ranging from Puerto Rico and then Florida to northern Mexico (which latter became the U.S. Southwest), represented the fourth early cultural group in the formation of the American family. These diverse Latinos were already in place long before the Pilgrims landed at Plymouth Rock. But it is only much later that their territories were annexed by the United States. It is also only toward the end of the nineteenth and early twentieth centuries that other immigrant groups, largely from Europe, began contributing to the landscape of American families. For their part, Hawaiians chronologically constitute one of the last indigenous cultural roots of family life in the United States, although their influence has remained largely localized, both because of conquest and long distance.

Other than the Europeans, the cultural groups are now minorities in the United States. The specific, historical trajectories of their family lives are discussed in Chapters 3 and 7. These trajectories are unique, as they have often been marked differently by the same historical events. For instance, the Civil War carried different implications and consequences for African Americans compared to whites (Burton and Snyder, 1998). Furthermore, the life courses of minority families have been deeply affected by developments among majority families. For example, Franklin (1993) discusses the role that white males played during slavery in African-American families and in the formation of black masculine identity. Although southern white women were affected by this reality even as mothers, overall, the historical causality flowed from whites to minorities. As well, the personal development of slave children was impacted by their situation; for instance, they grew up with the knowledge that they could be sold away from their families. Alston (1992) describes how some black children used to simulate slave auctions in their games.

The Colonial Period

The 20,000 Puritans who arrived from England between 1620 and 1640 brought with them the traditional, nuclear family of father, mother, and children. Their dream was to establish a Godly family based on the teachings of the Bible (Mintz and Kellogg, 1988). Families raised six or seven children who learned to read the scriptures at home and worked together as a unit of production. As the years went by and the colonists aged, grandparents usually resided with one of their adult children. But this extended family system at the household level never constituted the main form of family structure. The reason lies in the fact that life expectancy was low: Relatively few elderly parents survived until all their children were married. Furthermore, elderly parents had many children; thus, when they lived with one, all the others constituted separate nuclear families.

In terms of gender stratification, the colonial society was a masculine one, where women were subordinate to men, particularly their husbands and fathers. Fathers were responsible for the moral character of their children as well as their families' honor (Pleck and Pleck, 1997). They were the primary parent, although mothers were the main caregivers. For instance, it was only in the eighteenth century that mothers replaced fathers in the area of religious instruction (Vinovskis and Frank, 1997). Sexual relationships outside of marriage were condemned but nevertheless occurred and frequently led to legal proceedings (Norton, 1996). When the early moral standards of the small cohesive communities eroded somewhat, masculine infidelity became relatively more acceptable and, in the South, common between white men and slave women (Franklin, 1993). Divorces were granted on a very limited basis (Demos, 1974; Mintz, 1998), but when they were, fathers typically retained custody of children (Cherlin, 1998). Widowed women were regarded as replacing their deceased husbands and so could receive some land and manage their families (Kessler-Davis, 1981).

In the period roughly between 1620 and 1780, before industrialization, adults and children used to participate in the household economy. Families were **units of production,** and much of what they needed was produced at home or in the vicinity. Children contributed from an early age and were regarded as useful and responsible members of the family economy (Hanawalt, 1993; Vinovskis, 1995). Skills were acquired in one's immediate environment; children observed what their parents or host families were doing and learned by imitation as well as direct teaching. Families formed an integral part of their communities; many functions fulfilled by various social agencies today were taken care of at home, particularly education and social control. Fathers were responsible not only for their children's behavior but also for that of their live-in servants as well as slaves (Norton, 1996). Religion was a constitutive element of the family dynamics of these early Americans and was largely a masculine domain.

Families Become More Diverse and Stratified

As the conquest of the vast country moved southward and westward, families began to diversify depending on the geographic location of settlement and the nature of their work. Small cities became stratified along *social class* lines that later extended into the countryside. Social classes then largely consisted of three broad categories of families. In order of importance, they were large merchants and plantation owners, artisans, and the laboring segments of the population (Farber, 1972). At the botton of this stratification system were the slaves. After 1780, with the advent of industrialization, the merchant and landowner class was enlarged by entrepreneurs, and the artisan class expanded to include various types of clerical workers as well as army personnel. The lower class of workers was exploited for its labor. American families were becoming more socially diversified and rigidly stratified, their economic base was evolving, and their lifestyles were becoming more varied.

In poor households, children contributed to their families' economic survival well into the twentieth century. Thus, the social reconstruction of children's role did not reach all social classes simultaneously.

In the eighteenth century, children often left home by the age of 10, particularly in poor families, to become apprentices or even servants. They were incorporated within their host family. In the late nineteenth century until World War II, lodgers became part of the households of the poor, while servants lived in the homes of the more affluent, just as was the case in Victoria Leeds's past. Thus, although the European-American family was always predominantly nuclear rather than extended, the household unit often contained additional, unrelated persons (Laslett, 1971).

The seventeenth- and eighteenth-century family formed an economic unit, generally working together on a farm. The nineteenth-century family, although still predominantly agricultural, became more diversified as production gradually shifted outside the home to an urban landscape of factories and office jobs (Spigel, 1992). Around 1820, the United States witnessed the development of a middle-class ideal where the family became a site of comfort. A distinction was made between the home as a private domain and the public sphere of work, the economy, and politics from which women and children were excluded. The role of the father became less intimate and more externally oriented toward the public domain (Rotundo, 1985).

Industrialization and New Social Definitions

With the rapid growth of industrialization and urbanization in the nineteenth century, the condition and **social definition of childhood** began to change. The new economy no longer needed old forms of child labor, and concerns grew about the working conditions of poor children who toiled 12 hours a day in unsanitary environments. Moreover, romantic definitions of children as naturally innocent combined with the movement to control idle youth in urban areas resulted in a perception of children as needing protection and education (Degler, 1981). A consequence of these social developments resulted in child and adolescent schooling becoming the norm. Farm children as well as many children of immigrants escaped this rule for a long time, however, for they were needed to help their families economically (West, 1992). Thus, the social reconstruction of children did not reach all social classes nor all ethnic groups simultaneously.

The new attitude toward children as objects of emotional gratification rather than coworkers (Zelizer, 1985), as well as the generally declining birth rate among the white middle class, occurred concurrently with a new ideology of domesticity. It was characterized by an emphasis on **intensive mothering** and the privacy of the family (Hareven, 1994b). Mothers were seen as naturally endowed to pursue the moral education of their children and to nurse their sensitivities. Women's role in life was to invest their energies into the care of their children. As a reflection of these social reconstructions, after 1860, children were more frequently placed in their mother's custody following divorce (Grossberg, 1985).

The Twentieth Century

Husbands' and wives' emotional relations and companionship had become more important aspects of marriage by the early 1900s. The division of labor by gender solidified, particularly among the middle class. Mothers were relegated to the **domestic sphere** while fathers became the exclusive breadwinners and their families' representatives in the public domains (Cott, 1977). But again, these developments occurred unevenly throughout the social class system: The working class could not exactly afford to live without the wife's economic contribution, nor could African Americans. Boarders became more common in cities, particularly in immigrant households until the 1940s, in order to supplement families' income. Thus, the separation of the domestic sphere from the public domain was at first a white middle-class phenomenon.

As the nineteenth and twentieth centuries unfolded, most families had become **units of consumption:** Productivity took place elsewhere and basic necessities had to be purchased. Family heads worked for wages or occasionally had an office or business attached to their homes. Working-class children and particularly adolescents continued their contribution to the family economy as wage laborers until the 1920s (Haines, 1985) and on farms until much later (Parr, 1980). White women entered the work force in great numbers during World War II in order to replace men who went abroad as soldiers. But when the war was over, women were encouraged to stay home. This situation lasted until the 1960s, after which women's labor-force participation continued to rise to this day. However, African-American women had long preceded their white counterparts in this respect, as over 40 percent were employed by 1900, and this figure is probably an underestimate (Amott and Matthei, 1991).

Then, in the 1970s, adolescents reentered the work force in part-time jobs in the service sector, in order to acquire discretionary spending money. By 1990, 61 percent of tenth-graders and 90 percent of eleventh- and twelfth-graders worked at some time during the school year (Mortimer and Finch, 1996). By the close of the twentieth century, the requirements of the labor market in terms of education had given rise to two new life stages: that of young adulthood, which stretched adolescent dependence on parents longer, and that of preadolescence, largely the result of consumerism and media influences that sold expensive lifestyles to children. Thus, children became more differentiated along age lines and more isolated from other age groups, including adults.

ARE CHILDREN BECOMING DEFAMILIALIZED?

In addition to becoming more age differentiated, another important change pertaining to children occurred. This change first began with industrialization when the family lost its production function, which was one of its foundations of solidarity and of child integration (Martin, 1997). This change accelerated around 1960 or slightly thereafter in the United States and continues to this day. It resides in the fact that children's lives became more defamilialized. The concept of **defamilialization** was introduced by European sociologists. It refers to the fact that children are increasingly being taken care of by nonfamily members who earn their living doing so. Children spend less and less time at home interacting with their parents and enter care or educational institutions at an earlier age than was the case before the 1980s. Thus, the defamilialization of children is a relatively recent historical development.

North Americans, and for that matter, most people in other societies as well, define children and situate them socially through their families. For instance, a child's social class is that of his or her parents. Furthermore, the family is the child's first and main world. It is the child's first agent of socialization and source of attachment. This combination of factors constitutes what is referred to as the **familialization** of children. However, children's lives take place outside the home more and at an earlier age than before.

Childhood is changing from yet another perspective: It has become more structured. That is, children's lives are more organized, institutionalized, and regimented, and less spontaneous, free ranging, and adult-child interactive than in the past (Adler and Adler, 1998). Institutions such as day care centers, kindergartens, schools, organized extracurricular activities, day and overnight camps, and so on contribute to child socialization, leisure, and experience. Not only do these institutions regiment children's lives into organized time segments, but as the child spends less time within the folds of the family and is increasingly "serviced" by other adults and institutions, he or she becomes defamilialized.

Consequently, children are an important source of economic activities in postindustrial societies because they create childwork. *Childwork* refers to service work done by adults as they care for and educate children as well as organize and control their activities (Oldman, 1994). These adult workers include various teachers as well as day care personnel, social workers, clinicians, and various other child specialists.

Thus, childhood as a structural category creates employment opportunities for adulthood outside of the familial realm. As British sociologist David Oldman (1994) puts it, it is one of the paradoxes of the current economic situation "that parents need non-familial supervision of their own children so they can be paid for providing that non-familial supervision for other children." For instance, parents hire child care workers so that they can become teachers to other adults' children.

Danish sociologist Jens Qvortrup (1995) defines children as useful members of the economy, not only because they create what Oldman calls "childwork" but because children themselves *do work:* Their labor consists of schoolwork. Children participate in the societal division of labor by obtaining a solid education. In preindustrial societies, children were useful like most adults by their manual labor, but today, they are useful by attending school, preparing themselves for their future as citizens, adult workers, and taxpayers. As well, by remaining in school longer, children prevent the large-scale unemployment that would inevitably occur were they to enter the labor market prematurely.

German sociologist Angelika Engelbert (1994) describes children's lives as worlds of differentiation. Not only are children's worlds differentiated because of their class position vis-à-vis other children but children's worlds are also differentiated from those of adults. Children are separated from adults in day care centers, schools, and other supervisory settings. "Children are directly or indirectly excluded from environments that are not specialized to satisfy their needs' [such as the world of adult work and entertainment]" (Engelbert, 1994:289). This exclusion serves to protect the standard of efficiency required in the work environment. It also serves to protect children from the physical and moral dangers of, as well as exploitation by, the adult world. Furthermore, children are actually restricted to their special environments. Within this analytical framework, educational institutions are *institutions of exclusion,* even exclusion of children from their parents' world.

In contrast, children living in the villages of Africa and many Asian countries are fully integrated in the life of the community and in their parents' world, including work that is basically familial. Children learn their adult roles by imitating their parents as they help them. They are totally familialized, even though they may attend the village school. Moreover, these children play in mixed-age groups, the 6-year-olds or 10-year-olds watching over the babies collectively.

Thus, in U.S. society, not only are children segregated into age groups but they are also especially segregated from many of the activities carried out by their parents. As mentioned earlier, this **age segregation** is promoted by consumerism and is often self-chosen and reinforced by the peer culture that has evolved along age lines. For instance, even when they are at home, children may watch different television programs in their rooms or may be served dinner by their mothers rather than sharing in its preparation. Hence, children themselves contribute to their defamilialization which, in North America, is often referred to as the process of **individuation,** a psychological term referring to children's gaining a sense of identity separately from their connection to their parents. Individualism is largely absent as a notion in many more collectivistic societies of the world and even in ethnic groups in the United States that are more oriented toward their families.

THE AUDIOVISUAL MEDIA AND FAMILY LIFE

Perhaps one of the most salient historical developments for society and its families has occurred relatively recently. It resides in the introduction of the audiovisual media, particularly television and the Internet, on the cultural landscape. Major events are now experienced and socially constructed through the prism of the televised media, whether it is the news, sports, talk shows, or sitcoms. At its origins in the 1940s, television represented a mode of "family entertainment" that was to prove radically different from anything in the past. It had no historical precedent in terms of its ability to inform, influence, and structure daily life. Between 1948 and 1955, nearly two-thirds of the nation's homes acquired a television set. By 1960, almost 90 percent had at least one set and, at that point, the average person watched television about five hours a day. An analysis of magazines such as *American Home* and *Better Homes and Gardens* indicates that, by the 1960s, television had replaced the piano in American family rooms (Spigel, 1992).

Television Restructures Family Life

As people watched television, less time became available for the development of skills, such as musical abilities and creative play, and for family entertainment that might involve all the members. Early studies summarized by Andreasen (1994) indicate that, by 1952, 44 percent of families reported that they regularly ate with the television on, which meant less interpersonal exchange during dinner. Families with a television set went to bed later, talked less, and often ate separately while watching different programs at different times. These trends were reinforced in the 1970s and even more so in the 1980s. Television viewing could no longer be considered a form of "family entertainment," as multiple sets were brought in each home. By 1980, 50 percent of families owned at least two sets (Andreasen, 1994). Now, children and particularly middle-class adolescents have their own personal entertainment centers in their bedrooms, where they choose what they want to watch or which video game to play: Television became a solitary activity (Larson, 1995). However, family members who view television together find the experience more pleasant than when they watch it alone (Kubey, 1994).

Nearly all college students today have lived with television, video games, and the Internet. Few know what family life is without these audiovisual media. For most, the comparatively low level of time spent talking and sitting on the porch or in the backyard just enjoying each other's company seems normal. Nevertheless, one can still find students who feel lonely, at times because of a lack of familial time:

> *"One bone of contention in my family at this stage of my life seeing that I still live at home is that everyone is too busy watching television each in their own room, my father and brother with sports . . . my mother with soaps and movies, and I am left alone with my school work because I have no one to talk to."*

> *It really upsets me that my boyfriend is so hooked to sports on TV. I don't know if I can live with that because now with all these channels there is sports every night. We're only in love and he isn't ready to make concessions in this so I won-*

> *der how it will be if we get married. I can't live with a TV set on all the time, it just breaks any attempt to have a regular conversation. Maybe that's what he wants after all. So yes I am a little less than happy right now because I may be in for a nasty surprise. So may be I should split."*

Furthermore, *not a single one* of the writers of the 1,400 or so autobiographies ever mentioned television as a happy salient recollection in his or her past life. In contrast, most placed their parents in this category as well as their friends. In other words, television fills time but it does not create happiness. It can also create tension and an interpersonal void, as illustrated in the preceding quotes.

The Family on Television: A Historical Overview

The first television show geared to children, *Howdy Doody,* ran from 1947 to 1960, and with it, the debate about the effect of television on children began and has continued to this day (Wilcox and Kunkel, 1996). It has not, however, been accompanied to the same extent by debates over the impact of television on adults and on family life, although the research done for advertising and marketing firms indicates strong media effects on adult lifestyles and even beliefs as well as on family life. *Howdy Doody* also marked the beginning of the impact of audiovisual advertising on children (Stark, 1997:18).

Situation comedies, or sitcoms, as a lasting form of television entertainment for the entire family began with *I Love Lucy* in 1951. This was also the first show with a woman as its superstar. Except for sports and newscasts, women are the prime television audience, and the orientation of Lucille Ball's show around themes that concern couples, and particularly wives, contributed to women's devotion to this medium. A little later, *Leave It to Beaver* became the family show par excellence. It ran from 1957 through 1963 and represented the ideal American family: white, middle-class, a working father, a stay-at-home mother, and two sons. The program was child centered; that is, it offered a perspective on family life from a child's point of view. Not only did *Leave It to Beaver* become a cultural icon in later decades when the American family had changed from the idealized type of the 1950s but it also set the stage for the nostalgia of what Stephanie Coontz called, *The Way We Never Were* (1992).

The public, but particularly women, were used to soap operas, as these had long been a staple of radio programming. Therefore, it is not surprising that television adopted this genre (soaps) early on in the 1960s, such as *As the World Turns* and *Peyton Place.* These melodramas generally ran during the afternoons, which meant that they largely targeted a feminine audience. The programs included a mixture of largely traditional gender roles and family life, on the one hand, with powerful examples of sexually liberated women on the other hand. Others soon followed: *All My Children, The Young and the Restless, The Bold and the Beautiful, Dallas,* and *General Hospital,* among many (Walters, 1999).

The soap or melodrama genre is very particular. Although the plots generally revolve around couples or families, the children who are born are not especially nurtured; in fact, they soon disappear, generally resurfacing only when they are old enough to be wrapped up in romantic dramas of their own. Children's daily lives are not presented, thereby giving the impression that children inhibit passion and excitement. These shows contain many weddings, love triangles, breakups, and more adopted children than exist in reality (Wegar, 1997). Soaps focus on feelings, melodrama, and talk. They present a sharp contrast with real-life families, which is their attraction, as they allow women an escape from domestic reality.

Sesame Street, which has been running on the Public Broadcasting Service (PBS) since late 1969, is watched by over half of the nation's 12 million children between the ages of 3 and 5 (Stark, 1997). This program emphasizes the acceptance of differences based on ethnicity, as well as values of cooperation and environmentalism. It is devoid of commercialism, violence, and sex. Its goal is to provide skills to help prepare children for school, and research shows that children from varied backgrounds do learn by watching it (Children's Television Workshop, 1991). Accordingly, *Sesame Street* is highly appreciated by parents of all ethnic groups, many of whom grew up with it. It complements parents' role as educators, it does not conflict with family values, and it does not antagonize religious groups. However, the program has surprisingly little to do with family life; for instance, characters such as Big Bird have no parents and neither do the child guests.

Another family-related show that has remained popular, mainly through reruns, is *The Brady Bunch* (1969–1974). Its cast consisted of a widow with three girls who marries a widower with three boys. Like *Leave It to Beaver,* the young actors provided a child's view of the world and child-sized problems. Any child between 6 and 12 years of age could identify with a same-age character, as there were offspring of various ages in this television family. This reconstituted family anticipated the coming wave of real-life stepparenting situations created by divorce, which may explain why reruns of *The Brady Bunch* have remained popular: The show offers a rather pleasant formula for reconstituted families, a safe refuge for those whose families had failed to be so successful.

In the 1970s, *The Mary Tyler Moore Show* represented a turning point in sitcoms—it focused on single adults, particularly in the workplace. Families were not involved, and this in itself was an interesting perspective, especially in view of the fact that the main character, Mary Richards, was a woman. The U.S. Commission on Civil Rights (1977) found that, in the period between 1969 and 1972, almost one-half of the female characters portrayed on television were married, yet less than one-third of the males were. At about the same time, McNeil (1975) revealed that 74 percent of the female interactions on television took place within the context of problems associated with romance and family, compared to only 18 percent of male interactions. Thus, *The Mary Tyler Moore Show* was overcoming many gender stereotypes. For the first time, work was shown as salient in the life of a woman—albeit a single woman, not a married one with children—just as more and more women were entering the labor force.

The Cosby Show, running from 1984 to 1992, represented another milestone, as it introduced a black family headed by two professional parents. Although the family came closer to approximating a two-paycheck family than any other show had done before, traditional values were emphasized. In the mid-eighties, it was still quite unusual to think of a black family as well-to-do and stable. Thus, the racial context was an important element in its success. It was also probably the first national sitcom with which black families could identify, at least in terms of race if not necessarily lifestyle.

The last sitcom to be mentioned here is *Roseanne,* which began in 1988: a blue-collar family, a hard-working mother, three kids, loud-mouthed parents, and issues of teen sex, among others. *Roseanne* also departed from the usual tendency of representing the feminine body in terms of slimness (Fouts and Burggraf, 1999). All these factors combined reflected changes in the depiction of family life. Parents and children alike could be unpleasant creatures! Deplorable aspects of family life were also being reflected in the many talk shows that began appearing in the mid to late eighties, such as *Donahue, The Oprah Winfrey Show, Jenny Jones, Geraldo, Sally Jesse Raphael,* and so on. These programs placed the spotlight on the self-disclosure of what could be called deviances and dysfunctions, with much sex and vulgarity thrown in for good measure (Fox, 1999).

> *A July 1999 episode of* Ricki Lake *had four teen mothers learn who their babies' fathers were: DNA results were revealed on the show. Participants included willing and unwilling young prospective fathers, a mother, an aunt, and two teen "stepmoms" attached to the putative fathers. One teenage girl learned that neither of the two putative fathers were her baby's father and tears welled in her eyes. There was much arguing and swearing between the parties, even involving some of the adults, with the audience taking sides.*

The therapy session format is often utilized in these shows, although one wonders what happens to these couples and families after they leave and return home to face the repercussions of the confessions made on stage. The previously mentioned *Ricki Lake* show was particularly problematic in this respect because of the participants' young ages, their lack of maturity, and their obvious temperamental fragility. One does not need to be a sociologist to be concerned about the future of the babies that were behind these family revelations and quarrels played out on national television.

Effects of Family-Related Programs on Children

One must look at the form and contents of televised programs to understand how they influence family members and particularly children. Weiss and Wilson's (1996) analysis of the emotional contents of family sitcoms applies to soap operas, as well: It reveals that negative emotions, such as fear and anger, are more prominent than either positive or neutral emotions. Negative emotions "sell" better. This can lead children to believe that "real" family life (i.e., their family life) should be more dramatic because what they see on television is like that. However, the negative emotions expressed by television family members are largely ignored by the other characters in the play. This may further suggest to "a child viewer that negative feelings are unimportant to other family members" (Weiss and Wilson, 1996:19). Although children can learn that conflict is generally resolved, it is done quickly at the end of the show. Children may then expect fast resolutions in their own lives. On the positive side, they can learn to use humor to solve interpersonal problems.

Family sitcoms are among young children's (ages 2 to 11) favorite programs, perhaps in part because they portray or include a range of child actors (Weiss and Wilson, 1996). Young children can identify with these child characters and often view the world from the optic lens of these programs. For instance, Dorr, Kovaric, and Doubleday (1990) find that children aged 6 to 16 perceive approximately half of the families in America to be like the families in their favorite television series. For children, the real world should look like the world on television, because children see more about the world, as commercially constructed, on screen than in real life. In one night, a child can "visit" 10 virtual families, but in real life, that child belongs to only one. Not surprisingly, children often want to behave or be like the characters portrayed in the sitcoms (Austin, Roberts, and Nass, 1990). All in all, children think of these sitcoms as closer to reality, and children's retention of emotional information is higher from family sitcoms than from cartoon or muppet programs (Hayes and Casey, 1992).

In a study on children's imaginary or wishful identifications with favorite television characters, nearly all the boys chose male characters as favorites, and about half the girls chose females. When male characters were chosen, the children aged 7 to 12 reported identifying with them because of the characters' intelligence as well as humor, although attractive males were also selected. Female characters were chosen as objects of identification only on the basis of their attractiveness (Hoffner, 1996).

The Evolution of Sexual Contents and Effects on Adolescents

At another level, Lowry and Towles (1989) compared the sexual contents in soap operas in 1979 and 1987. They found that there were more episodes depicting sexual behaviors per hour in 1987 than in 1979—and, I might add, more now than in 1987! An increase was also seen in sexual behaviors between unmarried rather than married characters. The researchers concluded that the 1987 contents gave the following messages:

- Nonmarital sex is the most exciting.
- Spontaneous sex is very romantic, especially between unmarried persons, and carries no consequences.
- All unmarried people engage in sex, and promiscuity is the norm rather than the exception.
- Unplanned pregnancy and sexually transmitted diseases (STDs) are not presented and therefore cannot be a problem related to sex.

Sapolsky and Tabarlet (1991) also found that the majority of sexual action and language depicted on television involved unmarried characters. All in all, it may not be surprising that adults who are heavy soap-opera watchers believe that there is more sex among single than married persons and even that there are far more doctors and lawyers than actually exist. In contrast, the responses of adults who only occasionally watch such programming are far closer to reality.

On a related issue, Bryant and Rockwell (1994) have found that early adolescents who watch many programs in which nonmarital sex is involved develop a more lenient attitude toward sexual improprieties. They also judge victims of sexual infidelities and wrongdoings as having been less harmed than do two control groups. One control group had watched little television, and the other had watched only television programs involving marital sex.

The evidence is mounting to the effect that children interpret media presentations as a source of information. For many children, and even adults, television has become what the critical sociologist Habermas (1987:16) called an insulating expertise that splits children off from "the context of everyday practice" and leads to cultural impoverishment. Although children are active social actors and participate in the reconstruction of the messages they receive from the media, they can be empowered to gain a realistic perspective. However, this can be done only to the extent that the real world around them, particularly their families and their peers, offers them this alternative.

Children and Television Violence

Much of the research concerning television has been devoted to the effect of violence on the development of aggressiveness. For instance, the average child has witnessed well over 8,000 murders on television by the end of elementary school (Waters, 1993). The first studies in the 1960s and even the 1970s established that the more violence children watched, the more aggressive were their behaviors on average (Liebert and Sprafkin, 1988). For a while, it was believed that aggressive boys selected programs that were more violent—an explanation that is certainly valid to some extent—just as peaceful people are often repelled by violence and therefore refuse to watch it (Friedrich-Cofer and Huston, 1986).

In the 1980s, researchers began to harvest the results of longitudinal studies and found that young adults who tended to act more aggressively had watched more violence as 8-year-olds. In fact, the linkage between adult aggressiveness and childhood viewing of violence on television was even stronger than it had been at age 8. Boys who had *not* been aggressive at age 8, but who had watched more television violence, had become more aggressive young adults than a similar group of nonaggressive boys who had watched fewer episodes of violence (Huesmann et al., 1984). Such results indicate that it is not only a predilection for aggressiveness that leads children to select television violence but that this violence also leads to aggressiveness. By age 30, men who had watched more television violence as children had, on average, been convicted of more serious crimes, were more likely to treat their children harshly, and were more aggressive when drunk than men who had watched fewer violent programs as youngsters (Huesmann, 1986).

In an intriguing study (further described by MacBeth in Family Research 2.1) Joy, Kimball, and Zabrack (1986) compared three Canadian towns, one of which did not receive television transmission until 1974. The researchers tested the children before the introduction of television and two years after. The children in the town that had received television two years earlier showed a substantial increase in aggressiveness that was not observed among the youngsters in the other two towns. They also exhibited a sharp increase in sex-role stereotyping (Kimball, 1986).

Television violence may foster aggressiveness in a proportion of children, and later in adults, via several possible routes. First, violence may teach children that conflict can be resolved only with verbal or physical aggressiveness. Second, it may teach children to develop a lower threshold for frustration, so that they tolerate irritants less easily and react to them more explosively. Third, television violence, and perhaps more so video game violence, may desensitize children and adults as to the severity of its consequences, so that even killing can appear routine. In fact, killing *is* the goal in video games. Furthermore, children learn *how* to punch, kick, and kill via these programs and videos.

In a large study of eighth-graders across the United States, Muller and Kerbow (1993) found that, during weekdays, African-American parents restricted television less than other groups, including Asian Americans and whites. As we soon see in Chapters 3 and 7, a disproportionate segment of black families live in poor neighborhoods with high rates of criminality. Thus, children in these districts are subjected to real-life

FAMILY RESEARCH 2.1

Experimenting with Real-Life Situations to Determine Causality

In the fall of 1973, Tannis MacBeth (1998) initiated a study on the effect of television on children. She creatively exploited a naturally occurring social situation: At that time, a Canadian town, renamed Notel, was to receive television transmission for the first time. Notel was not isolated but was located in a valley, which prevented transmission. A nearby town, called Unitel, had already been receiving one Canadian channel for seven years, and a third town, called Multitel, had been receiving several U.S. channels in addition to a Canadian one for about 15 years. Notel (no television) became the experimental town; Unitel (one channel) and Multitel (several channels) became the two control towns. In Phase 1, in 1973, students in grades 4 and 7 from the three towns were tested on a wide range of behaviors and skills. In a longitudinal design, they were retested two years later (Phase 2), when in grades 6 and 9, to measure the effects of television. In order to rule out maturation or growing up influences, additional students in grades 4 and 7 were also included in Phase 2.

violence as well as violence on television and video games (Myers, 2000). This combination represents a potentially dangerous socialization experience.

Whenever experts give conferences on these issues, they unavoidably remind the public that parents have to exercise control over what children view, and that they should discuss potentially detrimental programs with children. The entertainment industry follows suit and shamelessly places the entire responsibility on parents' shoulders—one more family function. How this responsibility affects parents and their relationship with their children is not addressed. At least one observational study has shown that, in a supermarket, 65 percent of all parents' refusals to buy food items advertised on television instantly resulted in parent/child conflict or arguments (Atkin, 1978). Frequently seeing such occurrences in public places, one can only wonder about the level of conflict that takes place in the privacy of the home when parents attempt to curtail television viewing (Alexander, 1994:52).

The New Cultural Revolution: The Internet

Close to 50 percent of U.S. households have a personal computer and at least 30 percent are connected to the Internet—and these statistics change monthly and are certainly outdated by the time this book is printed (NTIA, 1998). Of course, far more individuals have *access* to the Internet, whether at school, at work, or in libraries. Computers and the Internet are now considered to be such a key economic feature and such a potent cultural influence that, in 1999, the journal *Family Relations* initiated a special section on the effect of information technology on family life.

There are indications that the use of the computer displaces television to some extent (Kohut, 1994). As is the case with television, the Internet also contains many dangers. First, it is far from an unmitigated blessing in terms of providing reliable information, because it is generally mixed with advertising and it is often difficult to assess the origin and accuracy of the information presented on websites (Hansell and Harmon, 1999). Indeed, anyone can create a website and pass on erroneous and misleading information that will be accepted as factual, for far too many people believe in the power of the Internet to inform accurately. Second, it is estimated that there are thousands of websites throughout the world with pedophilic and pornographic contents. The exploitation of children becomes more widespread because the Internet is not easily policed. Furthermore, adult pornographic websites are so easily accessible to children and adolescents that some schools have had to monitor closely the use that their students make of the Internet during class time. Finally, the 1998 and 1999 school massacres, especially in Littleton, Colorado, have awakened the public's consciousness about websites that, for example, allow anyone to learn how to manufacture bombs.

What does the Internet do in terms of family life? So far, the only reliable, although limited, study on the topic is that of Kraut and colleagues (1998). Their longitudinal research includes 73 households with 231 participating individuals who were tested at Time 1 when given a computer and free Internet access. Time spent on the Internet was recorded automatically. The individuals were tested on well-being and social involvement first and then again after one to two years of Internet use (Time 2).

The authors found that greater use of the Internet was related to a small but noticeable increase in depression, stress, and loneliness, with a concurrent decrease in family participation and size of one's real social network. Teenagers were more affected than adults in terms of loneliness and social support. However, several of these teenagers' parents believed that the Internet had had a positive outcome on their offsprings' education and that this advantage outweighed the decline in their social interactions. On the positive side, there were many families that took advantage of e-mail to keep in touch with their children in college and other relatives, and teenagers who exchanged messages with their classmates after school. As well, some parents have recourse to the Internet in order to find information about various aspects of family life, including parenting (Morris, Dollahite, and Hawkins, 1999).

Internet use is an even more individualistically oriented activity than television. It follows that extensive Internet exposure by family members, often in their own separate bedrooms/studies, may contribute to lack of interaction and a loss of communication skills. The Internet segments people as well as family members into interest groups and consequently prevents the growth of a sense of membership in a real community constituted of diverse individuals (Calhoun, 1998). But when properly used, the Internet also constitutes both a social (interaction) and a cultural (access to knowledge) resource. As with other types of resources in a stratified society, access to the Internet is still a privilege reserved to those who can afford it. This has been called the "digital divide" between those families that are information rich and those that are information poor (Hughes, Ebata, and Dollahite, 1999). Soon there will be repercussions on the ability of poor children to succeed at school and particularly to find jobs later on because of this additional divide. The next few years will indicate the direction the Internet is taking culturally and the type of use family members will make of it.

FAMILY CHANGE OR DECLINE? THE DEBATE

The contents and dynamics of family life have evolved considerably over the centuries and again since the mid-1950s. As well, since the 1950s, the structure or form of the family has changed dramatically, including substantial increases in births to single mothers, increases in the divorce rate, and increases in the advent of same-sex-parent families. Such changes occurring in an institution as basic to the foundation of society as the family raise warning flags of impending doom. It is therefore not surprising that there is a great deal of concern over family values and family decline expressed by religious leaders, by politicians during campaigns, in public opinion polls, and among scientists. On one side of the debate is the issue that the family as an institution is perceived to be in decline and in the process of losing its functions.

Is it? The answer to this question rests in great part on readers' values. U.S. society is heterogeneous and includes a wide range of opinions. Those who are morally opposed to same-sex couples and unwed births see these types of family structure as representing a decline in family values and in the ability of families to function adequately. However, those on the other side of the debate simply celebrate family change, particularly what they see as the liberation of women, children, and gays.

These debates have appeared in scholarly books as well as in the *Journal of Marriage and the Family* and *Family Relations*. Morality and religious beliefs are not the question of this chapter and cannot be disposed of respectfully within the confines of a few pages. These are not matters that can always be debated constructively without giving rise to bruised feelings. However, there are more easily analyzable aspects of the debate and so I begin with the much heralded loss of family functions.

Has the Family Lost Its Functions?

There is no doubt that the family has lost some of its functions if one compares today's situation with that of the preindustrial period. As Hareven (1994a:41) states, in those days, "the family not only reared children but also served as workshop, a school, a church, and a welfare agency. Preindustrial families meshed closely with the community and carried a variety of public responsibilities within the larger society." But society has evolved immensely since and the family adapted to this evolution. Many of the functions it has given up, such as training workers, were tied to a specific type of economic and technological tradition that has vanished long ago. Thus, these familial functions are no longer necessary for the survival of society and for the success of family members.

The Family's Functions: More Gains than Losses

A fact that is evident throughout this text yet one that is often overlooked is that the family has acquired other functions (Gubrium and Holstein, 1990). Above all, the family has become more specialized in certain domains. Furthermore, it is recapturing some traditional ones as the social safety net and social policies fail to care for society's most vulnerable members, particularly its children and elderly.

1. The family has retained its **reproductive** function. It is true that a large proportion of children are born to single mothers (Chapter 5). However, this nonmarital sexual reproduction serves as the foundation to a family form: the mother-headed nuclear family through which the child is reproduced culturally and socially.
2. The **socialization** of children still begins within the family. Other institutions soon complement parents or even take over this role in some domains.
3. Thus, another family function emerges: Parents become the coordinators of the education and the services that their children receive from various institutions.

Thus, the family has acquired the function of **coordination** or **management:** Parents must make the extrafamilial environment (whether schools, child care, or the media) accessible to and safe for their children. They must interpret these contexts to their children within the perspective of their own values.

4. By the same token, the family prevents the fragmentation of its young members' lives that would unavoidably occur in view of the numerous and often conflicting sources of socialization to which children are subjected. The family serves as an agency of **psychological stabilization** while providing a sense of identity and **belongingness,** particularly for its children.
5. The family fulfills many *affective* needs. It is within its boundaries that young children learn to love and be loved, where attachment first develops, where trust is built. The family is one of the prime movers in **personality development** for children and adults alike. The combination of the other functions described thus far means that parents contribute to the development of their children's personalities via the home environment they provide and the neighborhood into which they move. When adults become parents, their personality development continues as they extend themselves into this new role. However, the family shares this function with a person's genetic background and with other social systems, such as schools, work, and the peer group.
6. The family continues to **shelter** its members (housing), to attend to their basic nutritional needs, and to ensure their physical **health** according to their means.
7. The family still contributes to confer to its members their **place** within the social stratification or economic system, at least until children are old enough to be on their own.
8. A significant number of families provide the entire **special care** needed by their children who are intellectually, psychiatrically, or physically challenged and, in some cases, by frail elderly parents.

Many families fulfill additional functions for their members, depending on their means, social class position, racial/ethnic membership, religion, and citizenship status. This will become particularly obvious in subsequent chapters. For instance, some families are the center of worship and religious education and some provide at-home schooling. Others continue to serve as the center of leisure activities, both for their children and adult members. Amish families are a good example in this respect (Hostetler, 1993). Many families, particularly on farms and among owners of small enterprises, still form a unit of production: They train, employ, and pay their members. Finally, immigrant families serve important functions for their members, as many subsidize the immigration of their kin and support their resettlement to the United States.

Can All Families Equally Fulfill Their Functions?

In short, the American family, in general, is not always a haven and is far from being a perfect institution, but the functions that it fulfills cover an amazing range of personal, social, cultural, and economic needs. As imperfect and at times limping as it is, the American family still does better and more than any other social institution for its members. Actually, the term *family functions* is somewhat of a misnomer in the sense that *parents* are responsible for most functions.

The concern over the so-called decline in family functions is probably the result of an analytical and social policy misunderstanding: equating *individual* families' inability or failure to fulfill certain functions to a loss of functions by the family as an **institution** (Stacey, 1996). People correctly observe that more children are delinquent, problematic, unhappy, and in foster care than was the case 20 years ago. But the error begins when this is seen as a failure of *the* family as an institution rather than of individual families. The fact is that the family as an institution is burdened by functions while at the same time more individual families fail at these than in the past. Families are more unstable structurally, more isolated socially, and less well supported by other institutions at the cultural, economic, and political levels. Economic deprivation, segregation, social isolation, singlehood, and members' personality deficiencies are among the elements that prevent individual families from fulfilling their functions adequately. Most of these are socially driven problems, not family-produced ones. The structural conclusion is that the family as an institution certainly requires far more assistance from other institutions to fulfill its numerous functions adequately. If this assistance was forthcoming at the institutional level, most individual families would benefit and fewer would fail in this respect.

Are Traditional Family Values Necessarily under Attack?

Sociologists look at two other cultural as well as political realities concerning family change in American society. First, in an individualistic, democratic society, everyone is entitled to his or her religious and moral beliefs about family life. Except for abusing one's children or one's partner, or practicing polygamy, an *individualistic democracy* in North America ensures families' rights to live their lives and their relationships according to their personal beliefs (Glendon, 1989). But this *democratic right* of families also presumes an obligation: the tolerance of the different ways and values of other families.

This leads us to the second reality: the diversity of family life in the postmodern era (Stacey, 1996). Not only are there more divorces today than in 1950 (but less than in the mid-1980s), more children living in stepfamilies, and more babies born to single mothers, but same-sex couples are now raising and even reproducing children. A new wave of immigration has also contributed to further diversity in the familial landscape. Nevertheless, these culturally and structurally diverse families not only fulfill similar functions but also share some common concerns, such as the desire to see their children do well and, for many, the hope that they will have a better life than their parents—all cherished American values.

Concerns over Same-Sex-Parent Families

The movement among homosexuals and lesbians to form families and be recognized legally and religiously as couples involves two ideological contradictions. One is internal to the development of the homosexual community, whereas the other exists in the society at large. First, in recent history, particularly in the 1970s and 1980s, the gay and lesbian cultures were countercultures. They rejected motherhood and natality as well as traditional family values. Some of their banners read "Smash the Family" and "Smash Monogamy" (Stacey, 1998:17). This rejection of tradition was

A structural-functional analysis suggests that society would benefit if all family types were equally supported. Children in same-sex-parent families need stability and security, as do other children, in order to grow up to become functional members of society.

particularly strident among radical, feminist lesbians. In the midst of this rejection, a movement toward integration within the *mainstream family culture* emerged, with a focus on stable couple formation and family life. The movement's current family policy goals include legal marriage and legal rights for the nonbiological parent.

The second contradiction that surrounds same-sex parenting stems from the fact that, although many gays and particularly lesbians are becoming more pro-family and pro-marriage—values that average citizens cherish—this cultural conversion has been largely rejected by the rest of society. Gay and lesbian families are often stigmatized as abnormal and immoral and the parents are denied the right to marry at a time when concerns are raised about the decline of marriage.

A structural-functionalist analysis could suggest that the collective good requires tolerating other forms of families and fostering a cultural and policy climate within which all types of families can successfully fulfill their functions—that is, get on with the business of leading healthy lives and raising responsible citizens. A battle of family types is a no-win situation within the multicultural context of the new millennium, as it will simply create social problems and economic burdens for the entire society down the road.

Should It Be a Different Debate?

It could be suggested that the debate over "family decline," the "loss of family functions," and "the erosion of family values" should be refocused (Gubrium and Holstein, 1990). Perhaps it could be oriented toward asking why is it that a culture that can afford to spend billions in exploring outer space cannot afford to sustain its families that are more fragile or are at risk of so becoming?

While most sociologists are not particularly concerned about the diversification of family forms—that is, about the various arrangements of parents and children along with kin—there are clear indications, as we see in Chapter 5, that certain types of family structures are more vulnerable than others and fail to fulfill their institutional functions. For instance, in many families, one of the two parents, usually the father, has abdicated his responsibilities. At this point, the further away one goes from marriage, the lower the paternal investment (Seltzer, 1998): Paternal involvement diminishes after divorce and becomes particularly lacking in never-married families.

Hence, sociologists are concerned that certain types of family structures are not sufficiently supported by the economy and society in general. This lack of support leads to socialization failures and thus problematic life courses for children and for never-married, mother-headed families (Coley and Chase-Lansdale, 1998). One can also be concerned about the consequences for same-sex-parent families' ability to stay together and to nurture their children because of a lack of legal and social support (Kurdek, 1998). Such unions are not scaffolded by laws and this lack of legal structure contributes to their instability. Lack of support stigmatizes the children and could be detrimental to these parents' ability to fulfill ordinary family functions.

CONCLUSIONS: THE PACE OF CHANGE

Family life was relatively stable for centuries and then began to change in several aspects following industrialization. After that, the pace of change accelerated with technological innovations and the economic restructuring they heralded. By the last decades of the twentieth century, unplanned change may well have occurred too rapidly for the good of the family as an institution. As a result, although the family has been replaced for some of its old functions, such as the schooling of its children, it suddenly inherited a stockpile of new functions and responsibilities. Unfortunately, this pileup took place at the same time as drastic changes were occurring in family structure. These changes have actually reduced the number of adults or parents available to children, thus diminishing many families' ability to fulfill their functions adequately, particularly in terms of child socialization. For instance, a single mother who lacks adequate economic and social resources is likely to encounter far more difficulties in keeping her small family running smoothly than a two-parent family with a reasonable income.

A corresponding, major problem has been occurring along with accelerated changes in technology and family structure. It resides in the fact that the government has failed to plan or even keep up with change. Political institutions have failed to create social policies favorable to families of all types as well as policies protecting families, particularly children, against the potentially harmful impacts of technology. One could think here in terms of the structure of the work week and the workplace, the relative lack of child care centers, and the noxious contents of the media. But one can also think in terms of failure to assist near-poor and poor families, a topic frequently emphasized in this text.

SUMMARY

1. The historical roots of U.S. families are found in several different civilizations, from Natives, English colonialists, African Americans, Latinos, and Hawaiians.

What was to become the foundation of the mainstream American family began with the arrival of the Puritans in 1620, who brought the traditional nuclear family of father, mother, and children. The family was then a unit of production, with all members participating from an early age. Fathers were responsible for their wives, children, and servants. As the country expanded, families began to diversify, particularly after the advent of industrialization, and later on in the nineteenth century after the rapid growth of urbanization and wage labor. The definition of children began to change toward one of protection and objects of love, rather than coworkers. The social construction of motherhood slowly evolved toward one of intensive mothering and staying at home to raise children. Families were then transformed into units of consumption as productivity took place outside the home. In the twentieth century, schooling became mandatory, the birth rate declined, adolescence was invented, and mothers began entering the workforce in large numbers beginning in the late 1960s. Later on, adolescents began joining the workforce part time while in school, and young adulthood and preadolescence were created as social categories.

2. Children spend more time outside of their families and have become defamilialized. Childhood has become more structured in terms of activities than in the past. Children produce "childwork"—that is, work that adults do to educate them and organize their activities. Thus, children are useful to society via their schoolwork and the childwork they produce for the employment of adults. But children in industrialized nations are separated from adults, whereas in nonindustrialized societies, they are fully integrated in village life and their parents' work and they are totally familialized in contrast to a high level of defamilialization in many Western countries.

3. An important historical development took place at the cultural level as nearly two-thirds of the nation's homes acquired a television set between 1948 and 1955. As people watched television, less time became available for the development of certain skills and family sociability. A historical overview of the trends in television programming pertaining to family life and norms highlights the changes in the contents of programs as the decades went by. Family sitcoms are among young children's favorite programs, as they can identify with the child characters. For adolescents particularly, the tone and depiction of sexual contents in soap operas has changed and carries messages favoring nonmarital sex.

4. Television violence is well documented. Research also indicates that it can contribute to child and even later on adulthood aggressiveness. This is particularly problematic for disadvantaged children who live in high-poverty areas, as they tend to watch more television and are also exposed to more real-life violence.

5. The Internet, the latest cultural revolution, contains both positive and negative seeds in terms of child socialization and family relations. It can lead to an increase in social isolation and lack of family participation. The Internet is an even more individualistically oriented activity than television viewing is.

6. The debate over the so-called decline of the family centers on structural changes and loss of functions. But, although the family has lost a few traditional functions, it has gained a number of new ones. Its main functions are those of reproducing,

socializing the child, coordinating and managing external services children receive, stabilizing personalities, meeting affective needs, and providing a sense of belongingness, health care, a place to live, and care of family members who have special needs. However, too many individual families are unable to fulfill their functions, which should not be taken to mean a loss of functions by the family as an institution.

7. Families are changing in the sense that more are divorced, single-parent, and same-sex-parent families. Same-sex-parent families present two ideological contradictions. One is internal to the homosexual community and represents a movement away from a radical past toward the acceptance of traditional family life (i.e., a two-parent family). The second contradiction resides in that this pro-family stance is largely rejected by those in the population who are themselves very pro-family.
8. Sociologists are generally concerned that certain types of family structure are not sufficiently supported by the economy and the polity. Another concern is the potentially negative impact of the rapid pace of technological change.

KEY CONCEPTS AND THEMES

Age segregation, p. 37
Childwork, p. 36
Comparative approach, p. 31
Defamilialization of children, p. 36
Definition of childhood, p. 34
Development of aggressiveness, p. 43
Domestic sphere, p. 35
Familialization of children, p. 36
Family decline, p. 46
Fulfillment of family functions, p. 47
Individualistic democracy, p. 48
Individuation, p. 37
Industrialization, p. 34
Intensive mothering, p. 35
Internet, p. 44
Loss of family functions, p. 46
Pace of change, p. 50
Same-sex-parent families, p. 48
Sexual contents of television, p. 42
Social class, p. 33
Television, p. 38
Unit of consumption, p. 35
Unit of production, p. 33
Violence on television, p. 43

STUDY AND REVIEW QUESTIONS

1. What are the two dimensions of the comparative approach to the study of the family?
2. What are the multiple cultural roots of families in the United States?
3. Differentiate the American family of the colonial period from that which came after industrialization, say in the nineteenth century.
4. What is meant by the *defamilialization* of children?
5. What are some of the changes that have marked the development of television programming since its beginning? Add others you can think of that are not included in the text.
6. In the past, longitudinal studies have shown that television can lead to aggressiveness in some children. Why might it be more difficult methodologically to do similar studies today?
7. How does the Internet affect family life? What are the differences with television in this respect?

8. Has the family lost its functions? Justify your answer.
9. Why should a distinction be made between the family as an institution and individual families?
10. Place same-sex-parent families within the debate about family values.

SUGGESTED READINGS

Bird, G. W., and Sporakowski, M. J. (Eds.). 1994. *Taking sides: Clashing views on controversial issues in family and personal relationships.* Guilford, CT: Dushkin. This collection of articles presents opposite perspectives on various issues pertaining to family life and intimate relationships.

Blankenhorn, D., Bayme, S., and Elshtain, J. B. (Eds.). 1990. *Rebuilding the nest: A new commitment to the American family.* Milwaukee, WI: Family Service America. This collection of articles presents a variety of viewpoints on the current condition of the American family, on what ails it, and on what some solutions might be.

Norton, M. B. 1996. *Founding mothers and fathers: Gendered power and the forming of American society.* New York: Knopf. The author presents a well-documented historical account of the colonial period with a focus on family and community organizations along patriarchal lines.

Popenoe, D., Elshtain, J. B., and Blankenhorn, D. (Eds.). 1996. *Promises to keep: Decline and renewal of marriage in America.* Lanham, MD: Rowman & Littlefield. This collection of articles focuses on the decline of marriage and its perceived effects. It includes religious and legal dimensions. An entire section contains suggestions for rebuilding a marriage culture.

Stacey, J. 1996. *In the name of the family: Rethinking family values in the postmodern era.* Boston: Beacon Press. The focus here is on the postmodern family, with change and diversity as key characteristics. The author responds to critiques of family change and recognizes the instability inherent to current structural arrangements. She makes some interesting points concerning gay and lesbian families.

Van Enra, J. 1998. *Television and child development.* Mahwah, NJ: Erlbaum. This book presents a balanced review of the domain as well as some theoretical perspectives.

Zillman, D., Bryant, J., and Huston, A. C. (Eds.). 1994. *Media, children, and the family.* Hillsdale, NJ: Erlbaum. This is a collection of research and review articles on various aspects of family life related to television consumption, including some information on the effect on family interaction. The effect of television contents on children is also examined.

SUGGESTED WEBLINKS

Canadian Families Project provides some information about the historical approach to the study of families. **<http://web.uvic.ca/hrd/cfp>**

Children Now: The goal of this site is to improve the quality of news and entertainment both for children and about children. **<http://www.childrennow.org>**

Electronic Policy Network is a collection of member organizations that focus on policy and research concerning the Web. Click on *Media.* **<http://tap.epn.org/cms>**

SafeSurfer: This site provides information on how to make the Internet safer for children and to improve the quality of programming in the media. **<http://www.safesurf.com/>**

CHAPTER 3

Family Diversity and Adaptation

Immigration and Minority-Group Status

Immigrant Families
Immigrant Families' Diversity
Immigrant Families' Adjustment: The Environmental Constraints
Immigrant Generations
Intergenerational Conflict
Intergenerational Continuity

Native-American Families
Native Families: Diversity and Adaptation
Sources of Poverty among Native Families
Native Intermarriage and Family Types

African-American Families
Single Motherhood and Marriage: A Historical Perspective
Impacts of Prejudice, Discrimination, and Segregation
Middle-Class Families
Residence Problems of Middle-Class Families
The Contrasting Networks of Black Families
School-Related Problems
Residential Mobility
Discrimination

Latino-American Families
Mexican-American Families
Generations and Fertility
Types of Extended Families
Puerto Rican Families
Cuban-American Families

Asian-American Families
Chinese-American Families
Parents' Socialization Practices
Intergenerational Aspects of Chinese-American Families
Korean-American Families

Conclusions: Minority Families Pay a Heavy Price

Summary
Key Concepts and Themes
Study and Review Questions
Suggested Readings
Suggested Weblinks

OUTLINE

"The most painful part of my life was when I had to leave my grandmother in Jamaica and come here to my mother I had seen only a few times in ten years. I didn't know her and I hated her and I refused to do anything she asked. . . . Even to this day we aren't close but at least I can feel for her terrible situation." [This student's brother is now in a penitentiary.]

"At that age [10 to 14] it was total rebellion at home: My parents were first-generation immigrants but I was born here and I wanted nothing to do with being different, poor, them having an accent, not being allowed out at night with the others. . . . Now looking back I realize that it must have been a horrible time for my parents: They only wanted the best for me."

"The children at school wouldn't hold my hands when we played in circles because they said I was dirty. I felt so rejected." [Caucasian girl from an Arabic country]

"Three years ago, my parents made the 'big move' to an all-white suburb. I thought they were crazy and I was very apprehensive and that's putting it mildly. But all the neighbors have been accepting. I don't know if it helps that we have the largest house on the block." [Black student from the United States]

"At that age, I thought I was cool and being cool meant talking black. The teachers didn't allow it and I hated them for it but it gave us a good reason to fight them off. My parents were pretty upset at me because they just talked plain English and so did my grandparents."

"I can't say I have ever felt discriminated against and I have a very positive attitude as a result compared to my friends and right now I feel very good about life because I am the first in my family to get a university education and I'll have the kind of job my mother always dreamt of having." [This student's mother cleans homes for a living.]

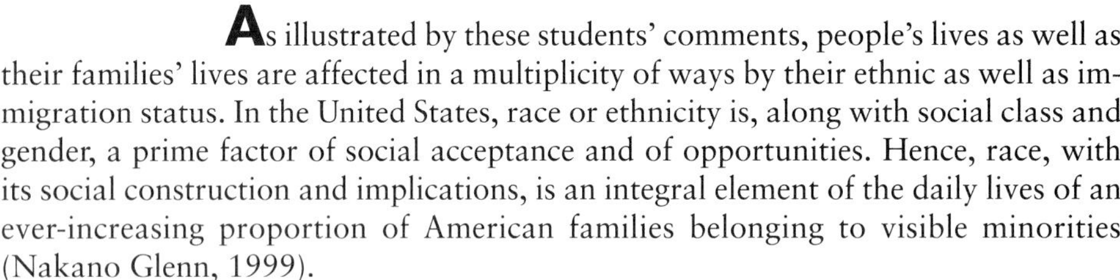

As illustrated by these students' comments, people's lives as well as their families' lives are affected in a multiplicity of ways by their ethnic as well as immigration status. In the United States, race or ethnicity is, along with social class and gender, a prime factor of social acceptance and of opportunities. Hence, race, with its social construction and implications, is an integral element of the daily lives of an ever-increasing proportion of American families belonging to visible minorities (Nakano Glenn, 1999).

IMMIGRANT FAMILIES

This chapter begins with a brief introduction to immigration in order to highlight the diversity of families that are arriving in the United States. Immigrant families' varying levels of adjustment and their intergenerational consequences are then discussed. Compared to 50 years ago, most of the new arrivals belong to *visible minority groups*.

A **minority group** is one that is given inferior status in a society, has less power, and is often deprived of resources and opportunities taken for granted by the group or groups that are in the majority or in power. A minority group, under this definition, can be a racial, ethnic, or even a religious one. At times, discrimination forces minority-group families to live separately; they are segregated.

African-American families are the prime minority group in the United States. They also constitute a *racial group* in the sense that they are socially defined by certain physical characteristics, such as skin color, facial features, and hair texture. Finally, African-American families are also an ethnic group. An *ethnic group* is not necessarily one that is different racially, such as whites, blacks, or Filippinos. It is, above all, a group that is set apart from others because of national origin or unique cultural patterns as well as a sense of distinctiveness (Schaefer, 1998). Diverse ethnic groups can exist within one racial group; a case in point are "ethnic whites" such as Italians and Germans.

Immigrant Families' Diversity

Apart from Native Americans, the United States is a country of immigrants. In 1998, there were over 27 million immigrants and nearly 28 million children of immigrants who, together, constituted one-fifth of the nation's population (Rumbaut, 1999). Several waves of immigration occurred after the colony was transformed into an independent country. By that time, American families were already quite diverse racially, but became even more so with the twentieth-century patterns of immigration, as illustrated in Figure 3.1. Currently, Europe contributes only a minority of immigrants and Mexico constitutes the majority. Therefore, the cultural and ethnic profile of U.S. families is changing drastically.

Not only are immigrants varied ethnically and culturally but they also encompass the entire educational spectrum. They consist of groups that have the highest average educational levels in the country, even higher than in the U.S.-born population, and other groups that have the lowest schooling levels (Rumbaut, 1997:23). For instance, 65 percent of people from India hold a college degree, compared to 22 percent for U.S.-born citizens. In other words, a majority of Asian Indians originate from educated families. Immigrants from the Philippines, Taiwan, Japan, Iran, Korea, and China also have high educational levels (U.S. Bureau of the Census, 1993a). Among those with the lowest educational levels are Mexicans, Guatemalans, Dominicans, Italians, Laotians, and Haitians.

As illustrated in Figure 3.1, at the end of the nineteenth and the beginning of the twentieth centuries, most immigrants were white, but they spoke a variety of languages, such as Italian, Polish, Yiddish, German, and Spanish. They were discriminated against because of their clothes, improper English, skin color, lack of education, and rural origins. Even the Irish were singled out for prejudicial treatment because they were largely poor, unskilled, and Catholic. Early in the twentieth century, children of immigrant families, including Jewish, did not attend school as long as old-stock American children, nor did they do well. Many had high delinquency rates, and some of the adult immigrants were involved in criminality because of blocked educational, occupational, and residential opportunities after arrival. For instance, in 1905 in New York, over one-third of correctional institution inmates were Jewish (Gold and Phillips, 1996). Yet, this group did not have a history of criminality in the old countries, but their opportunities in the United States were limited because of discrimination. Therefore, each century witnesses discrimination against immigrant families of different origins. Currently, the focus is on racially visible minorities rather than religious or cultural ones.

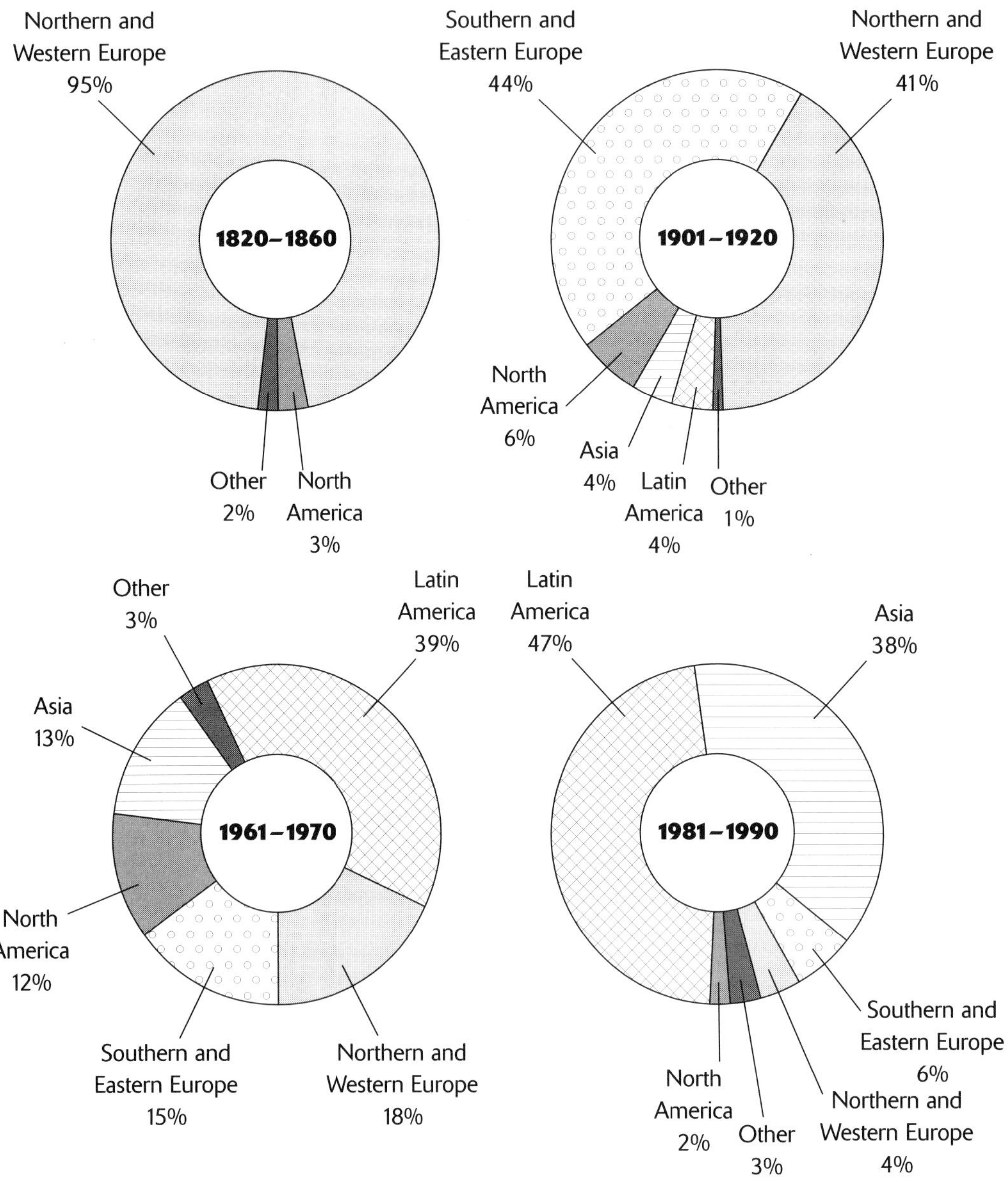

FIGURE 3.1

Legal Immigrants Admitted to the United States by Region of Last Residence: 1820–1990

Source: From Leon F. Bouvier and Robert W. Gardner, *Immigration to the U.S.: The Unfinished Story* (Washington, DC: Population Reference Bureau, 1986); and R. T. Schaefer, *Racial and Ethnic Groups*, 7th ed. (New York: Addison Wesley Longman, 1998), p. 105. Data for 1981–1990 are Schaefer's estimates based on Immigration and Naturalization Service data. Reprinted by permission of Addison Wesley Educational Publishers Inc.

Immigrant Families' Adjustment: The Environmental Constraints

Successful immigrant families whose children do well combine economic and educational adaptation while retaining core family and cultural values as well as a sense of ethnic identity. These families become **bicultural**—that is, fluent in two cultures—at least for a generation or two (Kim and Choi, 1994). They encourage their children to respect teachers and learn English. But other families experience what sociologist Alejandro Portes has termed **downward assimilation** (1995). This concept describes what happens when immigrant families are poor, belong to a visible minority, and have to settle in segregated and high-poverty neighborhoods harboring social problems. These areas, which are the topic of Chapter 7, often have elevated rates of criminality, school dropout, nonmarital pregnancy, and unemployment. As a consequence, these children of immigrants do less well than others and than the American average.

Parents migrate to secure a better future for their children and they have high aspirations. While they work hard, often at minimum wages, their children may attend schools where attitudes toward education and work are "adversarial," as Portes and Zhou (1993) have put it, where language skills are not mainstream, and where hanging out at the corner, courting trouble, is the main form of social activity. These immigrant children learn about U.S. culture through their neighbors' social isolation from mainstream society. Thus, they learn and accept the norms and ways of behaving of locally born children who are themselves members of discriminated visible minorities and as such have been cut off from mainstream society.

The opposite process occurs when the second generation moves into a neighborhood or a school where mainstream English is spoken and where students expect to go to college and consequently have low rates of early parenthood and school dropout. This could be called mainstream assimilation; it is likely to lead to **upward** rather than **downward social mobility.** Upward mobility takes place when children do better than their parents and "move up" in the social class system. Downward mobility is the opposite: Children "move down" socially and economically, compared to their parents.

Downward assimilation may also occur among **internal migrants,** such as rural blacks who move north or Natives who move to large cities. This type of assimilation plagues many Puerto Ricans, whose rates of poverty and single motherhood in the mainland are higher than in Puerto Rico (Carrasquillo and Sanchez-Korrol, 1996). Black immigrants from Haiti, the Dominican Republic, and Jamaica are particularly at risk of downward assimilation because segregation forces them to settle in areas that have too many negative role models for their children. Their children are assimilated at the racial level and often have no choice but to lose their identity as Jamaicians or Dominicans because society simply imposes on them the same constraints that it imposes on blacks in general (Waters, 1996).

Immigrant Generations

When speaking of generations of immigrants, the first generation refers to immigrants. Their American-born children constitute the second generation, and the third generation is composed of the immigrants' grandchildren. The economic situation of immigrant families is briefly discussed because one of the objections to immigration is that these families burden society and particularly its welfare system. In 1994, there was no difference in the overall poverty level of the foreign born when compared to that of the rest of society: Both stood at 15 percent (Jensen and Chitose, 1997). Nevertheless, in 1994, an immigrant family's average income was $6,000 lower than that of a third-generation family. Its household size was substantially larger, which means that most immigrants have to support more family members, including distant kin who have just arrived, on a lower income.

A proportion of immigrants send whatever little they can save to their extended families back in their country of origin. Thus, many immigrant families remain poor for a long period, at times over two generations, because of responsibilities to their larger kin, whether here or abroad. They are poor because of family-centered values rather than failure to work hard. For example, adolescents might drop out of school to help their families financially. This occurs among many Mexican Americans, for instance. Although this is helpful for the families, it blocks opportunities for advancement for the second generation.

Overall, immigrant families, although poorer than their third-generation counterparts, do not fall disproportionately under the poverty level and do not have exaggerated rates of welfare recipiency. They are willing to work hard, even at minimum wage, and pool their resources together. Furthermore, immigrants have relatively low rates of divorce and single-parent families, two sources of poverty, as we will see in Chapter 6. They would be much poorer were their rates as high as those found in the general population.

Intergenerational Conflict

At the risk of simplifying matters, there is less conflict between parents and growing/grown children when the family originates from an urban area of an economically advanced society. Such families have less adaptation to make and fewer aspects of their lives require change. The various facets of American society resemble to some extent what the parents had already been exposed to in their country of origin. But when families originate from rural areas of impoverished countries, the fit between the United States and the country of origin weakens. A great deal of adaptation is necessary, and not all the family members adapt at an equal rate and on the same matters. In some contexts, parents adapt faster than children, especially if they are educated. But generally, children and adolescents adapt more quickly, for they are culturally immersed through the school system and the peer group as well as television.

Rumbaut (1996a) reports that parent/child conflict is more likely when parents are less educated and struggle financially, and when the child prefers English, watches a great deal of television, and does not do well at school. Adolescents who experience discrimination may also have more conflict with their parents. The parents believe in the results of doing well at school, but these children's only desire is to be accepted by their peers. At that point, there is a divergence of immediate goals between the two generations. Indeed, immigrant children have perhaps a greater need than others to be socially accepted; consequently, they are eager to immerse themselves into the new American lifestyle. Girls in particular crave the freedom that their locally born peers enjoy. This may not be so acceptable to parents, and thus parent/daughter conflict occasionally arises, as described in a student autobiography:

> *"The unhappiest time in my life is when we moved here and I left all my friends and relatives behind. It was so hard for a 12-year-old girl who came from a small town to fit in this big city in a school where every child was so different than the children back home. They all seemed to have more freedom, clothes, money. I felt so deprived and lonely because no one accepted me. I was dressed weird by my parents and I wasn't allowed to go out like the other teenagers. I began rebelling against my parents but this didn't improve my situation because I lost the support of the only people who truly loved me. But at the time all I wanted was to be accepted by my peers and my parents didn't count in this picture."*

This brings us to the **gender** of the child. The majority of current immigrant families originate from societies that are patriarchal, thus male dominated. Girls are often more closely supervised than boys, especially in terms of contact with the opposite sex, activities outside the home, and clothing. The following quote relates sibling conflict brought about by parental gender-role expectations. The student in question was not only more supervised than her brother but also had to "pick up after him and do his bed":

> *"Till this day I am convinced that a [southern] European's belief that a son is the ultimate gift will never change. I did not only feel a difference of treatment between my brother and myself but this difference was openly expressed. Many a times when I questioned my unfair treatment, as compared to my brother's, I got the old dry statement: 'Well, it's different because you're a girl.' Most of the fighting that occurred between my brother and myself was a result of my parents' attitude."*

In other instances, adolescent males have more conflict with their parents than their sisters have. This generally occurs when they integrate themselves into peer groups that have low educational aspirations, have high rates of dropout, and may even be delinquent.

Intergenerational Continuity

In contrast, other immigrant children experience little intergenerational conflict, and adolescents continue to adhere at least in part to their cultural heritage. This happier situation often is the result of living in a community of the immigrants' group, whether Korean, Chinese, Cuban, or Mexican. This community provides adolescents with a great deal of contact with similar peers and with nonfamily adults of their ethnic group who become role models. These contacts reinforce what their parents teach them at home. Although these youths may attend a school that has a wide diversity of students, their community provides them with the security of same-culture peers whose parents' expectations are similar to that of their own parents. Thus, some collective socialization takes place, as these children belong to a **functional community** (Coleman and Hoffer, 1987). A Chinese student from a poor family explains this situation in her autobiography:

> *"There were several other Chinese students at my school and we all clung to each other desperately because we didn't fit in with the other students. They were all rich or so it appeared but we were all poor and had to help our parents and*

worked long hours during weekends in addition to doing our homework. This could have been the worse time of my life if I had gone to another school. But my Chinese friends all had the same problems and we all wanted to make our parents proud of us while too many of the other students who were popular didn't seem to respect their parents. We studied hard, learned English diligently and visited at each other's homes. I know that everyone thought that we were eggheads, but we made it and we were basically happy because we had each other for moral support and to look up to."

A certain degree of cultural continuity between parent and child generations is functional both at the familial and individual levels. Children who do not reject their parents' culture benefit from emotional support at home. These same children retain a greater respect for parental authority than do their more assimilated peers. This allows them to work harder at school and do better to meet parental expectations. Such children are in turn more likely to go on to postsecondary education and earn high incomes later on.

Bilingualism, or the speaking of one's language at home while being fluent in English, is an indicator both of generational continuity and ability to adapt. Children who are thoroughly bilingual, whether they are Mexican American or Asian American, do better at school than those of the same origins who no longer speak their language or who do not know English well (Blair and Qian, 1998). For instance, the dropout rates are higher among Latinos who are totally assimilated at the linguistic level and no longer speak Spanish at home (Rumberger and Larson, 1998). Children's bilingualism may be the most functional when their parents are not yet fluent in English. By retaining their native language, children can communicate with parents and absorb their aspirations (Mouw and Xie, 1999).

NATIVE-AMERICAN FAMILIES

Natives have been in North America for at least 40,000 years. They are the First Nations, the first Americans. They spoke at least 300 languages in a population that has been estimated at around 18 million when the colonists invaded (John, 1998). They were decimated by wars, genocides, diseases, and poverty, and today the Native-American population stands at about 2 million, including the Aleut and Inuit in Alaska. This is a large increase since the 1960 census, which enumerated only 523,591 American Natives. One reason for this increase is that more people of Native ancestry are willing to disclose their roots than in the recent past because there has been a renewal of ethnic identity and pride (Nagel, 1995).

Nearly one-quarter of Native-American families live in over 300 reservations or Indians lands, the largest of which is the Navajo Reservation with 124,000 members. In terms of tribes, there are at least 300 that are recognized; the most numerous are the Cherokee (over 300,000), Navajo, Chippewa, and Sioux. The states of Oklahoma, California, Arizona, New Mexico, and Alaska have the largest Native populations, and substantial groups live in New York City, Los Angeles, Oklahoma City, Phoenix, Tulsa, Albuquerque, Minneapolis-St. Paul, and Anchorage (Thornton, 1996). The majority do not live in traditional communities.

Native Families: Diversity and Adaptation

There is much diversity in Native family practices and structure: Many tribes are still matrilineal, whereas others are patrilineal. The former trace their line of descent on their mothers' side, and the latter trace it on the fathers' side. In the past, families could range from monogamy to polyandry and polygamy. Divorce was not uncommon; neither were premarital and extramarital sexuality, wife lending, spouse exchange, and adoption (John, 1998). Many Native women played a key role in the affairs of their band or tribe (Spencer and Jennings, 1977). Young women typically mated soon after puberty (around age 16) and families were small due to high rates of child mortality and because mothers often nursed their babies for several years. Children were generally treated with kindness and affection.

Perhaps the main characteristic that cuts across Native diversity is their **kin orientation.** Until the twentieth century, kinship ties actually constituted the main structure of their societies. Each family is part of an extended kinship system, which in turn is part of a clan and a tribe with which individuals identify. Thus, their recognized familial group is much larger than that of other Americans (Shoemaker, 1991).

In some Native languages, such as Iroquois, maternal aunts are called by the same word as one's mother and paternal brothers are called fathers. This terminology reflects basic family worldviews and values (Bonvillain, 1997). Indeed, traditionally, Native families have been characterized by the **sharing of parenting,** which is still in evidence on most reservations (Mintz and Kellogg, 1988). Tasks that are usually performed by the mother or father in the rest of U.S. society are generally spread across the extended family system (Machamer and Gruber, 1998:358). Supervision and discipline in particular tend to be the domain of aunts, uncles, or grandparents, or even the community at large. Elders are especially important in families and in communities. For their part, the role of parents is to be supportive and warm, which minimizes parent/child conflict.

Native-American families are, on average, larger and younger than other families in the United States. In Native communities, many of the childrearing functions fulfilled by parents in the U.S. society at large are shared with relatives. As Natives become urbanized, the extended family support diminishes and families often encounter difficulties with adolescent adaptation.

But when families move out of Native communities, they are often deprived of the child socialization support of their kin; they lose their functional community. Parents may not know how to assume the control aspects of childrearing, nor may their children be ready to accept this form of parenting. As a result, family functions that were performed by the kin system go unfulfilled and, in the already difficult process of integration, many Native youths lack guidance. One of the consequences is that these adolescents are at risk for a variety of problems, including school dropout, drug abuse, and delinquency. Another is that they feel less connected to their parents than do youths who live on reserves with an intact kin system (Machamer and Gruber, 1998). However, despite the support of the extended kin system, Native adolescents are similar to others when they live in families marred by domestic violence and substance abuse: They develop higher rates of delinquency and related problems (Zitzow, 1990).

Sources of Poverty among Native Families

After kin orientation, a second characteristic of Native families resides in their poverty. On average, Natives are certainly the most economically disadvantaged group in the United States and in Canada. This is particularly the case for those who live on reservations, although there is considerable variation in this respect. Natives are poor, first of all, because of historical circumstances, such as loss of self-determination and territory as well as cultural subjugation. Flowing from these historical causes, additional systemic sources of poverty have appeared related to discrimination and segregation. For example, in the area of education, the Native level is low—many children never attend school or drop out while still in elementary school (James et al., 1995). Only about 5 percent of Natives were enrolled in college in 1992, half of them at two-year institutions.

A second source of poverty resides in the scarcity of jobs on reservations and the fact that a great proportion of these jobs are in farming, forestry, fishing, and repair (Schaefer, 1998). These occupations do not pay well and are seasonal. The Native poverty rate is at 31 percent, ranging from 27 percent in Alaska to an astronomical 66 percent at Pine Ridge in South Dakota (Sandefur and Liebler, 1997). Consequences of poverty are relatively low life expectancy and high rates of debilitating ill health. For instance, in the 60 to 64 age bracket, 41 and 36 percent, respectively, of Native men and women suffer from at least one disability. This contrasts with only 14 percent among Asians and 24 percent among whites (Hayward and Heron, 1999). Thus, Native families' elder generation is less able to sustain younger ones. In fact, both because of low life expectancy and high fertility, compared to the rest of the U.S. population, Natives are, on average, younger and their families are larger, particularly on reservations, as illustrated in Table 3.1.

Native families are poorer, younger, and larger, three interrelated phenomena. High fertility contributes to low per-capita income in any group (Schiller, 1995). Furthermore, the comparatively larger Native family size exists despite the fact that only 55 percent of children live with two parents. One-parent Native families are a relatively new phenomenon and, as is the case among African Americans, this situation is directly related to poverty and involves both divorce and never-married motherhood (McCloskey, 1998). However, there are sharp differences among the various reservations as well as urban dwellers in the relative contribution of divorce and single motherhood to the formation of single-parent families. Single-parent families are

TABLE 3.1 Age and Family Size Characteristics of American Natives: 1990

Median age for the U.S.	33 years
Median Native age	27 years
Median reservation age	22 years
Average family size for the U.S.	3.2 persons
Average Native family size	3.6 persons
Average reservation family size	4.2 persons

Source: Based on Sandefur and Liebler, 1997.

not necessarily problematic within the context of reservations, where children are in great part raised with the help of the extended kin system. In cities, however, a one-parent family is more detrimental for Native than for other children because of the absence of kin who fulfill functions that, in the rest of U.S. society, are parental ones.

Native Intermarriage and Family Types

Another noteworthy aspect of Native family life is the high rate of intermarriage, particularly with whites. (These rates differ by region, however.) This feature of Native family life dates back to the beginnings of the colony and was often promoted for political and economic reasons (Sandefur and Liebler, 1997). Indeed, there were no feelings of antagonism between Natives and Europeans during the first decades of the colony, in great part because the colonials had not yet began expropriating Native lands on a large scale. Intermarriage has increased from about 39 percent in 1970 to 60 percent in 1990, with both men and women marrying out at about the same rate. Sandefur and Liebler's analysis indicates that younger Natives intermarry more than did their parents' cohort.

This mixture between Natives and other ethnic groups explains the ability of urban Natives simply to disappear in the melting pot, so to speak, if this is convenient for socioeconomic reasons. Although this situation brings flexibility, it can also create marginality among those who are not successful at integrating themselves within either the Native or the white communities. Thus, Gonzales (1992) distinguishes five theoretical types of Native families:

1. The traditional-reservation family has a strong ethnic identity, is close to ancestors and nature, and is oriented toward the traditions of the tribe. (This first type in turn subsumes a wide variety of tribal cultures and lifestyles.)
2. The transitional-urban family has recently left the reservation and is trying to adapt to urban life. These families are similar to immigrant ones in the sense that their main preoccupations center on finding employment and housing.
3. The marginal-anomic family has settled in an urban center but experiences difficulty with employment and housing. Many of these families "feel rejected and depressed, as they have abandoned their traditional ways and now find that they cannot accept nor integrate themselves into the ways of the city and Anglo-American society" (Gonzalez, 1992:308). They have no true cultural home.

4. The bicultural-urban family has been successful in its transition. It is similar to successful bilingual immigrant groups.
5. The exogamous-assimilated urban family is not only intermarried but has blended into the dominant culture. Other Natives at times call these "white Indians."

There are few indications in the statistics as to how prevalent each of these family types is. However, a nuclear family may pass through two or three of these types and experience them as developmental stages, whether in terms of a progressively greater level of assimilation or as a return to more traditional ways of living. Furthermore, extended families are likely to contain nuclear units that belong to a variety of family types. For instance, grandparents may be traditional along with one son's household, but a daughter's family may belong to the transitional-urban type, and another son's family may be totally assimilated into the dominant culture.

AFRICAN-AMERICAN FAMILIES

African Americans are the second largest U.S.-born racial/ethnic group. In 1997, they numbered 34 million and constituted nearly 13 percent of the American population. Blacks began arriving in the United States as slaves in 1619; they labored through slavery, and after the Emancipation Proclamation of 1863, they struggled to reconstitute family lives of their own (Genovese, 1976; Gutman, 1976). Between 1910 and 1970, 6.5 million African Americans moved from the South to the North. Of these, 5 million moved after 1940 (Lemann, 1991). This was called the **Great Migration.** Actually, another type of migration was also occurring in the South, as black Americans moved from urban to rural areas. The unstable cotton industry and the mechanization of agriculture increased the attraction toward the North, where the labor needs of industries created jobs during both world wars (Marks, 1996). In 1910, over 90 percent of the black population lived in the South; in 1997, only 55 percent remained in the South, where they comprised 20 percent of the population. Currently, only 14 percent of the black population is rural.

The movement north led to the establishment of blacks in segregated areas of inner cities, generally those areas that whites did not want. Following fair housing legislation in 1968, many black families of professionals and small entrepreneurs fled to less segregated rings of suburbs. After 1970, employers moved out of inner cities as industries shut down or relocated (Wacquant, 1995). As a result, the supply of well-paid jobs available to inner-city residents slowed down to a trickle. Increased unemployment among the working class followed and poverty rose. At the same time, and partly as a result, single motherhood and criminality increased in these neighborhoods.

Single Motherhood and Marriage: A Historical Perspective

It is frequently a surprise for nonblacks to learn that large-scale single motherhood among African Americans is a relatively recent phenomenon. During slavery, most children had a mother and a known father, although slave fathers were frequently separated from their children (Kolchin, 1993). The husband-wife family was the norm in the South after the Civil War, although black children still were 2.5 times more likely to reside without one or both parents than white children (Ruggles, 1994). Keep in mind that, in those days, both white and black children were frequently orphaned, as life expectancy was lower and mothers died of complications related to childbirth. Furthermore, because of economic hardships, life expectancy for black fathers was lower than that of white fathers. But, overall, the fact remains that a majority of black families had two parents.

Therefore, the current 70 percent rate of single motherhood among blacks is an anomaly, as detailed in Chapter 5. Various explanations have been offered but most are not historically sound. For instance, some explain that recent high rates are attributable to the heritage of slavery. But if this were the case, the rates of single motherhood would have been higher in the past, closer to the period of slavery, than in the present. Furthermore, even during slavery, children had two parents—although they were not allowed to marry. Nor can the high rate of single motherhood among blacks be attributed to black cultures originating from Africa. First, once again, the rates would have been higher in the past. Second, single motherhood has never been part of any major African culture, even though, in some countries, young women could bear a child before marriage. But this was a prelude to marriage, a proof of fertility, not a form of single parenthood.

Thus, current rates of single motherhood are more adequately explained by the recent socioeconomic developments described in Chapter 7. The result is that black women marry later and far less than white women, which means that fewer new black households have two married parents. On the basis of census data, Tolnay (1997) shows that, for the period between 1940 through 1990, black families who had migrated to northern cities from the South had more children living with two parents, more married women, and fewer never-married mothers than nonimmigrant blacks. However, like northern blacks, these rates changed throughout the years. Tolnay concludes that "the search for explanations of the dramatic change in family structure among inner-city African Americans during the last fifty years should focus on processes internal to northern cities—rather than on the introduction of a deviant family culture from the South" (Tolnay, 1997:1244; Tolnay and Crowder, 1999).

Evidently, however, there has always been a greater tolerance for nonmarried motherhood among African Americans. No adequate explanation for this greater tolerance, which can be observed as early as the mid-nineteenth century, has been provided. In this case, then, perhaps the best explanation does indeed reside in the institution of slavery itself. Slavery made maternity far more visible and important than paternity. For over two centuries, the value of a slave woman resided in her ability to reproduce healthy babies, particularly after 1807, when the trans-Atlantic transportation of slaves was prohibited. At the same time, slaves could not marry, although many owners encouraged stable families to facilitate reproduction. Many slaves held secret weddings and established permanent unions that they legalized after Emancipation (Gutman, 1976). At that point, marriage became widespread (Degler, 1981). It seems most likely that two centuries of slave maternity have acclimatized people of African origins to single motherhood. In view of this history, a more relevant, meaningful, and less biased question might be: Why were so many African Americans able to reverse this trend both during slavery and after Emancipation in 1863? There are probably two reasons. First, blacks were coming from marriage-oriented countries. Second, as a form of rebellion *and* assimilation, they wanted the same family formation rights as those held by whites.

Impacts of Prejudice, Discrimination, and Segregation

The combination of prejudice, discrimination, and segregation exacts an incredible burden on African-American families. This burden is shared by other minority groups, although not quite to the same extent. Members of African-American families build resilience or strengths against these conditions from the time their children are small. This is not a situation that can easily be understood or appreciated by whites in general (Reddy, 1994). The adaptation mechanisms employed by well-functioning and hard-working blacks do work but at a great cost. This cost is at times paid at the psychological level, and may include sadness, rage, and feelings of unfairness, hopelessness, and lack of control over one's life (Cose, 1993). These costs, added to the disadvantages of segregation, may help explain why African Americans' health status is inferior to that of whites, even when comparing well-to-do blacks and whites (Williams and Collins, 1995). These costs also explain why African Americans' life expectancy is much lower. Furthermore, the overall quality of life among blacks is inferior to that of whites, even after social class is taken into consideration.

The example of Dominicans is an enlightening one because people from the Dominican Republic come in all colors. Rumbaut (1996b) calculated, based on data from the 1990 U.S. census, that married Dominican-American women had different poverty rates depending on their visible race:

Among whites	12 percent are poor
Among racially mixed	16 percent are poor
Among blacks	37 percent are poor

These statistics indicate that, on average, the darker the complexion, the fewer the resources these mothers can utilize to raise their children. In fact, at least one other study has shown that darker-skinned families experience more discrimination than lighter-skinned ones (Keith and Herring, 1991). One result may be that the former families probably live in more disadvantaged segregated neighborhoods.

Black children are raised in densely populated areas with many other black children; in contrast, more white children live in single-home dwellings in suburbs with lower child density. Black children are surrounded by siblings, cousins, young aunts and uncles, same-floor neighbors, street peers, all of whom contribute to their socialization. In contrast, white children have more adults around them. The following black woman student brings up some of these issues when describing her relationship, at ages 10 to 14, with her parents:

> *"We all had a hard time together mainly because our parents couldn't cope with us three children. We weren't bad or anything of the sort but we lived in a cramped apartment near a subsidized project and there were kids, kids, kids everywhere.*

We were always with kids and I think that after a while our parents couldn't tell us apart [smile!]. We had a lot of fun some days but my parents didn't. They were trying to raise us well but the other kids we were always hanging around with would have none of it and their parents weren't always the best either, they'd let them stay out late at night, go wherever, invade and control the hallways, parking lots, you name it. They were up to no good but my sister brother and myself couldn't appreciate that our parents were trying to protect us from this mayhem. I resented my parents but at the same time I loved them and we had the only father on the block and that made us special also."

One survival strategy that children learn in many neighborhoods is to be "cool," what Richard Majors and Janet Billson (1993) refer to as the *Cool Pose*. It is a front, a self-presentation with the purpose of establishing one's style and one's status, and giving black males a sense of self-confidence. The authors find that this cool pose, which emphasizes posturing, shuts out life alternatives as well as contributes to wife or girlfriend abuse and to detachment from obligations toward one's children. The "cool" black male is also less likely to value school and go into legitimate occupations. The following black mother is part of a racially mixed support group for parents who have difficult adolescents. At the outset of her interview, she was reserved, but as two hours went by, she opened up to the way she saw it:

"Oh my boy is soooo cool [she imitates her son's language here]—you know, I don't think he even knows who he is. There's nothing real in him and all the dudes around him. I tell you I really resent these boys; they get away with everything. They act tough so all the other children are afraid of them at school and let them do what they want. . . . Then their parents, mothers really—ah I don't know what they think or do. Some of them act real cool, too, so what can you expect from the boys and even the girls? Now these girls are tough, real tough too. . . . So between these girls who act cool and these stupid white-trash girls who are wannabees and want a black baby, well my boy thinks he's God's gift to girls, so he struts his stuff and the police know his stuff, see what I mean?. . . A mother can't do a thing, and even my brother has tried to talk some sense into him, but he's sooo cool that my brother feels like punching him. So, yeah, I see jail time soon—that's cool ain't it?" [shakes her head sadly]

Parents' approach to child socialization differs according to the place they occupy in the resource structure of their society and the cultural tasks that the realities of their environment place on them. Black parents face the fact that, on average, their children's chances in the opportunity structure of society are fairly low, especially in comparison to what white parents, on average, can expect for their children. Many have accepted alternative strategies of child orientation to success through unconventional means. Raising children to be competent inner-city adults involves different skills than raising children to be competent, middle-class, white, suburban adults. For instance, and this is what the mother in the quote complains about, inner-city poor black parents may actually raise their children to develop "attitudes," to be defiant, self-reliant, able to fight back, and acquire a certain dose of mistrust (Ogbu, 1985). Thus, there is likely to be a great deal of difference in the ways blacks raise their children, depending on their own socioeconomic status and neighborhood situation.

Middle-class black families too often live in areas that present many socialization risks for their children. In such areas, parents may have to involve themselves more in their children's day-to-day lives.

Middle-Class Families

One aspect of black families that is misunderstood and for which not enough research exists resides in the fact that many are quite affluent in terms of income. There is an African-American middle class, upper-middle class, and a small upper class. It is true that, nationally, only 18 percent of black families have incomes over $50,000, compared to 37 percent among whites (Smith and Horton, 1997). Nevertheless, this 18 percent is largely ignored. For example, in Harlem, about 12 percent of individuals earn more than $50,000 and at least another third earn between $22,000 and $50,000. Keeping in mind that these are individual earners, one can easily imagine that their families' income is higher when there are two wage earners. For this same reason, the black middle class probably has a larger proportion of its families that are headed by married parents, while the reverse occurs among disadvantaged families.

However, these affluent incomes are somewhat dampened by another reality. Black families have either been unable to accumulate enough savings to buy real estate, particularly their own homes, or they have been forced to buy homes that have low real-estate value because of their location (Horton and Thomas, 1998). Very few families have been able to inherit expensive property and other assets, such as stocks and bonds. The result is that very few in the older generation can transfer wealth to their children. Thus, black families are, on average, poorer, not only because their income is lower but also because they have little wealth, inherited or accumulated, compared to other U.S. families. This situation limits their lifestyle options. For instance, whereas many white families take out second mortgages to pay for their children's education, few black families are able to do so. Their lack of accumulated assets often leaves them vulnerable to poverty when a crisis such as unemployment arises (McAdoo, 1988).

Residence Problems of Middle-Class Families

Black middle-class families face two major problems in terms of residence. The first arises because a large proportion are forced to live in poor neighborhoods, which is a topic of Chapter 7. The second arises when they live in a black middle-class neighborhood. Most of these neighborhoods are adjacent to high-poverty areas that often have elevated crime and homicide rates (Anderson, 1990; see Family Research 3.1). This means that their children are as easily introduced to gangs and the drug business as they are to legitimate employment opportunities. Patillo (1998) has carried out an observation study of a neighborhood where 60 percent of the population is white collar, the average family income is a comfortable $40,000, and most families live in single-dwelling homes on well-maintained streets. A majority of the residents have lived in the area, located on the south side of Chicago, for several decades.

Despite positive neighborhood socioeconomic characteristics, these middle-class black families do not live in a context that is ecologically equal to that of same-class whites, and that is the rule rather than the exception (Sampson and Wilson, 1995). Even most affluent blacks are not able to escape from crime, for they reside in communities as prone to crime as those housing the poorest whites (Logan and Stults, 1999). Indeed, "Groveland," as Patillo (1998) called the area, is also the home of gang leaders who grew up in the neighborhood and want to keep it safe for their own families. Therefore, most of the drug selling is done outside of the immediate area, and gang leaders join with the legitimate leaders who went to school with them to keep the area clean and safe.

The Contrasting Networks of Black Families

The length of residence and the fact that the children went to the same schools result in the interlocking of legitimate and illegitimate networks. This mutual familiarity means that residents, especially youths, are exposed to antisocial networks as well as legitimate ones—a mixture of influences that white middle-class parents do not have to confront. Furthermore, because a large segment of blacks are disadvantaged, a greater proportion of their middle-class families than is the case among whites have poor relatives (Billingsley, 1992). Others have relatives who have done time in jail, are on welfare, or are drug addicts. Therefore, even within the families themselves, it is often difficult to insulate children against negative socialization forces.

FAMILY RESEARCH 3.1

Race: Naturalistic Observation and Participant Observation

Elijah Anderson (1990) did fieldwork from the summer of 1985 to the summer of 1989 in an area containing two communities: one black and low income, the other racially mixed with middle- to upper-income families. He spent many hours on the streets, just talking and listening to the people who lived in the areas. He also videotaped street-corner scenes, did recorded interviews, "and got to know all kinds of people, from small-time drug dealers to policemen, middle-class whites, and outspoken black community activists" (p. ix). Anderson went to bars, laundromats, carryouts; he attended meetings; he even became an active board member of an education-oriented group. This is referred to as *participant observation*. Much of the information he obtained focused on the effect of ongoing economic changes on individuals and families. He also studied family life among youths and the impact of drugs and race relations.

Moreover, because of their kinship orientation, many well-off African-American families feel pressured to help relatives financially, monitor promising cousins educationally, offer legal advice, mediate with various authorities, and find jobs for other cousins who may be unreliable. A black woman student, who describes an affluent family situation in her autobiography, makes the following points when discussing her parents and their values:

> *"My parents came from a good family, value religion, hard work, education, and helping kin and neighbors. All I can say is that the latter has caused a lot of grief in my family because we have cousins who don't share these values, to say the least. . . . Throughout my life, we have had an assortment of cousins, some very distant, just come in and live with us as if we owed it to them and live off the fat of the land while they don't even bother looking for a job. People who don't even know how to behave in a nice house. . . . My parents have loaned money they have never seen again. . . . Once we had to call the police because this cousin's friend was selling dope out of our basement. . . . I could go on. My parents were solid pillars of their church, still are, but as far as I'm concerned, I have told them and my sister has too that they'll have to carry on their charity work at church and not at home. I don't care that these people are our cousins. Do we owe* them *anything? No."*

Again, such situations are less frequently encountered among well-off white families. Their residential area, geographic mobility, and lifestyle effectively erect a barrier between themselves and relatives who might be an embarrassment or might place demands on them.

School-Related Problems

The average African-American family is faced with many problems foreign to the average white family. Besides having to contend with prejudice and discrimination, they have to shelter their children against negative peer behaviors at school and neighborhood dangers. Many solve this problem by enrolling their children in private schools, which they often do at great personal sacrifice, because their income is, on average, lower.

Unfortunately, the private school may be in another neighborhood. This means that black students often have few or no friends they can socialize with in their immediate neighborhoods. Their parents have to become overprotective and cannot let them play in the streets for fear that they will meet bad peers, or that they will be picked on by gang members, or that they will be caught in the cross-fire of street violence. These parents have to be constantly vigilant and find alternative leisure activities for their children outside their neighborhoods or else keep them at home. Maton and Hrabowski (1998) report that African-American males who do very well in school are raised in families that are very involved in their children's lives, so as to counterbalance the negative influence of the neighborhood and peers as well as social stereotypes. These parents are strict, nurturant, and well connected to a community of teachers, church members, and extracurricular activities.

Residential Mobility Discrimination

Another set of problems arises when black middle-class families move to better areas. First, there is the matter of discrimination that is encountered.

Ellis Cose (1993) recalls that when he and his wife, who is Puerto Rican, decided to move out of their Fifth Avenue apartment, his wife first made a few calls to listings advertised in newspapers. In one case, she asked if the address was in a good neighborhood. The reply: "Yes, it's a very good neighborhood. There are no black people here" (p. 42). Then, when she contacted a real estate agent, the agent insisted on showing her slum apartments or extremely small ones. By the end of the day, Cose's wife was totally outraged. She said: "Next time I go looking for an apartment, I'm taking somebody white along with me" (p. 43).

If the black family succeeds in buying into a predominantly white neighborhood, the reception may be good, or it may be cool, or it may be downright hostile. The children become the school's "token blacks"; they may be lucky and make white friends or they may rarely be invited to their peers' homes. Perhaps a few other black families also live in the area, which gives them more opportunity to socialize. But, again, white neighbors may fear that "too many blacks" are moving in—even though these black families may actually be more educated and earn incomes superior to theirs. Thus, the "white flight" may begin, with a consequent reduction in real estate values.

In some of the whiter neighborhoods, black residents may be stopped by a suspicious police officer: "We have learned that there are cars we are not supposed to drive, streets we are not supposed to walk on. We may still be stopped and asked, 'Where are you going, boy?' whether we're in a Mercedes or a Volkswagen" (Cose, 1993:103). This is frightening and humiliating. Or, if the husband goes out for a walk, he may find that other residents who have never seen him before cross the street, fearing that he may attack them. The mother walking to school to pick up her children may at first be taken for a maid or a nanny. Thus, it is evident that members of black middle-class families encounter many stressors, whether they live in a predominantly white area, a black middle-class neighborhood, or a disadvantaged neighborhood.

In conclusion, black families, in general, including middle-class families, suffer from discriminatory constraints that place an enormous burden on them. Consequently, black families are forced to be stronger and more adaptive than other families (Toliver, 1998). While the statistics emphasize their problems and deficiencies, the reality is that these problems do not originate from within these families but from the organization of society at large. Were African-American families to benefit from the same socioeconomic advantages as do white families, their rate of problems would, in all likelihood, be no different.

LATINO-AMERICAN FAMILIES

Nearly 11 percent of the U.S. population is of Latino origins. Of these, almost 30 million people, the most prominent group consists of nearly 19 million Mexican Americans. Figure 3.2 details the proportional representation of each Latino group in terms of its national origin. Latino-American families, despite their cultural diversity, share a key value orientation—that of **familism.** Familism is characterized by strong commitment to family obligation and loyalty, including support, and a preference for geographic closeness (Hurtado, 1995). The family is the primary source of both social interaction and care giving (Schaefer, 1998:286). This value system typifies

FIGURE 3.2

Origins of the Latino Population in the United States: 1997

Source: U.S. Bureau of the Census, 1998, p. 54.

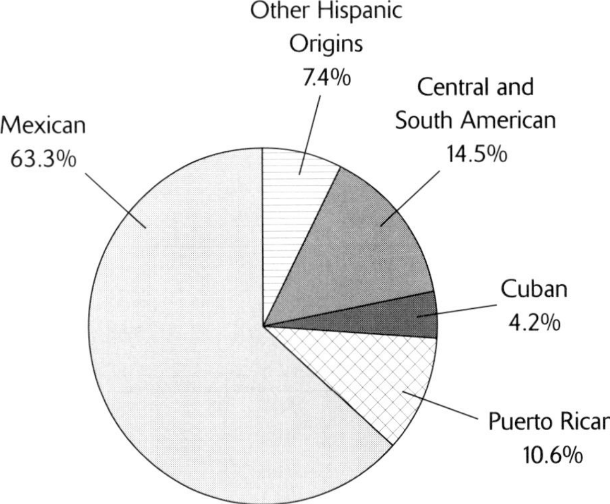

most Latino and Asian cultures and is reflected among their adolescents in the United States (Fuligni, Tseng, and Lam, 1999). However, there is little information concerning the extent to which familistic values are transformed into related family behaviors. As well, it may be an orientation that erodes somewhat under the more individualistic influence of the mainstream culture. Furthermore, divorce and single parenting contribute to weaken bilateral family ties. Thus, familism may diminish over the generations because of cultural assimilation and structural factors at the familial level.

Mexican-American Families

Mexican-American families constitute 63 percent of all Latinos and, with African Americans, are the largest minority group in the United States. In Table 3.2, the 1990 demographic characteristics of Mexican-American families are presented in comparison to those of the U.S.-born population and other minority families also discussed in this chapter. Mexicans appear in two sections of the table: those born in the United States (top panel of the table) and those who have immigrated (lower panel).

Adaptation in the United States has been difficult for Mexican families. First, many belonged to the southwestern states that were originally part of Mexico; at the conclusion of the war between Mexico and the United States in 1848, they became conquered citizens. Second, later on, those who immigrated were not always welcome as "real" immigrants but as stop-gap laborers. They were tolerated as long as they were useful. Furthermore, their "mixed race" status did not endear them to Anglos. They became a visible minority group.

Mexican family heads, lacking educational skills (column 3, Table 3.2) and not yet proficient in English, have had to accept low-paid, unskilled jobs. Such jobs have not allowed very many to achieve supervisory positions at work, particularly among recent arrivals, and to accumulate assets other than a home (column 6, Table 3.2).

Mexican immigrants' overall poverty at 30 percent is high, compared to the lower 14 percent among U.S.-born Mexican Americans. However, it is worth noting in

TABLE 3.2 **Familial and Socioeconomic Characteristics of U.S.-Born and Foreign-Born Individuals: 1990**

Origins	(1) Fertility of Women[a]	(2) Two-Parent Families	(3) College Graduates	(4) Poor	(5) Social Assistance	(6) Home-owners
U.S.-Born						
Whites (non-Hisp.)	1.8	80%	22%	9%	5%	68%
Natives	2.5	56	9	31	19	54
Blacks	2.2	37	11	30	20	43
Asians	1.5	86	36	10	4.5	63
Puerto Ricans	2.5	47	10	32	27	26
Mexicans	2.5	69	9	25	14	54
Foreign-Born						
Mexicans	3.3	73	3.5	30	11	36
Cubans	1.8	72	16	16	15	56
Chinese[b]	1.8	81–87	31–62	13–17	4–11	56–66
Koreans	1.8	87	34	16	10	48

[a] Average number of children ever born per woman age 35 to 44 years (an approximate measure of completed fertility).

[b] Depending on the country of origin.

Sources: Rumbaut, 1996b, Tables 3, 4, pp. 34–37; and U.S. Bureau of the Census, 1993a, Tables 1, 2; 1993c, Tables 1, 2; 1993d, Tables 1, 2; and data drawn from a 5 percent public use microdate sample (PUMS) of the 1990 U.S. census and subject to sample variability. Reprinted by permission of Thomson Learning for Wadsworth.

columns 4 and 5 of Table 3.2 that only one of every three poor Mexican-American immigrants utilizes welfare, whereas nearly all poor whites do. These figures may be related to ethics of hard work and pride.

Generations and Fertility

The comparison of first generations and other subsequent generations of Mexican Americans indicates that a proportion of these families have progressed economically with their U.S.-born children: lower birth rate, more college education, more home ownership, and less poverty. Another proportion, however, may have acquired American habits that are more problematic, such as higher rates of single mothers, youthful parents, and welfare assistance. For instance, beginning in 1995, the Mexican-American teen birth rate surpassed that of blacks (Mathews et al., 1998). Thus, a segment of Mexican-American children have assimilated downwardly. As they become more Americanized, second- and third-generation Mexican-American youths identify less with their country of origin and have fewer contacts with relatives in Mexico. They also report less interaction with their non-Americanized grandparents (Silverstein and Chen, 1999). A proportion reject their parents' work ethics and some of their family's values (Buriel and De Ment, 1997). They lose valuable aspects of their culture of origin and replace them with patterns that are considered problematic in mainstream America and are not conducive to success in U.S. society (Rumbaut, 1996b).

Mexican-American women have a higher fertility rate than blacks, whites, and Asians (column 1, Table 3.2). It stands at 2.5 per woman born in the United States. Immigrant Mexican women have even larger families, at 3.3 per woman (Mathews et al., 1998). In fact, except for some smaller groups of Southeast Asians, such as Laotians, immigrant Mexicans have the highest fertility of all foreign-born women. Several consequences flow from this simple demographic feature. First, more children mean less per-capita income available within each family, particularly in view of the fact that the group's overall income is already low. Second, the combination of high fertility and immigration means that this is the fastest-growing group in the United States. Third, as many Mexican Americans intermarry, a greater proportion of U.S. families than in the past will contain one parent of Mexican origin. Fourth, Mexican-American children have a larger number of siblings than others and fewer are only children. Consequently, their own children will be inserted in a more extended kinship system than is the case in the rest of society, with a potential for a more effective support network.

Types of Extended Families

Overall, over one-third of first-generation Mexican-American families are of the extended family type: They include children, parents, and grandparents in the household. But there has also been a sharp increase in what is called the *horizontally extended family.* This concept refers to family members from a same generation, as when adult brothers or sisters form a household along with their spouses. Nearly one-fourth of all new immigrant families from Mexico belong to this type of household (Glick, Bean, and Van Hook, 1997). Such a living arrangement is helpful to young immigrants, particularly when their salaries are minimal. In contrast, only 5 percent of all American households are of the horizontally extended type.

Second- and third-generation Mexican-American families have a larger kinship system available to them than immigrant ones. They have relatives already established in the United States. This network may be useful in terms of spreading around the responsibilities of child care and youth socialization. On the other hand, Buriel (1993) finds that subsequent generations of Mexican-American mothers and fathers agree less among themselves about childrearing goals and practices than do immigrant parents. New immigrants have fewer kin to help them, and as a result, parents have to rely on each other and support each other more. Furthermore, first-generation Mexican-American adults experience less stress in their parental role and have a closer relationship with their children than second-generation Mexican-American parents. The latter have children who are less and less Mexican in terms of family values, thus opening the door to greater parent/child conflict.

Puerto Rican Families

There are about 3.5 million Puerto Ricans on the island itself and over 3 million on the mainland. Large-scale immigration from Puerto Rico did not begin until the mid-

1940s. The Puerto Rican culture is marked by a heritage of colonialism, both Spanish and American, and, in terms of ethnicity, combines elements of former indigenous populations as well as Africans, whites, and Creoles. Unlike other immigrants, Puerto Ricans are free to move without visas, and relocation to the mainland is often a temporary economic measure. This also means that more Puerto Ricans who are less skilled can move to the mainland than is the case for other Latinos. As a result, perhaps, Puerto Ricans have the highest poverty rate of all Latino groups on the mainland.

Because of their lower labor-market skills and education (column 3, Table 3.2), Puerto Ricans at first established themselves as blue-collar workers in industries that were soon to decline or were being relocated to developing countries (Carrasquillo and Sanchez-Korrol, 1996). As a result, male unemployment quickly grew. Many women had to take low-paying jobs in the service sector. For others, their traditional skills, such as sewing, were in greater demand than those of their husbands, so that more and more Puerto Rican wives were forced to become their families' breadwinners. Overall, the economic situation of Puerto Rican families deteriorated on the mainland: They have the highest recourse to social assistance and the lowest level of home ownership of all minority groups (except for Laotian and Cambodian refugees).

One result of this economic precariousness is that single-mother households increased. In 1990, close to half of mainland Puerto Rican families were headed by mothers. However, in a substantial number of these families, the mother has a cohabitor, who may be the child's father. Consensual unions have had a long tradition in Puerto Rico. At least a third of all unions were consensual in the nineteenth century, but their prevalence had diminished to less than 5 percent by 1980 (Landale and Fennelly, 1992). These unions are now more concentrated among the poor. On the mainland, many of the consensual unions are long term and considered marital.

For mainland Puerto Ricans, the processes of immigration, downward assimilation in poor neighborhoods, loss of jobs among males, and general poverty all contribute to a reduced familial, social capital. As a result of assimilation and poverty, second- and third-generation Puerto Ricans have higher percentages of mother-headed families than that of the first generation. In fact, they experience sharply higher increases of single-parent families than second-generation Cubans, for instance (Rumbaut, 1997). The loss of male-headed families is particularly detrimental in a culture where fathers have traditionally held a salient role. Puerto Rican children without resident fathers, particularly in conditions of poverty, may be far more affected and less well socialized than in similar African-American families, where patriarchy has never been so much in evidence.

Puerto Rican families, along with most other Latino families, are of the extended type, although households are generally nuclear. Fictive kinship of adopted uncles and aunts as well as godparents are part of this system. Among them, the group takes precedence, and young individuals develop their identities within this kin system rather than separately. The latter represents the model of individuation developed on white samples by white researchers and clinicians; it does not apply to most Latino- and Asian-American families (Dilworth-Anderson, Burton, and Turner, 1993). In this respect, Contreras and colleagues (1999) have found that Puerto Rican teen mothers who are not acculturated and are dependent on their mothers experience much less parenting stress. In contrast, those who are acculturated experience more problems when they receive much help from their mothers because they no longer subscribe to cultural norms of familism.

The extended kin network provides support during and after immigration. However, because poverty is so widespread in this population, the extended family network does not have the resources available to provide for the families' needs for employment, child care, housing, and health. Thus, in a way, the extended kin is a burdened network and families are at times overwhelmed and defeated by its demands (Roschelle, 1997).

Cuban-American Families

There were approximately 1.3 million Cubans in the United States in 1997. Most are classified as white and most are located in the Miami area where they form a substantial part of the population and constitute an important political block. A majority arrived in the 1960s, before large-scale immigration from Latin America and Haiti. The first waves of Cubans consisted of business people and professionals, families with education and money, who were fleeing Fidel Castro's communist regime. More recent immigrants are mixed economically and a certain percentage are black (Suarez, 1993).

What characterizes Cuban-American families is the fact that, for decades now, an unknown percentage have lived in the United States hoping to return to their country of origin when Castro dies or is overthrown. No data exist on how such expectations vary by generation within each family. For instance, 60-year-old parents may still hope to return to Cuba, but their 35-year-old children, who have spent all their lives in Florida, and their own children, who are even more Americanized, may not share the same dream.

Perhaps because of the political situation that compelled Cubans to leave, families live in tightly knit communities with many formal organizations that provide services and opportunities for their members and mediate with the rest of the American economic and political structure. Their enclaves have created occupational, economic, and political opportunities. Cuban families are therefore well integrated in Florida's economic and political systems (Kelly and Schauffler, 1996). Close-knit communities also mean that families can maintain the use of Spanish longer than would be the case for another less politically cohesive immigrant group. Hopes of returning to their country also keep Cuban culture alive in a way that does not occur for other immigrant groups.

Cuban families have one of the lowest fertility rates in the United States: 1.8 children per woman. The proportion of households headed by women is only slightly higher than average. Their poverty and welfare percentages are not as low as those of the U.S.-born white population but are not exceedingly high, and over half of the families own their homes. Children often attend Cuban schools, which encourage bilingualism, thus their English proficiency is quite high (Portes and Schauffler, 1996). They have fewer dropouts and far less teenage pregnancy than most other immigrant groups from Latin American and the Caribbeans. Cuban children tend to be friends with peers of their nationality far more than is the case for other children of immigrants. All in all, Cuban communities constitute a strong socialization experience for children and youths. They reinforce parents' goals of economic success and preservation of Cuban identity.

ASIAN-AMERICAN FAMILIES

Asian and Pacific Islander families are even more different among themselves than are Latino families, because they do not share one language, religion, or culture of origin. They represent a variety of ethnic groups with large differences in terms of immigration or conquest (Hawaii), history, education, socioeconomic resources, and even level of segregation. All in all, there were about 10 million people of Asian and Pacific Islander origins in the United States in 1997, a majority of whom were foreign born. The Asian-American population grew by 141 percent between 1970 and 1980 and by another 99 percent between 1980 and 1990. During this period, the overall American population grew by only 10 percent each decade.

Chinese (1.6 million), Filipinos (1.4 million), and Japanese (850,000) have a long history of immigration to the United States. Koreans (800,000) and other groups, such as Vietnamese (600,000) and Asian Indians (815,000), have immigrated in large numbers more recently. This occurred after the 1960s, following U.S. military involvement in their respective countries (except for people from India).

For their part, Pacific Islanders constitute a Bureau of the Census category rather than a true racial or ethnic group. Among Americans, they include individuals who identify themselves as Hawaiians and who live mainly in Hawaii or have moved to the West Coast. They number 211,000, in addition to American Samoans and Guamanians. Hawaiians have intermarried with whites and Asian Americans so that their ancestry is somewhat more widespread than their relatively small numbers indicate.

Chinese-American Families

At 1.6 million, Chinese Americans are the largest group of Asian origins in the United States. They are heavily concentrated geographically in urban areas; 40 percent live in California. Those who are less concentrated are more likely to live in suburbs (Sun, 1997). They are upwardly mobile and have entered various professional, financial, and academic fields. The Chinese, along with the Koreans and the Filipinos, are a successful group at the educational level—the concept of *model minority* is often used. Depending on their region of origin, 31 to 62 percent of the recent Chinese immigrants have a college degree, compared to 22 percent among all Americans. Many came to the United States as graduate students and remained (Min, 1995).

Chinese mothers have a high labor-force participation, as is the case for most Asian-American women (Espiritu, 1996). At the more educated levels, husbands help more at home, although the division of household work remains traditional (Chen, 1992). At the lower end of the educational scale, women toil long hours in the garment industry, for instance, and return home to housework and at times to help their husbands with the family business. In certain industries, such as garment and the service sector, wives find jobs before husbands do. In these instances, fathers may have to do more child care than acceptable in their countries of origin. Thus, often in disadvantaged Chinese families, as is the case for many other immigrant groups, it is the wives who are the most employable, and their earnings may be equivalent to those of their husbands. Disadvantaged Chinese-American wives see their work as a means of sustaining their family rather than as a pathway to individual autonomy.

The fact that the Chinese tend to be highly concentrated in a few key cities, such as San Francisco, provides a great deal of social capital for arriving parents. Zhou (1995) describes how Chinatowns' organizations provide support networks to new immigrants that reinforce cultural identity and shield them against the processes of downward assimilation that could occur in view of their proximity to neighborhoods ridden with social problems. In this sense, the community serves to help parents guide children's behavior and maintain traditional values, as explained by a student:

> *"My peers' values have always been similar to those of my family's because I have always hung around with other Asians. Living in Chinatown has made my life easier. . . . We are different but I do not think that we ever cared much because there always were so many of us."*

In this manner, Chinatowns may constitute a form of **shared parenting** and social control.

Parents' Socialization Practices

Chinese parents tend to be lenient and indulgent until their children reach school age. At that point, children fall under stricter control (Buriel and De Ment, 1997). However, there has been some misunderstanding among non-Asians concerning this parenting style. There is actually some widespread "knowledge" that is more myth than fact. Many non-Asians believe that Chinese-American parents are overbearing. Although Chinese Americans do espouse more controlling attitudes than whites but less than Chinese in Asia (Lin and Fu, 1990), the Chinese parenting style is one of training or teaching rather than control (Chao, 1994).

Another myth is that Chinese-American parents push their children to do well at school, but studies indicate that these parents are less concerned about their children's school activities and homework than others (Steinberg, Brown, and Dornbusch, 1996). Rather, Chinese families are, on average, successful at inculcating familial and educational values in their children. The children do not want to disappoint their parents and will find a supportive peer group in this respect, as illustrated in the student quote on pp. 61–62. Nor is there any truth to the report that Chinese- and Japanese-American youths have high suicide rates and a low level of mental health. It is possible that these myths have racist overtones, in that some individuals believe that nonwhite immigrants simply are "not supposed to" do well so quickly, and the success of some Asian groups may give rise to resentment. In turn, this resentment may bring disparaging explanations in the form of the price that these so-called model minorities allegedly pay for their success.

Chinese-American families generally retain core cultural values that contribute to achievement. Feldman and Rosenthal (1990) have compared the age expectations for autonomy in various life domains of 15- through 18-year-old adolescents, including a sample living in Hong Kong, first-generation and second-generation samples in the United States, as well as a sample of white Americans. They found that white American adolescents had the earliest age expectations for the initiation of dating, boy-girl parties, and so on. First-generation American Chinese and Hong Kong students had the latest age expectations, with second-generation Chinese being somewhat in the middle. Chinese youths are generally more conservative sexually (Masten, Trapnell, and Gorzalka, 1998). Feldman and Rosenthal suggest that Chinese-American adolescents are slow to shift their expectations toward the American model of early autonomy because of the effectiveness of the family in transmitting its values. The following student was born in Toronto and was not part of the recent wave of affluent Chinese immigration to this city; her Chinese peer group had therefore been limited:

> *"I am still a virgin and I am 22 and there are times when it seems that I am the only one left here except for the few Chinese friends I have and they are like me. We talk about it even though it's not what our parents would expect us to talk about. If it wasn't for my friends I'd think I am abnormal, that there's something wrong with me or that I am not attractive enough because all the other students here sleep with their boyfriends or even live with them. At times I feel left out but I have different family values. I want sex with my husband to be special (I have someone nice in mind that my parents like) and I think that the other students don't have so much to look forward to because they've already done it all. I think it's cheap sex, but still it's hard to be the only one around who thinks like that. I keep my mouth shut."*

Intergenerational Aspects of Chinese-American Families

Chinese-American students experience less external pressure than whites because they are often excluded from the activities of their more emancipated white and black peer groups. These combined factors in turn contribute to reduce intergenerational conflict within these families. But Chinese-American teenagers do perceive their family environment as less accepting and more demanding than do white teenagers (Rosenthal and Feldman, 1991). However, the difference is not large and could be the result, on the part of the Chinese, of an unconscious comparison between their families and what they perceive to be an ideal norm in the United States (Pyke, 2000). Overall, the level of life satisfaction is as high among Chinese Americans as that of the rest of the population (Ying, 1992).

As among other immigrants, Chinese children often play the role of **cultural brokers** (Buriel and De Ment, 1997). This concept refers to what occurs in many families in which one or both parents are not English proficient. Children have to translate instructions to their mother, for instance, or help her at the checkout, or make phone calls for her. Later on, the more educated sibling tends to be the one who is the most relied on by parents or grandparents for information or as an interpreter. These children act as "go-betweens" linking two cultures.

Asian parents and children, in general, value filial piety, but parents have greater expectations of help from their first-born child than subsequent children (Uba, 1994). However, as is the case among the rest of the U.S. population, variables such as financial resources, distance, and parents' needs are important determinants in the financial support that Asian-American children provide to their elderly parents (Ishii-Kuntz, 1997). The end result is that Chinese-American adult children who have few financial resources are unable to help their elderly parents. Therefore, structural factors come into play that prevent the activation of the cultural emphasis on filial piety.

Korean-American Families

Nearly 75 percent of Americans of Korean origins were born in Korea. The Korean-American population has grown from 100,000 in 1970 to over 800,000 by 1997. More than half of the immigrants were already affiliated with Christian churches before arriving here. In contrast, only about 20 percent of people in Korea are Christian. This means that a selection process takes place whereby Christian Koreans may immigrate to the United States in part because similarity of religion makes adaptation easier.

Korean and Chinese Americans, as indicated in Table 3.2, have the highest proportion of two-parent families of all the ethnic groups in the United States. Not only does this situation reflect cultural values but it also stems from the relatively high educational levels of these families—at least a third of Korean Americans have completed college. Korean Americans have a lower home ownership rate than the Chinese, in part because they are more recent arrivals to the United States. These families tend to be young, on average (Ishii-Kuntz, 1997); a substantial proportion have children under age 18 or young adult children. Their strong sense of ethnic community provides social capital to parents as well as children and contributes to adolescents' academic success and subsequent upward social mobility (Portes and Zhou, 1993).

A singular aspect of Korean-American families is that they are disproportionately self-employed in small businesses where they put in long hours and family labor is a constitutive element. A majority of Korean mothers are employed in the Korean ethnic economy, often in their husbands' or fathers' businesses. Wives are thus very important for the economic stability of these families (Park, 1989). Self-employment is not necessarily a choice but often results from the lower chances of finding jobs that match educational levels and pay accordingly (Min, 1996). Indeed, despite their educational credentials, Asian men are less likely to be hired as professionals and managers and they are also less well paid than whites (Ong and Hee, 1994).

A great proportion of these small entrepreneurial families are located in black neighborhoods, where they fill needs in the grocery, dry-cleaning, and retail businesses that are not met by local entrepreneurs. As a result, a great deal of black hostility is generated against Korean Americans, although some of this has been exaggerated by media coverage (Min, 1996). At this time, unfortunately, there is no research information on how family life is impacted by this type of economic situation and by minority-within-a-minority existence in neighborhoods that have high rates of poverty and social problems (Norman, 1994). One could perhaps expect that parents orient their children's education toward career goals that are different from theirs.

Most Korean elderly parents are first-generation immigrants. In comparison, those of Chinese and Japanese origins are likely to be the children or even great-grandchildren of immigrants. Thus, elderly Koreans still suffer from adjustment problems, which may be one reason why they receive more help from their adult children than do other Asian seniors (Ishii-Kuntz, 1997). Their children are also recent arrivals, compared to the Chinese, and may more closely adhere to values of filial obligations. The adults have young children, and grandparents may consequently be more actively involved with their family life. Both senior and middle generations might engage in reciprocal exchange that might be necessary in small business ownership.

CONCLUSIONS: MINORITY FAMILIES PAY A HEAVY PRICE

Historical conquests and immigration have made U.S. society very diverse. There is no longer one type of American family but a great variety of them. These same elements of diversity, however, exact a price on minority-group families that are more or less put aside, forgotten, and segregated because they are socially defined as inferior. For other families, the price is one of prejudice rather than outright discrimination. Overall, however, the most obvious price paid by many minority groups as well as immigrants is that of economic marginality and even hardship as well as all the consequences that flow from these for their families.

Family adaptation to the larger social and economic context is deeply affected by marginality and discrimination for minority groups. Furthermore, immigrant families also have to shoulder additional tasks in terms of adaptation as they move into a new culture. Thus, while family diversity enriches the cultural mosaic of American society, being "diverse" or "different" carries connotations that too frequently constitute hardships for the families involved.

SUMMARY

1. Several waves of immigration have succeeded each other; Europe has been replaced by Latin America as a major source of immigrants.
2. Immigrant families whose children do well combine economic and educational adaptation while retaining core family and cultural values. But many families arrive poor and, particularly when belonging to a visible minority, have to settle in neighborhoods with high rates of social problems. Their children are then downwardly assimilated and do not meet parental expectations of a better future.
3. The first generation of immigrants is generally poorer than subsequent ones but does not have a high reliance on welfare. Immigrant families have lower rates of divorce and of female headship than is the case in the general population, and this reduces their poverty level.
4. Conflict between immigrant children and their parents is higher when parents are less educated and struggle financially, and when the child prefers English, watches a great deal of television, and does not do well at school. The gender of a child is an important variable in terms of intergenerational conflict. The support of peers from one's cultural group who have values congruent with those of one's parents helps adolescents retain their identity and contributes to family cohesion.
5. Native Americans are varied historically and culturally. Nearly a quarter live in over 300 reservations. Despite their diversity, they share a kin orientation: Each nuclear family is part of an extended family and a tribe. Uncles and aunts often fulfill functions that are considered parental in the rest of American families. Natives are the most economically disadvantaged group in the United States because of historical circumstances. Native-American families are poorer, younger, and larger (higher fertility)—three interrelated phenomena. They also have high rates

of single-parent families. About 60 percent of Native men and women marry interracially. Gonzales (1992) distinguishes five types of families, depending on their level of distance from their traditional culture and their integration into mainstream society.

6. The recent history of African Americans is marked by the Great Migration toward the North, particularly between 1940 and 1970. Blacks were established in segregated areas when they moved. Large-scale single motherhood is a recent phenomenon, in part caused by more recent economic disadvantages based on a history of discrimination. The current living conditions of black families are inferior to those of whites, even when incomes are equal. This is due to their segregation in less favorable areas and the burden of discrimination and prejudice. It is far more difficult to be a black than a white parent because it is far more difficult to raise children well in areas that seem to promote negative attitudes and behavior rather than encourage successful adaptation to mainstream society.
7. Black middle-class families are largely forced to live in poor neighborhoods. When they live in a black middle-class area, they are still located near districts that have elevated crime and homicide rates. They also encounter discrimination when they move to a white or mixed neighborhood.
8. Familism is a salient cultural feature of Latino and Asian groups. Mexican-American families constitute 60 percent of all Latinos; they are characterized by a high fertility rate and mixed economic success in subsequent generations. Their level of education is quite low, which prevents their penetration into the professional classes. Downward cultural assimilation too often occurs because of the neighborhoods in which their children are raised. Over one-third of first-generation Mexican-American families are of the extended type. Family obligations and loyalty are salient cultural features.
9. Puerto Rican families share familistic values with Mexican Americans. The economic situation of mainland Puerto Ricans is less stable and their rate of single-parent families is very high. Unlike Cuban Americans, their families have generally been assimilated within the context of deprived neighborhoods. A majority of Cuban families arrived in the 1960s and tended to be economically advantaged. Cuban families have one of the lowest fertility rates in the United States. Cuban children are raised within fairly self-sufficient ethnic enclaves that reinforce their parents' socialization goals of economic solvency and the preservation of Cuban identity.
10. Chinese- and Korean-American families share similar values of familism, respect for their elders, and education. However, Korean families have arrived here more recently and a substantial proportion have dependent children, whereas a higher proportion of Chinese families now have several generations residing in the United States. Mothers have a high labor-force participation. Despite cultural differences, both groups seem to be successful at giving their children the tools with which to be educationally successful while retaining some core cultural values. Children of Asian origins often experience less negative peer pressure than whites because they are often excluded from the activities of their more emancipated

white and black peer groups. A characteristic of Korean-American families is that many own small enterprises located in black neighborhoods.

11. Prejudice and discrimination exact a toll on minority families; consequently, their adaptation becomes more difficult.

KEY CONCEPTS AND THEMES

Bicultural, p. 59
Bilingualism, p. 62
Cool pose, p. 69
Cultural brokers, p. 81
Discrimination, p. 68
Downward assimilation, p. 59
Downward social mobility, p. 59
Ethnic group, p. 57
Extended family, p. 76
Familism, p. 73
Fertility, pp. 64, 75
Functional community, p. 61
Gender, p. 41
Generations, pp. 60–61
Great Migration, p. 66
Horizontally extended family, p. 76
Intergenerational conflict, p. 60
Intergenerational continuity, p. 61
Intermarriage, p. 65
Internal migrants, p. 59
Kin orientation, p. 63
Minority group, p. 56
Model minority, p. 79
Neighborhood quality, p. 71
Residential mobility, p. 72
Segregation, p. 68
Sharing of parenting, pp. 63, 80
Single motherhood, p. 66
Upward social mobility, p. 59

STUDY AND REVIEW QUESTIONS

1. Why does one speak in terms of immigrant "waves"?
2. What factors lessen the possibility of intergenerational conflict within immigrant families?
3. What role does gender play in immigrant family solidarity?
4. Urban Native adolescents have high rates of juvenile delinquency. Give at least three explanations for this phenomenon on the basis of the material presented in this chapter, even though juvenile delinquency is not mentioned.
5. What can explain recent large-scale single motherhood among African Americans and what cannot be used to explain it?
6. What are some of the problems faced by middle-class African-American families that their white counterparts do not encounter?
7. Apply the concept of downward assimilation to Mexican-American families.
8. Relate the economic situation of mainland Puerto Rican families to their family structure and dynamics.
9. Recall the theme of the effective community presented in Chapter 1. How can it be applied to Cuban-American children's outcomes?
10. Name some similarities and differences between Chinese- and Korean-American families.

SUGGESTED READINGS

Billingsley, A. 1992. *Climbing Jacob's ladder: The enduring legacy of African American families.* New York: Simon and Schuster. The author documents the history of African

Americans, including an examination of family life in West Africa, from where most slaves originated, and relates this history to current conditions of black families.

Franklin, J. H. 1993. *The color line: Legacy for the twenty-first century.* Columbia: University of Missouri Press. This is an analysis of historical developments that have impacted on the current condition of blacks and black families.

Greenfield, P. M., and Cocking, R. R. (Eds.). 1994. *Cross-cultural roots of minority child development.* Hillsdale, NJ: Erlbaum. This sociopsychological collection of reviews of the literature focuses on child socialization and development among diverse American minority groups. A few chapters are devoted to children in Africa, Mexico, and Asian countries.

McAdoo, H. P. (Ed.). 1993. *Family ethnicity: Strength in diversity.* Newbury Park, CA: Sage. This collection of articles examines various ethnic and racial groups in the United States, mainly but not exclusively with a focus on family life. Emphasis is on African-American, Native, Hispanic-, and Asian-American families.

Mindel, C. H., Habenstein, R. W., and Wright, R., Jr. (Eds.). 1998. *Ethnic families in America: Patterns and variations* (4th ed.). Upper Saddle River, NJ: Prentice-Hall. This collection of articles covers the family situation of a variety of ethnic groups, ranging from socioreligious groups such as the Amish and the Mormon, to white, Asian, and Hispanic ethnic groups.

Pedreza, S., and Rumbaut, R. G. (Eds.). 1996. *Origins and destinies: Immigration, race, and ethnicity in America.* Belmont, CA: Wadsworth. This is a most complete volume covering aspects of the history and current situation of diverse racial and ethnic groups in the United States. Among some of the groups discussed are Natives, African Americans, Mexican Americans, Japanese, Filipinos, and Koreans. Much of the material is relevant to families.

Portes, A., and Rumbaut, R. G. 1996. *Immigrant America: A portrait* (2nd ed.). Berkeley: University of California Press. The authors present analyses and theoretical perspectives on immigration in general, with an emphasis on more recent immigrants who belong to visible minority groups. This book contains a great deal of material on the education and socialization of children as well as on generations. Various minority groups are compared.

Rubin, L. B. 1994. *Families on the fault line: America's working class speaks about the families, the economy, race, and ethnicity.* New York: HarperCollins. The subtitle well describes the contents of this study of a group of families. The author's sample includes families of various ethnic and racial groups, many of which are white ethnics.

SUGGESTED WEBLINKS

About Immigration provides a long list of features, some practical, some scholarly, from a variety of sources, including newspaper reports. **<http://immigration.about.com>**

Center for Immigration Studies (Washington, DC) is a nonprofit organization devoted to research and policy concerning the impact of immigration on the United States. Click on *Backgrounder* to obtain a list of recent publications, including Ph.D. dissertations. **<http://www.cis.org>**

Office of Minority Health Resource Center is a government website. Click on *Welcome* and the site provides information on policies and initiatives regarding minorities. **<http://www.omhrc.gov>**

The Urban Institute is a nonpartisan economic and social policy research organization that investigates social and economic problems. It is relevant to families and welfare, immigration, violence, crime, and health care. **<http://www.urban.org>**

Women of Color Web explores the intersection of gender and race. It provides material on blacks as well as Chicanas. This website includes research, other Internet resources, and articles. **<http.//www.hsph.harvard.edu/grhf/WoC>**

CHAPTER 4

Partner Selection, Sexual Relations, and Reproduction

Dating
Heterosexual Dating
Same-Sex Dating

Date and Partner Selection
Heterosexual Mate Selection
Same-Sex Partner Selection
Same-Sex Marriage
Arranged Marriages

Sexual Relations
Early Sexuality
Ethnic Group Differences in Early Sexuality
Gender Differences in Early Sexuality
Early Sexuality and Health Risks
Marital and Cohabitational Sexual Relations
Frequency of Sexual Intercourse and Aging
Frequency of Sexual Intercourse and Cohabitation
Frequency of Sexual Intercourse and Relationship Quality
Extracouple Sexual Relations

Family Planning, Fertility, and Abortion
Family Planning
Fertility Rates
Abortion

New Reproductive Technologies
Types of Reproductive Alternatives
Artificial Insemination
In Vitro Fertilization and Transplantation
Frozen Embryos
Surrogate Mothers
Multiple Births

Singlehood and Married Childlessness by Choice
Types of Singles
Factors Facilitating Singlehood
Advantages and Disadvantages of Single Life
Childless Marriage by Choice

Conclusions: The Changing Profile of Reproduction

Summary
Key Concepts and Themes
Study and Review Questions
Suggested Readings
Suggested Weblinks

OUTLINE

"Besides finishing my studies, what's most important in my life right now is my boyfriend. The best part of my life is when I am with him."

"The most painful aspect of my life at this age [about 21] is that I don't have a steady boyfriend. I haven't had one in two years and I am worried that life is passing me by."

"I rate myself as very happy. . . . Before I broke up with my boyfriend of two years I had no life. I was entirely wrapped up in a relationship that denied my identity. . . . It's freedom now and time for me to use it to mature."

"In this age bracket [since age 18], what has been the most painful thing has been my girlfriend of nearly two years leaving me. Rationally, it shouldn't be painful

because she did me a service: she just was too self-centered to ever be a good wife or mother but I just kept clinging to her, hoping against hope."

"I am still a virgin and it has its inconvenience socially [popularity]. . . . I am proud of myself because I have stuck to my principles and my parents' and one day the full discovery of sex will be a very exciting experience to share with my husband. It will add something to our marriage and he will know that I have waited for him."

"The girls at my school were boy-crazy and there was nothing they wouldn't do to get one and sleeping around was the main instrument of capture. I just couldn't fit in this sort of crowd."

"I don't see children on the horizon. I've got too many plans for my life and all that I can fit in there is a wife to share these projects with. Children are too time consuming nowadays."

"I hope to have had two children by then [in 10 years]. I guess it would be too much to think of having three because I'll need to keep my job."

"I had an abortion two years ago and that was rather draining emotionally at the time because it would have been nice to have had the baby, but it would also have ruined my plans for school and perhaps getting married. So now I am thankful for it."

"Abortion is much easier than birth control" [from a student who had had three abortions].

The preceding students reveal how they feel about dating, sexuality, and some aspects of family planning—all main topics of this chapter. These quotes were chosen among many to reflect the variety of personal experiences and expectations that are generally found in a student population. Readers may perhaps be able to identify with some of these thoughts. This chapter starts with the chronological beginning of family life: individuals select partners, become couples, and initiate sexual relations.

DATING

Boys and girls in the United States begin dating much earlier than children in the rest of the Western world. Dating is an American institution that emerged after World War I. In contrast to the traditional *courtship* system, which was a prelude to marriage, dating represented a shift in terms of control over couple formation—the control shifted from parents to the youths involved. This American invention has evolved somewhat over time. As the period of adolescence lengthened and age at marriage was delayed, dating was separated from marriage as a goal; its purpose became recreational and sexualized. Nowhere is dating as ritualized and institutionalized among adolescents and college students as it is in the United States. In addition, nowhere else does it exist at the preadolescent level, as documented by Merten (1996) and Adler and Adler (1998).

Heterosexual Dating

It is commonplace in the United States for children as young as age 7 to be asked if they have a girlfriend [boyfriend] yet. Thus, children learn very early that a friendship with a member of the opposite sex is labeled *dating*. The friendship is, in effect, sexualized. Americans have been the first to organize school dances, even in grade school. A couple culture pervades American social life, which makes it difficult for unattached adolescents and adults to feel that they "belong" if they do not have a steady date or partner. Particularly among teenage and college women, the quest for a steady boyfriend may be an all-consuming pursuit—even among adults, particularly after a divorce. This quest brings both happiness and misery.

When this preoccupation with being part of a couple occurs early in a child's life, it may supplant other experiences and sources of self-definition. It brings adult preoccupations to the fore. Among adolescents, dating often becomes a form of social pressure and a key source of popularity. Coincidentally, popularity is a far more important feature of U.S. and Canadian youths' lives than it is in other nations. Overall, it is not surprising that adolescents and young adults seek steady dates, because they represent a measure of social and personal security. Dating also serves the function of socializing youths, both positively and negatively, for the role that they will play when they cohabit or marry. For many, it is a prelude to marriage.

Young women tend to be more invested in their dating relationship than are young men and work harder at maintaining it (Sacher and Fine, 1996). This pattern of **gender roles** in the emotional domain is pursued at all levels of romantic relationships (Kirkpatrick and Davis, 1994). The greater female investment stems in part from their socialization, which has taught them to be more nurturant and dependent on males. Young women also tend to perceive that they have access to fewer desirable alternatives outside their relationship than do males (Floyd and Wasner, 1994):

> *"The most painful experience at this stage has occurred three months ago when I broke up with my boyfriend of three years. It was the hardest decision to make in my adult life. I should have broken up with him two years ago because I could see then that things were not going to work out in the long run,*

he was too independent, not communicative, and he liked to control me by telling me as little as possible about his life. . . . But I was afraid to be left alone, that I wouldn't be able to go out without a boyfriend, that I couldn't find another one, but now I realize that I have wasted two years of my life, and that's terrifying."

This perception of a lack of alternatives contributes to reinforcing young women's tendency to work harder at relationship maintenance. In practical terms, it implies being "nice" to their partner, anticipating his needs, and planning activities for the couple. However, in terms of **exchange theory,** females with the most desirable resources (generally defined by males as attractiveness, social status, personality) can "afford" doing less maintenance work, as their alternatives may be more numerous and desirable than those of their date. But, overall, several studies confirm that dating interactions are nonegalitarian, at least at the beginning (Laner and Ventrone, 1998). This pattern is pursued in cohabitation and marriage, as discussed in Chapter 10.

Same-Sex Dating

It is not yet possible at this point to provide solid information on same-sex dating, because little research exists on this topic. Gay youths are often difficult to identify and are not readily accessible for research purposes (Anderson, 1998). Not only do they shun publicity so as to avoid stigmatization but they also constitute a small minority of all adolescents.

Although there is a certain overlap in terms of homosexual and heterosexual self-identity, it is nevertheless a myth that 10 percent of the population self-identifies as exclusively homosexual. This myth evolved from the hastily interpreted results of the poorly designed 1948 Kinsey Report. The Kinsey sample was not representative and was largely self-selected. But even then, Kinsey and his colleagues estimated that only 4 percent of males are *exclusively* homosexual (Kinsey, Pomeroy, and Martin, 1948:651; Laumann et al., 1994). Yet, this figure was overlooked, because the Kinsey Report also included men who had had at least one homosexual encounter, generally in their youth, but did not consider themselves to be gay (Michael et al., 1994)—all in all, for a total estimate of 10 percent of the population. It is this latter figure that caught the media's attention, became entrenched in the public's perception, and accepted by gays themselves. Kinsey's subsequent 1953 report on female homosexuality did not present exact numbers.

Young homosexuals tend to be more visible in metropolitan areas, such as Los Angeles, San Francisco, and New York. In these large urban centers, homosexuality is more acceptable than in other areas and gay and lesbian activities are quite visible, thus attracting gays from other parts of the country. In turn, this localized visibility, often enhanced by the media, lends credibility to inflated rates of homosexuality.

This being said, one can presume that coupling or dating may fulfill for gay and lesbian teens and young adults emotional functions similar to those among heterosexuals. Same-sex dating may, however, be dysfunctional in terms of high school acceptance and popularity as well as social acceptance in colleges located outside of key metropolitan areas. The high school environment is often homophobic or anti-gay, as is also the case in some colleges. As a result, gay youths are often harassed (Savin-Williams, 1994), which in turn can lead to mental health problems (Waldo, Hesson-

McInnis, and D'Augelli, 1998). Given this homophobic environment, it is not surprising that gay adolescents have higher suicide rates.

Gay adolescents and young adults, then, might not be able to date as do their heterosexual peers for fear of bringing social stigmatization on themselves. This situation thereby prevents them from gaining the experience in intimate relationships that their heterosexual peers acquire via the institution of dating. Furthermore, for many, "coming out" (revealing their sexual identities) may occur only when they reach adulthood. In the meantime, it is not uncommon for gay and lesbian youths, particularly women, to date members of the opposite sex (Schwartz and Rutter, 1998).

DATE AND PARTNER SELECTION

At the adolescent level, dates are largely chosen from schools, neighborhoods, churches, and social clubs to which adolescents or their parents belong. Parents and their friends may constitute a source of dates, particularly in some religions or ethnicities among whom marriage within the group is preferred, and at the upper-class level where adults are more likely to initiate introductions. Overall, **propinquity,** or physical proximity, is the first rule that explains how adolescents choose dates and, later on, partners. In young adulthood, proximal availability continues to be an important factor, but its scope broadens to include the worlds of college and work. Friends and siblings also serve as go-betweens.

Young adults become more selective because the relationships they initiate have the potential of leading to cohabitation and/or to marriage in the near future—a more serious step. Therefore, the pool of eligible dates and partners narrows because each individual then tries to select only certain types of persons. At this point, theories discuss mate selection in terms of **assortative mating,** which should now be relabeled

Date selection is largely endogamous in terms of race, particularly for black people. This situation reflects the fact that race is the prime element of social stratification in the United States.

assortative partnering. This term refers to choosing a date on the basis of certain characteristics similar to one's own rather than accepting anyone who is available nearby. Assortative partnering leads to compatibility of interests, values, and lifestyle (Surra, 1990). It facilitates an equitable exchange of resources, both personal and social.

Assortative partnering is related to **homogamy,** a concept used when two persons choose each other on the basis of some elements of similarity. When homogamy is analyzed at the level of the demographic characteristics or resources that are important in a society's stratification system, the term used is **endogamy.** That is, people date and marry within their own status group. Although no statistics are available on this topic, one can presume that people cohabit within their status group, as well. But one can also expect that a greater proportion of cohabitations, particularly when they are casual, than marriages are exogamous (defined below). People may be more willing to experiment and take risks for cohabitation than for marriage because personal investment is generally lower in cohabitation than in marriage.

Heterosexual Mate Selection

In the United States, the first element of stratification, or grouping, is **race** and **ethnicity.** Thus, race is the first source of assortative mating and endogamy. Intermarriage is synonymous with *exogamy,* which means marrying out of one's group—in this case, race or ethnicity. Intermarriages, however, can involve partners who, except for race, are very similar or homogamous in terms of religion, lifestyle, and values. Intermarriage has increased across all ethnic groups. As we learned in Chapter 3, Native Americans now marry out more than within their own groups. Asian Americans, particularly women, also have high rates of intermarriage, especially on the West Coast and in Hawaii. By 1994, there were over 1.2 million racially mixed *married* couples in the United States, or 2.4 percent of all married couples (U.S. Bureau of the Census, 1995a). Of these, 296,000 were black-white married couples—196,000 with a black husband and a white wife, and 100,000 with a black wife and a white husband. Although black women–white men marriages remain comparatively infrequent, they have increased proportionally more than for black husband–white wife couples since 1980.

Social class, or socioeconomic status (SES), as well as educational endogamy is widespread, particularly in marriage. In other words, people tend to marry within their social class or very close to it. This is partly explained by the fact that the proximity factor is driven by parents' social class. Parents' social class dictates where their children live and which schools they attend. Even at work, people are attracted to each other because of common interests and shared topics of conversation that are partly related to their resources, including education.

Religious endogamy is more important in some groups, such as Jewish and Amish, than others. Nevertheless, Jews intermarry in about half the cases (Schaefer, 1998:369), especially after a divorce. Jewish people marry out more often when they live in cities where the Jewish population is small. Under such circumstances, their social network may be largely non-Jewish, plus their ethnic group does not provide enough internal selection. These internally restrictive factors are conducive to intermarriage.

Age homogamy is another important mate selection factor in *first* marriages, because people often marry school or college peers. The male-female age difference at first marriage is generally around two years (Darroch, Landry, and Oslak, 1999). However, when men marry later or remarry, they remarry women considerably younger than they. The age gap increases with subsequent remarriages. This trend has not received an adequate explanation, but it could stem from men's opportunities to meet younger women in the workplace. Because there is a double standard of aging, men often prefer younger women to their agemates. In general, men are less receptive than women to the idea of marrying someone older than they; they are also less accepting of the notion of choosing someone who is not good looking (South, 1991).

Both from a functional perspective and exchange theory, endogamy and homogamy make sense; this is reflected in the observation that interreligious, interracial, and interclass marriages have higher divorce rates than endogamous ones (Laumann et al., 1994:502). Perhaps the same situation occurs among cohabitors. Similarity or complementarity of resources strengthens equity. It is also easier to fit in with someone who is similar than to adapt to someone who is from a different background. Similarity of lifestyle, values, and interests means that couples have a larger pool of experiences they can share and activities they can engage in together. It strengthens mutual feelings, we-ness, and companionship—key elements in American marriages nowadays.

Same-Sex Partner Selection

Once again, we are in the realm of perspectives rather than facts when it comes to same-sex partner selection, for there are no "hard" data from which to generalize. Thus, it is difficult to know to what extent the principles that dictate mate selection among heterosexuals apply to the formation of lasting relationships among same-sex couples. Homosexuals are nonconformists in at least one area of their lives—their sexuality (Bell and Weinberg, 1978). This may well lead them to be nontraditional in other domains, as well, including the criteria that dictate choice of partners. In their search, they may have to cast a far wider net than do heterosexuals, considering they constitute a minority of the population and suitable mates may not be readily available nearby. We have learned that males are less willing than women to select dates who are not good looking (South, 1991). There are also indications that partner selection among gay men may be more influenced by physical appearance than that among gay women.

As mentioned earlier, there are dating rituals that young gay men and women do not have the opportunity to engage in as do their heterosexual peers. This lack of rituals in the traditional form of "boy-meets-girl, boy-dates-girl" may deprive them of a structure for partner selection as well as experience in the processes that lead to this selection. It may be for this reason that lesbian relationships frequently break up: Lesbian women more readily move in with each other than do heterosexuals and gay men alike. As a result, their dating experience takes place within cohabitation—that is, after they have become a couple. When this occurs, it makes living together more unstable, because the partners were not sufficiently well acquainted before. This situation is likely to change as society becomes more tolerant of same-sex relationships.

Same-Sex Marriage

No country in the world has yet legalized same-sex marriage. This said, some religious congregations bless such unions, but this recognition varies largely from place to place and provides no legal rights. However, by the time this book goes to press, Holland will probably have become the first nation in the world to recognize and legalize same-sex marriages, and Hawaii may also have done so.

Other countries—such as Canada, France, and Germany—are eliminating most differences between same-sex and opposite-sex unions (Van Cleve, 1999). Several countries, beginning with Denmark in 1989, have established a new category called **registered partnership.** Van Cleve explains that this partnership is a giant step forward, as it recognizes the special nature of lesbian and gay relationships that are committed and it offers some of the benefits and guarantees of marriage. The benefits granted tend to be largely at the economic level, such as inheritance, pension plans, and health benefits. They do not, however, extend to matters such as adoption or artificial insemination paid by socialized medicine.

The 20 states that allow same-sex-couple adoption have a two-step process whereby one parent first adopts and then the second one can petition for joint rights. New Jersey allows both partners to adopt together. In other states, only one of the two partners can adopt as an individual (Partners Task Force, January 1999: <www.buddy.buddy.com>). Therefore, Americans are more liberal in terms of permitting some form of legal adoption than are other Western countries. That is, the United States seems more ready to legitimize same-sex *family* formation, whereas other countries are coming closer to recognizing the legality of same-sex *couple* formation, or marriage. It would seem that couples who are allowed to adopt a child legally, even with the two-step procedure, should be given the opportunity of being recognized as married, especially since Americans have always valued the sequence of marriage first and babies later.

Furthermore, as discussed in Chapters 5 and 10, the legalization of a union as marriage constitutes a more serious step than cohabitation. In turn, legalization constitutes a **barrier** preventing couples from breaking up for futile reasons (Kurdek, 1998). One can less easily walk out of a marriage than a cohabitation, because there are more legal and social strings attached to the former. Same-sex couples who have children constitute a family. These children would benefit if their parents had social and legal incentives that would stabilize their relationship (Schwartz and Rutter, 1998).

Arranged Marriages

Because of immigration from Asia, particularly India, and from Muslim countries, arranged marriages occur more frequently in the United States than used to be the case just a decade ago. They also take place among some Orthodox Jews. Such marriages are interesting sociologically because the contrasts they present highlight the demands placed on freely chosen relationships. Furthermore, there are *degrees* of arranged marriages; many U.S. marriages that appear to be freely chosen are actually arranged. This situation occurs particularly at the upper-class level.

At one extreme are marriages that are arranged by parents or brokers (intermediaries) without the input of the concerned offspring and without their ever having met or interacted before the wedding ceremony. Some of these arrangements are called *forced* marriages when the bride more or less becomes a captive of her parents and her groom's family. In some cases, bride giving and bride-price, or giving gifts to the bride's family, are still practiced, as are dowries to the groom's family (Tapper, 1991). In other instances, young people are consulted and allowed to meet, although chaperoned, in order to get acquainted. In theory, one of the two can refuse to proceed with the marriage, but such a refusal results in an embarrassing social situation whereby the rebuffed party and kin may be humiliated socially.

Currently, many well-educated American men from India ask their parents to find brides for them in India because they prefer this traditional arrangement. Islamic and Hindu Marriage Bureaus exist for the purpose of arranging suitable unions in the United States and Canada. The Internet is involved, too—an indication of the families' high level of education; also, ads are placed in newspapers. A sample follows from the February 1998 issue of the newspaper *India Abroad*. Similar ads exist for sons and even brothers.

> Agarwal parents seek MD residents match for their beautiful, talented daughter, 25/5'4", U.S. citizen starting residency July 98. Send biodata and photo.
>
> North Indian, Hindu parents invite correspondence for only son, MD, U.S. educated/citizen, 35/5'7"/170 lbs, handsome, likes East/West values, family values. Brief issueless marriage. Prefer Doctors with similar interests.

Arranged marriages are not necessarily homogamous, because, in some societies or groups, a woman's education may not be given much importance in the choice of a bride (Smits, Ultee, and Lammers, 1998). Her reproductive potential is more valued. Arranged marriages are driven by family duty and custom rather than by individualism. They serve as a link between two families. These institutional elements encourage stability and do not preclude love. The mother and father roles are clearly delineated and so are those of the husband and wife, with the wife generally seconding her husband. When the young couple accepts these values, stability is increased, in comparison to marriages that involve renewed bargaining over roles and the division of labor as the relationship develops and as the family grows in size.

Marriages that are arranged before immigration takes place may be particularly fortuitous for the wives who are freed from their onerous duties to their husbands' extended families (Sheth, 1995). However, there is a danger that, as women age and become better acquainted with U.S. customs, they may refuse to go along with the traditional roles, particularly when a double standard of sexuality exists (men are allowed freedom) and physical "punishment" of a wife takes place. Many of my students have described such circumstances in their own families:

> *"When my father arrived in Canada he corresponded with old friends who lived in another Asian country and asked them to find a wife for him. So that's how my mother arrived. . . . I think that she desperately wanted to leave her family because she had too many sisters and there was no future for her in her country. Here she had to work hard with my father and this was not a problem because she was used to hard work. But then she came to understand that women in North America don't have to obey their husbands, that they get some affection*

> *from them, that the husbands don't order them around or don't even beat them. I think that when these realities hit her when we were small she became even unhappier and keep in mind that she had never been happy before. But she put her maternal duties ahead of her marital happiness and we all survived but we really did not have a happy family life."*

In contrast to this description, one very modern and indulged student discussed her own arranged marriage. She had been married for three years, was in her mid-twenties, and had no children yet. They had seen each other socially before, and both sets of parents had allowed them to meet alone before a proposal was formally made:

> *"My parents would not have forced me if I had not wanted him. . . . I know that no one else in this class has a marriage like mine but I must tell you that I am very happy. . . . I have always known from the time I was a teenager that my parents would find a husband for me and I felt far more secure than most of the other non-Orthodox [Jewish] girls at my school who were so hyper about finding a date and then later on a husband. I trusted my parents and sure enough prince charming came along. I did not have to struggle with dates and pretend I loved them. I did not have to suffer rejection. And now we are both committed to our marriage and to our two families and we had a wonderful wedding and a great honeymoon and it has been so wonderful ever since. He is so romantic, I can't believe it."*

SEXUAL RELATIONS

The focus of this section is on *relations* rather than sexuality in general, sexual identity, or even the mechanics and "plumbing" aspects of sexuality. Sex tends to be defined as **premarital** if it occurs before a person marries. Any sex that occurs is socially constructed and labeled in comparison to married sex, which is the normative sex—particularly in a family textbook. When discussing the sexual activities of young people, the term *premarital* implies that they will eventually marry (Sprey, 2000). Yet, knowing that people delay marriage more and more, this labeling tradition may well in the future lead to farcical questions: Will the never-married continue having "premarital" sex for 15 years? Are they still having "premarital" sex while they are cohabiting? And if they choose to remain sexually active singles into their golden years, will they have been engaging in "premarital" sex all their long lives?

Early Sexuality

The question generally asked is: At what age do young Americans begin having sexual intercourse? The median age is about 16.6 years old for boys and 17.4 for girls. By the time they reach adulthood, as many as 20 percent of young men and 24 percent of young women have not yet experienced sexual intercourse (Kowaleski-Jones and Mott, 1998). Besides gender and race, the following variables contribute to a *later* sexual initiation: higher parental social class, two-parent family, school achievement, and religiosity (Beeghley, 1996). Higher social class and school achievement are two mutually reinforcing variables, because high-achieving adolescents are far more likely to come from a higher SES. The activities of such children, particularly those that could endanger their future success, are more supervised by their parents than is generally the case at other class levels. These parents are reasonably successful at inculcating a sense of sequencing in their youth's life course that places education first, sex later, and procreation last.

Ethnic Group Differences in Early Sexuality

The median age at first intercourse is younger among blacks than whites and Latinos, in general. A study of Los Angeles County youths reported similar results: Black males had the lowest median age at 15 and Asian American males the highest at 18 (Upchurch et al., 1998). As explained in the previous chapter, the Asian Americans' later age is partly explained by cultural expectations that delay adolescent autonomy in various domains (Rosenthal and Feldman, 1991). It is also partly explained by the fact that a larger proportion of Asian males than others are education oriented, which tends to delay early introduction into sexuality (Kowaleski-Jones and Mott, 1998).

Overall, there has been no adequate theory to explain why African Americans initiate sex earlier. Recent research suggests that one of the explanations may lie in segregation in disadvantaged neighborhoods. In contrast, whites are far less likely to live under such circumstances. Brewster (1994) shows that when black and white adolescents are compared by the type of neighborhood in which they live, similar proportions of their age groups are sexually active. Put otherwise, black adolescents who live in less racially and economically segregated neighborhoods initiate sexual intercourse later, just as do white teenagers, even if their own parents are poor. Conversely, white adolescents who live in disadvantaged neighborhoods initiate sexual intercourse earlier.

Gender Differences in Early Sexuality

In 1960, only 23 percent of women age 18 had had sexual intercourse; this proportion grew to 46 percent in 1975 and 67 percent in 1990 (Beeghley, 1996:23). Rubin (1990) points out that just three decades ago, a teenage girl who was sexually active had to pretend that she was a naive innocent. Today, it is the uninitiated who must play the role of the sexual sophisticate. However, were it not for general **peer pressure** and, in many instances, rape or psychological coercion, perhaps as many as 50 percent of young women would initiate sexual intercourse later than they currently do (Abma, Driscoll, and Moore, 1998). Even some males obviously feel pressured as well as "left out":

> *"I always felt left out in high school just because I didn't get laid. I was the only guy still a virgin at graduation. [Note that this was probably his perception rather than a fact.] The counselor told me there was nothing to worry about and he was right but to a 16-year-old that's not what you want to hear."*

Thus, simply mentioning the median age at first sexual intercourse camouflages an important reality: the degree of voluntariness and wantedness of the experience. This matter is further discussed in the next chapter.

There is also a great deal of difference by gender in the quality of the experience at first intercourse among adolescents. In part, this may stem from the fact that sexuality is now more goal oriented toward intercourse, and rather quickly, which may be more a male than a female vision of sexuality (Schwartz and Rutter, 1998:94). Girls might have a more satisfactory experience with a diffused sexuality involving much petting and stimulation over a long period of time. For their part, males describe their first intercourse as exciting and satisfying, whereas females report more fear, anxiety, embarrassment, and even guilt. Three women students' recent memories are presented:

> *"The first time I had sex was both most exciting and most painful."*

> *"I did not enjoy my first sexual experience at all because I was not ready for it and that's why I mention it here because it became something I regretted for a long time after and made me feel dirty. It took me three years after that, until with my boyfriend, to consider it again and the experience was so different because I felt loved."*

> *"The first time we made love was one of the nicest 'firsts' in my life. I had been so worried about it but it was the right thing at the right time with the right person."*

Obviously, the element of control is important and may be lacking in many cases due to peer pressure and lower self-esteem, compared to what is the case among males. Kowaleski-Jones and Mott (1998) report that, often, sexually active male teens feel more in control of their environment and express lower levels of depression than male teens who are not sexually active. The contrary is reported by many young females.

Early Sexuality and Health Risks

One problem concerning sex among adolescents is the high rate of sexually transmitted diseases (STDs). For instance, in 1998, a Johns Hopkins researcher found that over 25 percent of inner-city girls ages 12 through 19 were infected with chlamydia. This infection does not have overt symptoms, but it leads to infertility or tubal pregnancy (reported August 12, 1998, in the *New York Times*). Adolescents who take risks by having multiple partners and little use of contraception tend to have other problems, as well, such as more frequent alcohol consumption, lower school achievement, and a more difficult parent/child relationship (Perkins et al., 1998). They are also less likely to receive a great deal of supervision; permissive maternal attitudes about sexuality are equally related to having multiple partners (Miller, Forehand, and Kotchick, 1999). Family Research 4.1 further discusses this particular study.

Overall, the greater the number of partners in the past, the greater the chance that a person reports having had at least one sexually transmitted infection, and this is especially so among women. For example, of those with one partner since age 18, only 3 percent of men and 5 percent of women had had a STD, compared to 14 percent of men and 33 percent of women with 5 to 10 partners (Laumann et al., 1994:183).

Marital and Cohabitational Sexual Relations

Interestingly enough, conjugal sex is not as popular a topic of research as is sex outside of marriage! In the Psychlit database, for instance, one can find hundreds of articles on human sexuality published in scholarly journals, but very few on marital sex. In the sociologically oriented literature, the few studies on marital sexuality tend

FAMILY RESEARCH 4.1

Interviewers Have to Be Trained: A Study of Adolescent Sexual Behavior

The goal of research conducted by Miller, Forehand, and Kotchick (1999) was to study adolescent sexual behavior in relation to family variables among black and Latino youths, including a sample in Puerto Rico. The adolescents were ages 14 to 16 and still enrolled in high schools from where they were recruited: 982 mother-adolescent dyads were contacted. Mothers and sons were interviewed separately at school or at a research office. Interviewers were matched to the respondents by sex, language, and ethnicity. Older women interviewed mothers and younger persons worked with the adolescents.

The interviewers' training took place over several days for about 25 hours. The project and its goals were explained and interviewing techniques were reviewed. The interviewers familiarized themselves with the separate questionnaires they were to use with mothers and sons and they practiced among themselves. Each one had to conduct an interview while being observed and received feedback on his or her performance. Training also "addressed the interviewer's legal responsibility to report any abuse of a minor revealed during an interview" as well as crisis management.

to focus on the following questions: How often do couples have sex? What factors differentiate those with a high frequency compared to those with a low frequency?

Frequency of Sexual Intercourse and Aging

There is agreement that the frequency of sexual intercourse in marriage diminishes with age (Call, Sprecher, and Schwartz, 1995; Laumann et al., 1994). This downward trend is illustrated in Table 4.1. But these authors caution the reader that averages are not the best measure of couples' sexual activity after age 50 because couples who stop having sex depress the overall average. For instance, for respondents older than age 75, the average stands at about once a month. But when only those who have sexual intercourse are considered, the average rises to three times a month.

The question to address here, however, is how to untangle the effect of age from that of marital duration. In other words, as couples age, so does their marriage. The reader could argue that age has little to do with the decline in sexual activity; instead,

TABLE 4.1 Average Frequency of Sexual Intercourse among Married Couples by Age

Age Bracket	Monthly Frequency
19 to 24	11.7
30 to 34	8.5
50 to 54	5.5
65 to 69	2.4

Source: Data from Call, Sprecher, and Schwartz, 1995.

habituation or boredom with the same sexual partner may be the culprit in this decrease over time. Call, Sprecher, and Schwartz (1995) have done the calculations to respond exactly to this objection.

First, they found that age *is* the main variable. Second, if habituation has any effect at all, it is a short-term rather than a long-term one and it occurs early in the marriage. That is, couples' frequency of sex was highest during the first two years of marriage, regardless of age. After two years, or what is called the *honeymoon period*, the frequency of sex declined sharply. Thus, habituation or the wearing off of the novelty has its strongest impact *early* on in the marriage. The researchers further reasoned that, if habituation kept producing an effect, sex would then keep diminishing in frequency as the marriage continued to last, which is not the case.

The same phenomenon is observed in remarriages. The frequency of sex is high at the beginning of the relationship, no matter the age, and drops after the initial period. After that, it becomes a matter of age rather than length of marriage. Generally, couples who are younger at marriage or remarriage have a higher frequency of sexual intercourse than couples who are older.

Frequency of Sexual Intercourse and Cohabitation

Laumann and colleagues (1994) as well as Call, Sprecher, and Schwartz (1995) find that cohabiting couples have sexual intercourse much more often than do married couples. For instance, Laumann and colleagues report that only about 7 percent of married men mentioned having sex four or more times a week, compared to nearly 19 percent of cohabiting men. The women's reports were similar. The reader may then perhaps conclude that, at least as far as sex is concerned, cohabitation is more enjoyable. Is it?

Unfortunately, most long-term cohabiting unions tend to last at best for the same duration of time as does the honeymoon period in marriage—about two years. In fact, half of cohabitations end within one year (Laumann et al., 1994:496). Therefore, it is entirely possible that a higher frequency of sex among cohabitors simply reflects the fact that they are mainly honeymooners. When the honeymoon is over among cohabitors, the union generally dissolves. When the couple remains happy together, most then go on to marriage and, at least at the beginning, may maintain a higher frequency of sex.

So far, there have not been sufficient numbers of cohabiting couples at older ages whose relationships have remained intact for 5 to 15 years to compare them with married couples. However, one cannot eliminate the possibility that sex plays a more important role in cohabitation than it does in marriage and constitutes a larger part of the mutual attraction. Laumann and colleagues (1994) would agree with this possibility, as they point out that the decision to marry involves far more issues than does that to cohabit, including finances and families. Nevertheless, sexual frequency must also diminish with age among cohabitors who remain together.

Frequency of Sexual Intercourse and Relationship Quality

Couples with a higher frequency of sexuality experience a happier conjugal relationship. The more vital couples are, the more likely they are to remain interested in each other, and this interest generalizes into the sexual aspect of their relationship. Couples who get along better and share a higher level of companionship are inclined to be more physically affectionate, which leads to a desire and opportunity for sexual activities. Another complementary process is also at play: Having intercourse leads to a greater satisfaction with the marriage and the partner. Sex is a valued activity, and when it is satisfying, it increases a person's sense of well-being and appreciation. The partner feels rewarded. In contrast, when frequency diminishes too much or sex becomes less pleasant, the overall relationship may be negatively affected. Furthermore, when a couple quarrels a great deal or is more distant, this in turn depresses marital satisfaction and contributes to a decrease in sexual activity (Call, Sprecher, and Schwartz, 1995). One actually encounters both processes when studying how divorced couples' marriages deteriorated. One woman put it this way about her ex-husband in my study on divorce/remarriage:

> *"He always wanted sex more than I did and he was always mortally offended that I didn't. But he was always so mean to me otherwise that I had developed a sense of physical, you know, I felt repulsed at the thought of even touching him. I mean, you can't just separate the two. He used to call me a cold bitch, frigid, and that explained it all [her lack of interest in sex] in his mind. But, you know, my husband [remarriage] will tell you that I am a very physical woman [laughs]. If someone, your husband, is wonderful to you, it goes without saying that sex comes easily."*

The next respondent, also remarried, is explaining why he stayed so long with his ex-wife even though he did not like her much:

> *"Don't take me wrong here, I am not a pervert [we both laugh] but sex is the answer. We didn't get along well at all and didn't share much, but our sex life was great. It's difficult to explain but it was a nice release at the end of a hard day at work and even at home. That's why I stayed: I had a lot to lose here."*

Extracouple Sexual Relations

Generally, no matter the type of union they are in, males engage in extracouple sex more than women, as indicated in the percentages provided by Blumstein and Schwartz (1990). The respondents were men and women who reported at least one instance of sexuality outside of their marriage or cohabitation:

Husbands	11 percent
Wives	9 percent
Male cohabitors	25 percent
Female cohabitors	22 percent
Gay unions	79 percent
Lesbian unions	19 percent

In the 1994 study by Laumann and colleagues, the results were essentially similar. Whatever their marital status, most men and women reported having had only one sexual partner in the past year (67 and 75 percent, respectively). Of those who were married, 94 percent had been monogamous, compared to 75 percent of the cohabitors. These authors also report that, for both men and women, people whose first union was cohabitational have had more sexual partners than those whose first union was marital.

Hence, there is general agreement in the various sources of statistics on this topic, and several salient conclusions emerge. First, heterosexual men and women are more similar than homosexual men and women in terms of fidelity. Second, among gay unions, men are overwhelmingly nonmonogamous, whereas the opposite occurs among lesbian women. And third, married spouses have the lowest rate of infidelities. Cohabiting couples are far less monogamous, but there is little difference between men and women. The least that can be said is that married couples are far less sexually unfaithful than portrayed in the media. In fact, there is a great deal of consensus among Western countries that extramarital infidelities are unacceptable. For instance, Swedes who are very liberal in other domains of sexuality nearly unanimously disapprove of conjugal infidelities: 96 percent compared to 94 percent among Americans (Widmer, Treas, and Newcomb, 1998).

FAMILY PLANNING, FERTILITY, AND ABORTION

Family planning changed a great deal during the past century, aided in great part by technological advances in medicine—preventive reproduction. Furthermore, the changing roles of women and children described in Chapter 2 have drastically altered couples' and individuals' desired family size.

Family Planning

Family planning refers to women's or couples' decisions concerning the number and spacing of children they desire. In 1965, the Supreme Court ruled that contraceptives could be legally sold to married couples. Although anyone can now obtain contraceptives, family planning still remains a more difficult goal to achieve among singles. It is particularly problematic for adolescent women whose first intercourse is nonvoluntary (Abma, Driscoll, and Moore, 1998). Family planning has become easier within the marital unit because couples are more open on this subject and family size is an important topic of discussion between spouses.

In general, couples now show a preference for a two-child family—ideally, one boy and one girl. Couples who have reached this goal stop childbearing more often than those who have two same-sex children (Yamaguchi and Ferguson, 1995). For example, some couples with two or three girls are more likely to "try one more time" in order to have a son. But, overall, couples' family planning intentions change considerably over time, depending on circumstances such as health, finances, and work requirements (Heaton, Jacobson, and Holland, 1999).

Family planning has also become easier because of medical technology. There is now a wider availability of techniques, from condoms and the contraceptive pill, to injectable (the "shot") and implant (Norplant) contraception, as well as vasectomies and tubal ligations. Fewer sexually active women than in the past report not using any method, and this decrease is particularly marked among African Americans. Nevertheless, women ages 15 to 44 in 1994 still experienced a substantial number of unintended pregnancies. For instance, Henshaw (1997) reports that 48 percent of women have had at least one unplanned pregnancy in their lives. The rate was highest among women who were between the ages of 18 to 24, were unmarried, had a low income, and were black or Latina. Between 1987 and 1994, the rate of unintended pregnancy fell from 54 to 45 for every 1,000 women in the reproductive years. Fu and colleagues (1999) report that the highest rates of contraceptive failures occur to adolescents and cohabitors.

Above all, the fact remains that U.S. families, schools, and the media are not hugely successful at teaching the advantages of family planning and prevention of STDs to adolescents (see Donovan, 1998). Most adolescents point to peers and television rather than parents and teachers as sources of sex education. When ill-informed teenagers are the ones who educate others, the results are less than optimal. Condom availability in high schools provokes much debate because of fears that it will encourage sex. At least one evaluative study comparing adolescents' sexual habits before and several months after the introduction of condoms has found no such increase; the study also revealed that those males who were already sexually active used condoms more than before (Schuster et al., 1998).

Fertility Rates

Fertility refers to the number of births per 1,000 women during their fertile years (ages 15 to 44). A total fertility rate, which is often estimated, refers to the lifetime average number of children per woman. In the Western world, family size began declining in the nineteenth century, although many countries lagged well into the mid-twentieth century. In the United States, the downward trend occurred after the 1880s, when the average number of children was 7. As illustrated in Figure 4.1, this average then declined to 2.1 in the 1930s, only to bulge again to 3.7 during the **baby boom** or anomaly of the late 1940s and 1950s families. Indeed, after World War II, there was a sharp increase in fertility, in part explained by the social and economic optimism then generated. This increase was also fueled by a return home of young women who had been employed during the war.

Recently, most Western European nations have experienced fertility rates below the 2.2 replacement value needed to maintain a population. In the 1990s, Germany's fertility rate was 1.4, as was Italy's (a Catholic country); China's rate was 2.2, Brazil, 3.1, Mexico 3.8, and Nigeria 6.5. In the United States, white women who are not Latina have a fertility rate of 1.9. This compares with 1.1 for Japanese Americans, 2.5 for African Americans, and 3.2 for Mexican Americans (National Center for Health Statistics, 1997). Thus, Mexican Americans have the highest fertility rate but it is nevertheless lower than that of their counterparts (3.8) in Mexico.

The very low fertility rate experienced in all Western societies and in others as well, such as Japan and China, is a result of the combination of industrialization and urbanization. Children are less useful to the family unit and more costly in industrialized and technological societies (Zelizer, 1985). In contrast, families tend to be largest in horticultural and agricultural societies, or in the countryside more than in the urban zones of these societies. Agrarian children are useful, as they contribute to the familial economy in ways that are often substantial. In these same societies, large families, particularly those with many sons, are a source of masculine pride.

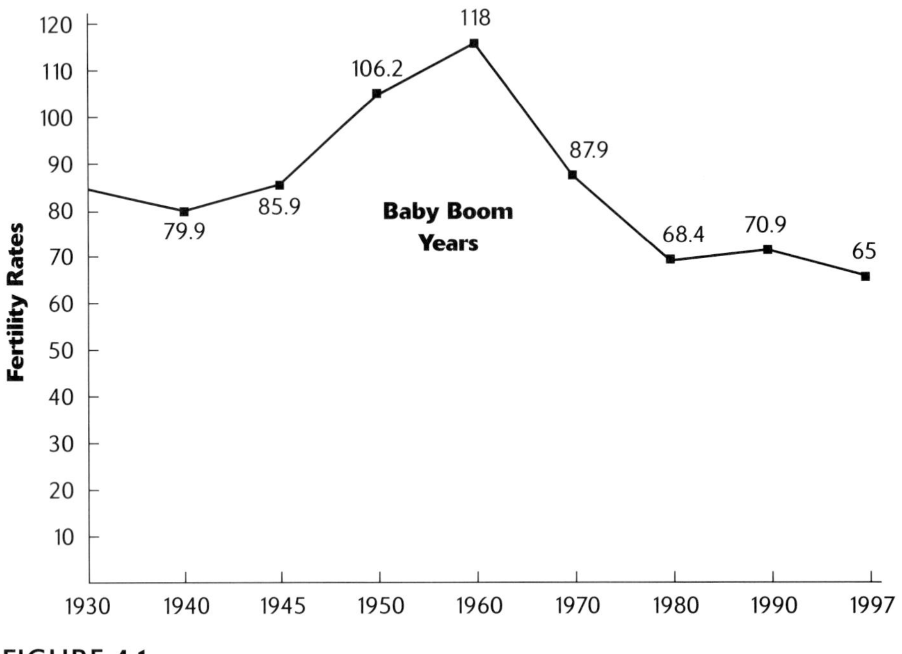

FIGURE 4.1

Fertility Rates per 1,000 Women Ages 15 to 44: 1930–1997

Source: Adapted from Ventura et al., 1999, Figure 1 and Table 1.

Abortion

Abortion is an extreme form of birth control; it occurs after other methods have failed or because no precautions were taken. The procedure became legal in the United States in 1973, with the famous *Roe* v. *Wade* case. The Supreme Court then ruled that states could not make abortion illegal during the first three months of pregnancy. Abortion has remained a topic shrouded in political minefields and emotional rhetoric from both ends of the ideological spectrum. At one end, abortion is synonymous with murder; abortion providers are viewed as child killers. At the other end are those who accept abortions as a woman's right over her body and claim that an abortion is "nothing."

In between these rhetorical extremes is the majority opinion that sees abortions performed in the first trimester of pregnancy as a woman's right while fully recognizing that it is not a decision to be taken lightly. For this majority, it is believed that abortions should not replace conscientious contraception and that late abortions are morally reprehensible because a premature infant born at the same gestational stage can survive with proper medical care. Thus, it is argued that perhaps late abortions to save a woman's life should take place by Caesarian section and the premature child's life saved. The child could be given up for adoption if not wanted. Then there are those who oppose all abortions because only God has the power to give and take human life. Those who do carry this belief do not, however, advocate retaliating against women clients at providing clinics nor against the clinics or their staff.

TABLE 4.2 Countries' Rates of Abortion per 1,000 Women Ages 15 to 44: 1990

Countries	Rates
United States	28
Sweden	20
United Kingdom	14
Netherlands	5

Source: Beeghley, 1996, p. 57.

In terms of factual data, abortions are relatively frequent in the United States compared to other Western countries, as illustrated in Table 4.2 for 1990. Rates in the United States have since been decreasing to nearly 20 per 1,000 women by 1999. In part, the relatively high U.S. rates reflect a lower access to contraceptive measures and a less successful education in this respect than in the Netherlands, for instance. Abortion is encountered among all religious groups, even if performed secretly, but not to the same extent. Catholics and some Protestant denominations have lower rates, whereas other religious groups and those not religiously affiliated have higher rates (Laumann et al., 1994).

Overall, it is estimated that one woman out of every four who has an *unplanned* pregnancy chooses abortion (Henshaw, 1997). Thus, about 43 percent of all women will have had at least one abortion by age 45. Women ages 20 to 24 have the highest rate of termination, at 53 percent. In fact, according to the Alan Guttmacher Institute (2000 website retrieval), 52 percent of all yearly abortions occur to women younger than age 25. Overall, 66 percent of all abortions are obtained by never-married women. Despite the fact that married women experience the lowest yearly incidence of abortion, they still constitute about 20 percent of the abortion cases, because they are the most numerous group of fertile females in the population. Married women have recourse to abortion either because they have had too many children, their health is precarious, the fetus is abnormal, or, more rarely, they wish to hide the result of an extramarital affair.

In 1992, 29 percent of pregnant Latina teenagers age 15 to 19 had an abortion, compared to 35 percent among non-Latina whites and 40 percent among black adolescents (Henshaw, 1997). In total, 60 percent of all abortions are performed on white women, because they constitute the majority of all women in the U.S. population. However, their rate is lower. For instance, black women are three times more likely to have an abortion than white women, and Latinas are two times more likely (Alan Guttmacher Institute, 2000 website retrieval).

There is agreement in the research that the decision to terminate an unwanted pregnancy rarely leads to serious and lasting psychological distress (Russell and Zierk, 1992), as expressed by a student:

> *"My boyfriend didn't want a baby so I had an abortion and I really hated myself for it eventually. I hated him because he could have left me with the baby, my parents would have helped. But he had said that no man should be forced to be a father against his will and that one day I'd ask for support when he couldn't*

> *afford it or the child would bounce up and sue him. . . . So it broke up the relationship. . . . Now with hindsight I know I am better off all around."*

When abortion is accompanied by a great deal of lasting distress, there generally were preexisting emotional problems. In fact, among adolescents, the long-term consequences of childbearing are more salient than those of abortion (Zabin and Hayward, 1993). Furthermore, children who were unintended at times suffer from negative outcomes later on, even as young adults, such as lower self-esteem. The mechanisms involved in this linkage are not known, however (Axinn, Barber, and Thornton, 1998). Above all, when legal abortions are denied, women turn to unscrupulous illegal abortionists and often pay with their lives; in other instances, their fertility is forever lost as the "surgical" procedure ruins their uteruses. In 1969, the number of illegal abortions performed in the United States was estimated to be around one million; between 5,000 to 10,000 women died yearly from complications (Kanowitz, 1969).

NEW REPRODUCTIVE TECHNOLOGIES

The issues surrounding reproductive technologies are sociologically interesting beyond the relatively small number of persons who have recourse to them. There has been a very rapid and generalized acceptance of or resignation to these technologies. Yet, these advances are problematic because they are generally occurring without any social planning, policies, and legal protection. For the medical researchers, biologists, and geneticists involved, discoveries represent progress as well as a source of income. However, families and the governments they elect are not given a chance to evaluate the social merits of these discoveries. Society has not retained its right "to determine how the achievements of science are used" (Strathern, 1995:33). Critiques further argue that these technologies have commercialized human reproduction, which has become a commodity—a service for a fee. In the long run, children may become commodities themselves, made to order in a catalogue (Rothman, 1989). Another critique is that, although single women as well as a few gay and lesbian couples have recourse to them, reproductive technologies and surrogacy are more available to married couples; they reinforce the traditional family structure (Cole, 1995). Physicians who sell these technologies often have a traditional construction of what a proper family is, so that relatively few are willing to offer their services to single women or homosexuals.

The number of American women who report some form of fertility impairment increased from 4.6 million in 1982 to 6.2 million in 1995 (Chandra and Stephen, 1998). This upward trend is largely the result of **delayed childbearing** among the baby boomers who then have difficulty conceiving when they finally try to do so during their less fertile reproductive years. Women are more likely to seek medical help for their impaired fertility when they are married, are white, and have higher educational and income levels. Men are also more likely to be implicated in fertility treatment than in the past. In a good proportion of the cases of "female" infertility, it is actually the husband who has the problem. Many instances of artificial insemination and in vitro fertilization occur as a result of low sperm count in men.

Types of Reproductive Alternatives

Let's review what is already available in reproductive technologies.

Artificial Insemination

Artificial insemination is a relatively simple and accepted procedure that was known by the end of the nineteenth century. Today, artificial insemination is often preceded by hormonal treatment, thus frequently resulting in the release of multiple eggs. Informal artificial insemination was followed by organized donor insemination whereby males donate or sell their sperm to a physician or to a sperm bank. In this instance, which constitutes one large step from the usual biological family, the husband is not the biological father; he is technically the *social father.* Donors are generally selected to match the social father as closely as possible. But potential parents can also request "designer" sperm by choosing a donor with certain characteristics, such as high IQ. One possible potential problem arises within the family unit as a result of social constructions of parenthood: The child is half adopted, half biological. Ethical questions that result are multiple:

- Should parents divulge to the child his or her biological background? After all, only one parent is not biological and this factor can easily be kept secret.
- What are the child's rights in knowing the biological father's identity?
- What is in the child's and the donor's best interest if the child, upon reaching adulthood, wants to locate the biological father?

A few European countries have already legislated on these three questions. For instance, in Sweden, when he or she reaches age 18, a child born as a result of artificial insemination has the right to know the identity of the sperm donor. The donor has no paternity rights or duties, however (Almond, 1995). Other questions are:

- What about multiple donations by the same man within a narrow geographic area? The possibility exists, however remote, that two half-siblings of the opposite sex could meet and have a child who may then suffer from a birth defect. In France, only two or three donations per man are allowed.
- With the American inclination to litigate, could a mother sue the donor for child support if the social father died or left?

In Vitro Fertilization and Transplantation

The next step in reproductive technologies occurred in Great Britain in 1978 with the birth of the first *test-tube baby,* Louise Brown. Her mother's egg was fertilized in vitro (in a test tube) by her father's sperm, and was then implanted into her mother's womb. This case is merely one of technology assisting nature rather than replacing any biological parent. Three kinds of in vitro fertilization then followed, each involving a further degree of biological distancing:

- The mother's egg is externally fertilized by donor sperm and then transplanted in her uterus. The birth mother is the biological mother, whereas her husband is the social father.

- A donor's egg is fertilized by the father's sperm and then transplanted in the wife's uterus. The wife becomes a nonbiological birth mother to her husband's and donor's biological child.
- A donor's egg is fertilized by a donor's sperm and transplanted in the birth mother's uterus. Neither the birth mother nor the birth father are biological parents. They are very similar to adoptive parents, except that the mother has carried the baby and given birth.

The last two techniques have recently been utilized for women over age 55; in fact, one birth mother was 63 years old. These cases have raised many questions concerning the future of a child who grows up with parents who may leave him or her orphaned at a young age. But it has been pointed out that older men often have children without encountering social disapproval (Schwartz and Rutter, 1998); older women, the argument goes, are discriminated against simply on the basis of their gender (van den Akker, 1994). Furthermore, there is no evidence that older women are less able mothers than women in their thirties (Berryman and Windridge, 1991).

In vitro fertilization carries higher risks of premature delivery, miscarriage, and multiple births. It is a fertility treatment that can be very stressful and even physically debilitating for the mother (Eugster and Vingerhoets, 1999). Fortunately, so far, the indications are that mothers whose embryos have been implanted are not negatively affected by their experience in terms of their parenting skills subsequent to the birth of *one* baby (Golombok et al., 1995). Nor are the children growing up differently compared to children conceived naturally (McMahon et al., 1995).

Frozen Embryos

Couples wishing to delay parenthood can freeze their biological embryos (i.e., fertilized eggs) so that they may have children of their genetic background when they are in their late thirties or early forties. However, there have already been cases in France and the United States of death and divorce of the potential parents. In France, despite sexual liberalism, single women are not regarded as ideal mothers:

> *A widowed woman requested to have one of her and her late husband's frozen embryos implanted in her uterus. The medical establishment refused; the courts upheld the decision, stating that it was not in the child's best interest to have a single mother. In the United States, a divorced couple is fighting for the "custody" of their embryos because the ex-wife wants to have a baby. Her ex-husband is afraid that he will be held responsible for children he does not want, particularly not from "that woman." The case is still in the courts at the time of this writing.*

Surrogate Mothers

A *surrogate mother* is a woman who carries a baby to term for a fee plus medical expenses and relinquishes it to the married couple or, more rarely, gay couple. Traditionally, the surrogate is artificially inseminated with the father's sperm (Bartholet, 1993). In order to avoid problems similar to that which made the headlines for so many months in the late 1980s concerning Baby M for whom the surrogate mother requested visitation and custodial rights, agencies screen surrogates more carefully;

in fact, most surrogates have children of their own (Ragoné, 1994). Other surrogate mothers carry a woman's ovum fertilized by either the father or a donor; surrogates are therefore not biologically related to the child, and cannot lay claim to the child on the basis of a genetic bond.

The surrogate mother phenomenon can be examined both from a class analysis and a feminist perspective, although there is a great deal of overlap between the two perspectives on this particular topic. Couples or gay men who avail themselves of a surrogate's services are unavoidably well off financially, and usually the surrogate is in some degree of financial need. Even though she may enjoy being pregnant, there is usually a social class gap between the parties involved, and this is seen as exploitative (Rothman, 1989). As feminists point out, this "rent a womb" arrangement exploits women and uses their bodies, although until now, another woman (the mother) has benefited.

On the other side of the coin, there have been cases of a mother carrying her daughter's baby because the daughter had no uterus (or sisters doing the same). In South Africa, for example, a mother carried all her daughter's children; in other words, she gave birth to her three grandchildren. The motives in these cases are purely altruistic. Therefore, although surrogacy is questionable from some analytical perspectives, it does fulfill several functions. The surrogate mothers themselves appreciate the small financial reward that comes with it and it allows them to stay home to care for their own children. Surrogate mothers generally adopt a professional and altruistic attitude and see the child not as theirs but as that of another woman. Compared to a woman who relinquishes her child for adoption, the surrogates have planned the pregnancy and its conclusion (Ragoné, 1994).

Multiple Births

Women are more likely to release multiple eggs when they are older. Delaying parenthood consequently causes a rise in the number of multiple births. But fertility treatment, including drugs and transplants of multiple embryos, are probably the main cause of the many multiple births that currently occur. Women who have recourse to fertility drugs have a 25 percent chance of giving birth to more than one baby (Wright, 1998). Normally, twins and higher-order births occur in the population at the rate of 1 or 2 percent:

One set of twins per 90 births
One set of triplets per 9,000 births
One set of quadruplets per 500,000 births

However, between 1972 and 1989, triplet births increased by 156 percent, quadruplets by 386 percent, and higher-order births by 182 percent among white women, who constitute the majority of fertility clinics' clientele (*Santa Barbara New Press*, 1992). In 1995 alone in the United States, 57 infants were born who were quintuplets or sextuplets, although not all survived (Adler, 1997). Multiple births to black women have increased far less because proportionately few can afford expensive fertility treatment; furthermore, black women do not tend to delay childbirth as often as do white women. However, black women's *natural* rate of twinship is higher than that of white women (Wong and Perry, 1998).

Twins and higher-order births now occur more frequently than in the recent past because of fertility treatment and delayed conception. These infants are generally born prematurely, weigh much less, and require more care from their parents than do singletons.

After the 1997 birth of the McCaughey septuplets and the less publicized 1998 birth of octoplets, the medical establishment finally began considering the ethical ramifications of such births following the implantation of multiple embryos or drug fertility treatment that allows the release of several ova. These pregnancies place the mothers' lives in serious danger. For instance, the woman who bore the octoplets had to spend several weeks on a hospital table that was tilted downward to her head in order to alleviate the pressure on her cervix and prolong the pregnancy.

Furthermore, nearly all multiple births have two immediate health consequences for infants: They have to compete for scarce resources in the womb and a majority are born prematurely because the womb becomes too crowded. Twins therefore have low birth weight, and babies of higher-order births can have extremely low birth weights—as little as or less than one pound. These infants are then at a far higher risk of neonatal death than singletons, particularly as a result of respiratory failure or the shutdown of some other of their tiny, immature systems. The danger period may last several months, during which the infants are kept in neonate intensive care units. Prematurely born infants are also far more likely than others to suffer from neurological deficits, whether learning disabilities or muscle coordination problems, although most of them make remarkable progress. For parents, twin and multiple births require a far greater adjustment to parenting than does a singleton birth: more time demands; less economic resources available per capita; the necessity to seek and accept help, even from total strangers; and more health-related concerns.

SINGLEHOOD AND MARRIED CHILDLESSNESS BY CHOICE

At this time, it is premature to state that a greater proportion of people than before are choosing to remain single and others who are married to remain childless. More people than before do live alone, but most of these individuals are simply delaying cohabitation, marriage, or even remarriage. Others are older widowed or divorced individuals, particularly women who, because of a better health and the unavailability of potential mates, live alone. At the very least, a prolonged period of singlehood before a first marital transition is becoming the norm and is a choice for many, particularly among whites and educated people of all races. For other persons, including a proportion of young women who give birth out of wedlock as well as minority women who are poor, singlehood may be imposed by socioeconomic as well as demographic circumstances, such as a scarcity of eligible partners within one's age group (see Chapter 6). For their part, a proportion of married couples chooses to remain childless, and another proportion postpones having children for so long that they effectively remain childless.

Types of Singles

A long while ago, Stein (1981) proposed four types of singles—a typology that is still relevant today, with some minor corrections. Stein's first two categories of singles are *voluntary.* Voluntary, temporary singles are simply delaying marriage, whereas voluntary, stable singles have chosen to remain single. The latter would include nuns and priests who accept celibacy. Stein, however, includes cohabitors in the category of voluntary singles. Cohabitation was relatively rare when he developed his classification and was not then, as it often is today, a substitute for marriage. Today, cohabitors are considered partnered rather than single. I suggest instead that voluntary, stable singles are individuals who choose not to be in a union that could become permanent. Under this definition, the voluntary, stable single category includes divorced and widowed persons, as well as persons who have cohabited, but who do not wish to marry or cohabit in the future.

Stein's two other types of singles are *involuntary:* Involuntary, *temporary* singles are still seeking a mate and would like to marry. They become involuntary, *stable* singles later if they have not been able to achieve the goal of marriage or cohabitation. Included here are some widowed and divorced persons who would like to remarry but will not find a mate. This category also includes individuals with mental, psychological, and physical disabilities that largely disqualify them as potential mates. It also includes women who are disqualified because of their age.

Factors Facilitating Singlehood

Certain structural factors make singlehood a far easier alternative than in the past. The most obvious is economic independence for a segment of women, especially the well educated and the professional. The second factor is the postponement of marriage that results in a greater number of singles in the population and thus makes singlehood a more acceptable status. The third factor is the high rate of divorce, which means that new singles of all ages reappear on the scene (some call this "recycling"), thereby making the single status a more fluid and less socially deviant one than in the past. And fourth is the greater social acceptability of giving birth out of wedlock or the possibility to adopt a child.

Urbanization is also a factor that has contributed to make the single life a more viable option than in the past; singles were both more isolated and visible socially when society was largely rural. In a city, in contrast, singles are less visible but they are also far more numerous, and this lowers the potential for isolation. They have access to a larger and more varied social network. The availability of a range of food- and household-related commercial services has also facilitated single life. Stein's (1981) typology applies both to heterosexuals and to homosexuals. Gays and lesbians basically can choose to remain single or to cohabit. Similarly, they may either be voluntary, temporary singles or involuntary, stable singles.

Advantages and Disadvantages of Single Life

For both sexes, remaining single is synonymous with various forms of independence. This involves flexible schedules, ability to engage in leisure activities spontaneously, being responsible only for oneself, and financial independence. For mature women, "going solo" may contribute to personal autonomy and growth (Gordon, 1994). In many instances, however, it is actually financial instability that leads to remaining single, particularly among men (Nakosteen and Zimmer, 1997). For these individuals, singlehood is not a blessing. For others, being single means a "revolving door" policy in terms of dating and sexual relationships, with no strings attached. Finally, many singles may actually fear marriage and family responsibilities. They may have friends or parents whose marriages ended catastrophically and they want to avoid such entanglements.

The main disadvantage of remaining single resides in the couple orientation and structure of society. Thus, single people lack a "built-in" partner for social activities. Other drawbacks are loneliness for some and a low income for others. Additional factors related to being single are alcoholism and dysfunctional health habits that persist, in part, because there is no spouse who provides some sort of structure and social control, as seen in the next chapter.

The disadvantages and advantages of remaining single are, to some extent, **gender** and **personality specific.** In general, single women maintain higher scores of mental and physical health and well-being than single men (Gove, Style, and Hughes, 1990). In fact, as we will see in the next chapter, single women are not all that different from married women in terms of happiness, although surveys have not taken into consideration the element of choice in singlehood. Furthermore, single women who choose not to have children may not be as disadvantaged as in the past, compared to their married counterparts with children, because children no longer constitute an unmitigated blessing in a woman's life (Ambert, 2001). Today, the benefits of having children vary greatly, depending on a number of variables (Menaghan, 1989). There is, however, a large difference between single and married men on all indicators of health and well-being in favor of the married. Therefore, although the status of a bachelor is still often portrayed as an enviable one and that of a single woman as problematic, the reality is different. Indeed, despite the double standard, it would appear that being single carries fewer disadvantages for women than men.

Childless Marriage by Choice

Official statistics make it impossible to determine how many couples are childless by choice and how many are because of fertility problems. The latter are generally called the *involuntary childless*. In 1995, nearly 18 percent of women between the ages of 40 and 44 were childless, compared to 10 percent in 1976 (National Center for Health Statistics, 1997). This 50 percent surge in so short a period of time cannot be explained by increased infertility; it is the result of choice or postponement until a point is reached where children are no longer desired or no longer possible to have (Heaton, Jacobson, and Holland, 1999).

As we will see in the next chapter, childless couples are more likely to divorce. Nevertheless, when controlling for number of years in a marriage, couples who are childless by choice experience greater marital satisfaction on some dimensions of their relationship (Somers, 1993). Couples are also happier before childbearing and after childrearing is completed. This has been called the **U-curve phenomenon** because levels of happiness start from high, then dip, then come up again. This U-curve phenomenon is not universally accepted among scholars. A few large-scale studies indicate that marital quality diminishes after a few years of marriage, children or no children, and that, on average, it does not pick up again after children are gone (Glenn, 1998). This question will be settled only when longitudinal studies of couples in their middle age to later years are carried out, comparing those who have children with those who are childless by choice.

Childless couples retain a more egalitarian division of household labor, for, as we will see in Chapters 9 and 10, the transition to parenthood leads to more traditional roles between husbands and wives. A couple alone has far less housework and does not have a schedule revolving around children. Consequently, the spouses do not have to renegotiate the terms of their relationship concerning who does what after the arrival of the first child, as is the case among couples who form a family. Childless couples have more freedom for work and leisure and fewer economic constraints. Their sexuality may be more spontaneously expressed. Their life choices as individuals are more numerous. For instance, they can more easily move without concerns about school and child care availability and the quality of the neighboring population.

CONCLUSIONS: THE CHANGING PROFILE OF REPRODUCTION

Change is the marking element in couple formation, sexuality, and modes of reproduction in North America. Many of these changes, particularly in the domain of reproduction, have no historical precedent and are controversial. Advances in genetics combined with new reproductive technologies could potentially give rise to abuse. For instance, in India and China, advances in the medical fields contribute to reinforce the traditional *devaluation of female children*, who are then aborted in great number. Scientific developments and their technological applications are revolutionizing not only the way in which families are formed but also the social construct of parenthood as well as human life.

SUMMARY

1. Dating is an American institution that replaced traditional courtship. Young women tend to be more invested in their dating relationship than are young men. Gay and lesbian students constitute a minority. Open, same-sex dating is a rarity at the high-school level, as students fear discrimination.
2. The choice of heterosexual dates (and later, partners) first follows rules of propinquity. Assortative mating becomes more prominent later on, and the term *homogamy* is used to refer to couples who are similar to each other on some characteristics. Homogamy becomes endogamy when couples partner themselves within their own group. Endogamy takes place largely along lines of race, social class, religion, and age.
3. Same-sex marriages are not yet a legal reality in the world. Registered partnerships are recognized in some countries for economic purposes. Arranged marriages are becoming more frequent in North America because of immigration. There are dangers that such marriages that are contracted before immigrating to the United States may be difficult as women become familiar with more liberal American customs.
4. The study of early sexual relations largely centers on factors related to delayed initiation into sexual intercourse. Variables that contribute to a later sexual initiation are high parental social class, a two-parent family, school achievement, and religiosity. Racial differences are largely explained by class and neighborhood variables. Young women's first sexual intercourse is not, on average, as pleasant as that of young men, and there are degrees of voluntariness and wantedness in the experience.
5. Within a marriage or a remarriage, couples' frequency of sex usually peaks during the first two years. It then diminishes drastically but remains stable in subsequent years, only to be gradually affected by age. Cohabiting couples experience higher rates of sexual intercourse, but there are no studies on long-term cohabiting couples. Frequency of sexual activity is related to marital happiness. Contrary to myths, a majority of married couples are sexually faithful. Cohabitors are less faithful. Least monogamous of all are same-sex male cohabitors. Lesbian cohabitors are less monogamous than wives but slightly more than cohabiting women.
6. *Fertility* refers to the number of births per 1,000 women ages 15 to 44. American fertility has diminished sharply since the beginning of the twentieth century, as has that in other Western countries. In the United States, women of Asian origins have the lowest rate. Family planning has become easier because of medical technology and more open communication on this topic among couples. Abortion is a controversial issue in the United States, even though abortion rates are higher than in other Western countries. It is estimated that one woman out of

every four who has an unplanned pregnancy has an abortion. Women in the 20 to 24 age bracket have the highest rate.

7. New reproductive technologies range from various forms of artificial donor insemination, embryo implantation, and surrogate motherhood. Children's and donors' rights are discussed, as are other ethical considerations. With fertility treatment, multiple births have increased astronomically. They do not represent an ideal developmental context for children, particularly while they are in the womb.
8. Singlehood is examined within its four subcategories: voluntary temporary versus voluntary stable singles, and involuntary temporary versus involuntary stable singles. The advantages of single life largely rest on independence and flexibility, whereas the disadvantages are age and gender specific. Married childlessness by choice is probably increasing and carries advantages. Marital happiness but not stability is higher among childless couples and the division of labor is more egalitarian.
9. Change is the marking element in couple formation, sexuality, and modes of reproduction in North America. Scientific developments in reproductive technologies could potentially give rise to abuse.

KEY CONCEPTS AND THEMES

Abortion, p. 106
Age homogamy, p. 95
Artificial insemination, p. 109
Assortative mating, p. 93
Baby boom, p. 105
Childlessness, p. 115
Cohabitational sexuality, pp. 100, 102
Courtship, p. 91
Dating, p. 91
Delayed childbearing, p. 108
Early sexuality, p. 98
Endogamy, p. 94
Exchange theory, p. 92
Exogamy, p. 94
Extracouple sexuality, p. 103
Family planning, p. 104
Fertility, p. 105
Gender differences, p. 99
Gender roles, p. 91
Gender specific, p. 114
Homogamy, p. 94
Homosexuality, p. 92
Intermarriage, p. 94
In vitro fertilization, p. 109
Marital sexuality, p. 100
Multiple births, p. 111
Peer pressure, p. 99
Personality specific, p. 114
Propinquity, p. 93
Race homogamy, p. 94
Registered partnership, p. 96
Religious homogamy, p. 94
Reproductive technologies, p. 108
Same-sex marriage, p. 96
Same-sex partnering, p. 95
Sexual intercourse and aging, p. 101
Sexual relations, p. 98
Singlehood, p. 112
Social class homogamy, p. 94
Surrogate motherhood, p. 110
U-curve phenomenon, p. 115

STUDY AND REVIEW QUESTIONS

1. What makes dating an American institution?
2. Are assortative mating and endogamy the same?
3. Analyze the variables related to early sexuality, both in terms of causality and consequences.
4. How do marital and cohabitational sexual lives compare?

5. Compare dating and sexual relations among heterosexuals and homosexuals.
6. How did family planning evolve in the last decades of the twentieth century?
7. Why do you think the United States has a higher rate of abortion than some other Western countries, particularly Holland?
8. What cultural and social issues relate to reproductive technologies?
9. Discuss surrogate motherhood from a class perspective.
10. Would you associate different personal outcomes with different types of singlehood or would the outcomes be the same? Why?

SUGGESTED READINGS

Anderson, C. M., Stewart, S., and Dimidjian, S. 1994. *Flying solo: Single women in midlife*. New York: W. W. Norton. This book is based on interviews of a large group of women who have never married. The contents take the form of life stories.

Cate, R. M., and Lloyd, S. A. 1992. *Courtship*. Newbury Park, CA: Sage. This text covers the history of courtship, discusses its functions, and traces the development of the relationship. It also looks toward the future.

Cohen, C. B. (Ed.). 1996. *New ways of making babies*. Bloomingdale: Indiana University Press. This collection of articles introduces the new reproductive technologies available and discusses their ramifications for the individuals concerned, including potential legal problems.

Laumann, E. O., Gagnon, J. H., Michael, R. T., and Michaels, S. 1994. *The social organization of sexuality: Sexual practices in the United States*. Chicago: University of Chicago Press. This book presents survey results in sexual practices on heterosexuality as well as homosexuality and in married as well as nonmarital sex. This book covers everything you ever wanted to know about sex, but does it within a carefully executed sociological analysis.

Rossi, A. S. (Ed.). 1994. *Sexuality across the life course*. Chicago: University of Chicago Press. This is a collection of scholarly articles on various aspects of sexuality and relationships.

Rothman, B. K. 1989. *Recreating motherhood: Ideology and technology in a patriarchal society.* New York: W. W. Norton. The author presents a thorough critical analysis, within a feminist perspective, of new reproductive technologies, including surrogate motherhood.

Smith, M. D., et al. (Eds.). 1996. *Sexuality and American social policy.* Melo Park, CA: Henry J. Kaiser Family Foundation. This collection of research and policy essays discusses a wide variety of topics and is quite informative.

SUGGESTED WEBLINKS

Alan Guttmacher Institute is devoted to reproductive health research, policy analysis, and public education. Topics range from pregnancy, abortion, STDs, and sexual behavior. **<http://www.agi-usa.org>**

Health and Human Services offers government statistics on topics such as birth rates and childlessness. **<http://www.hhs.gov>**

Surrogate Mothers Online is an informational site with a more personal focus. **<http://www.surromomsOnline.com>**

For various net links to parenting twins and higher-order birth children, consult **<http://multiples.miningco.com/home/parenting/multiples>**.

CHAPTER 5

Patterns of Family Formation

Single Motherhood, Cohabitation, or Marriage?

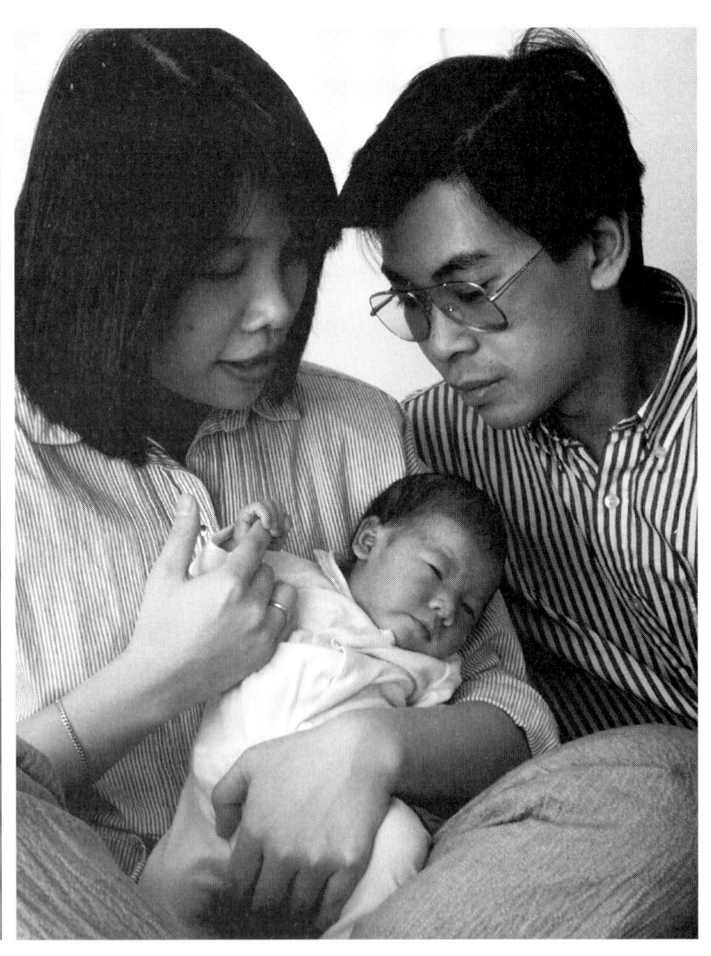

Single Motherhood
Trends in Unmarried Motherhood
Trends in Single-Parent Families
The Economic Perspective on Unmarried Mothering

Single Adolescent Motherhood
What Is Known about Teen Mothers?
The Adolescent's Life Course
Who Are the Babies' Fathers?
What Are the Effects of Single Adolescent Parenting on Children?

Cohabitation
What Is Known about Cohabitation?
Cohabitation and Children

Same-Sex-Parent Family Formation
An Overview of Same-Sex-Parent Families
Consequences for Children

Are There Advantages to Marriage?
Is Marriage Good for Adults?
Social Selection or Social Causation?
Are Marriage Benefits Gendered?
Is Marriage Good for Children?
Is Marriage Good for Society?

Adoption and Foster Families
How Do Adopted Children Develop?
What Is Involved in Stepchild Adoption?
What Are the Issues in Transracial Adoption?
What Is Open Adoption?
Reunions with Birth Parents: Functions and Consequences
Functions of Reunions for the Adopted Child
Functions of Reunions for the Birth Parents
Functions of Reunions for the Adoptive Parents
Foster Families: A Strained System

Conclusions: Family Formation Alternatives in Context

Summary
Key Concepts and Themes
Study and Review Questions
Suggested Readings
Suggested Weblinks

OUTLINE

"My sister had her first baby at 15, the second at 16, and the third at 18. She 'loves' babies but we've always had to take care of them and now she lives in our basement. I really resent her because sometimes I have to write a paper and there are these babies that I have to babysit. And now guess what, my brother's girlfriend is pregnant too and she's only 17. My mother should have never set a precedent by helping my sister."

"I come from a single-parent family and I wouldn't recommend it to anyone. My poor mom had too much of a hard time raising us three all alone, with no help and no respect from any one."

"My father left my mother before I even knew he existed so that I haven't missed out on much. The only drawback is that we weren't very well off but outside of

this I often think that I may just end up a single mother too one day if the right man doesn't come along. Beats not having children and besides I am very much like my mother and I would do very well thank you."

"I live with my boyfriend and I really like it for now but I worry about the future. I am 23 and want to get married one day but the way I see it, he likes it just fine the way it is and won't want to commit himself to something more serious."

"We're getting married this summer and we're both looking forward to it. We've lived together for one year because we could not afford the wedding and we felt that paying for one apartment as opposed to two would help us financially for when we get married. I would not however have lived with him had we not been engaged. That's a good way to get burned."

"It's a funny thing that I am getting married and my twin sister just started living with a guy. I don't know why she's doing it. I know what she says, she wants to play around a while longer and that maybe she'll end up marrying him. But it's all so superficial because my fiancee and I are talking about commitment, exclusivity, shoring up our finances, having two children. I mean, the two styles of conversation are just so totally different, it's unreal. I think my sister believes everything she sees on television, she's a soap addict."

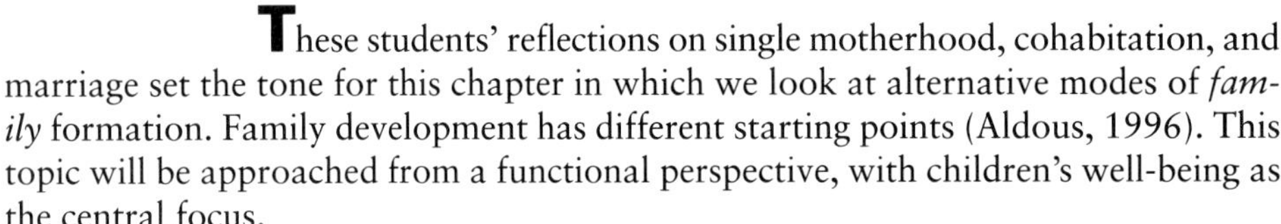

These students' reflections on single motherhood, cohabitation, and marriage set the tone for this chapter in which we look at alternative modes of *family* formation. Family development has different starting points (Aldous, 1996). This topic will be approached from a functional perspective, with children's well-being as the central focus.

SINGLE MOTHERHOOD

We saw in Chapter 2 that there is a great deal of alarm over the increase in single parenting in U.S. society, particularly that which results from births to unmarried mothers. If this concern is to be useful for the purpose of developing appropriate social policies, it must be accompanied by an understanding of official statistics and their implications.

Trends in Unmarried Motherhood

The *unmarried birth rate* reveals how many women out of 1,000 unmarried women ages 15 to 44 (the main reproductive years) have had a baby in any given year. In this and the next section, we will see that (1) the birth rate among unmarried women has increased since 1970 among whites and Latinas, but not among blacks; and (2) during the same period, the proportion of unmarried women giving birth, *compared to married women,* has skyrocketed. As a result, there has been a dramatic increase in the *proportion of children* born to single mothers, especially among blacks.

Let's start with item 1: If you look at Table 5.1 and compare the rates for the years 1970 and 1990, you will see that the birth rate for unmarried African-American women did not increase during this 20-year period; among them, the increase had taken place in the sixties. However, among whites, the rate nearly doubled, a fact that is significant in terms of numbers and policies, because there are far more whites than blacks and Latinas in the entire population. Nevertheless, by 1990, the rate for black and Latina women was over three times that of whites. But of equal importance is the sharp decline in the birth rate to unmarried African-American women after 1990.

As far as *unmarried adolescents* are concerned, their birth rate has largely followed that of adult women: It has increased for whites and Latinas. This was followed by a reversal later on in the 1990s, as seen in Table 5.2. In 1996, births to teen mothers declined by 12 percent overall and by 22 percent among blacks (Ventura et al., 1997). This decline continued in 1997, and was even more pronounced for repeat births (National Center for Health Statistics, 1998). The year 1997 witnessed the fifth consecutive yearly decline. This recent declining trend is explained by a more widespread use of birth control methods, particularly "the shot," and perhaps greater abstinence.

Actually, the *overall* rate of adolescent women giving birth reached its peak in 1957, with 96 births per 1,000 women of all races ages 15 to 19. Most of these adolescents

TABLE 5.1 **Birth Rates per 1,000 Unmarried Women Ages 15 to 44 for Non-Latina Whites, African Americans, and Latinas**

	Non-Latina Whites	African Americans	Latinas*
1970	13.9	95.5	NA
1980	18.1	81.1	NA
1985	22.5	77.0	NA
1990	24.4	90.5	89.6
1995	28.2	75.9	95.0
1997	27.0	73.4	91.4

*Includes all Latina women of any race.

NA = not available

Sources: Ventura et al., 1999, pp. 43–44, Table 18; and Bianchi, 1995, p. 85 for the year 1970.

TABLE 5.2 Birth Rates per 1,000 Unmarried Adolescent Women Ages 15 to 19 for Non-Latina Whites, African Americans, and Latinas

	Non-Latina Whites	African Americans	Latinas*
1970	10.9	96.9	NA
1980	16.2	87.9	NA
1985	20.3	87.6	NA
1990	25.0	106.0	65.9
1995	27.7	92.8	78.7
1997	25.9	86.4	75.2

*Includes all Latina women of any race.

NA = not available

Sources: Ventura et al., 1999, pp. 43–44, Table 18; and Bianchi, 1995, p. 85, for the year 1970.

were *married*, however. As the age at first marriage rose, fewer women married during adolescence, and the overall rate declined to 53 births by the mid-1980s. But, then, as births to unmarried teens increased, so did the overall teen birth rate. However, by 1996, the rate had declined to nearly 55 because of the recent decrease in nonmarital births. Thus, proportionately fewer teenagers now give birth than in the 1950s, but proportionately more *single* teens do. For instance, in 1970, 22 percent of 18- to 19-year-old women who gave birth were unmarried, compared to a staggering 72 percent in 1997 (Health and Human Services, 1998).

Trends in Single-Parent Families

While the rate of unmarried motherhood was increasing among whites and Latinas and had increased earlier among blacks, another process was at work. This fact refers to item 2 mentioned earlier: The *proportion* of *all* women (married and unmarried) giving birth outside of marriage has been increasing. As we will see in the next chapter, black women have been remaining single in disproportionate numbers because of economic reasons. This means that, although their birth rate among the unmarried was remaining stable or was even declining, fewer black women were marrying; thus, a larger proportion of children were born to single rather than married black mothers. By adding the overall rising divorce rate until the mid-1980s to this, then both the number and the proportion of children living in single-parent families have been increasing dramatically.

By 1991, 25 percent of U.S. children lived in a one-parent family, either following a parental divorce or because their parents had never married. Table 5.3 illustrates the spectacular increase in the number of one-parent families. Although the number of two-parent families also rose between 1950 and 1970 due to a general population increase, the number remained stable between 1970 and 1990 despite a further increment in the population. The sharp rise in divorce and the comparative

TABLE 5.3 Numbers of Two- and One-Parent Families with Dependent Children: 1950–1990

	Two-Parent Families (in millions)	One-Parent Families (in millions)
1950	18,316	1,531
1970	23,470	3,428
1990	23,495	7,383

Source: U.S. Bureau of the Census, 1992.

decline in marriage, particularly among blacks, as a mode of family formation explain this stagnation in the number of two-parent families.

Mathematically, the reader can understand what has occurred in terms of *proportions* of one-parent compared to two-parent families. While the number of two-parent families was remaining largely stable after 1970, the number of one-parent families kept increasing, thus increasing the proportion of all families that are of the one-parent type. By 1993, one of every four families was headed by a woman, with much higher rates among blacks (U.S. Bureau of the Census, 1995b:D22).

In 1940, nearly 18 percent of black families were headed by a woman, often following widowhood, compared to 10 percent among whites. The proportions among African Americans crept up to 22 percent in 1960, 28 percent in 1970, 40 percent in 1980, and shot up to 70 percent in 1997. Thus, contrary to some beliefs, and as already detailed in Chapter 3, the very high proportion of mother-headed families among blacks is a recent phenomenon.

The origins of single-mother families have changed over time. In 1970, only 7 percent of children living with a single mother had a never-married mother, compared to 35 percent in 1990; the remainder had separated, divorced, or widowed parents (U.S. Bureau of the Census, 1992). In 1970, 6 percent of all births to whites were to unmarried mothers, versus 35 percent for blacks. By 1996, nearly 20 percent of *all births* to whites were to unmarried mothers, versus nearly 41 percent among Latinas, and 70 percent among blacks—thus staggering increases in proportions.

In conclusion, since 1960, there has been a drastic decrease in the proportion of married families. Among blacks, and now Latinas, a majority of one-parent families are of the never-married type; among whites, they are of the separated-divorced type. Among blacks, the problem has been that, as fewer black women marry, the proportion of children born to single women has increased, even though single women's birth rate is declining.

The Economic Perspective on Unmarried Mothering

Never-married parenting, as well as parenting following separation or divorce, is problematic, because, as will be explained in Chapter 6, it more often than not stems from poverty and leads to poverty (Coley and Chase-Lansdale, 1998). In the short term, nonmarital motherhood makes relatively little economic difference in the life of an already impoverished teenager or young woman. But, generally, it *does* make a large, negative difference when the teenager or young adult belongs to a nonpoor family. In the long run, however, too many of the women who were already poor remain locked in poverty. Those who work at low wages have more expenditures (child care, health, transportation) and experience more hardships than those who remain on welfare—and welfare itself is difficult enough (Edin and Lein, 1997a; see Family Research 5.1).

Furthermore, age does not seem to make all that much difference at the economic level. Some exceptions aside, even single women between ages 25 and 40 who give birth tend to be or become poor nearly as often as adolescent mothers. They are more likely to be poor if their first birth occurred during adolescence (Foster, Jones, and Hoffman, 1998). Women who give birth during adolescence but have no subsequent births out of wedlock do somewhat better as adults than those who have nonmarital births in early adulthood (Hoffman and Foster, 1997). If you take two equally poor never-married sisters, one who has a first baby in her teens and the other in her early twenties, both are nearly as likely to still be poor by age 30. Both are nearly as likely to have been on welfare—except that the teen mother begins her life on welfare at a younger age (Luker, 1994).

From the individual point of view of the young mother, it makes short-term sense to have a child out of wedlock because there are relatively few males who could marry her and support her child, particularly if she is black (Coley and Chase-Lansdale, 1998). For many impoverished young women, having a baby out of wedlock may be the only form of social status they can look forward to (Fernandez-Kelly, 1995). Motherhood provides an important source of satisfaction and esteem for more than a third

FAMILY RESEARCH 5.1

Interviewing Is Easier Said than Done

Kathryn Edin and Laura Lein (1997b) wanted to resolve the discrepancy reported in large surveys that single mothers' expenditures are higher than their incomes. They interviewed 214 welfare-reliant and 165 wage-reliant, low-income mothers several times in order to track their unaccounted sources of income as well as types of expenditures. During the first meeting, the researchers asked mothers to detail all their monthly expenses. Edin and Lein point out that it was crucial to ask about expenses first and sources of income later. In their very first trial interviews, respondents who had talked about their incomes first had then adjusted their expenses downward to fit the reported income. Once the mothers had claimed that they spent nothing on clothes, for instance, it was impossible to make them retract, even if the interviewer saw the clothes on them! Thus, the order in which the questions are presented is extremely important in surveys.

Edin and Lein also emphasized that interviewers must listen carefully to the meanings that respondents attach to questions and words. For instance, the researchers learned that, when responding to large multiple-choice survey questions, most of the single mothers acknowledged receiving "child support" only when it was collected by the state. As a result, Edin and Lein found that the total value of money or gifts the women actually received from their children's fathers far exceeded what they reported in official surveys under the rubric of child support.

of all those living in poverty (Cohler and Musick, 1996). In such a context, motherhood, although unplanned, easily occurs, and certainly carries affective and social rewards. The young woman has someone very special to love, often gets a lot of attention from her family, and is the recipient of peer interest, at least in the short term.

On the other side on the coin, it makes no economic sense *for the child* who is born in poverty or who becomes at higher risk of poverty. Even when his or her mother exits poverty several years later, the fact remains that this child will have spent his or her entire formative years in poverty—and early poverty is most detrimental to a child's educational and occupational outcomes in life (Duncan et al., 1998).

Disadvantaged male and female adolescents who hold low educational and vocational expectations may feel that they have little to lose by engaging in unprotected sex that might lead to pregnancy (Furstenberg, 1992). This attitude is well expressed by a student:

> *"I am 28 and had my son at 16. At the time I was fed up with school and my mother and I didn't care to work and I thought the baby would be fun to have. I didn't go out of my way to have one but I certainly took no precautions. . . . It didn't end up being the rose garden I had wanted. . . . I was on welfare for many years . . . and bored. I went back to school at 23 and it has been a struggle."*

In contrast, whether they are poor or not, youths who are pursuing their education and who maintain reasonable expectations of finding a decent job after college or postsecondary training or who already have achieved these goals are generally motivated to avoid unmarried pregnancy and early pregnancy in general. As Devine and Wright (1993:139) state, "For the average middle-class girl, in short, having a baby is a quick path to downward mobility."

SINGLE ADOLESCENT MOTHERHOOD

Although single adolescent mothers constitute only 30 percent of all single mothers, they represent an important phenomenon on the American family landscape. It is a phenomenon that has no counterpart in terms of magnitude anywhere else in the major countries of the Western world, although England is rapidly gaining in this respect.

What Is Known about Teen Mothers?

Rebecca Maynard (1997) provides the following information: Each year, over one million adolescents become pregnant; approximately one-third have an abortion and 14 percent miscarry. A majority of the young mothers receive welfare at some point during the 10 years following the birth of their first child, and nearly half remain on welfare for more than 5 years. Only about 30 percent live with relatives. Until now, adolescent mothers have had an average of six-tenths more children than older women, and they have had their children over a shorter period, a situation that exacerbated their economic disadvantage and that of their children. But this situation is changing: Today, all women tend to have fewer children (Morgan and Rindfuss,

1999). At least 20 percent of teen mothers have experienced involuntary or **coerced sex** as have over half of those who became sexually active before age 15.

The 1995 National Survey of Family Growth asked 10,847 women ages 15 to 44 whether their first sexual intercourse had been voluntary. Of the women who had been age 13 or younger at the time of first intercourse, 24 percent reported that it had been involuntary, compared to 10 percent of those who were 19 to 24 years old at first intercourse (Abma, Driscoll, and Moore, 1998). Moreover, the larger the age difference between the young woman and her partner, the greater the level of coercion involved in the first experience with intercourse. Thus, evidently, a proportion of early teen mothers are set on the road to premature motherhood by child sexual abuse.

Abuse aside, it is still **sexual precociousness** that is most highly correlated with very early pregnancy. Indeed, sexually precocious females are four to five times more likely to have a teenage pregnancy than those who are sexually abused (Roosa et al., 1997). Teenage motherhood may occur after a single incident of sexual intercourse. Yet, in another study, some of the young mothers had become sexually active even before puberty; among blacks, 42 percent had been sexually active by age 13, compared to 21 percent among whites (Hardy et al., 1998). These data led the researchers to conclude that young males and females may not be very fertile early on; otherwise, pregnancies would occur more frequently before age 15.

The Adolescent's Life Course

The structure of adolescent motherhood contains the seeds of disadvantages rather than benefits. It is difficult in U.S. society to be both an adolescent, with all the activities that this entails, and a mother. Adolescence is often synonymous with acquiring rights and independence, whereas motherhood involves assuming responsibilities and being tied down. The two may conflict to the girl's detriment, but particularly to the infant's disadvantage. Nevertheless, single teen motherhood is far from a homogeneous situation resulting in similar outcomes for all mothers and children. Age is a source of differences. Motherhood that occurs between ages 11 to 15 is considered excessively premature for all parties concerned. Such early reproduction is more substantially correlated with poverty, sexual exploitation, other deviances, and faulty family processes than either middle (ages 16 and 17) or, especially, late adolescence (ages 18 and 19).

Another source of difference among teen mothers resides in their overall socioemotional development. Serbin and colleagues (1998) report that childhood aggressiveness is related to early pregnancy and dropping out of school. Before having a baby, adolescent mothers average more instances of suspensions, truancy, drug use, and fighting in school than other adolescent girls. Thus, single parenting is part of a nonnormative life course for a *subgroup* of adolescents who were problematic children long before becoming pregnant (Woodward and Fergusson, 1999). Even though they are still antisocial and impulsive, as are many of the fathers, they now have the responsibility of a helpless baby.

Outcomes for the babies of difficult teen mothers are generally more negative than those of nondeviant teen mothers. For instance, they are often unable to meet even basic child needs. As a consequence, their small children are more frequently brought to hospital emergency rooms because of injuries that suggest both neglect and abuse (Serbin, Peters, and Schwartzman, 1996). One would also expect that this type of "delinquent" motherhood is more related to poverty, both as a cause and as an effect, thus to its intergenerational transmission as well as to the intergenerational transmission of delinquent behaviors from mother and father to offspring.

The corollary is that parenting by older and well-balanced adolescents is less detrimental for all involved and may actually be based on a rational decision, especially when the young women pursue their education. In fact, adolescent mothers' educational level is the best predictor of small children's outcomes (Serbin et al., 1998). This line of reasoning is particularly applicable to single women older than age 30 who are financially secure and choose to become mothers, either because they prefer to remain independent or because of a lack of suitable marital partners.

Who Are the Babies' Fathers?

The rare studies carried out on young males who have a child while single highlight two salient points. The first is that a *process of selection* similar to that of young mothers takes place: These fathers tend to be more often unemployed, or in low-paid jobs, and they have fewer years of education than fathers who have a child after marriage (Hardy et al., 1998). Many have a history of childhood aggressiveness and other behavioral difficulties (Capaldi, Crosby, and Stoolmiller, 1996). More have deviant peers than same-age young men who do not become early fathers (Fagot et al., 1998). Second, either again as a selection process or as a consequence of single fatherhood, these males are more likely to cohabit than to marry later on. Even those who eventually marry tend to do less well economically than other men who begin paternity after marriage (Nock, 1998a).

In other words, both because of selection and the consequences of single fatherhood, young single fathers are similar to young single mothers: Both are generally of low socioeconomic status and come from single-parent families (Smith and Joe, 1994). Young males who are invested in higher education and in the labor market take fewer procreative risks because they stand to lose much by acquiring the support of a child before their financial goals are reached. As we have just seen, the same applies to women. Thus, in terms of partner selection, the principle of educational and **economic homogamy,** discussed in the previous chapter, applies to births outside of marriage.

Nock (1998a:261–262) reasons that premarital fatherhood may involve a set of attitudes and beliefs "that are inconsistent with the demands of the labor force. Unmarried fathers may associate with others who support and reinforce such beliefs." These same attitudes may be inconsistent with the model of a successful marriage that is accepted in U.S. society. As a result, even when they marry, these men's situation "does not totally ameliorate the effects of premarital fatherhood." This perspective joins that of Anderson (1990), who has suggested that men who are economically marginalized may pursue women to prove their masculinity. Young women may be manipulated or conned into sexual activity (Anderson, 1993). Children become a status symbol rather than a responsibility. Thus, a young father's involvement is greater when the child is an infant, in part because of the social status significance of becoming a father, particularly among disadvantaged youths.

However, even though the mother is a teen, the father is not necessarily an adolescent himself. The older he is, the fewer his contacts with his child, in some cases because he already has other children. According to one study, 15 to 18 months after the birth of their baby in 1983, 20 percent of the young mothers reported that the father had had a child by another woman. This is an underestimate because many mothers had little knowledge of the fathers' sexual activities (Hardy at al., 1998). Overall, fathers had no ongoing contact with their children and, when they did, it was infrequent. In a sample of 3,855 teenage mothers of 6,009 children, more than half of the fathers provided no support (but recall the cautionary remark in Family Research 5.1 on p. 126). More educated fathers (with at least high school) provided more support but not more contact with their child (Rangarajan and Gleason, 1998). Generally, single fathers pay less child support than divorced ones, in great part because the former are poorer: Compliance with child support payments is related to a parent's financial situation (Meyer, 1999).

What Are the Effects of Single Adolescent Parenting on Children?

The majority of all babies born to teen mothers are fathered by adolescent or very young men (Elo, King, and Furstenberg, 1999). Because of their age, adolescent parents are overwhelmingly poor and unschooled. They have yet to acquire the maturity that benefits small children. On average, a baby born to parents between the ages of 12 to 19 is at greater risk of suffering from *multiple disadvantages,* each disadvantage compounding the other. Nevertheless, one has to be careful not to overgeneralize here. As Cowan, Cowan, and Schulz (1996:10) point out, children can be at risk in one domain of life only. Others are at risk on a broader range of outcomes, and still others are at risk but are not affected.

A combination of problematic parental characteristics, vulnerable infants, and a deprived environment represents a **cumulation of risk factors** particularly detrimental to child development. Such a combination of disadvantages maximizes the likelihood that the child will develop negative traits, such as aggressiveness; it will also prevent the actualization of a child's innate competencies or abilities, such as a good IQ (Rowe, Jacobson, and Van den Oord, 1999). Sociologists Entwisle, Alexander, and Olson (1997:108) are concerned that, because "teen parents have had more problems in school than other teenagers," their children could experience adjustment difficulties. "Parents who had school problems themselves may be unable to coach children about how to behave in school," or may even be confrontational with teachers. It can also be argued that teenage parenting may now result in more negative consequences for mothers and children than was the case a decade ago (Coley and Chase-Lansdale, 1998). First, the demands of the current and future technologized labor markets are more exacting and require the development of greater skills for survival than in the past. Second, welfare benefits and length of recipiency have been drastically cut.

As Sandfort and Hill (1996) point out, adolescent mothers vary greatly among themselves, and many are quite competent. A good proportion of their children grow up normally, as do the mothers themselves. But, on average, a young mother is less likely to be as knowledgeable about child care or as psychologically mature as an older woman (Karraker and Evans, 1996). In fact, teenage mothers entertain more unrealistic expectations, are less perceptive of their baby's needs than older mothers, and are less qualified to help their child acquire those cognitive skills necessary for school success (Haskett, Johnson, and Miller, 1994). For example, young mothers frequently fail to reinforce language learning by their children (Culp, Osofsky, and O'Brien, 1996). On average, young mothers' children develop more behavioral problems and tend to be more impulsive than older mothers' children. In contrast, the children of older single mothers who are educated and earn a reasonable income perform academically as well as comparable children from two-parent families (Ceci, 1996).

Because teen mothers begin childbearing so early, they are more likely than older women to experience multiple transitions, such as successive cohabitations and separations, that make lives, including those of small children, less stable. Such frequent changes require a higher degree of adjustment than is needed in a stable family (Eggebeen, Crockett, and Hawkins, 1990). Unfortunately, for children who are vulnerable due to personal characteristics, a stable home environment is even more important for their optimal development than it is for children in general. Hence, a mother's multiple life transitions may present a danger to less resilient children. In general, children whose mothers experience multiple transitions tend to drop out of school and live independently earlier (Aquilino, 1996); they are thus more at risk of becoming impoverished adults.

COHABITATION

Cohabitation is a relatively short stage in the life cycle of most couples who soon marry or break up (Willis and Michael, 1994). Cohabitations are more likely to end in marriage when the male partner has economic resources (Smock and Manning, 1997). Nevertheless, this is a life stage that is becoming quite common, particularly among young people and the divorced, and one that has no historical precedent in the United States, although it is widespread in other Western nations, such as Sweden, Denmark, and Norway.

What Is Known about Cohabitation?

Cohabitation has increased dramatically at all age levels, particularly in the 25 to 29 age bracket. In 1994, among the unmarried in the 25 to 29 age group, nearly 24 percent were cohabiting (Waite, 1995). In 1997, there were approximately 4.1 million opposite-sex and 1.8 million same-sex households in which the couples were cohabiting (U.S. Bureau of the Census, 1997b). Currently, cohabitation often serves the function of delaying marriage, in part for economic reasons, to allow the completion of an advanced university degree, or until a wedding or a better lifestyle can be afforded (Clarkberg, 1999). Among the divorced, cohabitation is a substitute for remarriage more often than in the past (Goldscheider and Waite, 1991).

As seen in the previous chapter, cohabitors have more frequent sexual intercourse than married couples (Laumann et al., 1994). In part, this is because cohabitations are of shorter duration and because these relationships, being more individualistic, may be more invested in sexuality whereas marriage may be more invested in general commitment (Clarkberg, Stolzenberg, and Waite, 1996). Married spouses are happier with their relationships than are cohabitors (Nock, 1998c). However, when cohabitors plan to marry, the quality of their relationship is not much different from that of a married couple that has been together for the same duration (Brown and Booth, 1996).

Generally, male partners are less committed to their relationship than are married men, as first expressed by a cohabiting divorced man and then by a student:

> *"No, I don't know if I'll get married. Eventually, probably, but I am not yet ready for this. Right now I am not even sure that she's the right woman for me so that I prefer to take it easy; I have a wait-and-see attitude at this point."*

> *"I have lived with two different guys and that's* it! *No more! It's always the same thing: we just play at being married because they don't want to do anything except play. They couldn't get married because . . . the usual line is 'I'm not ready for such a commitment.'"*

Some individuals choose cohabitation because it requires, in their opinion, less sexual faithfulness than marriage (Bumpass, Sweet, and Cherlin, 1991). It may not be surprising, then, that so many of these unions dissolve. Furthermore, newly married couples who have cohabited before marriage have substantially higher rates of premarital violence than those who have not lived together. Premarital violence is, in turn, followed by more marital violence than when none had taken place before. Magdol and colleagues (1998) have reported that, in a group of 21-year-olds, cohabitors were significantly more likely than daters to be abusive.

Overall, the "role demands of cohabitation are less than those for marriage" (Thornton, Axinn, and Teachman, 1995:72). In other words, it is easier to enter into a cohabitational than a marital relationship because it is *less institutionalized.* For the same reason, it is easier to dissolve because there are fewer barriers against dissolution—whether legal, economic, or social—than is the case for marriage. Cohabitation appeals because it promises greater flexibility. Paradoxically, Brines and Joyner (1999) find that cohabitors are less tolerant regarding certain departures from convention than are married couples. For instance, married couples adopt a wider range of economic arrangements and divisions of labor, such as when a wife has a higher income than her husband, than do cohabitors, on average.

Cohabitation and Children

National statistics estimate that 6 percent of all children live in cohabiting families. Perhaps as many as 20 percent of children in single-parent families actually live with a parent and partner. Statistics on single-parent families do not generally inquire about cohabitation. Hence, when cohabitation is included in a specialized survey, a substantially smaller number of children actually live and spend less time in a single-parent family than is described in general statistics (Bumpass and Raley, 1995). Furthermore, a good proportion of children born to single mothers are born into a cohabiting unit, perhaps as high as 30 percent among whites, 40 percent among Mexican Americans, and about 15 percent among blacks (Bumpass and Sweet, 1989). These percentages were obtained in the 1980s and are certainly higher today, especially among whites, for whom cohabitation has been gaining in social acceptability. Thus, all the preceding statistics are tentative.

Children born to single but cohabiting parents are not generally at a large advantage, compared to those whose mothers do not cohabit. A reason is that cohabitation is a **more unstable union** than marriage; therefore, unless their cohabiting parents marry, children are at risk of living within an unstable family structure (Graefe and Lichter, 1999). In some families, there is a "revolving door" situation, whereby serial partners succeed each other over the years. Furthermore, couples who cohabit before marriage have a higher divorce rate (Axinn and Thornton, 1992). This implies that children are more likely to experience a parental divorce when their parents began their union as cohabitors. When a single mother goes on to cohabit, family poverty is reduced by close to 30 percent and as such benefits children (Manning and Lichter, 1996). However, children in cohabiting families have parents who are more similar to those in single than in married families in terms of education, employment, and earnings; for instance, male cohabitors earn less than married men. Better-off cohabitors are more likely to marry when or before they have children (Manning and Smock, 1995).

Very small children are more at risk when a mother cohabits with a man who is not the child's natural father. These couples are generally quite young and often disadvantaged. Unemployment is common. Such mothers are in a precarious situation, both conjugally and economically. These stressors can disrupt her parenting skills, and the children may suffer from neglect because the partner does not step in to compensate, as a married father often does when a mother is not sufficiently involved. One study has found that children living with their mother and cohabiting boyfriend had lower school performance and more behavioral problems (Thomson, Hanson, and McLanahan, 1994). *Physical abuse* is also more likely (Gelles, 1989), and cases of young children seriously injured or killed by a mother's live-in boyfriend are more frequent than in biological families. In addition, girls are at risk of being sexually abused (Gordon, 1989).

Cohabitation instead of remarriage after divorce may bring in a less involved stepparent. Furthermore, divorced nonresidential fathers who are cohabiting see their children less often than those who are remarried (Cooksey and Craig, 1998). Overall, in U.S. society, cohabitation currently is not a situation that signals *investment in children* as much as does marriage, although there are exceptions (Landale and Fennelly, 1992).

SAME-SEX-PARENT FAMILY FORMATION

The following presentation complements the sections on same-sex couple formation in the previous chapter. The focus here is on family formation by two gay men or two lesbian women.

An Overview of Same-Sex-Parent Families

The number of children raised by homosexual parents ranges from 6 to 14 million; these estimates are very tentative and include parents who remain single. What is known is that, so far, a majority of these children have been born to a mother-father family that ended in divorce and the lesbian or gay parent obtained custody (Green and Bozett, 1991). But more and more lesbian couples give birth following artificial insemination or adopt; some gay couples also adopt, and a few have had recourse to surrogate mothers. In other cases, gay and lesbian couples cooperate in producing (via artificial insemination) and raising children jointly, an arrangement that allows children to have parents of both sexes (Patterson and Chan, 1997). Some states do accept what is called *second-parent adoptions*. These involve the legal adoption of a woman's or man's biological or adopted child by the same-sex partner so that both can parent with equal rights.

But in those states that do not have second-parent adoptions, only the biological parent has any legal right to the child after a breakup. The other partner, who may have been very attached to and involved with the child, may not even have visitation rights. The child is thus suddenly cut off from half of his or her parental dyad, unless the two former partners are able to find an amicable solution. However, there are no indications that homosexual breakups are friendlier and more harmonious than heterosexual ones; therefore, the lack of a legal status for the nonbiological parent is quite problematic.

Lesbian women prefer to live in committed relationships far more than do gay men and are more monogamous sexually, as we saw in the preceding chapter (Fowlkes, 1994). As women, they are also socialized to be kin-keepers. These variables lead to the formation of a greater number of lesbian-based than gay-based families.

Consequences for Children

In the population at large, there are three main concerns regarding the children of same-sex parents. These are the fears that the offspring will grow up to be psychologically maladjusted, that they will be molested by their parents or parent's partners, and that they will become homosexual themselves. None of these concerns have been supported by the research so far (Ross, 1994). The reader should bear in mind, however, that same-sex-parent families have been excluded from large surveys on family life (Allen and Demo, 1995). As a result, studies on same-sex-parent families use small samples and tend to be nonrepresentative; researchers are forced to turn to advertisements or personal contacts to locate respondents. Consequently, it is difficult to assess to what extent the results can be generalized to all same-sex-parent families. Nevertheless, all the small studies put together are so far arriving at fairly similar results for children, adolescents, and young adults who have been raised in such families. The young adults and most adolescents in these studies, however, were originally born in heterosexual families that ended in divorce; one of their parents is not homosexual.

Children in same-sex-parent families, although often teased by peers and shunned by their peers' parents, do not grow up disadvantaged emotionally and may even possess certain strengths of character that other children do not have, such as tolerance and empathy (Laird, 1993; Patterson, 1992). A recent study comparing lesbian and heterosexual mothers—some single, some in couples—found no difference in chil-

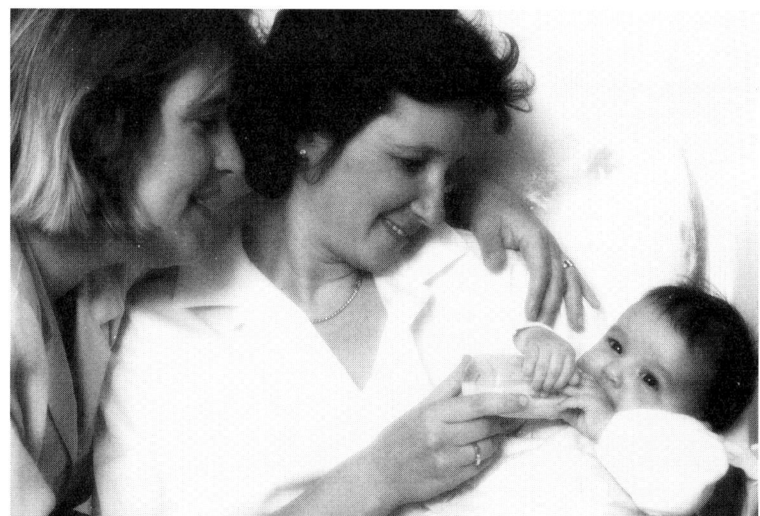

Two questions of interest to research concerning same-sex-parent families in which a child is born or adopted are: Will they be more or less stable than opposite-sex-parent families? Will male and female same-sex-parent families be equally stable?

dren's adaptation and development around age 7, even though all had been reproduced by artificial insemination, which is certainly an additional complication in a child's self-definition (Chan, Raboy, and Patterson, 1998). The sample was largely upper-middle class, so it is not known if the results would be replicated at a working-class level. Overall, as parents, lesbian mothers are similar to heterosexual mothers; it is not their sexual orientation that emerges as an important variable but their identity as mothers (Lewin, 1993). Their children show few differences from other children (Parks, 1998).

Children of homosexual partners usually adopt heterosexual identities. Bailey and colleagues (1995) compared adult sons who had spent many years with their gay fathers to sons who had lived only briefly with such fathers. There was no rise in homosexuality among the offspring with longer contact with fathers. A small study by Costello (1997) found that many homosexual partners consciously avoid pressuring their children to conform to parental sexual preferences. Although children raised in same-sex-parent families are more tolerant of same-sex experimentation (Stacey, 1996), they grow up heterosexual in pretty much the same proportion as do children in other families. As far as worries over child sexual abuse, gay men are no more likely than heterosexuals to abuse children, and the same applies to lesbian women (Jenny, Roesler, and Poyer, 1994).

But far more research is required on the topic of same-sex parents. For instance, little attention has been paid to reconstituted lesbian-headed families and the step-parent role that then occurs (Parks, 1998). In stepfamilies, the lesbian mother's partner is less involved with the children than is the partner of a donor-inseminated woman; in the latter case, the partner often becomes the "other mother," although her legal status is not recognized (Nelson, 1996). Couple breakup, its effect on children, and the consequences to the coparenting aspect have yet to be investigated.

ARE THERE ADVANTAGES TO MARRIAGE?

Of the possible trajectories to family formation, marriage is the most common one in North America, as it is in much of the world. It is the most **institutionalized** form of family formation; that is, it is legally accepted, it is supported by rules of behavior, and it involves duties and rights that are clearly delineated and on which there is much public consensus. Despite high divorce rates, marriage is still a valued goal and status. Even subgroups with low marriage rates, particularly African Americans and Puerto Ricans, value marriage. They are not turning away from it or refusing it; they simply cannot afford it. This failure to marry is a reflection of racial and economic inequalities rather than a rejection of marriage. This section discusses whether marriage carries advantages for adults, children, and society. From a *structural functionalist perspective,* what are the functions of marriage? What does it do *for* people and society?

Is Marriage Good for Adults?

Compared to cohabitation, marriage tends to last longer and it represents a higher level of commitment, particularly by males; therefore, marriage is a more secure institution than cohabitation. Marriage also provides more socially visible linkages between two families and has a greater potential to increase social support. At the emotional level, marriage is based, at least in theory, on love, commitment, interdependence, and the sharing of joys and sorrows alike. Spouses act as confidantes to each other and men confide in their wives more than they do to other persons.

Sexuality is a powerful ingredient in marriage, both physically and emotionally. We saw in the previous chapter that cohabitors engage in sex more often than married couples. Logically, this should make them happier. Yet, in their well-designed survey on sexuality, Laumann and colleagues (1994) show that men and women are by far happiest when they have had only one sex partner in the past 12 months and when they are married to that partner. On the basis of all the statistics they gathered, the authors conclude that "a monogamous sexual partnership embedded in a formal marriage evidently produces the greatest satisfaction and pleasure" (p. 364). Moreover, STDs are far less likely to occur within a monogamous marital relationship than under any other circumstances.

Research results in the domains of physical and psychological well-being, and even in the domain of longevity, are unanimous in finding that both married men and women, compared to men and women in any of the other marital status categories, score substantially higher on various scales of psychological well-being (Waite and Gallagher, 2000). They have lower rates of emotional problems, are healthier physically, and live longer (Coombs, 1991)—although the latter result may be equally a consequence of the fact that married people generally have higher incomes, which in turn are related to better health and lower mortality. In a study of 17 Western countries and Japan, Stack and Eshleman (1998) have found that being married is 3.4 times more closely tied to happiness than is cohabitation. Their results indicate that marriage, rather than cohabitation, increases both financial and health satisfaction, which in turn increase happiness. Naturally, the question that arises here is: Does marriage contribute to well-being (social causation) or does it simply capture people who are healthier, better balanced, and more attractive partners to begin with (social selection)?

Social Selection or Social Causation?

Let's first examine the evidence favoring the **social selection hypothesis** suggesting that there is a selection into marriage of the healthiest. Studies indicate that persons who suffer from serious mental illnesses, such as schizophrenia, are less likely to marry, particularly among men (Link et al., 1987). Highly dysfunctional persons either do not marry or, when they do so, their marriages do not last, after which it becomes difficult to remarry (Forthofer et al., 1996). Very ill persons as well as persons who are intellectually incompetent do not get selected into marriage as frequently as others. Therefore, there is a selection process that takes place, particularly among men. Once people are married, another selection process is activated: The marriages of disturbed, incompetent, or antisocial persons are less likely to last, as they become very difficult spouses. In contrast, psychological balance contributes to marital stability (Aseltine and Kessler, 1993).

Nevertheless, despite all these selection factors, most people still marry at least once, and a certain number of persons choose not to marry, yet they are fully functional. The positive effects of marriage are at least as important as the selectivity effects in explaining the differences in well-being by marital status (Daniel, 1996). In other words, the **social causation hypothesis** often explains far better the differences between the married and the others in terms of well-being. Indeed, marriage helps adults stabilize their personalities, gain self-esteem and personal security, and develop competencies and a sense of responsibility that were not necessary as single persons, particularly among men (Nock, 1998a). The rewards of a warm and supportive relationship enhance happiness, psychological well-being, physical health, and consequently longevity (Gove, Style, and Hughes, 1990; Hu and Goldman, 1990; Lillard and Waite, 1995).

Interestingly enough, there are indications in a rather old but still relevant study of homosexuality that gay men and lesbians who belong to a stable and monogamous cohabitation enjoy better mental health than nonexclusive homosexuals (Bell and Weinberg, 1978). Homosexual couples cannot yet legally marry; cohabitation is as close to marriage as they can get, and its benefits may approximate those of marriage among them.

Married men are more often regularly employed than other men, which provides them with greater personal stability (Daniel, 1996). When they change jobs, it is more to increase their economic gains than is the case among single and divorced men (Gorman, 1999). Furthermore, when his wife is employed, which has become the norm, a husband is now far better off financially than a single man. Married couples with an employed wife have an income advantage of $25,000, on average, over married couples with a wife who is not gainfully employed (U.S. Bureau of the Census, 1997a). Since most marriages that last at least a few years eventually result in children, a two-income family is a more secure basis than one with only one breadwinner. Therefore, men are generally far more secure with than without a wife. Waite (1995) calls marriage an insurance policy. Of course, the same applies to women financially.

Moreover, married adults are more likely to maintain a healthy lifestyle and diet than nonmarried adults. The former eat at home more, stay out late less, use alcohol and illegal drugs less, and are better organized to take care of their basic needs (Bachman et al., 1997). A cohesive marriage is an important social resource and brings an *informal element of social control* in the life of individuals. This may be the reason why married people drink less than cohabitors (Horwitz and Raskin White, 1998). Furthermore, Horney, Osgood, and Marshall (1995) as well as Laub, Nagin, and Sampson (1998) have found that a good marriage eventually contributes to the cessation of illegal activities among criminals.

Are Marriage Benefits Gendered?

Some literature indicates that marriage may be more advantageous to men than to women (Marks, 1996). Indeed, there is a larger difference between the scores of well-being of married men compared to divorced and single men than is the case among women of various marital statuses. Why would marriage benefit women less? To begin with, once children arrive, women have more responsibilities than men in marriage, particularly when both spouses are employed (McLanahan and Casper, 1995). Therefore, for many women, marriage is a mixed blessing, thus explaining in part why the scores of well-being of single women are not all that different from those of their married counterparts. These scores have actually become more similar in recent decades and, in some instances, by midlife the scores of single women are more positive than those of married women (Marks, 1996). Glenn and Weaver (1988) suggest that marriage may become less essential to women's well-being than in the past.

Within marriage, the quality of the relationship is an important determinant of well-being (Acock and Demo, 1994). All in all, marriage is beneficial to adults, but a troublesome marriage negates some or all of these benefits, particularly for women. Second, the benefits accrued in marriage may differ for men and women depending on the domains studied—emotional well-being, physical health, happiness, or security. These gendered benefits may also differ depending on the stage of the life course or age of the person. For instance, it is not clear whether marriage is more or less beneficial among young than middle-age persons (Marks and Lambert, 1998). Finally, the benefits of marriage depend on the time or cohort period that serves as a context for marriage. For example, more recent cohorts of women seem to benefit from marriage less than preceding cohorts, and this would be especially so for career women.

Is Marriage Good for Children?

In the following chapter, we will see that children who live with their married parents have the lowest poverty rate and therefore most avoid the deleterious consequences of poverty. Earlier, this chapter reviewed the impact on children of living in never-married and cohabiting families, and in Chapter 13, the effect of parental divorce and remarriage will be studied. The overall conclusion from these various sources of information is that children benefit more unequivocally than adults from their parents' marriage (Waite and Gallagher, 2000).

It is true that children who experience a conflictual parental marriage benefit less than children living with a well-balanced single parent (Jekielek, 1998). However, on the whole, highly conflictual marriages do not last long because of the acceptability of divorce as an alternative. Even among those who divorce, at best, one-third have highly conflictual marriages. Therefore, a relatively small proportion of marriages are detrimental to children and a relatively small proportion of divorces are beneficial to them (Amato and Booth, 1997). Furthermore, conflict aside, even when parents do not judge their marriage to be the happiest, children still benefit from it—especially if children find their parents' marriage satisfactory or do not perceive that their parents are dissatisfied with their relationship. Children benefit particularly in the area of health. For instance, infant mortality is lower in married families, and this demographic advantage is even found in Scandinavian countries, where there is less poverty among single mothers and more cohabitation than in the United States (Bennett et al., 1994; Oyen et al., 1997). Children also benefit in terms of economic security, school achievement, affective and emotional stability, leisure activities, prosocial behavior, and, later on as adults, in terms of work (Cooksey, Menaghan, and Jekielek, 1997).

In a society with a nuclear family system, children who have two parents—whether natural or adoptive, whether of the same or opposite sex—are at an advantage because they have two rather than one person *invested* in their well-being, *responsible* for them, and acting as **authority figures.** Children in married families also tend to be better supervised than others (Fischer, 1993). Additionally, two parents provide a greater repertoire of behaviors, attitudes, and knowledge from which children can draw and learn. In James Coleman's theory, two parents constitute a greater source of **social capital,** which then translates into more human capital for the children. With two parents, children have an alternative when the other has less time, is ill, or otherwise preoccupied. Two parents can also provide moral support to each other in their coparental duties and this benefits children (Grossbard-Shechtman, 1993). But all these advantages to children are more prevalent in *married* two-parent families.

Is Marriage Good for Society?

Inasmuch as the institution of marriage contributes to the emotional stability and overall well-being of adults and children, it becomes a very *functional institution* for society. It produces a great deal of social capital and serves as an **agency of social control** (Laub, Nagin, and Sampson, 1998). Children in two-parent families acquire more human capital: On average, they drop out of school less, get more education, and are less often on welfare (McLoyd, 1998). Later on, they contribute more in taxes than children who are not raised within the context of parental marriage. From a societal point of view, marriage contributes to the successful socialization of citizens, which does not mean, however, that a majority of children in other forms of family are less adequately socialized. It means that *proportionally more* children from married families are successfully socialized. From this perspective alone, it has been suggested that the legalization of marriage for same-sex couples who have children would be beneficial rather than detrimental to society. The legalization of these unions would contribute to their stability and to better outcomes for their children (Bell and Weinberg, 1978).

A married couple is a small, all-encompassing health and welfare agency staffed with volunteers. Marriage lowers health care costs, welfare outlays, and police and penal institution expenditures. It reduces costs related to alcohol abuse, drug addiction, and STDs. Moreover, as married individuals who have children become more vested in their neighborhood and schools, they contribute to the stability and betterment of their area and of the educational system.

Many people have come to believe that marriage is merely a matter of choice and has few overall consequences. The preceding clearly indicates that marriage, particularly a good and equitable marriage, carries many benefits for the spouses. It is, above all, highly beneficial to children, whether it is equitable or not between the parents. There is a school of thought whose proponents argue that what is important is not family structure (one versus two parents), but **healthy family processes.** Although it is certainly true that healthy family dynamics explain a part of children's positive outcomes, the fact remains that such dynamics are more likely to occur in two-parent families of the married type. Consequently, for society as a whole, marriage is an institution that deserves more encouragement (i.e., tax incentives, child care and health services, as well as a greater valorization of the role of parents [Ambert, 1997]). This topic is revisited in the last chapter of this book.

ADOPTION AND FOSTER FAMILIES

Adoption is an alternative mode of family formation. After having read the previous chapter, the reader may well ask why so many women subject their bodies to the misery of fertility treatment when adoption is available. There are four basic answers. First, the often negative **social construction of adoption** makes this option less "natural" and thus less desirable (Bartholet, 1993; Mason, Skolnick, and Sugarman, 1998). Second, most people prefer to have children who carry their own genes, who might look like them, who are "part of them." Third, there are not that many "suitable" infants available for adoption and the waiting list is a long one. Thus, white American couples who absolutely want an infant of their race often turn to international adoption. Others, however, choose to cross the racial line. And, fourth, many would-be parents are concerned about issues such as the preference given to birth parents by courts and children searching for their "real" parents later on.

Adoption agencies prefer couples with a stable economic outlook. As a result, adoptive couples tend to be of higher socioeconomic status than average. Single adults experience far more difficulty adopting and some even go abroad for this purpose (Bartholet, 1993). Same-sex couples are rarely accepted as potential parents—they are even less accepted in Europe. Singles and same-sex couples increase their chance if they are willing to adopt a "hard-to-place" child (Patterson and Chan, 1997). This label includes older children, many with a long history of foster care placements, children and infants with physical or mental disabilities, as well as minority infants and children.

How Do Adopted Children Develop?

The literature on adoption is divided between those researchers who have not found any significant difference in adjustment between adopted and nonadopted persons and those who do (for a review, see Sharma, McGue, and Benson, 1998). A few studies even find that adopted children show certain ego strengths and resilience (Benson,

Sharma, and Roehlkepartain, 1994). However, the deficits and strengths that are found largely depend on the methodology used, the type of adopted children included in the sample, the comparison group, and the outcomes measured. But, overall, adopted children and their parents do not show any consistent deficit that would warrant concern (Bartholet, 1993). Professionals who come into contact with troubled adopted children or adolescents may be too hasty to attribute the problems to adoption (Miall, 1996). This social construction of adoption may prevent these youngsters from being treated for the real problems that affect them.

Why is there a greater proportion of adopted than nonadopted children among the psychologists' and psychiatrists' clientele (Brodzinski, 1993)? The explanations that have been offered are twofold. First, some adoptive children may have a more difficult time growing up because of identity problems or because their parents have not properly bonded with them. Second, there may be no actual developmental difference between adoptive and nonadoptive children, but adoptive parents are of higher socioeconomic status and are more familiar with mental health services. Consequently, they may be more inclined to consult professionals as soon as their children evidence some problems (Warren, 1992).

But there is a third explanation that has not been sufficiently explored. Although adoptive children may feel as loved and as accepted by their parents as nonadopted children, their *peers* and even other adults often openly express doubts to them on this topic.

> *A respondent (adopted) in March's (1995:656) study said that outside the family, people "never believe that your adoptive parents love you like their parents love them. Because you aren't biological." One of my students recalls returning home one day quite distressed and asking her mother, "Is it true that you can't love me as much because I am adopted?" The mother was shocked and found it difficult to accept the cruelty or incomprehension of other children. Another student reported that, upon learning she was adopted, her peer on the school bus shrieked, "Oh, you poor poor child! You don't have any real parents."*

This **stigmatization** may constitute a heavy mental burden on some adoptees. Children are especially vulnerable to what their peers think. If their peers present them with a negative social construction of their adoptive status, then these children are at risk emotionally.

The view on adoptive parents is equally mixed (Groze, 1996). Some writers have suggested that adoptive parents may be less confident, more anxious, and stigmatized because of their infertility, whereas other researchers have not found any support for this "at-risk" perspective (for a review, see Borders, Black, and Pasley, 1998). Research questions, unfortunately, are framed within a pathological or deficit view of adoption. It is a *social construction of adoption* that creates problems rather than prevents them.

Adopted children fare equally well across a variety of family structures—when they are only children, have younger or older adopted siblings, or have younger or older biological siblings (Brodzinski and Brodzinski, 1992). Children adopted by single parents seem to be doing as well as children adopted by couples, which is the opposite of what occurs for births to single parents. Shireman (1995) reports on a follow-up of children with special needs placed in single and two-parent adoptive

The often negative social construction of adoption, and particularly that of transracial adoption, is detrimental to the children involved. Yet, most are happy and well adjusted.

homes. Contrary to expectations, children in single-parent families experienced fewer problems. This result may stem from the fact that the selection process of single parents is very demanding because single individuals are considered less favorably by adoption agencies. Therefore, it is likely that unsuitable singles are more efficiently screened out than are unsuitable couples. Singles may also have more time to devote to a child, as there is no one else vying for their attention in the family. They may receive more help from their own parents and they may be more willing to be trained to care for a child with special needs. Singles who accept such a parenting role probably have more financial and personal resources.

What Is Involved in Stepchild Adoption?

An estimated 100,000 stepchildren are adopted by their stepparents, generally a stepfather, each year (Levine and Sallee, 1990). This number far surpasses regular adoptions and should therefore be a more important topic of research. Although there are a few similarities between regular adoptions and adoptions by a stepparent, there are important differences as well as motives specific to each situation (Ganong et al., 1998). The main reasons for stepadoptions after divorce reside in a desire to be a "regular" family, to legitimize the roles and relationships within the reconstituted family, and to sever the relationship with the nonresidential parent, particularly when the latter does not contribute child support nor has much do to with the child.

The nonresidential parent either consents to the adoption or the case can go to court. A judge will rule in favor of the adoption only if the parent is deemed unfit or if it is in the child's best interest to sever the relationship (Mahoney, 1994). The long-term consequences of stepadoption after divorce are unknown. On the one hand, there may be a reaffirmation of the impermeability of the boundaries of the nuclear family. On the other hand, the situation may give rise to a great deal of pain and resentment when the child reaches adulthood, both on the natural parent's part and on the child's part. The latter may come to feel that his stepparent "stole" him from his nonresidential parent. The child may also resent the father for having given his rights away so easily. A better model might be that of the British Children Act of 1987, whereby stepparents can have responsibility for children without obliterating noncustodial parents' responsibilities and rights (Mason, 1998).

There are also legal issues involved when the remarriage breaks up. In theory, the stepfather has become the legal father. He is obligated to help support his adopted child. But, as we will see in Chapter 13, biological fathers too often fail to cooperate in this respect. Thus, one can well wonder what happens with adoptive stepfathers, particularly when they remarry again. Second, the child now has two fathers, both of whom divorced the mother. What if the first father decides to renew his relationship with the child or vice versa? This situation represents a legal minefield, but it also represents a certain level of security for stepfathers and children who are bonded: The relationship has been legalized.

What Are the Issues in Transracial Adoption?

Of the 50,000 children available for adoption, approximately one-half are visible minority children, primarily black (Child Welfare League of America, 1993). Currently, there is much research devoted to transracial adoptions, even though they constitute only a tiny fraction of all adoptions—about 4 percent in 1993. The saliency of race in the structure of American society gives rise to controversies and explains this research overrepresentation.

Much of the controversy around transracial adoption resides in the fact that most of the children are African American and most adoptive parents are white. Many blacks, including social workers belonging to the National Association of Black Social Workers (NABSW), have condemned this type of adoption as a form of cultural genocide. They have argued that black children placed in white families will lose their African-American heritage and will suffer an identity crisis. It has been counterargued that children need parents who love them to develop a secure sense of self; whatever their race, children simply need parents.

Amid this controversy, black social workers often refused to place children in white families even though the number of African-American children in foster care was increasing. The Multiethnic Placement Act was passed in 1994, in effect stating that children should not be deprived of the right to be adopted on the basis of their race, as this constitutes a form of discrimination. Since then, the NABSW has softened its stance, but many social workers, including white ones, are still afraid to place children transracially.

On which side of the debate does the evidence fall? There is absolutely no indication in the research literature that black children adopted by white parents turn out much differently than those adopted in black families (Silverman, 1993). The same results have been replicated in Great Britain (Bagley, 1993). Vroegh (1997) reports from a longitudinal study that, by adolescence, these children are still well adjusted and enjoy a high level of self-esteem—as is the case for children born to interracial couples (Stephan and Stephan, 1991). Most interracially adopted children grow up identifying as black, and most parents conscientiously promote their children's African-American heritage (Vroegh, 1997). This result should certainly allay the concerns of black activists.

However, there is yet another issue: Although African Americans are, on average, less affluent than whites, adoption programs run by blacks are more successful at finding same-race parents for their young clientele. Neal (1996) also points out that many white children with special needs languishing in foster care could be adopted by black families; but this reverse type of transracial adoption is generally blocked or discouraged—a discriminatory practice. In view of the fact that many children in foster care could be adopted and that a disproportionate number are black, greater efforts should be made to recruit African-American adoptive families, which is a goal of the NABSW (Hamm, 1997). Nevertheless, black couples also prefer infants, which does not help the many older or disabled children who are available for adoption. Even older white children are not as frequently adopted and remain in foster care.

What Is Open Adoption?

Many single mothers now relinquish their infants only under circumstances that allow them greater control over the adoption process and access to the child. To begin with, they participate in the selection of couples and may meet them. There are several types of agreements into which a birth mother (along with a birth father occasionally) and adoptive parents can enter, and much depends on the mother. She may simply request to receive pictures and letters explaining how the child is doing. She may request yearly visitations with the parents or the biological child. When the process is totally open, biological parents more or less enter the adoptive parents' family system as they obtain weekly visits and participate in decision making concerning their child's health (Grotevant et al., 1994).

The few studies that exist on open adoptions indicate that most of the adoptive and biological parents are satisfied with their relationship (Etter, 1993). But more biological than adoptive parents are happy about this arrangement, which concurs with Berry's (1991) conclusion that most of the benefits go to biological parents. However, adoptive parents are generally comfortable with the situation and may even gain a greater sense of permanency (Grotevant et al., 1994). Although most studies indicate that this arrangement is satisfactory (Gross, 1993), it is difficult to draw solid conclusions on the basis of the existing research. The samples are very small and do not allow for a comparison of adoptive families with low versus high frequency of contact with the biological mother to see how satisfaction and child outcomes are affected, if at all. In addition, some of the studies are carried out by social workers who are themselves involved in the process and favor open adoption. This preference could color their data-gathering process and the validity of the results.

Reunions with Birth Parents: Functions and Consequences

A combination of a greater emphasis on children's rights, on biological origins, and on biological parents' rights has led to an acceptance and even encouragement of reunion of birth parents and biological child. Today, some adoption agencies give basic information to an adult child about birth parents, whereas others openly encourage search and reunion. Registries exist in which birth parents as well as children and even siblings can enter information about themselves and indicate whom they are searching. Mothers and daughters are the most common clientele (Pacheco and Eme, 1993). This *gender* difference may be the result of women being more biologically involved in reproduction and birthing and because women are socialized to be more nurturant and family oriented than males. In fact, in some instances young women search for their birth parents only after they have become mothers themselves.

What functions do search and reunion fulfill and what are the consequences of reunions? The answer to this double question largely depends on which part of the family unit is considered. There can be functions and consequences for the child, the birth parent, the birth parent's family, and the adoptive family. The few studies that exist on this topic indicate that a majority of the adoptees who have been reunited with their biological family see this as a positive experience. But, as Pacheco and Eme (1993:55) point out, this high success rate is somewhat inflated; there is the possibility that the individuals who refuse to participate in surveys have had a negative experience. Furthermore, all reunions studied are initiated by the adoptees, and when biological parents initiate the reunion, the adoptees' responses is less positive (Sachdev, 1992). As well, most of the studies, including those of the three authors cited in this paragraph, have obtained their samples from support groups with a strong advocacy position in favor of the benefits of reunions. Adoptees who might believe otherwise or do not search are excluded.

Functions of Reunions for the Adopted Child

For the adopted child, the most obvious advantage is to gain knowledge about genetic factors that could predispose to illness or emotional problems and to integrate this information into his or her self-identity. In 1996, a young woman in a seminar recounted the day she met her birth mother for the first time:

> *"I was motivated by curiosity as I wanted to know if I looked like her and if I shared personality characteristics with her."*
>
> *"So what happened?"*
>
> *"I decided to bring my mom along so she would not feel left out because I could tell that she was more concerned than my father was; after all, I was not searching for my birth father, so he had no competition. So I met this woman at the Children's Aid Society and she was introduced to us as my birth mother. It was really awkward. I introduced myself and said to her, 'This is my mom,' and they shook hands and we all sat together. To make a long story short, I have met her alone a couple of other times but things just didn't click. I do look like her somewhat, but I think that I share my parents' values more. To me, she feels like a cousin, a distant family member. That's all."*

The reunion also allows adoptees to explain their background to others who may have stigmatized them because of their adoptive status (March, 1995). When a reunion is emotionally successful, another advantage is that it provides an additional affective outlet both for the child and the birth mother—an extension of the kinship system. Another woman student explained:

> *"Yes, I definitely found my biological roots with her. We are so much alike that it's amazing. But she is so much younger than my real [her word] parents that*

she feels more like a sister to me. I just can't think of her as my mom. My [adoptive] mom is really it, but it's a fun relationship because she has little kids, so this means that I now have half-brothers and I babysit for her once in a while."

For some adoptive children, a search is initiated because of a distant or conflictual parent-child relationship. The absent birth parents may have been idealized for years and the youth entertains notions that, "If only they [the adoptive parents] were my real parents, they'd love me more." Fortunately, studies also show that 90 percent of the adoptees who search feel loved by and love their adoptive parents (Sachdev, 1992). Half of the adoptees who initiate a search wait until they are older; they do not want to upset their parents. Perhaps at least a third of the adoptees keep the search secret from their parents, at least until after the reunion (Pacheco and Eme, 1993).

Functions of Reunions for the Birth Parents

For birth parents, the functions fulfilled by a reunion may be similar in terms of informing them about what their child looks like and how their child has grown up. A reunion also extends their kinship system. In addition, birth mothers may carry guilt feelings that can be alleviated when they see how successful in life the child has become. For others, however, suppressed guilt is reactivated (Sachdev, 1992). For example, when the young person is troubled, quite disturbed, and malfunctioning, a healthy birth parent suddenly acquires a load of guilt—"If only I had kept her with me, she would have turned out better." Many adoptees have admitted that they had held expectations that were unrealistic; several were reunited with biological parents suffering from an assortment of problems, such as alcoholism, poverty, and mental illness. In the Pacheco and Eme study, 71 percent of the respondents felt that the biological parent had reacted positively to the reunion, which is a lower figure than that of the adopted adults themselves.

Functions of Reunions for the Adoptive Parents

What about the adoptive family? Here, there is probably a far greater mix of functions and dysfunctions. Only about half of adoptive parents are perceived by their children as being entirely positive about the reunion. Sachdev (1992) found that 64 percent of the parents in his sample had reactions other than being "pleased." However, the parent-child relationship itself did not suffer; in fact, a substantial number of adoptees "realized that they had had a much better life than they would have had with the biological parent" (Pacheco and Eme, 1993:64). Although many adoptive parents are more accepting of this reunion than others, it nevertheless gives rise to a host of conflicting emotions. Parents tend to be somewhat apprehensive about the reunion because they are concerned about their child's well-being (Sachdev, 1992). In many cases, parents feel left out, even if this is only temporary. Their family boundaries as a system have to be readjusted but they may also fear losing their child emotionally—a fear that rarely materializes.

Foster Families: A Strained System

Fostering is an alternate form of family restructuration that is far more common than adoption. But the number of children in need of foster care far exceeds the availability of families. Each year, well over 500,000 children enter the foster care system in comparison to 260,000 in the 1980s. African-American children are overrepresented, tend to remain in foster care longer, and are less likely to be adopted (Hamm, 1997). Latino children are now more frequently entering the system than in the past. As a result, whites currently constitute less than 38 percent of this child population. A particular problem of foster children is that a majority have at least one sibling, yet most siblings are fostered separately because it is too difficult to find families willing to take in more than one child at a time (Phillips, 1998). As a consequence, these children face a second loss after that of their parent(s). They are also deprived of the social support they could provide each other. However, in many cases, some siblings fare better separately, especially when one is abusive or suffers from behavioral problems (Staff and Fein, 1992).

Children who have been in foster care and group homes generally have more negative outcomes than other children, particularly in terms of delinquency, mental health, and adult criminality. These children were neglected or abused in their families and the foster care placement represents for many an additional dislocation. Many of these children have been sexually active, are not using contraceptives, and suffer from STDs (Risley-Curtiss, 1997). Above all, many of the older ones find themselves on their own without a support group when they are discharged or run away from foster care. Intermediary programs are being established in some states to help them acquire skills for independent living and to provide them with peer social support (Mallon, 1998).

Who are the foster parents? A random sample of 218 foster parents drawn in Michigan by Kirby (1997) revealed that blacks were slightly overrepresented, considering their numbers in the general population, and Jewish foster parents were totally absent. All economic levels were represented. A majority were currently married. Kinship foster care is a growing phenomenon and accommodates, depending on the states, anywhere from 40 to 60 percent of the children (Bonecutter and Gleeson, 1997). African-American children are the most likely to be placed with kin, perhaps because of the tradition of shared childrearing among blacks. A majority of kin caregivers are single women who are related to the child's biological mother—as many as 60 percent are grandmothers. Kinship care generally lasts longer than regular foster care (Scannapieco, Hegar, and McAlpine, 1997).

Children in foster care often call their foster parents "mom" and "dad" and perceive them as their family, whereas their biological parents may be referred to by name or as the "other mother." Many believe that they are much better off than in their parents' homes and are even grateful to have been removed from the home when they were small (for a review, see Berrick et al., 1998). Many feel close to their caregivers, particularly foster mothers, but rarely as close as a comparison group of children in their own families. Length of care brings greater closeness and a sense of identity with the family (McAuley, 1996). On the other hand, regular contact and hopes of reunification with the natural family decrease closeness with foster parents.

The foster family is one that grows and shrinks in size depending on external circumstances. It is extensively scrutinized by child welfare agencies and receives occasional visits from the children's parents (Berrick et al., 1998). Adaptation is constantly required and equilibrium takes up to 18 months to be reestablished when a new child arrives (Seaberg and Harrigan, 1997). Somewhat like stepparents, foster parents lack clearly defined behavioral guidelines about their relationships with the children in their care (Erera, 1997).

CONCLUSIONS: FAMILY FORMATION ALTERNATIVES IN CONTEXT

Are cohabitation, marriage, and solo parenting equally functional modes of family formation? If one considers only childless adults, solo living is certainly becoming more advantageous than in the past, especially for women. As for cohabitation, it is a satisfying alternative for childless couples, particularly for men. In theory, cohabitation can also help a person rehearse some conjugal responsibilities before leaping unprepared into marriage. Yet, if cohabitation was such an excellent preparation for marriage, cohabitors would later on have lower divorce rates. But, as we have seen, the opposite occurs, although this situation may change as more couples enter cohabitation before they marry.

What about single mothering? There is absolutely nothing in the extensive research literature recommending unmarried motherhood for adolescents and adults alike. Nevertheless, for established and mature adults in their thirties and early forties, single parenthood may well be a positive alternative for both parent and child. This alternative is socially advantageous when an adult, generally a woman, adopts a child who would not otherwise have a family.

Despite high divorce rates, marriage seems to be the *current* optimal alternative when children are present. Since a good proportion of divorces do not involve children, the number of children benefiting from their parents' marriage is far greater than those who will be harmed by it. Most importantly, the research is unanimous to the effect that fathers invest far more in their children when they are in a marriage than either in a cohabitation or as a single parent (Cooksey and Craig, 1998; Doherty, Kouneski, and Erickson, 1998).

All this being said, however, a feminist analysis suggests the possibility that family formation via single parenting could become a far more functional alternative for children and adults in the future (e.g., Roschelle, 1999). This would be particularly so under the following circumstances:

1. If women earned incomes equal to those of men, then the poverty rate of families headed by women would diminish substantially, and so would children's problems.
2. If young males were socialized to be nurturant and equally responsible for their offspring, then even children in single-mother families would have two parents invested in them and supporting them.
3. If society was willing to invest in children, regardless of their parents' marital status, such a policy would prevent these children from even coming near the poverty line.
4. Once all these conditions are in place, delaying motherhood until adulthood and greater maturity would be the last necessary ingredient to making single parenting more functional for children and their parents than it currently is.

SUMMARY

1. Nonmarital fertility has increased dramatically beginning in the 1960s. But after 1970, the increase took place mainly among whites and more recently Latinas. Parallel trends occurred among adolescents. In the 1990s, however, births to unmarried teens decreased, particularly among blacks and for second births. Overall adolescent fertility peaked in 1957 at a time when marriage was more common in that age bracket. Since 1970, as the proportion of married families declined sharply, particularly among African Americans, the proportion of children living in a one-parent family increased.
2. Nonmarital births are more likely to occur to young women who are already poor. The birth generally keeps them in poverty, and, in this respect, there is not a large difference between teen and young adult mothers. In the short term, motherhood carries emotional and social status rewards for young women.
3. Very early pregnancy is related to sexual precociousness. The life course of adolescent mothers generally contains more transitions, and a proportion of them, as is the case for fathers, are deviant in terms of truancy, aggressiveness, and drug use. The babies' fathers tend to come from the same background of poverty as that of mothers. On average, these fathers do not constitute a substantial resource for their young families. Children of teen mothers are at high risk for negative outcomes, particularly when their environment represents a cumulation of risk factors. Nevertheless, adolescent mothers vary greatly among themselves and so do their children's lives.
4. Cohabitations have increased dramatically, so that by 1994, nearly 24 percent of unmarried individuals ages 25 to 29 were cohabiting. Most end within a year and perhaps half continue into marriage. Cohabitation is a less secure relationship than marriage; males are less committed to their partner than are married men. At least 6 percent of children live with a cohabiting parent. Such children are more similar to those in single-parent than married families. Although cohabitation boosts a mother's income, cohabiting couples are less economically secure than married couples. Small children are at a higher risk of abuse when their mother cohabits with a man who is not their natural father.
5. So far, most children who are raised in same-sex-parent families were born in a mother-father family that was disrupted by divorce. But more and more, same-sex couples are having children by artificial insemination and adoption. Overall, the results indicate that the public's concern for these children is unwarranted: They grow up normally, are not sexually molested by either parent, and most are heterosexual.
6. Marriage as an institution is advantageous for adults, particularly men, children, and society. Married adults benefit from social support, structure, and commitment. Married sexuality is more correlated to happiness than is cohabitational sexuality. Psychological and physical well-being is higher among married persons, particularly married men, than for any other marital status category. A certain degree of social selection into marriage explains these results. However, social causation is a more important explanation. Marriage itself causes positive adult outcomes. For women, however, marriage is a more mixed blessing than it is for men.

7. Above all, children who live with their married parents have the best outcomes of all categories of children. The only exception occurs in highly conflictual marriages. These, however, are a small minority, as most end in divorce. Furthermore, a marriage that is not quite satisfactory to the parents still usually benefits children. Marriage is advantageous to society because it presents a stabilizing factor for adults, acts as a volunteer welfare agency, and serves as an agent of socialization for children as well as social control for all.
8. Adoption is an alternate form of family formation that has been socially constructed as less "natural" than biological parenting. Adoptive couples and singles tend to be of higher socioeconomic status. The literature on the consequences of adoption for children tends to be divided between studies that show no disadvantage and those that indicate small deficits. Were the latter to be real, they would be most likely created by the less than optimal social climate surrounding adoption, particularly in children's peer groups. There are no indications that children adopted by single parents fare worse.
9. Stepchild adoption is the most common type of adoption. At this time, there is no research in terms of child outcomes, but it probably contains the seeds for rewards as well as problems as children age. Although only a small proportion of all adoptions are transracial, they are ideologically controversial because of the racial climate. On the whole, indications are that transracially adopted children succeed as well as others and identify with their own racial group.
10. It is difficult to evaluate the research on open adoption because of a variety of methodological considerations ranging from sample size and type as well as researchers' joint role as advocates and researchers. The same remark applies to the consequences of reunions of adoptive children with birth parents. In this case, reunions can have consequences for the child, the birth parents, and the adoptive parents.
11. Foster children generally have poor outcomes, mainly because of prior neglect or abuse and because of the dislocation in their young lives as they are shifted around.
12. Currently, marriage is the pattern of family formation that is in the best interest of children. The situation of children born to single mothers would improve with appropriate social policies and male gender-role socialization.

KEY CONCEPTS AND THEMES

Agency of social control, p. 139
Authority figures, p. 139
Coerced sex, p. 128
Cohabitation is less institutionalized, p. 132
Cohabitation is more unstable, pp. 131, 133
Cumulation of risk factors, p. 130
Economic homogamy, p. 129
Functional institution, p. 139
Healthy family processes, p. 140
Homogamy, p. 129
Informal element of social control, p. 138
Institutionalized form of family formation, p. 136
Investment in children, p. 133
Physical abuse, p. 133
Poverty, pp. 125, 127
Second-parent adoption, p. 134
Sexual precociousness, p. 128
Social capital, p. 139
Social causation hypothesis, p. 137

Social construction of adoption, p. 140
Social selection hypothesis, pp. 129, 137
Stigmatization of adoption, p. 141
Structural-functionalist perspective, p. 136
Teen mothers, p. 127
Unmarried birth rate, p. 123

STUDY AND REVIEW QUESTIONS

1. Explain how the birth rate to unmarried black women remained stable between 1970 to 1990, yet an increasing proportion of black children were born to unmarried mothers by 1990.
2. How is it possible that the teen birth rate is lower now than in 1957, yet the rate of birth to unmarried teens is so high?
3. Discuss coerced sex and sexual precociousness as factors in very early teen motherhood.
4. Explain how the process of selection among unmarried fathers is similar to that of young unmarried mothers.
5. How functional are cohabitations in terms of children's best interest?
6. Children in same-sex-parent families fare as well as other children, contrary to what many people think. Explain why this is so. (The answers are not necessarily all in the text.)
7. Discuss the relative merits of the social causation and social selection hypothesis in terms of the observation that married individuals have better health, income, and happiness than those in other marital categories.
8. How is parental marriage advantageous to children?
9. Enumerate the types of adoption discussed herein and explain the potential advantages and disadvantages of each.
10. What are the functions of adopted children's reunions with their birth parents?
11. Are all forms of family formation equally functional? Qualify your answer.

SUGGESTED READINGS

Behrman, R. E. (Ed.). 1993. *The future of children: Adoption.* Los Altos, CA: Center for the Future of Children, Davis and Lucille Packard Foundation. This edited collection contains many review and research articles on the outcomes of children who have been adopted.

Maynard, R. E. (Ed.). 1997. *Kids having kids: Economic costs and social consequences of teen pregnancy.* Washington, DC: The Urban Institute Press. This research book covers a wide variety of topics, including abuse and neglect, the children of teenage mothers, and the economic costs of adolescent childbearing.

Nock, S. L. 1998. *Marriage in men's lives.* New York: Oxford University Press. The author uses surveys to study the role that marriage plays in men's lives and in terms of their well-being. One of his theses is that marriage is at the root of adult masculinity.

Reigot, B. P., and Spina, R. K. 1996. *Beyond the traditional family: Voices of diversity.* New York: Springer. Chapters are based on interviews with persons who fulfill a variety of familial roles, including single mothers by choice and same-sex parents.

Tasker, F. L., and Golombok, S. 1997. *Growing up in a lesbian family: Effects on child development.* New York: Guilford. This book compares children in lesbian-mother and heterosexual-mother families. It provides both a review of the literature and results from a research done by the authors.

Waite, L. J., and Gallagher, M. 2000. *The case for marriage.* Cambridge, MA: Harvard University Press. This book focuses on the benefits of the institution of marriage for men, women, and children. It has chapters on physical health, emotional well-being, sexuality, careers, domestic violence, and children's outcomes, among others.

SUGGESTED WEBLINKS

Government websites provide some of the best information on family formation trends. Consult **<http://www.fedstats.gov>** for general statistics. Click on *A to Z* to obtain an alphabetical list. Other useful government websites are:

Bureau of the Census: Click on *People* and an index will appear. **<http://www.census.gov>**

Health and Human Services offers government statistics on topics such as birth rates and childlessness. **<http://www.hhs.gov>**

National Center for Health Statistics is an important source of information on family formation. **<http://www.cdc.gov/nchs>**

Minnesota Texas Adoption Research Project provides information on topics related to adoption. Click on *Findings,* where you will obtain material on open adoptions. **<http://www.fsos.che.umn.edu/mtarp/default/html>**

For additional information on adoption, consult the directory at **<http://www.go2net. com/directory/Home/Family/Adoption>** and, especially, **<http://www.calib.com/chexpress>,** a website provided by the **National Adoption Information Clearinghouse** on behalf of the Children's Bureau.

Treatment Foster Care On Line is a website sponsored by the Oregon Social Learning Center; it provides information and contacts for the specialized foster care of children with behavioral and emotional problems. **<http://www.oslc.org/tfc/tfconline/html>**

PART 2

Social and Cultural Family Contexts

Part 1 has helped us to begin understanding how family formation and dynamics are affected by large sociocultural forces. Gender stratification, discrimination related to ethnicity, and the media were analyzed as important contexts impacting on family life. We have also seen how these contexts often create problems impeding the fulfilment of family functions. Part 2 focuses directly on four additional, key environmental influences on family life. This focus allows us to pursue some of the themes that are central to this text—namely, those of social inequalities, family functions, as well as the role of the functional community.

Chapter 6 describes how the recent changes in the economy have affected both family formation and family members' life course opportunities. A special focus is placed on economic inequalities.

In **Chapter 7**, we return to the topic of families' neighborhoods and housing conditions for a more in-depth look at how these contexts affect families' lives, particularly child socialization.

Chapter 8 examines the role of two key institutions on family life: schools and religion. Both constitute cultural contexts by what they teach; they also constitute a social environment of interactions and potential communities.

CHAPTER 6

Effects of the Economy and Economic Inequalities on Families

OUTLINE

Overview of Economic Changes

Effects of Economic Changes on Families
General Effects of Economic Changes on Family Life
Effects of Economic Changes on Family Structure
The Dual-Income Family
Is Maternal Employment Detrimental to Children?
Parental Employment and Children

Causes of Family Poverty
What Are the Structural Causes of Poverty?
Is the Poverty Threshold Realistic?
Official Unemployment and Real Unemployment
Deficient Social Policies
What Are the Sociopersonal Causes of Poverty?
Divorce as a Cause of Poverty
Single-Mother Families as a Source of Poverty
Is Welfare an Incentive to Single Mothering?

Consequences of Family Poverty
For Mothers
For Fathers
For Children

Conclusions: The Costs of Poverty

Summary
Key Concepts and Themes
Study and Review Questions
Suggested Readings
Suggested Weblinks

"In 10 years from now I will be either a lawyer or a doctor. I want to make money, lots of it. That's my primary goal."

"In 10 years I hope to be out of this noisy apartment building and live in a modest house in the countryside. I hope to have travelled a bit and especially help my mother and sister out of here. I would want my mother to stay home and not to have to worry about money for the first time in her life."

"Coming to this university was a different experience for me after private schools and finishing off in Switzerland. I can't say I like the students all that much but I don't have to live with them and it makes me appreciate what I had always taken for granted."

"Right now my big problem is lack of money, nothing new here but now that I am getting close to becoming a teacher and having a bit for myself for the first time in my life, I can't stand it any longer!"

"This autobiography is going to be rather boring. I have lived the typical 'American dream' or should I say 'Canadian'? Born to poverty, hard working parents,

moves to better neighborhoods and now our dream come true: a big house on a street with other big houses."

"My father is a lawyer and when I turned 10 my mother became a stock broker. . . . We've always lived in the same lovely neighborhood in a fairly large home with lots of trees and flowers, in two homes actually because my parents at some point decided to have a house with a two-level foyer with French doors and matching staircase."

"At that age [10 to 14] all I can remember is being hungry most of the time but especially by the end of each month and never having something special or nice that belonged to me. I don't have one pleasant memory."

"I recall being very afraid all the time [ages 6 to 10] because my parents used to fight a lot and my father would then take all his frustration out on us kids and there were too many of us to begin with. . . . My mother looked ten years older than her age . . . she was constantly worried about feeding us and . . . I think her fears were contagious."

Students who want to become doctors or lawyers because their dreams include a lot of money, students who simply want to have just enough for a decent life, students who suffered from the deprivations and fears of poverty, and students who lived in affluence: As the preceding quotes begin to illustrate, economic circumstances and the economic system in which people live affect all facets of their lives as well as their families' lives. The new millennium, as if on cue, is characterized by an economy that has been radically transformed in the recent decades. These sweeping changes have contributed to the current profile of families and to what some see as upheavals in the nation's social and moral fabric. Without some understanding of the economy, we cannot fully grasp the root causes of the recent family transformations that we have discussed in the previous chapters.

OVERVIEW OF ECONOMIC CHANGES

We now live in what is called the postindustrial or even postmodern society. That is, the economy is now propelled by the **information technology,** high finances, and the service sector. The economy is no longer organized along regional or even national lines; rather, it is international or global (the **globalization** of the economy). It is driven by multinational corporations operating throughout the world. In order to increase their profits, these corporations—whether Ford, Microsoft, Sony, or Volkswagen—move production plants around the globe, depending on the availability of cheap labor (Thurow, 1999). Hence, national economies are at the mercy of worldwide fluctuations more than ever before. Thus, rather than each national government controlling its country's organization of the labor markets and financial sectors (Rhodes, 1996), multinational corporations' needs for profit dictate trade and commercial laws as well as who will work, where, at what wage, and under what conditions. Therefore, globalization has important consequences for families because governments can less easily than before step in to improve the economic opportunities of a disadvantaged neighborhood or of an area that is threatened by plant closure, for instance.

When profit margins fall, corporations **"downsize,"** a polite technical term for *lay off.* When demand for corporations' products and profits soar, then employees are courted, as they were in 2000. When that point is reached, families benefit, particularly at the upper levels. Many others are hurt because this economic restructuring favors high-technology corporations that, in turn, favor a very skilled work force (Nelson, 1995). The result is that families with less educated and skilled members struggle or even sink economically while, all around them, the economy is flourishing.

Until the 1970s, the largest U.S. employers were industries producing materials such as steel, and goods such as cars. Manufacturers provided well-paying entry-level jobs, employment security, and, later on, benefit packages to young workers fresh out of high school. These industries hired large numbers of youths who became heads of families and solid members of the working and middle classes in their communities. With such jobs, youths, especially males, could marry and support a family. After the 1970s, as technology progressed, fewer low-skilled workers were needed. Plant closures, downsizing, relocation, and imports from abroad, particularly Asia, followed and the proportion of males working in manufacturing declined from 30 to 19 percent. For instance, between 1970 and 1985, Chicago alone lost 250,000 manufacturing jobs (Skogan, 1990). All of these and other factors began to restrict working-class American families' ability to earn decent wages and, during certain periods, such as the early 1990s, to secure a job.

While this was occurring, another phenomenon also arose that changed the entire employment profile: the **service sector** expanded, a large segment of which offers only low-paying and part-time jobs—for example in the restaurant, hotel, and retail domains (Sassen, 1994). All in all, a 50 percent increase in low-paying jobs occurred in the 1980s alone. Furthermore, in the face of a more competitive and high-tech economy and the requirements of corporations, many jobs have been downsized into **part-time positions;** they, of course, pay less and provide no health or pension benefits—and ultimately lead to poverty. In 1996 alone, over four million Americans who worked part time wanted full-time jobs but could not find one (Schwarz, 1998). Part-time jobs are overwhelmingly held by women who turn to them in order to combine work with maternal duties. Yet, 44 percent more women than men in such jobs would prefer full-time ones (Handler, 1995). Thus, the traditional gender division of labor and of income, with women earning less, is continued in the new economy. This detrimental feminine wage and labor situation contributes to poverty in single-mother families and in those in which it is necessary to supplement the father's income.

Another consequence of the emerging postindustrial economy has been an **inflation in educational requirements.** About two-thirds of all new positions created—even some low-paying ones—require at least 13 years of formal education, and 45 percent require more that 16 years. In this type of economy, school dropouts and youths with only high school diplomas face a life of part-time or low-wage jobs, especially if they live in the inner cities. An examination of *median* annual incomes illustrates this point. (The median income is the one that falls in the middle of the income distribution.) In 1992, *employed* dropouts' median annual income was $14,200, compared to $21,700 for high-school graduates, and $40,000 for college graduates (Schiller, 1995:156). By 1996, householders with college degrees had a median income of nearly $62,000, compared to $38,000 for those with high school diplomas, and $21,000 for dropouts (U.S. Bureau of the Census, 1997a). The gap in terms of wealth (assets such as real estate, stocks, bonds, savings accounts, and business ownership) has also increased, particularly as a result of the soaring success of information technology stocks. These two gaps between families in terms of income and wealth are still growing.

EFFECTS OF ECONOMIC CHANGES ON FAMILIES

The economic changes just described have had many consequences, both for family structure and family dynamics. As well, the family situations they have created, such as the widespread participation of women in the labor force, have given rise to concerns about children's well-being.

General Effects of Economic Changes on Family Life

The first effect of economic change on families over the recent decades resides in an **increase in feminine employment** and in **two-income families.** Gardner and Herz (1992) estimate that an additional 50 to 70 percent of families with two incomes would fall below the poverty level without the earning of the second worker. In two-parent families, mothers' wages became increasingly important. In 1996, for instance, when both a husband and wife were employed, the median income was over $58,000, compared to nearly $34,000 when the wife was not employed (U.S. Bureau of the Census, 1997a).

Feminine employment would have grown, however, despite this economic necessity, although perhaps to a lesser extent, because of the liberalization of attitudes concerning women's roles in society and the direct impact of the 1970s wave of the Women's Movement. This combined cultural change has allowed women to enter the labor force in greater numbers and, perhaps more significantly, to penetrate occupational fields that had been traditionally masculine, such as law, medicine, and the physical sciences. In two-parent families, two wages have also become important because of a rise in consumer expectations: Parents and children are influenced by advertising and they develop costly "needs" that can be fulfilled only with two incomes.

Furthermore, higher divorce and single-parenting rates make it necessary for divorced and unmarried mothers to be employed.

A second effect of economic changes on families consists of what is called the **time crunch:** Too many activities are crammed into two few hours. Both parents work and, in comparison to the 1970s, they work longer hours. Spouses have less time for each other, especially if they work different shifts, and parents can devote far fewer hours to their children (Hofferth et al., 1998). As an illustration of this time squeeze, let's hear what two young professional couples, with both spouses employed full time, said when interviewed in 1998:

> *One 28-year-old mother sighed helplessly when she finished giving me her little family's crowded schedule:*
>
> > *"It's like a spinning wheel that never stops, uh, the more we work the more afraid we are that if we work less we won't be able to afford a better life for Jenny later on and for us when we are older [the 2-year-old is at home with a nanny]. But then in the meantime we don't get to enjoy her. I have already missed out on all the cute things that a baby starts doing. Uh, soon we'll turn around and she'll have grown up and we won't have seen it happen. I wish there was a better way for career couples nowadays."*
>
> *Another young couple in their early thirties both complained during their separate interviews that they had "no time for each other; it's even difficult to put some sex in our lives because we are always on the run" [wife]. For his part, the husband felt that the wife "could work fewer hours; that way, it would be easier to arrange our schedules so that we can take some time out for our relationship." He did not mention that he could also work fewer hours, a realistic possibility, given that he stayed at the office daily until 8 P.M. This was a very affluent couple with extremely high material expectations—costly expectations. In contrast to the four other couples interviewed, this couple was not concerned about having practically no time for their 4-year-old son. Fortunately, the little boy appeared to be good natured and easily contented. He made no demands during the two hours I spent at his home and he occupied himself peacefully.*

A third effect of economic changes on families resides in an increase in poverty, particularly among the working poor. The **working poor** are those whose wages are too low to raise their family above the poverty line or the income-to-needs ratio determined by the government. When wages are minimal, many families become or remain poor despite the fact that both parents are employed. Part-time work and minimum-wage jobs are largely responsible for this situation.

A fourth effect of economic changes on family life stems from increased educational requirements: *young adults remain at home* with their parents longer and *delay marriage.* Remaining at home allows youths to pursue their education, even if they attend college elsewhere. Once employed, free parental room and board allows those who earn low salaries to afford the luxuries of life that are now defined as necessities, such as cars, electronic equipment, regular changes in clothing styles, and even traveling. In disadvantaged families, particularly among immigrants who sponsor the arrival of other members of their kin group, young workers may stay home to pool their resources with those of their parents or, at the very least, to help pay for household expenses. Other youths remain home because of unemployment, and a large proportion of teen single mothers stay home for a few years, often with their mothers, either to complete their education, to work, or simply because they are too poor and inexperienced to live on their own.

Effects of Economic Changes on Family Structure

Another effect of economic changes has been an increase in the **creation of families headed by unmarried mothers,** as illustrated in the previous chapter. This effect has resulted from the combination of the decline in entry-level manufacturing jobs and the increase in service jobs. From 1979 to 1989, for instance, the proportion of males aged 18 to 24 who worked full time in low-paying jobs jumped from 18 to 35 percent, and for same-aged women from 29 to 43 percent. Moreover, youth unemployment has grown since the 1960s and is only now beginning to diminish (Nasar and Mitchell, 1999). As a result, young men with little education have become less attractive marital partners. Indeed, there is strong evidence that male employment, in general, and male employment in well-paying jobs, in particular, lead to higher marriage rates. In contrast, male unemployment and entry into jobs that carry only the minimum wage contribute to the creation of single-parent families. This situation applies across all races, but is particularly acute among blacks and Puerto Ricans, as seen in Chapter 3 (Tucker and Mitchell-Kernan, 1995).

I even found reflections of this situation when asking students to predict where they will be at 10 years from now. Each year, there are several black women students in my classes and what is so striking in their answers to this general question is how rarely they mention marriage; in contrast, most of the other women students expect marriage as a matter of course, although they are certainly not rushing into it, as was the case in the 1970s. The black women's answers vary but most are totally silent on this subject. Only a few are more or less explicit: "It is difficult to tell if I will be married or not but I am sure that I will have or will be planning my first child." One woman points out, "It would be foolish of me to expect to be married even though I'd love it. But I can't see who I could marry who could support me and my child when I have one." Another gets closer to the matter: "It's sad that I can't tell you that I'll be married because I bet that's what all the white and Asian girls in the class write. Sure, I can have a guy but I'll have an education and a good job and I won't settle for just any man who needs me to support him."

The next woman is even more sociological in her analysis of her prospects; she bitterly resents the fact that "white people always complain about us because we have children out of wedlock, as they call it. Don't they understand that a lot of us would like to get married too but many of our men can't marry us because they are too poor to support us? If our men could have jobs and be respected the way white men are then they'd respect themselves and we women would be able to turn to them for support. Our children would have fathers at home."

These autobiographies sadly support the statistics presented in this and the previous chapter: Black women's lower marriage rates are more a matter of economics than negative attitude about marriage (Sassler and Schoen, 1999).

The reputed sociologist William J. Wilson (1987) was one of the first to discuss the effect of unemployment and low wages on family formation, in his case on the black family. Following his example, demographers, such as South (1996), have studied the impact of men's and women's wages on marriage formation for all races. They found that both men's and women's marriage rates rise with each additional thousand dollars that men earn. A related study established that an employed black male is more likely to marry his girlfriend when she becomes pregnant or gives birth than is an unemployed black male (Testa et al., 1993). Overall, what this research suggests is that decent masculine wages contribute to marriageability and the formation of two-parent families.

The Dual-Income Family

In 1995, nearly 75 percent of mothers with dependent children, including 58 percent of mothers with children under 2 years and 62 percent with children under 6 years, were employed (cited in Hofferth, 1996). Thus, a majority of mothers with even very young children work. Strangely enough, as we saw in Chapter 2, this shift toward maternal employment has occurred during a time period when the care of small children has become more labor intensive and the pressures on women as mothers have mounted (Hays, 1996).

The net result is what sociologist Arlie Hochschild has called *The Second Shift* (1989). That is, although society has become more liberal concerning women's status and role in the workplace, this development has not been accompanied by a similar liberalizing or liberating one on the domestic front. In the "second shift," women come home from work to work even more. After picking up children at the day care center or at the sitter's, they cook and serve dinner, prepare lunches for the next day, perhaps do laundry, and help the children with their homework and bedtime (Hochschild, 1997). True, fathers participate somewhat more than in the past, particularly when the mother is employed, but their participation is still minimal. The end result is that full-time women employees toil more hours per week than men when housework and paid work hours are combined, a topic that is discussed at greater length in Chapter 10 (Demo and Acock, 1993).

Although employed mothers (and fathers) are healthier mentally and physically than stay-at-home mothers, they nevertheless encounter problems specific to their combined triple role of workers, mothers, and housekeepers (Glass and Fujimoto, 1994). They experience role conflict and stressors. In turn, these problems differ markedly across the social classes, between what is called the *two-wage-earner families* versus the *two-career families*. The latter families are in a far better financial situation to buy services, mainly quality child care, that can alleviate maternal role strain (Lennon and Rosenfield, 1992).

Still, overall, employed mothers, whether married or single, have little time for themselves, are overworked and stressed, frequently worry about their children and often feel guilty, even more so when child care arrangements are not optimal or when their children are alone at home after school or in the company of problematic peers. Despite these problems, it is interesting to note that mothers are often happier and more relaxed at work than at home, in part because of the enjoyment they derive from their achievements and social interactions (Hochschild, 1997). Furthermore, for women who shoulder most of the burden at home, paid work outside is often less stressful than housework and childrearing (Larson and Richards, 1994).

A related consequence of dual incomes on family life also applies to single-parent families: Children, even as infants, are more and more in the charge of persons other than their own parents. Since child care is discussed in Chapter 8, suffice it to say here that children spend fewer hours per week than before with any parent or with any adult in authority. The U.S. Bureau of the Census has estimated that, between 1960 and 1986, parental time available to children has diminished by 10 hours per week for whites and 12 for blacks (Fuchs, 1990). The phenomenon of "latchkey" children comes to mind here, as well as older siblings taking care of a younger one after school. It is, therefore, important to look at the effect that parental employment may have on children.

Is Maternal Employment Detrimental to Children?

The research literature, public policy debates, talk shows, and magazines focus on the effects of *maternal* rather than paternal employment. (For an exception, see Harvey, 1999.) Why is so much attention devoted to maternal employment and its presumed negative consequences on children? Why not consider fathers' employment in these respects? The answer to this question resides in the overall gender stratification and in consequent social constructions of motherhood and fatherhood, further discussed in Chapter 9. Under the existing gender-based division of responsibilities, mothers are still viewed as children's primary caregivers and fathers as chief breadwinners. But the notion that only mothers are children's best caregivers is unscientific. If mothers were "by nature" the best caregivers, why would an army of social workers be needed to watch over those hundreds of thousands of children abused or neglected by their biological mothers? Being a competent child caregiver is more a matter of training, personality, and social encouragement than femininity versus masculinity.

Evolutionists may point out that mothers' nursing and caregiving were essential to children's survival at the beginning of humanity and thus have come to constitute part of human nature. However, both historically and cross-culturally, the fact remains that *shared* child care is the norm rather than the exception (Scarr, 1998). Throughout the world, mothers share the care of their young ones with female relatives, older children, co-villagers, and even elderly men. The same situation probably prevailed during evolution. Shared care ("other mothers") is often encountered among African Americans and people from the Caribbean, perhaps a remnant of long traditions that continue to exist in African villages (Collins, 1992; Hunter and Ensminger, 1992).

Because of the traditional beliefs in the necessity of constant maternal care for children, studies originally carried out in the 1940s through the 1970s were biased or flawed from the start. They were set up to find problems and failed to consider important variables, as we see in the next paragraph. This research took place at a time when mothers were encouraged to leave work after the World War II effort in order to give back jobs that "naturally" belonged to returning male veterans. Not only were women "sent home" but child care centers built during the war were dismantled, thus making it difficult for mothers to continue their employment activities.

Despite these combined factors, very little in the way of negative impact of maternal employment was ever found (Harvey, 1999; Menaghan and Parcel, 1991). It took decades of additional studies with improved methods and less biased or slanted theories and social perspectives to tease out fact from fiction. Now, when the impact of maternal employment on children is studied, mothers' work circumstances and the quality of care children receive have to be considered—and this was not done in the early studies. For instance, maternal employment carries more risks among poor than nonpoor children because there often is no quality substitute care, mothers earn too little to make ends meet, their jobs are boring, and they are too exhausted to be enthusiastic parents when they return home (Ali and Avison, 1997:358). These difficulties may increase when families live in a dangerous neighborhood (Sampson and Laub, 1994).

So what can we conclude? All things being equal, children whose mothers are employed do not have more negative outcomes than children of stay-at-home mothers. Maternal employment is in fact advantageous for some children, particularly girls, in terms of school achievement and self-esteem. This is particularly so when mothers' occupations are highly skilled and complex (Cooksey, Menaghan, and Jekielek, 1997). Even for poor children, a mother's salary may raise the family's standard of living and thus provide compensations amidst risks for children (Harvey, 1999).

Parental Employment and Children

It is important to reframe the question within the context of parental employment rather than restricting it to mothers' employment. The effect of the employment of one parent cannot be separated from the effect of the employment of the other parent when the family is analyzed within a systems theory perspective. To begin with, no matter what their social class, when *both* parents work *long* hours and there are no adult substitutes at home, children and adolescents may not have sufficient interaction with caring authority figures. A recent study looking at the effect of both parents' employment found that, when mothers' hours at work increased, fathers became more aware of their 8- to 10-year-old children's activities, as a compensating mechanism (Crouter et al., 1999). But the researchers also found that children were less well monitored when fathers had very demanding jobs (Bumpus, Crouter, and McHale, 1999).

In situations where parents are overworked, children are deprived of social resources, or **social capital,** according to James Coleman's rational theory. Possibly, children will go unsupervised, which is a risky matter in this society where opportunities for problematic and even delinquent behaviors abound. Depending on their personalities, some adolescents may take advantage of negative opportunities and use drugs, become prematurely active sexually, or even engage in delinquent acts. Actually, there is a direct *correlation,* or correspondence, between delinquency and lack of supervision by *adults,* in general, including parents (Mekos, Hetherington, and Reiss, 1996). In other words, as seen in Figure 6.1, the better supervised adolescents are, the less likely they are to commit delinquent acts. (The figure allows the reader to see what correlations look like.) When no adults are in charge, children may fail to learn certain coping skills, others may not do their homework, and still others may not learn how to communicate effectively. In other words, even when their parents are relatively affluent, many of these children may not develop sufficient human capital and may

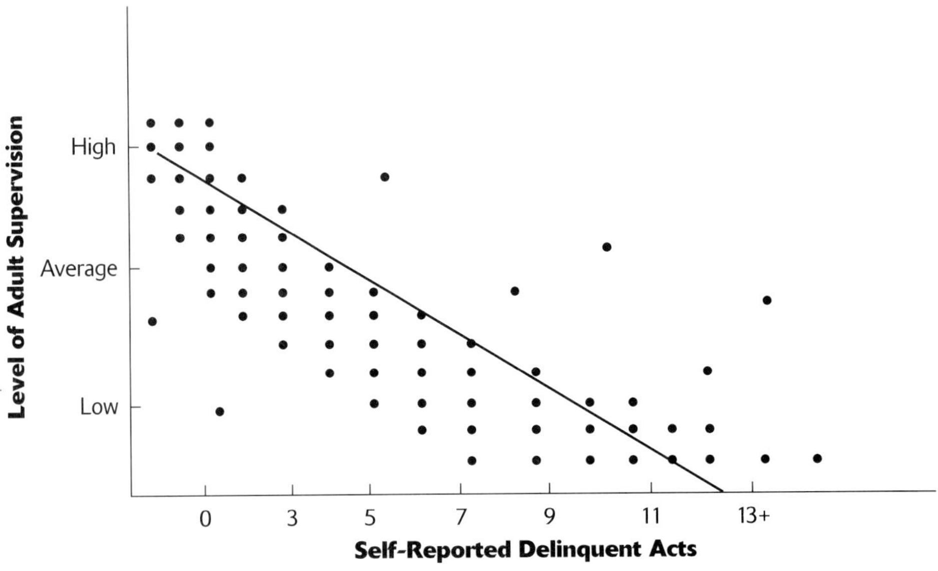

FIGURE 6.1

Correlation between Adult Supervision and Number of Delinquent Acts

Each dot represents an adolescent who is placed on the diagram depending on how many delinquent acts he or she reports and how well supervised he or she is by adults (parents, teachers, neighbors, etc.). When the dots fall in a well-ordered pattern, this is an indication that a good correlation exists. The straighter the line, the higher the correlation.

be **undersocialized.** That is, they may not learn what one is required to know at a given age in order to function effectively and ethically in this society.

Another potential problem related to parental employment resides in the combination of materialistic values with a *preoccupation for* **upward mobility,** or "moving up socially." These parents (who also have a high divorce rate; see Clydesdale, 1997) spend many hours at the office or on business trips and, when at home, often pursue their career-related activities rather than engage in family interactions. They do not have the time to relate to their children authoritatively or to teach them appropriate values. Also, the lives of working parents' children are sometimes hectically packed with activities and their days are lived at a frenetic pace. Let's look at the example of another young, affluent family from my 1998 home interviews of two-career couples.

> *This suburban family consists of two parents aged 35 (husband) and 33 (wife), both professionals in large brokerage firms, and two boys of 3 and 6 years. The family rises at 6:00 A.M. The parents alternate taking the boys to the day care center where they arrive at 7:00 A.M. Glenn, the oldest, is picked up by minivan at 8:45 and brought to a nearby school, where he is in first grade. The parents take turns fetching the children at 6:00 P.M. at the day care, where Glenn has been since 3:15 after another ride in the minivan. Once a week, a taxi drives him to*

music classes after school and returns him to the center. One parent takes the hungry children home and promptly serves them supper; the other parent arrives at 7:00 P.M., equally hungry and tired. The children are in bed at 8:00, quite exhausted by then.

Saturday morning, the father takes the boys for swimming lessons; the mother takes them for skating lessons in the afternoon. Sunday is spent going to church, shopping, and visiting with friends and relatives. Both parents are intelligent, attractive, and sociable. The boys get along well and play together in the few hours of unstructured time they have. They are apparently intelligent. However, Glenn's report card indicates that his verbal skills are below grade level. His visiting grandmother explains that this is due to the fact that the children are always in the company of other children and are rarely alone with adults who, at any rate, are obviously of no interest to the child-oriented boys. The boys basically spend only two hours daily with their parents, all the while busily engaged in housework activities. Little conversation takes place. Life is fast paced.

CAUSES OF FAMILY POVERTY

One other key by-product of the economy resides in poverty, which, in 1996, afflicted at least 14 percent of the population for a total of 36.5 million persons, or 11 percent, of all families. Why are there so many disadvantaged families amidst affluence in America? What are the causes of families' poverty? We began addressing this question earlier on in this chapter while examining some of the major changes in the economy and how they affect families' ability to be self-supporting.

At the risk of oversimplifying what is a highly complex issue, the causes of poverty fall into two categories: the **systemic**, or structural, causes at the social level and the **personal** ones. Both of these categories are explored separately. *Structural* and *systemic* refer to overall social conditions, whereas *personal* refers to attributes and behaviors of the poor. As a general rule, the personal causes are preceded by the large-scale socioeconomic or structural causes that generate both poverty and the personal sources of poverty (Haveman and Wolfe, 1994). If the economic and social causes of poverty were eliminated, the personal causes, while not vanishing entirely, would be radically reduced.

What Are the Structural Causes of Poverty?

Within the postindustrial economy, social inequalities, in general, and the gap between rich and poor families, in particular, have widened (Schor and Menaghan, 1995). In the United States, poverty is the result of an unequal distribution of wealth among families rather than an overall lack of riches (Ambert, 1998a). Among affluent Western societies, only the United States combines a large and entrenched population of very disadvantaged families, many of which are residentially segregated and are therefore more or less forgotten or out of sight. The plight of these families is heightened by the fact that the United States is also the only Western country that does not provide universal health care—unless families go on welfare.

At this time, the following structural aspects of the organization of the American society probably constitute the major causes of family poverty:

- Low-paying and part-time jobs, particularly among women and minority groups
- The decline of well-paid entry-level jobs in manufacturing
- Discrimination and segregation, which prevent various population groups from accessing good schools and job opportunities
- Unemployment related to low educational qualifications in some segments of the population
- Pay inequity by gender (women are paid less than men for comparable job qualifications)
- Lack of social benefits and health insurance for families

Is the Poverty Threshold Realistic?

We already understand how part-time jobs and low-paying work create poverty. A Roper survey conducted in April 1994 revealed that Americans felt they needed \$25,000 for a family of four "just to get by" and \$40,000 "to live in relative comfort." The government poverty threshold or cut-off point before poverty for a family of four was around \$15,000 (Schiller, 1995). Thus, it seems that American families' needs exceed by \$10,000 the official poverty line. This is understandable because this poverty line does not reflect reality: It is 40 percent lower than what Americans actually required in order to survive in 1998 (Schwarz, 1998). The poverty line established by the government is actually based on 1950s needs, when housing was less costly and life, in general, was less expensive.

Therefore, there are far more "real" poor families in United States than what shows up in statistics based on the official poverty line. Although "only" 15 percent of the population may be poor according to official statistics, at least another 10 to 15 percent hover precariously above the somewhat unrealistic threshold. These families constitute the near poor, or the economically marginal, as we will see later in Table 6.1. Any crisis can send them tumbling below the poverty level—crises such as a dental emergency, an illness, the birth of an additional child, or the loss of even one of the many part-time jobs these families may hold.

Official Unemployment and Real Unemployment

When *unemployment* rises, poverty becomes more widespread, especially visible poverty in the form of homelessness. In 2000, the unemployment rate in the United States, at about 4 percent, was the lowest in several decades, particularly compared to what it reached in the early 1990s (close to 10 percent) and the lowest compared to other Western nations. Unfortunately, the "full employment" of the new millennium has not reached all population groups equally and does not compensate for the proliferation of low-paying, unskilled jobs. Full employment has certainly not reached the youth population with less than some postsecondary education nor high-poverty rural areas and Native reservations. Only now is full employment beginning to make a dent in inner cities that are heavily populated by African-American families.

For instance, in 1993, the unemployment rate for white males was 7 percent, but was nearly 18 percent for those aged 16 to 19 years (i.e., the less educated). For black

The working poor include families in which both parents are employed in low-paying jobs. One parent may even hold two jobs. These families are hovering precariously just one slippery step above the poverty level, and even more so as few can afford health insurance.

males, in general, the unemployment rate was about 14 percent—double that among whites—and was as high as 40 percent for young African Americans aged 16 to 19 years (U.S. Bureau of the Census, 1994). By 1999, this percentage was finally creeping down. The overall black unemployment was near 9 percent, compared to 3.8 among whites. Nevertheless, it should be noted that **real unemployment** is even higher among black males in their prime (16 through 35 years of age). This is because a large number of inner-city black males have stopped looking for jobs and are therefore not counted as unemployed; only individuals who are actually looking for a job are counted as unemployed. Second, young black males' incarceration rate is high and the institutionalized population is not included in statistics on unemployment. Hence, it becomes obvious that one of the main sources of family poverty and single parenting in black families resides in the widespread *real* unemployment and low-paying jobs among black males and particularly among those who are at an age when they should be supporting small children.

Deficient Social Policies

Three deficient social policies are examined that contribute to either creating poverty or maintaining it. First, a recent study by the AFL-CIO has shown that, on average, women would earn over $4,000 more each year if they were paid as much as men who hold comparable job qualifications (Lewin, 1999). This is referred to as **pay inequity.** An example is a social worker (now a largely feminine occupation) who earns $35,000, compared to a probation officer who is paid $55,000. The educational

FAMILY RESEARCH 6.1

A Qualitative Study: "They Think You Ain't Much of Anything"

Seccombe, James, and Walters (1998) interviewed 47 women who were AFDC recipients in 1995 in order to study their interpretation of welfare use. They began with volunteers who were waiting in line to pick up their food stamps in northern Florida communities. Black and white interviewers were matched with same-race respondents.

The authors' approach was drawn from symbolic interactionism, particularly Blumer's (1969) notion that people actively construct their own realities through social interaction and the symbols and meanings involved. What was important was to allow the women to express themselves. The researchers had certain broad research questions in mind, such as why the women were on welfare. The interviews were taped, transcribed, and common themes were identified.

The authors found that the respondents blamed their welfare recipiency on structural factors out of their control, but they attributed welfare use by other women to personal deficits such as laziness. They believed in the popular, negative stereotypes, but not for themselves, a result also obtained by other researchers. This individualistic perspective on the causes of poverty may be more widespread "than previously assumed and may run deep in the psyche of the poor within our nation" (p. 862).

requirements are equivalent and the work demands are quite similar. If women were paid equitably, the poverty rate in families where the mothers are employed could be cut by half.

Unwillingness to work and welfare recipiency cannot be explained as reasons for family povery. Not only do most poor people work at least some months during the year, but only a minority of the disadvantaged receive cash welfare benefits at any point in time. Therefore, social assistance benefits cannot create poverty directly (although they create stigma, as described in Family Research 6.1). However, when families are already poor and receive minimal benefits, and for only a restricted period of time as is the case currently, these **deficient social assistance benefits** contribute to keeping them at or below the poverty level (Edin and Lein, 1997b). If benefits were somewhat more generous and if they were maintained in the form of child care and health care assistance once the breadwinner has found a low-paying job, poverty would diminish. Thus, from this perspective, it can be said that the welfare system contributes to familial poverty. For instance, the nation's food stamp rolls dropped by 30 percent from 1994 to 1998 as a result of tighter regulations. Among those who dropped out, it is estimated that three million would need that help to survive without going hungry (Revkin, 1999a).

Another policy related cause of poverty among families with young children resides in the *lack of universal assistance for parents*, which is quite a contrast to what occurs in most other Western countries. Let's digress for a moment to look at poverty among the elderly. As recently as 1959, 35 percent of the American elderly were disadvantaged, compared to about 11 percent in 1995—although here, as well, there are differences by race, ethnicity, and gender. For instance, 33 percent of the black elderly are poor (U.S. Senate Special Committee on Aging, 1992). The main reason why elderly poverty has declined so drastically is directly related to Social Security provisions. It is estimated that, without Social Security, nearly 48 percent of the elderly would be poor (*The New York Times*, April 9, 1999). Such a reduction in poverty could also occur for children in the form of child or maternal subsidies.

Knowing what other Western countries do places U.S. policies in perspective. Western governments provide parents with three types of financial help; most provide paid maternity and even paternity leaves. The United States and Australia are the only two Western countries that do not provide *paid* maternity, or even paternity, leaves. Some nations provide a mother's allowance—an income allocated to mothers, regardless of their marital status, depending on the number of dependent children. A few societies dispense a one-time cash outlay at the birth of a child, say $500 (which is increased for each additional child in some cases), to help defray the initial costs of baby clothing and furnishings. Thus, as will be discussed later, poverty rates for families headed by a relatively uneducated parent and those headed by a mother are comparatively low in most other Western countries. Paid maternity leaves, combined with free access to health care and subsidized child care, are key reasons for this lower familial poverty in Western countries and Japan (Corsaro, 1997).

What Are the Sociopersonal Causes of Poverty?

The personal causes of family poverty are generally the ones favored for discussion by the public, the media, and the policy makers. These personal causes imply that individuals who bear certain demographic characteristics, such as single motherhood, are responsible for their poverty and for all the consequences flowing from it, including a child's delinquency, for instance. An emphasis on the personal causes of poverty leads to the reasoning that, were these persons to change their attitudes and behaviors, poverty would be eradicated. In other words, this emphasis precludes a consideration of the larger socioeconomic causes of poverty and eradicates the political will to change them. This is why, in decades of budgetary restraints, welfare programs for mothers with dependent children are popular targets of suspicion and cuts. Yet, as we have seen earlier, this is a misguided notion because social assistance prevents poverty or, at the very least, prevents poor families from starving.

At the personal level, there are three basic causes of poverty: low educational level, which was mentioned earlier, divorce, and single-parent families.

Divorce as a Cause of Poverty

Divorce is a direct cause of poverty for women and children, although a sizeable proportion of divorces are themselves caused by economic hardship (Smock, Manning, and Gupta, 1999). Indeed, families under economic pressure are more likely to experience negative interactions, spousal conflict, domestic violence, and child abuse. Any of these problems can lead to divorce; thus, disadvantaged families are more likely to break apart (Aseltine and Kessler, 1993). Once separation takes place, the mother and child unit becomes even poorer.

Studies carried out by Smock (1994) as well as Bianchi, Subaiya, and Kahn (1999) clearly indicate that, in the year after divorce, and adjusting for family size, women's household income falls by about 40 to 60 percent, whereas men's income increases slightly. Hao (1996) has documented that divorced fathers accumulate about $23,000 in wealth, compared to a paltry $600 for divorced mothers. Below, divorced women from my study on divorce/remarriage explain their economic situation and express their feelings on this topic:

> *"Her father pays support but it does not begin to make up for what I lost because of the divorce. It keeps us off welfare, that's all."*

> *"I had never thought about money before I divorced. I tell you that it has been a shock; you can't imagine how hard it is to raise two children on no income so to speak [she is a secretary] while their father is living the good life. What I can't give them, he gives them and it makes me look bad. My sons use this as leverage to get their way."*

> *"If it was not of my parents' help we'd be very poor; at this stage we are barely above the poverty level. [She has three children.] . . . No I have not been employed since I first got pregnant, so that's 16 years ago. I don't know what I am going to do. Right now I am just scared stiff and I run from one grocery store to another with coupons. My daughter is really upset because I just can't afford as much as we used to have. I just don't know" [tears trickle down her cheeks].*

When divorced mothers become poor, however, they remain so or stay on welfare less long than never-married mothers (London, 1996). This is in part a matter of age and education as well as previous work experience. For those women who were comfortably middle class before divorce and fall into poverty after, this usually constitutes a transitory period; after several months to a few years, they are generally able to lift themselves out of poverty through employment, their parents' help, fathers' child support, and remarriage.

Single-Mother Families as a Source of Poverty

If current trends continue, over half of the present generation of children will at some point live in a single-parent family before age 16 (Rodgers, 1996). Whether children in single-mother families have divorced or never-married parents, two salient facts emerge. First, these children are much more likely to be poor than those who live with both parents. In 1991, 53 percent of mother-headed families were below the poverty level, compared to nearly 22 percent for single-father families, and 10 percent for two-parent families (Bianchi, 1995:88). Second, the combination of a single mother and ethnic minority places children at an extraordinary risk for poverty because of discrimination and segregation.

For its part, family formation by never-married mothers is both a result and a personal cause of poverty. To begin with, as seen in the previous chapter, a majority of disadvantaged never-married mothers already belonged to a poor family before becoming mothers, and so did their babies' fathers. As we descend the socioeconomic ladder, the number of new births to unmarried teenagers and young adults increases spectacularly, both for whites and blacks (Morris et al., 1996).

Once an already disadvantaged young woman has a child, the new situation merely entrenches her poverty or makes it last longer, and her chances of marrying decrease (Bennett, Bloom, and Miller, 1995). Her motherhood also creates poverty: The woman essentially gives birth to a child who becomes poor. Gottschalk and

Danziger (1993) calculate that, had the proportion of female-headed families compared to two-parent families remained at the 1960 lower level, poverty would now be one-third less among blacks and one-fifth less among whites. In other words, if most parents were married, as was the case in 1960 both among blacks and whites, poverty would be less widespread.

When a single mother is employed, not only is she the sole wage earner for herself and her child but she is also far more likely than a male worker to earn a very low salary (Edin and Lein, 1997b). She generally also earns less than an employed divorced mother, even though the latter does not earn as much, on average, as a male breadwinner. Therefore, the economic disadvantage of *women in general* (gender inequality) is especially detrimental to single mothers' families, both divorced and never married, but particularly the latter.

Surprisingly perhaps, in the past a majority of these mothers have eventually left poverty while still young—although one has to be careful here because economic conditions have changed drastically since these studies were carried out in the 1980s. In the future, it may become more difficult for such young women and their children to leave poverty, both because of the educational requirements of the labor market and lower social assistance payments. This said, admittedly, while relatively few become affluent, a good proportion never need to have recourse to welfare or, for others, never will again. For their part, Menaghan and Parcel (1995) find that single mothers who are employed in well-paid occupations provide their children with a home environment equivalent to that available in similar two-parent families. Unfortunately, among those who have never married, these mothers are the exception, unless they had their first child later in life and were able to accumulate both social and financial capitals.

Although single teen mothers account for only one-third of all single mothers, their situation is of great concern because a majority are poor. About 50 percent of all single teen mothers go on welfare within a year, and 77 percent do so within five years of their first child's birth. Often, they go on welfare as a result of a second birth (Congress of the United States, 1990). About $22 billion is spent through programs such as the former Aid for Families with Dependent Children (AFDC), food stamps, and Medicaid to women who were or are teen mothers (Haveman, Wolfe, and Wilson, 1997). However, single mothers in their early twenties who come from poor families are not much better off than adolescent ones, particularly when they had had a first child during adolescence (Foster, Jones, and Hoffman, 1998).

Is Welfare an Incentive to Single Mothering?

A much debated question in family policy is the following: Do young women become mothers because of the "easy availability of welfare"? The answer, contrary to what is believed by many, including politicians, is a *qualified no.* Rather, it seems that poor women, in general, are less likely to marry than nonpoor women, in part because of a scarcity of economically marriageable potential partners (McLaughlin and Lichter, 1997). Furthermore, Lichter, McLaughlin, and Rebar (1997) document that women's own higher earnings and education encourage marriage rather than single motherhood.

Economists and sociologists have addressed the question asked here using both government statistics and interviews with young women. They have found that, once women have a baby out of wedlock, welfare recipiency *may* discourage about 20 percent of them from marrying (Bennet, Bloom, and Miller, 1995). But they are not saying that welfare availability causes women to have children out of wedlock in the first place—just to remain unmarried for a proportion of them. Using a different set of statistics, McLaughlin and Lichter (1997) also agree that the prospect of welfare receipt is only slightly related to women's fertility outside of marriage.

Other statisticians have established that single mothering, compared to married mothering, has increased dramatically at a time when welfare benefits, then called AFDC, were being drastically reduced. (AFDC had its origins in 1935. The new program, established in 1996 following the Personal Responsibility and Work Opportunity Reconciliation Act, is called Temporary Assistance to Needy Families, or TANF.) If welfare payments were an inducement for nonmarital motherhood, the latter would have declined when payments declined and eligibility rules tightened. But the opposite occurred, suggesting that other causes are involved.

McLaughlin and Lichter (1997) have also documented that each $100 change in welfare benefits is related to a mere 1.3 percentage drop or increase in female headship (unwed and divorced). They have calculated that, even if welfare payments were cut in half, female headship among African Americans would drop by only 5 percent. Moreover, welfare availability does not explain why whites, particularly white Cubans, have a lower proportion of never-married mothers than blacks, Puerto Ricans, and Mexican Americans, for instance (Forste and Tienda, 1996). In the next chapter, we see that segregation in poor neighborhoods explains this difference far more adequately. Furthermore, we should not forget that European nations, with far more generous social benefits than provided in the United States, have lower rates of nonmarital births.

In a nutshell, nonmarital childbirths cannot be explained by the availability of welfare benefits. Poverty, the sex ratio (many young black males are in jail, thus unavailable to marry), segregation, a high proportion of young people in an area, cohabitation, and a liberalization of norms concerning out-of-wedlock pregnancies constitute *together* a more potent explanation than welfare availability and level of welfare payments. Decreasing payments as well as imposing a time limit on receipt *may* result in a slight increase in marriage rates, but better education and reasonably paying jobs are more important factors in this respect (McLaughlin and Lichter, 1997). One also has to consider that these are important factors in fostering *quality* marriages, a key element that is generally overlooked in the emphasis on marriage *rates*. The overall reality is that poverty, not welfare availability, largely creates unwed motherhood, prevents marriage as a means of family formation, and destabilizes existing marriages.

CONSEQUENCES OF FAMILY POVERTY

Poverty affects mothers, fathers, and children differently, in part because of gender roles (mothers versus fathers) and in part because of life stage: Children are affected early in their life course, whereas fathers and mothers are impacted as adults. However, in the case of teen mothers, the effect can be a recurrent one, as they generally were poor as children and are poor again as young mothers. This section is linked to

Chapter 3 and is complemented in the next two chapters, where we will see that the consequences of poverty at the family level are compounded or alleviated, depending on the case, by race as well as neighborhood factors and educational opportunities.

For Mothers

Impoverished mothers who live in neighborhoods, especially in housing projects, with a high concentration of poverty and criminality, are particularly vulnerable to failure as mothers because the circumstances under which they raise their children are simply unfair (see Kotlowitz, 1991). The deck of cards is stacked against them from the very outset. Their ability to supervise their children effectively is impaired by the conditions imposed by poverty (Sampson and Laub, 1994). In view of this situation, it is not the elevated rates of negative child outcomes that are surprising, but the fact that they are not higher. That so many of these mothers' children grow up to be decent citizens is a tribute both to the resilience of some children and to their mothers' extraordinary diligence and devotion.

These mothers are deprived of the resources that a middle-class woman takes for granted in raising her children (Edin and Lein, 1997a). In addition, they often lack credibility in their children's eyes due to their poverty and, in some cases, due to their never-married status. When such women are members of a devalued minority group that is segregated in decrepit neighborhoods, their burden is magnified because they have far fewer opportunities for employment. Discrimination and consequent segregation prevent them from moving to a better area.

As Cook and Fine (1995:132) note, low-income mothers have few childrearing options and cannot afford to make errors. In many neighborhoods, they have to be more strict and vigilant because "errors" lead to delinquency, drug addiction, early pregnancy, and even death. Therefore, success in socialization goals are seen in terms of "sheltering their children from the pitfalls of self-destruction, such as drugs, crime and cyclical government dependency" (Arnold, 1995:145). Loftier goals, such as the development of children's verbal and reading skills, are a luxury in such environments. The basic tasks of feeding, housing, and shielding their children from danger are at the forefront of these mothers' thoughts and energy.

> *When Alisha, a student, was small, her mother immigrated from Jamaica to Baltimore, where she and her two younger brothers joined her. Alisha was then 10 years old and was 13 when the family relocated to Toronto. In both cities, they lived in a poor neighboorhood. She recalls her life in the Baltimore "ghetto":*
>
> > *"In the morning, we were often late for school and I had to get my brothers ready because my mother had left a long time ago; she had to commute to her job. . . . After school, we'd go back home minding our own business and careful to stay away from the older boys as my mother had told us to do. We'd get something to eat and then watch TV and my mother would come home around 8:00. When it was dark in the winter months we used to be real afraid alone and sometimes Jamal would disobey and leave the apartment and get into trouble with the boys down the hall. I was so scared that my mother would blame me. . . . During weekends my mother would take us grocery shopping and then we'd stay home. We didn't have friends because my mother was afraid that we'd run with the wrong crowd. . . . We were not doing well*

at school and when we got to Toronto we were put back two years. I was so lonely in Baltimore . . . my mother was no fun to be with because she was real strict with us because she was afraid we'd go wrong or we'd get killed."

Granted, as they become single parents, women and their coprogenitors do perpetuate and even create poverty. But this result occurs mainly in countries that have very limited profamilial and prochild social policies. Although Table 6.1 does not actually cover very young families, it clearly indicates that, in countries such as Sweden, single mothers' poverty rates are not any higher than that of married mothers. (The limitations of Table 6.1 are discussed in Family Research 6.2.) Why? First, as seen earlier, Sweden and other Western governments provide adequate subsidies, universal health insurance, maternity leaves, and child care arrangements that allow mothers to be employed, whatever their marital status. A second reason why the poverty rate in single-mother families is not much higher in some countries is that most of these "single" mothers, particularly in Sweden, actually cohabit with their child's father: Cohabitation is more widespread than marriage among young couples of all social classes. These mothers are actually part of a two-parent family, and they benefit from the father's income if they are not themselves employed. And, finally, first-time single mothers are older in these countries: Rates of single teen childbearing are very low, thus further reducing the potential for poverty.

For Fathers

The effects of poverty on fathers have been less extensively studied than those on mothers, in great part because fathers are often absent in indigent families. Fathers are affected by poverty differently, depending on the place they occupy in their families of

TABLE 6.1 International Comparisons

Combined poverty and economic marginality percentages in one-parent and two-parent families in industrialized societies in 1987*

	Poor/Marginal Two-Parent Families	Poor/Marginal One-Parent Families
U.S.A.	24%	53%
Canada	16	45
U.K.	17	28
France	10	16
Holland	7	7
Sweden	5	6

*These statistics include families below the poverty level and those that were only slightly above (marginal). The family heads are 25 to 55 years of age (see Family Research 6.2). Although this table is over 12 years old, the trends described are entirely applicable today.

Sources: Canadian Institute of Child Health, 1994:21; Oderkirk, 1992.

FAMILY RESEARCH 6.2

Table 6.1 Does Not Tell the Whole Story

The percentages in Table 6.1 present a good opportunity to sharpen our methods analytical skills. First, this table includes only those families whose head is between ages 25 and 55. This is a problem in terms of our discussion. Why? Because very young families are excluded from these statistics, and we know that, in the United States, Canada, and even the United Kingdom, a great proportion of the poor families are headed by parents who are younger than age 25. In fact, most single mothers who are poor have their first child either in their teens or early twenties.

The second problem flows from the first one and concerns the international comparisons. Countries such as France, Holland, and Sweden have proportionally far fewer very young families. Therefore, Table 6.1 represents these countries' poverty profiles more accurately than it does for the United States or Canada. In the latter two countries, the combined poverty and near-poverty percentages for one-parent families are actually much higher than presented in Table 6.1, because many such families' heads are younger than age 25 and do not appear in the table.

procreation. In this respect, at least four categories of economically disadvantaged fathers exist:

1. Fathers who are part of two-parent families and are gainfully employed (their salaries are low and they may have to combine two jobs, or their work is seasonal)
2. Unemployed fathers in two-parent families
3. Separated or divorced fathers with minimal income or who are unemployed
4. Men who have fathered children out of wedlock, do not reside with them, and are either unemployed or earn inadequate wages

The first two categories of fathers are the most negatively affected by poverty, particularly when they are unemployed. They experience a great deal of pressure, even if only from within themselves, to support their family more adequately. In addition, they may be working at two jobs, in itself a source of stress and a potential for ill health. Society defines fathers as the chief breadwinners and this assigned role can be a heavy psychological burden on the shoulders of an economically disadvantaged man. His self-esteem may be badly bruised; he may feel that he has little control over his life or that he is failing his children and wife (Rubin, 1994). In stark contrast, a man who earns a decent income is proud of his ability to support his family.

Unemployment is a particularly painful situation for a man who has a family to support. It becomes a source of friction, general tension, and irritability between husbands and wives (Elder et al., 1992). Men feel diminished, experience psychological duress due to their unacceptable status and their humiliating and fruitless job searches, and may react more abrasively and withdraw emotionally from their wives. These behaviors may undermine the spousal relationship and contribute to marital instability. Wives may become resentful of their lack of financial resources and, when employed, may complain that they are shouldering the entire family's economic burden.

For their part, divorced or separated fathers who are too poor to contribute child support may distance themselves from their children. Their ex-wives may also prevent them from seeing their children, either because they fail to support them, they are a "bad example" or a "bad influence," or were abusive before. As for those men who have fathered children nonmaritally, do not live with them, and are too poor to support them (which may well be a majority of adolescent mothers' boyfriends), very little is known as to how poverty affects them *as fathers*. How poverty affects single fathers and their relationship with their offspring as well as the mother(s) constitutes a very interesting field of research that is largely unexplored (Tamis-LeMonda and Cabrera, 1999).

For Children

Child poverty denies human beings the chance to develop adequately and securely from the very beginning of their lives. However, not all children are affected in the same way by poverty. How they will be affected is contingent on a *combination of factors*, including:

- The age of the child (the younger, the worse the outcome)
- The extent and length of the poverty episode
- Family structure and functioning
- Race/ethnicity (segregation and discrimination)
- Neighborhood quality
- Parental education and mental health
- Parental monitoring of child's activities, particularly during adolescence
- Presence of antisocial peers
- Child personal characteristics and resources

At their negative level (e.g., low maternal education and lack of parental supervision), all of these variables represent risk factors: The greater the number of risk factors accompanying poverty, the more negative the effect (Sameroff and Seifer, 1995). Mounting evidence shows that, in terms of IQ development and school achievement, poverty has the most devastating impact when children begin life in poverty (Pagani, Boulerice, and Tremblay, 1997). Thus, early child poverty is the most detrimental in terms of a child's future status in society as an adult (Caspi et al., 1998; Duncan et al., 1998).

Any problematic child characteristic, such as low birth weight or deficient cognitive abilities, can combine with poverty to produce additional negative effects for the child, both currently and in the future. In contrast, a similar child raised in an economically secure family generally has a more positive life course (McLoyd, 1998). Young children who live in persistent economic hardship develop more problems, particularly at the cognitive level, than those whose poverty is temporary. In turn, the latter have more problems than children who have never experienced disadvantage (Duncan and Brooks-Gunn, 1997). The *depth* of poverty also exerts a dramatic effect on children's abilities and performance: Children in families with an income that is 50 percent below the poverty level are at a great disadvantage.

Children born into indigence or who are poor for many of their formative years are denied the opportunity to actualize their abilities, to receive a good education, often to live in a safe neighborhood, and even to be fed adequately. It is estimated that 12 million American children go hungry at some point each month. In turn, these cumulative disadvantages can later produce deficits in employment and health that persist into adulthood. For instance, poor health caused by poverty imperils health and well-being in midlife and old age, and ultimately reduces life expectancy. Children who experience poverty *at any point* are three times more likely to be poor in adulthood than children who have never been disadvantaged, and are also more likely to earn less—even when the economy is flourishing (Corcoran, 1995). In other words, the consequences of child poverty and its accompanying misfortunes far outlast the initial period of poverty itself and may be life long.

The most visible and consistent deficit related to poverty is that disadvantaged children, on average, have lower IQ, academic skills, and school achievement than nonpoor children. On average, therefore, poor children repeat grades, drop out of school, and become unemployed or enter dead-end jobs more often than children who have never been poor. Studies also agree that poverty during the preschool years is more pernicious than later poverty in terms of the previously mentioned consequences (McLoyd, 1998). Unfortunately, small children have higher rates of poverty than older ones because the latter have older parents who earn more. Thus, one can see why it is so important to prevent infant and preschool poverty, both for the short and long term.

Disadvantaged children have more frequent accidents than other children because their surroundings are less safe; they are also less healthy (Chase-Lansdale and Brooks-Gunn, 1995). Even poor children covered by Medicaid rarely receive proper medical attention because, in some states, Medicaid does not cover the entirety of needed expenses. Moreover, children on Medicaid are less likely to experience continuity of care, as they often go from one emergency room to another and do not have access to a physician who would provide follow-up services. The level of psychiatric problems among disadvantaged children far outstrips that of other children (McLeod and Shanahan, 1996). Moreover, children who are poor are more often than other children identified by teachers for conduct disorders. Even if one reduces this figure by half to account for possible teachers' prejudice against disadvantaged children or their parents (or against minority children or children in single-parent families), the difference remains substantial and is confirmed across the world.

As illustrated in the following student quote, disadvantaged children often stand out from others in a multitude of ways that are psychologically painful. For instance, some live in a housing project and may be ashamed of it. They may not want to let their peers know about their predicament and may not invite them home. Furthermore, poor children are unlikely to have the pocket money received by their schoolmates. They may be unable to participate in extracurricular activities with their peers, which can lead them to be ostracized. In fact, low-income children in economically mixed schools are less popular than more affluent children (Pettit et al., 1996). Their parents may be less well dressed, may not have a car or may have an old and rusty one, and may be unemployed. They may receive free meals at school. All or any of these visible social stigmas are humiliating and painful to bear, although they may be less so in a school where a great proportion of the children are equally disadvantaged.

> *"What I recall as having been the most painful between the ages of 10 and 14 is that we were poor. At least that's when I realized that we were poor, until then I guess I had not noticed and I had had other problems on my mind [her father's drinking and violent outbursts]. At that age kids can be cruel and they found out that I lived in a dump and even the other little scums as poor as me would pick*

on me to make themselves look superior. My mother was trying very hard to raise us well and always sent us to schools in the other neighborhood. That's probably why nobody found out or made me notice [that she was poor] until that age. . . . There were so many days when we were hungry, what can I say, my father drank every bit of money we could get. . . . I am ashamed now to think that I dreaded it when parents had to meet the teachers because my mom looked so tired, so old, her clothes were so out of style. She was so so tired and so so sad and often so ill but she hung on for us. . . . What I recall as having been the happiest time since 15? It's when my mom and older brother told my father to leave and dumped all his stuff outside and she got a better job and my brother got off school for a year to help her. We moved to a better place, I mean not rich but better and things started picking up from there. We were still poor but we were on our way and didn't have to tiptoe around my father." [When this autobiography was written, the siblings were in college and doing well.]

CONCLUSIONS: THE COSTS OF POVERTY

When all the consequences (both short term and long term) of child poverty are taken into account, it becomes obvious that it is much more economically advantageous for a society to invest in children and *prevent* child poverty—a topic to which we return in the last chapter of this book. Otherwise, society has to keep paying throughout the decades for poverty's multiple, recurring consequences. This means that subsequent generations will pay for the current societal neglect of poor children in terms of illness, mental hospitals, remedial schooling, juvenile courts, prisons, drug rehabilitation programs, and, later on, unemployment and Medicare in old age—to name only a few of the long-term economic costs on society of child poverty.

Today, people live in a society and in an era in which the economy, broadly defined, is probably one of the most determining features of family life, along with gender and race, although people are rarely conscious of this effect as they go about their daily activities at home. The economy and its accompanying technology determine job and income availability, which, in turn, impact on family life and even family formation and structure. Frequently, one fails to see how these same larger, structural forces contribute to poverty that then creates a fertile ground upon which personal causes of poverty (such as divorce, single parenting, and low educational level) can grow. In turn, the personal causes of poverty reinforce the effect of the larger economic forces that cruelly bear down upon the poor. When residential segregation (discussed in the next chapter) is added to this cauldron of forces, there is, on the one hand, a potent recipe for an enormous range of familial problems or dysfunctions, and, on the other hand, an even wider range of familial resilience, survival, and success against all odds.

SUMMARY

1. Economic and technological developments have contributed to the current profile of families. Manufacturing has become a less important source of good entry-

level jobs for youths with only a high school education. The service sector has expanded to provide jobs that require high educational credentials yet pay little and are often part time. The latter are disproportionately held by women, particularly minority women. As a result of the changes in the economy, the gap between poor and rich families has widened.

2. Economic changes have had the following effects on families: They have resulted in an increase in feminine employment and in two-income families, a reduction of familial as well as individual time, and an increase in poverty among the employed (i.e., the working poor). In turn, male unemployment and low-paid jobs have contributed to the creation of single-parent families. Furthermore, young adults remain at home with their parents longer and delay marriage to complete more years of education or because their jobs do not pay enough for independent living.
3. The dual-income family creates a second work shift for mothers. The main question asked concerning the effect of parental employment is this: Is maternal employment detrimental to children? Past studies were largely biased by historical circumstances, a traditional social construction of motherhood, and a social construction of childhood emphasizing the necessity of constant maternal care. More recent studies have found no detrimental effect of maternal employment on children. However, the possibility remains that when both parents work extremely long hours, children are deprived of adult attention and may not be adequately socialized.
4. At the structural level, the causes of family poverty, in addition to the general ones mentioned earlier, include discrimination, segregation, pay inequity for women, and lack of adequate social benefits to families. Other societies provide more resources to families, including mother allowances and paid maternity leaves. The two main sociopersonal causes of family poverty discussed in this chapter are divorce and the formation of families by single women.
5. After divorce, women's income plummets, and a good proportion become poor, as they have to support their children on a reduced family budget. Families formed by never-married mothers are both a result and a cause of poverty: A majority of the mothers are issued from poor families. However, a substantial proportion escape from poverty, particularly if they do not have any other nonmarital births, complete their education, secure a reasonably paying job, and/or remarry. Contrary to what is generally believed, welfare payments are rarely an incentive to single motherhood. Various studies are presented that refute this notion. For instance, while welfare benefits were decreasing, rates of single motherhood were increasing.
6. The consequences of poverty for mothers reside in the difficulties inherent to raising children within a very negative environment, particularly for those who live in high-risk neighborhoods. Men have not been studied in terms of how poverty affects them as fathers. We know that their unemployment becomes a recurrent source of friction within the family and that divorced fathers who cannot afford to pay for child support often become alienated from their children.
7. The consequences of poverty for children are more numerous and more severe when they are poor during their early childhood, when they are poor for a long

period, and when they live in an unsafe neighborhood with a high ratio of delinquent peers. Poor children are particularly affected in the domain of cognitive development, school progress, and conduct problems.

8. It would be economically advantageous for society to eliminate child poverty.

KEY CONCEPTS AND THEMES

Consumerism, p. 158
Corporations, p. 157
Correlation, p. 164
Deficient social assistance benefits, p. 168
Divorce, p. 169
Downsizing, p. 157
Dual-income families, p. 161
Globalization of the economy, p. 156
Human capital, p. 176
Inflation of educational requirements, p. 158
Information technology, p. 156
Low-paying jobs, p. 157
Maternal employment, p. 162
Part-time jobs, p. 157
Pay inequity, p. 167
Preoccupation with upward mobility, p. 164
Real unemployment, p. 167
Shared child care, p. 162
Single-parent families, pp. 160, 170
Systemic causes of poverty, p. 180
Time crunch, p. 159
Two-income families, p. 158
Unemployment, p. 166
Welfare, p. 171
Working poor, p. 159

STUDY AND REVIEW QUESTIONS

1. Explain the linkage between the expansion of the service sector and low-paying jobs.
2. What role might unemployment and low wages have played in the increase of single-parent families, particularly among blacks?
3. What has led to the myth that maternal employment is detrimental to children?
4. Critically discuss the official poverty line for families.
5. Is the unemployment rate accurate? Why?
6. What is the two-way relationship between poverty and the formation of families by single mothers?
7. Refute the myth that welfare benefits create single mothering.
8. Why is single mothering not related to poverty in countries such as Holland and Sweden?
9. Why is early poverty more detrimental to children's life course than is poverty that occurs late in adolescence, for instance?
10. Why is investment in the prevention of child poverty a good long-term social policy?

SUGGESTED READINGS

Ambert, A.-M. 1998. *The web of poverty: Psychosocial perspectives.* New York: Haworth. This book focuses on the consequence of poverty for neighborhoods, schools, families, mothers, childrearing, as well as child and adolescent outcomes.

Duncan, G. J., and Brooks-Gunn, J. (Eds.). 1997. *Consequences of growing up poor.* New York: Russell Sage Foundation. The various articles are quite readable. The contents present state-of-the-art information on the consequences of child poverty.

Hochschild, A. 1989. *The second shift.* New York: Avon. The author documents the disproportionate amount of work that employed mothers do, their exhaustion, and, often, the strain that the lack of father sharing in housework brings to the dual-income marriage.

Hogginbotham, E., and Romero, M. (Eds.). 1997. *Exploring race, ethnicity, and class.* Thousand Oaks, CA: Sage. The articles contain original research on the work lives of women by race, ethnicity, and class.

Rifkin, J. 1995. *The end of work.* New York: Putnam's Sons. For students interested in the effect on society of high-tech and international corporations, this book offers intriguing insights and information. It is well documented and intellectually stimulating.

SUGGESTED WEBLINKS

The National Conference of State Legislatures provides information on economic issues and reforms, many pertaining to the family. **<http://www.StateServ.hpts.org>**

The New York Times' website is one that should be consulted regularly, as this newspaper often carries articles related to the effects of the economy and poverty on families. **<http://www.nytimes.com>**

The Urban Institute's website offers special sections related to the economy. **<http://www.urban.org>**

CHAPTER 7

Impacts of Neighborhoods and Environments on Family Life

OUTLINE

Types of Urban and Suburban Areas and Family Life
Diversity of Urban and Suburban Areas
Families' Class Differences and Neighborhood Location
Upper-Upper-Class Families
Lower-Upper-Class Families
Upper-Middle-Class Families

Inner-City Neighborhoods
What Is a High-Poverty Neighborhood?
How Did Inner-City Poverty Come About?
The Addition of Social Problems
Risk Factors of High-Poverty Areas for Children
Inadequate Mainstream Socialization
Inadequate Supervision and Protection
Well-Functioning Families in High-Risk Areas

Homeless Families
What Are the Causes of Homelessness?
What Are the Effects of Homelessness on Mothers and Children?

Rural Areas and Family Life
Characteristics of Farm Families
Farm Families' Adaptation to Economic Crises
Kinship and Gender Roles

Families' Housing Conditions
The "Mansionization" of Suburban Housing
Family Privacy
Overcrowding

Residential Mobility

Conclusions: The Meaning of Neighborhood as Context

Summary
Key Concepts and Themes
Study and Review Questions
Suggested Readings
Suggested Weblinks

"We lived in three different places since my birth moving each time to a bigger better house. The first was a rented semi-detached that I lived in until I was 5, then we moved to a semi-detached we owned on a better street also downtown and then we moved to where we are now when I was 12 in our own house with three bathrooms and a big yard."

"My parents bought a three story semi-detached house downtown one year before I was born and we still live in the same house today. My family occupied only two rooms, a kitchen and a washroom. Every other room in the house was rented [to pay for the mortgage]. In four years, we started taking up more rooms for ourselves."

"I have always lived in the same house but the area around me changed. Until about [age] seven, the area was rural. Ever since that age, the surroundings have become more and more urban."

"I grew up on a farm that we still own. We could see the neighbors' farmhouses but we could not see the neighbors themselves. Except for the road turning into a

near highway with more traffic coming through nothing has changed much. Some neighbors have died and some farms have been sold but we know everyone even though we do not see them often. I like the feeling of community and I miss it here where I live during the school year. Everyone is in a rush and no one knows who lives where."

"My family has always lived in a two-bedroom apartment except that we have not lived in the same one all the time. I think we have lived in eight different ones. According to my mother we have moved because we were evicted once, we couldn't afford the rent. Then the other times we moved because the neighbors were either too noisy or too rough or too criminal. Now that we are older we are thinking of buying a townhouse just north of here [beginning of an inexpensive suburb]."

Housing and neighborhoods constitute a family's first immediate context. As the student quotes well illustrate, families' economic conditions and lifestyles are expressed through their dwellings and surroundings. Additional quotes later on in the text show how families' daily lives—and, in turn, their children's opportunities, health, and behavior—are affected by these surroundings. Although rarely encountered in family textbooks, the study of neighborhood effects on families is a domain of sociological inquiry with a long tradition. This tradition has recently been renewed, and has become particularly visible in sociologically oriented sections of child development publications. It is a field inspired by the Chicago School of Sociology (Park and Burgess, 1925) and by current concerns about the social problems families encounter in some inner-city neighborhoods. In this chapter, the inquiry is extended to an entire spectrum of families' living conditions.

The countryside and towns of less than 2,500 inhabitants are considered rural (Flora et al., 1992). Between 1957 and 1990, the farm population decreased from 15 million to less than 5 million, so that today only 2.5 percent of the population is employed on farms and ranches, compared to nearly 38 percent at the beginning of the twentieth century (Hoffman, 1993). For its part, the nonfarm rural population constitutes a little over 22 percent of the U.S. population. By this account, American families are largely urban and suburban.

TYPES OF URBAN AND SUBURBAN AREAS AND FAMILY LIFE

Most of the currently available research focuses on urban families, and, in recent decades, there has been little research on family life in smaller cities. The focus has been on large urban aggregations and particularly their inner-city neighborhoods.

Diversity of Urban and Suburban Areas

During the past decades, the 25 largest urban areas in the United States have experienced three phenomena. First, the central cities lost many of their functions, particularly commercial and industrial, which have shifted to the suburbs. Second, a larger proportion of the population now lives beyond the boundaries of the city itself—for instance, 80 percent of the Boston, Atlanta, Minneapolis, and Cleveland population now lives in suburbs (Minshull, 1996). Third, suburbs have evolved and many have become cities themselves; thus, suburbs have diversified and are no longer strictly residential.

The types of families residing in these various areas differ by social class, race, and household composition. For instance, singles and empty-nesters who have sold their houses are rarely encountered in the residential parts of suburbs and their extensions, preferring the more diverse lifestyle of the city or of suburbs that have become satellite cities into themselves. In contrast, families with small children tend to gravitate toward residential suburbs, if they have the means to do so. But even these suburbs are fast changing, as many include industrial zones, office and commercial areas, high rises, and mega-malls complete with hotels, restaurants, and entertainment centers (Minshull, 1996).

One concern that preoccupies Americans, particularly seniors and parents, is the issue of security. This essentially means being away from property crime, violence, and drugs. As a result, *gated enclaves* designed to shelter relatively affluent families have sprouted. Children in such areas grow up segregated from the less pleasant realities of life in the rest of the country. Such enclaves provide families with a distinct material lifestyle and at the very least the possibility of forming a close community. Children particularly have the potential of turning a set of streets into a community, but only if they have time to play outside and establish linkages between families, as was the case when this student was growing up in the 1970s:

> *"I also remember how much fun I used to have playing on our street. When my family moved into our house, the housing area was new and just starting to develop and many young families also moved into the area. The street was full of kids in the same age group, and we would get together and play games such as hide-and-seek, and almost everyone would play. There used to be something to do almost every night, especially in the summer. If it wasn't baseball, it was football or road hockey. As I now realize today, it was the kids of this age group which linked our street together, and as we got older we spent less and less time with each other."*

But communities, particularly the phenomenon of gated enclaves, have not been studied by sociologists and ethnographers since the advent of video games and the Internet, which, along with television, have been changing children's patterns of play and social interactions in their neighborhoods (Chapter 2). Furthermore, in middle-class and affluent areas, children's after-school lives are far busier and more structured than in the early 1980s (Hofferth et al., 1998). Hence, children now engage in less outdoor play in these neighborhoods (Adler and Adler, 1998). Therefore, their role as informal community organizers and links between families may have eroded.

Families' Class Differences and Neighborhood Location

It is an important underlying aspect of this chapter that a neighborhood reflects a family's position in the social class system; families select certain neighborhoods according to the position they occupy or wish to occupy in the social structure. In the United States, social class is the second largest source of family diversity, along with racial and ethnic distinctions. A family's position in the class system is the result of a combination of three key socioeconomic factors: occupational prestige, education, as well as income and wealth.

Upper-Upper-Class Families

In this section, as a contrast to the sections that follow, the focus is on the first three social classes in the stratification pyramid—that is, those containing the smallest proportion of the population. The upper-upper class, which is often referred to as the *capitalist class*, includes only 1 percent of all American families. What distinguishes these families is their very high income (over $1 million yearly), largely derived from returns on assets rather than income from a job (Gilbert and Kahl, 1993:18). Much of this is inherited wealth (Kerbo, 1996). These families own a majority of the means of production in the society. They are heirs, investors, and top executives of large corporations. The scions of these families have attended the best private schools, then went on to Harvard, Yale, Brown, or Princeton, among a few others, for a college degree (Karen, 1990). Their power is based on their wealth, ownership, and interconnections with similar other families or class members. "Old money" is very important (e.g., Rockefellers, Mellons, Carnegies, DuPonts, Fords, and, more recently, Kennedys) but new money is included (e.g., Bill Gates and Ted Turner), although the lifestyle of the latter may be somewhat more ostentatious and public.

These families congregate in two types of neighborhoods. One type is the center of cities, such as New York, where they own large brownstones, vast apartments or penthouses in condominiums and cooperatives at prestigious addresses. They also live in suburbs' extensions in mansions surrounded by greenery. These neighborhoods are exclusive and well secured, and their residents shun publicity. The homes contain recreational facilities (pools, billiard rooms, libraries, exercise rooms, tennis courts) that most other families encounter only at the community level. Moreover, the families maintain residences in several cities or even rural areas (such as vast ranches) as well as abroad. They are part of an international network of connections.

Lower-Upper-Class Families

At the next rung of the stratification ladder, the lower-upper class consists of chief executive officers (CEOs), bankers, successful stock brokers, officials elected to key government positions, chief justices, generals, highly educated persons in the civil service, owners of small private corporations or large businesses, and a few particularly successful scholars, physicians, lawyers, writers, artists, as well as some actors. These families derive their power largely from their knowledge base, their ability to manage, educate, or entertain. Their incomes are in the six figures or more and stem from a mixture of salary and returns on assets. These families may constitute 3 to 5 percent of U.S. households. They tend to reside near the first stratum and, in the center of cities, the two classes may be largely mixed residentially. Their homes are elaborate and often new. Some are now living in gated enclaves and many also share neighborhoods with upper-middle-class families or are adjacent to them.

Upper-Middle-Class Families

The upper-middle class, which is larger than the other two (10 to 15 percent of the population), is characterized by a high level of education or technological expertise. Among them are physicians, lawyers, pharmacists, university professors, some civil servants and businesspersons, as well as mid-managers in larger corporations (Rossides, 1990). This is essentially the professional class that provides skilled services. Families' income are in the $70,000 to $200,000 range. These families share neighborhoods with the successful segment of the remainder of the middle class, whereas others live in enclaves that are largely populated with families at their income level.

Home ownership tends to be the rule among top-earning families, but what is of particular significance among the more affluent is that ownership occurs early on in family formation and remains stable thereafter. In contrast, home ownership occurs later in the family life cycle among other social groups, including the middle class (Clark and Dieleman, 1996). Thus, at the higher-income levels, children grow up in homes that are owned by their parents, whereas children in other families reach this goal at a later age or never.

INNER-CITY NEIGHBORHOODS

We now leave behind this spacious lifestyle to enter the world of the inner cities. The centers of metropolitan areas often tend to be polarized between very rich families as well as fashionable shopping arcades and far larger areas where a disproportionate number of families are poor and belong to disadvantaged minority groups. Poverty and racial segregation prevail (Kasarda, 1993).

What Is a High-Poverty Neighborhood?

An area is defined as poor when at least one of every five households falls under the poverty level. When at least two of five households, or 40 percent, are so classified, this becomes a high-poverty area. Since the 1970s, the number of American families living in poor neighborhoods has more than tripled. The number of disadvantaged individuals residing in segregated poverty areas in the five largest American cities (New York, Chicago, Los Angeles, Philadelphia, and Detroit) increased by 58 percent from 1970 to 1980. This number grew by 70 percent in the high-poverty areas, and by "a whopping 182 percent in the extreme poverty areas" (Wilson, 1987:46). Therefore, some areas in inner cities harbor a very substantial **concentration of poverty.** This concentration is compounded by another one: About 87 percent of residents of poor urban areas are members of *minority groups*. That is, census tracts with a high concentration of poverty tend to be predominantly black or Latino—in the latter instance, Puerto Rican or Mexican American (Massey and Denton, 1993).

In 1989, 71 percent of blacks who were poor lived in areas of poverty, compared to 30 percent of whites who were poor—the latter including a large proportion of

FAMILY RESEARCH 7.1

SURVEYS: Panel Study of Income Dynamics (PSID)

This longitudinal survey is one of the most frequently utilized in statistical research on residential mobility, neighborhoods, poverty, employment, income, as well as racial and marital status differences in life outcomes. It contains information, mainly of a demographic and economic nature, on all the members of each family. The study began in 1968 as a nationally representative sample of about 5,000 families, with an oversampling of low-income families. It has grown to include over 7,000 families representing about 40,000 individuals. As children leave their parents' home, they are placed in the sample as new household units. This survey, then, is also intergenerational.

In studies where housing and neighborhood are important variables, researchers often link the data in the PSID to aggregate or group data from the census tracts in which the respondents live. These aggregate data are obtained from the Bureau of the Census. This method allows researchers to separate family variables such as income from the overall average income of all the families in the neighborhood, for instance. Each family's characteristics can be compared with those of *all* the other families combined in their neighborhood.

Latinos (Goldsmith and Blakeley, 1992:48). Whether or not they are poor, 57 percent of black children but only 7.5 percent of white children who are not Latino live in poor neighborhoods (Brooks-Gunn, Klebanov, and Duncan, 1996). Therefore, a majority of whites who are poor live in districts that provide them with social resources, whereas nearly all African Americans who are poor live in neighborhoods lacking such advantages. For whites, the consequences of poverty can be softened by positive community factors, although there are many exceptions, particularly in isolated pockets of white rural poverty. For blacks, the disadvantages of personal poverty are usually compounded by a concentration of detrimental neighborhood conditions (Sampson, Morenoff, and Earls, 1999). Therefore, it is practically impossible to compare the effects of poverty on black and white families, because, more often than not, black poverty is shackled to a deprived urban area. Viewed in this context, it can be said that black poverty is worse than white poverty, and current black urban poverty is worse than that of the 1950s (Wilson, 1987:57).

How Did Inner-City Poverty Come About?

At the beginning of the twentieth century, many inner cities already contained neighborhoods populated by recent European immigrants who were struggling to escape poverty. From the 1920s through the 1960s, large migrations of southern African Americans took place toward these same industrialized cities of the Northeast (and only much later on to the West Coast). Black workers were hired in stable blue-collar jobs. As the black population increased, whites moved out. The black working and middle classes solidified and African-American neighborhoods, although racially segregated, were not rigidly stratified by social class. Following fair housing legislation, many middle-class black families fled the inner cities after 1968, seeking more favorable living conditions and leaving behind the more disadvantaged families.

But by far the most powerful factor in the creation of inner-city poverty resulted from the scaling down after the 1970s of the industries that had traditionally employed African Americans and the moving out of urban areas to the suburbs of other employers, as discussed in the previous chapter. As a consequence, the supply of well-paid jobs available to inner-city families slowed down to a trickle, and increasing unemployment among the black working class followed, particularly among young black males just coming out of high school. Job prospects were destroyed. The advent of an increasing proportion of low-paying and part-time jobs also contributed heavily to poverty in the inner cities.

The Addition of Social Problems

As legitimate opportunities for employment were lost, and segregation closed all doors, many young people turned to illegal activities. Therefore, the neighborhoods with a large concentration of impoverished families inherited a strong element of criminality that became more violent with the easy availability of firearms and the expansion of gangs into the drug trade, particularly cocaine and, later on, crack cocaine. More and more inner-city census tracts in major American metropolises became poor and black or, more recently, Latino. This means that, as adjacent census tracts fell like dominoes to this concentration of poverty and segregation, it became more difficult for their inhabitants to be in touch with institutions and individuals who could help them find legal employment (Kasarda, 1993).

While these phenomena were occurring, the quality of the physical environment deteriorated and the prevalence of single motherhood was increasing in these same neighborhoods, in part related to the unemployment of young African-American males (Taylor and Harrell, 1996). Thus, the districts developed a quadruple concentration of disadvantages, each feeding on the other: poverty, deteriorated housing, criminality, and single-parent households (Sampson, 1992). By 1990, in high-poverty census tracts, 57 percent of the families with dependent children were headed by single mothers, a rate that is now probably closer to 70 percent (Jargowski, 1997:108).

It is important to keep in mind, in this discussion, that neighborhood poverty characterized by **social disorganization** is a recent phenomenon. As Wilson (1987) points out, even poor areas of inner cities exhibited all the features of social organization before the 1960s. There was some joblessness, as well as some criminality, and some black families were headed by women. But the streets were relatively safe, there was little welfare recipiency, and most adult African Americans were married as well as legally employed, even though salaries were low.

Sociologist Robert Sampson (1993) suggests that social disorganization follows when a community is no longer able to maintain **social control** and to supervise teenage peer groups. The concentration of female-headed households not only means that children are less well monitored when their sole parent is employed but also that large numbers of unattached young males roam the district with few responsibilities and too much free time on their hands (Land, McCall, and Cohen, 1990). A heavy concentration of out-of-school and unemployed young males generally precludes effective social control of their activities and those of male children who grow up imitating them. These young males, neither responsive to their mothers' demands nor to their children's needs, are the most important element of community disorganization.

These children, in an economically devastated area, creatively make use of the meager resources in their environment. They perhaps benefit from free play more than do children in middle-class neighborhoods.

The most obvious deficit of poor, segregated areas is criminality and its accompanying effects: *victimization* and *fear* (Garbarino, 1995). When there is a large concentration of female-headed families in a neighborhood, the rate of victimization is two to three times that of areas with a predominance of two-parent households (Sampson, 1993). The absence of adult males in the households often leads to the perception of women and children as more accessible targets for theft and sexual assault; adolescents become easier recruits for delinquency, as they are less supervised. All in all, children who live in neighborhoods devoid of *social resources*, such as positive role models in the form of steadily employed citizens, and direct or indirect community supervision are labeled "at risk."

Risk Factors of High-Poverty Areas for Children

Inadequate Mainstream Socialization

Children in neighborhoods that are both poor and beset by social problems, especially when their parents are also poor, are often *not adequately socialized;* that is, they fail to develop the social skills needed in the workplace, personal life skills, and general habits expected in mainstream society (Wilson, 1996). Where large housing developments are located, and fear and mistrust reign, parents cannot establish linkages among themselves and collectively monitor the whereabouts and activities of each other's children (Sampson, Morenoff, and Earls, 1999). Thus, parents in such areas are deprived of adequate power of supervision over their children.

Steinberg and colleagues (1995) point out that parenting "appears to be more than the individualistic process that contemporary society makes it out to be." It is a group phenomenon. This also ties in with the concept of the **functional community** that encourages parents to become involved in school activities, to supervise their children's behavior and associations, and to get acquainted with other children's parents (Coleman and Hoffer, 1987:7). For their part, Brooks-Gunn and colleagues (1995) suggest that, in more affluent areas, **collective socialization** may be operating. Families enjoying a decent income generally sustain better links to mainstream society's opportunities, and maintain more socially appropriate values and ways of behaving than families whose members are chronically unemployed. The following student's description of her privileged neighborhood is offered because of the stark contrast between two worlds that it allows us to portray:

> *"Everyone in Upper Point had money and lots of it. I didn't feel rich—just normal. I had a horse. Every girl there did. There were more stables around than gas stations. There were other differences as well. People slept at an earlier hour. Private parties were preferred. . . . People moved slower. Everything took forever. Everyone's life was planned for success since oh, age 5. Everyone knew what college they would apply to, what company they'd work for after graduation, and how much money they'd be making. Heavy thoughts, for twelve year olds."*

The type of socialization these affluent children receive contrasts sharply with what is available in far less privileged areas. In segregated and poor neighborhoods, there is a collective socialization taking place, but it is often in opposition to the values and behaviors of mainstream or middle-class society (Ogbu, 1994). For instance, Kupersmidt and colleagues (1995) compared children with familial vulnerabilities living in relatively low-socioeconomic areas to similar children living in somewhat more affluent neighborhoods. They found that the latter neighborhoods served as a protective shield against the development of aggression in high-risk children. These areas do not tolerate street and school aggressiveness. Therefore, children are less likely to associate with deviant peers; consequently, inadequate parental supervision is not as detrimental as it would be in a low-income area.

In a social program designed to improve families' living conditions, inner-city families were relocated, some to the suburbs, others to another area of the inner city. These households were followed up by researchers over time. The children who had moved to suburban apartments were more likely to go on to college and, once adults, to earn higher salaries than children who had moved to apartments in the city (Rosenbaum, 1991). Thus, it seems that a certain percentage (a **critical mass**) of low-income neighbors increases the risk for behavioral problems and then subsequent school difficulties in children as young as age 5. In contrast, a critical mass of affluent neighbors raises a child's chances of completing high school (Brooks-Gunn et al., 1993). More recent research indicates that low-income neighborhoods begin producing a negative effect on the develoment of a child's IQ by age 3, above and beyond the family environment (Klebanov et al., 1998).

However, in some middle-class and affluent neighborhoods, no collective socialization by adults takes place and there is no functional community in evidence. Parents are largely absent, permissive, and even uninvolved. A segment of adolescents spend their time in cars, at various "hot spots," or partying with drugs in otherwise empty homes, and even engage in gang activities leading to break-ins and thefts. Hence, one should not err in the direction of attaching an aura of superiority to a district simply on the basis of material affluence and lack of visible street criminality. An affluent neighborhood is not automatically a "good" one in which to raise children.

Inadequate Supervision and Protection

It is apparent, then, that poor children in dangerous districts are generally not as adequately supervised as children in other neighborhoods. Peers often belong to gangs that rule the area, and therefore largely escape the supervision of responsible adults. Moreover, these neighborhoods are also disproportionately populated by single-parent families. On average, children from such families are less well monitored (Fischer, 1993), particularly when the mothers' educational level is low (Quane and Rankin, 1998). Single mothers are frequently beset by problems that worry them and that take away attention and time that could be devoted to their children. When they are employed, the children may return to an empty home after school, or to the homes of equally unsupervised peers, or they may "hang out" on street corners or abandoned buildings where risks abound. Supervision—discussed at greater length in Chapter 11—is one of the elements that is generally found to be lacking in cases of early childbearing, drug use, and juvenile delinquency. However, as has been emphasized earlier, supervision by parents in individual families may no longer be a sufficient element. Rather, it is a collective level of supervision that is necessary (Sampson, 1997).

Finally, children and adolescents who live in areas of poverty are often not adequately protected. Lack of collective supervision leaves them free to roam buildings and streets that are dangerous. It also allows them to be prey to temptations that may be too difficult to resist, particularly because they are exposed to peers who may not resist the lure of deviant activities. These children are not sufficiently protected from bullying, sexual abuse, substance abuse, delinquency, and early childbearing. Even when parents monitor them adequately, the neighborhood violence these children witness still affects them, creating stressors against which there is no protection (Miller, Forehand, and Kotchick, 1999; Miller et al., 1999). Adolescents in low-income areas perceive their neighborhoods as more threatening and hazardous (Aneshensel and Sucoff, 1996). In the following excerpt, a black student describes her childhood neighborhood:

> *"My area had developed a reputation of being full of poor non-white crime related people. . . . I lived in a large dirty very unsafe apartment with thirteen floors that had no security or superintendent. Each apartment had a small balcony that was shared by two homes, and every home had two stories. . . . I specifically remember one night when our family was home and we heard people yelling and scuffling at the front door and in the hallway, it was intense and loud. . . . I peeked out of the mail slot and saw two guys fighting, they looked about 18 but I knew they were much younger than that. As I continued to look I saw more guys were fighting, it had turned out to be a huge gang fight. . . . In the morning as I left to go to school . . . there was blood all over the walls and on the doors, pieces of clothing and knives were all over the floor. I wasn't as much horrified by the blood, it was the violence of such young people that had got to me. It was a sight and a feeling that I would never forget."*

In Chicago, in 1993, 67 percent of homicides occurred in public places (Garbarino, 1995:76). In disrupted inner-city areas, one-third of all school-age children have witnessed a homicide, and as many as two-thirds were present during an assault (Bell and Jenkins, 1993). In Los Angeles, 45 percent of seventh-grade Mexican-American boys and 34 percent of Mexican-American girls know of someone close to them who has died violently; 65 percent can name friends who are in gangs; 39 percent of boys and 63 percent of girls have a close relative in jail (Rumberger and Larson, 1994:147). This visible form of violence becomes a salient part of the community's experience and consciousness, often creating a war or siege mentality among children and parents alike (Garbarino, Kostelny, and Dubrow, 1991). The woman student just quoted reminisces on the contrast between her old and new neighborhoods:

> *"Well at this age the happiest moment I remember was when we moved away from the apartment and into our new house. . . . I remember finally being able to feel the freedom to play out in the streets whenever I wanted. In the summer we would stay outside until eleven o'clock and I wouldn't be scared, that was something we wouldn't even think of doing at the apartment, so it was nice to know I could be safe."*

Well-Functioning Families in High-Risk Areas

The focus of research and social policies is on poor families and their problems and dysfunctions; consequently, very little is known about those families that succeed despite all the risks surrounding their children's socialization. Poor neighborhoods still contain a majority of families that are not poor but are forced to remain in disadvantaged areas because of discrimination. Therefore, poor areas contain both poor and nonpoor families that function well.

High levels of parental monitoring are particularly protective for children in poor neighborhoods (Pettit et al., 1999). These families try to protect their children from the negative influences that pervade their area. Their tasks are numerous—they have to keep their adolescents in school and ensure that they make good grades. This must be difficult to achieve in neighborhoods with a high dropout rate and the presence of street groups whose lifestyle may appear exciting to a teenager from a good family, "where nothing ever happens." Parents also have to delay or prevent early sexual activities that could lead to premature parenting. Then, they have to shelter their adolescents from the attraction of drugs and criminal activities. And they have to orient their youths toward the job market.

All these tasks are relatively easily accomplished in regular neighborhoods, and particularly in affluent areas where it is simply expected that adolescents will eventually go to college. But these tasks are a tall order in a district that lacks social resources, even for middle-class black families (Massey, Gross, and Shibuya, 1994:443). How do parents manage? Many succeed only by using drastic measures. If they are poor themselves, these measures will be costlier and far more demanding—practically heroic. As we saw in Chapter 3, one survival tactic consists of sending children to private schools, often religious ones.

Many parents walk their children to and from school, even high school, to protect them against bullies and the hazards of street life, and also to make sure that they do, in fact, attend. Above all, diligent parents control their children's activities outside the home. They may take them to public libraries, to swimming pools and parks in other areas, or to lessons at church. The church is an important element of social resources for these parents—poor and nonpoor alike. It serves as the hub of a functional community. Many children (and even adolescents) are often kept at home after school hours and during weekends. Overprotection is necessary to weed out bad peers, negative influences, and physical dangers. A student describes his reaction to his parents' efforts:

> *"At the time I didn't appreciate having to be home early and not going in the schoolyard to play ball with the other guys. My parents were afraid that I would get into drugs, that I would get a girl pregnant and whatever. I don't know if any of this would have happened but I know that it did happen to most of my old buddies so now I can appreciate their devotion and the fact that they put up with the fuss I stirred up."*

Some of these parents help organize support groups, crime prevention patrols, and other constructive activities in their immediate neighborhood. Furstenberg and colleagues (1994:243) appropriately write of the "supermotivation" that such parents need in order to protect their children and to create opportunities for them.

HOMELESS FAMILIES

Homelessness is not entirely unique to high-poverty neighborhoods, because homeless people often sleep in public parks and retail areas in affluent districts. But shelters for the homeless are generally located in or near areas of concentrated poverty. As such, homelessness becomes a problem of disadvantaged neighborhoods, particularly because abandoned buildings are often used by "squatters," and street life serves as a focal point for "vagrants."

At any point in time, there may be as many as 700,000 homeless persons; perhaps as many as 1 to 6 million Americans each year experience a period of homelessness. One out of five homeless persons remains so for several years (Aday, 1993). It has been estimated that anywhere between 12 and 26 million people are homeless at least once during their lifetimes (Link et al., 1994). Thus, homelessness touches a large percentage of American families, directly or indirectly, particularly families that are economically marginal. Families represent 40 percent of the homeless (Shane, 1996); the majority are headed by single mothers.

What Are the Causes of Homelessness?

The homeless are the most destitute among the poor, even though theirs may be a transitory condition, particularly in the case of two-parent families. A majority of the homeless have either been poor all their lives or poised at the margin of poverty. Many have never been on welfare, perhaps because of the inability to secure benefits (Toro et al., 1995). Families are homeless because of a lack of affordable housing. They can no longer pay rent and are evicted. Others have left their homes because of domestic violence or family breakdown (Shinn, Knickman, and Weitzman, 1991). Among adolescents, running away is a contributing factor. Runaways generally have a conflictual relationship with their parents, although this does not unavoidably involve bad parenting (Shane, 1996:5). Many youths from foster care also run away. Other adolescents are forced to leave their homes after disclosing that they are gay or lesbian (Mallon, 1997). Whatever the causality, homeless youths experience more problems with their parents (Wolfe, Toro, and McCaskill, 1999). But compared to the other homeless, youths do not uniformly originate from the disadvantaged class, although a majority do. A student from a well-to-do family describes her former street life after she was "kicked out" by parents who had, until then, tolerated all her drug and sex-related activities:

> *"I went and stayed at various friends' houses. I continued this for some weeks, but I soon ran out of friends. When one lives nowhere, on the street, one loses common ground with one's old companions. They want to talk about things they've done or seen. You're more concerned with basics. A shower for the first time in days. Some socks. Perhaps eating or actually washing your clothes. Frankly, you turn into a bum. 'Hey, what's happening man? Like, can I have your clothes, shoes, underwear, food, money, cigarettes? Cool! Blankets! Like, I've been sleeping in this stairwell, you know. It's not so bad, ya don't get caught or nothin, ya just gotta get out before the mall opens in the morning. Ya got a smoke?'. . . . I spent nine months as a street kid. My experiences were, for the most part, fun. I think this is partly because I knew that I could always go home. I still don't know why I kept it up for so long. . . . It's a complete sub-culture and many kids simply don't want to leave even if they do have somewhere to go."*

In addition to poverty, disabilities and addictions contribute to retaining people into homelessness once it has begun. Over 50 percent of the homeless adults have never married; most others are either separated or divorced (Rossi and Wright, 1993). Most have no relatives or even friends who can take them in during hard times, possibly because their families are equally poor or because they have lost touch with them. The magnitude of the personal problems many suffer from may have worn out their welcome with their families or depleted the support they could receive from them. It is also possible that many of their families are equally maladapted. At the very least, the personal problems of many of the homeless certainly prevent their reintegration into society at large.

Psychiatric problems as well as various addictions are endemic and certainly contribute to social isolation (Shane, 1996). Moreover, the decades-old trend to deinstitutionalizing the mentally ill, without the safety net of community care that had been promised by politicians, has exacerbated the problem: Too many families are unable to shelter and care for their mentally ill relatives. For many former mental patients, the streets become the only place they have. Domestic violence, rather than psychiatric or substance abuse, is often a cause of homelessness for women and their children, and may serve to isolate them from at least a part of their family. In fact, homeless mothers often have a long history of victimization (Bassuk et al., 1996). Once homeless, mothers' mental health easily deteriorates (McChesney, 1995). In other words, homelessness is a risk factor for emotional disorder. Nevertheless, many mothers develop coping mechanisms in order to keep their young family together and to reduce the effect of the daily stressors they encounter.

What Are the Effects of Homelessness on Mothers and Children?

According to Rafferty and Shinn (1991:1175), "Homeless parents often encounter difficulties balancing their own physical, social and personal needs and those of their children. The loss of control over their environment and their lives places them at increased risk for learned helplessness and depression." In fact, a large proportion of homeless mothers suffer from mental disorders (Zima et al., 1996). Several researchers have documented the difficulties that mothers encounter in fulfilling their parental role in shelters. They no longer have control over the daily routine of their family life, whether it is bedtime or other rituals. They are not able to be effective parents because of interference from other residents or staff—even though the children themselves may enjoy all this attention. In their study of homeless families in New York City hostels, Rafferty and Rollins (1989) found that 60 percent had been in at least two different shelters, 29 percent in at least four, and 10 percent in seven or more.

> *"The most painful event in my life occurred two years ago after my husband left me with my two preschoolers. I became very depressed, didn't do much of anything and ended up evicted. I had no family here and we ended up in a shelter. I got even more depressed, was briefly hospitalized, my children were in foster care, and back into the shelter where I finally bounced back or else I was going to lose the children. A social worker helped me find a job and day care and then a small apartment. But it had been a nightmare: we couldn't sleep, the children were totally out of it and went berserk, it was awful."*

Despite the difficulties described here by a woman student on welfare, mothers often report a sense of becoming closer to their children while in the shelter (Lindsey, 1998).

In order to separate the effects of homelessness from those of poverty, studies have compared homeless children in shelters to impoverished children who live in their home (e.g., Schteingart et al., 1995). The two consistent disadvantages of homelessness reside in health and education. In terms of *health,* homeless children are ill more often than other poor children. Their incidence of respiratory infections is especially elevated as a result of crowded conditions and the sharing of inadequate sanitary facilities. One can also presume that noise, overcrowding, and parents' distress depress children's immune systems so that they easily catch viruses. This health crisis is exacerbated by a lack of medical care among homeless children compared to other poor children.

The second domain in which homeless children are at a particular disadvantage is *schooling.* For one thing, their rate of absenteeism is higher. They are also more likely to repeat grades (Rafferty and Shinn, 1991). We know from the previous chapter that poor children do not, on average, achieve as well in school, and homeless children are even more adversely affected in this respect. This may lead to increased dropout rates in the future, especially among those who have repeated one or more grades.

Homeless children's disadvantage in school stems from a variety of interlocking causes: They change schools and are sick more frequently than other children. The crowded conditions in which they live are not conducive to homework, and may even deprive them of sufficient sleep. Their nutrition is inadequate; many go hungry and are not able to focus in class. Their parents may be too distressed or emotionally unbalanced to help and guide them. Older children may not want to go to school because they fear the ridicule of peers who, even though poor themselves, at least can claim a permanent address. Frequent school changes isolate homeless children socially, lead to disengagement from school, and even to falling in with a crowd of antisocial peers. Moreover, schools are unprepared to address these children's multiple problems.

RURAL AREAS AND FAMILY LIFE

The lives of rural families have undergone substantial change in recent decades because of increased proximity to urban areas, technological development, and economic uncertainty. In some regions, young people migrate to larger cities, thus leaving many rural communities populated by seniors, middle-aged householders, and, in some cases, young families. In others, fathers and mothers commute to their work to the nearest city or even metropolitan area, sometimes an hour or more each way. Rural couples are generally willing to tolerate long commutes to remain in their rural towns where housing and land prices are lower and where they feel that it is easier to raise a family away from the dangers of the big cities.

Of course, many rural residents make their living without relying on nearby cities. However, when heads of rural families lose their jobs, it is more difficult for them than for urbanites to find another occupation at reasonably close proximity. This stems in part from the fact that rural areas are less diversified at the economic level: They contain a higher proportion of blue-collar workers than do urban zones (Swaim, 1995). White-collar workers with more education tend to move out of rural areas so that this selective outmigration reduces the diversity of human resources available to all rural families (Lichter, McLaughlin, and Cornwell, 1995).

Rural areas offer families a better chance of being members of a true community as well as the benefits of a more egalitarian lifestyle that narrows socioeconomic differences. Greater social cohesion may offer family members advantages from which urbanites do not benefit (Hayward, Pienta, and McLaughlin, 1997). Some rural areas not only serve as residences to rural families but they also function as vacation spots for urbanites who can afford a second property: a cottage, a hobby farm, or other form of rural property where the family can choose its lifestyle and replenish its relationships, as well described by a student:

> *"I was especially happy there [at the cottage] because my family was always around, and there was a certain air of freedom that we could not find anywhere else. This is probably due to the fact that the cabin had no electricity or hot or cold running water. So essentially we were roughing it. We received water from a manual pump in the kitchen, and we got light from oil lamps and warmth from blankets and each other. We never knew or cared what time it was or what anyone else was doing, just as long as our little world was happy, and we only had guests on the rare occasion. It seemed like a different world because we were the only ones [in the area] with no means of communication, such as telephone, radio, television, or close neighbors to rely on. . . . For instance, we counted on catching fish at least three dinners of the week, so it became a matter of survival."*

This quote is interesting from yet another perspective: It illustrates the lifestyle contrasts that may exist between urban families on vacations and the neighboring rural families. The former embrace a temporary poverty lifestyle, whereas the latter often have to struggle to avoid it. In many areas, rural families make a living by offering goods and services to these tourists and cottagers. The two types of families coreside during the summer months and, in the South, during winter months. This coresidence is at times only wearily accepted by the resident families whose quiet lifestyle can resume after the busy season is over. Often, urban college students find summer jobs in rural resorts, representing their first experience away from their parents.

Characteristics of Farm Families

Farm families are far from being a homogeneous category. They vary in terms of their economic circumstances: Some are tenants, and others are migrant workers; some own small acreage and are struggling financially, and others are involved in large-scale agribusiness and ranching. Moreover, there are differences in the farming lifestyle, depending on the crops produced—from grain farms in Iowa, to cattle ranches in Montana, to fruit groves in Florida, to vegetables and grape-wine production in California, to dairy farms in New York. The level of technology utilized determines the daily activities of farm families, from the Amish in Pennsylvania who generally do not have recourse to fuel- or electricity-propelled machinery to farms where computers dictate levels of feed, fertilizers, and pesticides. Farm families also vary with respect to their degree of isolation. Many farms cluster along well-traveled rural roads, yet others are more remote and connect with neighbors in their area only via long drives, the telephone, and for a few the Internet.

Farm families are characterized by three additional demographic features. First, they constitute a tiny minority of the total American population, even though they feed the entire country and many other parts of the world as well. Their productivity increased tremendously in the twentieth century. Second, a growing proportion of the farm acreage is leased and a majority of land owners are 55 years or older (Janssen, 1993). Therefore, fully owned and operated family farms are less likely to have small children growing up in their midst than was the case 30 years ago. Third, farm families can be differentiated by their labor-force participation. There are families where neither spouse works "off-farm," a category that is rapidly becoming a minority because farm income alone is no longer sufficient to sustain a family. In other cases, one spouse works off-farm while the other works the farm. A last category is made up of husbands and wives who both work off-farm (Janssen, Stover, and Clark, 1993). These categories can be further divided into those who work off-farm full time versus part time.

Farm machinery does not require as much physical strength to operate as before, thus many wives work in the fields and even prefer this lifestyle to staying home (Salamon, 1992). Children raised on farms are used to large machinery and are initiated early on in life. It is not uncommon for 12- to 15-year-old boys to drive combines alongside their fathers in the fields.

> *Sonya Salamon (1992:52) reports the amusing anecdote of a farmer watching a combine no one was driving come toward him.*
>
> > *"When the machine stopped, his three boys, ages three, four, and five jumped out. They were all driving—one at the wheel, one at the gas pedal, and the third working the clutch."*

The Great Farm Crisis of the 1980s saw land prices plummet at a time when many families were heavily in debt because they had bought expensive farm equipment (such as large combines) and many had added to their acreage, only to see the prices go down afterwards. Many farms failed as a result. Some families remained on their former land as tenants, or sold at a loss and kept only a small acreage, whereas others left farming entirely and started life again as blue-collar workers elsewhere. Many went on welfare. By the early 1990s, the situation began slowly stabilizing again, with more agribusinesses controlled by fewer persons. The family farm had changed drastically and many families had broken up as a result of economic hardships. The nation has yet to see the long-term effects of the floods and droughts that plagued many agricultural regions in the late 1990s and endangered the viability of still more family farms.

Farm Families' Adaptation to Economic Crises

A few researchers have studied farm families' stress, survival, adaptation, and defeats in the face of mounting economic pressure. They have found that mothers who have to seek off-farm employment benefit their families financially and gain personal and occupational skills as well as social contacts. Most miss their previous lifestyle and long to return to work alongside their husbands, however (Elder, Robertson, and Foster, 1994). This finding is duplicated in other studies describing how a wife's satisfaction with life decreases when she is employed off-farm, in part because she has too many tasks left to do at home when she returns from her job (Bokemeier and Maurer, 1987). In some families, even adolescents increase their off-farm employment hours or leave school and take a job in order to help the family financially or to be self-supporting, thus minimizing family expenditures. In other families, both boys and girls increase their on-farm economic activities or work for relatives (Elder, Foster, and Ardelt, 1994). Thus, children and adolescents living on farms are far more familialized than urban children. A woman student explains how her contribution to her family's economic survival as an adolescent had shaped her sense of self:

> *"Between the ages of 10 to 14 I recall being very happy because I really felt that I was important in my family. I helped my mother with cow milking before I went to school and we enjoyed each other's company. After school, I helped my father feeding the same cows and cleaning up. It was dirty work but it was meaningful because we all had to pitch in as we were afraid to lose the farm."*

Economic pressure leads parents to become more preoccupied with survival and less involved in parenting. When adolescents transgress, these parents are more likely to react harshly and with hostility. This situation occurs less frequently when the parents' relationship has remained warm and supportive (Simons, Johnson, and Conger, 1994). In families that experience serious economic pressures, husbands often become more hostile toward their wives, and wives become more depressed. The quality of the marriages decline, both because of the wives' depressed moods and the husbands' increased hostility. Husbands are also particularly upset when their wives are irritable toward them: "This difference may be the result of social norms that are more accepting of male than female aggressiveness" (Conger, Ge, and Lorenz, 1994:202).

Kinship and Gender Roles

Despite the hazards of farming, Swisher and colleagues (1998) found that marital and familial conflict was less frequently reported by farm than nonfarm men in Iowa. However, when conflict exists, it is particularly detrimental, because it threatens the normal pattern of interdependence of kin among farm families. Nonfarmers, in contrast, establish more obligations based on friendship and can escape, to some extent, from the potentially negative impact of family conflict. The potential for conflict and the experience of stress is especially great for a daughter-in-law in two-generation farm families, particularly if she feels left out of the decision-making process and perceives her relationship with either of her in-laws as deficient (Martoz-Baden and Mattheis, 1994).

As is the case in the rest of society, the gender division of labor that has liberalized women has not carried over to the male side in terms of household tasks, despite the fact that fathers are present at meals and at home during the winter months and the mothers often work in the fields. Farm families tend to be patrilineally oriented because the property is generally acquired via the son's inheritance. In fact, his parents frequently live nearby. Consequently, although grandparents play a more salient role than in nonfarm families, paternal grandparents are particularly important (King and Elder, 1995). This is in contrast to the usual urban situation where maternal grandparents play a larger role.

The pattern of inheritance is a long one across the two generations and involves decades of shared familial work, which leads both to family cohesiveness and stress (Wilson, Martoz-Baden, and Holloway, 1991). The intergenerational situation can become problematic when middle-aged parents begin to think about their will (Zimmerman and Fetsch, 1994). If they decide the inheritance should favor the son who is interested in farming, if he is to survive at all economically, the bulk or even the entirety of the estate has to go to him. Perhaps very little can be passed on to the other children—a situation that may create sibling conflict later on in life.

FAMILIES' HOUSING CONDITIONS

Much has already been said in this chapter about families' housing conditions. But the focus so far has been on the external conditions. In this section, we look at the quality of the interiors in which families live. Not only are families affected by their neighborhood surroundings but their functioning is also impacted by the size of the lodging, the state of its maintenance, the personal space it allows, and the level of noise.

The state of maintenance or deterioration of a dwelling can have an impact on family atmosphere as well as on health. Old houses often contain asbestos or paint laced with lead—hazards for young children that have been related to intellectual and behavioral deficits (Boivin and Giordani, 1995). For instance, a study by Brody and colleagues (1994) reveals that small children living in cities have blood lead levels associated with cognitive impairment and behavior problems: Nearly 37 percent of black, 17 percent of Mexican-American, and 6 percent of white children were affected. The houses in which low-income families live may be poorly ventilated in the summer and inadequately heated in the winter, and the plumbing may have so deteriorated that leaks frequently occur. Of course, such instances occur mainly in rental housing and in poor neighborhoods, thus further adding to the diminished state of well-being of disadvantaged families.

Overall, the burden of housing costs has increased since the 1970s. This burden has become particularly difficult for renters, compared to homeowners, as well as for single-mother and minority families with three or more children (Chi and Laquatra, 1998). Americans value home ownership more now than 50 years ago. Before the Second World War, the ownership rate hovered around 45 percent; today, it is around 64 percent (Clark and Dieleman, 1996). In addition, the size of the family home has been increasing steadily. By the mid-fifties, the average new house had about 1,100 square feet and two bathrooms; by the 1970s, it had increased to 2,000 square feet, with the addition of a half-bathroom (Clark and Dieleman, 1996). This expansive private space has been fostered by middle-class families (Bird and Melville, 1994).

The "Mansionization" of Suburban Housing

Currently, among the well-to-do, particularly the new rich, the tendency is to build suburban homes with over 5,000 square feet. One of the reviewers of this text referred to this phenomenon as the "*mansionization*" of housing. This tendency toward extremely large homes would make an interesting study: The space per capita is vast and family members may be scattered throughout the house with only minimal contact with each other. Researchers might focus on how families who live in large dwellings (where each member has his or her separate suite, often on different floors) develop mechanisms that contribute to family cohesiveness and interaction as opposed to isolation and interpersonal distance. Such families may have more clearly delineated boundaries within their system than others; the parents on one side and each child separately on the other side. Currently, very little is known about how family space contributes to increases or erosions of intimacy as well as parents' ability to socialize their children.

One cannot help but compare this photograph with the previous one on page 190. The children shown here benefit from a well-manicured space. Yet, one knows very little about the effect, particularly on adolescents, of living in very large houses.

Family Privacy

Family privacy is both a characteristic within the family itself and a situation of the family toward the rest of the world. To begin with, we note the creation of a historically new stage in the life course: solitary living arrangements between the ages of 20 and 29. Despite the fact that young people reside with their parents longer than in the past (see Chapter 11), 27 percent of males and 20 percent of females live outside of any form of family arrangement, although half of those share a residence with an unrelated individual. In contrast, in 1950, fewer than 3 percent of young adults lived this way (Nock, 1998b). Goldscheider and Waite (1991) find that parents who had lived independently before marriage tend to raise their children more individualistically and with a lower sense of family orientation than parents who had stayed home until marriage.

In modern societies, parents need some privacy, and children need space where they can do homework, play games, talk on the phone, and interact among themselves. Many researchers believe that children need space that is their own and that they can control. The separate space occupied by each family fulfills certain functions, but it can also be problematic. As reviewed by Berardo (1998), family privacy allows couples to resolve their problems without external pressure. It serves to protect family members against the pressures of the external world. In this sense, privacy functions as a buffer as well as a protection. On the other side of the coin, as each couple and each family leads its life separately, they have few points in comparison that would allow them to improve their family functioning or even appreciate how good it is compared to that of others. Privacy also means that abuse and neglect can go on for extended periods of time without external detection and/or intervention.

Family life is much less public than it used to be when homes were designed with front porches, for instance. Now, the family has retreated inside or to the backyard (Bird and Melville, 1994). Families have become more individuated, as individualism is closely related to the concept of privacy. Nock (1998b) emphasizes that technological change has also enhanced privacy. Examples are home air conditioning (the windows of the house are closed); few, if any, trips to the laundromat (most homes have washers and dryers); and even a reduction in neighborhood grocery shopping (as on-line shopping increases in popularity). Functionally, families have become more self-reliant and isolated.

Overcrowding

Overcrowding is not an American value, so American-born or raised families do not accept it as a fact of life and may find it highly stressful. When too many family members congregate in too little space, the following is likely to happen.

First, parents may not be able to spend time alone, thus their level and quality of communication and intimacy may suffer. Second, personal hygiene may become problematic when the facilities have to accommodate too many persons. Third, contagious illnesses, such as colds and flus, may spread more easily in families living in cramped quarters, so that work or school days are frequently missed. Moreover, neither children nor adults may get enough sleep; as a result, their physical and mental health may suffer. Fourth, the noise level may distract children and prevent them from doing schoolwork, particularly when the television is on at all times in the small dwelling. Children with an attention deficit disorder may be particularly affected. Fifth, family members unwittingly compete for scarce space so that conflict may arise; in some families, siblings may quarrel more, parents may yell at them and tell them to "shut up," and the atmosphere is one of exacerbation. Nevertheless, some families do cope well in cramped quarters. These are often immigrants who were used to very little space in their home country because of weather, culture, or poverty. Others came from high-density areas—such as Hong Kong, where small apartments are the norm, or Moscow, where several families may share a few rooms. Tolerance of overcrowding therefore depends on cultural norms.

RESIDENTIAL MOBILITY

Moving from one home to another and, particularly for children who are already in school, from one neighborhood to another, is an important transition in a family's life. Not only does it require adjustment to a new interior spatial configuration and functioning, but all the members have to become acquainted with a new neighborhood, town, and even state. Americans, it is said, move far more than most other national groups (Long, 1992). Young adults are more geographically mobile when their educational level is higher (Clark and Dieleman, 1996).

A family move does not benefit its members equally. In fact, several studies have documented that the number of moves experienced by children and adolescents correlates with lower school achievement and rates of high school completion, and even to behavioral problems (Wood et al., 1993). This may be related to the fact that school-age children who move the most come from single-parent (Astone and McLanahan, 1994) as well as low-income families, thus children already at risk of poor school performance (Pribesh and Downey, 1999). When divorced families relocate, they tend to go from being owners to renters because their economic situation has deteriorated. Their mobility is particularly elevated in the first two years after separation (Clark and Dieleman, 1996). Consequently, the adjustment that children and adolescents have to make may be too demanding, for they incur three losses simultaneously: their old family structure, their former peer group, and their house (Maccoby et al., 1993). A male student describes part of this dilemma:

> *"The most painful thing that happened to me was when I had to move. I lost all my friends and had to leave my school but the worst part wasn't even leaving. The worst part was coming to a new school with new kids. They aren't very nice in grade 6 if you don't wear the same clothes as them or have as much money, etc. This was truly one of the hardest periods of my life. I remember going into the cafeteria at lunch and having to sit by myself or with some other losers who were in the same position as me. I was bothered and picked on by a lot of people because I was small and it took me a long time to adjust to my situation. Of course I eventually made friends but I never quite made it with the people who I most wanted to be friends with."*

(As an aside, it is interesting to note that the student labeled other children in the same situation as "losers." This evaluation reflects cultural norms of what is entailed in being successful in one's peer group [Adler and Adler, 1998]).

Adjustment may be particularly difficult when a move leads to an unstable neighborhood where the social control of youths is largely nonexistent. In such contexts, an adolescent from a family that has just suffered a breakup may be particularly susceptible to opportunities for delinquency (Sampson, 1997). School performance suffers with mobility, but this impact applies more to one- than to two-parent families. Children in one- or stepparent-families seem to suffer from any mobility (Tucker, Marx, and Long, 1998). The reason is that such families have less social capital or time that can be devoted to children to counterbalance the potentially negative impact of moving. In general, however, school-age children move less than preschoolers, because parents are aware of the adaptational difficulties inherent to a school change (Hensen, 1993).

When a family relocates in order to enhance a father's position on the job market, the mother may not benefit; she may actually have to abandon her own job and, if the move is an out-of-state one, she may lose her social support network (McCollum, 1990). The parallel occurs to the children, who then have to adjust to new schools and new peer groups. Elder's (1995) developmental or *life course theory* offers a new perspective on this situation. What is an advantage for the father becomes a dislocation in the children's lives: the two generational stages in the life course of a family do not mesh and the goals of one are incompatible with the needs of the other. However, this disparity in the life course timing of the family members can be mitigated in several ways. Husbands can compensate to some extent for their wives' loss of social support, and may even accept a promotion requiring relocation only after their wives have also found a new job.

As far as children are concerned, a harmonious home (Stoneman et al., 1999) as well as the continued or even increased involvement of both parents in their lives is an important stabilizing element. Mothers' involvement helps, but the *combined* paternal and maternal involvement mitigates the disruptive effects of mobility on children more effectively (Hagan, MacMillan, and Wheaton, 1996). When only one parent is involved, the social capital from which children can draw on may not be sufficient during a transition period. When neither parent is involved, because of financial or career pressures or because of personal problems, children are at high risk of failing to integrate themselves in a positive way in their new neighborhood and school.

CONCLUSIONS: THE MEANING OF NEIGHBORHOOD AS CONTEXT

Children and unemployed youths are often the most visible persons in a neighborhood, the ones who are the most affected by its social climate, and the ones who impact it most heavily. For many children and youths, the streets are a nexus of same-age sociability and of linkages between families. In other neighborhoods, the homes and the backyards fulfill this purpose; close acquaintances and friends often come from other areas. Thus, a family's social life may be located within its spatial framework or neighborhood or may extend to other areas and may even include several residential spaces.

Neighborhood structure and housing conditions not only have an impact on people's lives but also reflect a society's values concerning social diversity. This chapter reinforces and extends the findings presented in Chapters 3 and 6 on racial and economic inequalities, including segregation. It also serves as a link between these chapters and the next one, on education and religion, two institutions that constitute additional contexts influencing family life—in some cases, limiting family members' opportunities and, in other cases, enhancing them.

SUMMARY

1. Neighborhoods constitute families' first immediate, external context. Urban areas vary widely, ranging from metropolises to small towns, including a great variety of suburbs. The types of families residing in these various areas differ by social class, race, and household composition. The three upper levels of the class system are described.
2. Inner cities are either polarized between the very affluent and the poor or contain a disproportionate number of near-poor and poor families. The number of high-poverty neighborhoods in large cities has increased drastically since 1970. Concentration of poverty tends to go with minority group membership. For instance, a majority of black families that are poor live in areas of poverty, compared to about 30 percent of whites who are poor. Therefore, the effect of poverty among African Americans is compounded by neighborhood disadvantage. Large-scale inner-city poverty is largely the result of social segregation in areas that have been abandoned by industries after the 1960s. Loss of entry-level jobs resulted in unemployment, single-mother families, criminality and drug problems, as well as physical deterioration. Poor areas of inner cities exhibited all the features of social organization before the 1960s. After, communities were no longer able to maintain social control and to supervise their youths and children. In these areas, there are not enough social resources at the disposal of parents and children.
3. Neighborhoods that are poor and disorganized present several risk factors for children. First, they receive an inadequate, mainstream socialization: There is no effective community helping children develop the social and academic skills needed for the current labor market. Instead, there is a critical mass of low-income neighbors, a factor that is related to behavioral problems and low school achievement. Parents' conscientious childrearing is often defeated by the negative peer context and adult example. Second, children are not adequately supervised and, third, are therefore not protected from the dangers of their areas. Even when parents do their very best, children are still victims of or witness to violence.
4. Poverty areas nevertheless contain a high proportion of families that function very well and are highly resilient. But the task facing parents of successful children are enormous, as they have to be far more vigilant than similar parents in middle-class areas. These parents have to ensure their children's physical safety,

moral development, school success, and conformity to norms amidst a social climate that provides opposite models and opportunities.

5. Entire families have joined the ranks of the homeless and are generally found in hostels or shelters. Poverty, lack of subsidized housing, mental illness, and addiction are some of the key forces leading to homelessness and/or domestic violence. Family life in shelters is severely disruptive, and mothers encounter many difficulties in the fulfillment of their parental duties. Homeless mothers are often depressed as a result, and the general health of both mothers and children suffers. Compared to poor children living at home, homeless children also have more health- and school-related problems.
6. Rural areas vary in their settings and in the employment opportunities they offer to heads of families. Farm families are now in the minority and many are severely stressed economically. Today, most farm couples combine off-farm work with farming to make ends meet. In most families, adolescents contribute to the family economy. Patterns of farm inheritance lead both to family cohesiveness and stress.
7. Home ownership is a prime American value. The type of home owned or rented reflects a family's class position. The state of maintenance of a dwelling can have an impact on family atmosphere and health. Family space connotes with privacy in North America and the trend is toward larger space (square footage) at a time when family size is relatively small. There are problems related to overcrowding but one has to consider that certain cultures tolerate tight living space better than others.
8. A family's residential mobility does not benefit its members equally. Children and adolescents who experience many moves are more likely to suffer from school difficulties and disruptions in their social networks. Particularly affected are children in one-parent families.
9. Neighborhood structure and housing conditions affect families' lives and reflect society's values concerning social diversity.

KEY CONCEPTS AND THEMES

Collective socialization, p. 191
Collective supervision, p. 192
Concentration of poverty, p. 188
Critical mass, p. 191
Fear, p. 190
Functional community, p. 190
Gated enclaves, p. 185
Homelessness, p. 194
Inadequate mainstream socialization, p. 190
Inadequate protection, p. 192
Inadequate supervision, p. 192
Life course theory, p. 204
Mansionization, p. 201
Minority groups, p. 188
Residential mobility, p. 203
Social class, p. 186
Social control, p. 189
Social disorganization, p. 189
Social problems, p. 189
Social resources, p. 190
Victimization, p. 190
Well-functioning families, p. 193

STUDY AND REVIEW QUESTIONS

1. Link families' social class position and neighborhood.
2. What are the distinctions between a poverty area and one with social problems?

3. Discuss the theme of the effective or functional community with respect to children and parents living in high-poverty areas that are socially disorganized.
4. What other concepts are related to that of the functional community?
5. What risks do inner-city children encounter when they are not sufficiently supervized and protected?
6. How different are well-functioning families living in high-risk areas compared to those living in middle-class neighborhoods?
7. Relate family poverty to homelessness and compare the two conditions.
8. What are some of the characteristics of farm families?
9. What changes occurred in the last half of the twentieth century concerning families' housing conditions?
10. Distinguish between the social and personal functions of residential mobility for families.

SUGGESTED READINGS

Baumohl, J., for the National Coalition for the Homeless. 1996. *Homelessness in America.* Phoenix, AZ: Oryx Press. This large collection of articles deals with the history, causes, dimensions of, and responses to homelessness. Some chapters have a family focus. One deals with homelessness among blacks and another among Latinos.

Conger, R. D., and Elder, G. H. Jr., with Lorenz, F. O., Simons, R. L., and Whitbeck, L. B. (Eds.). 1994. *Families in troubled times: Adapting to change in rural America.* New York: Aldine de Gruyter. This book reports the results of the Iowa Youth and Family Project on various aspects of family life on farms.

Jencks, C. 1994. *The homeless.* Cambridge, MA: Harvard University Press. This book studies the socioeconomic causes behind the more recent waves of homelessness and offers potential solutions. Although there is some material on the family as background, the focus is on homeless individuals.

Wilson, W. J. 1987. *The truly disadvantaged.* Chicago: University of Chicago Press. This book is a historically grounded classic; it is still very relevant and influential concerning the formation of high-poverty, inner-city neighborhoods. It relates to the segregated family life of poor urban blacks and all the disadvantages that follow.

SUGGESTED WEBLINKS

The Urban Institute is an economic and social research organization focusing on problems confronting the nation and the search for appropriate social policies. One concern is poverty, both rural and urban. **<http://www.urban.org>**

Websites for major news chains include **<http://cnn.com/US>**, **<http://dailynews.yahoo.com/headlines>**, and **<http://www.foxnews.com/national>**. These websites regularly provide information about events that occur to urban and even rural families as well as homelessness. Most have archives of past news on given topics.

CHAPTER 8

Roles of Education and Religion in Family Life

OUTLINE

The Educational System: An Overview

Child Care: Quality and Child Outcomes

Extent and Quality of Child Care

The Effects of Child Care on Children

The Effects of Child Care on Parents

Early Childhood Education for Children in Low-Income Families

Familial Factors Related to Children's School Success

Parental Involvement

Parents' Higher Social Class and Involvement

Barriers to Low-Income Parents' Involvement

Families' Social Class and Children's Achievement

Family-School Compatibility

Summer Activities

Native Children

Poor Families and Poor Schools

Description of Poor Schools

Consequences for Children and Families

Private Education

Private Schools

Home Schooling

Are Objections to Home Schooling Valid?

Religion and Family Life

How Is Religiosity Measured?

Demographic Factors Related to Religiosity

Parents' and Children's Religiosity: The Socialization Aspect

Secular Society, Religious Parents

Factors in the Successful Transmission of Religiosity

Religiosity and Parenting Practices: Conservative Protestants

Is Religiosity Functional for the Family?

Religiosity Correlates with Well-Being

Religiosity Relates to Marital Stability

Religiosity Supports the Parental Role

Limitations of Religion for Nontraditional Families

Conclusions: The Balancing Act of Family Functions

Summary

Key Concepts and Themes

Study and Review Questions

Suggested Readings

Suggested Weblinks

"Between the ages of 14 to 18 the hardest part was school, school, school. I was not a good student, not motivated and a shit disturber, it seems I did my best to be the worse. . . . I ended up suffering for this and dropped out and back in at my parents' pleadings so that I was still in high school at age 20. . . . It wasn't all my fault because the school was the pits, the teachers didn't care, they just gossiped about their divorces and whatever and the students were more or less like me so we all deserved each other except that our parents didn't deserve this and it took them four years after that to convince me to go to a community college from where I enrolled here."

"High school was my best experience, better than my friends because my teachers were supportive and I got involved in about 10 clubs and participated in various contests and won and my parents were proud of me. It was an exciting time for all

of us because both my parents volunteered, my father as a coach, and my mother helped organize many school functions. They were well liked by all the teachers and even the students and it was just great, I felt at home everywhere I went."

"For sure the cornerstone of all my values and of my life for that matter is my faith in God. We're very religious by today's standards in the younger generation and at times I used to be teased by kids in high school about it so I like the freedom of university life in this respect. The only problem is that university life says nothing about religion. I haven't had a single prof in sociology who even went so far as to say a single word about it."

"I get along reasonably well with my parents now that they accept my lack of interest in religion and a few other deviances on my part. But I've never been religiously inclined and I don't feel I miss out on anything."

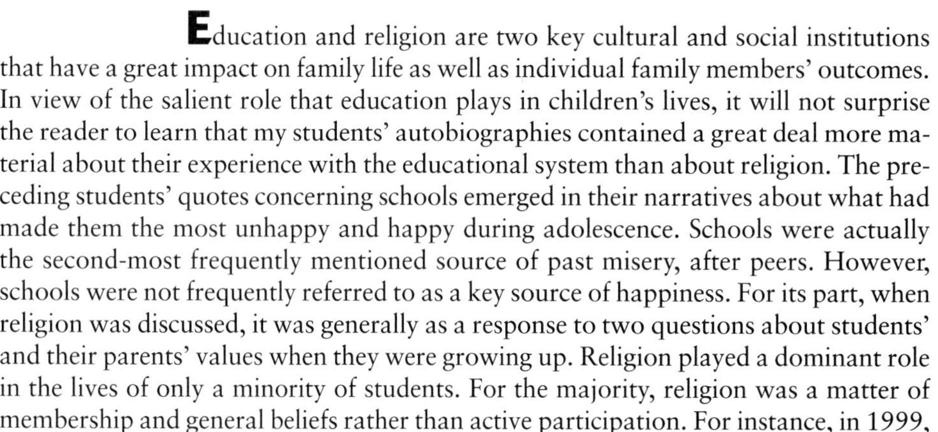

Education and religion are two key cultural and social institutions that have a great impact on family life as well as individual family members' outcomes. In view of the salient role that education plays in children's lives, it will not surprise the reader to learn that my students' autobiographies contained a great deal more material about their experience with the educational system than about religion. The preceding students' quotes concerning schools emerged in their narratives about what had made them the most unhappy and happy during adolescence. Schools were actually the second-most frequently mentioned source of past misery, after peers. However, schools were not frequently referred to as a key source of happiness. For its part, when religion was discussed, it was generally as a response to two questions about students' and their parents' values when they were growing up. Religion played a dominant role in the lives of only a minority of students. For the majority, religion was a matter of membership and general beliefs rather than active participation. For instance, in 1999, Ehmann reports that 45 percent of 18- to 29-year-old Americans state that religion is very important in their daily lives, but only 23 percent attend church once a week.

THE EDUCATIONAL SYSTEM: AN OVERVIEW

Although schools existed over 2,000 years ago in ancient Greece and Rome and later in China and Japan, they were the prerogative of a select group of students. The remainder of the child population worked alongside adults. In western Europe, North

America, and Australia, primary school attendance became compulsory between 1840 and 1890. Middle-class children were the first to benefit, whereas working-class and rural parents had some difficulty adjusting their economic circumstances to the loss of their children's labor and wages. In 1869–70, for instance, 57 percent of all U.S. children between the ages of 5 and 17 were enrolled in schools, but only 35 percent attended regularly (LeVine and White, 1994). Several decades elapsed, well into the first part of the twentieth century, before mass schooling spread to all social classes equally. Today, there are 52 million children in U.S. schools from K to grade 12.

After parents, schools have traditionally been considered, the main agent of socialization. In essence, the educational system pursues family goals of gender-role differentiation and of the social integration of children in society. The majority of children begin school earlier today than they did 30 years ago. Currently, most attend kindergarten, and a substantial proportion participate in preschool programs. Moreover, about a third of preschool children whose parents are employed are in institutional child care or minischools, some as early as 6 weeks old. Therefore, the educational function traditionally assigned to families has been taken over by institutions at younger ages. Child care has become a key family context with which we begin in order to follow the chronological order of a child's life.

CHILD CARE: QUALITY AND CHILD OUTCOMES

Child care generally refers to the care given to a child by a person other than his or her primary caregiver. In this society, the primary caregiver is usually defined as the mother (see Chapter 9). The roots of child care began with the reform and welfare movements of the nineteenth century. Day nurseries, which were the precursors of today's establishments, first started in Boston in 1840 for the children of widows and seamen's wives (Scarr, 1998). Other day nurseries were founded in the Northeast for poor or immigrant children. The primary purpose was to feed and protect children while mothers labored outside the home.

In the twentieth century, child care was provided during the Great Depression of the 1930s, and again during World War II for all working mothers. But since the war, federal or state day care has been provided only to a proportion of low-income mothers. This lack of universal availability makes it difficult for nonpoor working- and even middle-class families to afford quality child care, particularly in day centers, as the demand far outstrips the supply.

Extent and Quality of Child Care

More than half the mothers of babies under age 1 are employed. Therefore, the necessity for early child care arises in a majority of American families (Behrman, 1996). (In contrast, in European countries, *paid* parental leave from work allows infants to be cared for at home.) Not only are a majority of children in care during the day, but about 25 percent of all children under age 6 spend 40 hours or more a week in care—excluding kindergarten and school (Joesch, 1998). Of those children in care of someone other than their mother, about

21 percent are cared for at home by a relative
4 percent are cared for at home by a nanny or sitter
15 percent are cared for in another woman's home
31 percent are in a child care center (Hofferth, 1996)

The remaining children in child care experience a combination of care arrangements, including alternating shifts between mothers and fathers. Care in another woman's home is not always state licensed but centers are. Both types of care vary widely in quality and have been rated as mediocre, on average, ranging from disastrous to excellent (Cost, Quality, and Child Outcomes Study Team, 1995). Child care is therefore a cause for concern both for parents and society. Compared to the 1960s, proportionally more children are in centers rather than with female relatives, because the latter tend to be employed. Furthermore, affluent families are the least likely to choose care by relatives.

Child care of high quality includes a low child-to-caregiver ratio that allows for more adult/child interaction (Volling and Feagans, 1995). The qualifications of the caregivers, the availability of activities, toys, and educational materials, as well as the amount of space are other indicators of quality. Nutritious food and the functional structuring of daily activities, including naps, are also important elements of quality. Furthermore, we should consider low salaries as an indicator of quality: Low salaries lead to high turnover rates, thus instability in children's lives. In the United States, caregivers' salaries are much lower than those in Europe, and their turnover rate consequently is around 40 percent per year (Corsaro, 1997).

African-American children enter care by someone other than their mothers earlier and for longer hours than do white children. Children of high-income parents generally enter care only after three months following their birth, whereas poorer children often begin before they are three months old. However, high-familial income is related to spending longer hours in care, due to the demands of work responsibilities on professional and managerial parents. In poor families, in-home care by someone other than the father or grandparents is of lower quality in terms of the attention devoted to the child. As far as center-based care is concerned, both poor and affluent children receive better quality care than children from families with incomes above the poverty level. This may be explained by the availability of subsidies for disadvantaged families and programs such as Head Start (National Institute of Child Health and Human Development, 1998).

The Effects of Child Care on Children

Poor-quality care has been related to child disadvantages in the domains of cognition and language as well as social and emotional adjustment (Lamb, 1998). Unfortunately, research on the effect of nonfamilial care on children has until now largely failed to take family characteristics into consideration. It is entirely possible that some of what are believed to be negative consequences of day centers are actually results of certain family characteristics, such as a mother's low educational level or a difficult housing situation (Scarr, 1998). Naturally, to some extent, parents choose or are forced to accept a quality of care correlated to some of their own characteristics, such as income (Singer et al., 1998). In studies that have controlled for family variables, the quality of day centers still produces a small but evident difference in terms of language, cognitive development (Wasik et al., 1990), and overall adjustment (McCartney et al., 1997).

A review of large-scale studies of hundreds of centers carried out in the United States, Bermuda, Sweden, and Holland concludes that the differences found in children raised at home versus in day care do not have *persistent* consequences. Furthermore, day centers have no major impact on children's development when they come from average homes. "These results may differ for the children from socioeconomically disadvantaged homes, for whom quality child-care programs may supply missing elements in their lives" (Scarr, 1998:105). Basically, while children from disadvantaged families may benefit from quality day care, particularly in terms of school achievement later on, children from high-socioeconomic-status families probably derive the same benefits they would obtain at home, at least at the educational level (Ramey and Ramey, 1992).

Several studies find that children in day care are more self-confident, outgoing, assertive, verbally expressive, and helpful, as well as less timid in new situations. But the same studies also report that many of these children are less polite, agreeable, and compliant with mothers' or caregivers' requests, and more irritable, aggressive, and boisterous (reviewed by Clarke-Stewart, 1992). These results are particularly evident for children who have been placed in care when very small (Belsky, 1992).

Therefore, children who have too much peer contact and too little adult attention early in their lives may be at a deficit in terms of social adjustment. We already know from other studies on family size that such children are at a disadvantage in terms of language skills and intellectual development (Downey, 1995). There is nevertheless one important question that is still being debated: Are children who are in care from an early age for over 30 hours a week less influenced by parents' teachings and other family characteristics than children who are in care fewer hours (National Institute of Child Health & Human Development, 1998)?

In comparison, not enough research has been carried out on at-home child care in terms of its impact on children. The following student quotes reflect the wide variety of conditions that small children can encounter:

> *"At first I didn't like being separated from my mother but the lady was so nice. She took in two other children who were more or less my age and she gave us such a great time. She really loved children and looking back on that I wonder where she got all her ideas because she had dropped out of school after grade 9. She used to take us on long walks and we went to the park where we collected 'treasures' such as pine cones, leaves, bugs and she taught us things and then she had all these story books from the library, always different ones. It was never boring and we all learned to read with her and count and when we got to school I was placed in grade 2." [woman student]*

> *"What I hated the most [during ages 4 to 5] was this old woman who came home to babysit us each morning. She was like an old witch, nice with my parents but a real sulk as soon as they were out. She had nothing to do with us for the entire*

> *day except to feed us and stuff her own face. She knitted and watched TV and ate some more. . . . My parents noticed that we were becoming withdrawn and shy and my mother became concerned. We were too small to tell her much. . . . but my mother probably guessed that something was wrong and found another woman." [male student]*

The Effects of Child Care on Parents

As Mason and Duberstein (1992) point out, care should also be studied in terms of its effects on parents, particularly on their well-being. Care that is too expensive reduces parents' well-being as well as that of the entire family. Too great a proportion of the domestic budget that goes into child care depletes resources that could be utilized for other aspects of family life, such as better housing and nutrition. Furthermore, expensive care may prevent some parents from having a second child, or, when a second baby arrives, one of the two parents (generally the mother) may be forced to leave her employment. Thus, indirectly, via the expenses required, child care may reduce parental well-being.

Mason and Duberstein (1992) point to a second path via which child care can lessen parental well-being: Low-quality care not only impacts negatively on children's development, but parents are worried about their child as they attend to their job during the day. They may feel insecure and guilty. In other instances, the child is well cared for, but by relatives or sitters who exact a psychological price from parents, particularly mothers, by being intrusive or quarrelsome. Also, parents may feel that their child needs more attention but mothers may be afraid of antagonizing relatives if they make additional requests.

Thus, child care availability, affordability, and quality are key ingredients in contemporary children's development. But they are also key ingredients in parents' well-being. From a societal perspective, quality and affordable child care increases productivity, lowers employee stress and absenteeism, and offers a wider pool of potential workers. It also contributes to a healthier family situation. Hence, child care availability should be a prime target of social policies directed at improving family life.

Early Childhood Education for Children in Low-Income Families

Children from low-income families living in disadvantaged areas are often unprepared when they enter first grade and consequently fall behind at each subsequent level. Many such children repeat grades and then drop out of school to join the ranks of the unemployed and underpaid. Programs such as Head Start, which began in 1965 during the War on Poverty, were created to raise the level of disadvantaged children's school readiness. By 1998, over 40,000 Head Start classrooms served close to 800,000 children, or one-third of those eligible (Administration on Children, Youth, and Families, 1998). Figure 8.1 illustrates the ethnic distribution of Head Start's tiny clientele. This distribution reflects the fact that minority children are, on the whole, poorer than white ones.

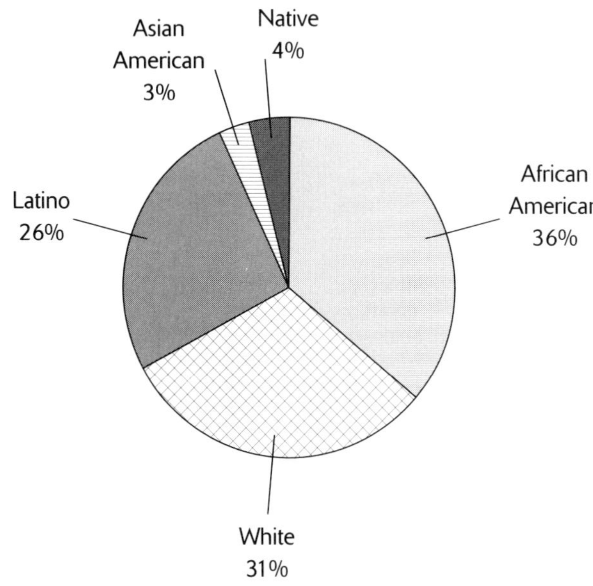

FIGURE 8.1

Ethnic Distribution of Children Enrolled in Head Start Programs in 1994

Source: Based on Administration on Children, Youth, and Families, 1998.

A solid body of longitudinal research concerns children who are enrolled in a Head Start type of preschool. What are the results? According to Barnett (1998), Gamble and Zigler (1989), and Raver and Zigler (1997):

1. Children experience a short-term boost in IQ scores that may last for a few years.
2. Once they are in first grade, these students do better than comparable students not previously enrolled in Head Start programs.
3. Only a small group is eventually placed in "special education."
4. Only about one-fifth are eventually retained in a grade, compared to one-third of a control group that did not attend Head Start.
5. More Head Start children graduate from high school.
6. More of these children are eventually employed than those children in the control group.
7. Children show an improvement in family interaction, health and nutritional status, as well as socioemotional adjustment.

Mothers are also more satisfied with the children's school performance and develop higher occupational aspirations for them later on. Quality Head Start programs generally provide a great deal of parent/teacher positive contact that encourages mothers to help their children remain highly motivated. When children arrive in first grade free of behavioral problems, not only are they more attentive in class and better able to learn but they also impress their teachers and peers more favorably (Ladd, Birch, and Buhs, 1999). In contrast, children who exhibit difficult and antisocial behaviors have a more conflictual and distant relationship with their kindergarten and first grade teachers (Birch and Ladd, 1998). The children's behavioral style makes them less adaptable to school, teachers, and peers.

Head Start children are more likely to arrive in first grade better prepared and their school adjustment is smoother. Teachers, in turn, are better disposed toward and expect more of them, which then carries through the rest of their school years, even though their initial IQ gain eventually disappears. As Entwisle, Alexander, and Olson (1997:18) remind us, "It is key to realize that only modestly better achievement in the first couple of grades might be enough for children to avoid retention or Special Education."

Full-day programs carry longer benefits than half-day ones. In fact, the longer children stay in school daily and the less they miss school, the better they do on aptitude tests (Ceci, 1991). Similarly, a longer school day seems to raise reading and math scores (Frazier and Morrison, 1998). Most child development experts now agree that disadvantaged children who are segregated in poor neighborhoods would do far better if they were to start preschool as early as possible, even at age 2 (Kagan and Neuman, 1998). They also agree that such an early intervention should extend through grade school to build on the initial progress and to involve other aspects of these families' lives (Reynolds and Temple, 1998). Such an extension would prevent the loss of early gains, which currently occurs as a result of the low-quality school environments in which disadvantaged children find themselves after Head Start.

Head Start programs for low-income families are thus an excellent investment for a society with a large pool of disadvantaged families. It is an investment in education, in children's present and future, and in families, including these children's future families. Inasmuch as such programs are both remedial and preventive, they are cost effective and save taxpayers enormous burdens in the long run, in terms of lower rates of delinquency, unemployment, ill health, and even adult criminality. Such programs could in the future contribute to the formation of two-parent families by increasing the pool of economically stable, thus marriageable, males in populations at risk. Therefore, such programs constitute the greatest return on investment that a society can make.

FAMILIAL FACTORS RELATED TO CHILDREN'S SCHOOL SUCCESS

In this section, we investigate family variables that promote or impede school success. Three interrelated variables are discussed: parental involvement, social class, and family-school compatibility.

Parental Involvement

Parental involvement in education is related to children's achievement and is consequently a key concern of teachers who expect parents to support them and to prepare children for school. Education manuals emphasize the "partnership" that exists between teachers and parents. Yet, the word *partnership* implies equality and this is generally not what teachers seek. Teachers approve of meetings with parents but only when they, and not parents, intitiate them (Steinberg, Brown, and Dornbusch,

1996:129). Moreover, as Kerbow and Bernhardt (1993) point out, the traditional concept of parental involvement implies that it rests solely on parents' motivation. In practice, there are several elements that either encourage or discourage parents from being involved, as we see later on.

Parents can involve themselves directly in school activities—for instance, by volunteering—or they can follow closely their children's education from home by showing interest, maintaining high expectations, and supervising homework. Parental participation and empowerment is related to children's school performance (Griffith, 1996). All in all, a great deal of research indicates that parents can have a positive effect on raising their children's school achievement as well as educational expectations and personal aspirations (Carey and Farris, 1996; Trusty, 1998).

Parents' Higher Social Class and Involvement

Building on Coleman's (1988) **theory of resources,** Lareau (1989) demonstrates how parents' social class position equips them with an unequal set of resources that can differentially impact their ability to be involved in their children's education. In her sample, upper-middle-class executive or professional parents have the competence to help their children when they encounter difficulties with the curriculum. These parents also feel self-confident with teachers and do not hesitate to request changes that could benefit their children or to question teachers' decisions. At the negative level, it is not uncommon for such parents to flatly reject teachers' suggestions concerning behavioral difficulties children are encountering. This situation is described by a student teacher who is doing her practicum at a school in a new upper-middle-class neighboorhood where parents are upwardly mobile and are extremely busy with their careers:

> *"Right now I can't wait to get out of that school because some of these parents aren't used to money and what comes with it and they treat you as if you were their maids. Most kids are fine but we have a few bad apples and the parents are high on denial, perhaps because they are never home to see what's wrong with their precious children. There's nothing that their Danny Boy or whoever can do wrong yet the boy is a regular delinquent. Oh no, he doesn't steal, how dare we complain,* accuse *him of this! More or less they tell us to learn manners which they don't even have themselves. It ruins your life as a teacher."*

In their own social networks, upper-middle-class parents often have access to professionals, such as pychologists, and other teachers whom they can consult on school matters. These parents are also better equipped to meet teachers' requests, because they have more material resources at their disposal (Zill and Nord, 1994). They can provide their children with educational supplies, computers, tutors, arts or music lessons, and perhaps summer camps. Lareau (1989) also mentions that these parents often bring work home from the office. The visibility of their work expands children's educational horizons, gives them at least some preparation for the adult world of work, and may serve as an incentive for homework.

Barriers to Low-Income Parents' Involvement

Disadvantaged parents generally value education as much as do their wealthier counterparts; Muller and Kerbow (1993) report that minority parents value postsecondary education more than white parents. Unfortunately, they often have low achievement expectations for their own children because several problems stand in their and their children's way that prevent the actualization of these parental values and consequently lower their aspirations. This is unfortunate, since studies indicate that parental expectations are key predictors of school achievement, starting in first grade. Entwisle, Alexander, and Olson (1997:93) point out that raising parents' expectations could affect performance indirectly for several years after first grade. As we have seen, programs such as Head Start often lift parents' expectations, which in turn contributes to their children's success.

Disadvantaged parents encounter several problems that prevent them from actualizing their high value for education. First, they often lack the skills to help their children when they have school problems. Second, they often feel intimidated or stigmatized by teachers, as discussed by a mature student on welfare:

> *"Currently, one of my worries is my daughter's school, rather, her teachers. They know that I am a single mother on welfare and it does not matter to them consequently that I have as much and even more education than they have. I can't talk to them, any of them, because they have subtle ways of putting me down, of making me feel that I am not a competent parent and person because I am poor. I wanted to get them involved in making sure that the children spell correctly . . . well, what a mistake because they can't spell themselves! But, of course, I am the problem: I am poor. Who am I? How can I have an opinion about my daughter's education, least of all spelling?"*

Third, teachers make more frequent requests for involvement from disadvantaged parents, but these requests are often negative, in part because poor children have more learning or behavioral problems (Sui-Chu and Willms, 1996). In fact, when children's grades are low, parents have more contact with the school (Muller and Kerbow, 1993). Otherwise, low-income parents attend parent/teacher conferences far less frequently. Often, lack of child care prevents them from doing so. Others may not have a flexible work schedule that would allow them to participate in school activities, such as volunteering. This is unfortunate, for volunteering would give them the opportunity to become informally acquainted with teachers and other parents. Such activities would, in turn, give their children an advantage within the system—an "inside track."

A fourth aspect of a family's low position in the class system that affects parents' expectations and children's education resides in the fact that, when these parents want to help their children with school work, they often meet resistance because the youngsters lack confidence in their competence. A student, reminiscing on her own experience growing up in a disadvantaged family, makes this point:

> *"When I look back on that period what I regret the most is the way I treated my mother, just because we were poor I felt that she was not as good as other mothers and whenever she'd try to help me with homework, I'd turn to her and give her my most despising look. Not only I hurt her a lot and made her feel useless as a mother but I made her feel worthless as a person because even then she was more educated than I am now especially when it comes down to writing proper sentences."*

Families' Social Class and Children's Achievement

Children from families of higher socioeconomic status (SES) do better academically; this observation holds across cultures. Furthermore, children who attend schools enrolling greater percentages of students from higher SES backgrounds do better academically (Gamoran, 1992). Using data from the National Educational Longitudinal Study, Pong (1998) found that children attending schools where a high proportion of the students enrolled are from single-parent families had lower mathematics and reading scores in grade 10, in great part because of the disadvantaged economic resources in these children's environment.

Furthermore, Pong (1998) found that, at the group level, high parental participation in educational activities to some extent alleviated the economic deficit by providing a positive community effect on the school and its students. Thus, students did better when parents' participation was high, in general, even though their own individual parents may not have been involved. The same findings applied for the extent to which parents were acquainted with each other. When parents knew many other parents, they served as sources of information and reinforcement for each other. This, in turn, helped them create a proeducational climate within the school for the benefit of all students. These results support Coleman's (1988) theory of **social capital** and the positive effect of a **functional community** above and beyond a family's social class and structure.

Social class is not always a good predictor of school success when other **cultural and language factors** are involved (Stanton-Salazar and Dornbusch, 1995). Several studies, including that of Rumberger and Larson (1998), have found that, for Latinos, school completion is more related to **bilingualism** than to social class. For instance, Mexican-American students who are proficient in English but have retained their Spanish language do better than those who know only English and than those who do not know English well. In fact, the dropout rates are higher among third-generation Latinos who are assimilated at the linguistic level than among second-generation Latinos who are still bilingual (Rumberger, 1995).

It is surmised by these authors that bilingual students have more social capital allowing them to access a greater variety of resources in their community. Having retained part of their culture of origin, they are more influenced by higher parental aspirations on their behalf and less by peers who have lost their heritage. These conclusions have been supported among bilingual Asian-American students, compared to those who no longer speak their language at home (Blair and Qian, 1998).

Family-School Compatibility

Children are more successful at school and better adjusted to its requirements when family life is similar to the middle-class climate of school organization. Children in families that have a schedule—where they eat breakfast, where rules are followed, and where educational activities are encouraged—are more easily integrated into the school system (Rumberger et al., 1990). Households with no employed adults are less likely to provide such a structure. In homes where everyone gets up whenever he or she wants, does not dress until later or not at all, eats meals whenever hungry, watches unlimited hours of television, and where reading material is absent, daily life is a world apart from school routine and even goals.

As a result, children from these families may experience more difficulty fitting in at school, as well as more trouble learning, because the two lifestyles actually clash. A student describes her experience in first grade as the most painful situation of her young life because of family and school incompatibility:

> *"Going to school for the first time was supposed to be a wonderful experience and I had so much looked forward to it: at last I was going to have something special that my four younger brothers and sisters didn't have. But things turned out differently than expected. . . . I was always late in the morning because my parents never got us up on time and we were too tired because we had watched TV late, even the babies. Then I would often fall asleep at my desk so that I missed out on a lot of things and most of the children seemed to know what to do and I didn't and I didn't know what to ask my parents to buy for me and they had other things on their minds anyways; for them my being at school was just one fewer child in the house but as far as the rest was concerned they were hopeless. Then I dressed differently than the other children or my clothes were dirty because we didn't have a washing machine in the apartment and my mother had to go to the laundromat. . . . I tried to fit in by copying the other children's behaviors and even watching what their parents did for them when they picked them up. Slowly by the end of grade 1 I had learned my way around school in terms of expected behavior and I've wanted to be a teacher ever since."*

Summer Activities

Several researchers have emphasized the differences that exist between children of diverse social classes in terms of summer activities. Middle-class children benefit from summer activities that are compatible with school routine. In contrast, disadvantaged children often spend their vacations in pursuits that increase their distance from what is required for school performance (Heyns, 1988). A knowledge vacuum is created and they have more difficulty than advantaged children in readapting themselves to school work once classes resume. Not surprisingly, these children lose a few points on the IQ scale as well as on tests of mathematical ability during vacations.

Entwisle and colleagues (1997) tested children and examined their school grades at the beginning, middle, and end of the school year. They found that, although disadvantaged children begin the school year with lower scores and less knowledge than those from more affluent families, they gain as much proportionately. In other words, some of the yearly difference in test scores between poor children and children of higher SES is caused by summer loss for the former.

Native Children

Family and school compatibility may be particularly important for Native-American children. In this respect, tribally controlled schools often value their culture more and understand their family dynamics better. For instance, Wall and Madak (1991) have found that Native high schoolers who attended tribal schools reported that their teachers and parents held higher educational aspirations for them than did Natives who attended regular public schools. In the latter case, their cultural heritage may be substantially diluted and the staff may lack an understanding of Natives' family processes. These two factors, combined, place children at a disadvantage in terms of school achievement.

Furthermore, family characteristics (parents' education, employment, and marital status) do not necessarily have the same impact on school success on reservations as they do off reservations and in the population at large (Ward, 1998). As we saw in Chapter 3, reservation Native parenting style is less supervisory than is the case in the rest of society, because it is their custom to rely on assistance from their extended kin for child supervision. For these parents, then, how well their children do in school may depend more on the social capital the community makes available to the children than their own socialization practices. When the tribe controls the school, parents and other community members can voice their concerns and have a greater impact on the curriculum (Ward, 1998). When a school has a very high proportion of its students who are Natives, they are more likely to participate in extracurricular activities and to develop an attachment to their school. Both variables, in turn, prevent drop out (Swisher and Hoisch, 1992).

POOR FAMILIES AND POOR SCHOOLS

The location of a school determines its resources. Schools in poorer districts are disadvantaged because of the local funding system based on property taxes. In 1991, the 47 largest urban school districts received $875 less per pupil annually than suburban districts; in a class of 25 pupils, this results in a $22,000 shortfall. As the Panel on High-Risk Youth (1993:7) notes, "When the relatively greater need of urban children for special services is taken into account (for health needs, language instruction for non-English-proficient students, etc.), the resource differences are even more critical." Many rural areas suffer from the same problems.

Description of Poor Schools

In *Savage Inequalities,* Kozol (1991) describes district after district where, within one urban area, schools serving primarily students who are both poor and members of minority groups receive much less than schools in affluent districts. For example, in 1988, Chicago spent $5,000 per inner-city high school student, compared to $9,000 per suburban student (p. 54). In Illinois, $2,100 was spent per child in the poorest district, versus over $10,000 in the richest (p. 57). The range in the state of New York in 1987 was from $5,500 per pupil in New York City to above $11,000 in many suburbs of Long Island (p. 83). In Texas, a state that has since taken some steps to remedy school inequality, a very wide gap existed between poor and some particularly well-endowed schools—from $2,000 to $19,000 (p. 223).

But these numbers are not sufficient to describe the often dreadful conditions of these underfunded institutions. Lack of finances translates into classrooms without teachers; classrooms where nearly 20 substitutes succeed each other in a semester; and teachers who are so unqualified that they neglect their pupils academically and

Minority-group parents whose children are enrolled in "at-risk" schools have to invest far more of themselves in their children's education than other parents whose children attend good schools.

destroy their self-esteem. Lack of finances also translates into word processing being taught without a computer; 200 students sharing 30 textbooks or using a textbook that is outdated by over 20 years, or having no textbook at all; courses that have to be held in lavatories; several classrooms sharing a noisy gym for want of space; 1,000 students crammed into a school designed for 500; science labs without water or even electricity; heaps of garbage behind the school yard; sewage backing up in the toilet and kitchen facilities; holes in the roof; ceiling tiles falling down. Unfortunately, this list could go on.

Consequences for Children and Families

The destruction of young minds in poor-quality schools is so systematic that, in some areas, only a minority of students graduate and even fewer achieve a high enough SAT score to qualify for college (Kozol, 1991:149). Children who attend these institutions are often treated as if they were expendable, as if they were lost before they entered the schools, while, in reality, it is the dreadful poverty of these places that puts them at further risk. As Polakow (1993) points out, these "at-risk" schools destroy the human potential of their students. Bowles and Gintis (1976) already observed 30 years ago that schools in high-poverty areas did not encourage their students to develop the self-presentation skills that are favored by employers, and thus, from the start, disadvantage their students on the labor market.

Orfield (1993:166) points out that the isolation and inequality of segregated minority students in poor-quality schools can mean that these students have "no way of assessing their performance relative to suburban students" with whom they will later compete for college acceptance. He also concurs that these schools totally fail to prepare their students for the labor market, which is often located in suburbs. This may be why "inner-city black youth often express high occupational aspirations that turn out to have no relationship to what happens to them later." Furthermore, parents may also be completely unaware of the low quality of education that their children receive, because they do not have a good basis for comparison: "At a certain point the system of ghettoization becomes so powerful that its victims have no way of comparing their experiences to those of the rest of society" (Orfield, 1993:170).

When a school is predominantly populated by students from single-parent families, the children's test scores are significantly reduced (Bankston and Caldas, 1998). Children from female-headed families who attend a school where most peers have two parents, and therefore have more resources, will be positively affected in their test scores. In contrast, children from two-parent families who attend a school where most families are headed by mothers will do less well in terms of test scores. But no one knows exactly what percentage (**critical mass**) of students from disadvantaged families tips the balance toward a negative influence. This is the same question that was asked in the previous chapter regarding neighborhood poverty.

This effect of a critical mass of poor parents on a school climate is clearly evident in a student's autobiography. She is a freshman taking Sociology 101. The spelling errors have been edited and the sentence structure has been improved by adding missing words between brackets:

> *"I am real unhappy at my age [because] I have much difficulties at school, I want to make it do something for myself and I thought university [would] be easier. . . . In high school my grades were good but I got here and find I cannot take notes because we [were] not doing this before and there's so many books I have to read and I have much difficulties with the tests."*

From what this student wrote in other segments of her autobiography, she lived in a self-contained world, within a low-income nuclear family surrounded by an even poorer extended family. Her neighborhood was disadvantaged, her peers devalued education, and the school educational climate had deteriorated. She was the only one in her peer group to attend college. Even with all the remedial help extended her, her obvious good will, and her aching desire to make it, she had dropped out before the year was over. Even though she had no learning disability, it was impossible for the university to bridge the gap that existed between the requisites of a basic college education and her family and peer background.

In normal situations, the more schooling children have, the larger their cognitive growth (Huttenlocher, Levine, and Vevea, 1998). Years of schooling tend to increase IQ levels, and absence from a good school for a prolonged period results in lower scores (Neisser et al., 1996). For instance, black children who had moved to Philadelphia from abysmal predesegregation schools in Georgia benefited from an IQ boost of one-half point for each year of schooling in Philadelphia (Lee, 1951).

PRIVATE EDUCATION

We look at two different alternatives to children's education: private schools and home schooling.

Private Schools

Private institutions enroll 6 of the 52 million children in schools today. They are loosely divided into three categories. First are schools that are sponsored by religious groups. This is probably the most common type and often the least expensive. Furthermore, such schools cater to children of all social classes, and the Catholic ones in large cities include visible minority children. These schools contribute to social mobility. Coleman (1990b:242) states, "The evidence is strong that the Catholic schools function much closer to the American ideal of the 'common school,' educating children from different backgrounds alike, than do public schools." Parental involvement is often high and a **functional community** (Coleman and Hoffer, 1987) develops based on shared religious beliefs and educational goals. Such a community, in turn, contributes to a more effective child socialization and integration into mainstream society, including higher educational levels (Evans and Schwab, 1995; Neal, 1997).

The second category is constituted by private schools that also foster academic excellence but are, above all, a means for rich families to raise their children within an exclusive environment. Boarding schools, or residential education, are included in this category; one can think of Groton, Choate, and St. Andrew's among the most prestigious. Students who attend these schools tend to have higher occupational and social class outcomes later on than students in public schools (Persell, Catsambris, and Cookson, 1992). This result remains even after family selection factors are controlled (Brewer, Eide, and Ehrenberg, 1999); it may stem from the critical mass factor mentioned earlier. A third type, at times called alternative schools, serves children whose parents are ideologically opposed to certain tenets of mass schooling (i.e., sexism, competitiveness, individualism) or children who have not adapted to regular schools because of behavioral, emotional, or intellectual problems.

Parents expect that private schools will pass on their values to their children, as well as their lifestyle, whether religion or class inspired. From this perspective, such schools serve as an **extension of the family** far more than public schools can:

> *"I had a wonderful adolescence! My parents put me in this wonderful private school in grade 7 and I just bloomed. It was like one very large family that sheltered us from the bullies we had had at the public school. I was a nerd and there certainly was no problem with this at this school. I was actually encouraged to read, explore new fields, ask questions, and tag-along the teachers. We were all nerdy and it was just great. Both boys and girls were like that so that even dating was not a problem even though the teachers and our parents all made us understand that this was a stage of life that could wait. So we waited. We did not have to conform to the 'peer culture' (some Culture!) at other schools. We never envied them and all of us grew up to be very well rounded, sociable, and athletic nerds. If we had gone on to public high schools, we would have grown up screwed up or most of us would have given up being intelligent just to fit in." [male student]*

The staff of a private school are hired on the basis of how well they conform to the school's ideology, which in turn reflects parental ideology. The compatibility between the two is particularly evident in the preceding student quote. Parents and teachers were encouraging their adolescents along similar lines of intellectual and social development.

Home Schooling

Home schooling is where the worlds of children and parents are most intertwined. It is the most clear-cut example of parental resistance to the defamilialization and institutionalization of children, discussed in Chapter 2. Home schooling is currently considered somewhat unusual. Yet, when one examines human history, home education has always prevailed until recently. Parents who resort to home schooling react against the philosophy, structure, and functioning of the formal educational system. Many also react against what they perceive to be dangerous peer influences.

During the closing years of the last millennium, home schooling of children was growing by about 15 percent a year and is expected to reach an estimated one million children soon. The timing of this growth is somewhat paradoxical: It occurs while most married families have two wage earners. Yet, most home teachers are mothers, which means that they in effect have to sacrifice their own financial independence.

Home-schooling parents do not generally function in a vacuum. Several national and statewide organizations exist for the purpose of offering instrumental and moral support to the families involved: Family Centered Learning Alternatives, the National Homeschool Association, and the National Center for Home Education are among the main organizations. Similarly, several magazines are published; jointly, they probably reach most of the home-school parents (Mayberry et al., 1995).

Are Objections to Home Schooling Valid?

Objections to home schooling, especially by the educational establishment, largely fall into three broad categories: (1) worries that the education provided by parents may not meet national standards, (2) concerns that "zealot" parents may brainwash their children ideologically and religiously, and (3) criticisms to the effect that these children will lack peer contact, will not develop appropriate social skills, and may become social isolates.

In order to examine the validity of the first objection, the question is: Do parents who school their children have certain deficits that would prevent them from being at least adequate teachers? Mayberry and colleagues (1995) have summarized the social profile of the fathers: The majority are white, religious, and tend to engage in occupations at the professional and technical level three times more than is the case nationally. On average, the fathers' income is higher, situating them at the middle- to upper-middle-class level. There are two types of parents involved in home shooling. The majority are religiously motivated and are devout Christians, primarily fundamentalists. The smaller group consists of parents motivated by lifestyle, pedagogic concerns, or a desire to strengthen their bond with their children (Van Galen, 1991).

Overall, assuming that mothers are similar to fathers, these parents are educationally qualified, even though they have not generally been trained as teachers. At any rate, research fails to find any significant relationship between fathers' educational level and home-schooled children's achievement scores (Ray and Wartes, 1991). In other words, the children of fathers with a high school education are doing as well as those with fathers who graduated college, which is the opposite of what occurs in regular schools. What probably counts for children's achievement in home schooling is parents' unusually high involvement. The children perform at the national average and frequently exceed it on standard tests. Many actually accelerate while being home schooled and enter college at a younger age.

As to whether parents brainwash their offspring and offer them an education that is, for instance, so religiously oriented that it closes the door to children's options in the future, there is no direct research that could answer this critique scientifically. However, it would seem that "brainwashed" children would not do very well on the standard tests they have to take to enter college or that researchers have given them. Yet, we have seen that the contrary happens, although there are certainly exceptions to that rule. Furthermore, parents themselves have an answer to this particular objection. They point out that secular humanism taught in public schools does brainwash children into values and beliefs that go against their principles.

In terms of growing up socially inept and isolated as well as emotionally maladjusted, the tests that have been carried out indicate normal development. But the samples employed may not have been representative, so no generalizations can be made. Nevertheless, it can be argued on the basis of other material presented in this chapter that the potential for maladjustment exists for too many children who attend regular schools. As we will see in Chapter 14, studies unanimously indicate that U.S. children are often bullied and victimized by peers. These statistics and experiences actually lead many parents to begin home schooling.

Furthermore, children who are home schooled generally have at least one sibling. As well, children meet others who are in similar circumstances; they know their peers in the neighborhood and many participate in extracurricular activities, such as sports teams and scouting, which put them in frequent contact with regularly schooled peers. At the high school level, as many home-schooled teens have jobs as other youths (Ray and Wartes, 1991). Overall, although home schooling is unusual, it does not appear to produce negative effects for families and children, and perhaps quite the opposite occurs.

RELIGION AND FAMILY LIFE

Religion constitutes one of the most important cultural domains in any society. It plays an important role in the lives of a substantial proportion of American families, even though its institutional role and moral authority have declined. Its impact on family life is therefore likely to be more obvious among the observants.

How Is Religiosity Measured?

How is the importance of religion to a family or to some of its members measured?A great deal of controversy revolves around this matter, as one can well imagine, because religiosity is difficult to define and measure. The most obvious and commonly used *indicator* of or way of measuring religiosity is attendance at religious services (see Family Research 8.1). Generally, phone or door-to-door surveys ask questions such as: "Did you, yourself, happen to attend church, mosque or synagogue in the last seven days?" This is actually a Gallup survey question (Smith, 1998). The problem with these and similar questions measuring religious activities resides in the double matter of truthfulness and of errors of recall. People forget that they did or did not go to church or synagogue in the past week; others may do some "forward telescoping"—that is, remembering having gone recently while in reality they went several weeks ago.

Furthermore, people may feel put "on the spot" so to speak by the question. This refers to what is called the *social desirability bias*. It means that people want to look good or proper in the eyes of the interviewer (recall symbolic interactionism here). Individuals may then exaggerate their behavior or that of their family toward the positive. (For the same reason of social acceptance, people might say that they drink two beers a day when they actually have five.) Therefore, there is quite a debate going on among sociologists concerning the impact of social desirability and memory or accurate recall on measures of religiosity (Hout and Greely, 1998; Woodberry, 1998). The reader should keep this methodological problem in mind when reading the following sections.

Demographic Factors Related to Religiosity

Each week, anywhere from 30 to 40 percent of Americans attend religious services, half the percentage of the 1940s. In a longitudinal study spanning the years from 1965 to 1982, Clydesdale (1997) found a one-third decline in frequency of attendance at religious services over that period. This decline in church or synagogue attendance is less pronounced in the South and is more widespread among Catholics than among other denominations (Hout and Greeley, 1998).

FAMILY RESEARCH 8.1

Large-Scale Canadian Survey Includes a Question on Religiosity

Statistics Canada conducts an annual General Social Survey from a sample of 10,000 Canadians. Since 1985, two questions about religion have been included. One question concerns religious affiliation and the other pertains to religiosity: It inquires about the frequency of attendance at religious services or meetings. Clark (1998) first controlled for or took into account income, family structure, education, age, sex, and employment because it is well known that these variables are related to various aspects of well-being. Then, with these controls in the background, the researchers found that persons who attend religious services or meetings weekly are half less likely to feel stressed and 1.5 times as likely to have a very happy marital relationship than those who do not attend religious services at all. Weekly attenders' marriages are also far more likely to last, regardless of which decade they were married. Overall, weekly attenders hold more traditional family values and adopt better health practices. For instance, in the 1996 survey, only 18 percent of weekly attenders aged 15 to 35 smoked, compared to 38 percent among those who never attended.

Worshiping together constitutes a form of social capital. Religious participation can also be the basis of a functional community, which contributes to child and adolescent socialization and buttresses the parental role.

Considering all the religious indicators together, but particularly attendance at services, women are more religious than men, the older more than the younger, "conservative" Protestants more than "liberal" Protestants, the married more than the single and divorced, southerners and midwesterners more than other regional groups, and whites who are not Latinos less than blacks and Latinos (Presser and Stinson, 1998). Among two-parent families, those where the wife is a homemaker or is employed only part time tend to attend religious services more frequently than families where the mother is employed full time (Hertel, 1995). It is not known whether this is a matter of beliefs or perhaps because housework needs to be done on weekends and thus competes with religious attendance in terms of time availability.

Among African-American families, religious attendance as well as participation in other religious activities are far more frequent than among non-Latino white families (Aldous and Ganey, 1999). Overall, there is a greater mixture of secular and religious functions in the black community (Lincoln and Mamiya, 1990). Indeed, black churches have been very active in addressing and redressing the social and political injustices suffered by their brethren. This closer linkage between blacks' everyday reality and organized religion probably explains African-American families' commitment to their churches (Taylor et al., 1996). Furthermore, their churches are the only institutions that blacks control entirely. African Americans have traditionally been prevented from fully participating in the economic, social, and political life of the majority society. Thus, their churches fulfill many functions for them that whites can normally find elsewhere. Segregation has therefore contributed to tie black families more closely to religion, and their churches have developed more culturally sensitive activities (Patillo-McCoy, 1998). For many African-American families, churches are the only center of an effective community to which they may have access.

Parents' and Children's Religiosity: The Socialization Aspect

Parents transmit their beliefs to their children by their teachings and their example (Myers, 1996). The family's church or synagogue attendance is itself a powerful socialization situation, and the example given by mothers who are warmly accepting toward their children is particularly powerful in the transmission of religious beliefs (Bao et al., 1999). So far, studies on the impact of parental religiosity on children have been carried out within the confines of one society, in this case the American society.

Secular Society, Religious Parents

Using a cross-cultural perspective, Kelley and De Graaf (1997) have classified 15 Western societies on the basis of the overall level of their citizens' religious beliefs and attendance. They ranked societies from most secular (East Germany and Norway) to most religious (Northern Ireland, Poland, and Ireland). The United States and Italy were just somewhat less religious than the last category. The researchers then examined the level of church attendance and religiosity of parents compared to that of their adult children. They found that in religious societies, people tend to report themselves to be religious even when their parents are not, thus showing the influence of the general cultural climate on socialization. However, even in these religious societies, adults were more religious when their parents also were (score of 85 out of a possible 100 in Figure 8.2) than when their parents were secular (score of 60). In a secular society,

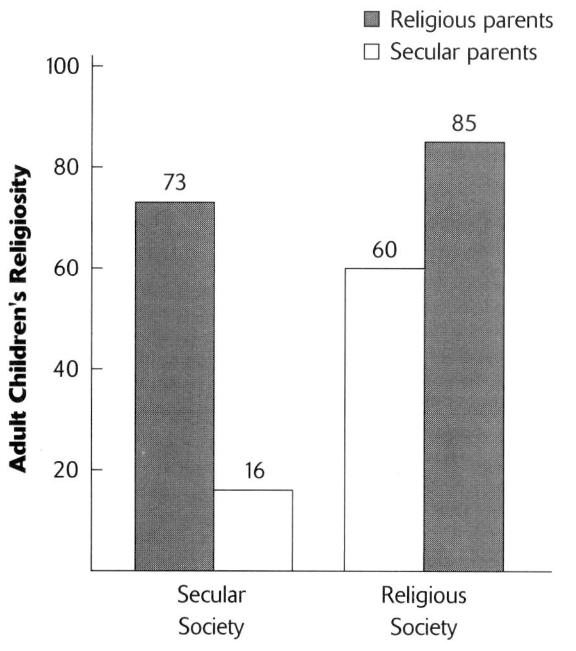

FIGURE 8.2

Adult Children's Religiosity by Society's and Parents' Religiosity

Source: Based on Kelley and De Graaf, 1997.

people report themselves to be less religious; nevertheless, adult children with devout parents were far more likely to be devout themselves (score of 73) than those whose parents were secular (score of 16).

In religious societies, religious parents' beliefs are simply reinforced by the general cultural climate. In a secular society, the familial climate is also quite successful at transmitting religious beliefs to children. However, religious parents have to be far more vigilant and invest far more effort in their example and their teachings than similar parents who live in a religious or fairly religious society. In secular societies, religious parents have to find means to insulate their children against the general secular climate; they are not always successful in this endeavor because there are too many social pressures against them.

In a religious society, secular parents probably do not see any harm in their children's religious participation and therefore do not discourage them from following cultural norms. But when both society and parents are secular, most children end up secular themselves. Thus, in a society such as the United States, which is considered to be quite religious, devout parents do not have to fight against a climate of secularism that is as strong as that of other societies. Nevertheless, because religion and state are separate, and because the media themselves are secular, American parents who are religious have to be fairly vigilant.

Factors in the Successful Transmission of Religiosity

Myers (1996) tried to see what characterized religious American parents who were the most successful at transmitting their beliefs to their children. Parental religiosity was measured in 1980, when the offspring were still living at home and thus under direct parental influence. In 1992, the offspring, who by then had reached adulthood, were interviewed. Myers's results showed that highly devout parents had children who, on average, were less similar to them than were the offspring of parents who were either moderately religious or not religious. In other words, the religious standards of many devout parents may have been too high to emulate, hence their children became only moderately religious later on, thus less similar to their parents on this dimension. A student describes a pertinent experience:

> *"One constant source of unhappiness throughout childhood and adolescence was religious observance. My parents are extremely religious, you call that 'holier-than-the-Pope.' I hated having to go to church weekly and say family prayers and having to go to religious school knowing full well that even the teachers thought that my parents were overdoing it. My parents and I fought constantly over religious issues and even theological matters. The end result is that I am religiously atheist."*

Myers (1996) also found that parents who both agreed on religious or secular beliefs had been more successful at transmitting them, which makes a great deal of sense because children learn better in a consistent environment. In families characterized by high marital happiness, offspring were more likely to resemble their parents in religious beliefs—whether these beliefs were orthodox, moderate, or lukewarm. This is related to other findings described in Chapter 10, indicating that a harmonious parental relationship constitutes a positive child socialization context.

Religiosity and Parenting Practices: Conservative Protestants

Conservative Protestants stress parental authority and child obedience more than other religious groups, perhaps with the exception of Muslims (Bartkowski and Ellison, 1995). They are more likely to want to keep their children within the faith than is the case among more liberal denominations (Danso, Hunsberger, and Pratt, 1997). Studies have also found that corporal punishment is used more in fundamentalist than in other families (Ellison and Sherkat, 1993). However, there is no evidence that conservative Protestant parents use harsh (as opposed to mild or moderate) corporal punishment more than parents from other religious orientations. Furthermore, there is little evidence that they disproportionately use it on adolescents (Ellison, 1996). This distinction is important because, when the *entire* parent/child relationship is considered, there is no evidence that occasional "fair" corporal punishment harms children developmentally (see Chapter 11). It is, however, more likely that corporal punishment may be detrimental to adolescents; it may be more harshly applied, is out of step with their developmental level, and may be indicative of a poor parent/child relationship.

Religiosity enhances well-being, improves the quality of the parent/child bond, and is related to authoritative parenting as well as adolescant competence (Gunnoe, Hetherington, and Reiss, 1999). Wilcox (1998) researched parenting books destined to conservative Protestants as well as childrearing practices found in the population at large. He discovered an ideology of love, warmth, and expressiveness in the parenting books. Then, he found that conservative Protestant parents were more likely to praise their children and give them physical affection, such as hugs, than other parents. Thus, on average, conservative Protestant parents use both corporal punishment *and* warm parenting. These parents seem to be more engaged in their children's lives and education as well as more expressive. This pattern of childrearing may, in turn, explain conservative Protestant adolescents' lower rates of risky behaviors. But otherwise, these parents may, on average, be more successful at socializing their children according to their values without a reduction in the youngsters' psychological well-being.

IS RELIGIOSITY FUNCTIONAL FOR THE FAMILY?

Does religious participation fulfill any function for family life and for the individuals concerned besides the transmission of beliefs and related behaviors? From a functionalist perspective, the question is: Is religion good for the family and its members? What does it do *for* them? Religious beliefs can be analyzed as a form of capital, **religious capital** as Iannaccone (1990) calls it, from which families can in theory draw cohesion as well as strength. Religious activities that include participation within a congregation may constitute a form of **social capital** in the guise of informal networks of social support (Ellison, 1994).

Religiosity Correlates with Well-Being

A substantial body of literature indicates that religious involvement and strength of beliefs are related to general feelings of well-being (Levin, 1994) as well as psychological and physical health, including lower adult mortality (Hummer et al., 1999). Religiosity provides internal coherence; it serves as an explanatory platform that enables individuals to make sense of everyday life and its adversities. It may help individuals integrate their personalities, give them guiding principles of action, and make them less individualistic and more duty bound. Religiosity serves as an internal and external **agent of social control** so that religious commitment lowers health risks, such as alcoholism, drug addiction, and precocious sexual activity, and may serve to prevent depression. In fact, there are indications that religiosity may deter drug use among adolescents, in part because religious adolescents are less likely to associate with peers who use drugs (Bahr et al., 1998). Church attendance itself, because of its social nature and the level of commitment that it requires, facilitates adjustment and also leads to positive evaluations of one's health (Broyles and Drenovsky, 1992).

Religious participation contributes to extend a family's social network and sources of social support (Ellison and George, 1994). Frequent churchgoers have somewhat larger non-kin social networks than others and enjoy more frequent person-to-person contacts. Furthermore, frequent churchgoers receive more help and report feeling cared for and valued (Ferraro and Koch, 1994). Therefore, religious participation becomes an important social resource or social capital for families:

> *"My mother is a concern to me at this stage because she is 65 and widowed and unemployed [but not poor]. But I think that her church activities and all the friendships she's made there help her a lot and will sustain her for some years to come. Sometimes I even go with her because I like meeting all these people of all ages. Anyway, my mother says that religion keeps her in good health and she is far from being a zealot."*

Religiosity Relates to Marital Stability

Adults who declare a religious affiliation are more likely to see marriage as a lifetime commitment than adults who profess no religious affiliation. They are also less likely to engage in extramarital sex (Treas and Giesen, 2000). Call and Heaton (1997) find that couples who regularly attend church together have a lower rate of divorce than those who attend infrequently or not at all. However, couples in which only one spouse attends are even more likely to divorce than couples who never attend. The latter finding can probably be explained in terms of religious similarity, or homogamy, described in Chapter 4. Couples who differ in religious matters may have one additional source of conflict. In contrast, couples who attend church together benefit from the sharing of a social and spiritual activity that reinforces their solidarity. They may also benefit from exposure to more *altruistic values* than nonchurchgoers, and this would in turn contribute to a less individualistic pattern of marital interaction (Pearce and Axinn, 1998):

> *"My problem right now is that my girlfriend is not religious and this worries me a lot because I know from my parents' experience that sharing beliefs and especially [going to church]. . . give a couple a lot in common. Above all I am con-*

cerned that my girlfriend may miss out on the importance of values that help keep a marriage together, like learning how to be committed and think in terms of the good of the relationship and not just about your own personal desires."

Similarly, mutually shared religious beliefs strengthen marital stability as religions tend to be pro-marriage rather than pro-divorce.

Amato and Rogers (1997) report that frequent church attendance may reduce the likelihood of divorce through a reduction in marital problems. Why would couples who attend church frequently experience fewer marital problems? Their explanation is congruent with the ones just presented. They reason that church attendance allows for the internalization and thus acceptance of norms of behavior that encourage couples to get along. They also refer to the social aspect of church attendance: It serves as a **support group** as well as a control group or an effective community. The sum of these studies therefore indicates a salutary effect of religiosity on the quality of the marital relationship as well as on the stability of the family unit.

Religiosity Supports the Parental Role

On another level, religious beliefs strengthen parents' involvement with their children, even when the latter become particularly difficult and stressful. Pearce and Axinn (1998:824) surmise that "exposure to religious themes such as tolerance, patience, and unconditional love" through religious activities constitutes a resource that helps parents and children maintain a good relationship. Mother/child similarity in religiosity strengthens the bond between the two.

Following a *family developmental perspective,* Stolzenberg, Blair-Loy, and Waite (1995) demonstrate that people often become more religious as they age. But the addition of children to the family unit further enhances this increase in religious participation (Nock, 1998c). In contrast, as childless married adults age, their religious participation does not increase to any great extent. One explanation for this finding may be that adults with children seek religious membership and participation in order to become better anchored in the community and as a means of social support in their parenting role. Along this line of reasoning, a student projects a greater role for religion later in her life:

"Right now I don't go to church often but I intend to become active again as soon as I have children, just as my parents did. I think that a bit of religion is very helpful to children: it teaches them values other than what they see on TV. The few times I go to church I am always struck by how civilized people behave and it gives you a warm feeling of humanity."

One could perhaps speculate that many parents *need* religion nowadays in order to feel more secure in their role in a very demanding and confusing world. Chaves (1991) points out that conventional families form the mainstay of organized religion. This would mean that parents may get gratification for their role within the context of religion, which would serve as a compensatory mechanism for the blaming and disempowerment they receive from so many quarters (see Chapter 15). Parents may also use religion as an agent of socialization and as a source of support for their children.

Limitations of Religion for Nontraditional Families

Organized religions have been culturally developed by men several millennia or centuries ago and support gender stratification (Sered, 1999). It follows that families headed by women and men who have a heightened sense of inequalities based on gender may not find spiritual sustenance and stability in religion as much as do other families. Furthermore, most religions frown on nonmarital forms of sexuality, and individuals who regularly attend religious services tend to disapprove of nonmarital sex (Thornton, Axinn, and Hill, 1992). They also often strongly disapprove of homosexuality.

Therefore, while faith and religiosity are very functional to the faithful's well-being on many levels, they are less functional for the well-being of those who engage in nontraditional forms of family life, such as families headed by same-sex couples. Religious communities by and large exclude them so that these families are deprived of a powerful instrument of child socialization and a powerful source of family stability. There are indications that many gays and lesbians are deeply religious but fear rejection, as explained in a student autobiography:

> *"My lover and I both come from religious families and this has probably contributed to our mutual attraction. We're basically both moderately religious but we can't go to church. I suppose we could go separately and I could even join the choir . . . and he might volunteer in the child care. But we can't do this because we'd stick out like sore thumbs and we might even be discouraged from participating. We could go with my parents but what if they were ostracized as a result? I'm sure that there must be other gays out there who are religious but Bob and I don't mix much with the gay community because we're a monogamous couple."*

(It is probably not a coincidence that this couple is planning to adopt children; their overall values are mainstream.) In many areas, various congregations are opening their community to homosexuals (see Ammerman's Chapter 4, 1997). But overall, it can be concluded that religious establishments do not serve the entire spectrum of families equally well.

CONCLUSIONS: THE BALANCING ACT OF FAMILY FUNCTIONS

Children and adolescents served by educational facilities and child care centers come to school from their families and return to their families when the school day is over. Children serve as a link between the educational and familial systems. Their parents must manage this linkage and remain vigilant so that the best interest of their child is well served. In particularly deficient schools, parents have to supplement their children's education. When schools harbor a critical mass of antisocial and aggressive children, parents have to step in, if they can, to protect and even shelter their children. Thus, although schools have taken over some of the functions previously fulfilled by families, schools have also forced an extension of family functions into the public domain. Furthermore, depending on family structure and place within the social class system, schools create a host of demands on parents.

Thus, to return to the discussions in Chapter 2, the educational system often expands family functions and may even burden the family system. For families that are religiously oriented, however, religion seems to offer them support in their socialization role—support of the parental role and support for adolescents and youths who wish to lead a life devoid of lifestyle risks. Therefore, at least for religious families, the practice of their faith generally strengthens their ability to fulfill their functions in a society that often provides pressures against this goal.

SUMMARY

1. After parents, schools are a main agent of child socialization. Children today begin school earlier, and for many, this includes child care other than maternal. Among the several types of nonmaternal child care are centers or minischools, a woman who takes in one or several children in her home, relative and father care, and a nanny. Poor-quality care has been related to disadvantages in cognition, language development, as well as social and emotional adjustment. However, care in quality centers does not generally result in negative outcomes that persist. But questions still remain concerning potentially negative effects of very long hours, too much peer contact, and too little interaction with adults. Child care availability, affordability, and quality are key ingredients in contemporary children's development and in their parents' well-being. Head Start types of programs benefit poor children living in disadvantaged areas, as they prepare them for school, both cognitively and behaviorally. It is suggested that such programs be expanded.
2. Parental involvement in their children's education contributes to school success. However, parents' social class largely determines the extent as well as the effectiveness of their involvement. Parental social capital benefits children's access to social as well as material resources that help them increase their adaptation to school. Overall, children from higher SES families do better academically, as do children who attend schools with greater percentages of students from higher SES backgrounds (a critical mass). Disadvantaged parents value education as much as others but practical problems often prevent this valuation from translating into higher aspirations and then achievement for their children. Incompatibility between family life and school routines often prevents children from adapting successfully at school. The summer activities of low-income children are often incompatible with learning, and they usually return to school even farther behind higher-income students. Family and school compatibility is particularly important for Native children in the guise of tribally controlled schools.
3. Children who live in disadvantaged areas are at risk of attending schools of inferior quality. These children then have high rates of school dropout, do not learn basic skills, and are not adequately prepared for college or employment. Their

families can be so segregated that they do not even realize the extent of the lack of progress in their children's education.

4. Private schools are selected by parents who can afford them and who expect that their values will be reinforced. Private schools, particularly religious ones, constitute an effective community that enhances children's academic abilities. Home schooling is another system that parents turn to in order to ensure the passage of their values to their children as well as their educational success. It is a growing phenomenon, and official concerns for the children's well-being and academic success do not seem to be warranted.
5. Religion plays an important role in the lives of many American families. The most commonly used indicator of religiosity is church or temple attendance. Each week, anywhere from 30 to 40 percent of Americans attend religious services, down by half since the 1940s. African Americans are generally more religious by this definition, in part because their churches are very relevant to their daily lives.
6. Parents transmit their religious beliefs to their children by their teachings and example, but the overall religious climate in a society also contributes to child socialization in this respect. Parents are more successful at passing on their beliefs within the context of a supportive religious climate. Parents' marital happiness may also be a factor contributing to the transmission of their religious values to their children. Still in the domain of socialization, conservative Protestant parents use both corporal punishment of young children and warm behaviors more than other parents. Their children, on average, engage less in risky behaviors. Overall, religious involvement seems functional in terms of health, psychological well-being, marital stability and happiness, as well as child socialization. Religiosity supports the parental role. However, religions are generally not supportive of nontraditional families.
7. While the educational system often increases the functions that families have to fulfill, the religious system may offer a supportive framework for the fulfillment of family functions.

KEY CONCEPTS AND THEMES

Agent of social control, p. 232
Bilingualism, p. 219
Consequences of child care, pp. 212, 214
Corporal punishment, p. 231
Critical mass, p. 223
Cultural and language factors, p. 219
Extension of the family, p. 224
Family developmental perspective, p. 223
Family functions, p. 234
Family and school compatibility, p. 219
Functional community, pp. 219, 224
Head Start programs, p. 214
Home schooling, p. 225
Indicator, p. 226
Marital stability, p. 232
Marital status, p. 219
Nontraditional families, p. 234
Parental involvement, p. 216
Poor schools, p. 221
Poverty, p. 218
Quality of child care, p. 211
Religiosity, p. 226
Religious capital, p. 231
Resources theory, p. 217
Social capital, p. 231
Social class, p. 217
Social desirability bias, p. 227

STUDY AND REVIEW QUESTIONS

1. What are some methodological difficulties involved in the study of the effect of child care on child development?
2. How can early childhood education for children in low-income families affect their entire life course?
3. What are the main family variables related to children's school success?
4. Utilize resources theory to explain the linkage between social class and children's progress through school.
5. Discuss the impact of isolation and inequality of segregated minority students on their school expectations and performance.
6. Use private schools to illustrate how educational institutions reproduce families' class position.
7. Why do you think that school officials and even some researchers are worried about home schooling? (Note: The question is *why* they are worried, *not what* they are worried about.)
8. With the help of research results, explain factors that contribute to parents' ability to transmit their religious beliefs to their children.
9. Studies show that religiously conservative parents use corporal punishment more than other parents. Does this mean that their children will grow up with more problems? Justify your answer on the basis of the research presented.
10. What is the relationship between religiosity and marital stability?
11. Overall, is religiosity beneficial to families? Explain your answer.
12. How does religion relate to family functions?

SUGGESTED READINGS

Dryfoos, J. G. 1994. *Full-service schools: A revolution in health and social services for children, youth, and families.* San Francisco: Jossey-Bass. This book provides a description and an analysis of programs that can be included in neighborhood schools to meet children's and families' educational, social, and health needs.

Entwisle, D. R., Alexander, K. L., and Olson, L. S. 1997. *Children, schools, and inequality.* Boulder, CO: Westview. The researchers marshal an impressive array of data to study the effect of schooling on children as well as the effect of social inequalities (parents' social class, for instance) on children's progress and test scores.

Houseknecht, S. K., and Parkhurst, J. G. (Eds.) 2000. *Family, religion and social change in diverse societies.* New York: Oxford University Press. This collection of articles focuses on religion and the family in various cultural contexts of social change. It includes sections on gender as well as economic factors.

Lareau, A. 1989. *Home advantage: Social class and parental intervention in elementary education.*New York: Falmer. The author, an educational sociologist, reports the results of her qualitative research on parents from varying social class levels in order to study the impact of social class on parental involvement in children's education.

Steinberg, L., Brown, B. B., and Dornbusch, S. M. 1996. *Beyond the classroom: Why school reform has failed and what parents need to do.* New York: Simon & Schuster.

These scholars review cross-cultural information to refute certain myths concerning American education as compared to education in other countries. One of the provocative questions raised is the lack of teenagers' investment in their own educational process.

SUGGESTED WEBLINKS

National Alliance for Safe Schools focuses on school safety and antiviolence programs. This website provides practical as well as research information. **<http://www.safeschools.org>**

National Child Care Information Center has a website sponsored by the U.S. government to provide mechanisms for enhancing the quality of child care. It offers comprehensive resources for parents and children. **<http://nccic.org>**

National Parents and Teachers Association is a policy-oriented volunteer organization with the goal of fostering children's and adolescents' education. **<http://www.pta.org>**

PART 3

Family Relationships

Family relationships are examined within a largely interactional-transactional perspective that includes strong elements of gender-role analysis as well as some aspects of behavior genetics. In other words, although the emphasis is on interactions, it is again obvious that families, in their intimate relationships, are impacted by their genetic inheritance and environment. The latter includes the society's gender stratification.

Chapter 9 describes family developmental stages as they mesh in with the life course of its individual members.

Chapter 10 examines the diversity and dynamics of marital and partner relationships.

Chapter 11 focuses on the parent/child relationship and parenting across the life span.

Chapter 12 looks at sibling relationships and situations in a variety of familial contexts. This topic also allows us to study how differences and similarities between siblings arise, affording us a more in-depth understanding of the complementary roles of genes and the environment.

CHAPTER 9

Family Developmental Stages

OUTLINE

The Gendered Social Construction of Parenthood
Motherhood
Fatherhood

The Prebirth Stage

The Infant's Arrival
Among Married Couples
In Other Family Structures
Young Unmarried Mothers
Mature, Older Unmarried Mothers
Same-Sex Couples
Delayed Parenthood
Generational Compressions and Successions

Subsequent Stages
The Early Years
Parents' Transition to a Second Child
The Older Child's Transitions
Parents' Transition to Child Schooling
Pets as New Family Members
The Adolescent Years
The Empty Nest: Or Is It?

The Grandparent Stage
Grandparenting as a Role
Grandparents Who Provide Child Care
Grandparents Who Raise Grandchildren
Effects on Grandparents
Effects on Grandchildren
Grandparenting after Divorce
Stepgrandparenting

The Death of Adults' Parents

Conclusions: Family Development in Context

Summary
Key Concepts and Themes
Study and Review Questions
Suggested Readings
Suggested Weblinks

James and Heather Austin, born in 1918 and 1920, respectively, married in 1938 after an unplanned pregnancy. They had four children within eight years and barely made ends meet; these were hard times. James, a construction worker after the war, spent most of his free time playing cards with his drinking buddies. The couple fought a lot and eventually grew apart, and Heather was lonely. James never allowed her to work for pay. The eldest two children left home to get away from it all when they were ages 16 and 18 and, by their sixties, had accumulated a grand total of seven divorces and six children who followed the same pattern. The youngest two children stayed in school somewhat longer, married later, and, by the year 2000, had two children each. Now in their fifties, they remain close to their mother, Heather, and help her with daily chores so she can remain at home in her modest bungalow. She largely depends on social security payments for support: James died 10 years earlier of lung cancer. Heather rarely sees her eldest daughter, still divorced; her eldest son died at age 60 in a car accident. Heather's life has been a difficult one, with few domestic pleasures except for the relative success in life of her two youngest children and their own children.

Walter and Marian McCall (also born in 1918 and 1920, respectively) were high school sweethearts but waited until the end of World War II to marry. He then completed his college education while she contributed to their support as a surgical nurse. They had their first child in 1948, when Walter was age 30 and Marian age 28, which, in those days, was considered late for a first birth. Their second child was born in 1952. The couple was companionable and happy together. When their younger child was 6 years old, Marian returned to college, after which she was promoted to nursing supervisor in a large hospital. Neither children were in any hurry to leave home and attended college locally. The son became an engineer and the daughter a pediatrician. They had two children each, both when they were in their early thirties. Walter and Marian retired, Walter first, and Marian at age 70. Both are in good physical health, although Marian suffers from arthritis and cannot do as much housework as before. But Walter has always contributed his share and now a housekeeper comes in three times a week. They have traveled together around the world and, to this day, socialize extensively with their four grandchildren.

The two couples in these fictive vignettes lived through the same historical periods, including the Great Depression and World War II. But their families' development had little in common and their personal life courses diverged because they came from dissimilar backgrounds, married and started their families at different ages, and followed divergent educational paths. Different vignettes could have shown the life course of two families from two different time periods, in which case we would have seen another set of differences emerge—this time based on the effect of cohort or time period. Victoria Leeds, in Chapter 2, would be a relevant example.

Ideally, within the life course perspective, family stages are studied in relation to parents' chronological age and to the stage in their relationship and work history, for instance. The introductory vignettes illustrate two different outcomes, in part related to these connections between a person's age as well as education and the timing of family transitions. The life course approach also requires that the interweaving of family transitions with the life trajectory of each member be analyzed within its historical context (Hareven, 1994b). That is, as the culture and the economic situation of the decades change, so do the roles attached to certain family transitions, such as marriage, and especially the timing of these transitions as well as their sequencing.

The precursors to family development include dating, cohabiting, and marrying. This is what we referred to as *couple* formation in Chapter 4. Then, in Chapter 5, we saw that there are different ways of starting a *family*. In this chapter, we focus on the family from first pregnancy all the way to the death of aged grandparents.

THE GENDERED SOCIAL CONSTRUCTION OF PARENTHOOD

One of the most important influences on individuals' experiences of family development stems from the gendered social construction of parenthood. The overall social stratification by gender dictates that mothers and fathers fulfill different functions in their respective parenting roles. As we see in the next chapter, the household division of labor is largely unequal and gives far more flexibility to fathers and husbands in the activities they choose to engage in at home. However, changes in the economy and at the cultural level have considerably altered the framework within which fathers and mothers interpret their roles.

Motherhood

Probably the most salient metamorphosis that occurs in the formation of a new nuclear family is the transformation of a girl or a woman into a mother. Motherhood is not only a biological state; it is, above all, a social and cultural phenomenon. Motherhood is socially constructed to serve the culture of the time and the economic system of a society. It is also defined according to the prevailing definition of childhood and of children's needs and roles within a particular economic system. As we have seen in Chapter 2, the "nature" of childhood is socially constructed and thus differs from culture to culture and from century to century (Prout and James, 1990). Parenting, and particularly mothering, is defined along with the nature of childhood, as the "needs" of children differ culturally (Ambert, 1994b).

For instance, in the United States, it is believed that small children need to be talked to, given affection, allowed some autonomy, and prepared for school (LeVine, 1994). As well, their self-esteem has to be nurtured. Such beliefs about children's needs place specific demands on how women mother (Hays, 1996). In other societies, such as the Efe foragers and the Lese farmers of Zaire, small children are defined as needing assistance from older children, needing to learn how to help in and around the house, and having to learn to get along with others (Morelli and Tronick, 1991). Such needs place fewer demands on mothers.

Once there is agreement in a society on what is "in the best interest of the child," what mothers should do and should be is implicitly and explicitly constructed. For instance, LeVine (1994) has found that the Gusii in East Africa, an agrarian people, focus on the health and survival of their infants because of high mortality. The role of caregivers is accordingly scripted around child safety and feeding. Notions pertaining to the development of self-esteem, attachment, and intellectual abilities simply do not exist. Thus, the role description of Efe, Lese, and Gusii mothers does not include activities and concerns about these aspects of child development. For instance, Whiting and Edwards (1988:94) have found that, in some societies, mothers initiate very few nurturing acts, such as cuddling; they leave these aspects of child care to older children. This observation led Whiting and Edwards to suggest that current stereotypes regarding the nature of the maternal role should be revised.

Furthermore, in Western societies, it is believed that mothers are absolutely essential for children's well-being, and that women have a natural, rather than learned, aptitude for mothering (Eyer, 1992). Although it may be that mothers are indeed the most important persons and parents in a majority of children's lives in modern, urban, and technological societies, this should not be taken to mean that *one* mother is a necessity of human nature. Indeed, the Western focus on individual mothers at the core of children's development is not universal. Many anthropologists question it as an *ethnocentric* phenomenon (LeVine, 1990). That is, motherhood is defined according to Western criteria. The reality is that multiple mothering and even **multiple parenting** are in the majority in many agrarian and gathering societies such as the Efe of Zaire (Morelli and Tronick, 1991). This means that several women in a small community share in the care and supervision of children (Rogoff et al., 1991); all the members of the village are responsible for all the children; older siblings or other youngsters are often small children's caregivers as well as their main source of psychological comfort and discomfort (Harkness and Super, 1992). To some extent, one encounters multiple parenting among African Americans (Collins, 1992) and even more so in some Caribbean communities. The care of small children by older ones was widely practiced in black families during slavery (Alston, 1992).

In contrast, most Western societies require **intensive mothering**—mothering that is expert-guided, is labor intensive at the middle-class level, and emphasizes the child's psychological development, particularly the promotion of self-esteem. Hays (1996) discusses the cultural contradictions of what is involved in this type of motherhood. She points out that this social construct requires mothers to expand a tremendous amount of time, energy, and money in raising their children. Yet, in expensive Western economies, two salaries are often necessary, so mothers can no longer afford to stay home and care for their children 24 hours a day. Besides, there is the fact that children do not need mothers at home because they are in school (Eyer, 1997).

Thus, at the same time that the economy propels men and women into an ever-competitive workplace, it also requires of these parents that children be raised intensively at the psychological level and prepared to become efficient workers later on. The end result is that the requirements of the current social constructions of motherhood and childhood compete. Furthermore, this cultural mothering perpetuates outdated assumptions regarding the "proper" relationship between mothers and children (Hays, 1998:782).

Another anomaly inherent to the social construction of intensive motherhood in a society where women are employed resides in the division of labor between fathers and mothers. As we see in the next chapter, even a mother who has a career as demanding as that of her husband spends more time in child care and housework than he does (Ferree, 1991). This division of labor includes 24-hour-a-day maternal availability if the child is ill or needs special attention. Even the tasks of hiring nannies or locating day care facilities usually are a woman's responsibility. Mothers also worry more about their children (Hays, 1996:104) and, as we see in Chapter 15, are blamed when a child "goes wrong" or develops problems. Children themselves internalize the cultural definition of motherhood and behave accordingly: They demand more of their mothers than of anyone else in society, including their fathers.

Therefore, the transition to parenthood presents a complex situation for both parents, however much a child is wanted. But this transition affects a **woman's role** in terms of daily activities and preoccupations far more than a man's role. A new father retains his primary identity as a worker, whereas a new mother acquires another identity that may supersede identities that she has devoted years to acquire by going to professional school, for instance. No matter how successful a woman is in her career, she may be ultimately judged by her maternal role, at least while her children grow up.

Fatherhood

The role of fathers is changing. Although fathers are still defined as the chief breadwinners in two-parent families, the reality that mothers contribute heavily to the family's economy contradicts this traditional social construction and brings considerable unease among a segment of men. Thus, there has been a shift in the social construction of fatherhood, in great part as a result of women's increased participation in the labor force (Lamb, 1997). The ideal father is now often described as the one who is involved with his children and shares household responsibilities with the mother (Wilkie, 1993). But reality clashes with this cultural shift, as paternal involvement in children's daily lives remains comparatively low (Acock and Demo, 1994).

Furthermore, a dual practice of fatherhood exists: one for intact families and one for what are called absent fathers. The more remote the *legal* paternity linkage to children, the less involved fathers are. Most are less involved after divorce, even though they may share custody, and are even less involved when the custody is not shared (Seltzer, 1998). When fathers remarry and have other biological children, their first set of children living elsewhere is often displaced or, as Cooksey and Craig (1998) put it, "crowded out." Finally, as seen in Chapter 5, men who father children out-of-wedlock, especially when they have not lived with the mother, are the least involved of all parents.

Therefore, it can be said that the male peer group and fathers themselves encourage involvement with and support of their children when the familial context is a *traditional* one and a fully legal one. Thus, the social practice of fathering and fathers' self-definitions, which influence their level of involvement with their children and even with their children's mothers, suffers from a double standard: one for traditional paternity within the two-parent family versus one for "new" paternities after divorce, in cohabitation, or out-of-wedlock. This double standard is problematic in view of the increase in alternate lifestyles, such as cohabitation and single parenting. "New" paternity includes same-sex male couples: Will they also become more or less delinquent fathers when their union dissolves?

Generally, mothers maintain a high level of emotional investment with children, even during marital conflict and divorce. In contrast, the role of fathers is less "scripted" (Parke, 1995) and is consequently more influenced by situational variables. Thus, **fathers' investment** in children decreases as fathers' relations with mothers deteriorate (Belsky et al., 1991). Thus, mothers constitute a key context for fathering. Husbands who perceive that their wives have confidence in their parenting ability are far more involved in the care of their children (McBride and Rane, 1998). These results clearly

Fathers' involvement in children's education is related to positive child outcomes. However, in general, fathers still spend relatively little time, compared to mothers, in character building and monitoring of child activities.

show another set of differences between motherhood and fatherhood. The latter depends to a large extent on the relationship with the children's mother. In contrast, motherhood exists on its own: A good relationship with the father helps, but it does not determine the presence or absence of mothering. Fathering is "a more contextually sensitive process than mothering" (Doherty, Kouneski, and Erickson, 1998:207).

This phenomenon is not a North American aberration. Throughout history, men have favored the children of their favorite wives or even mistresses. In polygamous societies, men prefer the sons of a favorite wife. This wife is then in a good position to see to it that scarce resources are bestowed on her children. Her sons receive more affection, attention, and wealth. This is particularly evident when polygamous kings choose a successor.

Much media attention has been devoted to "house husbands," or fathers who stay home and care for their children. However, this occurrence is, in reality, more one where mothers and fathers share child care because both parents have different work shifts (Casper, 1997). Furthermore, fathers are more likely to take care of their children when their own job schedule allows it (Brayfield, 1995). Casper and O'Connell (1998) also document that, in periods of recession, even though both spouses may still be employed, the specter of economic insecurity leads couples to economize: Child care by fathers in one form of economy.

THE PREBIRTH STAGE

Life during the months preceding the first baby's birth or adoption differs from family to family because there is such a wide variety of life course situations involved. The following prebirth structural arrangements are presented in their order of frequency in the population, first for married couples and then for other types of family structure.

For married couples, I first follow the typology derived from the Cowans' (1997) longitudinal study of couples experiencing their first pregnancy. This typology, illustrated in Figure 9.1, consists of the following situations:

Married Couples

- Married couples who have planned the pregnancy. Cowan and Cowan (1997) report that 50 percent of their couples were "planners." Both spouses welcome the pregnancy.
- Married couples who are expecting as a result of an unplanned pregnancy which they accept (acceptance of fate). Also included are ambivalent couples who are uncertain as to whether they want to pursue the pregnancy. For both sets of prospective parents, the pregnancy is an unscheduled or off-time event. One-third of the Cowans' sample fell in this combined category.
- Married couples who experience serious disagreement about the pregnancy. One spouse is enthusiastic or determined to have the baby, while the other accepts it reluctantly in order to save the relationship. Some 17 percent of the Cowans' couples belonged to this category.
- Married couples who are expecting as a result of various fertility methods, including in vitro fertilization and surrogate motherhood, or who are still in the process of negotiating such births. These couples, had they been included in the Cowans' sample, would have fallen under the rubric of "planners."
- Married couples who are awaiting the arrival of an adoptive child, a stage that may last many months and even years.

Cohabiting Couples

- Cohabiting couples may fall in any one of the first three preceding categories of expectant married couples but would be less likely to be planners. The union may be more or less stable and plans for marriage may be under way. Some of these

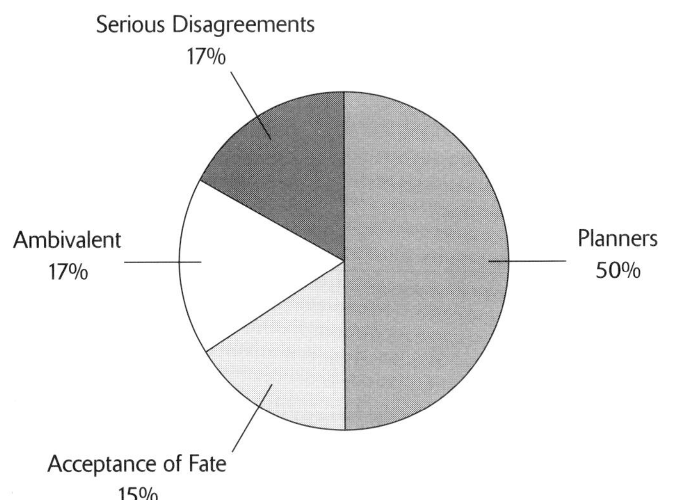

FIGURE 9.1

A Typology of Married Couples Expecting Their First Child

Source: Based on Cowan and Cowan, 1997, 1998.

cohabitors have been married before and one already has at least one child from the previous union.

- Lesbian couples who are expecting via childbirth or adoption.
- Gay men who are expecting via adoption or surrogacy.

Single Women

- Single women who become pregnant accidentally. This category is varied because it includes women who subsequently marry the child's father, others who remain with their parents, and yet others who will be on their own. Poverty is a frequent accompaniment of this transition.
- Single women who have planned a pregnancy in the hope of marrying the father.
- Single women, generally over 30 years old, who have planned a pregnancy or an adoption on their own.

This simplified classification represents a vast array of family planning activities and adaptations to the forthcoming birth or arrival of a baby. Therefore, the mental health consequences and the readiness to parent vary. Among couples, the conjugal relationship may be weakened or strengthened as a result of the pregnancy (Cowan and Cowan, 1998). The baby then arrives in a family that is prepared or ill prepared, enthusiastic or reluctant, harmonious or conflictual, well adapted or weakened by stressors. The prebirth level of readiness, in turn, affects how parents relate to each other and to the baby as well as to the baby's subsequent development, particularly when the infant is frail (Belsky and Kelly, 1994).

THE INFANT'S ARRIVAL

The infant's arrival, which constitutes the real beginning of a family, similarly differs in terms of impact and adaptation, depending on the marital status, the gender combination, and the number of available parents.

Among Married Couples

Longitudinal studies that have followed couples through the transition to parenthood find that about 50 percent of spouses experience stress and many experience some disenchantment with their marriage (Cowan and Cowan, 1992). In a society where companionship, intimacy, and romantic love are so highly prized, the infant unavoidably places a certain strain on these aspects, at least temporarily. During the pregnancy, the couple's sexual relations are less frequent at that stage (Call, Sprecher, and Schwartz, 1995). Similarly, couples experience a steep decline in joint activities that lasts throughout early childhood (Kurdek, 1993b). The demands of child care, particularly in the middle of the night, exert a physical toll; fatigue may be the norm rather than the exception for several months, as discovered by this student:

> *"Right now it is difficult for me to concentrate on anything with the baby. I think I had not expected to be so tired. I thought it would be a cinch because I am young but I just wasn't prepared for all that is involved in the care of a baby even though I had read books before. My husband was even less well prepared than*

me so you can imagine that the house is one big mess right now and I am very discouraged. When she starts crying I could lie down and cry with her. I just don't have any energy left. I can't imagine how we had this idea of having a second one soon after."

The level of adaptation required of parents in general is underestimated. This includes couples who were well aware of potential stressors ahead. Obviously, the simple shift from that of being a couple to becoming a family with a tiny infant is not without inherent problems. This transition is smoother for couples who were well adjusted before and for those who had planned the timing of their family. Variables that are particularly important are a husband's expression of fondness for his wife, his attitude of "we-ness," and the private, psychological time the couple retains (Gottman, 1998).

In the Cowans' study (1997:24), "the couples who stayed together but remained childless showed remarkable stability over the 7 years of the study in all five aspects of life that we assessed. By contrast, the couples who became parents described significant and often unexpected or disturbing shifts in every domain." By the time the children had reached age 5, 20 percent of the couples had separated or divorced. These divorces cannot, however, be attributed to the transition to parenthood. In fact, becoming parents was related to a lower divorce rate: 50 percent of the couples who had remained childless during the seven years of the study had divorced. Either being parents reduces the risk of divorcing (social causation) or couples who decide to have children have a more stable relationship to begin with (social selection). There is actually evidence supporting both explanations.

New mothers often wish that their husbands participated more in child care than they do (Belsky and Kelly, 1994). In a longitudinal study of couples who were interviewed the first two months after their weddings and then two years later, preferences about the division of child care tasks were evaluated and compared over time. Johnson and Huston (1998) found that, when wives' love was strong, their preferences changed in the direction of their husbands', but husbands' love for their wives did not translate into similar accommodating changes in their preferences. Thus, the traditional social constructions of motherhood and fatherhood are maintained throughout the transition to parenting by the emotional work that mothers put in.

For most women today, the arrival of the first baby interrupts their employment trajectory. Mothers stay at home after the birth for varying lengths of time. In another longitudinal pre- and after-birth study of couples, Volling and Belsky (1993) found that mothers who returned to work within the first three months after birth had higher levels of education, more prestigious occupations, and larger prenatal incomes than mothers who delayed returning to work. They stressed their career development and enjoyment as reasons for returning to work more often than those who were less educated. Nevertheless, 64 percent of all women who were back in their jobs so soon also mentioned that it was important for their family's financial stability that they return to work.

In Other Family Structures

The family development literature has largely focused on the two-parent unit, including families who divorce and then remarry. We know very little about the transition into parenthood in other types of family structure.

Young Unmarried Mothers

Even though much has been written about unmarried teen mothers, little is known of their family development except in terms of whether they stay in school, drop out, return later, go on welfare, and marry. And, of course, even less is known about this transition for the fathers. But the majority of women who are single mothers are not teenagers; yet even less is said about their own transition into parenthood.

Many young mothers at first bask under the sun of family support and love for the baby, peer support or curiosity, as well as the young father's temporary interest. For many, the baby represents someone who will love *them* unconditionally (Carlip, 1995). As well, for many mothers, including single ones, becoming a parent represents a transition away from the manner in which they themselves were mothered. Both Carlip (1995) and Higginson (1998) have found that teen mothers often wanted to be very different from their parents. They wanted to be more permissive and described their own parents as too restrictive. Others, however, felt that their mothers had neglected them or had not paid sufficient attention to them. Either of these themes should herald a great deal of mother/daughter tension among teens who continue living at home and who may be dependent on their families for support (Burton, 1996b).

For many teen mothers, the transition into motherhood is overlaid with the usual transitions that adolescents in this society make as they become more individuated from their parents. Teen mothers thus experience a double transition. Based on the literature we have reviewed in Chapter 5, it is more likely that many teen mothers had long emancipated themselves from their parents and had done this earlier than comparable girls who led a more normative lifestyle. This premature disaffection to parental rules may actually have been one of the immediate causes of their becoming sexually active and pregnant.

Young single mothers begin life transitions earlier than older mothers and experience more life transitions than mothers in two-parent families. For instance, single mothers are more likely to cohabit. Cohabitations are more transitory, so that these women may go through a series of household formation transitions. The interim between cohabitations may bring a return to poverty. Both the mother's and the child's life course is affected as transitions succeed each other. Until now, young mothers had a second child sooner than older mothers (Maynard, 1997): Theirs has been an accelerated fertility trajectory, although recent trends indicate a decrease in this respect. These young mothers can expect a different employment trajectory than mothers who return to childbearing at a later age. Teen mothers who have only one child are less poor later on than adolescent mothers who have subsequent children, even as adults (Hoffman and Foster, 1997).

Little is known about how women who mother on their own most of their lives and then become **single grandmothers** experience their personal development, identity, and old age. Their personal transitions may be far more linked to those of their children, grandchildren, and even great-grandchildren than is the case for mothers whose fertility transitions occurred later on in life and even mothers who were young at first birth but spent most of their lives with a husband. The phenomenon of widespread early mothering among some segments of the population, particularly among African-American women, originated in the 1960s. A sufficient number of such mothers has accumulated so that more research could be done.

Mature, Older Unmarried Mothers

For the mature single woman who is well established and has *planned* the pregnancy or the adoption, the arrival of a baby may actually require less adaptation than is the case among couples. To begin with, there is no conjugal relationship that needs readjustment and the household division of labor does not become less egalitarian as generally occurs among couples after the baby's birth. The older single mother may already have adjusted to a larger dwelling, have made contact with potential child caregivers, have assured herself of social support from friends and parents, and may expect far more difficulties than a couple generally does (Miller, 1992). Consequently, the mature single mother may actually find that the difficulties she encounters are less numerous than what she had been warned against. A mature student well illustrates this situation—two years earlier, she had adopted two infant girls abroad, aged 1 month and 11 months, respectively:

> *"Right now is the happiest stage in my life [around age 35]. Everything is perfect. I have returned to school and I am completing the requirements so that I can apply for a M.A. program. As I mentioned before, I have inherited quite a lot of money from my great aunt and that's what allowed me to fulfill my life-long dream of having children. I had it all planned and everything is working like a charm even though everyone had warned me that I would have a difficult time, you know, the usual b.s. But I have a wonderful day care and a nice elderly woman who babysits when I go out, which is rarely. I don't even have to ask anything from my parents, which they were afraid would happen I am sure, so seeing this they now volunteer to help me out. . . . Sure the girls have cried as is usual but I was ready and I wanted them so much that for me it's simply living in a dream."*

The older single mother encounters fewer structural family complications than couples do for the simple reason that her family structure is less complex: The parental subsystem consists of herself and she does not have to share her parenting role. She may therefore experience fewer internal pressures than couples do, although external pressures on family boundaries may be greater. But she may welcome the latter when they result in instrumental help and social support.

Same-Sex Couples

It would be interesting to know more about the adjustment process that takes place among lesbian couples when one of the two has a child. There are both potential structural advantages and ambiguities in this situation compared to heterosexual families. In terms of advantages, much evidence suggests that the role of the father presents a structural problem these days. This is a pitfall that lesbian couples avoid, because they can more easily share roles (Koepke, Hare, and Moran, 1992).

Two potential structural ambiguities exist in same-sex-parent families. First, the child is the biological child of only one of the two women, although creative alternatives, such as the insemination of one woman with her partner's brother's semen, alleviate this biological ambiguity (Stacey, 1998). The second structural ambiguity resides in the fact that two persons play the same role toward the child: Both are mothers, regardless of the terminology used in each household. The biological mother may be the "mom" and her companion the "other mother" or called by her first name

(Nelson, 1996). The same structural problem arises in the case of gay couples: Both are father figures.

Although a child may prefer his or her father or mother in a heterosexual arrangement, the less favored parent may not be much affected by this preference, as many explanations based on gender roles exist. Fathers who realize that their children are more attached to their mothers, as is generally the case, can easily accept this situation as a normal outcome of the mothers' primary caregiver role (Noller, 1994). But this rationalization may not be available in a same-sex-parent family. Thus, the potential for jealousy exists. This potential may differ in gay and lesbian couples.

Delayed Parenthood

One interesting aspect of the life course perspective is that it allows for the simultaneous consideration of a family's life trajectory with that of the individuals involved. This is further illustrated later with the help of Figure 9.2 on p. 254. Most families go through the transition into parenthood, but not all parents are at the same stage of their own lives when it occurs. On average, adults now have their first child four years later than in the 1970s. The proportion of women who have their first child in their thirties has increased spectacularly. In 1970, for instance, only 1 first birth in 25 was occurring to a woman between the ages of 30 and 35. Now, 1 in 5 first births is to a woman aged 30 to 35. Women aged 35 and older contributed to 1 out of 101 first births in 1970; this ratio is now 1 in 18 (Ventura et al., 1995). The phenomenon of delayed parenthood is far more common among white and Asian nationalities than among other ethnic groups.

In the *traditional* life course theories, adults who have their first child before age 30 are considered **"on time,"** whereas those who are older or very young are considered **"off time."** Consequently, concerns are raised about the potential for a more difficult adjustment among those who are off time because they are not in synchrony with their cohort or age group. These psychology-driven theories, such as those by Erikson (1968) and Levinson (1978), have not generally been supported by research. One reason for this failure may be their masculine orientation. A second reason is that the entire life cycle has since shifted upwardly in terms of what is considered the young adult stage. This stage now lasts into individuals' early thirties. Even "old age" has shifted to later years as longevity has increased (Sheehy, 1995).

Overall, the results are mixed but generally indicate a lower level of parenting stress, greater nurturance, and fewer interparental childrearing conflicts among older than younger first-time parents (Garrison et al., 1997). Mixed results are also illustrated in the following student quotes:

> *"At the time of my birth my mother was 33 and my father 38 years old. Today, people my parents' age have grandchildren and this is one reason why my parents regret marrying late in their lives. My father often complains that he is getting too old to have to worry about supporting us. . . . My mother does not want me to follow in her footsteps."*

> *"In 10 years from now? I will probably be thinking of getting married and having children but not before. I want to do like my parents and have children late*

when there is more time for them and more money. I just don't envy people my age who are getting married. I wouldn't be a good mother, not until I am older, satisfied with my life, more experienced, have seen the world. My parents did all of that and then after devoted so much more of themselves to us, they had more time for us two than my friends' parents who were much younger had because they were struggling financially and were often impatient with their lives and their children."

Heath (1995) replicated the positive results of late parenting and added that late-timing fathers are more nurturant and hold higher behavioral expectations for their children than young fathers. Cooney and colleagues (1993) report that late-timing fathers are more positive about their role, more involved with their children, and more satisfied with their marital relationship. By their late thirties and early forties, fathers are better established in their employment, more secure, and may be more able to devote time to their children without experiencing role conflict. Older parents often feel more competent, and their self-esteem is less tied to the vagaries of parenting (Cowan and Cowan, 1992). Greater personal maturity during the transition to parenthood implies a more stabilized sense of self, one that is less easily bruised by "failures" in the exercise of the parenting role.

The study of late-timing parenthood is a neglected field; in fact, longitudinal research generally fails to include such parents (see Family Research 9.1). Delayed first births on a large scale is a relatively new phenomenon, thus, some of its consequences are likely to change as society gets used to "older" mothers and fathers and even older grandparents. Furthermore, as illustrated in Figure 9.2, delayed parenthood decreases the number of generations present in a family. One also has to consider that many of the postponed first births may be so for only one of the two spouses when one of them had already been married before. In many of these families, however, the issue

FAMILY RESEARCH 9.1

The National Longitudinal Survey of Youth (NLSY)

The Center for Human Resource Research began the NLSY in 1979 when 12,686 males and females aged 14 to 21 were interviewed. The sample has been reinterviewed annually to follow the respondents on a variety of measures of quality of life. Beginning in 1986, the initial female respondents' children were included in the sample and were assessed every other year. This method allows researchers to link information gathered on children to what is known about their mothers. Thus, the study is not only longitudinal but also involves two generations.

Mothers' living arrangements (single, cohabiting, married, divorced, remarried) are followed over time, which provides a family developmental perspective on transitions. Furthermore, when mothers have more than one child, all are included in the study so that researchers can study siblings.

The main disadvantage of this survey is that its sample includes a disproportionate number of women who were young mothers and thus may not be the best instrument to do research on educated women who give birth later in life. But, overall, because of the richness of the data, the NLSY is one of the best instruments with which to study family life developments as well as child development.

FIGURE 9.2

Generational Successions: How a Woman Creates Generations Depending on Her Age at the Birth of Her First Child

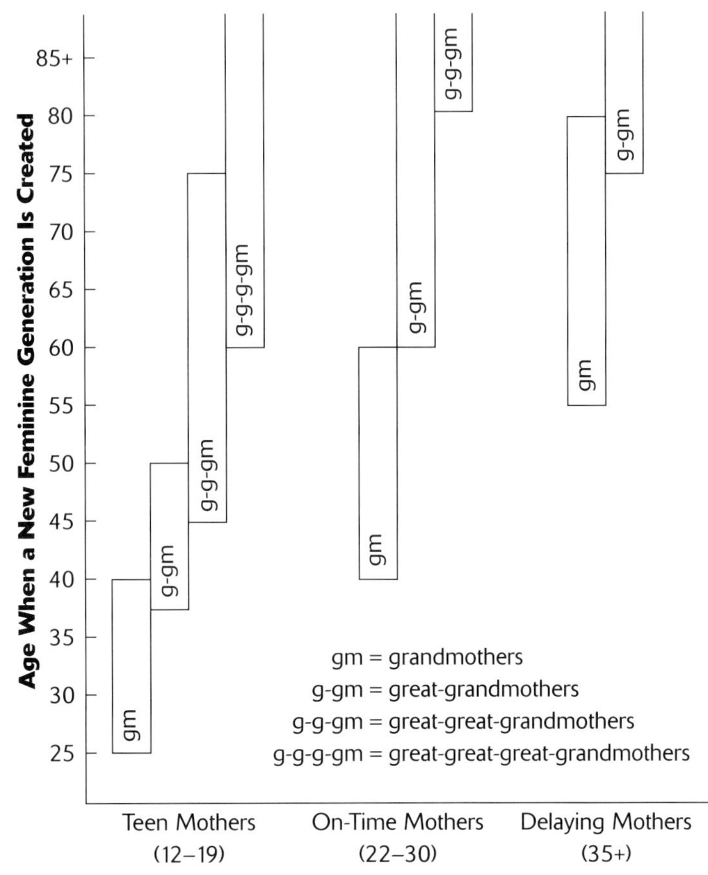

of stepparenting presents a confounding variable that makes it difficult to study the impact of the first birth as a life transition and a family development stage.

Generational Compressions and Successions

Generally, parents are at least 20 years older than their first-born child. When a 15-year-old has a baby, she initiates a generational chain of events in her family if she is her mother's first child to have a baby. She creates a young grandmother, as described in Figure 9.2, and may be creating a young great-grandmother and so on up the generational line (Burton and Bengtson, 1985). In other words, there is a generational compression with multiple successions, whereas in the case of an older mother, the opposite occurs. As well, with a young mother, the generational gap between mother and child is blurred, especially as the child grows up.

In U.S. society, grandparents are generally at least 40 years older than their first grandchild (see the midsection of Figure 9.2). Many teen mothers' own mothers were also teen mothers. This means that some new grandmothers may be anywhere from 25 to 35 years of age, thus creating a second generational compression within the same family. Great-grandmothers may be a mere 38 to 45. In effect, early births accelerate family stages and stack up several generations of *young* people within a same family—young people who have had little time to devote to their own developmental tasks (Burton, 1996a). They also have had little time to accumulate social and material resources that could benefit both the youngest and the oldest generations. The opposite is more likely to occur when adults become grandparents at an older age.

As the child ages, his or her young mother may be more like a peer or a sibling; unless another adult takes over, this child then lacks the benefit of having a parent who behaves like an adult, who assumes moral authority, and who can serve as a guide. A 12-year-old boy or girl may have a 27-year-old mother who dates and is obviously sexually active with men who are not the child's father. The father may be equally immature. Under such circumstances, the child may become a peer who is not monitored nor guided, so that the risks of delinquency and the transmission of nonmarital births are high. Such a child has a very different life, compared to a child in a two-parent family and compared to a child whose single mother is older, more mature, financially secure, and authoritative. On the other hand, for some young grandmothers whose teenage daughters largely relinquish their maternal duties to them, it may actually be the first time that they parent independently. Or it may be the first opportunity that they have to be able to enjoy parenting without the burden of youthful transitions and insecurities that had marred their own early mothering (Harvey, 1993).

SUBSEQUENT STAGES

Subsequent stages of family development include, in a majority of families that remain intact, the arrival of a second child. It may even involve incorporating pets into family life—pets that more or less become the children's companions and present additional responsibilities and joys to parents.

The Early Years

The early years of childrearing, including the school years, consolidate gender differences in how fathers and mothers live their roles. As well, the early years of childrearing temporarily draw men into greater contact with kin without diminishing the size of their overall network (Munch, McPherson, and Smith-Lovin, 1997). However, women's social networks decrease substantially, especially around the time the youngest child is age 3. This period seems to be very demanding in terms of parenting investment because of the requirements of the child's developmental stage as defined by society. Mothers' social networks generally return to their previous volume when the last child enters school. Therefore, the arrival of children and their young age present a multitude of transitions for mothers, which include not only an increase in workload but also changes in their employment patterns as well as a reduction in social contacts.

Parents' Transition to a Second Child

In most families today, but less so than in the past, another stage is reached with the arrival of the second child. Many adults choose to have their children in a rapid succession so that siblings can form close bonds and the labor-intensive period of parenting takes place over a short amount of time. The latter preference is often motivated by long-term family or conjugal goals and by employment or career considerations. For instance, a mother who has two children in two or three years interrupts her career only once if she chooses to stay home until the children reach kindergarten age. If she depends on her mother for child care, she has to consider the grandmother's age as well as her needs to resume her own life more freely.

Some couples think of their midlife and plan their family so as to have more years later on to devote to their relationship. In contrast, couples who space their children over several years spend a longer period parenting and have two or more offspring with different schedules and needs. This would suit couples who prefer to enjoy each child separately and relive the baby experience at different stages in their lives.

The transition required by a second child is probably easier than the transition for the first one. The structure of the family is not affected, because the partners have already crossed over the parenthood threshold. Furthermore, the second child presents less of an enigma, as parents already have some experience in caring for an infant and have accumulated social resources in the guise of pediatricians and caregivers. The arrival of a second infant, however, does further intensify the traditional division of labor, particularly when mothers remain at home.

The Older Child's Transitions

The transition to a two-child family is one that parents have to help the first-born negotiate. The latter now has to share his or her parents; the newborn is not always a welcome addition to the first-born's life (Baydar, Greek, and Brooks-Gunn, 1997). Children who are between 2 and 4 years of age are particularly affected, because their entire lives have been spent as their parents' only child (Dunn, 1994). Older children are more competent cognitively and can understand the situation better. Parents may be able to appeal to their sense of being "grown up," as explained by this male student:

> *"What I like best to remember when I was 5 is the birth of my little sister. I had wanted a brother to play hockey with but you can't be too choosy. What I liked best was that my parents made me feel so important, so grown up to be the big brother. I just loved to take care of her even though the novelty wore off after a while."*

Another milestone in the life of a family is the oldest child's entry into the school system. For each child individually, his or her first school day (generally, kindergarten) is of momentous importance. The child's transition also constitutes one for the entire family, particularly for mother and the younger siblings. Students recall this day with a wide range of memories:

> *"This was the worst day of my life. I cried and clung to my mother. I didn't want to go to school. I wanted to stay home with my brother."*

> *"At age five my best memories are of going to kindergarten. I had wanted this ever since my older sister had gone. I thought she looked so grown up and I couldn't wait to be just like her so that when the day arrived no one had to force me to go. I went marching proudly."*

Parents' Transition to Child Schooling

Formal schooling is certainly the most potent new context that young children encounter. It transforms their developmental path and affects the parent/child relationship. Children's social and cultural worlds expand and become more diversified. Thus, the fabric that constitutes the parent/child relationship is woven with threads of more varied colors and texture than was the case in early childhood. Several changes take place in the family's routine.

Today, children often attend preschool or a child care center before kindergarten, so the transition to school may be less momentous both for parents and children than in the recent past. However, for mothers who resume work when their last child enters school, this may be the most important stage for the young family since the first child's birth. With the resumption of maternal employment, the family routine is substantially altered for mother and children. It may well be at this stage that the couple renegotiates its daily practices concerning the division of labor on matters such as child care, housework, grocery shopping, and cooking. Research indicates, however, that even when negotiations do take place, they do not substantially alter the father's routine (Doherty, Kouneski, and Erickson, 1998).

Pets as New Family Members

Pets are often introduced in the family as companions to young children or even adolescents. Pets fulfill several functions for children. In fact, only children who have a pet spend more time with it than children who have both a sibling and a pet (Melson and Fogel, 1996). These same researchers even found that interest in pets was often a substitute for interest in babies in general, particularly among male children. Children establish a parallel between babies and pets: Both have to be taken care of and are somewhat entertaining. But babies become less interesting when a pet is available! Pets can serve as agents of socialization to teach nurturance (Davis and Juhasz, 1995). An animal requires care and grooming, and is in many ways at the mercy of its owner for survival, somewhat as a small child is. Thus, children can learn to put their pets' needs after their wants, which is a form of altruism. Unfortunately, violence against animal companions is frequent; it is often accompanied by other forms of family malfunctioning, such as conflict and abuse (Flynn, 2000).

Pets can also serve as a confidante and a source of attachment:

> *"When I was 17 I remember feeling a great sense of loss when my dog 'Topsy' died. She had been with our family since I was 4. I remember that when I was upset about something I would just go in the back and sit with her and often talk to her. She was very comforting when I had problems. She was a significant member of our family."*

Students often noted that being given a pet had been interpreted when they were small as a very special token of their parents' love; it was on a higher level than receiving even a large toy. The following quote from a student describes her delight upon receiving a pet and the opportunity to network afforded by the kitten's arrival:

> *"Dad said to go to my room. I did. When I got there, I found my mother sitting on my bed with the cutest, sweetest, softest little white kitten that one could ever see. I named her Fluffy (how original!) and I knew I'd love her for life. It felt great to care for something so helpless and gentle. I could feel the kitten respond to me and that felt so nice. I kept repeating 'She loves me!' I phoned all my little friends to tell them I just had a baby."*

Research indicates that pets have a positive effect on adults' well-being. Although children are generally attached to their furry friends, there is little research on pets' effects on children's well-being by gender, age, and family structure.

Some students recounted how they used their pets to apologize to their parents after having been disobedient. They would carry the pet to the mother or father, and when the parent picked up the cat or dog or patted it affectionately, the child took this as a sign of having been forgiven and that all was well again. A student recalled taking her cat with her in her mother's bed. The sharing of the fluffy creature was a symbol of love and security. Molnar (1996) describes how each year the assorted Freud family dogs presented birthday poems to Sigmund Freud. These poems had been written by his daughter, the future child psychoanalyst, Anna Freud. They were a means of communicating feelings that might not have been otherwise acceptable in that family. Thus, pets can become symbols of affection between children and parents or even between parents, as when a child asks quarrelling parents to take turns patting the dog. The child seeks reassurance that the parents still love each other while at the same time trying to pacify them.

The Adolescent Years

The transition to junior high school presents a key developmental stage for children and their parents. The latter may keenly recall their own passage into adolescence and high school. Parents' own past successes and failures at the same age, combined with their aspirations and fears for their children, may constitute a maturation process for them.

Pasley and Gecas (1984) found that around 62 percent of the mothers and fathers in their study perceived adolescence as the most difficult and stressful stage of parenting. Gecas and Seff (1990:943) conclude that for "the parents of adolescents, therefore, adolescence may indeed be a time of storm and stress, at least in modern times." This study finds resonance in students' autobiographies: Approximately one-third recalled experiencing a psychologically and socially painful adolescence; another one-third described this period as a happy one both for themselves and their parents; and the remaining one-third recalled an adolescence that included happy as well as unhappy periods. A majority of the adolescents' sources of unhappiness were located at the peer-group level. This was followed by school problems, and further down in the hierarchy of stressors were family problems. Interpersonal difficulties experienced with parents tended to have resulted from the adolescents' state of mind and particularly from peer-driven stressors (Ambert, 1994a):

> *"My behavior towards my parents during this period [ages 11–14] was that of resentment. . . . I blamed my parents for making me ugly. . . . I still blamed them for what was happening in my life. In this way, I had a negative impact on my parents. They had to deal with a child who was impossible."*

The adolescent years may require as much adaptation in terms of family dynamics as has so far occurred during the entire life span of the family. But the extent of this adaptation depends on the preadolescence quality of the parent/child relationship as well as on the various temperaments and frailties involved. Familial adaptation to adolescence is also contingent on the family's economic situation and race, because these two factors situate the family in neighborhoods, schools, and peer groups, all of which influence the course of adolescent development. The adolescent years are discussed at greater length in subsequent chapters.

The Empty Nest: Or Is It?

In centuries past, the nest was never empty. By the time the last child was ready to leave, both parents may have died, as women continued childbearing to the end of their reproductive years. When parents lived into old age, a substantial proportion remained in their home with one adult child or moved in with a married one. For instance, in 1900, 59 percent of the elderly resided with a grown child, compared to 14 percent in 1990 (Schoeni, 1998). The reasons elderly parents live with a grown child today differ from those in 1900. In those days, an adult child probably lived with an elderly parent because the farm property had passed to him and the mother remained in what was her own home (Demos, 1974). In other cases, a child stayed with or took in elderly parents to care for them. In contrast, today, it is as likely that a parent takes in an adult child because of that child's dependency as because of the older person's own needs (Hareven, 1994a).

As we have seen in Chapter 6, and will discuss at great length in Chapter 10, more and more young adults delay work and marriage in order to complete a long period of education. Furthermore, even when employed, the wages of young workers with no college education are low and many youths suffer from episodic periods of unemployment. These various factors mean that young people find it economically convenient to remain with their parents. This historic context, in turn, delays parents' transition to the empty nest. It also delays grandparenting.

A second change that has occurred in recent decades is that the family may go through **transition reversals:** children who have left home return following an illness, unemployment, new schooling requirements, and particularly divorce (White and Peterson, 1995). This has been referred to as the *revolving-door family.* These adult children's transitions actually alter the stages of their own parents' life course. The latter is therefore more contingent on these offsprings' own transitions. In some families, parents cannot retire as early as they wish, because they have to help a child who is financially dependent. In other families, parents have to abandon their plans of moving or traveling because they need to babysit for their grandchildren, or their son or daughter has just returned home despondent after a bitter divorce. In yet other cases, parents have to take in an adult child who is discharged from a mental hospital and has no employment prospects.

If we could total up all these cases, we may well find that over half of 50- to 65-year-old parents have had to make readjustments in their schedules and future plans to accommodate the transitions and needs of adult children and small grandchildren. In contrast, just two decades ago, these same parents would have lived in an empty nest with fewer obligations toward their children.

This situation represents yet another refutation of the pessimistic point of view of the family's loss of functions. Rather, active parenting is maintained well beyond what used to occur and is even reactivated, often repeatedly after all the children have left home for the first time. For many adults, active parenting has become a lifelong occupation because of changes in the economy, in family structure, and in the culture; these changes place their adult children and their grandchildren at the mercy of difficult circumstances. These include unemployment, drug addiction, divorce, single parenthood, criminality, as well as lack of social support for the mentally ill and the disabled.

THE GRANDPARENT STAGE

In the nineteenth century, adults who became grandparents for the first time were generally still busy raising their younger children. Today, grandparenting tends to be a separate family developmental stage, except in cases of early grandmothering, or unless one concurrently has small children from a remarriage.

Grandparenting as a Role

The role of grandparents is not rigidly scripted culturally; it leaves room for personal creativity as well as disappointments (Thomas, 1990). Overall, it has been qualified as a stabilizing force in the family and as a source of family continuity. There are indications that grandmothers enjoy their role more than grandfathers. They are also more involved. Cherlin and Furstenberg (1992) distinguish three styles of grandparenting: remote, companionate, and involved. Each probably has a different impact on the various relationships between the generations. For instance, remote grandparenting adds less to grandchildren's lives than a companionate or involved style. It is also less helpful to the grandchildren's parents. On the other hand, involved grandparenting may create a closer bond between the two generations and be helpful to parents, but it can also bring in conflicts when parents and grandparents disagree in terms of childrearing. Relatively little research exists on such topics. The role that grandparents play also differs according to their age and health as well as the age and gender of their grandchildren. For instance, adolescent grandchildren may prefer a remote or companionate style of grandparenting rather than an involved one.

Grandmothers have been described as **kin-keepers** and as persons who open the kin system so as to support members in difficulty (Dilworth-Anderson, 1992). This may be especially the case for African-American grandmothers: "Intergenerational exchanges are viewed as a coping strategy used by the black community to deal with the oppressive social environment" (Kivett, 1993:170). The feminine tie is very important, particularly among women responsible for children, as they can provide help to each other. Exchange between black grandmothers and the granddaughters they have raised is particularly meaningful and continues into the grandmothers' old age (Burton, 1996a).

King and Elder (1995) indicate that the quality of the relationship between grandparent and adult child significantly impacts on the grandparent/grandchildren relationship. Adult children who do not feel close to their parents or who perceive them to be meddlesome are less likely to encourage their children to visit them and to form close bonds with them (Rossi and Rossi, 1990). Similarly, it is possible that when children feel that their parents are not well treated by their grandparents, they may be reluctant to form close bonds, and may not trust the older generation as much (Hodgson, 1992). In another study, the relationship between adolescents and their grandparents was described by the youths as less close when their parents recalled that their own parents had been emotionally distant toward them during their own adolescence. These and other results indicate that parents act as mediators in the grandparent/grandchild relationship (Whitbeck, Hoyt, and Huck, 1993).

Grandparents Who Provide Child Care

For many women who become grandmothers, this transition constitutes an **extension** of their **maternal role.** Slightly over 40 percent of U.S. grandmothers provide care for at least one grandchild on a regular basis (Baydar and Brooks-Gunn, 1998). Grandmothers often babysit while their daughters are at work, whether they live with them or nearby. African-American grandmothers fill this role even more than their white counterparts, particularly when their daughters are single (Hogan, Hao, and Parish, 1990).

It is difficult to say whether more grandmothers are now babysitting than was the case in the past when fewer young mothers were in the labor force and the necessity for regular child care was less urgent. Now, grandmothers are needed more than before because their daughters and daughters-in-law are employed. In fact, one-third of low-income women report that lack of child care is the main reason why they remain unemployed (Kisker and Ross, 1997).

Baydar and Brooks-Gunn (1998) have studied the characteristics of grandmothers who provide child care. A majority live with their spouses, have more education than those who do not provide care—in part because they belong to the younger cohorts of grandmothers—and about 45 percent are employed. Babysitting grandmothers are busy women who combine several roles and are often active in their communities. Some even care simultaneously for their older mothers. Grandmothers who have several children and grandchildren have more opportunities to become caregivers. This opportunity increases when a teenage daughter who lives with them has a baby.

Grandparents Who Raise Grandchildren

In 1991, the U.S. Census Bureau estimated that 3.3 million children lived with their grandparents. This represented a 44 percent increase since 1980. In 1995, nearly 6 percent of all black children and 2 percent of white children were in the custody of grandparents (Pebley and Rudkin, 1999). Fifty percent of these grandchildren had only a mother, 28 percent had neither parents, 17 percent had two parents, and 5 percent only a father (Saluter, 1992). In a national survey, 11 percent of grandparents reported that they had raised a grandchild for at least six months in their lifetime (Pearson et al., 1997). In some states, and particularly among African Americans, over a quarter of children in foster care are living with grandparents, generally a grandmother (Bonecutter and Gleeson, 1997).

Effects on Grandparents

Jendrek (1993) has studied the impact that this caregiving role has on grandparents' lifestyles, especially the changes that grandparents have to bring to their own lives, the dreams they have to postpone or abandon altogether, and the physical and emotional demands that such a role places on them. Jendrek reports that, in 73 percent of their sample, grandchildren live with their grandparents because the child's mother suffers from emotional problems. Maternal drug problems are also involved in half of the cases, and alcoholism in 44 percent of the cases (Burton, 1992). In half of the cases, there is some overlap among the reasons, which means that these mothers suffer from a multiplicity of problems—not to omit the fact that fathers are absent. Obviously, such grandparents are taking charge of children who have lived in deteriorating family circumstances, a situation well described in this student's autobiography.

> *"I was raised by my grandparents who took me and my little brother in after my mother flipped after my father left her. We had had a hard life and all I remember about it is that my parents were scary [they were alcoholic]. Anyways we were better off with my grandparents and we knew them because they had often kept us over weekends. . . . Now that we're older it's harder on them in a way because my brother grew up with lots of problems but at least I turned out just fine and this just makes up for it. . . . I love them like my own parents and we owe them everything and I am planning on making a lot of money to take care of them because they are getting on in years."*

In contrast to grandparents who babysit, those who single-handedly raise one or more grandchildren tend to be poorer than the average for their age group, more of-

A substantial proportion of children in foster care live with a grandmother or grandparents. These children tend to stay in foster care longer and are less likely to be adopted than those placed in nonkin homes. No adequate explanation has yet been provided for this finding.

ten unemployed, and less educated (Solomon and Marx, 1995). A majority are African American, perhaps because of the higher rates of single motherhood as well as crack addiction among their children. In the Strawbridge and colleagues' (1997) longitudinal study, many of these grandparents had experienced negative life events in their own past, such as problems with marriages, finances, and health. Their new caregiving duties added up to the difficulties already caused by these old burdens. The life course of many caregiving grandparents differed from that of other grandparents for several decades, probably as a result of poverty. This is an example of how the consequences of poverty carry through the generations: from the grandparents, to their children, and now their grandchildren and back to the grandparents again.

Effects on Grandchildren

Given the reasons why they live with them, it can be expected that grandparents have to deal with grandchildren who are seriously at risk for emotional and behavioral problems. Solomon and Marx (1995) used the large National Health Interview Survey that included 448 households headed by grandparents to see how this type of family structure affected children's school and health outcomes. Children raised by grandparents were compared to children living with both biological parents and with children in single-parent families. In terms of behavior at school as well as indicators of school achievement, children in two-parent families had an advantage over the other two groups. However, children raised by grandparents were doing better than those raised in single-parent families, despite the generally low educational level of these grandparents. In terms of health, there were few differences between children in two-parent and grandparent families, but children in single-parent families were less healthy. Grandparents who raised girls had an easier time than those who raised boys.

In a nutshell, these results indicate that children raised by grandparents do quite well, considering the fact that many were often neglected or mistreated by their parents before. Thus, while being raised by a grandparent is a reasonable alternative for children, it is a more problematic one for the grandparents (Burnette, 1999); this is especially so when they are middle-aged and are encountering high demands from several generations as well as employment (Sands and Goldberg-Glen, 2000). They often have a multiplicity of roles to fulfill in addition to childrearing. Overall, foster grandparents find themselves out of synchrony with the normal developmental stage of family life: People of their age do not raise children. This anomaly deprives them of moral as well as instrumental support at their grandchildren's schools and in the neighborhood, particularly among whites (Pruchno, 1999). Hence, it is not surprising that support groups now exist for foster grandparents; these groups constitute an indicator of changing times.

Grandparenting after Divorce

Maternal grandparents' role often becomes involved as they help their divorcing daughters both emotionally and instrumentally, especially in terms of child care. But many other grandparents lose touch with grandchildren after a divorce, either because the custodial parent moves too far away or is not cooperative, or because their son, who is the visiting parent, more or less relinquishes his responsibilities. The latter probably occurs most sharply when a stepparent adopts the stepchildren, which means that the other parent has forfeited his or her legal responsibilities (Chapter 5). This is yet another example of how adult children's marital or parental transitions create related ones in the older generation: In the latter instance, grandparents lose their grandchildren (Ganong and Coleman, 1999).

Nearly all jurisdictions have planned third-party visitation rights, especially to facilitate the continuation of the grandparent/grandchild relationship in situations of separation, divorce, and remarriage. Although grandparents are overwhelmingly in favor of such rights, relatively little is known of their potential impact on the dynamics of the nuclear family. Besides money and help with child care, divorced parents probably most welcome moral support. In theory, in-laws, who are one's children's grandparents, should be a prime source of help. However, in my study, less than 20 percent of custodial parents actually talked to their former in-laws in a week's time, had visited them in a month's time, or had received some help from them (Ambert, 1989). Grandparents' visitation rights were opposed by over 90 percent of the divorced respondents, including those who had excellent relationships with their own parents and their former affines:

> *"Then what? I would have to juggle visitations with their father, their grandparents on his side, and why not my own parents? That's ridiculous. I couldn't survive so much stress, my life would be a nightmare and we would all end up hating each other. Whose welfare do they have in mind anyway? Theirs; not mine, not my children's." (Remarried custodial mother, age 38, with two children)*

Custodial parents generally pointed out that their former in-laws had stopped seeing them or saw their grandchildren only when the latter were visiting with the noncustodial parent. Consequently, so that their children did not lose half of their grandparents, custodial parents (and even their new spouses) often initiated a renewal of contact with their children's grandparents:

> *"I call them because I want my children to have a family. They don't come over but we visit them on their birthdays and Christmas. They're nice when we go but it always has to come from us."*

Some 60 percent of respondents talked of former in-laws who were hostile toward them, or potentially hostile; 35 percent of the respondents felt that their former in-laws projected their negative attitude, either verbally or behaviorally, to their grandchildren. Most prominent among these instances is the situation in which the ex-in-laws openly accused the custodial parent of having caused the failure of the marriage (48 percent). Second in order of frequency of mention were ex-in-laws' comments concerning custodial parents' fitness as parents (46 percent).

These accusations, gossips, and remarks ranged from stating that the parent was "unfit," was a "bad mother" or father, did not spend enough time with the children, left them alone too much, and was unfair or cruel to the father (or mother). These accusations were often extended into other areas of life, such as "poor money manager," "sexually loose," or "unable to hold down a job." Or grandparents would ask their grandchildren: "Does she go out? Whom with?" "Is she home when you come home from school?" "Does she drink?" One 14-year-old girl shouted at her mother, "Grandma says you sleep with anyone so I don't see why you can tell me that I can't go out tonight!" Even when words were not spoken, grandparents' refusal to talk to or see the other parent was a behavioral indicator that did not go unnoticed to the children.

It has been suggested that, when grandparents are granted legal access, they be advised of their *responsibilities*. The emphasis should be on the needs of the custodial family unit rather than on grandparents' rights. In fact, where relevant, grandparents should visit their grandchildren both at their custodial and noncustodial homes. Such visits would contribute to legitimize the two-home nuclear family. Grandchildren would retain a psychologically intact family and would not feel torn between the two sides of their consanguineous kin. Once again, I can only emphasize how regrettable it is that not enough research has been carried out on grandparenting after a child's divorce.

Stepgrandparenting

Becoming a stepgrandparent is not a role that most adults expect to fulfill. It is also a role that is even less culturally delineated than that of regular grandparenting, even though one-third of all American families include a stepgrandparent (Szinovacz, 1998). The few existing studies on this topic are reviewed by Ganong and Coleman (1994). They indicate that a child's young age upon entering a stepfamily facilitates the establishment of a true grandparenting situation and attachment. This relationship may become particularly useful and close if the child has more or less lost contact with one set of grandparents, generally on the father's side. A functional substitution can then take place.

However, when stepchildren do not accept their parent's remarriage, they may not wish to participate in family activities that include the stepparent's kin. It is particularly easy for a child to avoid contact with stepgrandparents when it is the noncustodial parent, generally the father, who remarries. The child usually spends little time with his or her father, even less with the stepmother, and none with her kin (Henry, Ceglian, and Ostrander, 1993). In fact, in my own research, stepmothers often went to see their own parents when their husband's children were visiting. In part, there was the desire to allow these children to receive as much attention as possible from their father without interference from the stepmother and her own children. In some cases, women knew that stepchildren and their mother resented them and they preferred to distance themselves from the situation. Thus, in many instances of noncustodial fathers' remarriage, the stepmother and her kin effectively remain in the background. Her parents are stepparents only in name and the termination of the son's remarriage affects them very little (Ganong and Coleman, 1999).

On the other side of the coin, it may be far easier for children and adolescents to accept a stepgrandparent when they rebel against having a stepparent at home. This is a less threatening and far more benign relationship. When the remarried custodial parent visits with the new in-laws and brings the children along, the latter may indirectly acquire a sense of normalization of family relationships. In this respect, stepgrandparents may contribute to the integration of the reconstituted family and fulfill the same functions as actual grandparents.

THE DEATH OF ADULTS' PARENTS

As new generations are born, couples become grandparents; a majority have a chance of becoming great-grandparents and many even see the birth of a fifth generation. As they age, parents are transformed into patriarchs and matriarchs. After they die, the mantle is passed on to their adult children who, if they themselves are grandparents, form a new branch of the family, each with the generations that descend from them. The very large family reunions that used to take place around the now deceased generation become smaller gatherings as the grandparent couples or singles head their own extended families separately from those of their siblings. The families become smaller because the birth rate has declined. The average 70-year-old grandparent today has 3 to 10 fewer grandchildren than his or her own parents' cohort had. The family tree becomes leaner.

Even though middle-aged and young senior adults fully expect their parents' death, this is an event that represents a transition both in their own individual lives and in the life course of the entire family system (Rossi and Rossi, 1990). Compared to the past, children and parents have a longer relationship because of a general increase in life expectancy. This means that both generations go through family transitions together or witness each other's transitions more often than in the early 1940s, for instance. A century ago, many parents did not even live long enough to see all their children marry. Most now do and even watch their children becoming parents; an increasing proportion see them become grandparents (Silverstein and Long, 1998). Thus, the relationship is not only longer but it also involves more shared experiences than in the past.

The end result is that adults, particularly females, have a more extended period of time during which to identify with their parents and delay the rupture of the knot by death than in the past. Female adults may have received more support from their mothers (Umberson, 1992). This may be even more the case in some groups than others, particularly among African Americans. Therefore, the death of the elderly mother, which occurs later than that of the father, on average, may represent a more significant marker event in adults' lives than in the recent past, particularly for women and African Americans. However, this death was probably a more significant passage in previous centuries when people's life expectancy was much lower: The older generation left young adults and even dependent children orphaned.

CONCLUSIONS: FAMILY DEVELOPMENT IN CONTEXT

As illustrated in the fictive vignettes opening this chapter, the family development perspective focuses on the intersection of the life course of the family with that of parents and children (Elder, 1998). Two families may experience exactly the same stage, that of the birth of a first grandchild, yet the transition carries different meanings and consequences for each family. In one family, for instance, the new grandparents are 45 years old and are employed. They may still have a child at home. In another family, the new grandparents are 60, beginning their retirement, have only one child, who is the infant's mother, and they are both keeping an eye out for an older mother who lives alone. The life course of these two families intersects with two very different personal stages in the life course of its adult members.

A second aspect of the developmental perspective is that the socioeconomic context of families largely dictates the timing and multiplicity of the transitions they experience. As we have seen, a substantial proportion of the poor actually experience accelerated generational transitions, beginning with teenage motherhood that often repeats itself across three generations. Family development in the United States is therefore contingent on socioeconomic status and particularly poverty. Not only is there an increasing economic gap between the rich and the poor, but this gap creates a divergent pattern of family development between the poor and the rest of the population.

Finally, the historical context or the decades in which a family is formed and experiences its transitions also sets limits or widens opportunities both on the timing of the stages and on their consequences. For instance, after the 1970s, women's greater educational opportunities and widespread employment contributed to adults' delayed passage into parenthood as well as a later timing of grandparenthood. At the same time, a longer life expectancy means that a family can now accumulate more generations and transitions in its developmental trajectory, unless a late passage into parenthood among families where a college education is the norm cancels out the results of the longer life expectancy.

SUMMARY

1. The social construction of motherhood and fatherhood greatly influences how family developments are experienced by men and women. Mothers are believed to have natural abilities to nurture children, who are socially constructed as needing their mothers on an intensive basis. Fathers have been defined mainly as breadwinners, although paternal involvement with children is a positive element in their development. Furthermore, there is a dual practice of fatherhood: Fathers in families other than intact and legally married are far less invested in their children. Even married fathers are less involved when the conjugal relationship is difficult.
2. The stages of family development begin during pregnancy. This situation is experienced differentially, depending on the family structure involved (number, sex, and marital status of parents). About half of couples experience stress and some marital disenchantment after the birth of a first child. This transition is smoother for couples who were well adjusted before and for those who had planned the timing of the birth. In other types of family structure, young, unmarried mothers generally experience more family transitions than married ones. Older, single mothers who plan the birth or who adopt may face far fewer disruptions than generally believed.
3. Delayed parenthood is becoming more common. Overall, the results are mixed but generally indicate a lower level of parenting stress, fewer interpersonal conflicts, and greater paternal investment.
4. A birth to an adolescent often leads to a generational compression whereby the young mother effectively creates premature grandmothers and great-grandmothers. Such families have rapidly succeeding generations that have had little time to accumulate social and material resources that could benefit both the youngest and the oldest generations.
5. The transition to a two-child family is less spectacular than the first transition into parenthood. However, it is a key transition in the life of the older child. The early years of childrearing consolidate gender differences in how fathers and mothers live their roles. Children's passage into the school system has traditionally been an important family transition that may be mitigated now by early day care and nursery experience. Another passage occurs when families acquire pets for their children. Pets fulfill functions of socialization and interaction. The adolescent years are generally perceived by a majority of parents as the most difficult stage of parenting.
6. Young adults now stay home longer than was the case in the 1970s; thus, parents are older at the transition to what used to be called the empty nest stage. Furthermore, the family often undergoes transition reversals as adult children return home following unemployment or divorce. The parenting role and family functions are extended over the family's life span.
7. The grandparenting role is not as culturally scripted as is the parental one. Grandmothers are more involved as kin-keepers. Slightly over 40 percent of U.S. grandmothers provide some form of care for at least one grandchild on a regular basis.

In addition, about 11 percent of grandparents raise a grandchild for at least 6 months in their lifetime. Custodial grandparents experience a great deal of stressors because, more often than not, they had already been through poverty, divorce, and single parenthood in earlier family stages. Children raised by grandparents do better than similar ones raised in a single-parent family but less well than those with two parents.

8. Grandparenting after an adult child's divorce may again involve a further extension of familial duties, or, if a son rarely sees his children, grandparents may lose contact with the grandchildren. Grandparenting visitation rights carry both advantages as well as difficulties, the latter particularly for custodial parents, Stepgrandparenting is the least culturally scripted role. It is a situation that can be beneficial to children, especially those who have lost touch with their original grandparents.
9. Compared to the past, children and parents have a longer relationship because of a general increase in life expectancy. Furthermore, they share more transitions together as several generations often succeed each other within a person's life span.
10. The age at which transitions occur reflects different meanings and brings different experiences. The socioeconomic context of families largely dictates the timing and the multiplicity of their transitions. Finally, the historical context in which a family is formed and develops sets limits or widens opportunities both in the timing of the stages and on their consequences.

KEY CONCEPTS AND THEMES

Delayed parenthood, p. 252
Ethnocentric phenomenon, p. 244
Extension of maternal role, p. 261
Fathers' investment, p. 245
Generational compression, p. 254
Grandparenting role, p. 260
Intensive mothering, p. 244
Kin-keepers, p. 261
Life course, pp. 242, 267
Multiple parenting, p. 244
"Off time," p. 252
Older mothers, p. 251
"On time," p. 252
Single grandmothers, p. 250
Social construction of fatherhood, p. 245
Social construction of motherhood, p. 243
Stepgrandparenting, p. 265
Transition reversals, p. 260
Woman's role, p. 245

STUDY AND REVIEW QUESTIONS

1. What are some cross-cultural findings that cast doubt on the universality of motherhood as understood in North America?
2. Discuss paternal investment contextually.
3. What are some structural variables that may impact on the effect of the arrival of a first baby?
4. What are key family development stages subsequent to the arrival of a first child?
5. How is the traditional division of gender roles pursued in grandparenting?
6. What may be some differences between families in which grandmothers simply provide child care and others in which they raise their grandchildren?

7. On average, what are the outcomes of children who are raised by their grandparents and how do you explain these outcomes?
8. What are the advantages of continued grandparenting after divorce for children and their custodial mothers?
9. Discuss stepgrandparenting as a role.
10. Analyze family stages from a developmental and historical perspective.

SUGGESTED READINGS

Aldous, J. 1996. *Family careers: Rethinking the developmental perspective.* Thousand Oaks, CA: Sage. The author utilizes the developmental perspective within a very broad range of family situations and contexts.

Belsky, J., and Kelly, J. 1994. *The transition to parenthood: How a first child changes a marriage.* New York: Delacorte Press. This volume presents the results of a short-term longitudinal study of couples expecting and then having their first child. It details the changes that are observed in the couples' lives.

Booth, A., and Crouter, A. C. (Eds.). 1998. *Men in families.* Mahwah, NJ: Erlbaum. Several researchers present data and perspectives on the role of husbands and fathers in contemporary American families. Historical overviews also presented.

Hays, S. 1996. *The cultural contradictions of motherhood.* New Haven, CT: Yale University Press. This book offers a critical feminist analysis, reviews of the literature, as well as qualitative sociology data on motherhood. The substantive focus is on intensive mothering.

Lamb, M. E. (Ed.). 1997. *The role of the father in child development* (3rd ed.). New York: John Wiley & Sons. This book contains chapters by specialists on fatherhood. The contents range from the history and social construction of fatherhood in the United States to father involvement and consequences for children at various age levels. There are chapters pertaining to divorce, stepfamilies, and family violence.

LaRossa, R. 1997. *The modernization of fatherhood: A social and political history.* Chicago: The University of Chicago Press. This book combines a history of fatherhood, motherhood, and childhood. It presents unusual information on the history of the social construction of fatherhood, particularly in the twentieth century.

Rossi, A. S., and Rossi, P. H. 1990. *Of human bonding: Parent-child relations across the life course.* New York: Aldine de Gruyter. This research on three generations in a family includes recollections of relationships with one's parents as well as current data. The research allows for the study of family transitions in the life cycle of individuals belonging to different cohorts.

SUGGESTED WEBLINKS

About Stepparenting contains a mixture of information and practical subjects. This site has a section on stepgrandparenting. It is a popular rather than an educational website. **<http://stepparenting.about.com/home/parenting/stepparenting/msubgran.htm>**

Alzheimer's Association's website provides research and practical information, support groups, and addresses by region. **<http://www.alz.org>**

American Association of Retired Persons. The website offers practical information on the later stages of family development, including grandparents who raise grandchildren as well as the care of elderly parents by their adult children. Regional resources are indicated. **<http://www.aarp.org>**

Zero the Three. This website for the National Center for Infants, Toddlers, and Families provides information for professionals as well as parents with a small child to help them understand this developmental stage. **<http://www.zerotothree.org>**

CHAPTER 10

Spousal and Partner Relationships

OUTLINE

Types of Marriages and How They Change
The Conflict-Habituated Relationship
The Devitalized Relationship
The Passive-Congenial Relationship
The Vital Relationship
The Total Relationship
Marriages Change

Division of Labor and Inequality
A Classification of the Domestic Division of Labor
The Egalitarian and Nongendered Division of Labor
The Equitable but Gendered Division of Labor
The Specialist Division of Labor
The Husband-Helper Division of Labor
The Traditional and Delegated Divisions of Labor
The Overall Perspective
The Effect of Marital Quality: Overview of Recent Changes
Division of Labor in Remarriages with Stepchildren
The Silent Division of Labor: Emotional Work

Aspects of Spousal Relationships
Marital Happiness, Satisfaction, and Success
Marital Quality through the Decades
Partner Conflict and Marital Problems
Partner Conflict
Marital Problems
The Conjugal Relationship in Later Life
The Next Time Around: Remarriage

Same-Sex-Partner Relationship

The Effect of the Parental Relationship on Children
The Effect of Parental Conflict
How to Explain the Effect of Marital Quality on Children
Marital Quality Fosters Supportive Parenting
The Role of Learning and Personality
Genes and Within-Family Environment
The Larger Environment Affects Marriage and Childrearing

Conclusions: Definitions of Marital Quality Are Culture Specific

Summary
Key Concepts and Themes
Study and Review Questions
Suggested Readings
Suggested Weblinks

"Right now, I'd rate myself as somewhat unhappy despite the fact that I just got married, which is what I wanted to do most in my life. It's just that marriage is so different than dating and becoming engaged. We used to do things together, special things, and had all the time in the world to talk. Now we're married and it's just like things are all settled for my husband; he has to work. I work, and I am finishing school and there's no time for the nice things in a relationship. Last year we were equally busy but he could find the time. I know that I may be too romantic and that I have to get used to this, but it is so disappointing."

"The past two years have certainly been the happiest of my life and mainly because I got married and even though I felt I was too young at the time it's the best decision I ever made. It's just the little things that make me happy like when I come home and he has the supper ready for me because he knows I have had a hard day and he knows that I am not used to cooking on a regular basis. What I like best probably is that we have so much to talk about, and we still talk about loving each other after two years but now we're also seriously planning the future as in having children. I can tell him that I am afraid to be cooped up in the house with two kids and no one to talk to and he takes it seriously and he says we'll have to find a way to keep me working and him doing a lot of fathering."

These two women students are at the beginning of their marriages and are of the same age—around 24 years old. Yet, their experience, level of happiness, and the extent to which their conjugal expectations are met are entirely different. Furthermore, their autobiographies indicate that they are fairly similar on many personal aspects, such as personality and values. They have, however, married young men who harbor radically different conceptions of conjugal life. As a social category, men are more powerful agents of the construction of reality than women (Ferree and Hall, 1996). This macrosociological advantage, as we see in this chapter, carries into intimate relationships.

Throughout the last half of the twentieth century, the relationship between spouses has become far more diverse than it used to be. To begin with, the explosion of divorce on the familial scene has meant that marital stability can no longer be taken for granted. Couples now enter marriage with a less secure feeling of permanency than was the case in the past, when only death could generally do them apart. Second, the massive entry of women on the labor market has resulted in more complex feminine expectations (and often more complex forms of masculine cooperation or resistance) in terms of the household division of labor. Couples now have to negotiate who does what at various stages of family development, and this situation can create a certain level of tension in the relationships. Third, couples' expectations of marriage concerning love, sexuality, and companionship have heightened. More is demanded of marriage in terms of relationship than in the past, while, at the same time, couples may be less patient when their expectations are not met (Amato and Booth, 1997). Perhaps the cultural focus of marriage as an institution has shifted from a collectivist and obligation axis to an individualistic axis emphasizing needs and gratifications.

The relationship between spouses has also become more diverse for the simple reason that it now includes more categories of couples. Today, the term *spouse* or *partner* has been analytically if not legally extended to all couples involved in living-together relationships, whether cohabitors, same-sex couples who live together, and remarried couples. However, certain qualifiers are necessary. Marriage is still the predominant demographic basis of family formation. Even though couples are now delaying marriage, appproximately 95 percent of the U.S. population marries at least once. This demographic reality, combined with the fact that comparatively more research exists on the marital than on any other form of partner relationship, means that a majority of the pages of this chapter are devoted to marriage.

TYPES OF MARRIAGES AND HOW THEY CHANGE

I wanted to begin this chapter with an overall classification of marital relationships, but I could not find recent in-depth studies of marriage types. This gap in the recent research is the result of sociologists having more and more recourse to large-scale surveys. These surveys, with their multiple-choice questions, do not provide sufficiently detailed and dynamic descriptions that would allow for a classification of marriages. In 1965, using a qualitative approach, John Cuber and Peggy Haroff proposed such a classification. Their typology was derived from in-depth interviews with 107 men and 104 women who had been married for at *least 10 years* and had never considered divorcing. This typology still applies today. The five types of marriage derived from their interview material were named on the basis of their central and distinguishing themes. They represent different configurations taken by the couples' relationship, or, stated another way, different levels of marital quality.

The Conflict-Habituated Relationship

The main characteristics of the conflict-habituated relationship are tension and unresolved conflict, some of which is overt and appears in the form of nagging and quarrelling. The spouses seem to argue for the sake of it. When on their best behavior, these couples are polite, particularly in the company of others. But they do not conceal their differences from their children and, during the interviews, emphasized their incompatibility and how tense they were in each other's presence. Many of these couples had already been conflictual at the dating stage. What holds their marriage together may be force of habit, the fact that the spouses have personalities that are combative or have been so chiselled by the marriage that they might have difficulty adjusting to a more peaceful situation were they to divorce. In other cases, they cannot afford to divorce because of poverty or shared wealth and/or social position.

Among *young* couples today, this type of marriage is conflictual rather than conflict habituated, and their relationship is likely to end soon. Even in the Cuber and Haroff sample in the early 1960s, this type of marriage was not the most frequently encountered. Today, it might cover 10 to 20 percent of long-term marriages. This is not a type of marital interaction that is valued in American society.

The Devitalized Relationship

In a devitalized relationship, the spouses had been deeply in love early on in their marriage, had enjoyed their sex lives, and had shared much together. Over time, the relationship lost its original "shine" and vitality. Now these couples simply take each other for granted but conflict is rare. Most of the time spent together is a matter of duty, to fulfill parental roles, to present a united front to the world, and to take care of each other's careers. These couples are often exemplary parents.

The relationship continues because of their commonly shared duties as well as absence of conflict. There generally are other rewarding aspects in their lives, in which they invest much. They celebrate anniversaries and appreciate each other as parents or as workers. Some hold values that supersede those of individual happiness and they respect marriage as an institution. Cuber and Haroff found this type of marriage to be very common in their sample, and may today constitute about one-third of all marriages of long duration.

However, these couples are quite susceptible to divorce because this type of marriage is considered less than ideal in the United States. It is a breach of romantic expectations of marital bliss. This risk is particularly high in view of the fact that these couples have, in the past, experienced greater companionship and pleasure in each other's presence. They are able to make comparisons; expectations for a happier relationship can arise and strain the status quo.

The Passive-Congenial Relationship

The passive-congenial relationship may be quite similar to the devitalized relationship, with the exception that couples do not have an early exciting past that has been hollowed out through the years. They may harbor deep affection and respect for each other and are not disillusioned as are the devitalized couples. In fact, they are quite comfortable with their situation. They emphasize what they share, such as their total agreement on a variety of political or religious issues, or the fact that they have similar leisure interests, parenting goals, and social network.

These couples' dating lives were generally uneventful, and a strong element of level-headedness rather than passionate love was at the basis of their decision to marry. For them, marriage is a secure platform from which to explore and develop other deep and even passionate interests, whether in parenting, politics, careers, or even volunteer work. Compatibility of background is often important. Many of these spouses believe that society is placing too much emphasis on sex and passionate love in marriage. Although some of these marriages end in divorce, the risk, by far, is not as high as for the two previous categories. This marriage fulfills many functions for the spouses and their families that are culturally acceptable. These unions may also be cemented by strong principles.

The Vital Relationship

The essence of the vital relationship marriage is sharing and togetherness. Such couples value their relationship, regularly discuss it, and, when alone, often think about it. A 35-year-old student describes some of the mechanisms at work in such a marriage:

> *"My husband really encouraged me to go back to school after our last son entered kindergarten. He has been supportive ever since and he has helped in the*

> *house and with the children far more than I ever thought he could. At dinner time, he always asks me to tell him and the children what I learned today and he shows a real interest. It makes me feel appreciated and the children treat me with more respect because of the example he sets. I love him so much."*

When these couples encounter conflict, they resolve it rapidly and move on. Differences are settled easily, even though with much discussion, but without verbal insults or humiliating put-downs, as would take place among the conflict-habituated couples.

This type of marriage comes very close to conforming to Americans' perception of an ideal marriage. Yet, it probably typifies only about one-third of couples who have been married for over 10 years. The vital marriage is not immune to divorce, although it is certainly less frequent among this category. But when a long-term vital relationship moves to a less involved one, such a marriage may become intolerable to one or both partners, even though it may still be a far better marriage than average. Divorce rather than adjustment may follow.

The vital marriage probably typifies the first years of a great proportion of marriages in North America as well as many marriages that are past the childrearing years. In other words, it is not only a type of marriage but, for many couples, it represents a stage in their relationship: the honeymoon.

The Total Relationship

Couples in a total relationship form a minority and are the "stuff of novels." They are in many ways similar to the vital couples—the main difference being that there is more sharing at the intellectual and psychological levels; more discussions take place for the sake of sharing their interests verbally as well as physically. In many instances, the couples have professional interests in common and help each other, attend conventions together, and confer on a wide range of issues. Whereas vital couples retain their individual existences, total couples seem to melt into the same existence, like identical twins.

These couples' sexual relationships are very important and are expressed in a multitude of settings and forms. Total couples define each other as lovers and best friends. Despite this, some do divorce because they have very high romantic and companionable standards. Experiencing less than what they have had, often after two or three decades, is not tolerable.

Marriages Change

Most students who have read these pages probably think that only the last two types of marriages would be good enough for them. This expectation is well expressed in the quote opening this chapter, where the young woman is devastated by what appears to be a rapid passage from a dating honeymoon into a devitalized marriage. Few approve of the conflict-habituated relationship and most hope that their marriage will never become devitalized. Although some see merits in the passive-congenial type, it certainly does not appear "very exciting," particularly in comparison to media portrayals in soaps and movies. Moreover, the studies of people who have divorced indicate that the first two types are at high risk for dissolution (Chapter 13). Clearly, in this society, some of these categories represent far less desirable states of matrimony.

Furthermore, marital relationships can evolve over time. Most middle-class couples probably begin at the vital stage, but a great proportion rapidly become conflictual or devitalized. Marital satisfaction plummets accordingly and divorce rates soar. In today's cultural climate, only a minority of marriages survive constant conflict. The others make a conscious effort to change or seek counseling.

One of the possible sequences between types that may occur throughout the years consists in a revitalization of the marriage after childrearing is completed. This is illustrated in the following student quote. She had described how the burdens of parenting and jobs had dulled her parents' marriage during her adolescence:

> *"Since then, my parents' happiness with their marital situation has been steadily rising. The business is great and my father's working less hours, Mary [a problematic adolescent] has a job, and I'm in college. They're happy with the whole family in general and they're like best friends. They're always getting all dressed up and they go out here, there, and everywhere. In fact, as I'm writing this down, they're on their way to Florida for a 2-week vacation—both from work and us kids. They're as close as a couple could be and are celebrating their 26th anniversary this year. They've made a lot of plans for the near future and they seem very happy and excited about it. Neither would be whole without the other."*

A devitalized marriage can also become a conflictual one over the years. At any point during these sequences, the marriage may break down, particularly when conflict and abuse occur. Furthermore, if we recall Cuber and Haroff's typology, marriages may remain of the same type throughout the years, except for the devitalized, which in itself represents a change from good to less satisfactory.

DIVISION OF LABOR AND INEQUALITY

One very important aspect in the spousal relationship is the household and child care division of labor as well as its perceived equity, an element that was relatively lacking in the Cuber and Haroff's typology. When they did their research, gender roles and the domestic division of labor had not yet become salient topics of research. These themes were soon to become far more discussed under the convergence of two trends occurring in the 1970s. One was the influence of feminism as a theoretical perspective and the second was the massive entry of wives on the labor market, thus placing into question the traditional division of labor that had prevailed up to that point. Men had been (and are still generally so considered) the families' heads and breadwinners, and women stayed at home with the children. This situation resulted from the social stratification by gender and conformed to its accompanying cultural values of feminine dependence and domesticity. The domestic division of labor is a perfect example of what was meant in Chapter 1 when I pointed out that microsociological phenomena (here, intimate domesticity) are closely related to macrosociological ones (in this instance, the overall social stratification by gender which pervades the entire society's organization).

A Classification of the Domestic Division of Labor

A classification of the division of labor between spouses has been derived from the sum of all the research carried out on this topic. The terms used are frequently encountered in the literature. The domestic division of labor involves two elements: who does what and who is responsible for planning or management—in other words, chores and responsibilities or availability. The traditional division of labor is most contested when wives are employed full time. In terms of equity, the more hours of paid work a woman engages in, the more likely she is to expect her husband to share domestic work (Potuchek, 1992). The classification presented here includes mothers who are not employed. It is one based on *behaviors* rather than attitudes, because far more couples believe in an egalitarian system than practice it (Pleck and Pleck, 1997). In other instances, daily necessities force couples to share child care equally, yet this egalitarian practice is not necessarily accompanied by egalitarian beliefs, in particular by husbands (Coltrane, 1996). Thus, the gap between attitudes and behaviors makes it preferable to focus on the latter.

The Egalitarian and Nongendered Division of Labor

In the egalitarian and nongendered division of labor, both spouses or partners participate equally in all aspects of the functioning of the household and in the care of the children. They come close to what Schwartz (1994) describes as *peer marriage,* and these couples are more likely to be encountered among the vital and total categories discussed earlier. Such couples may grocery shop and cook together, or they may alternate, with the husband cooking one week and the wife the next. Similarly, they may dress the children, get them ready for school, help them with breakfast, and so on together, or they may alternate—one week the father does morning duties while the mother does evening duties. The order is reversed the following week. If researchers went into such a household, they would add up the hours done by each parent on chores and responsibilities and would arrive at near identical totals.

Although many childless couples fit this description, relatively few couples with children do. As we have seen in the previous chapter, the arrival of the first child is generally the structural element that contributes to a change in the spousal division of labor toward the traditional. Couples who belong to this category often work shifts to avoid child care expenses or to provide a better quality of care to their children (O'Connell, 1993). However, there is some evidence that shift work is related to marital instability (Presser, 2000).

The Equitable but Gendered Division of Labor

The equitable but gendered division of labor involves a similar number of hours of work and child care but each spouse does different tasks largely based on what is considered appropriately male or female by this couple. It is another form of peer marriage but based on gender roles. For instance, the father may take care of the outside of the house, he may cook and do the dishes, but his wife does the cleaning and the child care and buys the groceries. They may both visit with their children's teachers; however, the father participates in coaching while the mother is responsible for sick days.

Researchers observing such a family would again arrive at a comparable number of hours for each spouse, but they would note that fathers and mothers generally engage in different tasks and have different responsibilities. Despite trends in this direction, relatively few families fit this description, which, although gendered, is judged as fair by employed mothers, even those who earn high salaries (Lennon and Rosenfield, 1994). What is important is that fathers participate equitably.

The Specialist Division of Labor

The specialist division of labor may be gendered or not: It resides in the recognition that one of the two spouses is better at cooking, while the other is more enthusiastic about cleaning or doing the laundry. One spouse or the other is better at putting the children to bed, while the other is more competent at supervising or helping with homework. In other words, things get done by the partner who is defined by the other or who self-identifies as the most qualified for the job. Some tasks may be occasionally shared or rotated depending on who is present when the necessity arises.

Researchers studying such families may come up with two vastly different sets of results. In one group of families, both spouses spend a same number of hours on their different tasks. This would be an equitable specialist situation, and is often encountered in lesbian-headed families (Nelson, 1996). Many of these women describe themselves as very conscious of problems stemming from the traditional division of labor and want to make sure that not one of the partners will become the traditional mother. In the other group of families, one spouse has specialized in minor chores (e.g., washing the car and taking out the garbage) so that the other is left doing everything else on a daily basis. The other could be the wife or the husband, depending perhaps on which spouse earns the most, is the strongest, or has the most power in the relationship. Here we see the beginning of inequity and of the potential for dissatisfaction by the spouse who carries most of the burden, generally the wife.

The Husband-Helper Division of Labor

The husband-helper takes no responsibility to ensure that dinner is ready, that a babysitter is available, that the children do their homework, and so on. The wife takes all the responsibilities and remains on a permanent state of availability for these duties. In some cases, it can be the reverse and it is the wife who is the helper, particularly if her job is demanding or if she has more power in the relationship. But the scenario that typifies perhaps a majority of American families sees the wife attending to most of the chores and child care responsibilities. She may ask, "Dear, I have left the grocery bags in the car—can you get them?" Or perhaps her husband may come in and ask what he can do to help or he simply does it. For instance, he might set the table or chop the onions. The wife's total number of hours devoted to child care and house chores will constitute 75 to 90 percent, and the husband's will constitute the balance, after the work the children do is factored in.

This division of labor typifies situations where the wife is not employed as well as cases of dual-earner couples. In families where the wife is employed, the husband's help is often perceived as fair because she feels that he appreciates her role by offering to pitch in. Husbands of nonemployed wives may, however, find their own help very generous and less fair. Thus, fairness in this respect is to some extent defined in a gendered way. When there is a discrepancy in perceptions, husbands' beliefs and perceptions are more likely to affect wives' than the reverse (Wilkie, Ferree, and Ratcliff, 1998:592)—a reflection of the greater masculine power in society at large. Husbands can generally choose the timing of their help, but wives are more bound to a schedule of tasks that have to be performed on a daily basis. Fathers often choose activities they like. This may be why Larson and Richards (1994) have found that mothers' moods are at their lowest when they engage in housework. In contrast, fathers often feel relaxed and cheerful.

The Traditional and Delegated Divisions of Labor

With the traditional division of labor, the mother does nearly everything and the father either watches television, tinkers with his car, or has a beer with his buddies after work. More often than not, the wife is unemployed or holds a part-time job. If she is employed full time, her husband may have objected to the decision. In his mind, and perhaps in hers as well, her place clearly is in the home. This division of labor is becoming less frequent but still occurs, particularly at the working-class level (see Harvey, 1993, for an ethnographic description). It also characterizes many families that have emigrated from countries where gender roles are patriarchal.

The delegated division of labor is generally a phenomenon observed among affluent families that can afford a housekeeper, a nanny, or a gardener. Although neither spouse actually does the work and child care consists of engaging in leisure activities with the children and visiting their teachers, the wife is generally responsible for finding, hiring, training, and keeping the help. This division of labor is a fairly traditional one. The wife may or may not be gainfully employed. When she is not, she engages in extensive community and volunteer work, organizes her husband's social activities, travels, and spends time shopping.

The Overall Perspective

When all these types of division of labor are put together, the husband-helper and the traditional types combined constitute a majority of couples. Whether the mother is married, divorced, part of a stepfamily, or single, she does most of the housework and child care. This is well illustrated in Figure 10.1. reproduced from a 1993 study by Demo and Acock. Bianchi (in Bianchi et al., 1999) has estimated on the basis of time-diaries that women do three times more housework and child care than husbands. Furthermore, unless they belong to the egalitarian category, fathers devote little mental energy worrying about household and children's daily needs or planning activities for them (Larson and Richards, 1994). However, on average, African-American husbands, compared to white husbands, do more child care and housework (Hossain and Roopnarine, 1993). Fathers who participate in the care of small children tend to maintain their involvement as the children get older (Aldous, Mulligan, and Bjarnason, 1998).

The Effect of Marital Quality: Overview of Recent Changes

In the 1950s and even in the early 1960s, middle-class wives' employment contributed to reduce marital satisfaction, especially among husbands, because it was

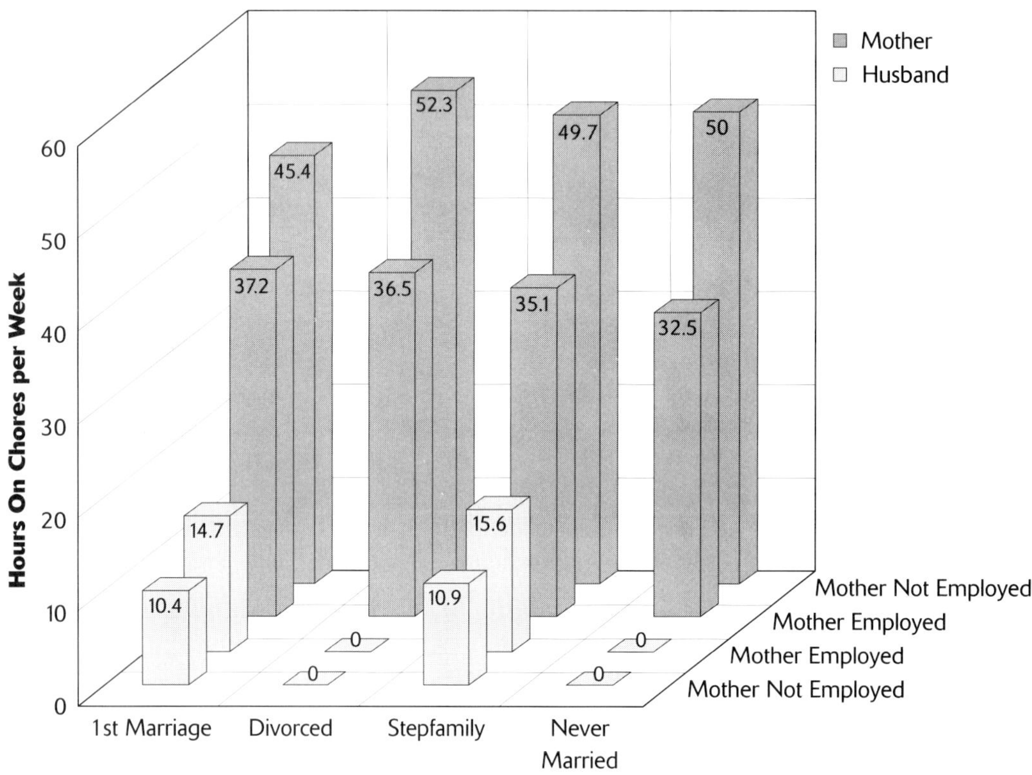

FIGURE 10.1

Mothers' and Their Husbands' Hours on Chores by Mothers' Work Status (Not Employed vs. Employed 30+ Hours)

Source: D. H. Demo and A. C. Acock, "Family Diversity and the Division of Domestic Labor: How Much Have Things Really Changed?" *Family Relations, 42* (1993). Copyright 1993 by the National Council on Family Relations, 3989 Central Ave. NE, Suite 550, Minneapolis, MN 55421. Reprinted by permission.

then an infrequent and unsual phenomenon (Burke and Weir, 1976). Appropriate changes in gender roles at the cultural level had not yet occurred among whites. (Black women were already employed far more often, but research on marital happiness did not include African-American couples back then.) In those days, there was no social support available to "working" wives (the term is set off in quotation marks because homemakers *do* work). For their part, husbands suffered a lowered sense of self-worth because wife employment often signaled that husbands earned too little and could not support their families on their own. Although this is currently still one of the main reasons why mothers work for pay, today it is a culturally recognized fact that two paychecks are necessary. Therefore, husbands do not generally feel diminished by their wives' employment, as used to be the case 40 to 50 years ago. Many take it for granted and are as proud of their wives' achievements as wives are of their husbands'.

African-American husbands often participate more in household activities than white husbands. This may stem from the long history of black women in the labor force as well as the hardships in their paid jobs, which have necessitated greater masculine household participation.

By the 1980s, a cultural shift had occurred, particularly among women, so that employed wives, especially highly educated ones, were more satisfied with their marriages than housewives (Houseknecht and Macke, 1981). Not surprisingly, husbands who held conventional beliefs about the division of labor and preferred to see wives at home reported lower levels of marital happiness when their wives were employed and earned high salaries (Perry-Jenkins and Crouter, 1990; Voydanoff, 1988). As time went by, husbands became more accepting of their wives' employment and started contributing more to housework, perhaps reluctantly. At the same time, researchers began to focus on the perception of fairness in the division of labor as it relates to marital happiness. The relative earnings of the spouses became an important factor influencing the power dynamics, even among minority group families that were quite traditional in the past, as Coltrane (1995) found for middle-class dual-earner couples of Mexican origins.

At the close of the twentieth century, researchers were seeing a correlation between marital satisfaction and the perception that the division of labor at home *and* at work is fair. In their overall evaluation of the quality of their marriage, the division of labor at home is much more important to women, whereas the division of labor at work is considered more frequently by husbands (Wilkie, Ferree, and Ratcliff, 1998). Furthermore, the division of domestic and paid work has positive and negative effects on marital satisfaction for both spouses, although the effects are still stronger for wives than husbands. These effects also have important implications for women's health (Bird, 1999; see Family Research 10.1). It is not only the relative amount of work that counts in affecting marital satisfaction but the perception of fairness or equity as well as the feelings that one's overall contribution to the family is appreciated (Wilkie, Ferree, and Ratcliff, 1998). The spouse who feels that his or her work, in and outside the home, is undervalued by the other is less happy with his or her marriage than the one who feels appreciated and supported.

FAMILY RESEARCH 10.1

Blood Pressure, High Job Strain, and Large Family Responsibilities among Women

This research method (Brisson et al., 1999) is interesting because it combines traditional sociological techniques with medical research. It was designed to test the effect of job strain and family work on women's health, and on blood pressure in particular. Samples of married women holding jobs with high versus low levels of strain, as well as high versus low levels of family responsibilities, were selected. Large family responsibilities were defined by the number of children at home, particularly young children, and much domestic work. All these were measured by means of questionnaires. The women's weights and heights were also verified. They wore Spacelabs monitors, and their blood pressures were recorded every 15 minutes as they went about their usual activities. Mothers with a university degree who had jobs involving strain and a substantial familial level of responsibilities had significantly higher blood pressure.

Division of Labor in Remarriages with Stepchildren

Some research indicates that decision making tends to be shared more equally in remarriages, yet studies on the division of labor itself show that it tends to remain traditional (Demo and Acock, 1993). With stepchildren present, the division of labor may constitute a key aspect of the spousal relationship. Visiting stepchildren often cause an enormous amount of work to stepmothers in terms of cooking and cleaning up. In some reconstituted families, fathers tend to contribute more. But in many others, the father simply entertains his visiting children, or he leaves with them after lunch for an outing while his wife inherits a load of dirty dishes. The following is a quote from a woman reminiscing about the problems created by visiting stepchildren in her previous remarriage:

> *"His kids kept coming here because he didn't want to visit them at their place, of course, because he hated his ex-wife. We had six kids here at times and his are the rough type; after they'd gone, the whole house was a mess for us to clean and the fridge was empty and I had to pay."*

This theme of inequity recurred throughout my interviews with stepmothers and was often exacerbated by complaints from the custodial mother to the father. Some complained that the children had not slept enough, had not been properly fed, or had watched too much television while visiting at their father's place. The stepmother felt particularly targeted because, after all, she was the one responsible for the smooth functioning of the household (O'Connor and Insabella, 1999).

> *"I feel like a glorified babysitter. I mean, she brings her boys here so that she can have a nice weekend of rest and go out. It's nice for her but I get nothing out of this except work, work, and more work, and the boys order me around like a slave."* [Their father?] *"Oh, he's so afraid of having further problems with*

her or that the boys won't want to visit that he says nothing. He pretends it's not there."

This stepmother did not intend to "stick around much longer."

In short, the matter of the division of labor seemed to bring in a great deal of conflict among these couples who had been together for only a few months or years at most. The wife's feelings of inequity may have been greater than in a first marriage with her own children. In these instances, the wife is at the very least laboring for her children, whereas in a remarriage, she is laboring for another woman's children—those of the ex-wife. One could add that a stepparent who feels burdened by an unequal division of labor may not relate so well to her stepchildren. In a few cases, another inequity was perceived by the stepmother: This occurred in instances where her husband's financial support of his children strained their budget and so plans for having a child of their own were accordingly delayed.

The Silent Division of Labor: Emotional Work

Another aspect to the division of labor is less discussed, although some research exists on this topic. It resides in the fact that, in general, women do more emotional or "love" work than men. Most exceptions to this rule would be found among the vital and total couples. We have seen in Chapter 4 that girls and women who date are more invested emotionally than males in the relationship. They work harder at maintaining it (Sacher and Fine, 1996), they initiate more conversations about the relationship, they express their love more frequently, they divulge more of themselves to their partner in order to show him their commitment, and they plan more of their activities together than he does. This pattern continues during cohabitation or marriage. We see in subsequent chapters that females nurture their relationship with their parents, siblings, children, and grandchildren more than males. Thus, all in all, whatever the familial roles they assume, from the time they are very young, females are socialized to become the kin-keepers, the expressive partners, and the emotional workers.

According to Hochschild, in *The Managed Heart* (1983), "emotion work" is a capital or an asset that women exchange for security in a relationship. In subordinate positions, the role occupants tend to rely on emotional capital. There are couples where the husband is subordinate because he wanted the marriage more than she or because she has more alternatives than he. This analysis fits very well with the exchange theories outlined in Chapter 1. In general, women have fewer alternatives, either because their maternal investment restricts their ability to work or to find other partners, or because there are many other women competitors "on the market." In other cases, women are disadvantaged because of the double standard of aging (note in Chapter 13 the tendency for men to remarry women younger than their previous wives).

For men, their marriage is a haven, yet for women, it is often both a haven and a source of work and insecurity (Hochschild, 1997). Wives are not necessarily more invested in the stability of their marriage than husbands, but they are more invested in its *quality maintenance*. This differential investment is a source of emotional insecurity for women, thus of subordination. It is also a source of marital dissatisfaction: Men tend to rate their current and past marriages more highly than women (Ambert, 1989). Men are not as observant as their wives are concerning the quality of their relationship. They tend to take it for granted, because they are not the emotional worker. In general, because of socialization and culture, women are more invested and sensitive in interpersonal relationships, and are particularly so in their marriage. However, women get more intrinsic rewards from these relationships, again a matter of gender-role socialization.

For instance, Larson and Richards (1994) report wives' moods to be more positive when they are with their husbands. Husbands' moods are also more positive when with their wives, but less so. Rook, Dooley, and Catalano (1991) have found that a husband's mood affects a wife's mood far more than the reverse. When a husband arrives home unhappy from stressors at work, he is more likely to transmit this state of mind to his wife, who is more attuned to his feelings and more dependent on them, than when a wife returns home unhappy. If a husband has any argument at work, this increases substantially the probability that he will have an argument with his wife later on (Bolger et al., 1989). In her autobiography, a mature student explains how deeply affected she is by this situation:

> *"The only reason that I take one course each year is that it gives me something to escape to when my husband comes home in a bad mood because of pressure at work. . . . He wants all of us to feel it or to suffer with him; he takes it out on us. But the few times that* I *have done this, he laughed it off and walked out. It's so unfair [when husband ignores her own bad mood]. I just hop in my car and come to the library to work on my paper. If I stayed home and went downstairs to type he would follow me and manage to pick a fight."*

Already 30 years ago, the reputed sociologist, Jessie Bernard (1972), talked of the two separate realities contained within one marriage—what she called a "his" and "hers"—two marriages in one. This differential still persists today and it is not a phenomenon specific to a particular social class or ethnic group; rather, it applies across the board. For instance, Coltrane (1995) found very similar patterns among middle-class Mexican-American couples in which both spouses were employed: his reality and her reality.

ASPECTS OF SPOUSAL RELATIONSHIPS

The type of relationship, including the division of domestic labor, that characterizes a union involves elements of happiness or disaffection as well as potential for conflict and conjugal problems. Furthermore, these elements have a threefold time dimension. First, they can be studied throughout the life span of a *couple* well into the later years. Second, marriages can succeed each other within a *person's* life span so that the sequencing of marital types, division of labor, and marital happiness constitutes an important research theme. Unfortunately, longitudinal studies, particularly those that would include in-depth qualitative material, are still scarce. Third, marital quality can be studied by *cohorts*—that is, for different generations.

Marital Happiness, Satisfaction, and Success

The concepts of marital happiness, satisfaction, and success have been very popular in the North American marriage literature ever since Burgess and Locke began their studies in the mid-1940s (see Burgess, Locke, and Thomes, 1963). The goal of this field of research is to define what a successful marriage is and compare the characteristics of couples who are satisfied and happy with their relationship to those of couples who are not. These various concepts are often used interchangeably, but there are different meanings attached to them. Marital happiness is an emotional state and is totally subjective and individual. In contrast, marital adjustment and success, while also subjective, depend much more on how the persons in the dyad perceive how they have achieved their goals, how well they communicate, and how companionable their relationship is (Glenn, 1998:570; see also Family Research 10.2).

Overall, studying marital happiness for both spouses is a complex undertaking, for it depends on a multitude of variables and it is impossible to include even most of them in a research. The variables that help couples achieve marital happiness can be found at several levels. Some, including economic situations, are derived from the macrosociological context and may account for lower marital satisfaction among blacks, who, on average, are economically disadvantaged (Aldous and Ganey, 1999). Others are psychological and involve personality characteristics, communication styles, and coping mechanisms. Furthermore, what makes for a happy marriage changes with the centuries and even the decades as couples' expectations evolve under various cultural influences that provide different social constructions of the conjugal relationship. It should also be mentioned that the emphasis on marital happiness as the foundation of a union is rather unique to Western countries. In most societies, the notion itself does not even exist at the cultural level.

As mentioned earlier, one can study what types of couples are happy together and what contributes to their dyadic satisfaction and even success. But it is also important to follow the trajectory of marital happiness longitudinally—that is, over time. Studying couples over time allows researchers to pinpoint types of personalities and of interactions existing in, say 1998, that may predict dyadic success or yet unhappiness by the year 2003 when they are reinterviewed. **Longitudinal studies** indicate to what extent marital happiness at Time 1 predicts that of Time 2 and what has happened in the interval to explain change or stability. Researchers can also predict with reasonable accuracy which marriages or relationships will end in divorce and verify this prediction with a follow-up study of the couples (Gottman, 1994). Furthermore, both psychologists and sociologists are interested in measuring parents' marital happiness to see how it relates to children's own development and adjustment.

In view of the importance of the parenting role in adults' self-identity (Thoits, 1992), it is surprising how few researchers have examined the effect of **parenting satisfaction** on marital happiness. In other words, not all adults are happy as *parents,* particularly when they have serious difficulties with their children (O'Connor and Insabella, 1999). Is it not possible that, when parents are happy in their role, this will reflect positively on their marital happiness? Sociologists Stacey Rogers and Lynn White (1998) have explored this question. They found reciprocal effects between marital happiness and parenting satisfaction, both for mothers and fathers. (*Parenting*

FAMILY RESEARCH 10.2

How Is Marital Satisfaction Measured?

Several measuring instruments have been devised to quantify marital adjustment and satisfaction. These instruments are generally called *scales* and are used during phone and face-to-face surveys designed to evaluate a couple's or even a family's functioning. Among the best-known is Spanier's Dyadic Adjustment Scale, which can be used for couples in general (see Spanier, 1976). The scale contains 32 close-ended questions testing for dyadic satisfaction and happiness, dyadic cohesion (shared activities and communication), dyadic consensus or perceived level of agreement, and perceived agreement on demonstration of affection, including sexuality. Examples of questions are:

- How often do you kiss your mate?
- How often do you confide in your mate?
- How often do you work together on a project?
- How often do you quarrel?

satisfaction was defined as parents' satisfaction with their relationship with their children.) Rogers and White (1998:305) conclude that "success in one family role primes an individual for success in other family roles . . . parents may include their own success as parents as one component of their marital evaluation."

Marital Quality through the Decades

Indications are that the quality of marriages has been declining, at least since 1969. In 1991, sociologist Norval Glenn first showed that the proportion of people reporting their marriages to be very happy had gradually declined between 1973 and 1988. This finding was unexpected, because divorce rates had increased during the same period. One would think that, on average, the surviving marriages would be happier than in the past, when even unhappy couples were forced to stay together. A complementary study carried out by Rogers and Amato (1997) used data gathered previously through phone surveys of two cohorts of individuals: those who had married between 1969 and 1980 and those who had married between 1981 and 1992.

Members of the 1981–92 cohort reported less marital interaction, more conflict and problems in their marriages, but not a lower overall marital happiness, than members of the 1969–80 cohort. Generally, there was greater conflict and less interaction when both spouses were employed and when there were preschool-age children at home. There was also more conflict when the spouses had fewer economic resources and the marriage had been preceded by cohabitation. The authors concluded that the decline in the quality of some aspects of marriage over the years can be partly attributed to changes in the requirements of the social context.

Partner Conflict and Marital Problems

Researchers evaluate the frequency of spousal conflict via self-reports and at times laboratory observations. They also investigate the mechanisms used by couples to resolve their conflicts. Overall, most of what is known about marital conflict and resolution comes from self-reports as well as spousal appraisals of the other partner's behavior. Same-sex and opposite-sex couples engage in similar conflict-resolution mechanisms (Kurdek, 1994). All report a relatively low level of conflict. Lesbian women are significantly more satisfied with their relationships and use more constructive conflict-resolution styles. They also report making greater effort to resolve conflict, perhaps because as women they have been socialized to be attuned to a partner's distress more than is the case among other couples that include at least one man (Metz, Rosser, and Strapko, 1994).

Partner Conflict

Conflict between partners and spouses arises from issues pertaining to the division of labor, communication, lack of attention to each other, sex, children, finances, and leisure time (Vangelisti and Huston, 1994). Finances involve not only how money is spent but who controls it as well as who earns it. In a marriage, there are usually more reasons for wives than for husbands to be dissatisfied, because women are more invested in their marital and parental relationships than men; also, when there is inequity in the division of labor, it usually favors husbands. Furthermore, in their role of emotional workers, wives are more involved in problem resolution (Gottman, 1998). For all these reasons, wives are generally less satisfied with their current and past marriages than husbands. Furthermore, wives are compelled to express more dissatisfaction to their husbands than the reverse and are therefore in the unpleasant position of initiating more conflict (Kluwer et al., 1997).

Styles of conflict resolution are often measured by the Styles of Conflict Inventory (SCI) scale. Conflict resolution falls along two basic dimensions (Metz, 1993). First, the engagement dimension includes assertion, aggression, and adaptation. Second, the avoiding style includes withdrawal, submission, and denial. In turn, these styles are either destructive (aggression, withdrawal, submission, or denial) or constructive and beneficial and lead to relationship satisfaction (healthy assertion and adaptation). Conflicts are least likely to be resolved constructively when, for instance, the husband withdraws from the interaction and this maintains the status quo (Gottman, 1994). Constructive outcomes occur when the communication of the dissatisfaction results in a better understanding of each other's feelings with a mutual search for a solution, including compromise.

Egalitarian couples tend to be more responsive to each other's disclosure of dissatisfaction and are more likely to engage in mutually satisfactory solutions (Rosenfeld, Bowen, and Richman, 1995). Traditional couples are more likely to avoid discussing their dissatisfaction with the division of labor. But conflict avoidance does not resolve the situation and may decrease marital happiness. However, were a researcher to ask these "avoiding" couples about conflict, he or she would be told that little exists—compared to what the researcher would find among couples containing at least one nontraditional spouse. Thus, a lack of reported conflict in this case simply refers to *overt* conflict; such couples may actually have a very high level of what could be called *covert* or simmering conflict, as described by a divorced woman about her previous marriage:

> *"My ex-husband always said to whoever would be present that we never had problems or quarrels. That's true, we never fought verbally and certainly not physically. But we could never talk about our disagreements and problems. As*

soon as I'd mention something, he'd smile, or laugh, or joke and walk away. He just left and things just kept getting bottled up; I mean we couldn't talk about money, about sex, about going out or not, his mother, nothing. Sure, we had no quarrels—we had no communication."

Marital Problems

Marital problems are more encompassing than conflict. However, the two overlap in the sense that disagreements and conflict constitute one type of problem reported by spouses. As is the case for the division of labor, there is a **gendered aspect** to marital problems: Wives report more marital problems than husbands and report more problems created by their husbands both during marriage and after divorce (Kitson, 1992).

A longitudinal study of married persons from 1980 to 1992 provided respondents with a list of problems and asked them to indicate which existed in their marriage and which person had the problem: the respondent, his or her spouse, or both. Amato and Rogers (1997) used this information to see if there were specific marital problems that could predict that a couple would be divorced at each subsequent reinterview. They found six problems, at times occurring as far back as nine years earlier, that predicted divorce. These were infidelity, spending money foolishly, drinking or using drugs, jealousy, having irritating habits, and moodiness. However, there might have been other equally good predictors of divorce, but they had not originally been included in the study. One can think here of problems related to an unequal division of labor or physical abuse, both of which are often mentioned by people after a divorce.

The Conjugal Relationship in Later Life

Older couples experience relatively high levels of marital satisfaction, with a great deal of closeness and little conflict (Carstensen, Gottman, and Levenson, 1995). At this point in time, it is difficult to determine if this elevated level of happiness in the later years is the result of the **U-curve phenomenon** or if it is a matter of cohort. The *U-curve* refers to those studies that have found a dip in the quality of marriages during the childrearing years followed by an upward trend after late adolescence. Such studies imply that the quality of a marriage varies during a couple's life span and is particularly affected by the negative aspects of the parental role. There is a great deal of support for this perspective: As we have seen in the previous chapter, companionship diminishes after the birth of a first baby.

But, in the case of a **cohort effect,** it would mean that older couples who married 30 to 70 years ago began their relationship in a social climate that emphasized mutuality or duty rather than personal gratification in marriage. These couples may have had lower expectations to begin with in terms of what marriage could do for them, focusing instead on what they can do for the relationship. They may, as a result, have been happier maritally (Glenn, 1998). When the U-curve applies, higher marital satisfaction in later years could reflect relief from the stress of active parenting as well as work-related problems (White and Edwards, 1990). Rather than being mutually exclusive, it is likely that both the U-curve and the cohort effect are implicated in the longitudinal dynamics of marital quality.

Retirement presents both opportunities and potential strains on the conjugal relationship. It reduces the pressure of commitments related to work as well as time

Mature couples often enjoy vital marriages. Some experience a renewal in the quality of their relationship, whereas others have maintained a high level of involvement with each other throughout the years. In-depth longitudinal studies are needed to research the dynamics involved over time.

constraints. Couples can then engage in more activities together and make plans that cannot be derailed because of role conflicts. However, increased togetherness may be stressful for some, particularly when their entire lives had revolved around parenting and working, and their relationship had not grown. They may find themselves with too much time on their hands and too little to say to each other, and thus some divorces occur at this stage. Many wives actually dread the day their husbands retire because "he won't know what to do with himself and I'll lose my freedom."

In an in-depth study, Robinson and Blanton (1993) asked 15 couples who had been married for at least 30 years to give their perception of the qualities that had sustained their relationship. The first qualities mentioned were intimacy and closeness, which resulted in the sharing of joys and activities and in mutual support in difficult times. These couples had enjoyed doing things together. They closely resembled the vital couples described earlier. The other quality that made their marriage endure was commitment to the relationship, to the spouse, or even at some points in the past to their marriage and children. The third aspect was communication or the sharing of thoughts and feelings so as to know the other's perspective. The fourth was called "congruence" by the researchers. This refers to the fact that most of these couples had similar perceptions regarding various domains of their lives, from commitment to religious orientation. Finally, the last salient quality was religiosity, which returns us to the contents of Chapter 8 indicating a positive effect of religiosity on the marital relationship and family life in general.

When both spouses live into very old age, one of the two may become frail. Physical impairment, such as difficulties walking, do not diminish closeness between the spouses. But a spouse's **cognitive impairment** lowers the degree of closeness between them, as perceived by the caregiving spouse (Townsend and Franks, 1997). This spouse also perceives that his or her efforts are less effective. Cognitive disabilities—such as dementia, senility, and Alzheimer's disease—bring changes in personality and behaviors that constitute a discontinuity in the pattern of the relationship. The caregiving spouse becomes more socially isolated because of the demands of his or her new role

(Barber and Pasley, 1995). It is then more difficult to cope with the conflicts engendered by the new dependency, such as when the afflicted spouse criticizes the efforts of the other, refuses the help offered, or even becomes aggressive. In contrast, when the frail spouse is supportive of the partner's efforts, the caregiver feels more efficient, less stressed, and is more satisfied with the caretaker role (Dorfman, Holmes, and Berlin, 1996).

The Next Time Around: Remarriage

Remarriages are as happy as first marriages, once duration is taken into consideration (Ganong and Coleman, 1994). Yet, remarriages end in divorce more than first marriages. How can this paradox be explained? Booth and Edwards (1992) suggest that it takes less deterioration in marital quality to precipitate a divorce among remarried than married couples. Along these same lines, Kurdek (1990) has found that marital satisfaction decreased more in remarriages than in first marriages.

In a remarriage, the spouses enter the union with more emotional baggage than in a first one. Their previous union may have raised or depressed their expectations and it may have made them more or yet less tolerant when expectations are not met. So far, the higher redivorce rate suggests that couples are less tolerant the second time around. Remarried spouses may be less willing to cope with what are considered to be smaller disappointments for others; these disappointments then bring ideas of divorce that might not occur so rapidly in a young couple who has never had to contemplate divorce. Obviously, there are processes involved in the second marital relationship that bring about a dissolution more readily than the first time around. Consequently, remarriages that are successful may require a deeper commitment and a conscious effort to avoid the downward spiraling trend. A reevaluation of what is and is not important in life is required, as expressed by a remarried man during his interview:

> *"I came to the conclusion that if marriage is to be successful, both partners have to work at it or at least spend time enjoying it. I had to rework my priorities and since I can't imagine myself married to your average Jane Doe I knew I was in for another career woman and I had to learn to give in a bit. Point of fact, my wife is very similar to my first wife and the reason is obvious: My first wife was fine. It's just that we failed to live our married lives. Now my career's less important, my marriage more. I even passed up a promotion recently. It's a shame that it took a divorce to come to this realization."*

Furthermore, redivorces occur even more rapidly than first divorce, as we see in Chapter 13. This rapid breakup may reflect the inability of many remarried spouses to establish a satisfying relationship very early on because of the complications of the structural factors involved (Tzeng and Mare, 1995). The presence of stepchildren, ex-spouses, and ex-in-laws represents for some couples a force that diverts their attention from the task of building their relationship and hampers their ability to invest in the dyad. A man reflects a similar perspective when trying to evaluate the quality of his remarriage during an interview:

> *"I think it's very difficult to start a remarriage on the right footing even with the best of intentions. There's always someone ready to make you trip over, especially her children. I find it hard to commit to this relationship—and I love her*

deeply, don't take me wrong here—because her children are so hostile. I can't separate them from her; they come in a package deal. One minute we're happy and I feel that I belong and the next minute they come in, throw stuff around, just ignore me, and it's so awkward."

Thus, when studying remarried couples' conjugal quality, it would be important to distinguish between those who have dependent stepchildren and those who were childless when they remarried.

SAME-SEX-PARTNER RELATIONSHIP

The research on the topic of the quality of the dyadic relationship among cohabiting same-sex partners is scant, and much of what exists is flawed methodologically. To begin with, it is impossible to draw large random samples of same-sex couples. The number of how many such couples exist and where they live is unknown. Therefore, most of the studies on same-sex couples have been small and many have relied on self-selection (i.e., researchers have placed ads in gay/lesbian newsletters and clubs to solicit couples' cooperation). Obviously, such an approach draws relatively educated couples who maintain links to the homosexual community, may be activists, and are fairly young. Less educated same-sex couples who have little to do with the homosexual subcultures or are older will not be represented in these samples (but see Yip, 1997). Moreover, gays and lesbians have suffered from stigmatization and may not wish to share the intimate details of their lives with researchers for fear of being further victimized or categorized (Nelson, 1996:10). As a result, only couples who are happy together may respond to such ads.

For instance, in a recent study, Kurdek (1998) admits to his sample's lack of representativeness. Nevertheless, despite this sampling deficiency, this research is well designed. Kurdek compared married to gay and lesbian couples on several dimensions of dyadic satisfaction. Gay couples reported more autonomy from each other in terms of activities, friendships, and decision making than married dyads. Lesbian couples reported more intimacy, autonomy, and equality than married dyads. (However, the researcher did not present comparisons between gay and lesbian couples.) Both gay and lesbian couples had higher rates of dissolution than married ones.

Kurdek explained this difference by the fact that nothing in the social world encourages same-sex couples to stay together, whereas the contrary occurs for married couples. The latter are supported by cultural values preventing them from leaving the relationship. Gay unions do not constitute an institution, as do marriages. Actually, for all types of couples in this longitudinal study, only the **absence of barriers to leaving** was a significant predictor of later high breakup rates. Indicators of barriers are statements such as:

- I would find it difficult to leave my partner because it would hurt those who depend on me.
- I would find it difficult to leave my partner because of pressure from my family, friends, or community.
- I would find it difficult to leave my partner because I feel obligated to keep the relationship together.

As Kurdek (1998) points out, there are no legal barriers preventing the dissolution of gay and lesbian relationships, and the same occurs for cohabiting couples who do not have children. Socially, same-sex relationship is already labeled deviant by many and few, particularly in their families, object if the relationhship breaks up. Despite this lack of social barriers, around 85 percent of the same-sex couples remained together for the duration of the 5-year longitudinal study. But they had already been together for an average of 10 and 7 years, respectively, for gay and lesbian dyads. In other words, they had survived the most unstable years, which are the first ones.

In the domain of conflict, Kurdek (1994) compared gay, lesbian, and heterosexual couples and found little difference in the rank order of frequency of conflict in six global areas regarding power, social issues, personal flaws, distrust, intimacy, and personal distance. Issues pertaining to intimacy and power were the most frequently mentioned sources of conflict by all three types of couples. This is interesting in itself because it indicates that problems related to power are not entirely explainable in terms of gender roles or the patriarchal order, for they exist in same-sex couples as well. For all three types of couples, frequent conflict was negatively related to each partner's satisfaction with the relationship. Conflict over intimacy and power was more related to a lower satisfaction than other conflict topics. During the one-year duration of the study, conflict over power was the most predictive of later relationship deterioration. These findings are in agreement with those of Gottman (1994) as well as Vangelisti and Huston (1994) for married couples.

As is the case among heterosexuals, saying "I love you," showing physical affection, giving gifts, and cooking for the other are frequently mentioned expressions of love among same-sex partners (Stiers, 1996). Gift giving is more often mentioned among males than females, perhaps as a substitute for verbal expressions of affection. Overall, as herein indicated and as seen in other chapters, there are more similarities than differences in the way homosexual and heterosexual couples live their relationships. The structure and requirements of daily life place similar demands on them.

THE EFFECT OF THE PARENTAL RELATIONSHIP ON CHILDREN

Most of the literature on the effect of the parental relationship on children has to do with parental conflict both during and after divorce. Nevertheless, researchers are interested in finding a theoretical explanation for the observed relationship between the quality of parents' marriage and children's well-being.

The Effect of Parental Conflict

The research focus on parental conflict is understandable in view of the fact that children who live with openly conflictual parents often have poorer adjustments than children in well-functioning single-parent families (Seltzer, 1994). Children are more disturbed when the content of the conflict relates to them. For instance, parents who openly fight about their children upset them more than if they are quarreling about money; the children may even blame themselves, especially when they are small (Grych and Fincham, 1994).

Parental disagreement by itself does not affect children negatively. In fact, children can learn functional ways of solving human problems by listening to their parents iron out their difficulties in a cooperative manner. Constant disagreement that is left unresolved or that simmers may be detrimental. Above all, parental conflict of the hostile type has the most negative effects (Buehler et al., 1998). Children exposed to repeated hostility between parents fail to learn adaptive modes of conflict resolution. But, as Fincham (1998:551) correctly remarks, there is more to a marriage than absence of conflict. Above all, "there has been no research on the impact of the spouses' supportive behavior on child development." When parents enjoy a good marriage, the mother's relationship with her small child is warmer and she is more nurturant. Fathering is even more affected than mothering by the quality of the marriage.

All in all, children whose parents get along well exhibit far fewer behavioral difficulties than those whose parents are in a conflictual marital situation (Morrison and Coiro, 1999). The advantage extends to adolescence and adulthood. Furthermore, a happy parental relationship is related to greater parent/child affection and consensus (Amato and Booth, 1997).

How to Explain the Effect of Marital Quality on Children

Several complementary explanations exist for the correlation between the quality of parents' marriage and their children's outcomes. But before we examine them, it is important to mention that such a correlation may not exist in cultures where fathers and mothers, men and women, live largely separate lives, and where the definition of the marital relationship is an institutional one rather than one that is largely personal. It may not include affection, companionship, and even discussions concerning the children. Instead, it might revolve around patriarchal authority and kin relationship. It is not known what effect, if any, the quality of the marital interaction has on child development or on parenting in these societies.

Marital Quality Fosters Supportive Parenting

In U.S. society, the correlation between a happy marriage, warm parenting, and positive child development is expressed by the arrows from left to right in the *center* of Figure 10.2. The most frequently mentioned explanation is that the supported and loved mother lives in a warm environment that translates into a close and attentive relationship with her child (Belsky, 1984). In contrast, when conflict exists, parents are stressed, feel unappreciated, and may be less able to transfer loving feelings to their child. Childrearing is disrupted and parents agree less with each other in terms of child care (Jodl et al., 1999). It becomes more difficult to use authoritative socialization practices. Parents' hostility toward each other often results in harsh parenting and rejecting behavior toward children (Krishnakumar and Buehler, 2000). In

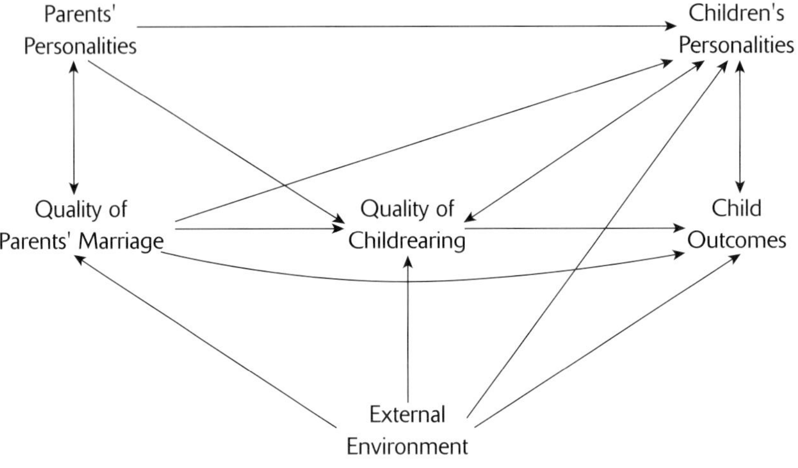

FIGURE 10.2

Variables Explaining the Correlation between the Quality of Parents' Marriage and Child Outcomes

some cases, parents use their children to get at each other, as had occurred to a male student who, in his self-description, grew up to be "out of control":

> *"I was more attached to my father because I always turned to him when my mother said no and he usually said yes so that I always ended up doing what I wanted. At other times he'd say, 'Ah, don't worry about her, she doesn't know what boys are like,' and I think that after a while my mother gave up on me. I remember that my father used to just ignore her or would tell her off and I didn't mind at the time because I was getting my way. It worked great during my adolescence, well, at first, but then it turned sour because I had become way out of control and it took my last girlfriend's leaving me before I finally realized what had happened to me. She just hated my father and she said I'd turn out just like him as a husband and she wasn't going to live with this."*

At its worse, a family environment can be filled with recriminations, sharp verbal exchanges, disrespect, fear on the part of the most vulnerable spouse, long periods of sulking silence, and even physical violence. The difficulties these mothers encounter with their partners may drain them so much that they are often inconsistent in their reactions to their children's demands and misbehavior.

The Role of Learning and Personality

With the second explanation, the focus shifts on what children can learn in this context: that quarreling and even being abused is a normal way of living and of resolving conflicts (Grych and Fincham, 1994). (This is expressed by the curve from quality of marriage to child outcomes in Figure 10.2.) Small children who are already predisposed to hyperactivity, nervousness, or aggression may be especially vulnerable to parental conflict; they may be particularly susceptible to acquiring dysfunctional behaviors by observing and modelling their parents' conflictual interaction.

The third explanation also resides in assumptions about personality and temperament, as shown at the top of Figure 10.2 (Erel and Burman, 1995). A conflictual marriage may arise because the two parents have problematic personalities, are difficult to get along with, do not like to compromise, or are aggressive. Even if only one of the two parents is so, the marriage is likely to be unstable. Furthermore, if a mother is impatient, irritable, and has little tolerance for frustration, she may exhibit these patterns in her parenting practices as well, and the same holds true for the father. This would explain why, in conflictual marriages, the parent/child relationship is less warm and more erratic *and* why the babies and children in these families experience more adjustment difficulties, anxiety, and behavioral problems. In contrast, in a peaceful and supportive marriage of the vital type, there are strong chances that the parents' personalities are conducive to good relationships, and the child's environment is accordingly regulated.

Genes and Within-Family Environment

A fourth and complementary explanation flows from the preceeding explanation. It resides in joint genetic and environmental considerations (Reiss, 1995). Parents who are aggressive, have little tolerance for frustration, are impatient, or are not easy to get along with may well pass at least some of these unfortunate traits via genetic inheritance to their children (Plomin, 1994; Rowe, 1994). The result is that some of these babies may themselves be more fussy and irritable, and may later become more oppositional, hyperactive, and aggressive than children who are born to parents who are warm, patient, and cooperative, and who consequently have a stable relationship.

Each person in a family constitutes part of the others' environment. Thus, the behavioral manifestations of parental characteristics become part of the children's environment, both as childrearing styles and as marital styles. At the negative level, children's own behavioral manifestations of their partly inherited traits, such as hyperactivity, elicit a negative reaction from parents, and this reaction then also becomes part of the children's environment. These partly genetically driven environments interact with each other and result in inadequate parent/child relationships as well as negative child outcomes or adjustment (Reiss, 1995).

The Larger Environment Affects Marriage and Childrearing

Finally, as shown in the lower part of Figure 10.2, marriages and childrearing can be strained by the environment external to the family—poverty and unemployment come to mind here (Elder et al., 1992). Thus, children's personalities and outcomes may be indirectly affected by these environmental strains. Furthermore, as they age, children whose parents have a conflictual marriage may be more at the mercy of deleterious neighborhood, school, and peer influences. A student unwittingly puts her finger on this causality chain when she points out the following:

> *"I stayed home as little as I could between the ages of 10 and 18 because my parents weren't easy to get along with and were fighting all the time, more my father*

than my mother, and a lot of the time they'd get mad at me or yelled at me or it would upset me to see my mother cry. My parents were too busy fighting and maybe it was a relief for them when I was out so that I was on the streets most of the time by [age] 10. Of course, I got into all kinds of trouble but they became aware of little of it and I ran around with much older children. . . . I think that all of this affected my personality because I am somewhat difficult to be with and I don't put up with much. I don't know if I got that from my parents or because I ran around peers who were like that or because the teachers gave me a hard time (after I gave them a hard time), I don't know. But the fact is that I'd like to have a nice relationship with a male but it's an uphill battle because I tend to fly off the handle."

CONCLUSIONS: DEFINITIONS OF MARITAL QUALITY ARE CULTURE SPECIFIC

A marital relationship consists of several dimensions, from the affective level to its power-sharing aspect. Some of these dimensions tend to be given a greater emphasis in different cultures, at different historical periods, and, within each couple, at different times in their life course. For instance, the romantic or love aspect considered so important in North America is not even taken into consideration in many countries of the world, particularly where marriages are arranged. Love often develops among a proportion of these couples, but it is not an aspect of marriage deemed necessary. The sexual satisfaction dimension was not given much emphasis in this country a hundred years ago, particularly not for women. Sex was certainly not something openly discussed concerning marriage. Within couples in Western countries, romantic love may be considered far more important at the beginning of the relationship, for instance, and so may sexual satisfaction. As time goes by and as the relationship develops, these domains may become less salient than value consensus, shared activities, the division of labor, and parenting.

Culture is a key factor in teaching men and women what to expect in marriage and in determining what constitutes a satisfying conjugal relationship. As culture changes, so do cultural definitions of marital happiness to some extent. Currently, in North America the media are a key source of cultural definitions. This includes books written by experts as well as what is depicted in films and on television programs.

The media focus entirely on heterosexual dating, cohabiting, and married couples. Thus, the general public inherits the cultural representations that depict ideal partner relationships only as opposite-sex couples. Yet, we have learned that there is a great deal of overlap between what makes a homosexual and a heterosexual couple satisfied with their respective relationship. What differs, naturally, are the mechanics of sex. But, otherwise, there is much similarity between gay, lesbian, and heterosexual couples. It would be interesting to gain a better understanding of how and from where homosexuals develop expectations concerning relationship satisfaction in view of the fact that they grow up in a heterosexual culture.

SUMMARY

1. The Cuber and Haroff typology of couples married for at least 10 years includes the conflict habituated, the devitalized, the passive-congenial, the vital, and the total. Changes in marital quality over the conjugal life may lead to conflict and divorce, or revitalization can occur.
2. The spousal division of labor includes not only who does what in the household and in child care but also who is responsible for what. The classification suggested includes the egalitarian and nongendered division of labor, the equitable but gendered, the specialist (the number of hours spent by each spouse may vary), the husband-helper (fairly widespread but typical in husband-earner families), the traditional, and the delegated among the more affluent. In general, gender roles dictate that the wife-mother does far more housework and child care and remains available for these responsibilities.
3. The effect of this unequal division of labor on marital quality seems to have changed during the last decades of the twentieth century along with the evolution of the cultural and economic climate concerning the employment of women. The spousal division of labor becomes a particularly thorny issue for stepmothers of live-in or frequently visiting stepchildren. An important aspect of the spousal division of labor resides in emotional work: Women generally work harder at maintaining the relationship and are more sensitive to its quality and to their partners' moods.
4. The concepts of marital happiness, satisfaction, and success are defined and differentiated. Marital adjustment and success is a predictor of divorce. There are reciprocal effects between marital happiness and spouses' satisfaction with their parenting role. The quality of marriages may have been declining since the 1970s as a result of changes in the social context of marriage.
5. Same- and opposite-sex couples engage in similar types of conflict and conflict-resolution mechanisms. Conflict arises from issues pertaining to the division of labor, communication, lack of attention to each other, sex, children, and finances. In marriages, wives are generally more dissatisfied than husbands and perceive more problems.
6. Older couples experience relatively high levels of marital satisfaction. At this time, it is not known if this is a matter of cohort or of revitalization of marriages after midlife (the U-curve phenomenon). Qualities that sustain long-term unions are closeness, commitment, communication, and similarity of perceptions and beliefs. The relationship is altered when one spouse becomes disabled, particularly at the cognitive level.
7. Remarriages are as happy as first marriages but satisfaction decreases more easily in remarriages. Remarried spouses may be less willing to cope with smaller disappointments. Furthermore, the structure of remarriages (e.g., stepchildren and ex-spouses) complicates the relationship.
8. The study of the relationship among same-sex couples is still in its infancy and requires methodological refinements. Lesbian couples report more intimacy,

autonomy, and equality than married couples, whereas gay couples report more autonomy. Same-sex couples have higher rates of dissolution than married couples. This may, in part, be due to an absence of barriers, particularly at the legal level, to leaving the relationship. All types of couples, however, experience similar sources of conjugal conflict.

9. Parental conflict that is perceived by children is detrimental to their development. Happy marriages are related to healthy child development. This may be explained by the secure environment provided by such parents; the children have more positive role models; parents' personalities are less problematic in happy marriages; the children may have inherited easier predispositions; and, finally, external environmental influences affect parents and children.
10. Culture is a key factor in teaching men and women what to expect in marriage and in determining their level of happiness.

KEY CONCEPTS AND THEMES

Absence of barriers to leaving, p. 293
Child adjustment, p. 294
Cognitive impairment, p. 291
Cohort effect, p. 290
Conflict, pp. 289, 294
Conflict-habituated marriage, p. 275
Delegated division of labor, p. 281
Devitalized marriage, p. 275
Egalitarian division of labor, p. 279
Emotional work, p. 285
Equitable division of labor, p. 279
Gendered aspect, p. 290
Husband-helper, p. 280
Longitudinal studies, p. 287
Marital adjustment, p. 287
Marital happiness, p. 287
Marital quality, p. 288
Parenting satisfaction, p. 287
Passive-congenial marriage, p. 276
Quality maintenance, p. 285
Remarriage, pp. 284, 292
Retirement, p. 290
Same-sex-partner relationship, p. 293
Specialist division of labor, p. 280
Total marriage, p. 277
Traditional division of labor, p. 281
U-curve phenomenon, p. 290
Vital marriage, p. 276

STUDY AND REVIEW QUESTIONS

1. Why did Cuber and Haroff study couples who had been married for a long time rather than newly married ones to arrive at a typology of marriages?
2. Considering the classification of the domestic division of labor, what can be concluded on the basis of exchange theory? (A return to Chapter 1 may help in answering this question.)
3. What are some of the methodological complications in the measurement of marital adjustment?
4. How can conflict and marital problems be used to predict divorce?
5. Link the first section of this chapter on the types of marriages to the section on marriage in later life to explain long-term marital success.
6. Remarriages are as happy as first marriages; why, then, are they more at risk of divorce?
7. What are some of the methodological difficulties inherent to the study of same-sex-partner relationships currently?

8. What are the differences and similarities between heterosexual marriages and same-sex partnerships?
9. Which explanation do you prefer for the correlation between the quality of parents' marriage and their children's outcomes? Justify your choice.
10. How does culture play a role in the definition of what constitutes marital happiness?

SUGGESTED READINGS

Alford-Cooper, F. 1998. *For keeps: Marriages that last a lifetime.* Armont, NY: Sharpe. The author reports on a study of couples belonging to two cohorts. One was married during the Great Depresssion and the other during World War II. She looks at the problems specific to each cohort of couples as well as their relationships.

Blumstein, P., and Schwartz, P. 1983. *American couples.* New York: Pocket Books. This is a relatively old but still relevant study on four types of couples: married, cohabiting, gay, and lesbian. Issues pertaining to their relationships are examined comparatively, including sexuality, money, and work.

Potuchek, J. L. 1997. *Who supports the family? Gender and breadwinning in dual-earner marriages.* Stanford, CA: Stanford University Press. This book presents a few statistics but is largely designed around the presentation of case studies of couples. The author studies husbands' and wives' social construction of breadwinning.

Rosenblatt, P. C., Karis, T. A., and Powell, R. D. 1995. *Multiracial couples: Black and white voices.* Thousand Oaks, CA: Sage. This book reports on the results of a qualitative study (in-depth interviews) of 21 couples. The focus is on relationships and their dynamics within a biracial context.

Schwartz, P. 1994. *Peer marriage: How love between equals really works.* New York: Free Press. The author presents the results of a qualitative study of couples who are in an egalitarian marriage. The relationships are examined, with a focus on the compromises and the necessity to radically alter traditional marriage patterns.

SUGGESTED WEBLINKS

National Council on Family Relations provides several sources and articles on topics related to marriage. **<http://www.ncfr.org>**

For further information, check *yahoo* search engine at **<http://dir.yahoo.com/Society_and_Culture/Families>** as well as *metacrawler* search engine at **<http://www.go2net.com/directory/Society/Relationships/Marriage>**.

CHAPTER 11

The Parent/Child Relationship and Parenting

OUTLINE

The Beginning of the Parent/Child Relationship

Parents' Socialization Practices
Authoritative Parenting
Authoritarian and No-Nonsense Parenting
Permissive and Uninvolved Parenting
Additional Parenting Styles

Determinants of Parenting Socialization Practices
Contextual and Cultural Determinants
The Question of What Constitutes "Proper" Parenting
The Debate over Physical Punishment
Parents' Personalities and Beliefs
Parental Adaptation to Children

The Parent/Adolescent Relationship
The Social Construction of Adolescence
How Do Parents and Adolescents Get Along?
Parental Influence
The Role of Historical Periods
The Role of the Human Qualities That Are Valued

The Role of Peers in the Parent/Adolescent Relationship
Peer Groups and Parental Isolation
Peer Spillover Effect

The Relationship between Parents and Adult Children
When the Child Is a Young Adult
Adulthood Comes Later
Why Do Young Adults Stay Home Longer?
Factors Related to Mutual Satisfaction
When the Child Is 30 to 40 Years Old
Senior Parents Help Their Adult Children
Adult Children Help Their Elderly Parents
Children's Marital Status
Children's and Parents' Gender

Conclusions: The Macro and Micro Aspects in the Parent/Child Relationship

Summary
Key Concepts and Themes
Study and Review Questions
Suggested Readings
Suggested Weblinks

If you stay a while in the nursery of a hospital maternity ward, you will see that each newborn is different from the very beginning of life. For instance, you may see one neonate such as Lucia, who cries constantly, even when picked up, and who is agitated and resists feeding. In the next crib, Jack is a total contrast: He sleeps contentedly, nurses avidly, and cries but stops as soon as he is fed or changed. A third baby, Latitia, is small, quiet, does not cry, sleeps most of the time, and drinks little milk. Each baby needs different types of care.

Baby Lucia requires more attention because she calls for more of it with her cries (what is called a child-driven stimulus*). In contrast, Baby Jack demands little attention and is easy: All he needs is to be fed, changed, and cuddled. Jack's parents have more free time and feel competent because it seems to them that everything* *they do for him is rewarded with success. From the beginning of his life, Jack and his parents establish a smooth relationship that is likely to continue in the future.*

Lucia's temperament presents at the outset the potential for problems. Her parents may feel less competent and more tense, especially if she is their first child. If they are poor and experience marital conflicts, Lucia may constitute an additional problem for them. Her parents' reactions may not always be positive because they are already frazzled by other preoccupations. As a result, she might grow up with less positive interactions and may not find interpersonal relations as rewarding as Jack will.

For her part, Baby Latitia arouses her caregivers' concern because of her low birth weight and minimal appetite. At the same time, her parents are likely to feel comfortable because she is an easy baby. If fed regularly, she will eventually thrive and will not make too many demands on them. But with a mother who does not know much about infant care, a neonate such as tiny Latitia may deteriorate and waste away because she may not cry enough to indicate that she is hungry.

THE BEGINNING OF THE PARENT/CHILD RELATIONSHIP

In this chapter, the parent/child relationship is studied within a combined interactional-transactional and life course perspective (Elder, 1995). Our three fictive newborns illustrate some of the mechanisms at the origin of this relationship. What emerges from these vignettes are interactions, or **transactions.** On a basic level, each baby has different needs to which parents respond; this means that infants initiate many of the parental gestures that form the cornerstone of the relationship. For instance, a baby who cries constantly (see Family Research 11.1) may elicit less positive reactions from his or her parents (Sanson and Rothbart, 1995). In turn, this reaction depends on parents' gender, personalities, perceptions, and life circumstances (Goldsmith, Buss, and Lemery, 1997). Then, these reactions (being fed, changed, cuddled, or discouragingly ignored) become part of the babies' environment and contribute to the shaping of their subsequent behaviors and, later on, their attitudes and beliefs.

A small child who is blessed with positive characteristics, such as having a good attention span and low impulsivity, finds it easier to comply to parents' socialization requests as he or she internalizes family rules and norms more easily. In turn, this child requires less supervision and less repetition, and receives fewer negative reactions from his or her parents. That child is less frequently disapproved of and scolded.

FAMILY RESEARCH 11.1

Can Mothers Accurately Judge Their Babies' Fussiness?

Lounsbury and Bates (1982) taped the hunger cries of infants who had already been described by their mothers as being either difficult, average, or easy. The tapes were played to other women, also mothers, who were unaware of the ratings. These women judged the cries of the infants who had been described by their own mothers as difficult to be more irritating than the cries of the other infants. The correlations between the biological mothers' judgments of their baby's difficultness and the observers' ratings were quite substantial. This study indicates that there are certain societal norms as to what constitutes child and infant difficultness.

Such children may form stronger attachments to their parents, both as a result of their personalities and of the way parents react to them. This attachment then further reinforces their willingness and ability to be socialized (Kochanska, 1995). Thus, within the **interactional-transactional perspective,** parents and children interact with and influence each other's behaviors and attitudes (Magnusson and Allen, 1983). First, from the very beginning, children contribute to the way their parents see them and treat them. Second, these interactions between parents and children become part of the children's environment. Third, these interactions are in turn affected and shaped by sociostructural variables (Bronfenbrenner, 1979; Lewis, 1997). These include the number of children and adults in the family, the family's economic situation, and how society defines children and good parenting.

This perspective stands in contrast with traditional views on socialization still held that describe children's personalities and behaviors as the product of their parents' childrearing. Although parental practices are indeed important, we see in this chapter that children and even more so adolescents contribute to the formation of their environment and of their own development. In other words, **children are coproducers** of their own development (Lerner and Busch-Rossnagel, 1981). They are coagents in their socialization process: They help their parents teach them the ways of behaving and thinking acceptable within their status group and society at large.

PARENTS' SOCIALIZATION PRACTICES

In contrast to the dynamics of the interactional-transactional perspective, the vast literature on parents' socialization practices is unidirectional and static. It purports to link proper ways of parenting causally to positive child outcomes. In the presentation that follows, only the more useful aspects of the study of parents' socialization practices are retained. We begin with Baumrind's (1967) initial typology: authoritative, authoritarian, and permissive styles of parenting. This typology is somewhat expanded here to meet criteria of cultural diversity.

Authoritative Parenting

Parents who are authoritative combine warmth, respect for their children's individuality, and psychological autonomy with monitoring of their activities and whereabouts (Gray and Steinberg, 1999). Authoritative parents are firm yet loving: They are involved. Such parents explain to their children the reasons behind their demands and the consequences of not complying. They insist on obedience and then follow through with enforcement of the rules and appropriate punishment. Some evidence shows that punishment, when necessary, increases the effectiveness of reasoning for small children. It may increase their ability to internalize rules of behavior so that, when older, they will no longer need to be punished (Larzelere et al., 1998).

Warmth and monitoring have been correlated with successful child and adolescent outcomes in all types of family structures in North America and other countries (Steinberg and Darling, 1994). More specifically, monitoring is related to lower rates of risky sexual activities among adolescents (Miller, Forehand, and Kotchick, 1999; Rodgers, 1999) and behavior problems among early adolescents (Pettit et al., 1999). The authoritative pattern correlates the most with good adjustment on all dimensions of development (Steinberg et al., 1995), but its various components (psychological autonomy, monitoring, and involvement) contribute in unique and independent ways to diverse child outcomes (Gray and Steinberg, 1999). However, within an interactional perspective, this research should not be taken to mean that authoritative parenting can prevent *all* problems, as illustrated here, in a male student's autobiography:

> *"I had continued to do drugs through grade nine and managed to keep a decent average in school. Pete's, John's and my parents had been comparing incidents and behavioral changes for a little while and finally figured that we were doing drugs. The straw that broke the camel's back was when Pete's mother found drugs in his room (I am sure my parents had searched mine). Pete admitted everything, including my participation. What followed was what was most painful to me and that was* reality. *I had hurt my family, my reputation, and who knows what else during my drug times and now I had to deal with all of this. Firstly, my parents sat down and talked to me. They were crying and told me I was not allowed to see any of those people again, that I was grounded, that I would be much more accountable now, and that I would improve my marks in school to meet my potential."*

In this incident, the parents could not detect drug use that was taking place behind their backs. But vigilance, communication with other parents, and then a firm but loving stand contributed to the adolescent's redress—along with his cooperative personality. Thus, again one sees the interaction between parental efforts and child characteristics.

Authoritarian and No-Nonsense Parenting

In contrast, what predominates in the authoritarian parenting style is the dimension of control, restriction, and, at the extreme, coercion. This type of discipline is not so effective for European-American adolescents, perhaps in part because it is not socially constructed as suitable within the broad cultural context; control and restrictions are better accepted in other cultures, where they are seen as guidance (Gorman, 1998).

Other authoritarian parents are characterized by inconsistency. They are arbitrary and erratic; they tell their children what to do and punish severely and indiscriminately, or they threaten, then harshly punish one day, but fail to follow through the next day. They "natter" a lot. This type of discipline is not as effective because children can take advantage of its inconsistencies; it neither stimulates the development of self-control nor does it respect children's psychological autonomy.

If Baumrind rewrote her typology today, she probably would include a socialization practice that falls between the authoritative and the authoritarian: no-nonsense parenting, often seen in African-American samples, particularly disadvantaged mothers. Brody and Flor (1998) describe this style as higher on control than in the authoritative pattern but also involving more warmth and nurturance than is the case in the authoritarian style. Control includes physical punishment that occurs within an otherwise affectionate context.

This no-nonsense pattern, first described in an ethnographic study by Young in 1974, "represents a functional adaptation to contexts that are more dangerous" (Brody and Flor, 1998:813); it signals to the child that the parent is vigilant and cares. So far, studies have found that this style of parenting promotes black children's sense of competence and regulation, and results in lower rates of detrimental behaviors and attitudes. These findings apply both in one- and two-parent families. This style of parenting is related to black teenagers' better school outcomes and taking personal responsibility—even though these adolescents find that their parents "hassle" them (Spencer et al., 1996).

Permissive and Uninvolved Parenting

For their part, permissive parents place very few maturity demands on their children, who can behave very much as they wish. Such parents do not actively socialize their children, because they fail to set rules concerning school, behavior at home, or activities with peers. Neither do they supervise their children. Permissiveness can be combined with either a high level of warmth and acceptance or with disinterest and even rejection.

Subsequent to Baumrind's description of permissive childrearing, another style of parenting was added: uninvolved parents (Maccoby and Martin, 1983). Such parents are both permissive and indifferent or permissive and rejecting. They do not pay much attention to their offspring and do not fulfill their socialization function (Steinberg, Brown, and Dornbusch, 1996). Low parental control and rejection are the opposite of support and monitoring (Crouter, 1994). They are a combination that has been consistently related to a host of negative outcomes, including delinquency and drug use (Baumrind, 1991b). Adolescents raised in such a context tolerate frustration poorly and are more likely than others to be underachievers. They lack emotional control and long-term goals as well as purpose in life (Lamborn et al., 1991). At one extreme, such parents are called *neglecting*, whereas others are *abusive*. Abusive parents, however, are often quite involved—the wrong type of involvement, however.

The well-known developmentalist, Urie Bronfenbrenner (1985), as well as Noller and Callan (1991), point out that parental permissiveness has more negative consequences than authoritarianism in times when there is cultural and social instability.

In such a fluid context, norms of behavior change rapidly, and a child needs far more guidance than in times when the entire community agrees on what constitutes proper and moral behavior. Baumrind (1991a:114) notes that "in a context of social instability, caregivers are required to sustain a higher level of supervision than would be needed in a period of stability." Today, there are more dangers that confront adolescents than was the case 30 years ago. Consequently, "premature emancipation is perhaps a greater threat to mature identity formation than delayed separation from family attachments" (Baumrind, 1991a:115).

A perfect example of permissive but warm parenting is described by a student whose parents were both highly trained professionals. She had initiated sexual intercourse at age 12, had had two abortions, had been "stoned" throughout high school, had sold drugs, and had lived on the streets by choice—all experiences she recalled fondly. Her parents allowed drug use and sex at home and finally bought a condominium to give her more freedom while she was a drugged teenager:

> *"We were allowed to toke in the house and grow pot plants in the basement. . . . My parents were completely straight, but extremely liberal. They allowed all manners of goings on. . . . School at this point was a joke. I was stoned every single day. I sat in the girls' washroom, the "English Can" because of its location, and smoked and toked. I had company since boys also partied in there. . . . I spent nine months as a street kid. My experiences were, for the most part, fun. I think this is partly because I knew that I could always go home. I still don't know why I kept it up for so long. . . . From ages 15 to 18 I simply didn't have any notably painful experiences. This was partly because I was constantly stoned and partly because I was having such an adventurous life. . . . I was now having the time of my life in a close-knit subculture."*

The two students quoted in this section shared one problem: drugs. The two sets of parents' and the offsprings' reactions to this problem are dramatically opposite. The results are also entirely different. These different outcomes and student appraisals of their situations are not caused just by their parents' socialization practices. They are also the result of environmental factors that both parents and adolescents created as well as of the interaction between parents' and adolescents' personalities. In these quotes, one detects some similarities of character traits that parents and their individual adolescent share (Plomin, 1994). The male adolescent and his parents seem more duty bound and emotionally connected. As a young man, he describes himself as cooperative and stable. The female adolescent and her parents are less tied to conventions, less emotionally involved, as well as more gratification oriented and individualistic. As a young woman, she describes herself as unstable, "depressed," and "highly critical" of other people's ways of living.

Additional Parenting Styles

There may yet be at least one other type of parenting style that has not been discussed by researchers. It overlaps somewhat with the permissive, and is tentatively called the *wavering-negotiating* pattern, for want of a better term. Parents who exhibit this style do not guide their children, even their toddlers, or make demands on them. Rather, they consult with their children about every step they undertake; when the parents make suggestions, they change them as soon as the child objects or disagrees. Such parents never punish but are very involved and loving. Here are two examples I recently observed:

> *The mother and a 2-year-old boy are getting in line at one of the checkout counters of a large food store.*
>
> M: *You want to follow the lady?*
> B: *No, no, want to leave!*
> M: *If you wait a minute, you'll get to ride the conveyor belt.*
> B: *Want a candy bar.*
> M: *OK, what about this one?*
> B: *No, this one.*
> M: *OK, now let's follow the lady.*
> B: *Want belt right away (stamps foot).*
> M: *Ask the lady [me] if she can push her cart.*
>
> *The conversation went on like this for the approximately three minutes I stood at the checkout counter. When I turned around to leave, the child was on the conveyor belt, to the clerk's obvious dismay.*

> *The mother of a 4-year-old girl is trying to buy a blouse in a department store.*
>
> G: *It's ugly, I don't like it.*
> M: *Of course, honey, you're right, but I really don't need a pretty one.*
> G: *This one is nicer (grabs one from the rack. Note that she is eating ice cream that is running down her hands.)*
> M: *Alright, I'll try it on if you want.*
> G: *No, I'm tired, I want to see the dollies.*
> M: *Alright, sweetie, let's go and see the dollies.*
>
> *The mother patiently followed.*

In all the numerous instances when this pattern of interaction was observed, the mothers appeared well educated and upper-middle class. Mother/child negotiating went on for extended periods and the mothers unavoidably lost each round with a weary smile or sigh. The children never appeared satisfied and, when the mothers finally drew the line somewhere, several of the children threw loud temper tantrums—all in public places. These observations are anecdotal, but it is my guess that if researchers carried out systematic observations in large food stores and malls in upper-middle-class metropolitan areas, they would encounter this pattern regularly.

DETERMINANTS OF PARENTING SOCIALIZATION PRACTICES

How do parents develop their socialization practices? Or what influences parents to adopt an authoritative or yet permissive approach? Three types of influences come to mind. They are complementary rather than mutually exclusive, and interact with each other: contextual and cultural influences, parents' personalities and beliefs, and parents' adaptation to their children's personalities and behaviors. However, we have already seen that society entertains vastly different social constructions of motherhood and fatherhood. It is therefore entirely possible that mothers and fathers develop their parenting styles somewhat differently; thus the mechanisms described here may not apply equally well to both genders at the same time.

Contextual and Cultural Determinants

Childrearing practices can become ineffective or harsh because of environmentally induced stressors. One can think here of poverty, unemployment, marital conflict, and divorce. These stress-inducing circumstances tend to disrupt parental practices and make parents less responsive to children's needs. For instance, fathers' warmth decreases and irritability increases following unemployment (Elder, Caspi, and Nguyen, 1994). Stress experienced by mothers because of marital problems or economic hardships often leads to a more erratic, punishing, and disciplinary relationship with their children (Conger, Patterson, and Ge, 1995). Lenton (1990:173) suggests that harsher disciplinary practices "are explained by insufficient resources and because parents may also experience an erosion of their authority." They then try to recoup their authority by becoming less flexible. Adults who experience work and stress overload feel easily harassed and impatient; they may therefore parent less effectively and happily (Galambos et al., 1995). Thus, the quality of childrearing may change over the life course, not simply in response to the different needs of growing children but also as a consequence of evolving contextual factors.

The Question of What Constitutes "Proper" Parenting

A particularly sensitive issue when discussing impoverished families as well as families from other cultures is the matter of what constitutes "proper" childrearing practices: the **social construction of proper parenting.** In North America, good parenting is synonymous with authoritative parenting. This approach is endorsed by professionals, especially psychologists and social workers as well as child advocates. However, some practices may be more acceptable in certain cultural contexts than others: "What may be experienced by adolescents as parental intrusiveness in some cultural groups may be experienced as concern in others" (Steinberg, Dornbusch, and Brown, 1992:729). Poor mothers, and particularly African-American mothers in disadvantaged neighborhoods, are, on average, more disciplinarian or no-nonsense than authoritative, as seen earlier (Mason et al., 1996).

This stricter type of discipline generally has positive behavioral outcomes among black children (Deater-Deckard et al., 1996). In dangerous neighborhoods, this style of parenting may be appropriate to secure compliance and to ensure safety and may be perceived as a form of concern (Lamborn, Dornbusch, and Steinberg, 1996). Hanson, McLanahan, and Thomson (1997:213) have found that poor children are less "negatively affected by yelling and spanking and more positively affected by hugging and praising and by living with parents who have high aspirations for them." When peers are problematic, more controlling measures are adaptive and act as a deterrent to detrimental behaviors (Mason et al., 1996).

Therefore, one needs to evaluate "proper" parenting practices within the context in which they are applied. Rather than value independence and creativity in their children, impoverished minority mothers frequently value obedience and respect for authority—as is the case in most countries of the world. For instance, this is reflected in Latina mothers' preferences (Harwood et al., 1996). The valuation of independence and creativity is a middle-class Western phenomenon (Chao, 1994).

The Debate over Physical Punishment

There is a related debate as to whether physical or corporal punishment leads to maladjustment in children and adolescents. Some research, in fact, documents a relationship between corporal punishment and low self-esteem as well as delinquency, aggressiveness, and other problems (Straus and Donnelly, 1994). However, this research corpus has several limitations. The first stems from the fact that these studies are not longitudinal; thus, one has no way of knowing if physical punishment caused the delinquency, alcoholism, and behavioral problems in some of the adolescents and adults who report having been spanked as children. A life course perspective suggests that some of the adults were probably difficult children: Parents of children with behavioral problems generally use more disciplinary methods of *all* kinds, including reasoning, spanking, grounding, and withdrawal of privileges (Robert Larzerele, quoted in *The Globe and Mail,* October 5, 1999). Thus, parents may have been responding to children who were already problematic and are still so as adults. Similarly, it is possible that troubled young adults recall their parents' behaviors more negatively than they were in reality (see Chapter 15).

These studies also fail to provide valid results because they they have little to say about parents' level of stress as well as psychological adjustment—all factors that could have contributed more substantially to their children's future problems. Furthermore, this research rarely inquires about the remainder of the parents' socialization practices. For instance, it rarely considers whether parents are or have been loving or rejecting in their punitive approach (Florsheim, Tolan, and Gorman-Smith, 1996:1229). Finally, this research does not tell us whether children perceive the punishment as a sign of parental rejection or concern (Baumrind, 1994; Simons et al., 1994). Basically, the meaning of physical punishment is a social construction. Its consequences will vary accordingly, within certain limits.

In English-speaking Western countries, there are indications that physical punishment is harmful psychologically when the child perceives it as a form of parental rejection (Rohner, Bourque, and Elordi, 1996) or when the overall parent/child relationship is negative (Larzelere et al., 1998). It is important to distinguish between parents who hit in anger and impulsively "at the drop of a hat," and parents who spank with regret and after having explained to the child how he or she disobeyed. In other words, physical punishment does not take place in a vacuum—its consequences will depend greatly on the *totality of the familial climate.*

Baumrind (1996) emphasizes that it is not a particular disciplinary practice that is important, but how it is applied and in which context. She mentions Sweden, where corporal punishment has been legally abolished (the *aga* law). In the following years, Sweden saw an increase rather than a decrease of adolescent violence: "The ban on corporal punishment in Sweden has not resulted in cultural spillover of the adult culture's nonviolent values to a segment of the youth" (p. 412). Clearly, Baumrind concludes, "the root causes of youth violence are to be found elsewhere than in the use of disciplinary physical punishment in the home" (p. 413). In summary, it is unlikely that occasional and fair corporal punishment of young children in itself causes any of the ills with which it has been associated. Nevertheless, even light physical punishment is not a parenting practice that is appropriate on a regular basis.

Parents' Personalities and Beliefs

Parents' personalities and beliefs constitute the second element that influences how they raise their children. A wide range of adult personality characteristics can lead to authoritative parenting. For instance, parents who are patient, calm, and affectionate, who have a sense of humor, or who are businesslike may be more inclined to use authoritative or even no-nonsense techniques. By the same token, another range of personality configurations makes it impossible for adults to become authoritative or no-nonsense parents. For example, think of a man who is easily frustrated, impatient, and impulsive. Such a man is more likely to become a harsh, rejecting, and perhaps abusive parent than an authoritative one. In turn, there is a good chance that his children will show some of these partly genetically influenced traits (Neiderhiser et al., 1999). Their irritating behaviors will trigger bouts of impulsive punishing, especially when he is under stress. In fact, a certain level of poor parenting results from parents' difficult personalities and deviant attitudes (Newcomb and Loeb, 1999).

Parents' beliefs about the proper ways of raising children are also important determinants. These beliefs can result from the way parents were themselves raised. For instance, adults who felt unloved as children because their parents were cold and nonexpressive may react by becoming warm and supportive parents. Others may have been influenced by cultural constructs of children as naturally good ("If you let them lead the way, everything will be fine"). Yet others have learned that "sparing the rod spoils the child" and behave accordingly. Parents' beliefs and notions about proper childrearing can be learned from books, professionals, or friends.

Parental Adaptation to Children

A third factor influencing parents' socialization practices is suggested by the interactional perspective: Many parents adapt their practices to fit their children's behaviors, personalities, and abilities (Bates et al., 1998). Several examples document this process of adaptation. For instance, when hyperactive children are successfully treated with the drug methylphenidate or Ritalin, their hyperactivity diminishes substantially, and mothers become less controlling (Tarver-Behring and Barkley, 1985). Similar reactions have been observed among teachers (Whalen, Henker, and Dotemoto, 1980). In other studies, mothers of normal and difficult-oppositional children were experimentally paired with a difficult child (not their own) and then with a cooperative child (not their own). Both types of mothers exhibited more controlling and intrusive behavior with the oppositional child than with the cooperative one (Brunk and Henggeler, 1984). In other words, adults may adapt their parenting practices to children's behaviors (Magnusson, 1990).

Pursuing this interactional line of reasoning, one can see that children and adolescents may influence their parents to become coercive or rejecting, even if they do so unconsciously. As Hanson, McLanahan, and Thomson (1997:208) state, "Parents may monitor children with behavior problems more closely than they do children without these problems." Simons and colleagues (1994:359) point out that "rebellious, antisocial children often punish parental efforts to monitor and discipline while reinforcing parental withdrawal and deviance." Patterson, Reid, and Dishion (1992:11) observe that it is difficult to monitor the whereabouts of an adolescent who is extremely oppositional. Hanson and colleagues (1997) also write about the possibility that lower-income parents may receive less admiration and respect from their children—and we have seen such examples in Chapter 8. This disadvantage reduces their effectiveness as parents, and in turn may lead them to adopt harsher practices or feel defeated and become permissive. From this perspective, it can be said that children coproduce the parental socialization practices of which they are the beneficiaries or the victims (see also Henderson et al., 1996).

THE PARENT/ADOLESCENT RELATIONSHIP

The parent/adolescent relationship is influenced by societal definitions of what adolescence is. North American research emphasizes conflict as well as lack of parent/adolescent communication. In this section, we also examine the limits and contexts of parental influence on adolescents.

The Social Construction of Adolescence

Much American research and literature has been devoted to parent/adolescent conflict, a focus not necessarily found in all countries of the world. In contrast, harmony is much less emphasized in the research. This interest in conflict derives in part from antiquated notions that portray adolescence as being necessarily a period of turbulence—the idea of "storm and stress." At the beginning of the twentieth century, the psychologist Stanley Hall was at the origin of this perspective on adolescence as a naturally turbulent stage. Sigmund Freud, who was very influential in North America, reinforced this idea that adolescence is unavoidably a period during which all youths undergo emotional turmoil.

The beginning of adolescence is generally determined by the onset of puberty—that is, hormonal changes and the development of primary and secondary sexual characteristics. The transition to adolescence exists in all cultures throughout the world, even though the age of onset varies depending on life conditions, such as nutrition. A poor diet, for instance, is likely to delay the onset of menarche. What is important to underscore is that this period of physiological puberty does not give rise to an identical psychological and social puberty throughout the world (Schlegel and Barry, 1991). But, despite the fact that the "storm and stress" ideology concerning adolescence does not apply universally, it still remains a widely held belief in North America (Holmbeck and Hill, 1988).

The social construction of adolescence as a period of storm and stress, peer-related activities, and growing independence from parents is at the core of society's treatment of youths. It also influences the type and quality of the parent/adolescent relationship.

The famed anthropologist Margaret Mead (1928) was the first to document the fact that the problematic type of adolescence frequently encountered in North America, and that has become more common in most Western countries, is a cultural rather than a biological entity. At that time, her research was going against the grain of prevailing social constructions. But in the last two decades, most qualified specialists have reached the same conclusion. "Teenagehood" is a **historical phenomenon** (Modell and Goodman, 1990). Historians Kett (1977) and Demos (1971) have placed the invention of adolescence as a social category between 1890 and 1920—after most middle-class youngsters were pushed out of the labor market and into the school system, separated from the adult world of which they had until then been part.

It is important to distinguish between the fact that U.S. society often presents a perturbing context for adolescents and the supposition that adolescence is in itself "naturally"—thus necessarily—a period that is difficult, stormy, and in opposition to the adult world (Steinberg, 1990). Adolescent crisis is in great part created by the type of environment that has evolved in North America and in other English-speaking countries—not by the nature of adolescence in general. In the United States, Montemayor (1986) estimates that over one-third of adolescents pass through difficult times. However, it should be noted that a good proportion of these teenagers are experiencing problems that were already with them in childhood (Carlson et al., 1999). One cannot therefore blame adolescence for all the problems encountered by youths. Many of these youths will remain problematic as adults—they are problematic persons rather than problematic adolescents.

How Do Parents and Adolescents Get Along?

As stated earlier, much of the literature on the parent/adolescent relationship focuses on conflict. The research indicates that conflict generally pertains to daily routines rather than key value issues (Smetana and Gaines, 1999). In other words, there does not seem to be too much serious conflict, although both parents and adolescents mention more of it now than in the past (Collins and Russell, 1991). Adolescents also report more conflict than do their parents. This low reported rate of conflictual relations appears paradoxical for two reasons. First, society is experiencing very rapid social change, and such periods often create new subcultures for each generation and are consequently accompanied by intergenerational difficulties and misunderstandings. And, second, the high prevalence of problematic adolescent behaviors—such as delinquency, violence, drug use, precocious sexual activity, and unplanned teen pregnancies—lead one to think that, surely, parents cannot be happy about these. Even if their own children are not involved, these activities may bring an insecure atmosphere to many parent/adolescent interactions: Parents may fear that their children will follow the example of other youths. It is difficult to reconcile these potentially conflict-producing facts with a low level of tension between adolescents and parents. However, more naturalistic studies based on day-to-day reports, such as the one described in Family Research 11.2, show higher levels of daily tension than survey questionnaires do (Larson and Richards, 1994).

Barber (1994:384) suggests that the absence of conflict over controversial topics such as sex and drugs most likely means that, although parents and adolescents differ in attitudes about them, they do not discuss these issues. In fact, a survey reported in *Time* magazine (June 15, 1998) supports the notion that parents and children rarely talk to each other about drugs and sex, two contentious issues in society. When asked from what sources teenagers learn about sex, only 7 percent mentioned parents, but 45 and 29 percent, respectively, mentioned peers and television.

Another related explanation, provided by Demo (1992:115), is that parents and adolescents "spend very little time together, often not more than one hour per day of

FAMILY RESEARCH 11.2

Naturalistic Self-Reporting: Daily Activities

In a study conducted by Larson and Richards (1994), adolescents and their parents were asked to carry a pager for one week. When beeped, each completed a report on their current activities, indicating what they were doing, where and with whom they were, as well as their thoughts and emotional states at the time of each signal. They were beeped once at random within every two-hour block of time between 7:30 A.M. and 9:30 P.M. This method was called the *Experience Sampling Method.* The focus was on the daily activities of adolescents and parents from single- and married-parent families. Adolescents were sampled from the fifth through ninth grades of a middle- and working-class Chicago suburb. In addition, parents and adolescents filled out many questionnaires about their family life and themselves.

This combination of methods allowed the researchers to study daily activities and accompanying moods of all the family members individually. But, above all, it allowed them to compare how each family member felt in the company of the others and how each felt while engaging in various activities together or separately, whether at school, work, home, with peers or coworkers. The researchers could also obtain on-the-spot reports of conflict, contentment, or boredom while family members were together. They could also, for instance, compare how each reported on the same conflict.

direct interaction." While parents' and adolescents' reports on time spent together are somewhat at odds, the fact is that both mention spending only a few minutes each day talking (Larson and Richards, 1994). There may be a wide variety of situations that adolescents experience and parents never know about, thus reducing the potential for conflict, but at the same time depriving adolescents of proper guidance. It is at least logical that, when adolescents' behaviors go against parental expectations, they try to carry on as much of their lives as possible without their parents' knowledge.

Moreover, parents are busier than previous cohorts of adults used to be, are generally employed, and many work even longer hours than just a decade ago to make ends meet (Schor, 1991). High rates of divorce and other problems, such as alcoholism, spousal abuse, and mental illness, mean that many parents are so preoccupied by their own personal difficulties that they overlook those of their children. These factors diminish parenting availability and monitoring, and henceforth reduce parent/adolescent friction.

Montemayor and Hanson (1985), as well as Larson and Richards (1994), report that adolescents experience less conflict with their fathers than their mothers, partly because mothers interact more with them concerning the basics of their daily lives. The household division of labor based on gender roles places mothers at a disadvantage over fathers in this respect. In this vein, Collins (1990) reviews studies illustrating that, when a mother interrupts her adolescent during a discussion, the youngster subsequently interrupts her even more, but does not do so for the father. Yet, all studies indicate that adolescents are closer to their mothers than their fathers (Noller, 1994), particularly in divorced families (Zill, Morrison, and Coiro, 1993). In married families, adolescents are both more attached to and in conflict with their mothers than with their fathers. They also seek her support and advice more.

Parental Influence

Parental influence or the ability to socialize children and affect their outcomes is a much discussed topic these days, particularly with regard to adolescents. This section discusses how parental effectiveness does not operate within a vacuum but is circumscribed by society and the child outcomes it values.

The Role of Historical Periods

Family relationships take place within a distinct cultural context, at a given historical period, and under specific economic conditions (Hareven, 1994a, 1994b). Families' social and cultural context has altered drastically within the past 20 years (Elder, 1995): Technological changes have occurred with an extreme rapidity that has had no precedent in history. The environment is now controlled by information technology, including the audiovisual media. The workplace, schools, homes, and leisure activities have all been affected by these changes and the evolution of the value systems that generally accompanies such transitions. Parents have had to adapt their role within this new context and raise their children accordingly, although much of this adaptation takes place unconsciously (Alwin, 1990). For instance, numerous parents have accepted television and video games as children's main sources of entertainment and often as babysitters. Many have become habituated to the violence and the values streaming out of these visual media.

For their part, children react to their parents according to what they learn about them and themselves through their environment. Their sources of information include their peer group and the messages they receive from the media as well as from professionals. Children are more aware of their rights than in the past. They have higher material expectations and requirements. They want more autonomy, and male children in particular are taught to separate themselves from their mothers and the feminine realm. As a result of all of these changes, children's and adolescents' receptivity to parental socialization efforts has evolved. Many no longer see their parents as legitimate sources of information or even of authority for their behaviors.

These changes in the external environment have all affected the extent of parental influence on their children. This is why it can be said that, as a general rule, the extent of parents' influence on their children, particularly on their adolescents, varies according to prevailing sociohistorical conditions (Bronfenbrenner, 1989). In other words, there are *historical eras* or time periods when it is easier for parents to influence their youngsters and others when it is far more difficult to do so. Social change ushers in new influences on children's lives while also reducing the impact of other influences. Just 50 or so years ago, there was no television, but that medium has long since been considered to be a prime agent of socialization or of influence. Often, as seen in Chapter 2, the contents of television and related media do not support parental efforts and may even undermine their moral and practical teachings. In contrast, religion, which generally supports parents and upholds their moral authority, used to be a more powerful influence than it is now throughout all regions and social classes. Thus, parents have lost a degree of legitimacy through these two changes alone.

The Role of the Human Qualities That Are Valued

As society evolves, it places a premium on certain specific human outcomes. Thus, parents are emphasizing autonomy and self-reliance in their socialization practices both because of the society's value orientation toward individuality and because parents who are employed need more self-reliant children (Rossi and Rossi, 1990). For instance, educated parents tend to encourage early residential independence (Amato and Booth, 1997). Mainstream American society also values the development of self-esteem and educational achievement. Although all of these outcomes are, to some extent, affected by parents, the outcomes are particularly influenced by peer interaction and the school situation. For instance, self-esteem is peer driven after a certain age. Television may also affect self-esteem, for that matter, as teenagers probably find it difficult to compare themselves favorably to their idols who are invariably rich, attractive, popular, and well developed physically while remaining slim (Spitzer, Henderson, and Zivian, 1999). Furthermore, self-esteem, achievement, and ability to be self-reliant are also affected by innate factors such as cognitive ability, hyperactivity, and locus of control. Self-esteem is a partly personality-driven element, and thus less easily influenced by parents.

In contrast, a few decades ago, the development of politeness, obedience, conformity, or patriotism was given more importance in the socialization of children (Alwin,

1990). These outcomes are more culturally influenced; they are thus subject to direct teaching and example, thus parental socialization. Therefore, parents were more influential in these respects than is the case for outcomes that are more personality driven, such as self-esteem and the ability to be independent. The topic of parental influence is continued at the end of Chapter 12, where we will take a critical look at the conclusions reached by some behavior geneticists in this respect.

THE ROLE OF PEERS IN THE PARENT/ADOLESCENT RELATIONSHIP

Today's parents have less control than in the past over whom their child associates with after a certain age, and they are also concerned about the quality of their children's peers. More peer interactions, especially among boys, take place outside the home than used to be the case. When children attend schools outside their neighborhood, or have a car, or live in a spread-out suburb or in an area where gangs rule, parents are fairly helpless (Brown and Huang, 1995). They cannot monitor what takes place and with whom their child or adolescent associates.

Peer Groups and Parental Isolation

The peer group may support parental teachings, but it may also conflict with parents' values. Children whose peers' behaviors and values are so different from what they are taught within their families experience **cross-pressures.** A child's socialization is considerably easier when both peers and parents agree, and is difficult, at best, when fundamental contradictions exist between the two systems. The greater the similarity between parents' values and those of their children's peers, the lower the level of parent/child conflict. Youngsters whose parents approve of their peers, and particularly of their close friends, will get along better with their parents. Not only do they have more in common, but parents need to exert less direct control over them, thus preempting conflict. In contrast, when parents disapprove of their adolescents' friends, a great deal of tension may exist if parents voice their concerns.

What parent has not heard, "But all the others are going!" "Everybody is doing it" and "Everybody has one" are powerful and often intimidating messages handed to parents (Ambert, 1997a). Thus, each parenting couple and, more and more, each single mother or father has to face what is presented by their child as a normal entitlement among youngsters. Parents are made to feel that, if they do not conform, they will do a grave injustice and deprive the child. This alleged consensus among youngsters allows them to speak with great authority to their parents, because parents are generally more isolated than children when it comes to tactical and moral support. Adolescent groups and subcultures are much more cohesive and less fragmented for each child than are adult subcultures for each individual parent. In reality, there is no such thing as a parental subculture or peer group, and this constitutes a disequilibrium that is detrimental to parents' role (Small and Eastman, 1991). A single mother expresses the situation thusly when attempting to understand with hindsight how her teenage daughter became delinquent without her noticing it:

"My daughter has a lot of friends, some I know, some I don't. They talk on the phone on a daily basis even after they have been to school together, they make plans, they exchange clothes, they cover for each other, they watch each other's back against their parents. They come and they go and it's impossible to keep track of all of this. New clothes that she wears are borrowed from Mindy and if I ask Mindy, she'll say, 'Don't I got good taste!' If Mindy's mother calls to find out where she is, all I can say is that they went to the movies together. That's what I was told. But they actually went to this boy's place. If Mindy's mother calls about clothes, I say that they exchange a lot while in reality they are all shoplifting. So you see you have to be a very very clever parent to keep track of all of this and to add it all up together to one conclusion: My child is a shoplifter and she's barely 15 and she's screwing around. But don't think for one minute that I added this up on my own; the police did it for me. These girls just protect each other. Protect for what? They're the ones who need protection against each other. Now I tell you that Mindy's mother, Jessie's mother, and I have all been fooled."

Along these lines, Steinberg and colleagues (1995:453) find that, when adolescents' peers have authoritative parents, the latter contribute to positive developmental outcomes above and beyond their own parents' authoritativeness: "We believe that this may be due in part to the higher level of shared social control provided by a network of authoritative parents." Yet, in the preceding quote, the parents are exhibiting all the "symptoms" of being authoritative, but their children's delinquent peer group is far more clever and better organized.

Many parents, especially more educated ones, make it a point of knowing their children's friends' parents (Muller and Kerbow, 1993). **Parent networks** can fulfill several functions both for parents and their children. When these are school based, they can contribute to a smoother socialization process, norms that are more closely adhered to, and better-informed parents. It is, however, far more difficult for adolescents' parents than for young children's parents to know their children's peers' parents—at a time when such contacts would be the most helpful.

Peer Spillover Effect

Many autobiographies of students underscore the continued impact of the peer group even after the child returns home from school. Once at home, the youngster keeps on reacting to what the peers did or said or failed to say. In other words, children and adolescents bring home the stress experienced via their peers, and this stress spills over into their interactions with parents (Ladd, 1992). Students frequently pointed out that they had used their parents as "scapegoats" and taken their peer-related frustrations out on them as soon as one parent had said or done something that the youngster could react to: "I used to sulk up and down the stairs, just to make them as miserable as I was," or "I would blow my top," or "I used to cry and yell and storm out." These adolescents would lash out at the surprised parent, who then tried to reason out the situation, only to unwittingly provoke a sharper outburst from the youngster.

Furthermore, peer maltreatment, discussed more extensively in Chapter 14, creates additional spillover effect into the parent/child relationship. The ill-treated child's parents often suffer with their child when they learn of the victimization, but they especially suffer indirectly. That is, the frustrated child often takes it out on his parents and siblings (Ambert, 1994a). Parents inherit what one student called "the flak." In addition, parents can even be blamed by clinicians for traumas that actually have peers at their source. A male student's recollections illustrate this latter phenomenon quite vividly:

> *"Up to that age [11 years] I had been quite happy at school but then something happened to me, I stopped growing and I became in no time the shortest and skinniest and soon the pimpliest little runt at my grade level. The other boys used to pick on me, hide my coat, steal my lunches and would never include me in their games. They'd laugh at me openly and the girls started avoiding me too because it wasn't cool to be seen with the most unpopular boy. . . . You can't imagine how many times my mother had to keep me home because I'd start throwing up. I became scared shitless. . . . The funny thing is that my parents had to send me to a psychiatrist and he turned around and blamed them for not being supportive and for whatever else. That's kind of sad when you think that my problems had nothing to do with my parents. My parents were sort of being made miserable because of this little runt I was and now by this psychiatrist and to this day they have never blamed me and have always been supportive."*

THE RELATIONSHIP BETWEEN PARENTS AND ADULT CHILDREN

The parent/child relationship changes throughout the various stages of family development as well as throughout the life course of each family member. In these respects, the following sections complement Chapter 9.

When the Child Is a Young Adult

The following quote from a student's autobiography reflects a thoughtful perspective within very painful contexts and illustrates the extent to which a person in her early twenties can reflect on her parents' life course. This student is married; her parents were immigrants from Europe. She also summarizes, in the first paragraph, what many students who had a good relationship with their mothers during their teens wrote:

> *"My feelings towards my mother 0–18 years consisted mainly of love. . . . When I was mad, she cheered me up; when I was sad, she made me happy; when I used to cry, she wiped my tears; when I was depressed, she lifted my spirits; when I needed a person to talk to, she listened; and when I needed love, she provided. . . . Throughout my early years, I also felt very sorry for my mom . . . because she had to carry the load of bringing us up when my father used to be away all of the time. . . . She had to raise and take care of my two oldest brothers and my oldest sister as soon as she got married. This was because my father's ex-wife left her children to my dad and got married. . . . I felt especially sorry for my mom when my dad separated from her. At that time, I think she experienced many emotional and economic difficulties. That's when she had to find a job as a cleaner in order to bring us up. She worked extra long hours just to make ends meet. She said that she would rather die than let us go on welfare. . . . As for my dad, I also love him very much regardless of the harm and pain he has caused*

> *my mom. . . . As I look back now, I have noticed that I became more and more attached to him as I grew older. . . . I just felt that he was becoming an old man much faster than I realized. And since my dad was much older than my mom, I knew that he would not live as long as my mom is going to live. I felt that I had to make up for the years he was away from us."*

Adulthood Comes Later

The timing of the passage into adulthood may be changing. Adolescence now extends into the early part of adulthood for the segment of the youth population that goes on to higher education or those who remain unemployed. As a social stage, adolescence starts earlier and finishes later than it did 50 years ago. Whereas adolescence as a social construct was the invention of the dawn of the twentieth century, young adulthood is the creation of the closing of that century. Because of the increasingly prolonged education that is now required to make a decent living, young adults, aged 19 to 25, often remain financially dependent on their parents. While parents have to give freedom to their adolescents, regarding sexuality for instance, earlier than before, they have to remain active in a supportive role for a far longer period than was the case previously.

This duality of freedom and dependence can result in a conflict-generating situation, both for young adults and their parents. Until now, families and researchers have accepted the problematic aspect of this situation for youths, but have failed to appreciate the fact that more and more parents are looking forward to acquiring their independence—from their grown children! Parents generally look forward to seeing their young adults settle down with a good job and later on with a family of their own. Adult children's departure is in some cases related to an improvement in parents' marital relationship (Suitor and Pillemer, 1991). Other parents look forward to becoming grandparents, since it is generally an enjoyable role to play.

Why Do Young Adults Stay Home Longer?

Young adults remain home longer than was the case two decades ago and more remain financially dependent on their parents for a longer period of time. In a substantial number of families, the parents' relationship with their young adult child is marked by coresidence. First, young adults stay home longer because they remain in the educational system longer. Second, the development of the service economy and the shrinking of the manufacturing base have resulted in an increase in part-time and low-paying jobs for young people without a college degree—jobs that force them to remain with their parents for financial reasons.

A third reason for the lengthening dependence of young adults may be related to the finding that high school seniors are increasingly endorsing consumerist values (Crimmins, Easterlin, and Saito, 1991). What were considered luxuries in previous cohorts—such as cars, computers, and home entertainment systems—have become necessities for current ones. Consequently, the earnings required to reach such heightened material expectations come later, and in the meantime young adults can afford them only when they remain with their parents. As Hareven (1994b:448) points out, whereas in the late nineteenth century, children remained at home to help aging parents or widowed mothers, now "young adult children reside with their parents in order to meet their own needs." In fact, 20- to 29-year-old young adults are the age group of grown children most likely to receive parental support (Cooney and Uhlenberg, 1992).

Factors Related to a Mutual Satisfaction

The research results are inconsistent and even contradictory when it comes to evaluating parental satisfaction with coresidence with their young adult children. The reasons for lengthened coresidence probably affect parents' satisfaction with it. For instance, parental stress is higher when children are financially dependent. Furthermore, the quality of the relationship is an important variable and parental stress is lower when interaction is positive and little conflict exists (Aquilino and Supple, 1991). There may be differences by social class and race in terms of satisfaction with parenting young adult children. For instance, black mothers perceive their children to be less supportive than do white mothers (Umberson, 1992). This contrast is possibly a question of income and resource differentials between the two groups, or it may result from the fact that African-American parents have higher filial expectations than do whites (Lee, Peek, and Coward, 1998).

As young adults leave the nest and enter roles that parents have occupied for years, particularly work and marriage, parents feel closer to their children (Aquilino, 1997:682). As young adults age, their relationship with both parents is still important for their psychological well-being (Barnett, Marshall, and Pleck, 1992). This includes a stepfather who might have been part of the family for several years. Nevertheless, in some families, parental pressure on children may still continue, often over a child's delayed passage into a status transition at an "appropriate age." This dilemma is well expressed by a 23-year-old student:

> *"In my religion, orthodox girls marry in their late teens or early 20's . . . my parents have lately been putting pressure for me to get married like the other girls in my class. . . . My mother would pester me and say 'Why can't you be like other girls your age?' 'Girls your age already have kids.' These comments have made me feel very depressed and lonely. She sees how my classmates are getting married one by one and she would like to see me settle down. I constantly argue with my mother that I do intend to get married when I meet the right person. She wants me to think about it now; however, I would like to finish school and find a good job before I go out and look for a husband. Marriage is not my number one priority at this time of my life and my mother cannot understand my reluctance."*

As young adults marry and enter full-time employment, the parental relationship becomes less salient for their well-being. Gender differences do exist, in the sense that females continue to feel more connected to their parents than males.

When the Child Is 30 to 40 Years Old

One key aspect of the *life course perspective* is that it brings attention to the development of the relationship over time as both parents and adult children age. But whatever their age, a majority of adults and their parents report having a good relationship and, when geographic distances are not too large, seeing each other fairly regularly. Adult children, particularly daughters, speak regularly with their mothers, although they do so less frequently with fathers (Amato and Booth, 1997). Generally, the affection that exists between parents and adult children is the chief motivator in continued contact and exchange with parents (Rossi and Rossi, 1990). The more parents and children see each other, the greater affection they have for each other, and vice versa (Lawton, Silverstein, and Bengtson, 1994:65). But these researchers have found that this reciprocity of affectivity does not always apply to fathers. They concluded that "the motivations for interaction between adult children and their mothers and fathers are different."

Studies tend to present demographic characteristics to explain the quality of the parent/child relationship: gender and marital status of parent and child, socioeconomic status, geographic distance, and parents' health status. But the interactional perspective suggests studies that would look at a child's and a parent's personality characteristics that could affect the relationship. One might also look at the matter of fit between the personalities. Is the relationship between parent and adult child closer and warmer when the two have similar or complementary personalities? What if they are similar on traits that are not conducive to harmony, such as restlessness, aggressivity, and disagreeableness? What happens when the personalities are different but not complementary? Here, one could think of poised, warm, and peaceful parents whose son is irritable and verbally combative. Do these personality configurations produce a similar result whether the child is a son or a daughter? In other words, parents may have more difficulty getting along with a restless son than they would a restless daughter, or the reverse. Or children can have more difficulty getting along with an intrusive mother than an intrusive father, or the reverse. These questions remain to be tested by researchers.

From a life course perspective, other researchers believe that, as adult children mature, their values become more similar to those of their parents because they have lived through similar experiences, such as getting married, having children, and shouldering work responsibilities (Rossi and Rossi, 1990). When children most closely resemble their parents in terms of values and beliefs, they also have a better relationship with them. In fact, Aldous, Klaus, and Klein (1985) found that adult children who shared interests and values with their parents were favored by them.

Finally, the interactional and life course perspectives accommodate structural variables in the parent/child relationship (Aldous, 1996). For instance, when there is a sharp distinction in professional standing, and therefore income, between father and adult child or mother and child, is the relationship affected? Rossi and Rossi (1990:299) comment that occupational success and social mobility may be attained at the expense of family solidarity and closeness between the generations. What happens, for example, when a child or several children have far surpassed their parents' social status—or, the reverse, when a child or all siblings have drifted downward socially? Do these families become fractured as a result of social mobility or does the generation with the most favorable position help the other? Differences among ethnic groups probably exist in this respect, particularly when immigration is involved and parents expect their children to surpass them in occupational prestige.

Senior Parents Help Their Adult Children

In a previous chapter, we have seen that a good segment of the senior generation contributes to their children's lives by raising or helping raise grandchildren. Generally, these are older women who see their maternal role extended into their later years.

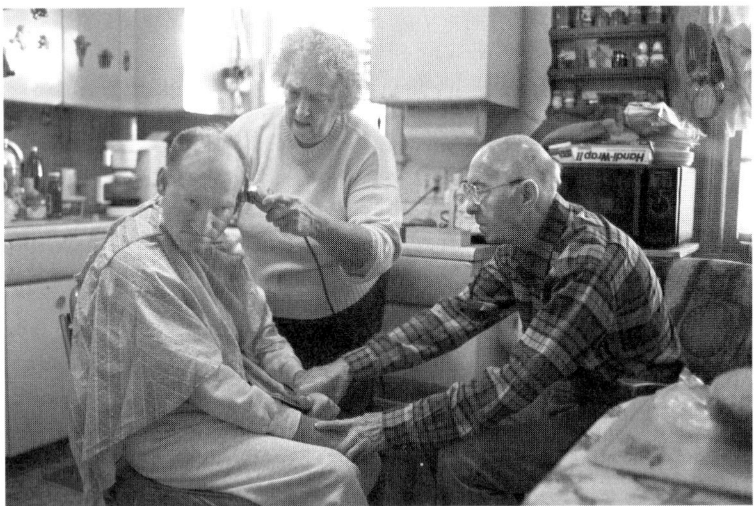

Social policies concerning adults with special needs are so deficient that even frail elderly parents often have to continue assuming the entire responsibility for the care of their middle-aged children with disabilities. They receive little help, exhaust their meager resources, and their own health may deteriorate.

They basically fulfill family functions that, given adequate social policies, should be dealt with by society—for instance, in the form of universal access to child care centers. In general, older parents, especially when they are still in reasonable health—and most are, particularly among whites and Asian Americans—provide a great deal of help to their adult children, including at the material level. The 1987 National Survey of Families and Households indicated that only about 5 percent of adult children had given money to their parents in the past five years. In contrast, 20 percent of white adult children and six percent of African-American and Latino adult children had received over $200 during the same period.

Perhaps the most intriguing result of that survey was that parents, particularly minority ones, tended to give more to children who had a higher educational level and larger incomes. Researchers Lee and Aytac (1998:440) concluded that parents "concentrate their resources on promising children"—that is, children "who are likely to yield greater returns." However, it is equally plausible that parents help their needy children differently. They may do so more by providing services such as babysitting, or giving them food, clothing, lodging, and gifts in kind rather than cash. In contrast, they may give more money to children who are doing well.

Another form of help that adult children benefit from is **coresidence.** About 30 percent of adults aged 25 to 54 who have never married and 13 percent of those who are divorced live in their parents' home (White and Peterson, 1995). The greater the number of children, the more likely senior parents are to have one who resides with them because of need. A few adult children have never left home, whereas others have returned. Parents over age 65 who have a coresident child (and about 15 percent do, according to Aquilino, 1990) usually receive relatively little in terms of household or financial help from that child. Da Vanzo and Goldscheider (1990) show that male children are more likely to return home than female children; moreover, males do 20 percent less housework than females when they live with their parents. Hence, coresidence generally benefits adult children more than parents, and male children more than female children.

As parents age, they often do not or cannot disengage from the problems experienced by their adult children. Pillemer and Suitor (1991) report that a quarter of senior parents mention that at least one of their children is experiencing serious physical or mental health problems or a high level of stress. These children's problems correlate significantly with depression in the older parents, and some studies find that older parents who have to provide a great deal of help to their children feel more depressed (Mutran and Reitzes, 1984). These parents may be particularly worried over children who fail to achieve a reasonable level of independence. In addition, when children have problems, they may receive advice that is not wanted or that they are unwilling or unable to put into practice. One can see that, at the very least, the potential for intergenerational ambivalence and even conflict is high.

Then, there is the fact that a certain proportion of parents of perturbed, troubled, or distressed and unsuccessful adult children are themselves problematic persons: They were difficult persons as younger adults and may have had an unsatisfying relationship with their children when the latter were growing up (Reiss, 1995). In addition, these children might have inherited temperamental disadvantages from them, such as tendencies toward irritability or depression. Hence, it is to be expected that a segment of distressed or difficult adults have parents who are or were similar to them. Research on such a theme would contribute additional perspectives on the family life course and adult development.

Adult Children Help Their Elderly Parents

When elderly parents become much older, a proportion experience diminished health, and limitations are placed on their ability to be independent. At that point, adult children often become their key instrumental and social support resources (Eggebeen and Hogan, 1990). Nevertheless, elderly parents are happier when they give than when they receive, and they accept help more readily when they can contribute something in return, particularly to their sons. When parents require a great deal of support from their children, they are less satisfied with the relationship. In part, this can be explained by the fact that contact with the child is necessitated by the parents' needs rather than by the child's desire to see the parents or by the spontaneity of a visit just to socialize. It is not surprising, therefore, that when older parents are in better health, they report a more positive relationship with their children.

When the entire family, and not just the parents, have always valued reciprocity, elders may be satisfied that their earlier parental efforts were appreciated. They may not be negatively affected if they are unable to reciprocate in their later years. Lee, Netzer, and Coward (1995) find that older parents who receive more help are more depressed. As they point out, American elders value their independence, and dependence on children may be troublesome for them. But they also suggest the possibility of a reversed causality; that is, children might respond to their parents' depression by helping them more.

In some families, a process of status reversal begins to take place when parents fall prey to mental disabilities such as senility and Alzheimer's disease. The relationship is totally altered: The parent becomes the child and the child becomes the parent. This is when the responsibilities of caregiving multiply for the child, while meaningful verbal exchanges diminish until even recognition disappears. For the parent, the world, including his or her own children, fades little by little until it has entirely evaporated. Children actually lose the parent long before biological death arrives.

Adult children who care for a parent are far more stressed when the parent suffers from cognitive-behavioral than physical disabilities (Starrels et al., 1997). In contrast, when the parent's handicaps are physical only, the parent/child relationship generally continues to include most of its previous elements. A popularized but misleading concept in this vein is that of the *sandwich generation*—that is, adults caught between raising their children and caring for frail parents. In reality, only a minority of adults provide care to both generations at the same time (Ward and Spitze, 1998). Those who find themselves in this situation have had children late in life, or their parent suffers from a premature disability, or they are grandparents who care simultaneously for a grandchild and a parent.

So far, the research literature has emphasized the stress experienced by adult children, especially daughters, as a result of their role as caregivers of disabled parents (Gerstel and Gallagher, 1993). In this respect, the concept of **burden** is frequently utilized. This, in itself, is a *social construct* worth analyzing, because it reflects cultural values about intergenerational relations. For instance, one does not encounter this concept when studying the care that parents give to their children, unless the latter are adults and quite problematic. The reason is that it is considered to be part of parents' role to care for their young children. However, when these same parents age and their health falters, help extended to them by their children is analyzed in terms of burden—when in other societies it is simply a duty or part of an adult child's role. Not surprisingly, there is also little research showing the positive side of caring for one's elderly parents. In this respect, Pruchno, Patrick, and Burant (1997) have pointed out the importance of distinguishing between caregiving burden and caregiving satisfaction.

Elderly adults who are childless are not unhappier or in poorer health than those who have living children, although both black and white seniors receive more help when they have children. But having children, especially if they reside nearby, may be a more important factor in the life satisfaction of older black adults (Taylor and Chatters, 1991). What seems to count for the emotional well-being of the elderly is not whether they have children but the quality of the relationship between them and their progeny. For instance, Silverstein and Bengtson (1991) find that a warm relationship with adult children may increase parental longevity after widowhood.

Children's Marital Status

Does the children's marital status make a difference in the help they provide their elderly parents? Results are inconsistent on this point. For instance, one study has found that divorced children give less help than married or single children and that they tend to overlook some of their parents' needs and feel less obligated to help them, perhaps because many are consumed by their own problems or have too many other responsibilities (Cicirelli, 1983). But Spitze and colleagues (1994) mention that divorced daughters continue to help their parents and also receive more help from them for babysitting than married daughters. Other studies report that unmarried children assist their parents less than married ones. However, White and Peterson (1995) found no difference in help by children's marital status.

Obviously, more research needs to be done to resolve contradictions between findings. These conflicting results may result from the types of samples utilized, the health of parents in these samples, and what exactly is measured as constituting help. Ideally, such research should include social class and ethnicity, for these variables have already been linked to several difference in family relationships. Older parents' marital status should also be considered (Ganong and Coleman, 1999).

Children's and Parents' Gender

Studies unanimously find that **daughters** are far more likely to become their elderly parents' helpers or caregivers than sons (Silverstein, Parrott, and Bengtson, 1995). When a son has the responsibility for his parents, his wife often assumes this duty or, at the very least, contributes to it. Sons provide help mainly in the domains of transportation and finances; but when parents become more needy in terms of personal care, sons frequently abdicate or delegate their role (Montgomery and Kamo, 1989). In fact, Spitze and Logan (1991) point out that the key to receiving help resides in having one daughter. This situation reflects the fact that women are generally assigned nurturant roles in society and learn to be responsible for the well-being of others from the time they are young. Consequently, parents may also expect more help from their daughters than their sons—although the reverse occurs in many other societies, such as China or Japan.

Starrels and colleagues (1997) have found that elderly parents who receive help from their children tend to reciprocate more with sons than daughters and provide less assistance to daughters than sons. Parents seem to appreciate their sons' caregiving more than their daughters' caregiving, perhaps because sons are still more valued in this society and also because it is taken for granted that daughters are nurturant. It is expected that they will help their elderly parents as part of their feminine role. This gender expectation and the greater reciprocity with or recognition accorded to helpful sons may be reasons why daughters experience more caregiver stress than sons.

Gender is a factor not only in who gives help but also in who receives it. As their health deteriorates, widowed mothers in their seventies to nineties receive more attention from their children than do widowed fathers. Silverstein, Parrott, and Bengtson (1995) report that affection is a stronger motivator for help to older mothers, while expectation of an inheritance is more frequently a factor for assistance to fathers, although this is more the case among sons than daughters.

CONCLUSIONS: THE MACRO AND MICRO ASPECTS IN THE PARENT/CHILD RELATIONSHIP

The parent/child relationship is best examined within the context of the life course of the two generations involved. Out of the small child's relationship with his or her parents is born the adolescent relationship and from both flow the adult child/parent involvement, closeness, or conflict and distancing. In addition, the life course is a road that is paved with both risks and successes, most of which originate in the extrafamilial environment. Therefore, social and cultural changes as well as economic situations can influence both the quality of parenting (which, in turn, influences child socialization and development to some extent) and of the parent/child relationship.

At a more micro level of analysis, we consider the effect of personalities both on the quality of parenting and on the parent/child interaction. Parents' and children's personalities influence their behaviors and their subsequent reactions to each other. No longer are children considered a blank slate upon which parents write the script of their offspring's personalities and outcomes. Children are social actors (Corsaro, 1997) who interact with their parents and contribute to the formation of their destinies. Children's personalities influence their familial environment just as do their parents' personalities. Personalities are the result of the interaction between nature and nurture and, in turn, the familial environment is also the result of this interaction between genetic and environmental forces (Reiss, 1995; Scarr, 1993). The future in the study of the parent/child relationship lies in the recognition of the combination of sociocultural and genetic influences on family members, a line of inquiry pursued in subsequent chapters.

SUMMARY

1. The beginning of the parent/child relationship is rooted in the intersections between the infant's personality and needs, the parents' reactions to these needs, the feedback between the two levels of personalities and reactions, as well as the familial environment that they create.
2. The main types of parents' socialization practices are the authoritative, authoritarian, no-nonsense, permissive, uninvolved, neglecting, or even abusive. Socialization practices arise from the combination of (a) cultural and environmental determinants, including poverty and norms about what is considered "proper" parenting; (b) parents' personalities as well as beliefs; and (c) parental adaptation to children's behaviors, needs, and personalities. In this interactional perspective, children contribute to the development of their parents' socialization style.
3. The parent/adolescent relationship is largely based on social definitions of adolescence. Adolescence is a social construct dating back to the 1890–1920 period. It is a cultural invention rather than an unavoidable and universal period of stress and turmoil. American parent/adolescent conflict is generally about minor issues of daily living rather than crucial issues, such as sex, drugs, and violence. This apparent paradox may stem from a lack of communication on these issues, the fact that adolescents and parents spend relatively little time daily in direct interaction, and the busy life of parents. Overall, about one-third of youths have a very difficult adolescence and parent/child relationship.
4. Eras or time periods as well as the human qualities that are valued within each make it easier or more difficult for parents to influence their adolescents.

5. Children's peers affect their relationship with their parents through the peer group spillover effect, the cross-pressures they place, and the relative solidarity of peer subcultures.
6. The timing of the passage into full adult independence is often postponed because of higher educational requirements. Therefore, young adults often remain home longer than was the case just 20 years ago. Coresidence is particularly difficult for parents when adult children are still financially dependent. Within the life course perspective, as children age and acquire new roles, the parent/child relationship generally remains strong, particularly with mothers, but changes to accommodate maturity and independence. Several demographic variables contribute to the frequency of interaction, including the sex of both parent and child as well as geographic distance. Values, attitudes, and lifestyles may also be important variables.
7. Overall, elderly parents help their adult children substantially and are happier when they give than when they receive. African-American elderly parents help their children less than their white counterparts probably because they have fewer resources. Finally, many adult children have personal problems that force parents to be their mainstay. Adult children help their elderly parents who become frail or disabled, but few actually undertake the entire care. The burden of care is highest when a parent becomes cognitively impaired, because the relationship is entirely altered. The results are inconsistent as to whether a child's marital status makes a difference in the ability to help a parent. However, daughters provide more help, particularly of a personal nature. Possibly because a woman's help is somewhat taken for granted, elderly parents at times appreciate and reward more the help provided by sons. Childless seniors are not unhappier than others but they receive less help than those with children.
8. The parent/child relationship has to be examined within the context of the personalities involved and the sociocultural situation in which the family is embedded.

KEY CONCEPTS AND THEMES

Adolescent subcultures, p. 318
Authoritarian parenting, p. 306
Authoritative parenting, p. 306
Burden, p. 326
Children as coproducers, p. 305
Children's marital status, p. 326
Contextual framework, pp. 310, 311
Coresidence, pp. 322, 324
Cross-pressures, p. 318
Daughters, p. 327
Delayed adulthood, p. 321
Environmental context, p. 310
Gender, p. 327
Interactional perspective, p. 305
Invention of adolescence, p. 314
Life course perspective, p. 322
Nature and nurture, p. 328
No-nonsense parenting, p. 306
Parent networks, p. 319
Parental adaptation, p. 312
Parental influence, p. 316
Peers, p. 318
Permissive parenting, p. 307
Physical punishment, p. 311
"Proper" childrearing practices, p. 310
Social construction of adolescence, p. 313
Spillover effect, p. 319
Transactions, p. 304
Uninvolved parenting, p. 307

STUDY AND REVIEW QUESTIONS

1. Analyze the levels of transactions that take place at the beginning of the parent/child relationship.
2. Discuss the no-nonsense approach to childrearing within its sociocultural context.
3. What is the place of parental monitoring within the authoritative, no-nonsense, and permissive styles?
4. What are the limitations of the research on the effects of physical punishment on children?
5. Explain how children and adolescents are coproducers of their parents' child-rearing styles.
6. Analyze the social construct of adolescence within a cross-cultural context.
7. What factors delimit parental influence?
8. What are the main mechanisms by which peers are influential in the parent/child relationship?
9. Is there a new construction of young adulthood in the making? If yes, what are the consequences on family dynamics?
10. What are some key variables affecting the help that adult children provide their elderly parents?
11. One the whole, which generation of adults benefits the most from the other in our type of society?

SUGGESTED READINGS

Ambert, A.-M. 1997. *Parents, children and adolescents: Interactive relationships and development in context.* New York: Haworth. This book discusses at greater length the parent/child relationship within a variety of contexts. The theoretical perspective amalgamates interactional, ecological, as well as genetic theories.

Bengtson, V. L., and Harootyan, R. A. (Eds.). 1994. *Intergenerational linkages: Hidden connections in American society.* New York: Springer. Several authors present research results and perspectives on parent/child relations, including economic exchange.

Bengtson, V. L., Schaie, K. W., and Burton, L. M. (Eds.). 1995. *Adult intergenerational relations: Effects of societal change.* New York: Springer. Collection of articles combining research results, commentaries, and perspectives on the adult parent/child relationship. There is an interesting section on African-American families that have teenage childbearers.

Greenfield, P. M., and Cocking, R. R. (Eds.). 1994. *Cross-cultural roots of minority child development.* Hillsdale, NJ: Erlbaum. This collection of articles contains a great deal of information on the parent/child relationship and child socialization by parents. Countries from Africa, Asia, as well as Mexico are included, along with minority groups in the United States.

Logan, J. R., and Spitze, G. D. 1996. *Family ties: Enduring relations between parents and their grown children.* Philadelphia: Temple University Press. This book provides a great deal of sociopsychological information.

Rossi, A. S., and Rossi, P. H. 1990. *Of human bonding: Parent-child relations across the life course.* New York: Aldine de Gruyter. The authors present the results of a three-generational research on parents and children and their relationships.

SUGGESTED WEBLINKS

The three scholarly organizations that are the most pertinent for online information about the parent/child relationship and parenting are:

American Psychological Association <http://www.apa.org>

National Council on Family Relations <http://www.ncfr.org>

Society for Research in Child Development <http://www.srcd.org>

Administration on Aging is a government agency offering information on the care of elderly parents, local resources, and other weblinks. **<http://www.aoa.gov>**

American Association of Retired Persons has websites and chat lines for elderly parents who care for dependent adult children and grandchildren. It has even more information on elder care by children. **<http://www.aarp.org>**

National Institute on Aging also has information on elder care, including by children. **<http://www.nih.gov/nia>**

National Parenting Center is a center for parenting information services. It offers information as well as chat rooms, all with the goal of promoting parenting skills. **<http://www.tnpc.com>**

CHAPTER 12

Sibling Relationships and Situations

OUTLINE

The Sibling Relationship Begins
The Only Child Becomes the Older Child
Consequences of Children's Spacing
Consequences of Family Size

Child and Adolescent Sibling Relationships
Older and Younger Siblings
Gender and Class in the Sibling Relationship
Linkages to the Parent/Child Relationship
Sibling Influence
Older Siblings as Role Models
Siblings Who Share Peers
Supportive Sibling Relationships
When a Sibling Has a Disability
During Parental Conflict, Divorce, and Remarriage

Differential Parental Treatment
Birth Order and Development Stage as Factors
Gender as a Factor
Developmental Impact of Differential Treatment
The Interactional Perspective
Situations That Cushion or Exacerbate the Impact

Adult and Stepsibling Relationships
Adult Sibling Relationships
Stepsibling Relationships

How Can Siblings Be So Different?
What Are the Sources of Sibling Differences?
Children's Different Perceptions of Familial Environment
Families That Provide a More Powerful Shared Environment

Sibling Similarities and Differences: Twin Studies
Twins as Natural Experiments
Is Parental Influence Really So Unimportant?

Conclusions: The Nature and Nurture of Parental Influence

Summary
Key Concepts and Themes
Study and Review Questions
Suggested Readings
Suggested Weblinks

1970

Ten-year-old Juan is sitting at the kitchen table helping his 6-year-old sister, Pepita, do a drawing for school. Both children giggle happily and the mother who is preparing dinner smiles at them. Al, age 13, walks in swaggering and drops his lunch box on the table with a bang. Both children quiet down. The mother sighs.

Al to Juan: *Youz such a sissy, always playin' with girls.*

Pepita: *No, he's no sissy. You're mean!*

Al: *Ah, shut up!*

Both children do as told while Al mockingly looks at the drawings, laughs, throws them on the floor and walks out. The two younger ones look at each other. Drawing is no longer fun. The mother sighs again.

2000

Juan Santiago, now 40, is a married high school teacher with two children. He lives near Pepita, who has three children. Her husband is wheelchair-bound following a car accident and she is the family's main breadwinner. They have difficulty making ends meet on disability payments and her job as an office receptionist. But Juan and his wife, also a teacher, are always there to help them out. They all see each other everyday and are close to their parents who live a few blocks west. Al, the oldest is now 43; he has three children from three different women, does odd jobs, and hangs around with his drinking buddies. On the rare occasions when he visits the family at his parents' place, he makes everyone ill at ease with his sarcasm and criticisms. He picks on Pepita, who has gained weight, and on Juan, whom he mockingly calls "the school teacher."

Some things change over time in the sibling relationship while others flow throughout the life course. Pepita stood up for Juan when they were children; now he is the one who helps her. The bond has remained close and supportive. Al used to break the family's peace and continues to do so. He was always self-satisfied, arrogant, and quarrelsome. He drew a wedge between himself and his siblings. Juan, the "sissy," with his good temperament and desire to help, has grown into a solid pillar of society. Al, in contrast, has not done so well in life.

This fictive vignette is the essence of the chapter: sibling relationships through the life course. In the United States, almost 80 percent of children have at least one sibling, thus, it is a very important type of familial relationship. It is also one that generally outlasts the parent/child relationship.

THE SIBLING RELATIONSHIP BEGINS

Generally, whether the first-born child recognizes it or not, the birth of a second baby transforms his or her life entirely, as well as that of the family as a system. With the arrival of each baby, parents spend more time interacting with their children altogether, but they have less time for each child individually. Furthermore, the family's economic resources available per person diminish with each new child. On the positive side, the arrival of a second baby generally means that the older child has a lower chance of experiencing a parental divorce, compared to only children of the same age who do not get a sibling (Baydar, Greek, and Brooks-Gunn, 1997). The reason for this is that happily married couples are more likely to add another child to their family than couples who are not happy together (Myers, 1997).

The Only Child Becomes the Older Child

With the new arrival, parents cannot maintain their exclusive relationship with the first-born, a factor that may become paramount in this child's life experience if he or she feels a loss of status as well as affection. The survival requirements of an infant are more urgent and constant than those of an older sibling. As a result, parents give more attention to younger than older children. With the arrival of the second child, the mother/child relationship often becomes less affectionate, particularly if the spacing between the two children is small and the family experiences a reduction in income per person. The mother's parenting style at times becomes more punitive and the older child may feel less securely attached (Teti et al., 1996). As a result of all these changes, the first-born child occasionally suffers from a variety of problems of adjustment, including anxiety, clinging behavior, bed wetting, and even aggressiveness (Baydar, Greek, and Brooks-Gunn, 1997).

The child's reaction to the baby's arrival is largely tailored by his or her personality as well as by the steps that parents undertake to reassure and involve him or her. Dunn (1994) points out that small children who are intense and less adaptable react more negatively to the baby's arrival than children with a sunnier and contented disposition. The former may even protest when the mother pays attention to the infant. The following amusing student anecdote portrays this situation:

> *"When my little sister was born, I was three, and when my parents brought her home I asked them to return her to the hospital. I did not like to see all the fuss over this little red faced creature that cried all the time. Then one day, seeing that my parents were not returning her, I tried to wrap her in giftwrapping paper and my mother caught me in the act. It's funny to think of this now because we are best friends and often laugh over it. My sister has had my mother tell this story over and over: she just loves it."*

Such an older child's reaction to the newborn often becomes part of the family culture: It constitutes a story everyone loves to hear. But in other families, when the child has hurt the infant, pushed it off the table, or has threatened to "kill the baby," this is held against the first-born as an illustration of his or her lack of love or her or his wicked nature.

Additional infants benefit from the experience that parents have acquired with their earlier-born children. Many first-born young adults, looking back on their past, feel that their parents acquired a great deal of skills at their expense:

> *"If I could relive my life, I would have wanted to be the second oldest child in my family. I disliked having to be the first to 'test the waters.' I wish that I had had an older sibling whose errors would have served as warning posts on what lay ahead. . . . I was a learning experience for my parents."*

> *"I changed my parents' views on a lot of things. I had to fight to get what I wanted and when my sister reached the same point in life, she didn't have to fight as hard as I did. I was jealous of her for the longest time, but now I have come to learn to deal with it."*

Obviously, the education that the first-born provides parents, while perhaps to the advantage of subsequent children, is often recalled as an injustice by the older child.

Consequences of Children's Spacing

During the newborn's first months, the infant's schedule is quite different from that of the older child, especially if the latter is already at school. With four years or more of spacing between the two children, the parents' relationship with the first-born may continue to be exclusive during a portion of the day as the baby sleeps. With this much spacing, each sibling is in a way an only child, and little competition takes place, especially if the older one likes to play at surrogate parenting:

> *"Surely the happiest memory I have of my mid teens is when my mother announced that she was pregnant. This took a bit to get used to, you know the idea that your parents are 'doing it' but my sister and I were really excited. . . . Then the best times arrived with my little sister. Oh how we loved that baby. She was spoiled as we would never leave her alone which somewhat worried my parents but then my mother was happy because she had less work to do as I always volunteered to take care of Kathy. . . . Now Kathy is seven and the brightest kid on the block because we provided her with an adult environment and each one of us in the family taught her different skills and she loved to learn from the time she was small. We read to her, made her read when she was three and took her skating, biking, rollerblading, swimming. She became incredibly well coordinated. She is also very sociable because despite all the spoiling she got from us older sisters and our cousins, we still insisted on good manners and no temper tantrums or anything of the sort. She had a whole batch of parents to raise her."*

In terms of educational achievement, children do less well, on average, when they are closely spaced, and this holds true both for large and small families (Powell and Steelman, 1993). For instance, when comparing families with two children, the children who are only one year apart do less well in school. Parents have less individual time for two children who are close in age, because they essentially follow a same routine. When one child is several years older, however, the two children have different needs at different times and receive more individual attention. The older child is an only child longer and the younger child then benefits both from having a sibling who is more developed and from parents who have more time for him or her. Much older siblings are more intellectually and socially stimulating for children than siblings closer to them in age (Zajonc and Mullally, 1997). A younger sibling benefits from a large age gap between him or her and older children simply because the latter know more, as is illustrated in the previous student quote. Smaller children tend to look up to their older brothers or sisters (Buhrmester and Furman, 1990).

Consequences of Family Size

In terms of number of children, those from large sibling groups generally do not do as well at school, on average, as children from small families (Downey, 1995). Neither do they advance as much professionally later on as do adults coming from smaller families. These results remain when parents' social class is taken into consideration: Even upper-class parents provide fewer resources per child in large than in small families. The concept used to explain this family size effect is the **dilution of parental resources.** In effect, this means that parents have fewer nonexpendable resources for each child individually, whether in terms of time, attention, and even economic means. Therefore, a large sibling group dilutes the quality of the home environment available to each child (Menaghan and Parcel, 1991). This occurs even more so when children are closely spaced in a large family, because they interact more among themselves and have less adult attention; they also learn less than they would with one or two much older siblings or alone with their parents.

But, of course, there are plenty of exceptions to the rule and there are large families, particularly well-to-do ones, where all the children do very well at school or become high achievers in their professions later on. Such families may benefit from other resources, such as the help of their relatives and the presence of a large community of parents' friends and colleagues who contribute to stimulate children's intellectual development and serve as individual role models. Some research supports such a perspective. For example, a large family size has a negative impact on most non-Orthodox Jews, but it has no effect for Muslim Arabs (Shavit and Pierce, 1991). For the latter, what counts is the *hamula,* or extended family, that supports the nuclear family. The extended family increases resources and compensates for the dilution of the resources at the nuclear level. These families, in other words, have more **social capital** to offer to each individual child.

Furthermore, as Zajonc and Mullally (1997:697) pointedly remark, there are advantages to large family size that are not measured by the traditional research perspective emphasizing achievement. For instance, it may well be that siblings growing up in a large family are more "affiliative, more affectionate, good leaders, less prone to depression, or otherwise healthier." They may be less individualistic and more cooperative. They are used to sharing everything and adjusting to a far greater number of personalities. They can compromise and overlook frustrating situations. However, the only reasonably recent and large-scale study on this topic has not found any family size advantage in terms of sociability and need to be with others (Blake, Richardson, and Bhattacharya, 1991). But this study did not test for the other possible advantages mentioned by Zajonc and Mullally. A final note: Despite having benefited from less individual attention, there is no indication that adult children from large families are less attached to their parents nor their parents to them than in small families (Spitze and Logan, 1991).

CHILD AND ADOLESCENT SIBLING RELATIONSHIPS

At the personal level, sibling relationships are determined by children's characteristics, their personality similarities and differences, parents' behavior toward the children, and siblings' perception of such. Given that most of these factors are reasonably stable through each childhood, one can expect a certain degree of stability in the sibling relationship. However, the availability of peers as alternate playmates in later childhood and early adolescence is likely to bring change in the relationship. Munn and Dunn (1988) report that brothers and sisters whose personalities are compatible or complementary experience a more harmonious relationship than those who are temperamentally incompatible. When one child has an intense or unadaptable personality, sibling interactions are more conflictual (McCoy, Brody, and Stoneman, 1994). High-activity siblings get into each other's way and their requirements clash quickly and frequently.

Older and Younger Siblings

Furman and Lanthier (1996) gave personality tests and a relationship questionnaire to 56 triads of mothers and two siblings, one age 9 and the other age 11. They found that it was the older child's personality that more strongly affected the distribution of power in the relationship. The dimensions of conscientiousness and agreeableness, particularly in the older child, were strong predictors of harmony and lack of power struggle.

To complement the above study, Dunn and colleagues (1994) found that older siblings tend to be fairly consistent over time in their behavior toward their younger brother or sister: Aggressiveness or friendliness persists. This means that, in some families, younger children spend their entire childhood with a friendly and supportive sibling, whereas in others, they are in a relationship that is hostile, disparaging, and physically aggressive. The impact on child development may be substantial, but it is a question that is rarely raised in research, because traditional theories focus on parental rather than sibling effect. It is possible that negative effects that have been attributed to parents and to their harsh or rejecting treatment actually result from the rough handling that a child has received from siblings or from siblings and parents together. Such a possibility makes sense from the perspective of genetics alone. Intolerant and irritable parents may produce some offspring who are like them and may jointly have a negative impact on the sibling who is different at the outset.

Younger siblings show less stability of behavior toward their older siblings than the older ones do toward them. As we have seen earlier, smaller children look up to their older siblings; the younger ones adapt their style of interaction in order to secure the older's good will. In contrast, the older child does not have to adapt, because it is the younger ones who do. Overall, older children tend to be more domineering, and younger ones are forced to be more compliant in the sibling relationship. Putting these variables together, it is therefore not surprising that, in terms of development, the older child has a stronger effect on the younger one than vice versa (Dunn et al., 1994). As children reach adolescence, their relationship generally becomes more even and, in some cases, more egalitarian and distant.

Gender and Class in the Sibling Relationship

Gender differences exist in the sibling relationship. By the time they were 12 or 13 years old, first-born boys in a longitudinal study by Dunn (1996) reported a more distant relationship with their younger siblings than did first-born girls. This difference was, in part, explained as a result of the older boys' growing ties with their peer group. As well, the second-born children were becoming more assertive and more willing to disagree with the older boys, and this in turn contributed to the cooler climate. These pitfalls were less in evidence with older sisters. Indeed, girls maintain more intimate relationships with both siblings and peers than do boys (Updegraff and

Obeidallah, 1999). Thus, females begin at an early age their function of **kin-keepers** (Stack and Burton, 1993) and emotional workers, as described in Chapter 10.

For a girl, having an older brother often represents a precious *social resource* in male-dominated peer groups. Older brothers serve as protectors and may also enhance a child's status among peers at school:

> *"It was great having an older brother with so many friends. I remember playing foot hockey with them. I would give all to the game so that my brother would be proud of me. . . . After a few games of hockey with the guys, I gained my proud nickname, 'The little green monster.' . . . When I was in fifth grade I was known among all the grades. . . . it helps to have brothers who are both younger and older than you, since you become familiar with the students."*

Later on, the older brother's circle of friends may include males who can accompany a younger sister to a dance or party without her having to "date." This circle of friends may, of course, also be a source of dates.

Another interesting aspect in the study of siblings is that they do not perceive their relationship similarly. Dunn and McGuire (1994:120) mention that only 23 percent of the siblings in their sample reported a degree of closeness similar to that reported by their brother or sister. This discrepancy may be explained by the age and gender differences between siblings. Smaller children may be more susceptible to feeling left out by older siblings who, for their part, may be more involved with peers and largely ignore the younger ones. Girls may find their brothers less supportive, whereas boys may not notice that they are being aloof from their sisters.

Dunn (1994) also found that, by early adolescence, a social class difference had emerged in the sibling relationship. The older children of higher-income families reported more warmth and closeness with their siblings than the older children of lower-income families. Negative behaviors toward younger siblings increased at the lower socioeconomic levels during the period of study. Dunn could not offer an explanation for this social class difference, but it could originate in the more stressful familial and neighborhood environments in which many low-income families live. In such households, siblings may have to compete for scarce resources. Parents' stress and behaviors may also affect family harmony and feedback negatively onto the sibling relationship (Brody et al., 1999).

Linkages to the Parent/Child Relationship

Children who enjoy warm interactions with their mother tend to have a warm and nurturing relationship with their siblings (Teti and Ablard, 1989)—a matter of temperamental similarity between parents and children may be involved in some of these cases. In other instances, the parental example may have a constructive modeling effect. As well, warm parents reinforce their children's positive predispositions and offset negative ones. For instance, warm parents are likely to discourage aggressiveness so that their offspring get along better than in a family where parents are far less nurturing and where aggressive predispositions can bloom.

The interactional perspective suggests that it would be important to inquire into the impact of the sibling interactions on the parent/child relationship. When brothers and sisters do not get along and are close in age, parents may initiate fewer activities as a family because of the constant fraternal bickering. They may actually distance themselves from the children in order to avoid unpleasant situations. As a result, quarrelsome siblings might receive less educational input from their parents. In turn, this may result in more negative outcomes for them later on, especially if they grow up equally quarrelsome with the external world of peers and teachers.

Sibling Influence

As we have seen in the previous chapter, peers are a powerful source of influence on children and adolescents. In contrast, sibling influence and pressure are rarely acknowledged. McHale and Crouter (1996) report that preteens spend 33 percent of their out-of-school hours with siblings, compared to 13 percent with friends. These numbers alone should predict a great deal of sibling influence as well as supportive relationships or, at the very least, the potential for such.

What information do researchers have? Overall, when a sibling is aggressive, the other tends to follow suit, so that siblings are important agents of socialization to each other in this respect, and probably in many others that have yet to be researched. Patterson (1986a) finds that the aggressive interaction style of the older boys in a family trains the younger boys to be equally coercive. Rowe and Gulley's (1992) results indicate that there is a significant level of concordance among boys in a family in terms of juvenile delinquency: When one boy is delinquent, there is a good chance that the other one also is. Furthermore, when one adolescent abuses alcohol, the other is at risk of doing so, as well (Conger and Rueter, 1996).

In terms of sexuality, Widmer (1997) reports that older siblings have an effect on the timing of first intercourse among their younger brothers and sisters. Adolescent girls who have a sexually active or childbearing adolescent sister, as well as similarly oriented peers, tend to be more sexually active (East, Felice, and Morgan, 1993), even when other family variables, such as education, are taken into consideration (Powers and Hsueh, 1997). East (1999) reasons that a birth to a teenager may make it more difficult for mothers to supervise their younger children, as the grandchild increases the new grandmother's work level. Brothers are even more influential than sisters in the timing of sexual intercourse. When older brothers are virgins, their behavior may reinforce parental teachings on sexual restraint by giving them validity in the mind of younger siblings. However, East, Felice, and Morgan (1993) point out that this fraternal influence is less important than parental attitudes and teachings on this topic.

Older Siblings as Role Models

These results together indicate that older siblings act as role models for younger ones, that the sharing of activities leads to an indirect form of influence, and that an older sibling's treatment of the younger one serves as an incentive to adopt this interactional style in other relationships. These results could also indicate that siblings share an environment that encourages certain behaviors over others, whether at home, school, or in the neighborhood. A complementary explanation is that siblings share certain personality characteristics that make them equally vulnerable or equally resilient to life's temptations and circumstances. The validity of this last explanation could be tested by studying siblings who are different. For instance, in situations where two brothers have different personalities and the younger one follows the example of the older one, a far more solid case of influence can be made than when two brothers have similar tendencies to begin with.

Older siblings are particularly important sources of information and general influence in families that have recently immigrated. This is especially so when parents do not speak English well (Perez-Granados and Callanan, 1997). In such instances, older siblings acquire an aura of authority as they are better able to introduce the American culture, or even the subculture of a neighborhood, to their younger siblings. This influence is strengthened when parents depend on their older children for translation, for instance, a phenomenon referred to in Chapter 3 as children assuming the role of "cultural brokers."

Siblings Who Share Peers

Sibling influence can be compounded by the sharing of friends. During adolescence, and more in adulthood, siblings' similarity of characteristics seems to increase friendliness and contact as well as the sharing of friends. In turn, frequency of positive contact contributes to an increased resemblance between siblings over the long term, especially with regard to ideas, values, and leisure activities (Bouchard et al., 1990). One would expect that the sharing of a prosocial peer group by siblings enhances their own prosocial behaviors. This, in turn, greatly facilitates parental duties as these prosocial children are probably easier to raise. This network of peers becomes a form of **social capital** to both parents and children (Furstenberg and Hughes, 1995). Prosocial peers are also more likely to have authoritative parents; when a group of peers have similarly oriented parents, the burden of supervision is lessened for each individual set of parents, given that they all participate to some degree in the monitoring process (Fletcher et al., 1995). This refers us back to the concepts of the **functional community** and group or **collective socialization.**

By the same token, when siblings who are already predisposed to deviance share a delinquent or aggressive peer group, this raises the chance that they will commit delinquent acts (Rowe et al., 1989). Consequently, parents must increasingly monitor such offspring and set more limits on their activities and whereabouts. This demanding level of supervision and alertness may go beyond the abilities of many parents, as indicated in the following passage from a female student's autobiography. It graphically illustrates the family dynamics that may occur during adolescence when siblings are closely spaced, get along with each other, and encourage each other and peers in activities that parents disapprove of:

> *"The problem with my family at that age is that there were four adolescent children, two boys, two girls, and we actually ran the house. There was nothing that our parents could do to control us. If we wanted some friends over for the night, we'd hide them and my parents would not notice. Anyway, they hated to come in our rooms which were an absolute mess. It may not come as a great surprise that my brother got a girl pregnant when he was only 15 and my sister became a drug addict at 16. The other two of us turned out alright, which is amazing considering the bad example we got from the other two and the fact that we used to encourage their misbehavior, side with them, and help them out*

when in trouble. We had absolutely no solidarity with our parents. It was just among us children, as we were one or two years apart. Our second solidarity was for our friends."

Supportive Sibling Relationships

The literature on the family is by necessity often oriented toward the study of problems rather than daily dynamics. One of the consequences of this orientation is that there is relatively little research on supportive sibling relationships during childhood and adolescence. The major exceptions pertain to children who have a sibling suffering from a disability and to brothers and sisters whose parents are conflictual, divorce, or remarry.

When a Sibling Has a Disability

Parents usually shoulder the responsibility of caring for or coordinating the care of a child with a disability well into adulthood. A cooperative sibling can greatly lighten the burden of the parents, who often develop particularly warm feelings for that helpful adult child, as illustrated in this situation:

"My older sister is retarded and has some heart problems so that my relationship with her is one of role reversal. She is 5 years older than me but I take care of her a lot to give some breathing space to my parents. When I was a bit younger . . . once in a while our needs clashed with hers or the demands our parents placed on us because of her. She does look normal and my mother often asked us to take her out with us to see a movie or something of the sort. Jackie loved it but it was different for us because we wanted to be with our friends and felt unpleasantly 'special.' . . . My parents really appreciate what we do for her and for them because they say that they trust that we will take care of her after they are gone, which is the biggest worry that parents of delayed adult children have. My brother and I will take care of her for sure although thankfully our parents are still young. But I think that of the two of us I may end of having to do most of the caring because I noticed that my brother does less than he used to do—he is a male!"

However, in reality, there is no indication so far that siblings become the primary caregivers of their disabled brother or sister when parents are no longer able to do so. Many of these disabled individuals have to turn outside the family for help (Pruchno, Patrick, and Burant, 1996).

Horwitz (1993) suggests that therapists should encourage adults who are mentally ill to develop mutual relationships with their siblings, given that people are more willing to help someone who reciprocates. The results of Seltzer and colleagues' study (1997) further indicate the necessity to help the mentally ill develop less confrontational behaviors with their siblings. The researchers found that adults had a higher level of well-being and a closer relationship with a sibling who is mentally delayed than a sibling who is mentally ill. Siblings, like parents, are affected more negatively by behavioral and attitudinal problems than by intellectual limitations. In other words, adults who experience better psychological well-being are those whose mentally-ill siblings are kept at a distance, which also means that the sibling with mental illness receives less support than the one with retardation, unless the latter also exhibits difficult behaviors.

During childhood and adolescence, having a brother or sister with special needs also carries costs (LeClere and Kowalewski, 1994). The literature is quite unanimous in this respect and the previous student quote nicely illustrated this dilemma. These children generally get less parental attention because so much is demanded of parents for the care of the disabled or chronically ill child. The family can less easily pursue leisure activities than other families, and friends cannot be invited home so as not to disrupt the routine of care. When a sibling with disabilities is aggressive toward the helping child or adolescent, the latter tends to be less well adjusted emotionally—and we have just seen that this also occurs in adulthood.

During Parental Conflict, Divorce, and Remarriage

Brothers and sisters, especially older ones who function well, can act as a buffer for their younger siblings at times of marital conflict or divorce, or in the event of a parent's illness or emotional problems. However, so far, the research indicates that this type of sibling support is not always forthcoming—for instance, divorce actually increases negative interactions between siblings (Kim, Hetherington, and Reiss, 1999). In fact, a conflictual relationship between parents is more likely to lead to, or be accompanied by, greater sibling conflict. Conger and Conger (1996:119) find that "it is the actual disruption of marriage rather than the degree" of parental conflict in intact marriages "that most adversely affects relations between brothers and sisters." This effect of divorce on the sibling relationship is one that is infrequently mentioned in the literature on the negative consequences of marital breakup.

This greater sibling conflict can be explained by a combination of variables. For one, conflict between parents, and even more so the divorce itself, dilutes familial resources so that stress and emotional deprivation pit each child against the other for

Fathers are more likely than mothers to treat sons and daughters differently. Fathers who treat their opposite-sex children more equally provide powerful messages to small children in terms of healthy gender-role development and feelings of security.

scarce parental attention. Second, the stressors experienced by parents spill over into their childrearing practices and lead to brother-sister friction. Third, a portion of divorcing couples may have difficult personalities and their children may have inherited these predispositions so that they develop conflictual relationships among themselves. Furthermore, the spacing between children has not been considered in these studies: Sibling friction may occur only when there is little age difference among them, which leads to competition for scarce resources, such as parental attention.

Hetherington (1988) finds that the presence of a stepfather is often accompanied by fractious sibling interactions. Overall, boys, particularly when they reach adolescence, disengage more from their siblings in remarried than in married families (Anderson and Rice, 1992). But among those siblings who remain cohesive, mutual support reduces the number of problems experienced when they are exposed to parental conflict (Jenkins and Smith, 1990). In families with two children, the presence of at least one girl increases the chance that a cohesive sibling relationship is established (Conger and Conger, 1996). Thus, once again, the children's gender is an important variable in this respect.

DIFFERENTIAL PARENTAL TREATMENT

As seen earlier, parents treat children differently depending on each child's age. The younger child is favored by both parents in some circumstances, yet the older one is in other matters (McHale et al., 1995). Furthermore, fathers show more interest in sons, particularly first-borns, and in children who have a more expressive personality (Crouter et al., 1999; see Family Research 12.1 for the methodology involved). There are also indications that parents who are stressed by poverty or marital conflict, or are depressed are more likely to treat one child better or less well than the other (Henderson et al., 1996).

Birth Order and Development Stage as Factors

It appears that mothers treat their children similarly at a given age within relatively small sibling groups and spacing—at least in the United Kingdom and North America. It is not known to what extent the following results apply in the case of larger families and other situations. A longitudinal study yielded high correlations between a mother's treatment of the older child at age 2 and her subsequent treatment of the younger child at the same age. That is, it appears that mothers treat children in a manner appropriate to each age level, so that both children are treated similarly at a given age, yet are treated differently in the present because they are of different ages (Dunn, Plomin, and Daniels, 1986).

But the correlations between the maternal treatments of the children at the same age are not perfect. This suggests, first, that mothers adapt their behavior to each child's individuality and developmental rhythm (Volling, 1997). Second, the later-born child enters the family system at a different point in the family's life course (Hoffman, 1991:193). The mother may be busier or more tired when the younger child is

FAMILY RESEARCH 12.1

Parents' Knowledge of Each Sibling's Daily Activities

Crouter and colleagues (1999) wanted to see if parents would be more aware of the older sibling's or the younger sibling's daily life, and whether this knowledge would depend on the children's sex, personality, as well as parents' employment hours. Letters were sent to the homes of fourth- and fifth-graders in 16 central Pennsylvania school districts. The 203 participating families were headed by two parents with at least two children, and the second sibling had to be younger by one to four years.

In a first step, family members were interviewed at home separately; parents and children also filled out questionnaires. Questions were read aloud when children's literacy skills required it. In a second step, both parents and children were interviewed over the phone on several different evenings during a two- to three-week period following the home interviews. Parents and children were queried about their daily activities; questions designed to measure parents' knowledge of their children's activities were included:

Did child X have English homework today? What was the assignment?
Did child X watch TV, videos, or movies at home today? What?
Did child X have any conflict or disagreement with a friend today? Which friend?
Was child X outside the home at 4:00 P.M. today? Where was he or she?

2 years old than she was when the older one was the same age a few years earlier. This difference in treatment could also be explained by any other factor that may have changed in the child's and mother's lives and environment. For instance, when child B reaches age 2, the parents may have separated and the mother may be under more (or less) stress than she was when child A was age 2. Her higher or lower level of stress could affect her parenting vis-à-vis the younger child.

To sum up, it seems that mothers tend to treat their children similarly at a given level of child maturity. But they are not necessarily as consistent toward the same child while he or she is growing up because children change with age, and some become easier or more difficult; as well, the parental context changes. In some families, it is obvious that parents treat their children differently, not simply because of age differences, but because one offspring may be less adaptive or need more encouragement or structure, as is illustrated in the following student quote:

> *"My parents have always treated my sister differently than they have me. My sister was the smart one, school came easier to her and my parents treated her as the smart one. They were much more concerned about whether I did homework or not and how my marks in school were; I was under much more scrutiny. . . . My sister was allowed to stay up later, go out for longer, do more things, and have more fun."*

Information concerning parenting consistency during adolescence and later ages is lacking. As children grow older, it is quite possible that parents treat them increasingly differently so as to respond to their delopmental needs. Children may contribute to this differential treatment as they try to differentiate themselves from their siblings in order to assert their own individuality.

Gender as a Factor

Gender is one of the most important variables in child socialization. Parents raise boys and girls to assume different roles in society, although families vary in the extent to which they do so and in the degree to which they treat boys and girls differently. Overall, fathers are more likely to make a distinction between sons and daughters and are generally more involved with sons (Harris and Morgan, 1991). There are also indications in the student autobiographies that parents treat sons and daughters increasingly differently as they age. Women students repeatedly complained that adolescent brothers were given much more freedom than they had been allowed at the same age. In some ethnic groups, a slightly older brother or even a younger one chaperons a sister whenever she goes out, especially in the evenings. Causing even more resentment is the fact that these girls have to do more housework, age for age, than their brothers, and some even have to clean up after them:

> *"In my family, there are two standards: one for my brother and one for my sister and I. We girls do everything in the house and work to pay for school whereas my brother does nothing and works to pay for his car and dates. I really resent it even though I try to rationalize it this way, that my parents come from a non-Christian background, but it does not erase the unpleasant reality. People who immigrate here should leave behind their unpleasant backgrounds and adapt to what families do here which is by and large to treat boys and girls the same."*

> *"My brother gets to go out without even telling my parents where he is going. My sister and I have to tell my parents everything, where we are going, what time we will be home and so on."*

The more males are valued in a culture, the greater the difference in parental treatment. (In fact, in some societies experiencing scarcity, sons are given the best food while daughters go hungry.) However, it is possible that, in large families, parents have less time to react to each child's gender and accordingly treat their offspring more similarly than do parents with fewer children. Or, alternatively, they may treat all the boys one way and all the girls the other way. In other instances, fathers feel closer to sons and mothers to daughters because they share same-sex interests and aspirations.

Developmental Impact of Differential Treatment

Several studies have discovered that the sibling who receives the most favorable parental treatment seems to be doing better than the other. Daniels (1987) reports that the sibling who enjoys more affection from the father has more ambitious educational and vocational goals. Children who are more controlled by their mother or perceive receiving less affection than their siblings are more likely to be anxious or depressed. These children also tend to be more difficult.

The Interactional Perspective

It may not be the differential parental treatment that necessarily produces these observed outcomes (Schieffelin, 1990). The interactional perspective suggests a reversed causality in many cases. For instance, a difficult child may require parents to become more controlling. It may also be that a more ambitious child attracts paternal attention and encouragement. That is, his or her ambitions *create* or evoke the favored attention rather than vice versa. It is also possible that it is the perception and interpretation of differences rather than the actual differential treatment that cause the problems for the child who feels deprived (Reiss et al., 1995). In other words, children may not be adversely affected when their parents give more attention to a sibling if they find that this is justifiable on the basis of a younger siblings's needs, for instance.

Therefore, differential parental treatment and its presumed effects have to be analyzed within an interactional model. In great part, except for gender roles, parents respond to their children according to their personalities and behaviors, as seen in the preceding chapter. Thus, Bank, Patterson, and Reid (1996) find that parents behave differently with a boy who is aggressive and oppositional than with his easy-going sibling. In their experimental study, one group of families had both a difficult and an easy-going boy while the other set of families had two "easy" children. The researchers observed family interactions when the difficult sons were present and then when they were absent. The two samples showed different parental treatment of their children when the difficult boys were included. But when only the parents and the easy-going child were considered together, there was no difference between the two samples of families in the way parents treated their children. This result illustrates the impact of a child on family dynamics and the creation of differential parental treatment. Children, in great part, create the differential treatment they receive from their parents—the concept of children as **coproducers** of their socialization experience (discussed in Chapter 11).

Situations That Cushion or Exacerbate the Impact

Volling (1997) makes a distinction between *differential favoritism,* which has negative consequences for family relationships, and *differential discipline.* Among preschoolers, she found that when the older child was disciplined more often than the younger one, the family functioned better than when it was the younger one who was more often disciplined. The reason for this observation is that, in the latter case, parents were not taking into consideration the children's respective developmental levels. They were probably as demanding of the younger as of the older one—a situation that creates difficulties because the younger child has not yet developed the ability to meet such maturity demands.

Differential parental treatment that does not appear fair to children causes jealousy and resentment on the part of the less favored child, and may well give rise to feelings of entitlement on the part of the preferred child, who becomes the little king or queen. The less favored offspring expresses his or her resentment toward the more favored one (Boer, Goedhart, and Treffers, 1992). This expression of negative feelings may be the result of justified jealousy or, alternatively, it may be the result of the more difficult personality of the less favored child, who behaves less pleasantly toward siblings and parents alike.

McHale and colleagues (1995) as well as Volling (1997) went one step farther in this type of research on differential parental treatment and grouped families depending on whether both parents were *congruent* (displaying more affection for the same child) or *incongruent* (each parent preferring a different child). Congruent parents predominated. Incongruence tends to occur among couples whose relationship is distressed: These parents at times form a coalition with different children against each other (Reiss et al., 1994). When this occurs, the parent/child boundaries melt away while boundaries between parents rise. This situation, in turn, makes it difficult to raise children authoritatively. In contrast, parents who get along maintain the boundaries of the parental system and tend to agree on which child needs more support.

Thus, one sees the importance of studying parents' differential treatment in the context of other variables, such as marital happiness as well as number and spacing of offspring. It is not known, for instance, if differential treatment has a more negative impact in a poor quality environment or in a more privileged environment, or in families that have children of only one sex or of both. Moreover, differential treatment may produce effects that vary according to parental personality, *relative parental power* within the family, and overall level of parenting involvement. For example, a parent who has little power or who is perceived to be weak may not have the same impact as one who is psychologically strong and is dominant in the family. Siblings may notice it more if they are treated differently by a dominant parent than by a weak one. As illustrated by the following mature student, children may seek attention more from a parent who is socially prominent than from a parent who has a lower profile:

> *"At home, I am in a rather unfortunate situation: although I am always available to the children and am really their maid, when their father is around I am just as good as not there. They hang on to his every word and find him so interesting. He doesn't even have to ask them to do something, they just do it. One or the other children gets very upset if he doesn't talk to him or her or gives equal treatment. They're like courtesans around a king. Me, what am I? Nothing! So if I yell at one, that one doesn't even notice it. If I give him a compliment, they shrug it off. It has more or less always been like that: my husband is quite the social butterfly, looks good, and is known to a lot of people. In contrast, I am the somewhat mousy wife about whom people wonder, 'Whatever did he find in her?' "*

The children seem to notice their mother's lower social prominence and "shrug off" her differential behaviors toward them, yet are affected when the father does not treat them equally.

ADULT AND STEPSIBLING RELATIONSHIPS

As children reach adulthood, the sibling relationship in industrialized societies, particularly those of Western cultures, becomes discretionary. That is, continuing the relationship is a matter of choice and is secondary to the spousal and parent/child relationships. Cicirelli (1994:16) points out that adult sibling interactions "do not have a major effect in family functioning or adaptation to the larger society." In contrast, in other societies, continuation of the sibling relationship into adulthood is the norm and is of fundamental importance for the family's integration into society at large. Sibling relationships, particularly between two brothers or two sisters, may actually be more consequential than their relationship with a spouse, both at the social and economic level.

Adult Sibling Relationships

Among adults in North America, proximity increases contact between siblings and the potential for both conflict and closeness (Cicirelli, 1995). When no other family member lives nearby, proximity also increases the exchange of help between siblings (Miner and Uhlenberg, 1997). Personalities and lifestyles must be fairly important in determining the quality of adult sibling bonds, particularly in view of the fact that these relationships are largely optional. Cicirelli (1996) points out that older persons like to reminisce about the past. They can do so far better with like-minded siblings than with their adult children, for instance.

We return here to the theme of **gender** in the sibling relationship. Overall, bonds are closer between sisters than between brothers, although there are many exceptions (Cicirelli, 1995). Furthermore, sisters provide more help to each other, as well as to other family members, than do brothers; this pattern is more obvious in some ethnic groups than others (Johnson, 1985). For males, a good relationship with their sisters is also important for their morale. Cicirelli (1989) reports that elderly brothers who have more sisters feel happier and more secure. This result probably stems from the greater familial cohesiveness that exists in families that have females and from the nurturing role to which women are socialized (Baines, Evans, and Neysmith, 1991). Sisters provide moral support to their brothers and this contributes to the latter's sense of well-being. Unfortunately, sisters may not benefit equally from fraternal support, as brothers have not generally been socialized to be nurturant and supportive. For both genders, ties with siblings are particularly important after widowhood and in periods of crisis (Cicirelli, Coward, and Dwyer, 1992).

However, differential parental treatment that was perceived to be unfair when the children were growing up often extends its negative consequences into adulthood and is reflected in the siblings' later relationships (Baker and Daniels, 1990). Siblings who were less favored or who perceived they were may feel that they have been cheated and, as they age, may distance themselves from the others. They may find alternative sources of moral support. These relationships may even be more conflictual. In some cases, jealousy continues into old age, even though there never was any factual basis for it—it was simply a matter of perception, as one male student deplores:

> *"I have never been able to understand why my older brother and sisters are still so jealous of me. It's very painful to me at this age [about 23] because I have never done anything and neither have my parents to attract this attitude. I was sick more often as a child and my parents had to worry about me more. But the older ones had a lot more freedom and they got much more financially: they didn't have to pay for school as I am doing. At my age they all had cars and I don't. I should be the one who is jealous, really. It's just in their heads and it's upsetting because they certainly don't go out of their way to encourage my little nephews and nieces to accept me."*

Less than 10 percent of adult Americans over the age of 30 live with one or more siblings. However, the percentages are nearly twice as high among African Americans and Latinos (except for Puerto Ricans), and the lowest among Asian groups. Blacks report the most contact with their siblings; Asians report the fewest. Whites report the most exchange in terms of help and resources. Riedmann and White (1996) conclude that, although racial/ethnic groups have different forms of sibling solidarity, no group is disadvantaged in this respect. Among Mexican Americans, adult coresidence with a sibling, even a married one, seems to occur more frequently among new immigrants and among the younger groups—this was referred to as the horizontally-extended family in Chapter 3, and probably serves an economic function. But among African Americans, help and exchange with siblings, including coresidence, is lower among the very poor and young adults.

Stepsibling Relationships

The literature on remarriage has been so focused on problems of adult and child adjustment that little attention has been devoted to the new relationships that are formed among children from the merging families (Ganong and Coleman, 1994). Not only is there little information on the relationship between stepsiblings, but there is equally little on that between halfsiblings (i.e., when new children are born in a remarriage)—apart from the fact that halfsiblings who share a mother tend to be closer than those who share a father (Bernstein, 1997).

Remarriages are often brief and stepchildren do not always live in a same household, so that many of these relationships simply do not have the time nor the opportunity to blossom. Each set of stepsiblings may simply be an element of curiosity for the other. A father's children may feel some degree of animosity toward those stepsiblings who live with him and are his new wife's children. This animosity or jealousy can be provoked by the fact that many noncustodial fathers see their own children rarely or do not support them:

> *"My feelings for my father . . . I can't say with 100% certainty that I love him because we have always been his invisible children. . . . I can't stand his wife's children after all those years because they have it all: my father has been very good to them and they've always been in the way, like we can't see him without these two being there and grabbing all the attention."*

> *"So I have a stepsister who is two years older than I am. At first, we hated each other . . . after all, her father was taking my father's place and when she visited my mother was taking her mother's place. . . . Now we are not close but we get along quite well now that we don't have to see each other often."*

When the remarriage lasts, stepsiblings often become companionable and supportive (Anderson, 1999), and maintain some level of connectedness into adulthood.

> *"My two stepbrothers were then 2 and 4 years younger than me and they looked up to me so that I soon ended up playing big brother. For a 10-year-old who is rather upset at what has happened to his parents, that was a great thing. We got along famously well and have been a team to this day."*

Being African American increases the likelihood of contact between stepsiblings (White and Riedmann, 1992)—so does being a female (and we note for the fourth time in this chapter the role that females play in sibling integration and solidarity). The stepsibling relationship is closer when there are no full siblings. Half and stepsiblings may be better able to bond when the type of solidarity that generally exists between two full siblings, whether biological or adopted, is absent. The former may then serve as substitute siblings and all accept each other as such. Even among older cohorts, more conflict is reported between halfsiblings and stepsiblings than between full siblings, perhaps in part because they have at least one parent they do not share. Halfsiblings and stepsiblings also help each other less in old age than do full siblings.

All in all, in adulthood, the longer stepsiblings have lived together as children, the closer the bond. Having lived with one's mother and stepfather also leads to more contact than having lived with one's father and a stepmother—again indicating the salience of relationships that are maintained by a mother.

HOW CAN SIBLINGS BE SO DIFFERENT?

In this section and the next, we investigate the ramifications of yet another aspect of the situation of siblings vis-à-vis each other: their differences. As I have already alluded to in Chapter 1, the question of why siblings can be so different rather than similar has been used to investigate the role that genes and the environment play in human development. Traditional socialization theories inform us that parents are extremely important in the formation of their children's personalities, behaviors, and well-being. However, most studies based on this premise find only weak or moderate correlations between various child outcomes and parents' socialization practices. It is not surprising that most results of behavior genetic studies find the same.

These results combined put into question the validity of many past and current sociological interpretations of the parental role, particularly when it comes to *personality development* as opposed to *behaviors*. Geneticists correctly point out that the traditional research confounds genetic and environmental influences (Scarr, 1993): It studies the family as if it were only an environment and ignores the fact that genes play an important role in the interaction between parents and children. In essence, what in the past has been assumed to be the result of parenting is now better understood as an interplay between parents' and children's genetic predispositions as well as between these and the general environment in which families are located (Luster et al., 2000: 145). This perspective meshes well with the interactional-transactional theories that analyze causality from a multidirectional framework.

What Are the Sources of Sibling Differences?

Dunn and Plomin (1990) have documented how dissimilar siblings generally are on at least some important personality characteristics and related behaviors. Everyday experience also presents the reader with many opportunities to observe such differences between two brothers or two sisters who are only one year apart. Yet, children in a same family are exposed to a **shared environment** that includes family structure, family routines and events, values and teachings emphasized by parents, as well as the effects of parents' personalities on family functioning (Plomin and McClearn, 1993). The traditional socialization perspective predicts that this shared environment should make siblings quite similar in terms of personality characteristics, values, behaviors, and even adult lifestyles. Furthermore, each child inherits 50 percent of his or her genetic makeup from the mother and the other 50 percent from the father. Thus, siblings inherit their genetic makeup from the combined gene pool of a same mother and father—hence, one more reason for them to be similar. Why are they not? There are three reasons.

First, siblings are different because each inherits a different *combination* of their *parents' gene pool.* Let's take two sisters, Linda and Jenny. Linda looks like the father physically but is also sociable like the mother; in contrast, Jenny looks like the mother but is shy and reserved like the father is. Second, siblings are different because of the **nonshared environment,** which essentially refers to environmental influences or experiences that differ for each child. These include birth order, peers, school experiences, and accidents and illnesses that affect one sibling but not the other. As we have seen, even their own relationship can constitute a nonshared experience: They often treat each other differently.

Children's Different Perceptions of Familial Environment

A third reason why siblings are different is that they transform much of their shared or familial environment into a nonshared one. Indeed, although siblings partake equally of their shared familial environment, such as parental teachings or even divorce, they attach **different meanings** to it because of their individual personalities and what they have learned outside the family (Monahan et al., 1993). For instance, Dunn and McGuire (1994) compared the impact on siblings of 256 events that had occurred in the families they had observed over a three-year period. These shared events affected the siblings differently in nearly 70 percent of the cases. Thus, only 30 percent of the events produced a common effect.

> *Let's take the fictive example of two fraternal twins. Although their parents treat them similarly, twin Bob* perceives *that he receives less love, whereas twin Harry does not see any difference in the way they are treated. This perceptual gap results from twin Bob being more sensitive, anxious, and rebellious than Harry (Baker and Daniels, 1990). This perceptual difference produces another consequence: Bob's sense of resentment and then distancing from parents.*

In effect, because of his reaction, Bob is creating for himself a family climate different from that of his twin. This divergent family climate will become part of their nonshared environment. In turn, this nonshared environment interacts with each twin's predispositions to create different ways of behaving toward others, including their parents. For instance, Bob becomes even more rebellious and anxious as a result of the nonshared environment he has in great part created—although he has done so unconsciously.

> *Another hypothetical example, that of a disadvantaged family with three daughters, further illustrates this mechanism. One sister is good natured and easily satisfied. She does not feel deprived and makes the best out of a bad situation. The other sister is materialistic, envious, and demanding. Consequently, she reacts to their poverty with stress, dissatisfaction, behavioral problems, and lack of respect for their parents. The last sister is goal oriented and industrious; she is determined to improve her lot.*

These siblings' **perceptions** based on their different personalities lead them to react differently to a shared environment of poverty. In turn, these disparate reactions not only strengthen their personality differences but also create a private environment—that is, one that they do not share with their two sisters. This nonshared environment contributes to maintaining or even widening the differences among these siblings.

Such examples fit very well within the perspectives of symbolic interactionism and interactional theories. In summary, siblings are dissimilar to some extent in terms of personalities, appearance, and physical constitution because of a different combination of genes. (By the same token, however, they are more similar among themselves than to unrelated persons of the same age in their neighborhood.) Second, siblings are also different because of the nonshared environment, such as different friends. And third, their different perceptions of and reactions to their shared environment reinforces their differences and creates new ones.

Families That Provide a More Powerful Shared Environment

The above having been said, the fact remains that some families provide more shared socialization experiences for their children than do most other families. This expanded family environment becomes more powerful and can make siblings similar, not necessarily in terms of personalities, but in leisure activities, lifestyle, beliefs, values, and even the skills they learn (Lykken, 1987). How do parents provide a more comprehensive or powerful shared environment?

To begin with, some fathers and mothers are quite similar to each other as a result of **assortative mating** (Chapter 4). Such parents are likely to reinforce each other's teachings and provide a more uniform home climate that leaves less room for differentiation among siblings than when parents hold different views. Second, we can use Thornton and Lin's (1994) theory of **family integration** as an explanation. Parents who engage in many activities with their children, both at home or elsewhere, provide siblings with a more cohesive and integrative learning experience. For instance, parents may take their children along on vacations and to the library or museums, and they may engage in specific sport activities as a family group. All these activities combined contribute to family integration, which enlarges the children's shared environment; the shared activities also limit the time the children spend in nonshared activities and in environments that could lead to a different learning experience.

Third, this shared effect becomes even more powerful when parents and children together engage in activities with other parents and their children as a group; the entire family then experiences more shared elements. These activities can include church or synagogue worship, sports, communal picnics, and visits to other families' homes. The end result is that parents and offspring interact with others their age within a same context that, in turn, reinforces parental teachings. Fourth, when parents are able to send their children to schools that replicate their own value system and lifestyle, siblings and parents have a more expanded, shared learning environment (Chapter 8). The school becomes an extension of the home, particularly when like-minded parents send like-minded children to the same schools. The school and the family essentially overlap in what the children learn, each agent of socialization reinforcing the other and, in rational theory's terms, offering *social closure* against the rest of the world.

Although each child in such families benefits from the common environment somewhat differently because of his or her personality, the fact remains that these siblings are surrounded by a "wraparound" lifestyle that is shared by parents, relatives, friends, friends' parents, parents' friends, and even teachers. This shared environment becomes a **functional community** where everyone more or less pitches in and socializes its children similarly. **Collective socialization** is a shared experience involving a large group or a village, as is the case in agrarian societies. It is a far more powerful agent of socialization than isolated parental efforts at home, which can be contramended by different sets of values and behaviors as soon as children step outside (Dornbusch, Ritter, and Steinberg, 1991). Therefore, when parents are able or can afford to provide their children with an extrafamilial environment that reinforces the home one, the shared environment becomes a more powerful source of influence on offspring. Siblings then become more similar, not in terms of personality characteristics, but with regard to lifestyle, education, values, beliefs, and occupational achievement.

One sees such examples among traditional Mafia families that interact among themselves and where the male children learn to engage in illegal activities, and among communities of rural Amish families where the children who remain home replicate their parents' specific rural and religious lifestyle. Among upper-class families, one can perhaps think of many of the Kennedy and Bush adult children who, despite different personalities, grew up to be politically and community oriented. This expanded shared environment can also occur by default in geographically isolated pockets of rural poverty, where all the children fall under the same influences that limit their life alternatives. They consequently grow up to replicate their parents' and their neighbors' poverty, despite having different personalities and innate abilities (Rowe, Jacobson, and Van den Oord, 1999).

SIBLING SIMILARITIES AND DIFFERENCES: TWIN STUDIES

Until the science of molecular or biological genetics is able to pinpoint exactly which sets of genes are causally related to specific personality predispositions as well as illnesses (the work of the Human Genome Project), behavior geneticists in the meantime have to rely on sophisticated statistical guesswork. The best natural experiment that life provides them at this point are twins as well as adoption situations.

Twins as Natural Experiments

The rationale behind research with twins and adoptive siblings is to take advantage of degrees of genetic closeness (Plomin et al., 1998; see Family Research 12.2). Identical twins share all of their genes; fraternal twins and other siblings share about 50 percent; halfsiblings about 25 percent; and stepsiblings as well as adopted children have no genetic background in common. The more closely related two persons are genetically, the more likely they are to be similar. Furthermore, research designs comparing identical

FAMILY RESEARCH 12.2

Potential Problems in Twin Studies

A recent Colorado Adoption Project study compared pairs of adoptive siblings with pairs of biological siblings on mild delinquency and aggressive behavior (Deater-Deckard and Plomin, 1999). For our purposes here, we are interested in the many potential problems of twin studies the authors raised in their discussion. For instance, the authors wondered whether it is valid to assume that twins' family environment is equivalent to that of regular siblings. This is a necessary assumption if the results of behavior genetics studies are to be valid. Yet, one can easily see that parenting two or more same-age children may create a different familial climate, which would violate the assumption of an equivalent family environment. Furthermore, identical twins may be more likely to copy each other's behavior than fraternal twins or even just regular siblings, a situation that could artificially increase the genetic influence. Thus, serious methodological problems may exist in the research on twins and may endanger researchers' ability to draw solid and generalizable conclusions about the role of genetics and environment in human development.

twins and fraternal twins reared apart in adoptive homes to twins raised together in their family of birth allow for the study of the separate and combined role played by genetics, shared environment, and nonshared environment (Kendler, 1996).

Thus, researchers "experiment" with degrees of genetic closeness along with degrees of shared environments: Twins who have been adopted into separate families present an ideal experimental situation. This particular twin research design is illustrated in Table 12.1. This table is fictive in the sense that the numbers are invented for teaching purposes (the statistics utilized by behavior geneticists are too complex for a family textbook). However, the numbers presented follow the general line of reasoning of such studies. This table focuses on personality characteristics because they are more likely to be genetically influenced than are lifestyles and activities; the latter depend more on the available environment.

To begin with, if genes were the main determinant in the formation of personality, the percentages for identical twins would be close to 90 percent to indicate near perfect similarity. But the highest figure in Table 12.1 is 40 percent, which more or

TABLE 12.1 Fictive Percentages of Overall Personality Similarity among Identical and Fraternal Twins Who Were Raised Together or Separately*

Identical Twins Raised Together (Group 1)	Identical Twins Raised Separately (Group 2)	Fraternal Twins Raised Together (Group 3)	Fraternal Twins Raised Separately (Group 4)
40%	35%	20%	15%

*The fictive subjects are four groups each containing 100 pairs of same-sex twins aged 14.

Identical twins constitute a natural "experimental" situation for researchers interested in the joint role of genes and environment in human development. Unfortunately, too little serious research exists regarding twins' development of their individual self-concepts and the dynamics of their relationships.

less means that around 60 percent of the identical twins' personalities is produced by the environment, both shared and nonshared. A second way of examining the role of genes and environment is to look at twins reared together (Groups 1 and 3). Identical twins are still much more similar than fraternal twins on personality characteristics: The percentages are 40 and 20 for identical and fraternal twins, respectively. This indicates a role played by genes. If genes played no role, identical and fraternal twins would be equally similar because of the environment they share: Their percentages would be the same.

However, one would expect no similarity between identical twins raised separately were the home environment the main determinant. Thus, a third way is to look at different family environments, in this case those in which twins have been raised separately (Groups 2 and 4). Identical twins reared apart are still more similar to each other in terms of personality than fraternal twins (35 versus 15 percent), but they are not quite as similar as identical twins who have been raised together (40 versus 35 percent). This indicates that genes are important but that the family environment also plays a role, although a small one, as can be seen by the mere 5 percent difference between twins raised apart and separately.

According to this line of reasoning, genes win over family influence, but not over the nonshared environment. Behavioral geneticists calculate the influence of the nonshared environment as being nearly everything else that is not accounted for by genes and family (or around 55 percent for identical twins in this table). Thus, because the percentage difference attributed to the family environment is so small in these statistics (5 percent), behavior geneticists believe that the nonshared environment is more influential in making siblings what they are than the familial or shared environment (Reiss, 1993). The conclusions derived from this line of reasoning are critiqued later on.

Identical adult twins who have been raised apart give many similar answers when they are asked to describe the homes in which they have been reared (Hur and Bouchard, 1995:339). Their **perceptions** are more similar than are those of fraternal twins also raised apart. In view of the fact that the homes were different, how can this be? This similarity of perceptions is the result of a combined genetic and environmental effect. To begin with, it is likely that these identical twins' different sets of adoptive parents were reacting fairly similarly to the twins' identical physical appearances and relatively similar personalities when they were growing up. (Parents adapt to their children, as discussed in Chapter 11.)

Although living in different homes, the identical twins may then have developed more similar relationships with their two sets of parents and thus naturally perceive these homes more similarly than do fraternal twins. The latter were less alike in terms of appearance and personalities, and consequently elicited **different reactions** from their two sets of adoptive parents. As the reader can see, these processes are also easily understood through both symbolic interactionism and interactional theories: People create reactions that then become part of their environment, and this environment in turn helps create their personalities and perceptions. All in all, these studies indicate that genes indirectly play a role in the creation of a person's environment—genes and environment act together.

Is Parental Influence Really So Unimportant?

As we have seen, the results of behavior geneticists' studies lead them to emphasize the effect of the nonshared environment over the familial one into the shaping of siblings' personalities and related behaviors (Plomin and Rutter, 1998). Unfortunately, these statistical results and conclusions have led a few researchers, and recently, at a more popular level, a writer such as Harris (1998), to conclude that parenting is largely irrelevant to children's development. Is this so?

No: This belief is a misunderstanding arising from the twin and adoption *methodology* (Monahan et al., 1993). The misunderstanding arises because the relative lack of similarity among siblings raised together is interpreted to mean that only a different thus nonshared environment is influential. Within this interpretation, parents (shared environment) consequently play practically no role in their children's development because, according to this way of thinking, parents should create similarity, not difference.

The fact is that whether siblings are similar or different is irrelevant in terms of parental influence. Parents influence their offspring, both biological and adopted, both similar and different, and they do so within the *limits* set by these children's genetic predispositions, perceptions, and reactions. Think of it this way: If parents had no impact on their children, whether they are similar or different in terms of personality, children would arrive in day care or kindergarten totally unsocialized—that is, as small, grunting animals. Yet, quite the contrary is true: Young children who have spent their first four years at home with their parents, even with no television and no peer group, arrive in kindergarten fully equipped with language, behaviors, skills, beliefs, expectations, and attitudes. These can only come from parental care and effect.

As seen earlier, some parents are more successful than others at influencing their children, in part because they have more personal resources and the social context they live in is more compatible (Lamborn, Dornbusch, and Steinberg, 1996). Furthermore, children unconsciously (and later consciously) filter their parents' teachings through their own predispositions or personalities. Rutter (1997:393), a behavior geneticist, correctly puts this into perspective when he points out that parents produce an effect but it is dissimilar or nonshared: It is different for each child because each child is different at birth.

For example, twin Mia is impulsive, quick to react, and pays little attention to what is said. With the help of her mother, Mia learns to become *less* impulsive than she would be were she living in a family that provides little structure. In the latter family, she would become *more* impulsive. Her twin Al is totally different: He is quiet, shy, and learns quickly. With the mother's help, he becomes more engaging socially, thus *less* shy. Because he is a quick learner, the mother can teach him many skills, so that Al learns even better than he would in a family with a less invested mother (Bronfenbrenner, 1994). Although both twins remain different, each improves under maternal influence, even though his or her basic personality remains (Fergusson, Lynskey, and Horwood, 1995:613). Unfortunately, this improvement (or worsening in other cases) is not measured by the behavior genetic studies described earlier (see also Cherlin, 1999).

Thus, it is false to conclude that parents and the shared environment have no influence, and that, for instance, as Harris (1998) concludes, only peers matter. On the other hand, it is equally false to conclude, as sociologists and psychologists have done, that parents hold *the key* to their child's development: Both genes and the nonshared environment (siblings, peers, media, schools, neighborhoods, etc.) contribute the other keys. Furthermore, as we have seen when discussing parental influence in the previous chapter, environmental forces today are far more powerful in child socialization than they were a century ago.

CONCLUSIONS: THE NATURE AND NURTURE OF PARENTAL INFLUENCE

Sibling interactions are far more varied and optional than parent/child relationships because they are less scripted culturally. The silbing relationship is affected by the familial context and later on by the peer network and other social alternatives. We have also seen that the influence of siblings on each other is underrated, and it is quite possible that, at least for the younger child in a family, it is greater than parental influence in many domains of life.

The study of siblings, particularly twins and adopted children, has been directed toward the goal of better understanding the role that genes and the environment jointly play in human development. For sociologists of the family, this new knowledge can be utilized to soften traditional views on the presumably all-powerful role that parents play in their child's socialization—and consequently to rectify the blame parents have received when a child turns out "wrong." So, on the one hand, traditional sociological and psychological theories have overrated parental influence on children's development and outcomes. On the other hand, behavior geneticists' results often lead to the conclusion that parents have relatively little to do in terms of their children's development. In this respect, we have seen that the methodology used by behavior geneticists is a stumbling block in understanding parental contribution to children's outcomes. The reality is that parents influence their children but they do so within a specific context (their social class, neighborhood, peer group, media) and in conjunction with the genetic material or predispositions inherited by their children. There is a constant, ongoing interplay between nature and nurture.

SUMMARY

1. The mother/child interaction changes with the arrival of a second infant. The older child's personality and parents' initiatives largely affect the child's adaptation to the arrival. Each new baby dilutes parental resources, but this is particularly so in large families with closely spaced children. In such families, offspring generally do not do as well at school, on average. There are advantages, however, to being part of a large sibling group, but studies have yet to measure these adequately.
2. Sibling relationships are determined by siblings' characteristics, personality compatibility, parental behaviors, as well as children's perceptions of how they are treated compared to their siblings. Older siblings tend to be fairly consistent over time in their behavior toward younger ones, whereas younger ones show less stability because they are the ones who have to adapt to the older's behaviors. It is possible that effects that have been attributed to parental practices are actually the result of the handling a child has received from siblings. Gender plays a very important role in sibling relations, with girls being closer to their siblings than boys. Overall, siblings do not perceive their relationship similarly.
3. Siblings influence each other, particularly older ones toward younger ones. This is documented in studies on aggressiveness, delinquency, early sexual activity, and even early childbearing. The sharing of friends contributes to sibling similarity and influence.
4. When a child suffers from disabilities, siblings often help parents care for him or her. However, adults' well-being is often negatively affected when the sibling has emotional problems compared to physical or mental delay. Although siblings can act as a buffer for each other in times of family distress, the research indicates that divorce and the arrival of a stepparent is often accompanied by sibling conflict.

5. Differential parental treatment of siblings is in part related to children's age, developmental stage, gender, and child personality. Mothers tend to treat children similarly at a given age, but at any point in time, siblings are treated somewhat differently. Those who receive the most favorable treatment seem to do better than the others. In terms of the interactional perspective, the causality path may as easily originate from the child as it does from the parents.
6. The adult sibling relationship in industrialized societies is discretionary. In North America, proximity increases contact and the potential for both conflict and closeness. Gender continues to be an important variable: Sisters form closer bonds and benefit even brothers. Perceived differential treatment from parents while growing up often contributes to the tone of the adult sibling relationship. Stepsiblings do not usually bond as closely when full siblings are present. The longer stepsiblings have lived together as children, the closer the adult bond.
7. The study of sibling differences returns us to the issues raised by behavior genetics. This theoretical perspective redressed some of the excesses of traditional socialization theories and meshes with the interactional framework. Despite a shared home environment and genes inherited from the same parents, siblings are different because each inherits a particular combination of their parents' gene pool and has a different nonshared environment, including birth order as well as peer and school experiences. Furthermore, because of their individual personalities, children perceive and interpret their shared environment (such as parental teachings) differently. Certain families are able to extend the shared environment and to make its impact stronger so that siblings become more similar, not in terms of personalities, but in terms of values and lifestyles.
8. In order to study the joint and separate effect of genes and environment on human development, twin and adoption studies are used because they present degrees of genetic closeness. Twins reared apart also present degrees of environmental closeness. Identical twins show more personality similarities than fraternal twins, even when raised separately. The similarity is higher when they are raised together. The totality of the studies indicates that environmental forces are more important than biology. However, the calculations used by behavior geneticists has led them to conclude that it is not the shared home environment that is the most important in human development but the nonshared one. They confuse a relative lack of similarity between siblings with a lack of parental influence. The fact is that parents influence their offspring, both biological and adopted, but they do so only within the limits set by the children's genetic predispositions, perception, and reactions.

KEY CONCEPTS AND THEMES

Assortative mating, p. 353
Birth order, p. 344
Collective socialization, pp. 341, 354
Combination of parents' gene pool, p. 352
Different meanings, p. 352
Different reactions, p. 357
Differential parental treatment, p. 344
Dilution of parental resources, p. 336
Evocative effect, p. 347
Family integration, p. 353
Family size, p. 336

Functional community, pp. 341, 354
Gender, pp. 338, 346, 349
Interactional perspective, p. 346
Kin-keepers, p. 339
Nonshared environment, p. 352
Perceptions, pp. 353, 357
Personality development, p. 351
Shared environment, p. 351
Sibling differences, p. 351
Sibling influence, p. 340
Social capital, pp. 337, 341
Social class, p. 338
Social closure, p. 353
Social resource, p. 339
Spacing, p. 336
Stepsiblings, p. 350

STUDY AND REVIEW QUESTIONS

1. What are the implications of the dilution of parental resources for child development?
2. How does the older child's sibling relationship differ from that of the younger child?
3. In what domains do siblings influence each other?
4. What factors help siblings be supportive toward each other?
5. Discuss differential parental treatment of siblings within the interactional framework.
6. How is the gendered division of labor pursued in sibling relationships at all age levels?
7. Why are siblings different?
8. What role do perceptions play in the distinction of what constitutes the shared versus the nonshared environment?
9. What research methods have behavior geneticists utilized in the study of the respective role of nature and nurture?
10. Why can we disagree with behavior geneticists when they rule out parental influence (or the shared environment) as a key element in children's development?

SUGGESTED READINGS

Berk, L. E. 2000. *Child development* (5th ed.). Boston: Allyn and Bacon. This comprehensive textbook on child development includes a clear introduction to behavior genetics.

Boer, F., and Dunn, J. (Eds.). 1992. *Children's sibling relationships.* Hillsdale, NJ: Erlbaum. The articles focus on the relationship between young siblings and utilize it as a vehicle for the study of child development within the family. Behavior genetics is an important perspective. Differential parental treatment is discussed.

Brody, G. H. (Ed.). 1996. *Sibling relationships: Their causes and consequences.* Norwood, NJ: Ablex. This is a collection of scholarly articles from a wide range of disciplines focusing on diverse aspects of the sibling relationship. Some of the studies presented are longitudinal. Various ages are considered throughout the life span. Sibling influence, family contexts, and behavior genetics are other aspects surveyed.

Hetherington, E. M., Reiss, D., and Plomin, R. (Eds.) 1994. *Separate social worlds of siblings: The impact of the nonshared environment on development.* Hillsdale, NJ: Erlbaum. As indicated by the title, this collection of articles is largely inspired by behavior genetics theories. Reviews of the literature as well as new research data are presented.

SUGGESTED WEBLINKS

For general information, I suggest two directories from the search engine *metacrawler:*
<http://www.go2net.com/directory/Home/Family/Parenting>
<http://www.go2net.com/directory/Home/Family/Large_Families>

Institute for Behavioral Genetics at the University of Colorado offers a glimpse into some of the issues in the science of behavior genetics. Consult their yearly workshops on the methodology of twin and family studies. **<http://ibgwww.colorado.edu>**

PART 4

Family Problems and Solutions

Part 4 emphasizes family problems and difficulties, including marital transitions. Although these situations are placed within their broader social contexts, Part 4 contains the most microsociological chapters of this text—that is, Chapter 15. A focus on social policies that could prevent some family crises and alleviate family problems in general is also evident.

The topic of **Chapter 13** is marital transition, particularly divorce and remarriage. Widowhood is also discussed. A distinction is made between the outcomes of these transitions for adults and children.

Chapter 14 examines violence, abuse, and child neglect occurring within the family. The discussion proceeds in the developmental order of family life, beginning with dating violence and proceding with abuse between spouses or partners who live together. Abuse of children by their peers, which is such a topical issue, is included. The theoretical perspective is largely structural but also includes elements of behavior genetics, interactional-transactional theories, and gender roles.

In **Chapter 15**, we reach the most microsociological level of analysis and link with the literature in psychiatry and clinical psychology within a combined interactional, genetic, and structural framework. The chapter examines the dynamics and the interactions that take place in families when parents and children are affected by emotional, behavioral, and delinquency problems. The maternal role is particularly in evidence.

Chapter 16 focuses on the future of families and on a reexamination of the main themes that have informed this text. Above all, this chapter returns to social policies affecting families and offers specific models of programs that could lead to a reduction in familial problems and an increase in familial well-being.

CHAPTER 13

Divorce and Remarriage

Divorce Rates
What Are the Overall Trends in Divorce Rates?
How Are Divorce Rates Measured?

What Are the Factors Associated with Divorce?
Sociocultural Factors
Demographic Factors
The First Four Years of Marriage
Low Income
Youthful Marriage, Prior Cohabitation, and Parental Divorce
Presence of Unmarried Women
What Reasons Do People Give for Divorcing?
How Do Marriages Break Down?

The Aftermath of Divorce for Adults
What Factors Are Associated with Adjustment?
What Is a Successful Divorce?
Changes in Ex-Spouses' Social Networks after Divorce
Custodial Fathers and Mothers

Serial Divorces
How Frequent Are Serial Divorces?
Who Are the Persons Who Divorce Serially?

What Are the Effects of Divorce on Children?
How Does Divorce Affect Children?
Do the Effects Vary by Age and Gender?
What Are the Effects of Multiple Divorces?
Theories Explaining How Divorce Affects Children
Economic Explanation
Disruption of Parenting
The Role of Parental Conflict
Preexisting Child Characteristics
Genetic Influence
Overview of the Effects of Divorce on Children

Widowhood and Bereavement
Stages of Bereavement
Consequences of a Parent's Death for Children

Remarriage
The Aftermath of Remarriage for Spouses
Adjustment to Remarriage: The Impact of Stepparenting
The Impact of the Ex-Spouse
The New Spouse and the Ex-Spouse
What Are the Effects of Remarriage on Children?
Boys and Girls May Adapt Differently
Children's Age May Matter
Advantages for Stepchildren

Conclusions: The Familial and Social Meanings of Divorce

Summary
Key Concepts and Themes
Study and Review Questions
Suggested Readings
Suggested Weblinks

OUTLINE

"I really didn't see it coming [his marriage breaking up]. I guess I was too busy."

"Oh, I was so unhappy with him, you have no idea. He has no idea either."

"My divorce was a pathetic waste, a waste of time and a psychological waste. We could have stayed together; instead we chose to subject each other to all manners of psychological warfare." [This man was happily remarried.]

"Am I better off now? I am not any happier. It's hard to raise children on your own when that wasn't in the planning. But at least I don't have to put up with his constant rejection and abuse."

"I couldn't afford a divorce but that's all I got in life, a lousy piece of paper that gives me no rights and all the burdens in the world." [Custodial mother on welfare]

"Surely, you do not expect me to tell you that I see my ex-wife every other day! [Laughs] If you have an ex-wife, it's because you don't want to see her!"

"I used to think that a woman my age was too old for me. I dated much younger women, you know the stereotypical bachelor. I liked the ego boost these girls gave me. But when the party was over and time came to face life, I went for a woman my age . . . otherwise the life goals, long-term life goals, would have been too different."

"He shares in the upbringing of our children whereas I had to do it all in my previous marriage. He is thoughtful and we plan everything together. In my first marriage, it was all his *life; his home was his castle. I was a fringe benefit."*

"I love my stepchildren. Now I have a very large family and more grandchildren."

"I'd rather not have my stepsons. Mind you, I care for them and I am attached to them but I never set out to have children, and having someone else's children is a burden, I often resent it."

I have chosen these quotes from the hundreds available in the files of my longitudinal study on divorce and remarriage to represent the various stages from divorcing, to remarrying or remaining single, and to stepparenting. These quotes offer a glimpse into some of the issues that are discussed in this chapter. They also illustrate that the experience of divorce is one that is both very individual and yet carries some similarities across cases: A first divorce is, at the very least, a marking event in a person's life.

In 1900, 25 percent of all children under the age of 15 had lost a parent by death. Until World War II, the death of a spouse remained the leading cause of family disruption, at which point it was surpassed by divorce. It is because of this historical shift that divorce, rather than widowhood, is the main focus of this chapter, along with remarriage. Divorce is a legal institution whose function is to separate spouses who can no longer live together. It also brings about, at least temporarily, the social relocation of the ex-spouses from one marital status category to another with consequently different opportunities for life as well as constraints (Cotten, 1999). Divorce carries implications for the life course of both adults and children. One of its results often includes family poverty, with consequently negative impacts on children. In this chapter, therefore, several pages are devoted to studying how divorce affects children in addition to exploring its ramifications for adults.

DIVORCE RATES

American divorce rates are particularly complex to discuss because perhaps as many as a third of divorces occurring each year are actually second or third divorces (U.S. Bureau of the Census, 1997b). Unfortunately, general statistics do not differentiate between first and subsequent divorces. The least that can be said is that repeat divorcers inflate the overall U.S. rate; in turn, this means that there are fewer *first* marriages that ever end in divorce than the overall rate suggests.

What Are the Overall Trends in Divorce Rates?

We begin by looking at trends of divorce over time per 1,000 population and per 1,000 married women, as illustrated in Table 13.1. Rates rose substantially after World War II as a result of the many hasty marriages that had been contracted before the troops left. These couples did not have time to solidify their relationship. Upon return, often after an absence of two or three years, many soldiers had difficulty readjusting to civilian life and to marriage. Both partners may have matured, each their own separate way. As a result, many of these unions broke up. Once these postwar divorces were out of the way, the rates dropped fairly abruptly and then began a steady climb in 1968. Divorce reached its peak in 1980, with a rate of 5.2, and then declined to the point where, in 1998, the rates were equivalent to those of the early 1970s.

Divorce rates differ by geographic region. Generally, they tend to be higher in the West and the South, lower in the Midwest and the Northeast. In 1995, Massachusetts, for instance, had a "mere" 2.2 divorce rate, compared to the 1995 national rate of 4.5 (U.S. Bureau of the Census, 1998:114). These differentials might be explained by lower levels of social integration and lack of an effective community brought about by a great deal of residential mobility; as well, cultural heterogeneity may produce circumstances that are conducive to divorce at the regional level.

As indicated in Table 13.2, American rates currently are the highest in the Western world. It is difficult to explain this American phenomenon, but perhaps some of the correlates of divorce just mentioned for the regional level also apply to the overall American situation compared to that of other Western countries. It is possible that the causes of divorce (discussed in a next section) are more active or in evidence in the U.S. than elsewhere in the world.

In both Tables 13.1 and 13.2, there are two missing ingredients that prevent us from grasping the entirety of the phenomenon of *marital dissolution.* The first concerns

TABLE 13.1 Divorce Rates per 1,000 Population and Married Women over the Years

		Divorce Rates per	
Years	Numbers*	1,000 Population	1,000 Married Women
1940	N/A	2.0	N/A
1945	485,000	3.5	14.4
1946	(postwar)	4.3	17.9
1950	385,000	2.6	10.3
1960	393,000	2.2	9.2
1965	479,000	2.5	10.7
1970	708,000	3.5	14.9
1975	1,036,000	4.8	20.3
1980	(peak years)	5.2	22.6
1985	1,190,000	5.0	21.7
1990	1,182,000	4.7	20.9
1994	1,191,000	4.6	20.5
1996	1,150,000	4.3	19.5
1998	1,135,000	4.2	N/A

*Numbers rounded.

Sources: U.S. Bureau of the Census, 1998; U.S. Department of Health and Human Services, 1999.

TABLE 13.2 Western Divorce Rates per 1,000 Population for 1996

Country	Divorce Rate per 1,000 Population
Canada	2.6
Cuba	3.7
France	2.7
Italy	0.5
Mexico	0.4
Sweden	2.2
United Kingdom	3.1
United States	4.3

Source: United Nations, 1998, pp. 383–385.

those couples who separate but never divorce. The second involves cohabiting couples who "split." Neither separation nor cohabitation breakups are included in divorce statistics. As cohabitations become more common, it would be important to learn more about their stability.

How Are Divorce Rates Measured?

Statisticians use four basic methodologies to measure or estimate divorce rates:

1. The most commonly used method to measure divorce, both nationally and internationally, has already been illustrated: It is the rate for every 1,000 or 100,000 people in the population. But there is a problem with this measure. The denominator (bottom figure of 1,000 or 100,000) includes the entire population—that is, children, as well as widowed, single, and already-divorced persons. These people cannot divorce: They are not even married! Furthermore, this measure may obscure cohort differences. For instance, as seniors become proportionately more numerous in an aging society, the number of divorces should go down. The presence of large numbers of seniors or of children in a population in effect lowers the overall divorce rate. It can, for example, hide the fact that young adults might be divorcing at a very high rate.
2. A more accurate method measures the rate of divorce per 1,000 or 100,000 *married* couples or even married women in the population: This method is also included in Table 13.1. The obvious advantage of this measure is that only those who are eligible to divorce are used as the basis of calculations. It removes children as well as widowed and single adults from the denominator.
3. An even more refined way of measuring divorce, as illustrated on page 371, is to look at couples who married at a particular time—for example, in the year 2000—and check what proportion have divorced by the year 2005. For instance, we could find that 30 percent of all couples who married in 2000 have divorced by 2005—that is, within a five-year time span. Or we could look at couples who married 25 years ago and find that 42 percent have divorced. This method has the advantage of indicating the number of years of marriage that present the highest risk of divorce. However, this method is not practical for the purpose of producing quick statistics because it requires complex calculations back into time. Therefore, it is not widely utilized.
4. The annual rate of divorces occurring in a year is placed over the rate of marriages contracted that same year. For instance, in 1995, the divorce rate per 1,000 population was 4.4 and the marriage rate was 8.9. With this ratio, it seems as if one out of every two marriages ends in divorce. This approach is misleading because, each year, both the numbers of divorces and marriages change, so that, if fewer marriages occur, for instance, the proportion or rate of divorce will rise even though the number of divorces may not have increased. All in all, the true proportion of new marriages in a year that will eventually end in divorce can be obtained only after one of the two spouses has died! The closest approximation of the true divorce rate resides in Method 3.

WHAT ARE THE FACTORS ASSOCIATED WITH DIVORCE?

Multiple, interlocking factors contributed to the spectacular rise of divorce in the United States in the second half of the twentieth century and to its maintenance at a relatively high level. In this section, both sociocultural and demographic factors associated with an increase in divorce are considered. We also look at the reasons that couples give to explain the breakup of their marriage.

Sociocultural Factors

As we have seen throughout this textbook, sociocultural factors are broad social and cultural variables that affect several aspects of people's lives and contribute to influence the ways in which families perceive and experience their relationships. One such a phenomenon occurred when society evolved from one where religious norms predominated to a **secular society.** Although religion is still important in the United States, it does not influence as many aspects of personal life as in the past. Overall, religious prescriptions concerning the conjugal relationship are no longer paramount in couples' lives. The religious aspect is now largely missing in the institution of marriage.

This evolution is at times referred to as the **desacralization of marriage:** Marriage is no longer a covenant or sacrament contracted before God but has become an individual choice. This change has contributed to the acceptance of the temporal nature of marriage. The loss of the sacred nature of marriage may particularly affect couples who are not religious; it may be one of the reasons why persons who are not religious have more elevated divorce rates than those who are (Thomas and Cornwall, 1990). Furthermore, divorce has become reluctantly accepted by most Christian clergies. It is also granted among Jews and Muslims. Only Catholics officially ban divorce, although the Catholic Church has considerably liberalized its grounds for annulment during the past decade, in effect resulting in more Catholic "divorces." (The latter are usually included in general divorce statistics.)

Secularization was accompanied by a **liberalization of norms** concerning individual life choices and, with these two factors combined, the **liberalization of divorce laws** ensued. Easier divorce laws, particularly of the no-fault category, are generally followed by an increase in divorce (Nakonezny, Shull, and Rodgers, 1995). Divorce lost its stigma and became socially accepted. Therefore, these cultural and legal factors have made it far easier for people to be less attached to marriage as an *institution* and consequently to divorce.

Individualism is an ideology emphasizing rights as opposed to responsibilities. Affective individualism emphasizes the emotional bonds among family members over reciprocal responsibilities (Stone, 1977). In the past, responsibilities were more important than emotions, particularly in terms of marriage. When individualism is coupled with an ideology of gratification, particularly sexual and psychological, where people are encouraged to be "happy" and "fulfilled," it follows that spouses' mentality about their marriage is affected (Glenn, 1996). Marriage is no longer seen as an institution centered on mutual responsibilities but is now based on the pursuit of happiness, fulfillment, and companionship. More is demanded of marriage in terms of personal gratification than was the case in the past and than is still the case in many countries of the world. As Simons and Associates (1996:219) put it, "If the raison d'être for marriage is mutual love and support, it is difficult for people to justify staying in a relationship where this is no longer present." In other words, marriage is **deinstitutionalized.**

Along with individualism and the pursuit of gratification, Americans have developed a **lower threshold of tolerance** when their marriage does not meet with their expectations for personal fulfillment (Amato, 1999). They are less likely to put up with unpleasantness than their grandparents' generation was. All things considered, while more is expected of marriage, couples are also less tolerant about its failings and less willing to shoulder the sacrifices it may require (Shorter, 1975). This cultural attitude may, in turn, contribute to explaining why American rates are higher than those of any other nation. At the positive level, the lower threshold of tolerance also means that women now leave abusive relationships that would have kept them captive 40 years ago.

Demographic Factors

Given the cultural variables facilitating divorce, we now look at demographic factors through which vulnerability to divorce is expressed.

The First Four Years of Marriage

The first four years of marriage are by far the most vulnerable to disruption, as illustrated in Figure 13.1. Of marriages contracted in the years 1980–84 (an example of previously mentioned Method 3), 23 percent of marriages among whites and 38 percent among blacks had resulted in divorce by 1988 (Bianchi, 1995). Over one-third of all divorces take place within the first four years of marriage, and nearly another

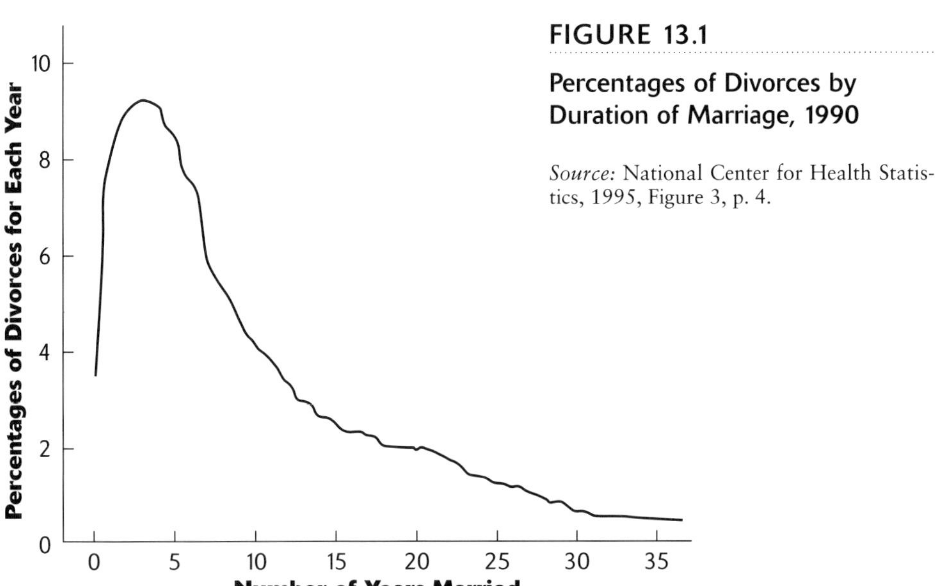

FIGURE 13.1

Percentages of Divorces by Duration of Marriage, 1990

Source: National Center for Health Statistics, 1995, Figure 3, p. 4.

one-third occurs during the fifth through ninth years of marriage (National Center for Health Statistics, 1995:4). Early divorces carry both advantages and disadvantages. The advantages reside in the fact that fewer children may be included; as well, the spouses are young and have a higher probability of remarrying. On the other hand, when children are involved, these early divorces may create more poverty, as parents may be less well established on the labor market.

Low Income

Low-income couples are at a higher risk of divorcing, and this may apply particularly to black couples who are poor (Shaw, Winslow, and Flanagan, 1999). The latest figures available by race are for 1991: White married women had a divorce rate of 15.9 per 1,000, compared to 37 for black married women. We have seen in Chapter 6 how poverty multiplies individual risks in general, reduces life opportunities, and increases stressors. All of these factors impact negatively on the marital relationship. But we have also seen that divorce contributes to poverty. This means that these two variables reinforce each other in the causality chain.

Youthful Marriage, Prior Cohabitation, and Parental Divorce

Another demographic characteristic that is related to an enhanced risk of divorcing is youthful marriage (Feng et al., 1999). This variable is partly related to the previous one; couples who marry during their teens are less likely to benefit from reasonable means of support. Moreover, they often marry for reasons that differ from those of couples who are more mature. For instance, Forthofer and colleagues (1996) find that adolescents who suffer from emotional problems are more likely to marry. Although comparatively few now marry because of a pregnancy, others marry to get away from an unhappy home situation. These youthful reasons for marrying do not form a solid foundation for a lasting marriage. We have seen in Chapter 5 that **prior cohabitation** is related to higher divorce rates (Axinn and Thornton, 1992), perhaps because of a selection factor or lack of commitment to the institution of marriage. We also see later on in this chapter that **parents' divorce** during childhood or adolescence is a factor that is related to more elevated divorce rates among children when they reach adulthood.

Presence of Unmarried Women

South and Lloyd (1995) have found that when a geographic area has a **high proportion of *unmarried* women in the labor force,** rates of divorce are more elevated among whites. This factor has nothing to do with the traditional notion that married women's own employment and financial independence enhance their chance of divorcing. (According to Rogers [1999], women may actually increase their employment efforts and income, thus financial independence, as a *result* of marital discord.) Rather, what South and Lloyd propose is that large proportions of unattached women in the labor force raise married *men's* chances of meeting a more attractive alternative to their current wife and later on to divorce. Wives are expendable.

What Reasons Do People Give for Divorcing?

Couples who are asked what led to their divorce mention irreconcilable differences, "didn't get along," "no longer loved each other," fighting and quarrelling about

FAMILY RESEARCH 13.1

Asking Both Ex-Spouses about Their Past Marital Happiness

You may recall reading in Chapter 10 that few studies examine the marital happiness of a *couple*. The same deficit occurs in studies of divorce. I have interviewed both ex-spouses and derived a classification of ex-couples depending on both ex-spouses' reported level of marital happiness in their past marriage:

High happiness ex-couples	13%
Mid-level happiness ex-couples (mixture of near high, average, near low)	52%
High unhappiness ex-couples	35%

In other words, in only one-third of the cases did both ex-spouses recall having been very to fairly unhappy in their past marriage. Furthermore, at least 1 divorce in 10 occurs to couples who were both happy.

money, children, and their relationship. Frequently mentioned also are physical abuse, mental cruelty, extramarital sex, religious differences, and alcoholism. Drug addiction, gambling, mental illness, criminality, "he's never home," and child-related problems, such as the stress of caring for a child with a disability, are occasionally mentioned. The spouse who has not initiated the divorce (and often very much wants to remain married) generally has a less extensive list of reasons or motives: "You ask me why I divorced? Ask *her*! *She* wanted it," replied one man bitterly, even though he was happily remarried.

South and Lloyd (1995) report that in over a third of divorces there has been at least one extramarital affair for one or both partners. In the study I conducted, there were several cases in which casual and unplanned extramarital affairs, such as those occurring at an out-of-town convention, caused an enormous blow-up when the other spouse accidentally learned of it; separation was practically immediate. I referred to these as "accidental" or "useless" divorces (Ambert, 1989). These divorces may never have otherwise occurred, because the relationships were sound and both ex-spouses reported a high level of marital happiness (see Family Research 13.1). It is commonly believed, with probably a great deal of truth, that only marriages that are not sound disintegrate following a casual affair. In many cases, however, the offended spouse simply cannot cope with this dilemma, even in a good marriage. An affair plants seeds of doubt and insecurity that are too difficult to overcome for persons who may have fewer psychological resources or may have other alternatives.

Many of the self-reported reasons for divorce stem from larger sociocultural factors described in the previous section. For example, without an emphasis on individualism, people would not divorce because they "fell out of love" or because they did not get along. In countries where marriage is strongly institutionalized within a context of family solidarity, these reasons would be considered frivolous. In a society where divorce is more difficult to obtain and less acceptable, only "strong" reasons, such as abuse and abandonment, are tolerated. Therefore, before people decide to divorce because of particular grounds, a **social and cultural climate** has to exist

that offers a legitimate framework for their reasons. Furthermore, personal grounds for divorce such as "didn't get along" and "fighting" tend to be mentioned more by couples with some of the demographic characteristics discussed in the previous subsection, such as youthful marriage and prior cohabitation. Thus, sociocultural and demographic factors related to divorce "push" people out of marriage into divorce via their own personal reasons.

How Do Marriages Break Down?

For a number of couples, the seeds of divorce already existed while they were dating. In some cases, the dating period was too brief and the partners did not have the time to get well acquainted, as is often the case with youthful marriages as well as with remarriages. Such couples may separate rapidly after marriage because they suddenly discover too many differences. The relationship had been brief and therefore relatively easy to terminate, particularly when no children were born and few joint assets were accumulated. Lacking in obligations toward each other and their families, these couples are less invested in their marriage; they are often young or are "on the rebound" from a previous divorce. Divorce is then a comparatively easy step that is unlikely to have large consequences for them, their families, or society—except from a moral climate standpoint in the sense that high divorce rates lower the institutional legitimacy of marriage. Such a scenario also helps explain the high rates of divorce in the very first years of marriage observed earlier.

However, the seeds of divorce often germinate into a marriage that lasts many years, results in children, and leads to a great deal of suffering for everyone involved:

> *Jan and Joe Smith were 18 and 19, respectively, when they married. Both came from very poor families. Jan said that she is responsible for the divorce "because I knew from the beginning that I would be unhappy." While they dated, "he was generally drunk, went after women, sometimes right in front of me," and she also knew that he was not a steady worker. But she hoped for a better life, hoped that the responsibility that went with marriage would change him. The opposite occurred. They remained married for 15 years and had five children. By the third interview, the eldest was in jail for assault, and the third child, a daughter, was pregnant at age 14; by age 17, she had had two babies and was divorced. One other son had behavioral problems. Jan was on and off welfare during most of her married life, including several years after her divorce. At the time of her third interview over a six-year span, she had not remarried. Her ex-husband, Joe, was in his fourth marriage.*

The Smiths' marriage was characterized by poverty, unemployment, welfare dependency, wife abuse, binge drinking, quarrels, and infidelity: a long list. He deserted. The divorce was characterized by more welfare, difficult and out-of-control children, a miserable life, and a father who really did not care for his children, and hopped from one marriage to the next.

Marriages are less likely to last when wives complain to their husbands, and the latter, instead of sympathizing with their wives' problems, escalate the interaction into a full-blown conflict (Gottman, 1998). A proportion of couples who eventually divorce threaten to do so or talk about it for a few acrimonious months or years be-

Women have been socialized to be the expressive and emotional partner. For their part, many husbands disengage from or avoid discussions pertaining to marital problems. Conflicts are thus not resolved and this situation often leads to divorce.

fore finally separating. Generally, one of the two partners is more active in this process. In most cases of divorce, one spouse wants out far more than does the other (Hopper, 1993). Women generally find more problems with their marriage than husbands do and decide to divorce more often than men, even though they are the ones who carry the larger burden afterwards (Furstenberg and Cherlin, 1991). Already in 1956, William Goode had explained this apparent contradiction as follows:

> We suggest, then, that in our society the husband more frequently than the wife will engage in behavior whose function, if not intent, whose result, if not aim, is to force the other spouse to ask for the divorce first. Thereby the husband frees himself to some extent from the guilt burden, since he did not ask for the divorce. A by-product of this process frees him still more: the wife's repeated objections to this behavior will mean that there are family squabbles, and one almost constant result of repeated family squabbles is a lessened affection between husband and wife. (Goode, 1956:136–137).

Many of the results and insights of Goode's pioneer study are still applicable. Today, though, the dynamics described by Goode can also be initiated by women, particularly when they stand to lose relatively little and gain much from the divorce. Women who would fit Goode's explanation are more likely to be young, financially independent, and remarriageable.

THE AFTERMATH OF DIVORCE FOR ADULTS

The ex-spouse who has the least personal, financial, and social resources, while at the same time having the most responsibilities, encounters more difficulties and may take longer to adjust to divorce and to life in general. The ex-spouse who has ample resources adapts more successfully. This does not mean, however, that he or she is less hurt than the other. In fact, the stronger person may suffer the most, yet be able to overcome the pain more effectively.

What Factors Are Associated with Adjustment?

In a nutshell, *adjusting to divorce is easier when:*

- A couple does not have dependent children.
- A couple does not share many assets, such as a house or a car (the division of assets constitutes one of the most rancorous aspects of divorce).
- The marriage has been brief—less than five years (the spouses have had less time to invest themselves in the relationship and less time to become habituated to being married).

For a woman, adjusting to divorce is easier when:

- She is under age 30, which gives her a much higher chance of remarrying and of having a family in her second marriage.
- She has been employed throughout her marriage or, at the very least, fairly recently (her economic situation will be less precarious and she may have a work-related social network).

In contrast, *divorce is much more stressful and requires a great deal of adjustment when:*

- A couple has children who still live at home.
- A couple jointly owns a home and shares other assets.
- A marriage was long and many habits have to be changed.
- A couple is older, thus less flexible, and perhaps no longer employed.
- A husband and wife share all their friends.
- One or both spouses is in ill health, an alcoholic, or a drug abuser.
- Respective families take sides (each ex-spouse then loses half of her or his extended kin group).
- Friends are lost (as discussed below, social support deteriorates at a time of emotional need).
- There is a loss of financial resources and economic status.

For a woman, it is generally more difficult to adjust when:

- She has not been employed in the past five years.
- She is over age 40 (at that age, a woman is less likely to remarry and it is more difficult to rebuild her social life).

Divorce drastically reduces the mental health of many adults (Aseltine and Kessler, 1993). This may be particularly so for men compared to women in the long term, in part because men have fewer close friendships, seek support less, and have not been socialized to take care of their domestic needs. Nevertheless, the first two years after divorce are the most difficult for women (Kitson, 1992).

What Is a Successful Divorce?

In theory, a successful divorce is one where *all* the parties involved are better off after than during the marriage. In practice, there are few successful divorces in the short term, because there is always someone who feels less happy or who is less well adjusted after divorce than during the marriage. We can discuss the success of divorce from three perspectives. A divorce is successful from an *individual's perspective* when he or she is happier and functions better after divorce—which does not mean that the same occurs to the ex-spouse. Second, a divorce is successful from a *familial perspective* when the children function better following the divorce and are adequately parented. There are fewer successful divorces from a familial perspective because parenting generally becomes difficult and children are often miserable about the divorce even when their parents are relieved to be rid of each other.

Finally, from a *societal perspective,* a divorce is successful when the individuals concerned (parents and children alike) are healthier than during the marriage; function better at work, at school, as citizens; and do not resort to any form of social assistance. A successful divorce is one where the children have a better chance to grow up healthy and are more adequately cared for than during their parents' marriage. Again, by this societal definition, most divorces are not successful, particularly in the short run, or are at best a "mixed blessing."

Thus, considering the three levels of analysis—the individual, the family, and the society—divorce tends to be a successful venture mainly at the micro or individual level. Once a period of adjustment has taken place (and it is longer for some families than others), adults and children build a new life. Yet, overall, the price for adjustment can be enormous.

Changes in Ex-Spouses' Social Networks after Divorce

One important factor in adjustment after divorce is a person's social network, but very little is actually known about this topic. In order to modestly remedy this lack of information, I am using qualitative data from my longitudinal study of divorce and remarriage. With divorce, most couples lose the in-law kin system, so that each ex-spouse now has a reduced kin network until remarriage. Women become single mothers and their supportive network is generally smaller (Cross, 1990). In my research, more women than men reported losing friends after separation. This may reflect the fact that women have more close friendships than men to begin with. Women tended to suffer the greatest loss of friendships in long-term marriages during which friendships had been shared as a couple. Mutual friends remained with the ex-husband more often than with the ex-wife. Two women explained this situation thusly:

> *"His wife [the male friend's wife] feels more secure with Paul I think than with me. As a single woman, I am a threat to her. . . . I just never realized that she'd be so jealous the minute her husband looked at me."*

> *"My ex-husband is more fun to be with because he has more money to do things and go out."*

Women reported a sharp decline in social activities involving friends they had had while married: fewer phone calls, visits, outings, and movies, for instance. Men reported either little change or an increase in visiting, particularly being invited over for dinner and for outings when their children were with them. Custodial fathers definitely received more offers of help from friends and colleagues, and even from their children's teachers, than custodial mothers. Friends seem to presume that a father needs more help because it is relatively unusual for men to have sole physical custody of their children. They received far more sympathy than custodial mothers.

However, very few women had lost those friends whom they had already had before their marriage or had maintained separately during the marriage. Few lost work-related acquaintances and the workplace actually became an important source of moral support at that time. As pointed out in a later quote, in a couple-oriented society, social support is more readily extended to coupled individuals and, after divorce, to men, generally with the help of friends' wives, unless women have a strong, independent network of female friends. Married men seem less threatened by their divorced male friends than married women are by their divorced women friends. However, there are instances when a divorced man experiences rejection:

> *"He used to be a good friend as friends go, but I think that he would rather stay away from people who divorce. The way I see it, I am a bad example or rather my ex-wife and I are a bad example. In case his wife gets any idea."*

At Time 2 and particularly Time 3 of the follow-up six years later, a great proportion of respondents had remarried. These remarriages provided an excellent opportunity to see if changes in social networks had occurred. Remarried women at both the working- and middle-class levels had seen a substantial increase in their social activities involving new friends. This increase was far more salient for women who had lost their friends to their ex-husbands. The change had been practically instantaneous for many. One woman sarcastically put it this way:

> *"Remarriage puts a woman back where she belongs; she's no longer a threat to other women, no longer a temptation to their husbands. But I also think that socially a woman has value because of her married status; I could feel it. I mean, I felt so bitter about it when I was divorced, it was so obvious. From a couple's point of view a divorced woman is more than useless, and all adults are couples so that leaves you nowhere." [Now?] "I am part of a couple again."*

Remarried men also reported an increase in social activity but a less noticeable one when they had maintained their original network. To begin with, when adults remarry, they gain another set of in-laws; then, they often acquire each other's friends and this explains in part their increased social network and activities. Again, to paraphrase the last woman's quote, this increase is also in part explained by the fact that a couple is a safer and more valued unit for friendship than a divorced individual for other couples. The **status of marriage** or of being part of a couple certainly enhances a person's social acceptability. Therefore, adults who need friends less (the married) have more, while those who could benefit from friends' social support, such as divorced mothers and the poor, often have fewer (Hughes, Good, and Candell, 1993). These are social inequities based on gender and coupling status.

Custodial Fathers and Mothers

A substantial increase has occurred in the number but not the proportion of custodial fathers. Basically, it is still the case now as it was 20 years ago that only about 10 percent of all fathers have *sole* legal and physical custody. There are many more cases where both parents share legal custody; however, in most of these instances, children live with their mother. In 1950, there were only 275,000 families headed by a father. By 1990, this figure had risen to 1,351,000 and constituted 14 percent of all single-parent families. The majority of these single-father families resulted from divorce, as only 89,000 were widowed (Greif, 1995). Overall, custodial fathers have fewer children in their care, and fewer younger ones, than custodial mothers. Fathers who have small children or many of them tend not to seek their custody. Furthermore, compared to custodial mothers, custodial fathers are more likely to have another adult living with them, whether a cohabitor, their own mother, or a housekeeper (Bianchi, 1995).

For men, coresidence with their child after divorce results in a better father/child relationship than would otherwise be the case and contributes to fathers' mental health (Arendell, 1995). They are less subjected to feelings of lack of control over their paternal situation, as is the case among nonresidential fathers (Umberson and Williams, 1993). However, fathers find their role constraining—they have less freedom and more demands are placed on them—and are less happy than visiting fathers (Shapiro and Lambert, 1999).

Cases of **joint custody** are increasing and fathers are particularly satisfied with this arrangement (Arditti, 1992). Joint custody may involve children living on alternate weeks or months with each parent, but it may also simply involve equal rights for both parents while the children remain with one parent. Mothers prefer sole custody, but are favorable to joint custody when they perceive their ex-husbands to be good parents (Wilcox, Wolchik, and Braver, 1998). Mothers generally obtain custody because of widely held beliefs that they are "naturally" better parents and also because they have been the child's primary caregiver. It is indeed less disruptive for children to live with the parent who has taken care of them, attended to their basic needs, and spent time with them on a regular basis (Maccoby, 1999). The parent/child fit is a better one than when a child is shifted to the custody of a father he or she rarely saw and who was far from being a primary caregiver.

This said, however, the evidence so far accumulated indicates that father and mother custody have equivalent results for children (Downey and Powell, 1993). This means that children who live with their mother, compared to those who live with their father, do not do worse or better overall, although they may fare slightly better or less well on specific dimensions of their lives. Actually, children in single-father and single-mother families are *both* outperformed in school by children in two-parent families. Single fathers have more financial resources available for their children than single mothers (Hao, 1996), but the latter compensate with a higher level of interpersonal resources (Downey, 1994). This includes more time spent in child care and monitoring (Maccoby and Mnookin, 1992).

There does not seem to be any particular overall advantage of **same-sex matching** between parent and child. Boys and girls by age 16 do as well or as poorly whether in a father's or a mother's custody (Powell and Downey, 1997). Similarly, there is no difference in well-being among adults depending on the sex of the single parent with whom they grew up (Downey, Ainsworth-Darnell, and Dufur, 1998). But the research is not unanimous, as some studies have found an advantage for children who live with a parent of their own sex (Zill, 1988). This may be a question of having an appropriate gender-role model, or of parental ability to understand a same-sex child better (Gately and Schwebel, 1991).

About 75 percent of mothers who are noncustodial are so by choice (Herrerias, 1995). Among them are mothers who relinquish custody because of financial hardship and a few in order to have more freedom or to remarry someone who does not want children at home. In other cases, the father has won custody after a lenghty and often costly legal battle. Other noncustodial mothers are involuntary as a result of ill health, mental problems, criminal conviction, child neglect, or because the child has been kidnapped by the father.

Nonresident mothers have more frequent telephone, letter, and extended visitation contacts than nonresidential fathers (Stewart, 1999b). However, both sets of parents exhibit similar low levels of in-person contact with their children. Moreover, both noncustodial mothers and fathers tend to engage largely in leisure activities with their children (Stewart, 1999a). Furthermore, neither mothers nor fathers pay all the child support they owe (U.S. Bureau of the Census, 1995a). This result has led some researchers to suggest that there is something in the structure of being a nonresidential parent that inhibits active parenting as well as economic support for children outside of marriage (Doherty, Kouneski, and Erickson, 1998:282–283).

SERIAL DIVORCES

Divorce became more prevalent in the 1970s and 1980s. As a good percentage of these divorces occurred before age 30, remarriage rates rose accordingly. Remarriages are more unstable, thus second or higher-order divorces became more frequent.

How Frequent Are Serial Divorces?

Each year, perhaps a third of divorces are actually second or third divorces for one spouse. These redivorces contribute to increases in the overall divorce rate. By late adolescence, nearly half of children in divorced families see their parents divorce again. Thus, 15 percent of *all* children in the population will see their custodial parent divorce, remarry, and redivorce before reaching the age of 18 (Furstenberg and Cherlin, 1991:14).

Table 13.3 indicates that even among very young women (20 to 29 years), around 15 percent of their divorces were following a remarriage; that is, these women had been divorced and remarried at least once before. Their young age returns us to the fact that youthful marriages are a risk factor for divorce. It appears that even youthful remarriages are at risk. Naturally, the proportion of redivorces increases with age. This can be explained by the fact that, as people age, they have lived more years during which several marital transitions could take place. Women ages 45 to 49 had the highest divorce rate after a remarriage; a small proportion of these remarriages might have followed a period of widowhood rather than divorce. This age bracket contains women who are older by 20 years than the first set of younger women. Their marital transitions have occurred later and at a less rapid pace. In contrast, young adults who go through multiple marital transitions experience them earlier and at a more accelerated pace.

In 1990, the median interval between a first marriage and divorce was eight years, whereas only six years elapsed between a second marriage and divorce and four years between a third marriage and divorce (National Center for Health Statistics, 1995:19). These statistics give the distinct impression that people who divorce more than twice may be in what South and Lloyd (1995) have called a state of permanent availability to any better alternative that comes along. For them, marriage is definitely not an institution.

Who Are the Persons Who Divorce Serially?

Very little research has been done with people who divorce several times, in part because surveys place them within the general category of the divorced. The serially divorced seem to differ on some dimensions from people who have divorced only once (Booth, 1999). For instance, they are more likely to suffer from emotional, alcohol, and drug-related problems (Counts, 1992). They may have more unstable personalities and may be more stressful to get along with (Kurdek, 1990). They are less committed to their relationship. They like being married but are not much willing or ready to make adjustments or concessions that could lead to stability, as illustrated in the quotes below:

> *"Women expect too much out of marriage. I sure as hell can't live out their dreams." [Man in his fourth marriage]*
>
> *"My wife says I have to work at our marriage. I don't agree with her. Marriage is supposed to be pleasant and if it isn't, well, it's not my problem." [Man in his third marriage]*

TABLE 13.3 **Percentages of All Divorces That Follow a Remarriage (Women)**

Age Bracket	1980	1990
20–24 years old	8.5%	13.1%
25–29	15.6	17.8
30–34	19.1	22.7
35–39	24.7	28.5
40–44	28.4	30.6
45–49	25.1	36.4
50–54	29.0	34.5

Source: U.S. Bureau of the Census, 1997b, p. 107.

These remarks were very different from whatever most respondents who had divorced only once said (Ambert, 1989). The latter expressed more feelings of hurt, guilt, and even regret. While interviewing persons who had divorced several times within a *short time span,* I often had the impression that their marriage was part of the throw-away culture: If it's of no use, then get rid of it. For instance, Joe Smith was in his fourth marriage by the third interview. He was asked to compare his wives, current and past. As for the first one, Jan, he said:

> *"Oh, the old bag. She wasn't even fit to be a mother. Look what became of the kids. I hear that one is in the pen. Does that have anything to do with me? No. I wasn't even there.* She *raised them. And she wanted me to support her, can you believe it!? . . . I mean, we've never been rich and she made* five *kids!"*

Joe takes absolutely no responsibility for the reproduction and the outcome of his five offspring. However, given that Jan herself was neither violent, alcoholic, lazy, nor emotionally unstable, it is quite likely that the children followed the father's example and/or had inherited negative predispositions from him, which their deprived environment exacerbated. Furthermore, during the rare periods of employment he enjoyed while still living with them, Joe drank away a lot of the money that the family could have used for food or clothing. This certainly had negative consequences for the children who experienced nothing but deprivation and parental conflict.

This case study should not obscure the fact that serial divorces also occur at the middle-class level. Although they are more frequent among the less affluent, they happen among high-income earners as well, particularly in the entertainment industry. It is difficult to know if serial divorce is so frequent among them because of a selection into acting and show business people with more difficult or individualistic personalities (social selection), or because the temptations inherent to their lifestyles are too great (social causation). It could also be that the media create many potential sources of friction between spouses.

In my study, the serially divorced did not all unavoidably differ from those who had divorced only once. Some had simply had the misfortune of remarrying a "divorce-prone" spouse. Moreover, there are persons who make a mistake early on and divorce in their twenties, remarry, have children, and divorce again in their forties or fifties. There is no research comparing such persons who divorce a second time after years of stability with those such as in my study who had divorced two to four times within 15 years or less. One can reasonably assume that the former may be more stable and more responsible spouses and parents than the latter. This assumption may be validated by the fact that Booth and Edwards (1992) have found only a weak link between personality characteristics and risk of redivorcing. Their sample probably included a mixture of timing at redivorce that was not available in the sample I studied.

WHAT ARE THE EFFECTS OF DIVORCE ON CHILDREN?

Each year, over one million, or about 2 percent, of all children in the United States experience a parental divorce (Forehand, Armistead, and David, 1997). With a lower birth rate and marriages that end in divorce earlier, the number of children per 1,000 divorces has been declining slightly from 1.22 in 1970 to 0.90 in 1990 (U.S. Bureau of the Census, 1997b:106).

How Does Divorce Affect Children?

In a nutshell, although most children do not experience developmental problems, divorce is certainly a strong risk factor (Cherlin, 1999) and a source of stressors (Emery, 1999). It is, above all, an emotionally painful transition. Although differences are not large, *on average,* children and adolescents whose parents are divorced tend to do less well in school and have more behavioral and emotional problems than children in intact families (Zill, Morrison, and Coiro, 1993). They are also at a greater risk for delinquency (Ambert, 1999; Coughlin and Vuchinich, 1996) and for premarital births (Wu, 1996). When children of divorce reach adulthood, their relationship with their parents is less likely to be warm than that of children whose parents remained in an unhappy marriage (Amato and Booth, 1997). Furthermore, their educational and occupational levels are, on average, lower than those of children whose parents have not divorced. They also tend to have higher divorce rates themselves. A new couple's risk of divorcing is even higher when their two sets of parents had divorced during their childhood or adolescence (Amato, 1996). When they reach young adulthood, children of divorce leave home earlier (Aquilino, 1991; Boyd and Norris, 1995). They generally do so as a consequence of their custodial parent's remarriage or cohabitation; they often cite family conflicts as the reason for leaving (Kiernan, 1992). One long-term negative result of divorce is that, at maturity, many adult children have lost contact with their father.

Recent longitudinal studies following children up to age 33 indicate that, where emotional problems develop, the effect of parental divorce may last and can even intensify (Cherlin, Chase-Lansdale, and McRae, 1998). Because these studies were longitudinal, the researchers were able to measure other family and child characteristics that could have influenced the development of emotional problems. Yet, even after they had considered these other influences, their results still showed that the divorce itself had increased the likelihood of emotional problems, even later on in adulthood.

Do the Effects Vary by Age and Gender?

The effects of divorce differ by the child's age and gender, depending on the outcomes that are measured. For instance, in terms of behavior, boys are more negatively affected than girls (Morrison and Cherlin, 1995). In other words, boys' behavior often becomes much more difficult after divorce than that of girls. Despite this difference, after divorce, both boys and girls tend to exhibit more acting-up problems during adolescence than during childhood (Baumrind, 1991a).

In terms of age, small children are not mentally equipped to make sense of what is essentially an adult transition (Jenkins and Smith, 1993). As a result, they may come to believe that the departure of their father is their fault. Adolescence may be a particularly difficult period for a parental divorce to occur, but at least adolescents are able to see reasons for divorce and in some cases appreciate its benefits. Furthermore, teenagers often distance themselves from family turmoil (Aseltine et al., 1994). Their interactions with peers can serve to insulate them from family upheavals, if these relationships are supportive. However, children of divorce and remarriage, as are those in unmarried families, are more at risk of falling in with a negative peer group (Kim, Hetherington, and Reiss, 1999).

What Are the Effects of Multiple Divorces?

As mentioned earlier, by age 18, nearly half of the children of divorce experience at least one of their parents' redivorce. There is little information on the effect of repeated parental divorce on children. However, the more marital transitions parents experience, the less well adjusted children are in some domains of life (Wu and Martinson, 1993). But it is possible that most of the damage caused to children stems mainly from their own parents' divorce. Remarriages end more quickly than first marriages, thus children may not have had the time to bond with their temporary stepparent to suffer from this loss.

However, repeated divorces affect adults, which in turn may affect their ability to parent adequately (Seltzer, 1994). Moreover, multiple divorces may constitute a **socialization experience** for children who see their parents divorce so rapidly and so often: They may fail to learn adequate conflict resolution techniques. Such children may learn to quarrel or to give up without resolving differences. In turn, they could later on experience more difficulties in their own marriage.

Theories Explaining How Divorce Affects Children

Several theories explain the negative consequences of divorce for children. All receive some support in the research. These explanations are complementary rather than mutually exclusive, because each fits some children better than others.

Economic Explanation

One of the theories that receives the greatest research support is the economic or material resources one (Ross and Mirowsky, 1999). As well documented in Chapter 6, a majority of children experience a reduction in their standard of living after divorce and many become poor. When all variables are considered, the studies reviewed by McLanahan (1997:47) led her to conclude that postdivorce poverty is at least as strong a cause of lower cognitive ability and school achievement as is the divorce itself. Hence, when poverty does not occur along with divorce, children may not be so adversely affected, at least in terms of cognitive development, depression, and school success (Aseltine, 1996).

A 40 to 50 percent income loss for women and children after divorce leads to many concurrent changes. For instance, the family often has to move to a more disadvantaged neighborhood in a small and crowded apartment. This means that children go to a different school, where many students may also be disadvantaged or less well supervised, and where the rates of juvenile delinquency and teen pregnancy may be higher. The sudden, reduced standard of living is often accompanied by a less than plentiful diet, fewer clothes, and little pocket money. In a consumer-oriented society, such a downfall may be felt acutely by children, particularly in the age group of 10- to 16-year-olds. All of these changes are a lot to ask of children, including adolescents who are simultaneously undergoing physiological puberty with its accompanying socioemotional risks (Hines, 1997).

Disruption of Parenting

The economic theory is not in itself sufficient to explain divorce effects: Living in a single-parent family still produces an independent negative effect of its own (Wu, 1996). Thus, a second theory, one that also receives a great deal of research support, sees parenting behaviors as either a direct causative variable or as a mediator variable (McLanahan, 1997). In a nutshell, this theory posits that parents who divorce experience a great deal of stressors and have to adjust to a new lifestyle that gives them less social support as individuals and as parents (Simons and Associates, 1996:89–91). As a consequence, their parenting skills and availability suffer (Lee, 1993). Many become less tolerant of misbehavior and are more prone to have screaming fits, while others become depressed and withdraw from their children (Forgatch, Patterson, and Roy, 1996). Divorced parents tend to be very preoccupied or extremely busy, which means less time for children—less time for advice, for love, and for monitoring children's whereabouts. Sons often become defiant, disobedient, disrespectful, and even abusive (Hetherington, Clingempeel et al., 1992).

Amato and Gilbreth (1999) suggest that children of divorce have better outcomes when nonresidential fathers are more than friends and entertainers and behave as parents—that is, when they provide emotional and instrumental support, make behavioral demands, place limits on what can be done, and administer consistent discipline. When nonresidential fathers remain **active parents,** as opposed to "Sunday daddies" or their children's "pals," they complement and reinforce custodial mothers' socialization efforts. The children receive a same message of support and authority from both parents—an ideal situation rarely achieved. Basically, what counts in child outcomes is neither the custodial arrangement nor the frequency of visitation, but the quality of parenting and parents' psychological functioning (Wallerstein, 1998).

The Role of Parental Conflict

The third theory overlaps with the second theory to some extent. It focuses on parental conflict both during marriage and after divorce. Conflict is so detrimental that children who remain in a conflict-ridden family have more negative outcomes than those whose parents divorce to eliminate the tension (Amato, Spencer-Loomis, and Booth, 1995). Parental conflict is particularly painful when adolescents or children hear their parents fight about them: They feel caught in the middle (Maccoby et al., 1993). In at least one study, boys who were in regular contact with their nonresidential parent in situations of high parental conflict tended to have more problems than boys for whom this contact was limited (Amato and Rezac, 1994). However, parental conflict after divorce diminishes over time and the research is not unanimous about its undesirable effects (King and Heard, 1999). Nevertheless, while it lasts, as expressed in the following male student quote, conflict is extremely painful for children of all ages, both while parents are married and after the divorce:

> *"When I was 11, my parents separated. This has been the most difficult period of my short life until now and it still hurts to this day. But when I was 11 it was worse because my life became so different. My sister seemed to cope better but I just couldn't stand the fighting. They'd fight over the phone about everything and when my father would pick us up for the weekend they'd go at it some more and I'd be shaken up for the entire weekend and it would start all over when he*

would drop us off and on top of it all, they used to talk against each other and say awful things about each other in front of me. To this day, my skin crawls when I know that they'll talk to each other which is rare now that we're older. My sister's wedding was a nightmare of tension and as far as I'm concerned I'll just elope one day because I just couldn't go through with it. I have been a nervous wreck since that time [age 11]."

In fact, Buchanan, Maccoby, and Dornbusch (1996) have found that the worst thing that can happen to a child is that his or her parents remain locked in conflict after divorce. In such cases, divorce fulfills no positive function for the child; rather, it exacts a heavy price for which there is no compensation. Parental conflict also means lack of authoritative and guiding parenting. In contrast, low parental conflict may shield children from the stressors of divorce (Amato and Booth, 1997). Unfortunately, children in low-conflict marriages that end in divorce lose a great deal. Overall, there is research consensus that pre- and postdivorce conflict is detrimental to children but that the divorce itself contributes an additional source of potential problems for children (Hanson, 1999).

Preexisting Child Characteristics

A fourth explanation resides in preexisting conditions and has evolved from longitudinal studies of children who were in intact families at the time of the first interview, or Time 1. Throughout the years, some of these children's parents divorced. This family development allowed the researchers at subsequent stages of the study to return to what they had observed at Time 1 and compare the behavior and mental health of children whose parents stayed together to those of children whose parents eventually divorced. Two of these studies found that long before the divorce occurred, children of divorce already exhibited more problems than children whose parents stayed together (Block, Block, and Gjerde, 1988). This led these authors to warn that some of what is interpreted to be consequences of divorce may have actually existed before the divorce or have been consequences of conflict within the marriage (Elliott and Richards, 1991). There is no doubt that this occurs in quite a number of families.

More recent studies, however, have established that the functioning of children and adolescents often changes negatively *after* their parents' separation, even when researchers control for the child's predivorce characteristics or difficulties (Aseltine, 1996; Morrison and Cherlin, 1995). In other words, the pre- and postdifferences "can be attributed to parental divorce and its accompanying disruption of family processes" (Forehand, Armistead, and David, 1997:157). This conclusion is reaffirmed by Cherlin and colleagues (1998), who in effect were retracting their conclusion from a previous study that favored predivorce characteristics. Their more recent data indicate that predivorce characteristics cannot entirely explain children's problems after divorce. Nevertheless, it appears that, in many cases, children are already more difficult before the divorce, which makes sense, considering that their parents may have been fighting or were at the very least preoccupied.

Genetic Influence

A fifth theory relates to the genetic inheritance of problematic predispositions. Offspring of divorce "are more likely to have an interpersonal style marked by . . . problems with anger, jealousy, hurt feelings, communication, [and] infidelity" (Amato, 1996:638). These interpersonal behaviors may be both learned and genetically transmitted. Genetic transmission would be particularly relevant to the offspring of parents whose divorce is caused by alcoholism, mental illness, and difficult personality characteristics (Kendler, 1995). When children are already genetically vulnerable, the environment created by the divorce exacerbates their vulnerabilities. They receive less attention, monitoring, and guidance, so that their genetic liabilities often find a fertile ground upon which to grow (Plomin and Rutter, 1998). In contrast, children who have more positive predispositions (Garmezy and Masten, 1994) and also have more stable parents are far less likely to develop problems after divorce.

Overview of the Effects of Divorce on Children

In summary, most children survive their parents' divorce quite well developmentally, even though they may be very worried and unhappy (Emery, 1999). But when children are adversely affected in terms of mental health, sociability, behavior, school and work achievement, and later on in their own marital lives, a combination of factors enters into play to explain these consequences. These are reduced financial status and poverty; disruptions in parenting skills and practices, particularly monitoring; parental conflict after divorce; and children's genetic vulnerabilities. To this, one may add that a parental remarriage often contributes another assortment of stressors.

WIDOWHOOD AND BEREAVEMENT

In 1994, there were 11.1 million widows and 2.2 million widowers in the United States (U.S. Bureau of the Census, 1995a:55). Of women ages 45 to 54, almost 5 percent were widowed and nearly 17 percent were divorced. In comparison, less than 1 percent of men of the same age group were widowed and 12 percent were divorced. Of women ages 55 to 64 years, almost 14 percent were widowed, compared to 3 percent among men. Widowhood occurs later among men, when it does at all: Men's life expectancy is briefer than that of women, and men tend to marry women younger than they. Widowhood is therefore a **gendered stage** that affects women far more than men. Widowed women are more likely than their male counterparts to become poor: 25 percent of elderly women who are living alone are poor (Quinn and Smeeding, 1994). Because widowhood occurs later in life than it did even 50 years ago, most young children are spared the loss of a parent by death. In 1994, less than 5 percent of all children were living with a widowed mother.

Stages of Bereavement

The death of a partner requires much readjustment in addition to the great emotional pain it brings. Age, health status, and level of independence may prolong or shorten bereavement. Adaptation to widowhood also depends on the income that is available, as sudden poverty may add a tremendous burden to the afflicted person (Brubaker, 1991). The widowed partner and his or her children go through stages of bereavement. These stages can include an initial period of shock and disbelief, particularly following a sudden death, and even denial. The grieving family members may then experience guilt if they feel that they have not shown enough love for the deceased while he or she was alive. "If only I had . . ." is a recurrent thought. Others go through a period of anger, especially when the death was accidental or was caused by another party, as in the case of drunk driving. The anger may actually galvanize them into social activism that can benefit other members of society later on.

The period of grief can include a stage of idealization of the deceased, even if the latter had caused much suffering. Among seniors, the loss of a spouse is often followed by some mental confusion, helplessness, depression, illness, and general physical vulnerability, as well as a loss of interest in life. The length of the grieving period very much depends on personal resources, the social support received, and how well prepared the bereaved spouse was for the death. With a long terminal illness, the spouse often begins mourning before death occurs and may be more resigned to it.

The quality of the relationship with the deceased partner is also an important element in the grieving process, but may produce different results. Some spouses may be relieved by the death of a partner who has made their lives miserable, whereas others may feel guilty. When a good relationship had existed, some spouses miss their partners and are inconsolable for a long period, yet others are thankful for the years they shared.

Consequences of a Parent's Death for Children

In terms of outcomes, children of widowhood do as well as those in two-parent families or, at the very least, far better than children of divorced and single parents (Axinn, Duncan, and Thornton, 1997). This is not to say that children do not grieve and miss their deceased parent terribly. But these children may benefit from several social, familial, and personal advantages over children of divorce. First, they are less likely to have been subjected to parental conflict before the death and are certainly not affected by it after. Second, the remaining parent is generally left in a more favorable economic situation and is also helped by social security benefits so that poverty occurs less frequently. This relative economic security also protects children from a host of accompanying stressors, such as having to move and change school. Third, following death, there are social rites of bonding through which sympathy and feelings of community are bestowed upon children, which is quite a contrast to what happens to children of divorce.

Fourth, the remaining parent's task of grieving, of caring for the children's own pain, and of behaving as a proper widow or widower delays his or her reentry on the dating and mating scene. Children are not immediately faced with a parent who is suddenly unavailable because of the demands of his or her social life (Seltzer, 1994). There is no immediate competition for their parent's love. A fifth element protecting children of widowhood is that a good proportion of the deaths occur to couples who had a stable marriage. Thus, the personalities involved may not have included so many parents with difficult personalities, as may be the case in situations of divorce (Simons and Associates, 1996). Consequently, the children themselves have greater chances of being stable individuals.

Remarriages are as happy as first marriages; they are, however, more fragile and likely to end in another divorce. The structural complexity of remarriages—the presence of children belonging to each partner—certainly contributes to their instability.

Children may also adapt better to their parents' remarriage later on when one parent has died, because this loss makes them more receptive to acquiring a substitute parent. Orphaned children do not have another parent, whether visiting or custodial, whose place seems to be usurped by a stepparent. No visitations are involved; there is only one home, one set of rules, and one family. With peers and teachers, a formerly widowed parent with a new spouse and the children more easily pass for a "real" family.

REMARRIAGE

Approximately 75 percent of men and 66 percent of women eventually remarry, generally within two years after divorce (DeWitt, 1994). Whites remarry more than blacks, although in the 1960s, blacks remarried nearly as often as whites (Cherlin and Furstenberg, 1994). Economic conditions have generally eroded blacks' ability to do so, just as they have eroded their ability to marry in the first place. Latinos also remarry less after divorce. As most Latinos are Catholic, a religious influence may be evident here.

Naturally, these figures say nothing of cohabitation after divorce. Many people cohabit rather than remarry, and a small proportion have a same-sex partner. As cohabitation rates increase, remarriage rates decrease, at least temporarily. Educated and high-income women may wait longer to remarry because they can easily support their children. But, currently, African-American women with a high educational level are more likely to remarry than their less educated counterparts (Smock, 1994).

The Aftermath of Remarriage for Spouses

A remarriage after divorce generally increases the quality of adults' lives, emotionally, socially, and financially, the latter especially for women. Many mother-headed families exit poverty through remarriage. When a remarriage endures, it may far outlast the first marriage. After years of remarriage, many spouses even forget that they have been married to someone else, particularly when there were no children from the first union.

Adjustment to Remarriage: The Impact of Stepparenting

When neither spouse has children, adjustment to remarriage is no different than in a first marriage. It becomes somewhat more complex with stepchildren, and the complexity increases when there are both live-in and visiting stepchildren. The period of readjustment takes several years before a surviving stepfamily is stabilized (Bray and Kelly, 1998). Being a stepparent is not a role one expects to occupy and for which one is prepared—it is not an institutionalized one (Cherlin, 1978). Stepparenthood is also a vilified role when one thinks of the "wicked stepmother" in fairy tales. The role is considered inferior to that of mothers (Nielsen, 1999). No norms or rules guide the behavior of a "good" stepparent, as is the case for a good parent. Each stepparent more or less has to reinvent the role and the relationship, which can be both an advantage and a disadvantage.

With stepchildren, the newlyweds have to adapt to two key roles simultaneously, parent and spouse, while these two roles are generally initiated separately in first marriages. The complexity of the adjustment requirements may contribute to making remarriages more unstable than first marriages (Booth and Edwards, 1992). Furthermore, when children are involved, their other parent constitutes an additional, structural complication for the newly remarried spouses.

The Impact of the Ex-Spouse

After divorce and remarriage, there is a wide spectrum in the quality of the parents' relationship and in the frequency of face-to-face and over-the-phone contact (Ahrons, 1994; Kitson, 1992). Masheter (1997) has compared divorced persons along two dimensions: their level of preoccupation with and hostility toward their ex-spouse. She finds that the divorced who are better adjusted in terms of emotional well-being fall into two categories: those who are friendly but not obsessed or preoccupied with their ex-spouse, and those who are also little preoccupied but are high on hostility. In contrast, respondents who are very preoccupied and friendly with the ex-spouse do not adjust as well to divorce because their attachment prevents them from forging ahead. Anger, combined with low preoccupation, may mobilize divorced individuals against depression (Clapp, 1992). In terms of coparenting, friendliness without preoccupation is more functional. Ex-spouses need to be mutually supportive for the benefit of their children (Madden-Derdich and Arditti, 1999). Ex-husbands are far more likely to remain involved if they feel supported by their ex-wives (Arditti and Bickley, 1996).

The New Spouse and the Ex-Spouse

Another effect of remarriage on adults resides in the fact that a remarried person whose spouse has children may need to relate to the children's other parent. Relatively little research exists on this complex relationship, so I have borrowed from my fieldwork. It is obvious from the quotes that follow as well as from the entire research data that the spouse's ex is not overly popular among current wives and husbands:

> *"We don't socialize. It's strictly business for the children's sake. I didn't marry my husband to acquire his ex-wife or her new husband, and my husband certainly does not want to be saddled with my ex-husband and his girlfriend. No. These relationships are nice on a TV screen but not in real life."*

The new husband or wife often resents the help the spouse has to give his or her ex, especially financial help (Nielsen, 1999). Noncustodial fathers frequently expressed serious concerns about their ex-wife's new partner who had become their children's stepparent. They worry about the way the new stepfather treats the children, the example he provides, as well as the potential for sexual abuse:

> *"My ex-wife's husband is a burden to me in a way [he is an alcoholic]. I told my wife, my ex-wife, that she's got to be very careful never to let the girls alone with him. She was offended but she got the point. I just don't trust him."*

In some instances, the new wife and the ex-wife have to cooperate in order to raise the other's children and to arrange visitation schedules:

> *"We have a lot of planning to do to arrange her children's visits. . . . So we have a lot to talk about. But I think she must appreciate me because I don't have to have his children over as often as I do especially so since I have three of my own, so actually I babysit for her. She doesn't [interfere], not exactly, but what can you expect with so many children, it's a real interference even if they're quite good."*

In a few cases, a new wife and her husband's ex-wife will develop a warm and friendly relationship. But, overall, the study unearthed a great deal of uneasiness about the possibility of having a close relationship with that person, in part because of the danger of instability it could create in the new marriage. In a monogamous society, the specter of a marital triangle looms large. It is not surprising, therefore, that a relationship with a spouse's ex is facilitated when the new spouse has not been the "cause" of the previous marital breakdown—that is, when the new spouse has not been involved with the other partner in an adulterous relationship. Obviously, boundary maintenance is a key element in the success of remarriages, and this issue arises more sharply than in first marriages (Ganong and Coleman, 1994).

When a friendship is involved, the two persons—ex and current spouse—generally avoid discussing the partner they have shared serially. Although there are no explicit ground rules that guide this relationship, respondents were very articulate and opinionated concerning what they should or should not do, should say or not say to their spouse's ex-husband or ex-wife. When the current spouse and the spouse's ex were asked what they talked about when they met, children were always mentioned first, especially by women. They exchanged information and gossip they believed could be mutually useful: recipes, television programs, films, work, and the like. Men mentioned "sports, news, cars, and the like." Conversations between a woman's two "husbands" were less personal than those between a man's two "wives." But, overall, this was generally a relationship people wished they could live without.

What Are the Effects of Remarriage on Children?

Do children benefit from their parents' remarriage? Research yields mixed results, in part because it has focused on the short term—that is, the first two years following remarriage. Although each case is different, one has to consider that most stepchildren have already undergone one difficult passage involving an incredible array of adjustments—their parents' divorce. They have lived in a single-parent family for a year or more and then their parents remarry, one after the other. Stepchildren do not generally have better outcomes than those who remain with their divorced parent, except perhaps financially while they live at home (McLanahan, 1997). However, parental cohabitation rather than remarriage may be associated with more child problems (Buchanan, Maccoby, and Dornbusch, 1996). This may stem from a lower stepfather investment in cohabitation. In contrast, there is a correlation between high stepfather involvement and mothers' reports of fewer behavioral problems among children (Amato and Rivera, 1999).

Boys and Girls May Adapt Differently

Some children who adjusted well to divorce with no or few adverse outcomes begin to deteriorate after the custodial parent's remarriage. This is particularly the case for girls who adjust better to divorce than boys, although the research is not unanimous on this point (see Cooksey, Menaghan, and Jekielek, 1997). When girls have problems with the remarriage, they are likely to fare poorly when they had a close relationship with their single mother. They miss the attention their mother lavished on them and may resent the intruder. For them, the remarriage constitutes a loss (Vuchinich et al., 1991).

Moreover, stepdaughters are more at risk of being abused sexually by their stepfather or their mother's boyfriend than are daughters in intact families (for a review, see Giles-Sims, 1997). This may stem from the fact that roles are more blurred than in biological families. Furthermore, stepfathers have a low involvement in child care, and low involvement in care increases the risk for sexual abuse, even among fathers (cited in Giles-Sims, 1997). As well, in many cases, stepfathers become acquainted with the child only when she is older and can be perceived as an object of sexual attraction.

In contrast, boys adjust better than girls to being a stepchild, perhaps because they are at home less or because many benefit from the presence of a stepfather. However, Pagani, Boulerice, and Tremblay (1997) have found that adolescent boys living with a recently remarried parent were the most hyperactive at school of all categories of boys ages 12 to 16. This latter result was replicated by Coughlin and Vuchinich (1996), who documented higher rates of early delinquency among boys who had lived in either a single-parent or stepparent family at age 10.

Cooksey and colleagues (1997) find that black children benefit more than white children from the presence of a stepfather. This may be because a live-in *male* parent is a more scarce, thus valued, person among African Americans than among whites; as well, a stepfather may be particularly helpful financially—we have seen that black males who marry are more likely to have a steady employment than those who do not. Furthermore, African Americans are more flexible at integrating other kin within their families. Cherlin and Furstenberg (1994) have observed that black children in inner cities rarely use the term *stepfather.* Rather, the term *daddy* refers to the man who assumes the responsibility for the children or cares for them, whereas the term *father* is the biological parent.

Children's Age May Matter

Stepchildren adapt better when they are very small and have more or less always known the stepparent (Marsiglio, 1992). For their part, adolescents frequently resent the intrusion of one or more authority figures in their lives at a time when they may be seeking autonomy from their family. In the autobiographies, there were students who "hated" the stepparent and had decided to break up their father's or mother's remarriage and succeeded. They made the stepparent's life so unpleasant that the newly married spouses were soon embroiled in conflict with each other as the adolescent played one against the other. One student admitted to being ashamed of her role in the breakup of her mother's remarriage

> *"because it had been my mother's only chance to rebuild her life and I ruined it. Today my mother feels very vulnerable after two failed marriages and is quite lonely. I feel quite guilty and go out of my way to make her happy."*

Advantages for Stepchildren

Stepchildren can harvest advantages, particularly in the long term. They belong to two nuclear families and, in times of illness or other emergencies, care can in theory be more easily arranged. They often acquire stepsiblings and even halfsiblings (Anderson, 1999). Children also acquire stepgrandparents. The kin system is expanding and the potential for establishing other rewarding relationships increases. Stepgrandparents can be quite a resource for a child who has lost one set of kin, often the father's side of the family.

Many stepparents actually become de facto parents when noncustodial parents distance themselves from their duties and others even adopt their stepchild (Ganong et al., 1998). Children who establish a good relationship with their stepfather benefit in terms of emotional stability, social relationships in general, and school achievement (Hetherington, 1993). In some cases, stepchildren replace biological children. Therefore, if stepparents are in many instances a child's second best chance of acquiring a parent, stepchildren may bring unexpected joys to their parent's spouse.

CONCLUSIONS: THE FAMILIAL AND SOCIAL MEANINGS OF DIVORCE

According to Furstenberg and Cherlin (1991:28), divorce creates a **structural ambiguity** in that "the social and psychological tasks of divorce directly collide with the normal expectations of parenthood." Divorce represents a solution to conjugal unhappiness and misery. But what is a solution for adults is not necessarily one for their children. Nevertheless, results on the effect of divorce on children have to be interpreted with caution. First, not all children are affected by their parents' divorce, whether positively or negatively. Some children had no problems before and acquire none after. Others had problems before and have the same or worse ones after. Yet others do better after the divorce of highly conflictual parents (Jekielek, 1998). Second, among children who *are* affected, the magnitude and duration of the effect differ greatly. Some children are affected in the short term only. Others may react belatedly when they reach adulthood and marry. There is also a great deal of difference in terms of the domains of life that are touched. For instance, some children are affected emotionally, others socially, and still others in terms of school performance. The most affected are impacted on all these and other fronts.

The factors associated with divorce may be evolving. For instance, as young people delay marriage, youthful marriages become a less salient correlate of divorce. As cohabitations increase in frequency, their dissolution may replace some divorces, and, for others, cohabitation before marriage may become a factor associated with an increased propensity to divorce. At a more global level, media influences may change and affect adults' mentality concerning their marriage and thus contribute to encouraging or discouraging divorce. Any unforeseen religious revival might strengthen the institutional aspect of marriage for a segment of families and contribute to a reduction in divorce. In a nutshell, marital breakdown is a social phenomenon that evolves within the changing sociocultural context in which the family system is embedded. It cannot be understood fully without an appreciation for this larger context.

SUMMARY

1. At 4.2 per 1,000 population in 1998, the American divorce rate is the highest in the Western world. Rates vary by geographic region. There are four methods of measurement: the rate per 1,000 population, per 1,000 married couples, for married couples within a given number of years after marriage (the most accurate but less frequently used method), and the annual ratio of new divorces over new marriages.

2. The sociocultural factors related to a high divorce rate are multiple and interlinked. They include the secularization of society, the desacralization and deinstitutionalization of marriage, the liberalization of norms and divorce laws, individualism, and a lower threshold of tolerance for marital failings combined with a high level of expectation of marital life.
3. At the demographic level, the first four years of marriage are the most vulnerable to divorce. Besides poverty, additional demographic risks include youthful marriage, prior cohabitation, parents' divorce, and a high proportion of unmarried women in the labor force. Reasons for divorcing vary but the most commonly mentioned are irreconcilable differences, conflict, and falling out of love.
4. The process of marital breakdown differs from couple to couple and, in many cases, begins at the dating stage. A proportion of couples who eventually divorce threaten to do so for many years. Generally, one of the partners is more active than the other in this process.
5. The many factors associated with an easier adjustment to divorce include a couple having no dependent children and no shared assets, a marriage that has been

brief, and each spouse retaining friends individually. Women who are younger and have remained employed are advantaged in the process of adjustment. The success of a divorce can be examined from an individual, a familial, and a societal perspective. A divorce that is successful for one spouse may not be for the other or for the children. From a societal level, a majority of divorces are probably not all that successful.

6. Fathers have sole child custody in only about 10 percent of cases. Father and mother custody seem to have equivalent results for children. In neither case are children as favored as those in two-parent families. Noncustodial mothers are more likely to remain in close contact with their children than noncustodial fathers.
7. Serial divorces have increased; 15 percent of *all* children will see their parents divorce, remarry, and redivorce before they are 18 years old. Indications are that individuals who divorce several times within a decade may have a few deficits in terms of personality that translate into difficulties in getting along and being committed to the relationship.
8. On average, children whose parents divorce experience higher rates of behavioral, emotional, and achievement problems, even into adulthood, than children raised by their two parents. The main theories explaining these negative consequences focus on the diminished family income and even poverty that too often follows divorce; disruption of parenting behaviors as a result of stressors; parental conflict both before and after divorce; and genetic inheritance of difficult personalities in some families. Preexisting negative child attributes and behaviors also contribute to problems after divorce, but problems specific to divorce arise, as well. At the individual level, children exhibit a wide range of consequences of divorce, from being very negatively affected all the way to benefiting from it.
9. Early widowhood is far less common than it was even in the 1920s. But widowhood is more common among women than men in middle age and after. It is a gendered stage. The stages and length of bereavement vary. In the long term, children of widowhood have outcomes similar to those whose parents remain together.
10. Approximately 75 percent of men and 66 percent of women who divorce eventually remarry. Stepchildren complicate the dynamics of remarriages in part because their presence necessitates contact with the ex-spouses involved. The relationship between, say, a man's wife and ex-wife is generally difficult and there are no norms that guide interaction. Although remarriage usually raises parents' level of well-being and a mother's familial income, children benefit differentially from remarriage. For many, it requires even more negative adjustment than had been the case for divorce. For others, there are few benefits but no disadvantages. Still others, particularly adolescent boys, may benefit from the presence of a stepfather. The acquisition of stepgrandparents may also be beneficial.
11. Divorce and remarriage are adult institutions that often create a structural ambiguity that collides with the requisites of effective parenting. The factors associated with divorce and remarriage may evolve over time.

KEY CONCEPTS AND THEMES

Adjustment to divorce, p. 376
Adult institution, p. 393
Bereavement, p. 387
Custodial fathers, p. 379
Custodial mothers, p. 379
Deinstitutionalization of marriage, p. 371
Desacralization of marriage, p. 370
Disruption of parenting, p. 385
Divorce rates, p. 367
Effects of divorce on children, p. 382
Genetic influences, p. 387
Individualism, p. 370
Liberalization of divorce laws, p. 370
Liberalization of norms, p. 370
Lower threshold of tolerance, p. 371
Parental conflict, p. 385
Preexisting child characteristics, p. 386
Remarriage, p. 389
Same-sex matching, p. 379
Secular society, p. 370
Serial divorces, pp. 380, 384
Social networks, p. 377
Socialization experience, p. 384
Stepparenting, p. 391
Successful divorces, p. 377
Widowhood, p. 387
Youthful marriages, p. 372

STUDY AND REVIEW QUESTIONS

1. Discuss the advantages and disadvantages of each method utilized to calculate divorce rates.
2. What relationships would you establish between the reasons people give for their own divorce and the sociocultural factors related to divorce?
3. Why can it be said that adjustment to divorce is a gendered phenomenon?
4. Discuss the finding that children who live with custodial fathers are no worse nor better off than those who live with custodial mothers.
5. What variables may be particularly related to serial divorces?
6. Are there gender and age differences in the effect of divorce on children? Explain.
7. Of the theories meant to explain the negative effects of parental divorce on children, which would particularly apply to children whose parents have remarried and why?
8. Children who lose a parent by death do as well as children in two-parent families. Explain why they are not more similar to children of divorce.
9. What are some of the latent rules of behavior or interaction in the relationship between a person's new spouse and the former spouse?
10. Why do children of divorce not benefit more than they do from their parents' remarriage in the short term?

SUGGESTED READINGS

Amato, P. R., and Booth, A. 1997. *A generation at risk: Growing up in an era of family upheaval.* Cambridge, MA: Harvard University Press. This book presents the results of a longitudinal study including intact families and families of divorce. This study considers, among others, the quality of the parent/child relationship along with the quality of the parents' marriage and timing of divorce.

Furstenberg, F. F., Jr., and Cherlin, A, J. 1991. *Divided families: What happens to the children when parents part.* Cambridge, MA: Harvard University Press. This relatively short book packs in a great deal of information and perspectives on the effect of divorce and remarriage on children.

Ganong, L., and Coleman, M. 1994. *Remarried family relationships*. Newbury Park, CA: Sage. This volume presents a thorough review of the literature on the relationships that develop after remarriage, including stepparenting.

Maccoby, E. E., and Mnookin, R. H., with Depner, C. E., and Peters, H. E. 1992. *Dividing the child: Social and legal dilemmas of custody.* Cambridge, MA: Harvard University Press. The authors discuss the process of divorce and then report on their study comparing divorced families with various types of child custody arrangements and the resulting consequences for family dynamics and children.

Simons, R., and Associates (Eds.). 1996. *Understanding differences between divorced and intact families.* Thousand Oaks, CA: Sage. Several researchers present the results of their studies. The topics covered are diverse and even include sibling relations after divorce.

SUGGESTED WEBLINKS

Bureau of the Census. Click on *People* and an index of topics will appear, including divorce. **<http://www.census.gov>**

Divorce Online. This is the website for the American Divorce Information Network. It provides articles and information on legal, psychological, and financial issues pertaining to divorce. **<http://www.divorce-online.com/>**

For a general directory of weblinks, consult: **<http://dir.yahoo.com/Society_and_Culture/Families>.**

The following directory contains a mixture of information, practicalities, as well as chat lines about stepparenting. It has an extensive set of weblinks. **<http://stepparenting.about/com/home/parenting/stepparenting>**

CHAPTER 14

Family Violence, Abuse, and Child Neglect

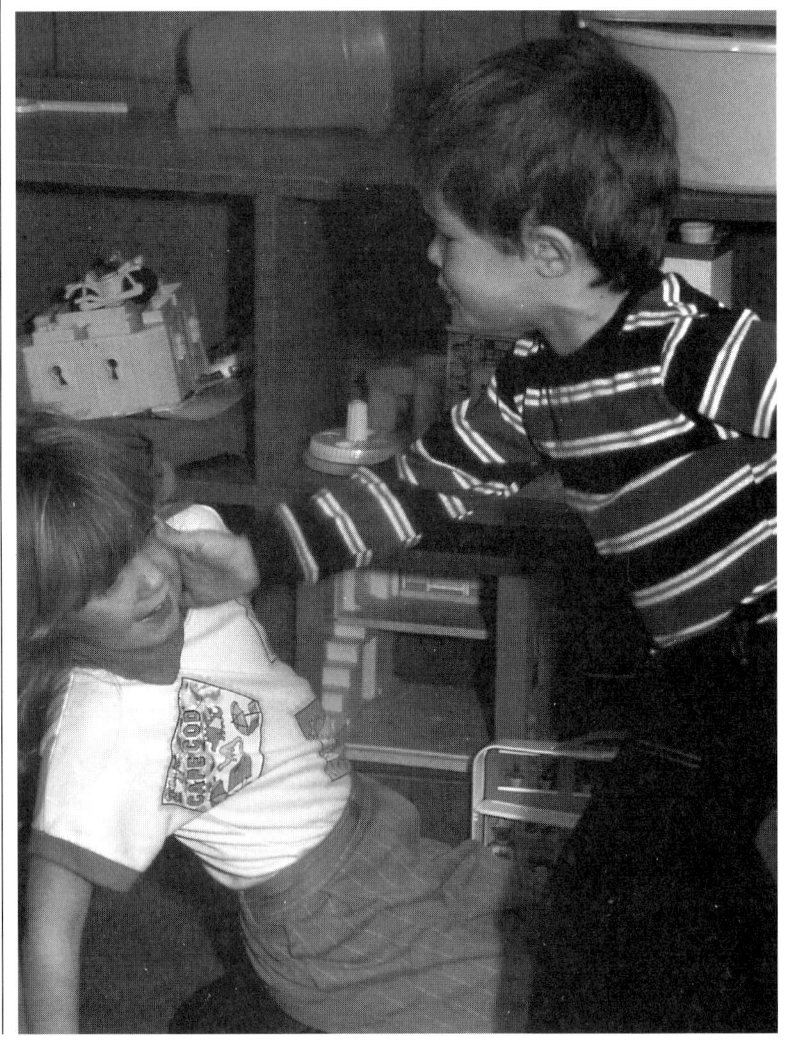

OUTLINE

Dating and Partner Abuse
Dating and Courtship Violence
Date Rape
Causes of Dating Violence
Verbal and Psychological Abuse of Partners
Spousal and Partner Physical Abuse
Range of Violent Acts
Factors Related to Spousal Abuse
Same-Sex-Partner Violence
The Effect of Spousal Violence on Children

Child Abuse and Neglect by Parents
Child Abuse by Parents
Factors Related to Child Abuse by Parents
Physical Punishment: The Question Mark
Consequences of Parental Abuse for Children
Do Abused Children Become Abusive Parents?
Child Neglect by Parents
Is Child Abuse by Parents Increasing?

Child Sexual Abuse by Adults
Who Are and Where Are the Abusers?
Consequences of Sexual Abuse for the Child
The Life Course Perspective
Overview of Consequences

Sibling Abuse
Sibling Violence
Sibling Sexual Abuse

Peer Abuse
How Common Is Peer Abuse?
Consequences and Context of Peer Abuse
Peer Sexual Harassment and Abuse

Abuse of Parents by Children
Physical Abuse of Parents by Children and Adolescents
Abuse of Elderly Parents by Adult Children

Conclusions: The Larger Context of Family Violence

Summary
Key Concepts and Themes
Study and Review Questions
Suggested Readings
Suggested Weblinks

A man stalks his wife after she leaves him for battering. Despite a restraining order preventing him from coming within 300 feet, he savagely stabs her as she returns home from work. She leaves two children.
(Source: 1998 newscast)

Social workers are called to a home where they find five children ranging in age from 2 to 10 in a filthy and barely furnished home. The children are hungry and cold, and the level of functioning of all but the oldest one indicates delay due to neglect. The two parents involved have been out on a crack-induced "trip" for three days.
(Source: 1998 newscast)

A man is beaten up by his gay partner so severely that he requires emergency surgery. The battering had been going on for two years.
(Source: 1998 newscast)

A 16-year-old rapes his 15-year-old girlfriend in his car on the way back from the movies. He felt that they had been going out long enough and it was time "to go all the way."
(Source: Abstract from student autobiography)

A police officer brings a 14-year-old girl back home after finding her doing drugs with two older males at a strip mall. It's 3:00 A.M. She lives in an affluent suburban home. Her parents did not know that she was out.
(Source: Abstract from student autobiography)

A 10-year-old girl has been fondled, kissed in the genital area, and convinced to "touch" the genitals of her father's best friend. He is "part of the family," and often babysits the two children, a boy and a girl. One day, he forces the girl to practice oral sex on him when the boy, age 11, walks in and later tells his parents who call the police.
(Source: Abstract from student autobiography)

What these vignettes share in common is either violence or neglect. When one adds sibling violence and peer abuse, which are the most common types of maltreatment, and child-to-parent abuse to these situations, then it can be said that abuse and neglect are regular features on the American familial landscape.

DATING AND PARTNER ABUSE

Family violence and partner abuse have belatedly become more socially and politically visible in the last four decades. Dating abuse is only beginning to emerge in the public consciousness.

Dating and Courtship Violence

For a substantial segment of American youths, dating is a fertile ground upon which to continue their aggressive behaviors toward their peers. For others, it is an opportunity to discover a new arena in which to exercise power. Few incidents of courtship or acquaintance violence are reported to authorities or to parents, and many youths consider them a normal part of the dating process (Sleek, 1998):

> *"We both have strong personalities and don't let people walk all over us and that goes for each other. I don't mind punching him in the stomach or kicking his legs*

> *if he's too fresh and he does the same, except that he's bigger and it hurts more. My mother goes on my nerves about this because she says, 'if that's the way the both of you behave now think what it's going to be like in 5 years.'"*

But other women students were not so complacent:

> *"I'd rate myself as unhappy at this point because I have to decide if I'll stay with my boyfriend of three years. Once in a while he calls me names but recently he's grabbed me and shoved me in the car and once against the wall another time and I am afraid that I'll end up a battered wife."*

> *"It so happens that I just broke up with my fiance. . . . He was slapping me on a regular basis and swearing at me. There's no way he would discuss it and he refused seeing a counselor. I'd rather stay single."*

Dating violence predicts domestic abuse later on in married life. Perhaps the most surprising aspect of courtship violence, as is the case for spousal abuse, is that both genders are involved in inflicting harm (Makepeace, 1997). However, women sustain most of the injuries (Stets and Henderson, 1991).

Date Rape

Currently, date rape is an issue that is belatedly receiving attention. Overall, about 20 percent of female college students surveyed mention having been forced to have sexual intercourse (Brener et al., 1999). But most of these students never report it to the authorities, as is the case for the following young woman:

> *"The most painful event in my entire life is having been raped. Wayne was a good friend. I had known him for a long time. One winter day I decided to call Wayne from school. He invited me to come over to watch movies, and seeing as I didn't feel like going to class, I went. When I got to Wayne's apartment everything seemed to be running smooth. We were watching movies. Wayne then suggested that I check out his bedroom, so, out of stupidity and perhaps curiosity, I went. He then locked the door and raped me. I really did try to fight him off but he's a football player. . . . I couldn't tell my parents, and they still don't know."*

The situation of date and even acquaintance rape worsened in the 1990s with the arrival of readily available chemicals that, when dropped in a woman's drink, secure her full "cooperation." The woman cannot later recall much of what occurred. These situations happen on campuses as well as in bars and nightclubs where the purpose is to meet members of the opposite sex. They include gang rape, even in college fraternities (Sanday, 1990). This is the ultimate in terms of a "power trip" and *patriarchal dominance.* These instances well illustrate young males' readiness to accept deviance in order to secure their own sexual gratification and to be able to justify their acts within a masculinist mentality (Sanday, 1996). National newscasts recently (November 1999) reported that 30 percent of male students admitted that they would force sex on a woman if they felt that they could get away with it.

Causes of Dating Violence

The origins of dating violence are still debated in the research literature. The reason for this is that most studies have **psychologized** and **familialized** the origins of dating violence and do not control for extrafamilial, cultural influences. By now, the reader has been sensitized to the fact that the quality of parenting explains only a small portion of children's current and future behaviors, and this also applies to partner violence. Omission of other influential factors, particularly at the macrosociological level, distorts reality and prevents one from acquiring a full understanding of how particular behaviors emerge. For instance, in certain peer groups, including athletes, the **social construction of masculinity** includes a level of violent attitudes toward girls and women as well as a mentality of sexual entitlement (Sanday, 1996). Thus, among heterosexual couples, the overall gender stratification leaves room for violence against women. This type of cultural climate is reflected in the *media*. As well, pornographic materials, to which many men and boys are exposed, do contain violent sex. Similarly, as we soon see, children in same-sex peer groups engage in a great deal of abuse that can be easily transposed into dating relationships. Other boys engage in sexual harassment, and lack of adult intervention leads them to perceive their own behaviors as normal.

Studies on childhood exposure to interparental violence as the key factor in the origins of dating violence are largely inconclusive: Some find a relationship between the two but others do not (Simons, Lin, and Gordon, 1998). The least that can be said is that exposure to parental violence during adolescence and young adulthood as well as having been harshly treated by one's parents certainly are *risk factors*. Furthermore, evidence shows that, on average, males who assault their dates were aggressive as boys (Capaldi and Clark, 1998). Many exhibited behavioral problems as children and may still be out of control; the same pattern occurs among some abusive females. Simons and colleagues (1998) find that males who engage in dating violence are more likely to have engaged in delinquent acts and drug use than other males. These results corroborate those of other researchers who report two categories of abusers among the married: those who limit their abuse to the home and those who are violent in other contexts as well (Edleson and Tolman, 1992). The latter often have participated in criminal activities and have a more antisocial personality. They may also be more likely to begin abuse at the dating stage.

Verbal and Psychological Abuse of Partners

Verbal abuse consists of repeatedly calling one's partner epithets, including much foul language, berating and demeaning—put-downs, in other words—threatening and criticizing, even in public. Its purpose is to dominate, to exercise *power*, and to show who is "the boss." It is also used to rationalize or excuse one's bad behavior by demeaning the other. Calling one's date an "idiot" once is unfortunate but it does not constitute verbal abuse; however, if such a behavior is repeated, then it is abusive. It also sets a precedent upon which physical abuse can be added once civility has been eroded in the relationship. In fact, physical abuse is generally accompanied or preceded by verbal insults and attempts by one partner or both at intimidating the other (Sugarman et al., 1996). Males particularly tend to practice both types of abuse in severe cases of psychological and physical assaults (Hamby and Sugarman, 1999).

Verbal abuse may be on the increase. For instance, verbal abuse is quite salient in music videos favored by adolescents and youths, and it is nearly always directed against women because, in a subtle way, culture defines women as legitimate targets of male violence. The word *bitch* is widespread in a growing segment of younger cohorts; it is often used as soon as a quarrel erupts. It is not unusual to hear young couples calling each other foul and demeaning names; such insults were rarely overheard just a decade ago. These exchanges represent a dangerous escalation, a **lack of civility,** part of what Garbarino (1995) refers to as the "toxic" environment in which people raise children. Many young couples are only at the dating stage, yet are already immersed in name calling.

As Renzetti (1997b) has discovered among same-sex couples, psychological abuse is often tailored to fit a partner's vulnerabilities. During my own study on divorce, ex-spouses, particularly ex-wives, frequently mentioned that such verbal violence had been a pattern in their past marriage:

> *One woman who was obese was repeatedly called a "fat slob" and a "pile of lard" by her husband. He would tell her to "move your fat ass" or "sit on your god-damn fat ass, I have something to tell you." At the dinner table, she had to eat like a bird lest he observed to the children, "There goes your mother, stuffing her fat face." Or he would yell, "You're just adding one pound of lard to your fat ass." The more he emphasized her weight, the more she ate, and the larger she became, until her health was threatened.*

This tailoring of verbal abuse can focus on facial features, body shape, clumsiness, lack of mental agility, as well as unemployment and financial difficulties:

> *One ex-wife had repeatedly taunted her unemployed husband in front of their children as "good for nothing" and "you're no real man." Renzetti (1997b:74) writes of two women with physical disabilities: "Their partners would abandon them in dangerous settings (i.e., an isolated wooded area) without their wheelchairs. Another woman who was diabetic stated that her partner would punish her by forcing her to eat sugar."*

Verbal abuse can also take the form of threats and become a form of psychological blackmail:

> *One divorced woman recalled that her ex-husband used to threaten to tell her children that she had given up her first-born for adoption—disregarding the fact that the infant had been his and he had not wanted it (this was before they married). Another was constantly threatened by her ex-husband of losing custody of her children: She suffered from bouts of depression, and the threats, which terrorized her, merely increased her sad condition. One ex-husband was threatened by his ex-wife of legal exposure if he did not "cough up" more monthly support; at some point in the past, he had defrauded his former employers but had never been caught. His ex-wife was fully aware of his past illegal activities and used them as leverage.*

One form of abuse that is unique to same-sex relationships is the threat of "outing," or revealing that the other is gay or lesbian, at his or her work, for instance, or to relatives who are unaware of the situation and might turn against the hapless person were they to be so informed.

Spousal and Partner Physical Abuse

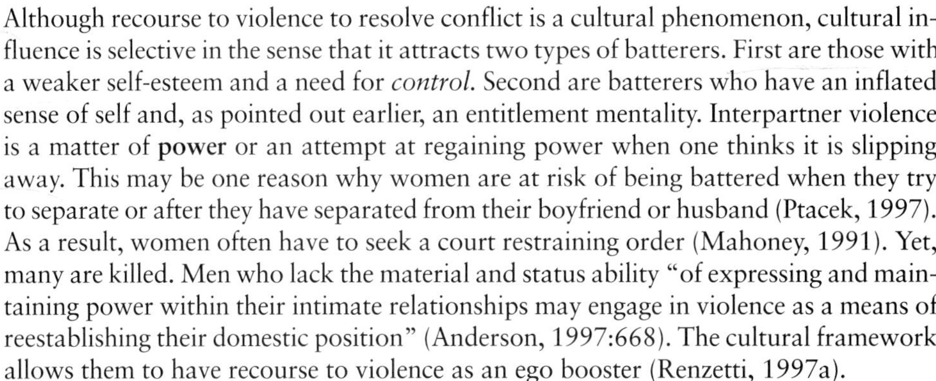

Although recourse to violence to resolve conflict is a cultural phenomenon, cultural influence is selective in the sense that it attracts two types of batterers. First are those with a weaker self-esteem and a need for *control*. Second are batterers who have an inflated sense of self and, as pointed out earlier, an entitlement mentality. Interpartner violence is a matter of **power** or an attempt at regaining power when one thinks it is slipping away. This may be one reason why women are at risk of being battered when they try to separate or after they have separated from their boyfriend or husband (Ptacek, 1997). As a result, women often have to seek a court restraining order (Mahoney, 1991). Yet, many are killed. Men who lack the material and status ability "of expressing and maintaining power within their intimate relationships may engage in violence as a means of reestablishing their domestic position" (Anderson, 1997:668). The cultural framework allows them to have recourse to violence as an ego booster (Renzetti, 1997a).

Many batterers are actually quite pathological (Coleman, 1994). However, one has to consider that pathology is culturally influenced, channeled, or even created. In many societies, it leads to interpersonal violence or abuse, among other things. As was the case for dating, both men and women who engage in spousal violence are more likely than nonviolent spouses to have been involved in delinquency and were considered troublemakers when adolescents (Giordano et al., 1999). Gottman (1998:153) found that violent men tended to reject their wives' influence in an experimental situation: They not only rejected their wives' complaints but they also escalated any attempt at discussion into a full-blown conflict.

Range of Violent Acts

Spousal or partner physical abuse covers quite a range of acts, so that one has to exercise caution when interpreting statistics. Straus (1979) devised the Conflict Tactics Scale that includes the following acts, in descending order of severity:

1. Threw something at spouse
2. Pushed, grabbed, or shoved spouse
3. Slapped spouse
4. Kicked, bit, or hit spouse with fist
5. Hit or tried to hit spouse with something
6. Beat up spouse
7. Choked spouse
8. Threatened spouse with a knife or gun
9. Used a knife or a gun on spouse

Most acts of violence committed by intimate partners tend to be at the less severe end of the scale. In the Gelles and Straus (1988) large survey, 28 percent of couples reported at least one instance of violence during their marriage, with the milder forms predominating. But once a wife becomes a target of abuse, she is likely to be a repeat victim—about three times each year. This is particularly the case when physical injury results (Brookoff et al., 1997). Women are even attacked during pregnancy.

The fact that wives also commit acts of violence does not mean that they are more violent than or even as violent as husbands or dates (Browne, 1997). Women who

Wife battering is often preceded by or accompanied with verbal abuse and threats. This pattern of violence also exists among same-sex couples.

are truly and forcefully violent and abuse their male partners are still the exception. Above all, women may fear damaging retaliation if they hit their partners. Women attack with far less force and energy than men. They are less muscular, tall, heavy, and strong, thus the results of their aggressiveness are generally inconsequential physically and their partners may not even take their assaults seriously. In contrast, when men attack, the effect on women is far more lethal and results in bruises, concussions, and broken bones (Feldhaus et al., 1997). At least one large survey has found that being the victim of domestic violence is a "qualitatively different experience for women and men" (Umberson et al., 1998:449). For instance, it results in a loss of feelings of personal control among women but not men.

Rape is one aspect of spousal violence. Men who are very violent toward their wives often combine physical battering with sexual assault (Browne, 1997). This is the ultimate way of establishing one's power over the other. Browne points out that women whose partners are sexually aggressive "have a higher risk of experiencing more severe and injurious nonsexual aggression than women with male partners who are physically but not sexually violent" (p. 50).

Factors Related to Spousal Abuse

A proportion of dating and domestic violence is committed under the influence of **alcohol.** Many batterers and even their victims construct alcohol as a socially acceptable excuse for violence (Gelles, 1993:184). The belief that men batter because drinking pushes them to it is so well ingrained in the collective mentality that cases have even been thrown out of courts because "he was so drunk that he didn't know what he was doing." Alcohol facilitates abuse, as it inhibits control. When both the batterer and the victim have been drinking, they may not even notice the presence of their children (Hutchison, 1999). In other cases, alcohol use follows a battering incident rather than precedes it (Gelles, 1993). Alcohol and drugs are involved in a majority of the cases when the police are called, perhaps because women are more afraid of the violence and, if they have also been drinking, they may be less inhibited and less inclined to excuse their partner (Brookoff et al., 1997).

Cohabiting couples have the highest rate of partner violence (Stets and Straus, 1989). This may in part be related to their greater level of disagreement on key issues, such as marriage, and to the feeling of lower commitment that exists in these relationships, particularly on the masculine side (Faurre and Maddock, 1994). As we have seen in Chapter 5, cohabitation is not institutionalized; consequently, there are fewer rules governing it, and thus it may not be a structural situation that is as efficient as marriage at preventing domestic violence.

Among very *low-income* couples and women with relatively little schooling, there is an increased risk for partner violence. Poor couples who live in **disadvantaged neighborhoods** are more at risk of spousal abuse (and, as seen later, child abuse) than similar couples who live in economically secure environments (Miles-Doan, 1998). Absence of visible violence in relatively affluent areas may act as a deterrent against domestic abuse. In fact, as we have seen in Chapter 7, poor neighborhoods exhibit higher rates of violence of all sorts, and this includes spousal abuse. However, this should not be taken to mean that domestic abuse does not occur among the more affluent: It does.

Few studies focus on **ethnicity.** In view of income differentials and segregation, which result in African Americans living in neighborhoods where more violence exists in general, it is not surprising that one study indicates substantial levels of cohabitant and spousal abuse among blacks (Uzzell and Peebles-Wilkins, 1989). However, is it quite possible that domestic violence among oppressed minorities has root causes that differ from those among whites. For instance, blacks are differentially located in society because of their devalued color. Prejudice and discrimination may be internalized among a segment of black males, who then demean black women and express their general rage toward them rather than projecting it onto society (Crenshaw, 1994).

The culture of Latino men gives them a great deal of power, compared to women (Fernandez-Kelly and Garcia, 1990). Yet, they feel powerless in society at large and may express their frustration within the safety of their families, where their remnants of power are located. The same authors have found that Mexican-American men born and raised in Mexico have lower rates of spousal abuse than non-Latino whites and than Mexican-American men born in the United States. This difference could be the result of socialization: Living in the United States perhaps teaches violence, particularly among low-income groups.

Same-Sex-Partner Violence

Same-sex-partner violence is as much a matter of power and control as it is in heterosexual couple violence, except that gender or patriarchal ideologies are not an issue. The rate of violence among same-sex couples approximates that of heterosexuals, between 12 and 33 percent, depending on the sample and measures (Straus and Gelles, 1990a). The research carried out strictly on gay and lesbian samples shows slightly higher rates (Elliott, 1996). Depending on the studies, as many as 50 percent or as few as 17 percent of lesbians admit having been abused by a female partner. Of those who have been victimized, the same proportion report having also practiced abuse.

But 30 percent of those who have not been abused report having been abusive. These statistics are tentative, because, as Renzetti (1997a:289) points out, no reliable study of the prevalence of same-sex-partner abuse exists yet.

Estimating same-sex-partner abuse is difficult because homosexuals may be reluctant to talk about their personal lives for fear of being misunderstood and further stigmatized. Domestic abuse is also a problem that the homosexual community often avoids, because it is often believed that it occurs only in male/female couples. In addition, same-sex-partner domestic violence receives less attention from the police, both because it is less reported and may be interpreted as violence of one man against another rather than as domestic violence. However, many police departments are now well trained and deal with these cases efficiently (Island and Letellier, 1991).

Bars have been important to this point in the social life of homosexuals, which leads to alcohol-related problems, including partner abuse. However, as happens among heterosexual couples, alcohol is merely a facilitator and is also utilized as an excuse, both for one's actions and for those of the abuser by the victimized partner (Renzetti, 1997a). Renzetti also found that partner abuse often went hand in hand with child abuse, particularly toward the child of the victimized partner. These cases, however, have been documented only among lesbian couples whose children were from a previous marriage.

One major drawback of the literature on same-sex domestic violence is that it does not study its effects on children. Lesbian and homosexual couples who have children together represent a new phenomenon and it will take a few years before these children are grown. However, it is reasonable to assume that same-sex couples who are involved in physical abuse are less likely to have children than similar heterosexual couples. Cohabitation is more fragile than marriage, and same-sex couples who do not get along and quarrel violently probably separate even before the thought of having children occurs to them.

Moreover, reproducing children is a far more complicated project to carry out among homosexuals than among heterosexuals. It is not something that happens accidentally, for instance. Therefore, it is possible that a process of **social selection** is at work: Those who decide to have children and are then able to achieve this goal may be a select group of more stable and devoted couples than are average heterosexual couples. Consequently, they would not fall prey to deviances, especially spousal abuse, that could endanger their relationship and their children's well-being.

The Effect of Spousal Violence on Children

It is estimated that several million children witness interparental violence annually. We have already discussed, in Chapter 10, the effect that parental conflict has on children, and we also saw in the previous chapter that it is an important factor in the negative outcomes of children before and after divorce. Here, we will explore what happens to children when they watch their fathers beat their mothers or see both parents throw projectiles at each other and engage in mutual slapping and punching, with much yelling and name calling. These scenes many times occur in full view of children or while the children are at home and can hear what is taking place.

Some effects are immediate; others are delayed until certain life transitions occur; and many are long lasting. One immediate effect is fear, an urge to run away or to help the victimized parent. Children may throw themselves between parents, and often older sons try to fend off a father; many children are injured in the process (Brookoff et al., 1997). Other children call for neighbors' help or even the police. A few others take the abuser's side, and it may be them that society has to fear, as explained by an older woman student:

> *"Ever since I can recall, my father always beat up my mother and in those days (1960–70) women had to put up with it. I used to hide when it would start and then I would run to my mother and hug her and kiss her and cry with her. As a result, I have always been a sad child and to this day I tend to be anxious and easily pessimistic. But perhaps the saddest part is that my older brother never felt sorry for my mom. He used to tell her like my father did, 'That serves you right, next time do as he says.' My brother used to kiss my father's ass and really worship the ground he walked on. He grew up just like him and he often beat me up too and a couple of times he slapped my mother. . . . [He] beat up his ex-wife and he's tried it on many women but he's such a hypocrite: At work he's a model citizen."*

On average, children of abused mothers have more behavioral and psychological problems and exhibit less interpersonal sensitivity (Rosenberg, 1987). Other long-lasting effects include lower psychological well-being in adulthood, increased risk for depression, as well as poor parent/child relationships (McNeal and Amato, 1998). These consequences on children may be exasperated by the negative effect of battering on the mothers themselves. Women who are repeatedly abused have high rates of sleep disorders, depression, illness, and even suicide attempts (Birns and Birns, 1997). It would be surprising if these severe maternal symptoms did not disrupt mothers' ability to parent and consequently negatively affect at least some aspects of many children's personal development.

The greatest negative impact of interparental violence occurs in those families where parents are the most violent toward each other and engage in the entire spectrum of abusive activities (Jouriles et al., 1998). By the age of 18, offspring from these dysfunctional families have generally been exposed to other adversities, including poverty, divorce, parental alcoholism, and even criminality and childhood abuse (Birns and Birns, 1997). Once these contextual circumstances are controlled for, the direct negative effect of interparental violence is substantially reduced but does not disappear entirely (Fergusson and Horwood, 1998).

The matter of the intergenerational transmission of violence—that is, from witnessing parental violence to committing dating and partner violence later on—is much discussed. As we have seen, the evidence is not unanimous, and even researchers who support the cycle of violence theory recognize that "the mechanisms by which violence is transmitted appear to be complex and multidimensional" (O'Keefe, 1998:41). O'Keefe distributed questionnaires to 1,012 high school students in the Los Angeles area. She asked them about parental violence, their own dating experience, their attitude toward dating violence, and the type and frequency of violence they witnessed in their community and at school. She then focused on the 232 students who reported a *great deal* of interparental violence in order to see what would differentiate students who abuse their dates from those who do not—in other words, what characterizes those who follow the parental example.

She found that 51 percent had never inflicted violence against a dating partner, and 49 percent had done so at least once. As well, 55 percent reported having been victimized at least once. Among males, those who had inflicted or been the victim of dating violence tended to be of lower socioeconomic status and reported more exposure to **community and school violence.** Among females, those who had followed the parental example or who had been victimized were characterized by exposure to community and school violence, poor school performance, and having been abused as a child.

Therefore, the exposure to a *high* level of parental violence places youths at a great risk of committing similar acts and being themselves victimized. But there are other risk factors at the social level that increase the likelihood of such occurrences in the students' own lives. The variable of exposure to community and school violence is particularly significant, because it appears as a risk factor for both sexes. Conversely, the protective factors that intervene to prevent the transmission of violence across the two generations are higher socioeconomic status and low community and school violence. Thus, O'Keefe's results on dating violence link with those studies that find more spousal and child abuse in those disadvantaged neighborhoods where a great deal of general violence exists.

CHILD ABUSE AND NEGLECT BY PARENTS

This section focuses on parents as the perpetrators of abuse and neglect of children. It is customary in textbooks to begin discussions of child abuse by parents, even though children are far more likely to be maltreated by their peers and their siblings (lower part of Figure 14.1). Only very small children who are abused are abused mainly by their parents or a caregiver (upper part of Figure 14.1). There are no reliable statistics on the combined sources of child abuse, but Figure 14.1 presents a reasonable estimate of the overall situation up to age 16 in terms of who tends to maltreat children the most frequently.

Child Abuse by Parents

Between 850 and 1,800 deaths result each year from child abuse, and particularly from neglect among children younger than age 5 (reported in Smithey, 1998). Shockingly, between one-third and one-half of these fatalities might have been prevented, as these children had already been brought to the attention of law enforcement and child protection agencies (Emery and Laumann-Billings, 1998). Infants are at a higher risk of fatal abuse from their mothers up to age 4 months, from their fathers between the ages of 4 to 10 months, and from their mothers' boyfriends or stepfathers from ages 10 to 25 months.

Child physical abuse at home has been estimated at a rate of nearly 6 cases per 1,000 children for 1993 (Kaplan, Pelcovitz, and Labruna, 1999). An estimate of the number of children abused in 1993 includes

638,800 cases of physical abuse
302,000 cases of sexual abuse
536,400 cases of emotional abuse

FIGURE 14.1

Estimates of the Main Sources of Child Maltreatment up to Age 16

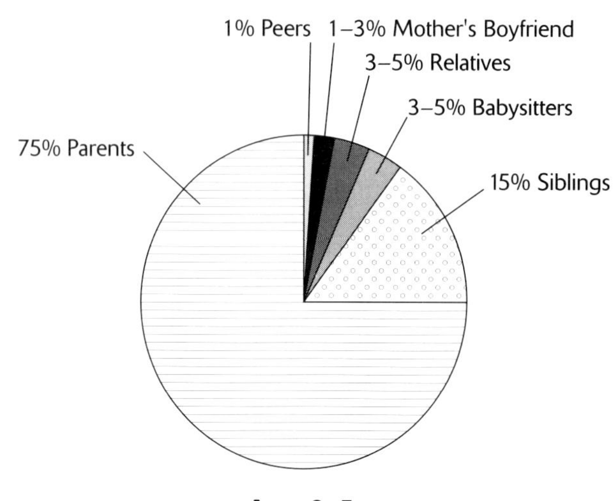

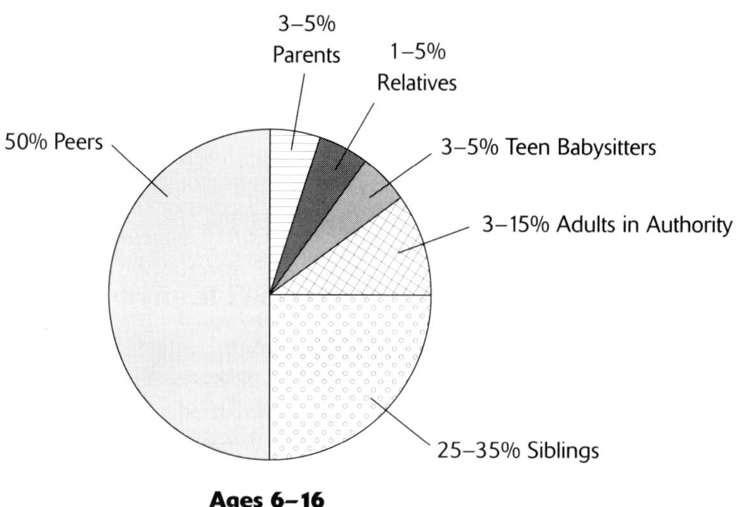

These figures include 572,200 cases of seriously injured children (Gelles, 1997:46). (Estimates for neglect, which are higher, are presented in a following section.) The Gelles data are based on population surveys. For their part, Weise and Daro (1995) used cases of child abuse reported by states, of which 33 percent were substantiated after investigation. Of these *substantiated* cases,

217,500 children had been physically abused
113,960 had been sexually abused
31,080 had been emotionally abused

With toddlers and preschool-age children, it is often difficult to distinguish a *first* occurrence of abuse from an accidental circumstance. For instance, day care workers or kindergarten teachers may notice bruises or a child who is limping. The child may not be able to establish a cause and effect between these physical symptoms and the fact that he or she was punched or thrown against a piece of furniture the day before. Parents generally explain that the child fell into the bathtub, off the toilet seat, or down the staircase. These explanations are plausible, because nearly all small children sooner or later have such accidents and some are more accident prone than others, particularly when they are active as well as impulsive (Schwebel and Plumert, 1999).

Factors Related to Child Abuse by Parents

Child abuse and neglect are more common in *low-income* families, especially in **neighborhoods** with a high **concentration** of **poverty** and **violence** (Bell and Jenkins, 1993). It is possible that child abuse is more easily detected among the poor—particularly those who are clients of social agencies—than among other income groups who may also harbor this problem (Appell, 1998). Despite this cautionary remark, a true relationship still exists between poverty and child abuse (McLoyd, 1995). In fact, already two decades ago, Garbarino and Sherman (1980) had found that living in a high-risk neighborhood correlated with child abuse, even after controlling for family characteristics. In these neighborhoods, the lack of an effective community means that each set of parents or each single parent is socially isolated, lacks support, and is deprived of elements of social control (Garbarino and Kostelny, 1992). Were all these missing elements present, parents would be prevented from lashing out at their children as often and cruelly as they do.

Many studies link parents' daily stressors and psychological distress to distant, rejecting, and punitive parenting. McLoyd (1995) shows that, among single mothers, the adverse effects of poverty increase maternal depression and, in turn, punishment of adolescents. All in all, the daily stressors of poverty exacerbate difficult temperaments and may activate predispositions to violence, while simultaneously inhibiting controls against violence. In conditions of poverty, coping mechanisms are unduly taxed by daily irritants that cumulate to form an explosive situation. Depending on the temperament of the individuals affected and the characteristics of the child who is targeted, explosive or apathetic behaviors may result (Elder, Caspi, and Nguyen, 1994).

Physical Punishment: The Question Mark

Physical abuse is part of a continuum, from severe to mild, and also from disciplining to excess. Physical punishment of children, such as spankings, is used by 84 to 97 percent of all parents at some point in their offsprings' lives (Straus and Donnelly, 1994). Most spankings occur to children below age 10. Mothers are more often the spanking agents than fathers, probably because they are the primary caregivers (Day, Peterson, and McCracken, 1998), and, as seen in the next chapter, because children are more difficult with mothers than they are with fathers. The intent of spankings is to stop disruptive behavior, often after all else has failed, to shock a small child into reality or to take him or her from harm's way (such as running into the street). This type of punishment as a form of family violence is considered abusive by some but appropriate by a majority (Flynn, 1994). Over 80 percent of college students, and even more so among blacks than whites, judge spanking as appropriate (Flynn, 1998). However, the recourse to spanking is associated conceptually with incompetent parenting by researchers.

The ideology behind the condemnation of "just" and occasional corporal punishment presents a dilemma to parents who live in dangerous neighborhoods or those whose children are difficult. Such parents are often compelled to resort to strict discipline in order to keep their children out of trouble, and they may find threats of a spanking very effective. This ideology is also baffling to many immigrant parents, in whose countries of origin, physical punishment is totally acceptable—as may be abuse and wife battering. Thus, the labeling of "fair" corporal punishment as a form of child abuse is controversial, as we have seen in Chapter 11. Reports of negative consequences for occasional and light spankings are probably unfounded, unless there are other risk factors present (Rosellini, 1998). These could include lack of overall parenting warmth, parenting aggresiveness, parents who are generally antisocial or criminal, detrimental peers, poverty, and child frailties, such as low impulse control or high anxiety and sensitivity.

Consequences of Parental Abuse for Children

The literature on child abuse tends to focus on children's developmental outcomes rather than on their current suffering, struggles, and small victories. The everyday life of these children is not well documented at all. What is known is that overall, children who have been or are abused, on average, do less well in school (Eckenrode, Laird, and Doris, 1993), are more frequently delinquent (Sternberg et al., 1993), have more peer-related problems (Howes, 1988), and are less reciprocal in their relations (Salzinger, Feldman, and Hammer, 1993). Understandably, they become hypervigilant to danger and threat, and, as a result, are often more aggressive and tend to attribute hostile intent to others (Dodge, Bates, and Pettit, 1990).

In other words, these children share some of the characteristics mentioned earlier among children who witness interparental violence. In fact, fathers who abuse their wives physically are more likely to abuse their children (McCloskey, Figueredo, and Koss, 1995). In turn, abused mothers use harsh punishment more often than nonabused mothers (Straus and Smith, 1990). Women who have been abused as children have a higher chance of marrying an abusive husband. Together, these factors mean that child abuse often coexists or overlaps with spousal abuse and related difficulties. This **combination of factors** may explain the similarity between the long-term effects of child abuse and those of interparental violence. It also makes it difficult to determine the effects specific to child abuse alone. However, children who have been abused generally fare less well than those who witness interparental violence (see Margolin, 1998).

Instead of becoming aggressive, adults who have been abused as children at times become depressed, withdrawn, and addicted to drugs (McCauley et al., 1997). Others may become warm and particularly altruistic. Certain types of abuse and degree of severity affect personal development, whereas other types of abuse affect subsequent parenting behaviors or interpersonal relations. Still other patterns of abuse are linked to antisocial behavior or are causally linked to all such negative outcomes. However, the initial "causative" factor (the abuse) may be outweighed by personality strengths or resilience, happy circumstances in the person's life course, and a general lack of subsequent stressors (Rutter, 1989).

Therefore, the path between a variable believed to be causal and its resulting outcome depends on many other factors, and may lead to a totally nonpredicted outcome depending on a person's life course. Salzinger, Feldman, and Hammer (1993) pointedly remark that protective factors must exist for severely abused children who turn out well, whereas risk factors must exist for children who are not abused but go on to become abusive as adults. These protective and risk factors may be found at the microsociological level (the child's personality), at the family level (supportive siblings or one parent who is warm), or at the macrosociological level (good schools and a neighborhood that is largely prosocial).

Do Abused Children Become Abusive Parents?

Just as is the case for interparental violence, one of the consequences of child abuse that is much studied and debated involves its reproduction in the next generation. As it turns out, abusive parents themselves, compared to nonabusive parents, have, on average, been more frequently abused or harshly treated as children. Abusive parents, especially those who are sexually exploitative, lack empathy for their child and entertain unrealistic expectations of what the child can do for them (Pianta, Egeland, and Erickson, 1989). Despite these parental drawbacks, most abused children do not grow up to be criminal or even abusive. However, many develop behavioral problems or psychiatric disorders that never come to clinical attention. Put otherwise, severe and persistent child abuse probably always leaves long-term traces of psychological misery.

Kaufman and Zigler (1987) and Widom (1990) have estimated the transmission rate of family violence to be about 30 percent or lower. Abuse is not unavoidably transmitted, because several factors enter into play in the causality chain of transmission. This includes the meaning that people attach to having been abused (Korbin, 1986): Some children who are beaten interpret this as justifiable punishment, yet, because it has hurt them, they decide later on to utilize other forms of punishment with their own children. Attachment to a partner and children as well as the perceived disapproval of friends and relatives concerning family violence also prevents individuals who suffered or witnessed violence in their families from committing it themselves. This explanation is related to social bonding theory (Lackey and Williams, 1995). In other instances, a potential abuser's spouse intervenes and resocializes her husband into utilizing more appropriate punishment.

Although some violent parents are more at risk of transmitting this pattern than others, the mechanisms through which this occurs are still poorly understood. In this respect, Simons and colleagues (1995) propose that a **parent's antisocial orientation** may well be one mediating factor in the transmission of violence to the next generation. Thus, it is possible that abusive parents who have other antisocial characteristics are more likely to transmit various abusive and violent behaviors to their children than adults who, except for being abusive parents, are otherwise prosocial (Frick et al., 1992). Antisocial parents might abuse their spouse, pick fights with others, or engage in criminal activity, for instance. In other words, they provide a stronger negative socialization experience for their children. In a small core of families, it may also be that physical abuse as well as other antisocial activities are transmitted across generations by heredity, that is, parents pass on to their children severe predispositions for aggressiveness or for other partly genetically influenced traits, such as low self-control or high impulsivity. However, one should be careful not to think that heredity means unavoidability or that it excuses the behaviors. Most people born with a predisposition to aggressiveness are not condemned or forced to act it out. But they are more likely to act it out when their environment encourages violence.

Parental stress induced by a child's disruptive behavior often precipitates abuse (Pianta, Egeland, and Erickson, 1989). Hence, another pathway to the transmission of abuse in some families is through a child's difficult behavior, to which impulsive parents respond inappropriately, and that children pursue later on as adults. In a previous section, we have seen that exposure to community and school violence represents risk factors in the transmission of violence. We have also noted earlier that spousal and child abuse more frequently occur in poor neighborhoods, along with many other forms of violence and antisocial behaviors. It is therefore quite likely that children who were abused *and* still live in a high-crime area will be more at risk of reproducing this pattern of violence in their own families than similar children who grow up in peaceful neighborhoods where visible violence is practically nonexistent.

Child Neglect by Parents

Neglect is a passive form of maltreatment. It involves not so much what parents do to their offspring but what they fail to do (Barnett, Manly, and Cicchetti, 1993). This includes failing to feed children, not clothing them adequately in cold weather, allowing toddlers to roam outside without supervision, failing to keep dangerous substances and firearms out of children's reach, and not sending them to school. At the more psychological level, neglecting parents fail to give their children a chance at getting an education or they neglect them emotionally by ignoring them most of the time and not interacting with them. Other parents fail to reprimand their children and their adolescents when they engage in antisocial or badly inappropriate behaviors.

Neglect is a situation that is less easily detected and less reported than abuse. For instance, adolescents are neglected when they are given all the freedom they want to experiment with sex, alcohol, drugs, and even criminal activities. Not surprisingly, many of these youths do not define their parents as neglectful; they often see them as being "understanding" and "cool." Parents may actually define themselves along the same lines. In fact, I heard one child advocate arguing that permissive parents "are simply respecting their children's rights." What was meant here were "rights" to engage in early sex, abusing drugs, and exploiting other children. Adolescents are far more likely to complain about supervisory than permissive parents, even though the former are more invested parents. Although child neglect, particularly at the adolescent stage, is less discussed than child abuse, it involves more children and it may carry consequences that well-intentioned persons do not think of linking to it.

Child neglect by parents is more common than child abuse (U.S. Department of Health and Human Services, 1996). It accounts for nearly half of child deaths related to maltreatment (McCurdy and Daro, 1994). Let's return to the 1993 survey reported by Gelles (1997:46): It contained 2,481,800 cases of child neglect divided into

1,368,200 cases of physical neglect
583,600 cases of emotional neglect
530,000 cases of educational neglect

In the Weise and Daro (1995) study of the cases reported by states and investigated in 1994, 507,640 were abjudicated as child neglect. All in all, over half of officially substantiated cases are of physical neglect.

Physical child neglect is related to parents' drug addiction and mental illness (DiLeonardi, 1993). Above all, it stems from **poverty** as well as the stressors and social isolation created by poverty (Pelton, 1994). Furthermore, when families are forced to remain in or move to a poor neighborhood, children are immediately at risk of physical and psychological harm as well as bad example. The dangers are so numerous that parents have to be extremely vigilant, which is not a normal state—for parents nor for children (Garbarino, Kostelny, and Dubrow, 1991). Therefore, it is easy for such parents to fail at being vigilant enough, although they may be doing everything they can. Pelton (1991:3) points out that poverty sets up a double standard of parenting "in that we implicitly ask impoverished parents to be *more* diligent in their supervisory responsibility than middle-class parents, because greater protection is required to guard children from the dangerous conditions of poverty than from the relatively safer conditions of middle-class homes and neighborhoods."

> *In the course of my fieldwork on divorce, one of the dilemmas I encountered as a researcher involved a deserted young mother of three children below age 8. Julie was, by all measures, an excellent mother and the children were well adjusted, happy, and pleasant. She was a recent arrival to Toronto and had no one who could help her. A strikingly attractive young woman, she had staved off poverty and solved child care during the day by becoming a highly paid stripper. She was ashamed of this but, without a high school diploma, she had had no other alternative. She had entirely childproofed the apartment, and left for work in the evening after the children were sound asleep to return at 3:00* A.M. *She was constantly terrified that something would happen to the children (particularly fire) or that they would be discovered alone and taken away from her. Alarmed, and with Julie's great relief at being helped, I immediately phoned another much older woman interviewee on welfare for whom babysitting at night was a great opportunity. Officially, and in one respect, Julie was a neglecting mother; serious harm could have come to the children. But all she needed was help. Indeed, the young family continued to do well and, by the last follow-up six years later, Julie had become a secretary after taking day classes. She was also seriously considering marriage.*

When parents are under stress or hold jobs that keep them away from home a great deal of the time, children go unsupervised. In other societies, leaving children home alone is not a problem. But this is often not the case in North America due to the potential risks involved. This, then, becomes child neglect unless parents supervise their children's activities by phone, for instance, and set strict rules of safety and behaviors to be followed during their absence. Dangers are less likely in a "good" area because the neighborhood offers fewer harmful activities for children to engage in and because the presence of other supervising parents helps (Kupersmidt et al., 1995). In a disadvantaged and dangerous area, however, such neglect can have serious consequences: It can lead to peer abuse, excessively premature motherhood, and drug addiction, for instance.

Too few studies document the negative effects of child neglect (Crouch and Milner, 1993). Children often suffer from abuse and neglect together or from physical and emotional neglect combined (Ney, Fung, and Wickett, 1994). This overlap makes it nearly impossible to attribute specific effects. The effects of neglect range from insecurity, to aggressiveness toward peers, behavior problems, and lack of school readiness (Eckenrode, Laird, and Doris, 1993). Neglectful families function less adequately than other families, in general. They often receive less social support from their immediate kin network, as was the case with Julie, and mothers perceive their children to be more difficult (Harrington et al., 1998). Yet, in spite of all these and their own problems, children who are neglected do not necessarily perceive their family differently than other children. They may have no basis for comparison, particularly if families in their environment are similar to theirs. In other instances, children do not wish to report neglect to social workers because they fear being placed out of their homes (Gable, 1998).

Is Child Abuse by Parents Increasing?

Child abuse was brought to the public's attention only in the 1960s by doctors who coined the concept of the *battered-child syndrome* (Kempe et al., 1962). It is therefore impossible to estimate how widespread a phenomenon it was before that date. Although others have registered an increase (Kaplan, Pelcovitz, and Labruna, 1999), according to Straus and Gelles (1990b), the period between 1975 and 1985 saw a decrease in the rate of child abuse. All estimates are probably somewhat lower than reality, but the increases recently apparent in statistics and social work caseload probably reflect the fact that society has become sensitized to child and wife battery as well as sexual exploitation, so that more cases are now **reported** than in the past. Therefore, social agencies are swamped by reported cases at a time when the rate of occurrence may be lower than in those days when no one spoke about the problem and it was more widely tolerated and practiced.

Demographic changes alone are consonant with the notion of decrease. Families have fewer children and especially fewer unplanned children than in the past. They are less burdened demographically and are less overcrowded. Parents, particularly mothers, spend fewer hours per week with their children, a situation that decreases the potential for child abuse—but not neglect. In the majority of the population, women now have their first child when they are older and more mature, and can put their children's needs ahead of theirs. Parents are more aware of some of the literature on child development, at least at the middle-class level, and may try to avoid any situation that could traumatize their children. Furthermore, parents certainly perceive that there is a greater likelihood that they could get caught and punished severely, including losing their children, and this perception may act as a deterrent.

However, there are three caveats here. Child abuse may increase when current violent children become parents later on. As well, child *neglect* may be on the rise. More children now live in families that are structurally burdened: They have only one parent and that parent often suffers from role strain and spends too many hours away from home employed. Second, one of the reasons that may have contributed to a decrease in child abuse—parental fears of being labeled as abusers—may have contributed to lower the authority of parents, in general, and have led to a reluctance on their part to intervene in some domains of their children's lives. This situation would leave youths unsupervised and unprotected, which are forms of neglect. Third, in the last few decades, there has been an upsurge in poverty and drug addiction among young mothers who then become unable to meet their small children's basic needs to the point where gross neglect becomes deadly.

CHILD SEXUAL ABUSE BY ADULTS

Sexual abuse is the commission of a sex act with a person who does not want it or is too young or immature to understand what is asked of or done to him or her. This broad definition involves inappropriate touching of erogenous zones as well as penetration for the perpetrator's sexual gratification.

Who Are and Where Are the Abusers?

The incidence of child sexual abuse is even more complex to estimate than that of physical abuse because of the element of victims' shame or ignorance, perpetrators' complete secrecy, and lack of visible physical symptoms. Overall, the consensus is that about one out of every four females is sexually abused before she reaches age 16. The median age for abuse is just under age 10. A late 1980s national survey revealed that 27 percent of the women and 16 percent of the men interviewed reported having been sexually abused as children (Finkelhor et al., 1990). Although no question was asked about this topic, the female students' autobiographies nevertheless revealed a range from 15 to 25 percent, depending on the year; rare instances surfaced among males.

Young girls are more often sexually abused within the family and boys outside of the family. Perpetrators within the family include stepfathers or mothers' boyfriends as well as older sisters' boyfriends more frequently than fathers. They are followed by siblings, grandparents, uncles, and cousins, as well as other relatives. Children are also sexually abused by fathers' friends; in foster care, day care, and group care institutions; by babysitters and coaches, as well as by peers. A majority of the perpetrators are males but victimization by a mother, a sister, or a female babysitter as well as a stepmother occasionally occurs.

In the students' autobiographies, not a single case of father/child incest came to light. It is possible that, if it occurred, students did not want to discuss it because it was too painful and private—but I doubt this because a great deal of other very sensitive material was divulged. Rather, such cases probably occur more in clinical than student samples, because this is a type of abuse that carries the most serious consequences (see also Hyman, 2000). In a clinical intervention for 50 adolescent girls who had been sexually abused, the fathers had been the offenders in 16 percent of the cases, whereas stepfathers and mothers' boyfriends had been in 32 percent of the cases (Morrison and Clavenna-Valleroy, 1998).

Furthermore, over half of these girls' mothers also reported having been sexually abused as a child, an extremely high rate that coincides with a high rate of these mothers' partners having abused their daughters. This double female victimization relates to other research findings showing that a proportion of women who are abused as girls marry partners who abuse them and may also abuse their daughters. The abuse carries from one generation to the next through the **transmission of victimization** from mother to daughter. In fact, children who live with an abused mother are over 12 times more likely to be sexually abused (McCloskey, Figueredo, and Koss, 1995).

Once again, children from low-income families are far more likely to be sexually victimized than others (Hollingsworth, 1998). This brings us back to Chapter 4, where we saw that a proportion of girls who become mothers by age 15 had been coerced into sex, and most were poor. In addition, Chapter 7 indicates that, in areas with a high level of poverty, children are less well supervised and thus more at risk of victimization. The presence of transient male adults in the family as well as overcrowding can also contribute to explain this difference in child sexual abuse by social class.

Consequences of Sexual Abuse for the Child

The consequences for the sexually abused child are generally analyzed within a psychogenic model of trauma: The more severe the abuse, the more negative the consequences (Finkelhor and Browne, 1985). Probably the most dramatic results follow **incest,** particularly if a father, mother, sibling, or grandfather is the culprit. The child is the most vulnerable within these situations because of daily availability, longer duration, and more extensive harm (Fischer and McDonald, 1998). Perhaps worse of all is the reality that the child is emotionally attached to her abuser and trusts him. Her abuser should be her protector and an agent of socialization but instead becomes her tormentor.

> *A student devoted many pages detailing the sexual abuse she began suffering at age 6 when her grandparents were babysitting her. Although her grandmother was nearby in the kitchen, the grandfather regularly coerced the child into performing oral sex in the family room because "it made him feel good and he used to tell me that I was his special girl." The poor little girl gagged and gagged and had to submit to further indecencies. "At the time I was convinced that I was special and he had me promise not to tell anyone so that I was essentially isolated and didn't know any better." As she grew up, she became more and more repulsed and begged her mother to find her another sitter. The abuse stopped when she was 10 years old. By early adolescence, she feared men, and by late adolescence, she had to seek therapy because sex disgusted her. She began suffering from depressive episodes. "I will never let any old man babysit my children."*

The conjugal unit and even the entire family can be destroyed by incest. Mothers may leave the perpetrator, although cases of mothers who turn against their daughters are not unheard of in clinical practice or among delinquents and street adolescents. In these instances, the daughter is seen as the trespasser within the conjugal subsystem, yet in reality, it is the father or boyfriend who initiated the coalition with the daughter. When mothers are not supportive or do not believe the daughters, the latter risk becoming very depressive, even during treatment (Morrison and Clavenna-Valleroy, 1998). Mothers who have been sexually abused themselves when they were children experience greater emotional distress than other mothers when they learn of their child's abuse. This maternal turmoil in itself reflects the long-term effects of child sexual abuse; these mothers are forced to relive their own abuse, which is very traumatic for them (Hiebert-Murphy, 1998).

The Life Course Perspective

Within a life course sociological framework, sexual abuse constitutes an **inappropriate sexual socialization.** One immediate consequence is that sexual contact with an adult focuses the child on his or her own sexuality from a less than healthy perspective very early on in life. The abuse constitutes a precocious initiation into sex. This life course brings a premature foreclosure in identity: The young girl begins to define herself in terms of sexuality and perhaps material gains. This opens the door to de-

FAMILY RESEARCH 14.1

In-Depth Interviews with Incest Perpetrators

Jane Gilgun (1995) recruited 11 incest perpetrators, 10 men and 1 woman, from two prisons and referrals from community-based treatment centers. Her goal was to use in-depth conversations with these informants to test hypotheses derived from the literature and to modify these hypotheses if they did not fit her data. Each informant was interviewed an average of six times for a total of 12 hours. The author proceeded through open-ended life history interviews.

Open-ended is the opposite of multiple-choice questions, which are *close-ended* and which do not allow respondents to add information and qualifiers to their responses. In contrast, open-ended interviews tend to be conversational in style and the researcher is free to probe issues in more depth. Again, this is not possible to do with a fixed questionnaire. With the respondents' consent, Gilgun tape-recorded and transcribed the contents of the interviews. She then analyzed the interviews to identify themes and variations within each theme. "My intent was to create as complete a picture of the moral discourse of the perpetrators in this study" (p. 270).

viant opportunities and closes the door to a normal life course. In turn, these "opportunities" may lead to early sexual relations with older peers and pregnancy. These children have more sexual partners among older peers, are at greater risk of contracting sexually transmitted diseases, and becoming homeless (Seidman, Mosher, and Aral, 1994). The same path may lead to early prostitution.

As Browning and Laumann (1997:557) explain it, adult sexual contact with a young girl "seems to provide access to sexuality without cultivating the emotional and cognitive skills to manage sexual experiences." The subsequent deviant behavior of the girls often results from the fact that their self-perception has been distorted as a result of the abuse (Dalenberg and Jacobs, 1994). Some of these young girls may grow up believing that others have the right to their body or that early sexuality is normal. As we have just seen in the previous case study, this is actually one of the *discourses* that child abusers hold with their victim. They explain that the act is "normal" or that the relationship is a "special" one to convince the girl to be victimized and later on to justify their behavior (Gilgun, 1995; see Family Research 14.1). Browning and Laumann (1997) find that, when child abuse does not give rise to an early risky sexual life, the women are less likely to experience adverse outcomes later in life. The authors conclude that the long-term effects of child sexual abuse are probably indirect, through the negative life course that it often generates; redirecting sexual trajectories at an early age might cancel most of the severe negative consequences of sexual abuse.

Overview of Consequences

Fortunately, most children who are sexually abused do not follow a deviant life course. Parental or peer support, personal strengths, as well as appropriate psychotherapy may be instrumental in resocializing children and helping them build their lives constructively. Nevertheless, many such children develop emotional and behavioral problems, both as children and later on as adults (Briere and Runtz, 1993). As illustrated in the student vignette, depression is a common sequela that can appear as early as adolescence

(Heger and Lytle, 1993). Sexual abuse may trigger problems in a child who may not otherwise be at risk or it may increase preexisting problems, even later on in life (Mancini, Van Ameringen, and Macmillan, 1995).

Many children grow up to forget or repress the abuse. For instance, Williams and Banyard (1997) followed up with men and women who, in the early 1970s, had been examined in a hospital emergency room for sexual abuse. After 17 years, 38 percent of the women and 55 percent of the men had no recollection of the abuse. Widom and Morris (1997) found similar numbers when they followed up court-substantiated instances of child sexual abuse that had taken place 20 years earlier. Perhaps the fact that the abuse has been forgotten means that, at the time, it had not been vested with tragic overtones by the child. Perhaps children who grow up to forget have particular resiliences. But, above all, as Browning and Laumann (1997) indicate, perhaps children who grow up to forget are also more likely to have had a normal life course.

SIBLING ABUSE

As is the case for child abuse, in general, sibling violence is divided between physical and sexual. (Psychological abuse was covered to some extent in Chapter 12.)

Sibling Violence

Straus, Gelles, and Steinmetz (1980) sampled 1,224 pairs of siblings ranging in age from 3 to 17 years. Pushing and shoving were the most frequently mentioned acts of physical violence at the less serious end of the continuum. At the other extreme, 14 percent reported having beaten up their sibling and 5 percent reported using a gun, either to threaten or to hurt. This survey took place in 1975. The level of violence among children, in general, has since risen substantially, and, because adult presence at home has diminished, these figures are probably higher today. The result that sister pairs were the least aggressive of all sibling pairs is probably still true today, but here as well, one can expect higher frequencies than in the 1970s, for violence perpetrated by girls is becoming more common.

The media, the public, professionals, and researchers have paid a great deal of attention to child abuse by parents when, actually, sibling abuse is far more common. This selective inattention to sibling abuse stems from widespread beliefs that it is simply part of growing up. It is considered normal (Gelles, 1997). Siblings hurt each other so frequently that no one pays much attention to it. Parents are very concerned, however, about sibling conflict (Kramer and Baron, 1995). They do not like the name calling, fighting, shoving, slapping, and hair pulling, but generally do not intervene (Perozynski and Kramer, 1999). Frequently heard comments from parents run like the following:

- "It drives me crazy; they're always at it."
- "I'm always afraid they'll really hurt each other one day, but it's better to let them resolve their problems on their own."
- "Parents shouldn't interfere in their children's lives; they have to learn on their own."

This type of reasoning leads to the conclusion that sibling violence is not "real" violence that one has to prevent (Gelles, 1997). These parents' beliefs about nonintervention are reinforced by the lack of professional concern. Because of this widespread **adult tolerance,** children are far less likely to report sibling abuse to their parents or other authority figures than is the case for abuse by adults. The stronger of the two siblings is likely to be encouraged on this path because he or she benefits from advantages over the other and no one intervenes. As a result, later on, adults who are asked about victimization in their past often fail to equate sibling beatings with assault. Once more, this leads to the underrepresentation of sibling violence in official surveys (Bachman, 1994). Furthermore, very little is actually known about the developmental consequences of everyday sibling abuse; nor is it known how it affects their relationship as adults.

Indications are that children who abuse their siblings often have poor relationships with their peers (Hetherington, 1988). Some children have learned to be violent and repeat this pattern in a multiplicity of contexts with others of their age. From a personality theory perspective, it could be that children who are predisposed to aggressiveness are likely to form conflictual relationships both with peers and siblings. A third explanation advances that the stress that children experience in their peer relations spills over into their sibling relations, or vice versa. One can also ask whether adolescents who abuse their siblings will also be more likely to abuse their dates, spouses, and children later on.

Sibling Sexual Abuse

The following student quote serves as an introduction to a topic that is also frequently overlooked: sibling sexual abuse or sibling incest, which is probably more common than parent/child incest (O'Brien, 1991):

> *"The most painful time in my life is the period between the ages of 6 to 10: my brother was six years older than me and my parents counted on him to babysit me. . . . At first I did not understand what was happening to me, however difficult this is to explain with hindsight, but my brother got me into performing intimate acts for him and later on after a year of this his best friend used to come over and they would both share me. This is all I can write here because this is very painful. This went on for two years until I became strong enough to resist and threaten to tell my parents which of course I never did because I was too ashamed. At school I was ashamed too because I saw this boy. . . . Now I harbor intensely negative feelings about my brother who seems to have forgotten all about these years. . . . It would kill my parents if I told them. I went into therapy when I got to this university and have come to terms with the situation, which is not to say that I accept it but I can live with it and go on with my life. But I know that I will be very very careful with my own children later on in life. Very careful."*

Sibling incest is a predominantly brother-to-sister initiated or coerced phenomenon, but incest between siblings of the same sex also occurs (Smith and Israel, 1997). Ascherman and Safier had placed the incidence of sibling incest at about 13 percent in 1990. A 1982 study found that it had occurred in 60 percent of psychiatric outpatients (Bess and Janssen, 1982). As is the case for all types of sexual abuse, sibling incest is found more in clinical than in survey populations. This would indicate that sibling incest results in serious psychological consequences for many abused brothers and sisters.

Sibling sexual abuse may perhaps occur more among dysfunctional families where other problems already exist, or among families that simply cannot supervise their children because of various burdens (DiGiorgio-Miller, 1998). It can also result from the way parental roles are carried out. Extramarital affairs, open sexuality between parents that children observe, for instance, are related to sibling incest (Smith and Israel, 1997): Children may copy what they see. A lack of parental supervision and involvement is especially evident in many of these families.

O'Brien (1991) compared adolescent sex offenders whose victims were siblings to other adolescent sex offenders whose victims were young peers outside of the family. Adolescents who had sexually abused a sibling had done it more often and for a much longer period of time (one year) than the adolescents who had abused a child outside of the family, because of the availability of the little brother or sister at home (as illustrated in the student quote). As well, their sibling victim was much younger, between 4 and 9 years of age, than the victim of other boys. This young age allowed for greater accessibility, because a small child can more easily be coerced by an adolescent than an older child. The frequency of the abuse resulted in nearly half of the sibling cases progressing to anal or vaginal penetration. This occurred rarely when the victim was not a sibling, for it is easier to progress to penetration within the context of long-term availability and within the secrecy of home.

In families of sibling incest, O'Brien uncovered a phenomenon we have already encountered for child sexual abuse by a father or a stepfather, where both mother and daughter have been abused: (1) Parents of incest perpetrators, particularly mothers, had been more often abused sexually as children than was the case among the parents of the other sex offenders and (2) 42 percent of the incestuous offenders had been abused sexually, although generally outside the family. Thus, in these families, many parents had themselves been vulnerable during their childhood. Furthermore, some of their sons had also been sexually abused, and of those many had gone on to abuse their siblings. The transmission from one generation to the next was one of *vulnerability* for sexual victimization in many of these families.

PEER ABUSE

As we have seen earlier with Figure 14.1, older children are now more likely to be abused by their peers than by any family member. Examples of cruel, destructive, and even violent peer behaviors are mentioned in the newscasts on a weekly basis, and in some cases, the results are deadly. Peer abuse is a situation that severely depletes a child's social capital outside the home and often endangers the development of his or her human capital. It also affects family dynamics.

How Common Is Peer Abuse?

Child and adolescent abuse at home has been estimated at around 3 percent, slightly more or less depending on the study (Finkelhor and Dziuba-Leatherman, 1994). In contrast, a conservative estimate might be that a minimum of 20 percent of all children are seriously abused by peers during their young lives—and this does not refer to normal conflicts, disagreements, and teasing (Eder, 1991). Moreover, recent surveys reported in the news media, both in Canada and the United States, present much higher estimates, often as high as 75 percent. Depending on what is included in the definition, Espelage and colleagues (1996) found a 90 percent victimization rate among adolescents. Such a rate implies that most adolescents are both victims and abusers, although not necessarily at the same time.

In my research on autobiographies, students recalled far more abusive peer treatment that they described as having had detrimental and *lasting* consequences on their development than was the case for parental treatment. That is, these experiences had affected them for several years, often up to the present time (Ambert, 1994a). Furthermore, there was an increasing trend from one cohort to another throughout the years. This result, corroborated by more recent studies, is startling, considering the often single-minded focus of child welfare professionals and researchers on abuse by parents, while neglecting what is becoming the most salient source of psychological misery among youths—peer conflict and maltreatment (Ambert, 1995).

Consequences and Context of Peer Abuse

In the autobiographies, as well as in magazines (*Time* and *Newsweek,* May 1999), one reads about students who had been happy and well adjusted, but quite rapidly began deteriorating psychologically, sometimes to the point of becoming physically ill and incompetent in school or even delinquent. For many, the impact of peer maltreatment leads to avoidance of school (Kochenderfer and Ladd, 1996). In other instances, it contributes to poor school performance (Hodges, Malone, and Perry, 1997) as well as anxiety and depression (Egan and Perry, 1998). As one student recalls it, even school work can be disrupted, as young victims become too distraught to focus on anything else and often too fearful:

> *"The years between 12 and 16 were the worst in my life. I was surely the most unpopular boy at my school. There was a group of boys with some girls too who used to pick on me and no one would have dared be nice to me after that. They'd steal my lunch, force me to hand over my pocket money, they'd laugh and snicker when I passed by. . . . It got to the point where I felt so terrorized that I couldn't even pay attention to what the teacher said in class and my marks suffered and of course my parents weren't too sympathetic because they hadn't a clue that this was going on until I got really sick with chronic stomach problems, but by then the years had gone by and my life had been ruined. I feel insecure to this day and always sit at the back to avoid being noticed."*

Studies of peer abuse should go beyond the matter of dwelling into *victims'* characteristics. This is akin to inquiring about the personal life of rape victims rather than prosecuting the rapist for his actions. Nowadays, a child can become the victim of peer abuse through no fault of his or her own or of his or her family (Garbarino, 1999). In other words, peer abuse is not merely a psychological situation created by a victim and an abuser because of two sets of personality characteristics. Nor it is merely a consequence of parenting practices, as often described in the literature (Finnegan, Hodges, and Perry, 1998).

Rather, peer abuse is influenced by the clique structure of schools and by what children have learned elsewhere, including the media—whether television or video games. For instance, Espelage and colleagues (1996) find that adolescent bullies watch more violent television, are more difficult at home, spend less time with adults, and have more exposure to gang activities than other children. A third had a single parent, and another third lived with a stepparent. Thus, it would seem that serious bullies escape adult influence and control. Their family structure is burdened in terms of its ability to provide supervision. Instead, they surround themselves with negative, virtual (as in videos), and real role models. At a more macrosociological level, the **culture of violence** in the society at large is implicated along with reduced social control. Peer abuse is, above all, a cultural phenomenon and a reflection of a **lack of a functional community** (Coleman and Hoffer, 1987). In a culture that rejects violence and that exerts effective social control over its children, even aggressive children will have few opportunities to indulge their inclinations, and the latter are likely to desist for lack of reinforcement.

Peer Sexual Harassment and Abuse

Sexual harassment, mainly by boys toward girls, is a particularly pernicious form of abuse that may begin early (Stein, 1995), as explained by a student:

> *"The boys of my elementary school were rude and disgusting and held no respect for any of the girls. They felt that whenever they wanted to, they could grab you wherever they wanted. In addition to this they loved to fabricate stories about girls and what they were able to do to them. . . . I'd walk down the aisle to the teacher's desk and while the teachers turned their head someone would grab me at the closest location."*

Peer sexual harassment generally goes undetected, may even be approved of by boys' parents ("he's *all* boy"), and some girls may be led to believe that it is flattering ("he likes you, silly") or simply the normal price one has to pay for popularity. It is the forecaster of date and partner abuse. Many adolescents and even preadolescent girls are coerced into sexuality by male peers. The degree of coercion ranges from outright rape to subtle pressure in a relationship where the girl is afraid to lose her date. Adolescents are particularly at risk when they score high on scales of conformity to peers (Small and Kerns, 1993): They become vulnerable because they need their peers' approval more than a less conforming adolescent does. While many girls are not raped, they nevertheless do not want sexual intercourse but comply because of peer pressure (Laumann, 1996). Some of this pressure comes from female peers who may already be sexually active or pretend to be. This creates a *cultural climate* that is very potent; as a result, a teenager eager for peer acceptance will follow suit.

Victimization from severe forms of sexual abuse, rape, or coercion into unwanted sexuality is more likely to occur to adolescents who live in neighborhoods that have a high rate of social problems and whose parents cannot supervise or protect them adequately. Thus, girls from single-parent families, particularly when they are disadvantaged, as well as those who have parents who suffer from alcoholism, for instance, are at a higher risk of sexual victimization, in general, including by peers (Moore, Nord, and Peterson, 1989). Peer sexual abuse, as is the case for peer abuse, in general, is very much a **crime of opportunity.** It is done by and occurs to children and adolescents while they are unsupervised by adults, whether at school, at home, in an abandoned building, or in the back seat of a car. Peer sexual abuse is the result of media influences and disengagement from adults, including teachers and parents—in other words, a generalized lack of an effective community.

ABUSE OF PARENTS BY CHILDREN

Two additional types of familial abuse exist: ill treatment of parents by their young children, particularly adolescents, and the abuse of elder parents by their adult offspring. The literature is lacking concerning both topics; yet, the matter of parent abuse by children may be timely because children and adolescents are, on average, less disciplined, more aggressive, and exhibit more behavioral problems than before (Ambert, 1997a). One could well argue that parents can easily become victims of aggressive and out-of-control children, particularly in decades when respect for parents is less valued than in the past, even by parents themselves (Alwin, 1986), and when peer groups, often of the deviant type, have become more influential.

Physical Abuse of Parents by Children and Adolescents

The relative absence of research on this topic is perplexing in view of the fact that people often witness verbal abuse of parents by children and particularly by adolescents. One can also witness physical assault of mothers by children as young as age 4 or 5. These observations are made in public areas—such as sidewalks, parks, and subway platforms—for everyone to see, a sign that children are no longer sensitized against this behavior and that they do not have to fear public condemnation in this respect.

> *I recently observed the following scene in a subway train. A well-dressed mother, age 25 to 30, walked in with an equally well-groomed little boy, age 4 or 5. The little boy was screaming at his mother at the top of his lungs:*
>
> B: *You hurt my feelings!*
> M: *(bending down to soothe him) I'm so sorry, honey, I apologize.*
> B: *I hate you, I hate you! (He was red in the face with rage and was hitting his mother with his fists.)*
> M: *(softly) Again, I'm sorry honey; it won't happen again.*
> B: *You're stupid (he kicked her with his booted foot).*
>
> *The mother had tears in her eyes. The boy was not in the least bit deterred by the staring disapproval from passengers as he continued punching and yelling.*

Moreover, my fieldwork for two separate studies has revealed mothers who were regularly assaulted by their adolescents, and even bore marks of recent beatings. The mothers were single and poor; one was in a wheelchair.

Several studies in the United States and Great Britain have obtained self-reports by adolescents of child-to-parent abuse, with a trend for mothers to be a somewhat more frequent recipient of physical violence than fathers (U.S. Department of Justice, 1994). In Massachusetts, between September 1992 and June 1993, nearly one-third of all restraining court orders issued were requested by parents against children, mainly by mothers against sons (reported in Gelles, 1997). In a 1996 British Crime Survey, 1 in 10 mothers reported having been assaulted by her children—some of these offspring were over age 18 (Mirrlees-Black, Mayhew, and Percy, 1996).

Among American university students, some mutuality of parent and young adult violence exists. There is some continuity of behavior from parents who have physically maltreated their children to the children who then maltreat parents (Browne, 1998). But, overall, there is more discontinuity than continuity across generations. Gelles (1997:112) points out that clinical observations of abusive adolescents reveal deficiencies in the authority structure of families whereby adolescents have been granted too much control and decision-making power. There may perhaps be a connection between permissive parenting and abuse of parents by their offspring.

Abuse of Elderly Parents by Adult Children

Women outlive men, and one of the consistent findings on elder abuse is that most victims are women—old mothers (Whittaker, 1995). Until now, the study of elder abuse has emphasized the dependent elderly's caregivers: The line of reasoning is that the frustrated and burdened caregiver lashes out at the frail dependent parent (Steinmetz, 1993). In addition, elderly parents are abused by an adult child who lives with them because of his or her own dependency (Wolf and Pillemer, 1989). In that case, the adult child depends on the parent financially or for shelter, because he or she is unemployed or is mentally delayed, physically challenged, or emotionally disturbed. Indeed, after discharge from hospital care, 85 percent of unmarried adult children who are mentally ill move in with their elderly parents (Greenberg, Seltzer, and Greenlay, 1993). The potential for abuse certainly exists (Lefley, 1997). Hence, Pillemer (1985) believes that research may have placed too much emphasis on the dependence of the elderly as a source of abuse and that those elderly who have a dependent and physically stronger spouse or child living with them should be considered at risk.

It is difficult to know whether it is sons or daughters who abuse their elderly parents the most. Daughters are more frequent caregivers; consequently, they have more opportunities to be abusive as well as more frustration to vent. They fit Steinmetz's (1993) theory better than sons. For their part, more sons live with their elderly parents due to sons' lack of independence. Males have been socialized to be more aggressive than females and are often not as emotionally attached to their parents as females are. These factors could contribute to more parental abuse by sons. One study in Florida discovered that males were more likely to practice physical abuse, whereas females were more likely to practice elderly neglect (Miller and Dodder, 1989).

Complicating the issue is the existence of verbal and material forms of abuse. The latter are motivated by greed, personal debts or addictions, or a spouse's or children's demands. It includes siphoning off parental revenues, walking out with parents' possessions, or controlling the parents' house (Korbin, Anetzberger, and Austin, 1995). Medical abuse is at times perpetrated when the caregiving adult child does not seek assistance for a sick or suffering elderly parent—to safeguard the entirety of the inheritance or precipitate its occurrence.

Elderly parents who are abused by their adult children rarely report the situation. They feel ashamed and may fear retaliation. Furthermore, they are often socially isolated and have no one in whom to confide.

Abuse of elderly parents is a relatively easy act to commit and can have even less social visibility than abuse of school-age children. The elderly who are most at risk are often socially isolated: They are no longer connected to their social networks, such as church, work, or even friends. No one may notice the abuse, and physicians who see bruises may be told that the senior person fell, which occurs quite often in old age. (The parallel with small children is obvious here.) Above all, elderly parents may be less likely to report the abuse than would a maltreated adolescent or even a child. Actually, perhaps as few as 5 percent report it (Tatara, 1993). Abused elderly parents may be ashamed of their situation and, at any rate, they may have no one else to turn to for help. An attempt to report the abuse might fail and bring retaliation. Moreover, while abused children grow up and may eventually denounce their parents, the elderly parent dies with the secret.

Little research exists on elder abuse among various ethnic and racial groups (Griffin, 1994). Comparisons between groups is important in view of the fact that black seniors, particularly grandmothers, take needy children and grandchildren into their homes more than whites do. Thus, at least in theory, they are at a higher risk of abuse, not only from their children but also from their grandchildren.

Whether the model of the intergenerational transmission of violence is a valid explanatory framework for elder abuse is under debate. At any rate, this perspective does not address larger sociological issues (Whittaker, 1995). Some of these issues relate to the double fact that, among the elderly, women are poorer than men and most of their caregivers are other women, generally their daughters. Both sets of women belong to two generations with a different history of employment and dependency, yet both suffer from structural gender inequalities.

CONCLUSIONS: THE LARGER CONTEXT OF FAMILY VIOLENCE

The literature on neglect and particularly physical and sexual abuse is one largely oriented toward the psychological causes of maltreatment of a family member by another. One cannot deny that these causes are present. However, from a sociological perspective, violence within the family is a reflection of violence within society, including its media. To begin with, difficult and out-of-control temperaments that lead to abusive situations would not be so prevalent in a society where civility, altruism, and a sense of communal responsibility were the valued forms of behavior. Second, within such a civilized and less competitive-aggressive environment, even impulsive parents, spouses, and children would learn to respect others rather than maltreat them.

Other larger sociocultural forces that are implicated in family violence include discrimination and poverty as well as the fact that the family is the only institution that is single-handedly responsible for the well-being of its dependent members—whether children, the disabled, or the frail elderly. The family fulfills too many functions and particularly too many caregiving functions while it receives too little social support from the very complex, expensive, and competitive society in which it lives. In other words, we have come full circle and these remarks return us to the discussion on multiple family functions in Chapter 2.

SUMMARY

1. Violence and abuse are negative family dynamics that are greatly affected by the sociocultural context in which families live. Verbal and psychological abuse of partners is not as easy to measure as physical abuse is. It has also been less researched. It is quite salient in music videos favored by adolescents. This form of abuse is often tailored to fit partners' vulnerabilities.
2. Few incidents of courtship violence are reported to authorities, and many youths consider such incidents as a normal part of the dating process. Both sexes participate in this phenomenon; however, women sustain most of the injuries. Most of the studies of the origins of dating violence fail to consider extrafamilial influences. Date rape is the ultimate form of violence.
3. At the spousal level, along with cultural influences, partner physical violence is an issue of power and it covers a wide range of acts from mild to lethal. Alcohol is often involved in domestic violence but it is also used as a convenient excuse. Cohabiting couples have the highest rate of partner violence. Poor couples, particularly those living in dangerous neighborhoods, have a higher risk of partner violence. Domestic violence among oppressed minorities may have causes that do not exist among whites. Same-sex-partner violence is as much a matter of power and control as it is in heterosexual couple violence, except that gender is not an issue. The rate of violence approximates that among heterosexual couples.
4. Several million children witness interparental violence annually. On average, children of abused mothers have more behavioral and psychological problems. How-

ever, the intergenerational transmission of violence depends on many variables, and only a minority of these children grow up to repeat the pattern in their own families. Factors that contribute to transmission include high levels of parental violence as well as exposure to community and school violence.

5. Child and adolescent abuse has been estimated at around 3 percent of households. Physical punishment is a much debated issue in this context and occurs occasionally in most families. Children who have been or are abused, on average, have more behavioral problems, particularly in terms of aggressiveness. Abused children are often surrounded by a climate of violence. Child abuse and neglect are more common in low-income families, especially in areas with a high concentration of poverty and violence. Approximately 30 percent of abused children grow up to repeat this pattern with their own offspring. Many variables enter into the risk of transmission, including the meaning attached to it by the children themselves, additional parental characteristics of an antisocial nature, and general environment. Parental stress often precipitates abuse, including that caused by a child's disruptive behaviors.
6. Child neglect is more widespread and involves not so much what parents do to their offspring but what they fail to do. It ranges from malnutrition to failure to supervise properly, and is not as easily detected nor as reported as abuse. Physical neglect is particularly related to poverty, and its consequences include early motherhood as a result of a lack of supervision. Neglectful families often function less adequately than other families, in general, receive less social support, and mothers perceive their children to be more difficult.
7. There may have been a decrease in child abuse by parents in the last two decades of the twentieth century, although there has been an increase in reporting. However, child neglect has probably increased.
8. Child sexual abuse tends to occur more within the family among girls and outside the family among boys. Approximately 25 percent of women and over 15 percent of men report having been sexually abused as children. A proportion of women who are abused as girls marry partners who abuse them or their daughters. Again, children from low-income families are at a higher risk of sexual abuse. The consequences for the child depend on the nature of the abuse and who the perpetrator is. Father/daughter incest is probably the most damaging; it may also destroy the family fabric. Sexual contact with an adult prematurely focuses the child on his or her sexuality, and this focus in turn often initiates a series of events in the life course of the child that deviate from the norm of other young persons' life courses. Sexual abuse constitutes an inappropriate sexual socialization. Most children who are sexually abused do not follow a deviant life course and many grow up to forget about it entirely.
9. Sibling violence ranges from mild to severe and is fairly common. Relatively little attention has been paid to it, and parents rarely intervene even though they are concerned. Children rarely report it. Sibling incest has been estimated to be at about 13 percent and is predominantly a brother-to-sister situation. It is reported more in clinical than in survey populations: It may happen more in families that are dysfunctional in other respects. Adolescents who abuse a sibling are more

likely to do it for a longer period and to have full intercourse than those who abuse nonrelated children.

10. Abuse of children by their peers is probably the most common form of abuse in society. It carries many negative consequences and can be explained by sociocultural factors. Peer sexual abuse also arises out of the society's general cultural climate of violence and exploitation of women.
11. A number of children and adolescents assault their parents, particularly their mothers, both verbally and physically, but this topic is not given much attention in the research. Among the elderly who are abused by their adult children, most are mothers. Some elderly are abused by their frustrated caregiving children, but perhaps even more are by children who depend on them because they have various disabilities. Furthermore, verbal as well as material forms of elderly parent abuse exist; the latter may be motivated by greed. Elderly abuse is a relatively easy act to commit and may be less reported than child abuse.
12. Violence within the family is a reflection of violence in the society at large. It also results from the fact that the family is burdened with functions for which it receives little societal support.

KEY CONCEPTS AND THEMES

Adult tolerance, p. 421
Alcohol, p. 405
Antisocial parents, p. 413
Cohabiting couples, p. 406
Combination of factors, p. 412
Community and school violence, p. 409
Concentration of violence, p. 411
Control, p. 411
Crime of opportunity, p. 424
Culture of violence, p. 424
Disadvantaged neighborhoods, pp. 406, 411
Discourse, p. 419
Ethnicity, p. 406
Familialized, p. 401
Inappropriate sexual socialization, p. 418
Incest, p. 418
Intergenerational transmission, p. 408
Lack of civility, p. 403
Lack of a functional community, p. 424
Life course, p. 418
Low income, p. 411
Media, p. 402
Parents' antisocial orientation, p. 413
Patriarchal dominance, p. 401
Physical punishment, p. 411
Poverty, p. 411
Power, pp. 401, 404
Psychologized, p. 401
Reported cases, p. 416
Risk factor, p. 402
Social selection, p. 407
Transmission of victimization, p. 417
Vulnerability, p. 403

STUDY AND REVIEW QUESTIONS

1. What are some of the individual motives for partner/spousal abuse?
2. The intergenerational transmission of violence and abuse is a recurrent theme in this chapter. What are the salient findings overall?
3. What role does culture play in partner abuse?
4. Cohabiting couples have high rates of partner violence. Explain why this is so, using information from this chapter and perhaps Chapter 5.
5. Is partner abuse less frequent and different among same-sex couples? Why or why not?

6. Various types of abuse are related to low-income families living in disadvantaged neighborhoods. Which types of abuse occur and how can you explain this relationship?
7. What are some of the consequences of interparental violence on children?
8. Make a case for and against physical punishment being a form of child abuse.
9. Why is permissiveness a form of child or adolescent neglect?
10. In families in which a child is sexually abused by a father, father figure, or older sibling, what indirect form of intergenerational transmission often exists?
11. Discuss child sexual abuse from a life course perspective.
12. Why is sibling abuse overlooked?
13. What factors encourage peer abuse?
14. Why does abuse of elderly parents have low social visibility?

SUGGESTED READINGS

Briere, J., Berliner, L., Bulkey, J. A., Jenny, C., and Reid, T. (Eds.). 1996. *The APSAC handbook on child maltreatment.* Thousand Oaks, CA: Sage. This collection of articles presents the latest facts on child abuse and neglect, on abusers, as well as on interventions.

Cardarelli, A. P. (Ed). 1997. *Violence between intimate partners.* Boston: Allyn and Bacon. This collection of research articles focuses on violence in marriage, cohabitation, same-sex partners, and during courtship.

Gelles, R. J. 1997. *Intimate violence in families* (3rd. ed.). Thousand Oaks, CA: Sage. This text updates the information on various aspects of family violence, from spousal abuse to child sexual abuse.

Gelles, R. J., and Loseke, D. (Eds.). 1993. *Current controversies on family violence.* Newbury Park, CA: Sage. Several scholars present research as well as reviews of the literature on partner and child physical violence.

Renzetti, C. M., and Miley, C. H. (Eds.). 1996. *Violence in gay and lesbian domestic partnerships.* New York: Harrington Park Press. Several studies and reviews of the literature form the contents of this book.

Sanday, P. R. 1996. *A woman scorned: Acquaintance rape on trial.* New York: Doubleday. This book provides historical perspectives as well as recent information on acquaintance rape, and includes material pertaining to student populations.

SUGGESTED WEBLINKS

Child Abuse Prevention Network provides resources for the prevention of child abuse and neglect and addresses their causes at the familial and community level. **<http://child.cornell.edu>.**

Children's Bureau Express is a website disseminated by the National Clearinghouse of Child Abuse and Neglect on behalf of the Children's Bureau. **<http://www.calib.com/cbexpress>**

Domestic Violence Resources offers advocacy and information but not clinical advice. This practical and research-oriented site also includes addresses of shelters. **<http://www.Silcom.com/~paladin/madv>**

Let's Stop Domestic Violence provides many sites of interest on the topic, both research and personal. **<http://famvi.com>**

CHAPTER 15

Family Dynamics and Emotional, Behavioral, and Delinquency Problems

OUTLINE

Parents Who Suffer from Depression
What Are the Causes of Depression?
Consequences of Parental Depression for Children
The Research Focus on Depressed Mothers
A Critique of Maternal Causality

Alcoholism in the Family
What Are the Causes of Alcoholism?
Consequences of Parental Alcoholism for Children

Children with Behavioral Problems
What Are the Causes of Behavioral Problems?
Environmental Factors in Behavioral Problems
The Life Course Perspective
Disruption of Parenting Skills: Interactional Dynamics
The Role of Children's Faulty Perceptions
Gendered Family Dynamics: Mothers and Difficult Children

Delinquency: Family Dynamics
The Life Course Perspective on Delinquency
What Are the Causes of Delinquency?
Inadequate Parental Supervision
School, Peers, and Neighborhood Influences
Delinquency and Family Dynamics
General Impact on Parents
Parental Social Isolation
Mothers Are More Affected

How Relatives and Experts Affect Family Dynamics
Relatives and Friends
Professional Authority over Parents
Professionals' Social Constructions
The Blaming and Marginalization of Parents

Conclusions: Family Vulnerability

Summary
Key Concepts and Themes
Study and Review Questions
Suggested Readings
Suggested Weblinks

"My dad is burning rubber," is Nick's sarcastic description of his 45-year-old father when he is in the manic stage of bipolar depression. Mr. Driscoll and his wife of 20 years have two adolescent children, Nick, age 15, and Nicole, age 13. When Mr. Driscoll is "high," the family is on "red alert," Nick explains, because he is so agitated that he can't stand still, can't go to work, and has to be watched around the clock—otherwise, "who knows what he'll do?" Nick resents his father and stays away from home as much as possible: "I party and hang out." His grades at school are not that great, his teachers are weary of him, and he gets into fights with his peers. Nicole feels sorry for her father, although his mood swings frighten her: "But when he's OK, he's real OK and he really loves us, and he's better than other fathers. I know he feels guilty about his trips after and then he gets real depressed." Nicole is a pleasant adolescent, well liked, with good grades at school, but is somewhat sad and a bit withdrawn. The mother, a physiotherapist, alternates between love and hate for her husband: "He isn't much of a husband because he is such a

responsibility. It's like having a third out-of-control child at times. But when he's well, things are relatively calm for about three months and we can catch up on all the bills that have piled up because he can't work." She is a lonely woman: "If I didn't have Nicole and my work, I'd just let go and have a nervous breakdown."

The Kowalevski family has a different problem. The only son had been "hard to control" since early childhood: He was given to violent temper tantrums, which led his parents to join a parent-effectiveness training group. The group helped the parents set some limits on Mike and he improved steadily for a few years. "But, you know, there has always been something lurking, ready to happen to him, so we'd been cautiously optimistic." Mike was arrested for shoplifting at age 12. "We thought the shoplifting was an accident, but apparently we hadn't been careful enough because he had been doing it for months we learned." Six months after the first incident, he was arrested for trying to steal a car. "Actually he did break into it but was caught. Too inexperienced, I guess." The Kowalevskis sought psychiatric counseling. It helped only temporarily. From ages 13 to 16, Mike was arrested six times and spent a year altogether in a detention center, "where he added more tricks to his trade." The father has given up on the 16-year-old and does not "even want to see him; I am so ashamed of him, he makes me sick." His mother is torn between feelings of responsibility, wanting to help, and yet "running away to the Bahamas and forget that I ever had a child like him. It's horrible, we just don't have a life. Even our friends are uncomfortable in our presence because they never know what we went through the week before and are afraid to ask." The couple even experienced a difficult period in their relationship: They began fighting about Mike and blaming each other. The couple sought counseling and are now close and mutually supportive. They go out as much as they can, "but Mike's always in the back of our mind. We constantly ask ourselves, How long is this going to last?"
(Source: my study on parents of difficult adolescents)

These two families are facing problems that are very different, yet produce many similar results: Tension. Insecurity. Fatigue. Never-ending worries. Social isolation. Recourse to professionals for help. Feelings of being caught in an impossible situation. Needs to escape that cannot be realized. Family dynamics that stop and go. These are the realities of this chapter, which introduces the reader to the psychiatric, clinical, and delinquency literature relevant to family dynamics. The clinical data and theories presented here are framed within a sociological perspective that includes social constructionist, interactionalist, and feminist analyses. This combined sociological framework is complemented with an emphasis on the partly genetic aspect of some of the afflictions herein covered.

PARENTS WHO SUFFER FROM DEPRESSION

Depression takes two forms. The most serious, as in the case of Mr. Driscoll in the vignette, is manic or bipolar depression and, when extreme, is a psychosis. Psychoses involve a loss of contact with reality. Bipolar depression is characterized by shifts over time from a depressed state to a highly excited (manic) state, or the predominance of such a state. In the manic phase, the afflicted persons are hyperactive, elated, at times loud and aggressive, may go on ruinous shopping sprees, and may need to be sedated to prevent harm to themselves or to others. In the depressed mode, the persons feel hopeless, helpless, alone, and may progress to suicidal thoughts.

Unipolar depression, generally known as *depression,* contains the elements of hopelessness and extreme sadness but does not generally involve a cognitive break with reality. It is not a psychosis, even though it can be quite severe and can lead to suicide. Depression is often reactive; that is, it is a response to environmental stressors. The lifetime risk for depression is estimated at between 10 to 30 percent, depending on the severity of the symptoms included in the definition (Kendler et al., 1992).

What Are the Causes of Depression?

Manic depression rarely occurs before puberty or even during adolescence and is partly hereditary (Harrington et al., 1993). For instance, adult identical twins' concordance or similarity for manic depression is over 65 percent, compared to 14 to 20 percent among fraternal twins. In general, depression occurring without obvious precipitants or environmental causes implies that the illness is more largely genetic than when causal environmental factors are present. Other relatives are then at a greater chance of being affected by the condition. When parents' manic depression began early in life (late adolescence and early twenties), this is a sign of stronger genetic origins, and their children run a higher probability of being afflicted than those of parents whose illness started later (Weissman et al., 1987).

In contrast, unipolar depression can occur in adolescence and even among very young children. The genetic influence is more modest or even absent (McGuffin and Katz, 1993). However, there are some indications that many individuals select themselves into situations that have a high probability of producing stressors (Kendler, Karkowski, and Prescott, 1999). Depression can result from rejection, social isolation, the loss of a significant other or social status, failures, and general distress. During difficult social and cultural transitions, the lifetime occurrence of depression may rise, even though the gene pool remains constant (Nigg and Goldsmith, 1994:349).

Consequences of Parental Depression for Children

Parents who suffer from *severe* depression place their children at a double disadvantage. First, these children are at greater **genetic risk.** Second, the children have a higher probability of suffering from a **stressful familial environment** created by their parents' illness, in part via detrimental parenting practices. Moreover, when one spouse is depressed, the chance of *marital disharmony* increases, which, in turn, impacts negatively on children, and particularly on children who are already at risk because of their own temperament. Cowan, Cowan, and Schulz (1996) report that, when a husband is depressed, his wife tends to be supportive and maintains a high level of care for their children. But when a wife is depressed, husbands are often hostile and rejecting; they do not necessarily step in to compensate for the care of their children.

For some children, another route from parental depression to negative outcomes originates from learning and developmental theories. It resides in an **inappropriate socialization** and consequent life course. Children who live with depressed persons are exposed to a certain type of body language and reaction to situations they may learn and adopt (Cummings and Cicchetti, 1990). They may simply model "acting depressed." This learned behavior may, in turn, deprive them of social skills; consequently, other children and teachers may not readily accept them or understand them. Social isolation results, along with the loss of important opportunities in life, including promotions. In other words, the *life course* of these children has been derailed and they may actually become depressed in their later years.

The Research Focus on Depressed Mothers

With very few exceptions (Ballard and Davies, 1996; Deater-Deckard et al., 1998), the large literature on the effects of parental depression on children focuses on mothers (Cummings and Davies, 1994). This emphasis stems from the **social construction of women** as children's psychological mainstay. Several studies remark on seriously depressed mothers' lack of childrearing skills (Zahn-Waxler et al., 1990), whereas others find no disturbance in the mother/child relationship (see Mowbray et al., 1995). Radke-Yarrow (1990) finds that depressed mothers tend to avoid confrontation with their children; thus, when children are not compliant, they can continue being difficult because no one steps in to set limits. When mothers are severely depressed, daughters are far less compliant than girls whose mothers are not depressed. The research methods utilized by Radke-Yarrow's team are particularly interesting and are presented in Family Research 15.1. Some of her key findings follow:

- Depressed mothers exhibit negative moods for longer periods of time than non-depressed mothers—27 percent versus 12 percent, respectively, of the minutes that were observed.
- When the interaction between child and mother is high on negative emotion, this negativism tends to be replicated between siblings when they are left alone to play.
- Mothers and 2- to 3-year-old children observed together are concordant in negative emotionality in 60 percent of the cases.

Radke-Yarrow (1990) concludes that these small children are not only subjected to their mothers' negativism but they also learn to feel and display patterns of negative

FAMILY RESEARCH 15.1

Naturalistic Observations in a Specifically Designed Apartment

An apartment was designed in a lovely old house to study parent/child interactions, sibling relationships, and other aspects of family dynamics in as natural a setting as possible. The families that are participants in the research can spend several days there so that the situation has a more normal "feel" to it than if they were just interviewed. Families go through their regular routines and, with their consent, are videotaped through viewing mirrors. For instance, mothers prepare lunches, siblings are left alone while the mother is busy in the other room, the family eats a meal, a "doctor" comes to examine a child, and so on. These routines and events allow for the observation of a wide range of family and individual behaviors and moods. The researcher, Marian Radke-Yarrow (1990), recognizes some of the limitations imposed by this approximation of a family's naturalistic setting. This includes the fact that, for families experiencing very chaotic lives, this apartment sojourn "may be a spot of peace and an imposed organization" (p. 177).

emotions (the socialization model discussed earlier). At least a few of these small children may themselves be genetically predisposed to depression and therefore more easily "absorb" the negativism: They are more vulnerable to it and learn it more readily. Within an **interactional perspective,** one also has to consider that difficult child behaviors (see Figure 15.1) probably exacerbate maternal depression (Brown, Brody, and Stoneman, 2000), which results in a further disturbance in parenting activities (Mash and Johnson, 1990). Other studies, such as those by Stein and colleagues (1991), indicate that depression does not unavoidably alter family patterns. Many children function quite well, perhaps because they are more resilient, have otherwise caring parents, benefit from other positive advantages present in their environment, or a combination of these factors, as illustrated in the following student quote:

> *"I love my parents very much. My mother is a gentle depressive and has been since after my brother's birth. She is sweet and harmless but she is deeply unhappy although she could make everyone envious because she has it all. Without antidepressants she could be worse. My father has never let her down and I admire him for that because even though she is so sweet she depresses us all and drags us down. We're all her mothers. There has never been much fun or laughter in our lives at home, only when we visit our grandparents who have always tried to compensate. My father has poured his heart into raising us and we all stick together to give each other some happiness in life. My brother wants to get married but feels bad about leaving my father behind and I am engaged and feeling the same way. He will be so lonely."*

A Critique of Maternal Causality

On the whole, the correlations between maternal depression and negative child outcomes—such as attachment difficulties, low self-esteem, and behavioral problems—consistently surface, but are *not large* (Downey and Coyne, 1990). It is difficult to

FIGURE 15.1

Maternal Depression and Children's Problems: Explanatory Models

The Traditional Perspective on *Simple* Depression

Maternal depression ⟶ Children's problems

A More Sophisticated Explanatory Model

Maternal depression ⟶ Parenting disruption ⟶ Children's problems

The Best Model: The Interactional Perspective

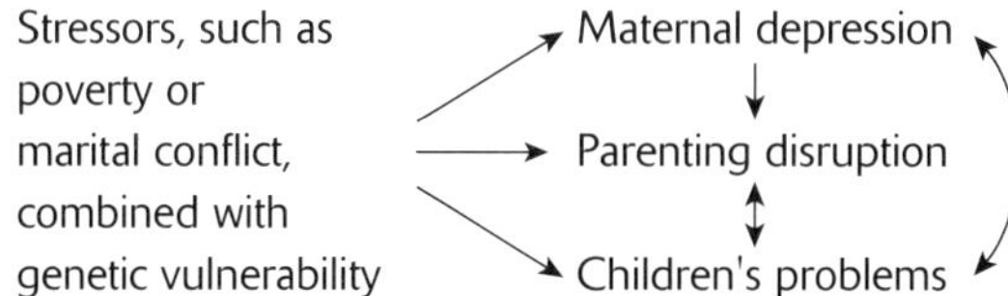

know how seriously one should take these correlations, because studies overlook too many variables that could be important and could affect the child even more than maternal depression. For instance, poverty is one key variable that is omitted in these studies. In addition, children and mothers both could have problems stemming from marital conflict: As we have seen in Chapters 10 and 14, parental conflict is detrimental to children's well-being at all age levels. This multiple causality pattern is diagrammed at the bottom section of Figure 15.1, which indicates both the inadequacy of simplistic models and the complexity of the interrelationships involved in the study of the effects of maternal depression.

A second broad critique resides in the fact that depressive mothers constitute a very heterogeneous group and should not be treated as if they were identical (Brown, Brody, and Stoneman, 2000). A particularly worthwhile aspect of the Radke-Yarrow (1990) study is that she differentiates between types of depressed mothers. One group tends to express more sadness and anxiety, a second is more apathetic, and a third shows mixed symptoms, including unpredictable displays of anger and irritability. Not surprisingly, there are some differences in the behaviors of these mothers' children.

A third critique resides in the role that fathers play: Few studies examine depression in fathers. Keller and colleagues (1986) represent one exception, among a few others, and report that only mothers' depression is statistically related to children's problems. If such results were replicated in other studies of a longitudinal nature, they might imply that mothers' depression is more consequential for children, probably because they have more contact with mothers than with fathers. Nevertheless, on the other side of the coin, one is still left wondering about the negative impact on a woman's mothering ability when she lives with a husband who is very depressed or manic depressive, as is the case with Mr. Driscoll. Furthermore, living with a depressed spouse can lead the other to become sad and withdrawn. Unfortunately, studies rarely consider the mental state of *both* parents: Children with two depressed parents are bound to be more affected as they are surrounded by more risk factors.

Finally, part of this maternal "causality" actually stems from a certain degree of parent/child genetic similarity. In other words, it may not be so much what depressed mothers or fathers *do* that affects their children's outcomes but the degree to which each child has inherited predispositions for depression or other related negative outcomes. Unfortunately, studies fail to consider this linkage. It is easier to focus on maternal behaviors—even though correlations are small and indicate that other variables may be more important.

ALCOHOLISM IN THE FAMILY

Alcoholism is a form of drug addiction; therefore, many of the discussions presented below apply to other addictions. For instance, binge drinking is a form of drug abuse with the difference that it is socially constructed as a popular activity on many campuses. Thus, some of the material in the causality section applies to student alcoholism and even eating disorders.

What Are the Causes of Alcoholism?

Alcoholism may be partly hereditary (McGue, 1993), just as may be the tendency for drug addiction (Cadoret et al., 1995). But how can alcoholism and drug addiction be partly genetic when they involve behaviors that are dependent on environmental influences—that is, availability of and exposure to substances as well as to role models? McGue (1993) reasons that three behavioral predispositions contribute to an inclination toward alcoholism, and perhaps other drug addictions as well. One of these is *alcohol sensitivity,* particularly a strong feeling of relief after alcohol consumption, that then leads the person to repeat the experience. Another contributor to alcoholism is being *aroused by alcohol* (becoming more outgoing or aggressive) so that the person feels happier or more powerful and is then inclined to want to drink more. A third contributor resides in *personality or temperament* variables, such as low impulse control or moodiness, that may contribute to the development of alcoholism. Thus, people who inherit all or some of these precursors may be more susceptible to alcoholism and drug use than others when they are placed in an environment that encourages such behaviors. This is another illustration of the combined role that genes and the environment play.

Furthermore, alcoholism has a high *comorbidity* with other psychological problems (Regier et al., 1990). That is, it is often accompanied by other emotional problems. So, it is possible that children inherit some of their parents' problems through other genetic pathways, such as a propensity for depression that alcohol may temporarily relieve. Thus, it may not be the direct propensity to alcoholism that is the inherited factor but other predispositions, such as depressiveness, that, given environmental influence and opportunities, can lead to alcoholism or eating disorders. A *transaction* takes place between a child's temperament and the environment (Brody et al., 1998). If parents drink too much—or eat too much, for that matter—this example provides an incentive and an opportunity for genetic inclinations to be activated in their offspring via modeling. Modeling can provide an example even when no genetic predisposition exists. The incentive is greater if the parents' attitude is permissive, if alcohol consumption is widespread, and if the peer group is likewise inclined.

But for most, the route to alcoholism is purely environmental or cultural. The family example or peer pressure may be too overpowering or appear too acceptable to resist. The acceptability of alcohol is further reinforced by advertising linking alcohol consumption to socially valued attributes, such as popularity and sex appeal. A similar cultural explanation applies to **eating disorders,** such as anorexia nervosa and bulemia. These two disorders were largely absent just 20 years ago and then "caught on like wildfire," as a result of media images of slimness and related bodily obsessions. One can therefore be concerned about the advisability of labeling eating disorders a "family problem." On the one hand, it is true that, when a person, generally a daughter, suffers from anorexia or bulemia, the entire family is affected. However, the term *family problem* generally implies a familial causality, thus a psychological problem, when in reality the causality resides in sociocultural forces (Harrison and Cantor, 1997). Binge drinking is largely a campus cultural phenomenon. However, it can have severe consequences for persons who are already predisposed to alcoholism or emotional problems.

Consequences of Parental Alcoholism for Children

Parental alcoholism places children at risk of developing problems and of becoming victims. The presence of an alcoholic parent often disrupts family functioning, impairs proper parenting, and increases the likelihood of divorce (Hawkins, Catalano, and Miller, 1992). Children of alcoholics are often affected by interparental conflict and violence (Fitzgerald et al., 1993). Families that combine alcohol and violence also tend to suffer from episodic unemployment and poverty, as well as erratic parenting practices—all situations that in themselves place additional stressors on children. Wives of alcohol-dependent men often become depressed, and their affective mood may impact negatively on their children in any of the pathways described earlier. Children may also be negatively affected by the suffering of the nonalcoholic who becomes the target of violence, as is described here:

> *"My father used to drink a lot and he'd scare all of us to death because he was real violent. Sometimes he'd get the kitchen knives out and pretend to go after us but then would go after my mother. We were too small to call the police or anyone else for help but once in a while a neighbor would hear the commotion and call the police. But in those days, they'd leave my father alone and take us to my grandmother's place. My mother had in her life with my father a broken nose, a broken jaw, lost some teeth, one leg broken, and her body was always covered in bruises that she would hide with pants and long sleeves. Most of the time she would get all of this punishment while trying to protect us children because he'd like to scare her by pretending to go after us and of course we thought it was for real. . . . Looking back I find it incredible that no one ever did anything to help my mother. To this day, she's still too shell-shocked to watch vio-*

lence on television. [Eventually the case came to the attention of a social worker; the mother left with her children.]

However, most alcoholic parents are not abusive. Jacob, Krahn, and Leonard (1991) suggest that children have normal outcomes when alcoholic parents are able to maintain a warm and supervisory relationship with them. This generally occurs in families where alcoholism does not result in temperamental or even violent outbursts, and parents are otherwise functional. Supportive parenting, either by the alcoholic parent or the sober parent, acts as a buffer to preserve children's mental health (Roosa et al., 1993). When parents use drugs or alcohol but are not dependent and maintain a nonpermissive role vis-à-vis their offspring, the latter are less likely to follow suit. However, when parental attitude is favorable to substances, children may be indirectly encouraged to seek a peer group with similar proclivities and to use substances themselves. The children are negatively influenced by their parents' behavior, permissive attitude, and the peer group they access. All of these sources of influence reinforce each other and provide a strong **socialization** context toward substance abuse.

Although a majority of children of alcoholics do well, a greater proportion of such children than of controls exhibit emotional problems, conduct disorders, and abuse alcohol or other substances (Chassin et al., 1999). As is the case for other emotional problems, when children have two alcoholic parents, they suffer from negative outcomes more often than children who have one alcoholic parent. Parents' drinking or use of illegal drugs when offspring are small can leave children vulnerable in yet another way. Daughters are more vulnerable to experiencing nonvoluntary sexual intercourse (Moore, Nord, and Peterson, 1989). Inebriated parents may not know the whereabouts of their children nor in whose company they are, so that daughters become prey to unwanted sexuality. Sons may well become abusers because the familial climate does not offer deterrents against such activities. Surprising as it may be, most adolescents of alcoholics manage to survive quite well. However, the price paid in terms of emotional adjustment and premature obligations has yet to be documented but can be glimpsed at in the following quote from a female student:

"The most painful aspect of my life for so long as I can remember, but I remember it better since age 10, is that my mother was/is an alcoholic. . . . No, she was a drunk and now she is just an alcoholic. . . . In those days we had to fend for ourselves, get food and cook it, do the laundry, clean up and do our homework and then my father would take over when he would get home. We had to do everything as if we didn't have a mother. . . . We couldn't have anyone over because we were all so ashamed. Sometimes we would come home and find our mother passed out on the floor anywhere in the house: she seemed to like getting herself under the rugs with a bottle and we would leave her there. It is terrible what it does to children. We hated her, we had all kinds of negative feelings for her until she sobered up some and could be a mother again to some extent. But by then my father could no longer cope with it and seeing that she could at least take care of herself he took us away, with my older sister staying behind to keep an eye on her. But my father always helped my sister and she came home nearly every day to be with us. For some reason she was better able to cope with our mother than anyone of us could and she did not have such negative feelings for her, rather she just felt sorry for her." [The sister was a mere 14 years of age when she took on this responsibility.]

CHILDREN WITH BEHAVIORAL PROBLEMS

Young children and adolescents' emotional problems are generally discussed at great length in abnormal psychology textbooks. Unfortunately, very few of these discussions utilize a sociological or even an interactional perspective. In contrast, the literature on behavioral problems includes a reasonable level of sociologically oriented analyses that make this topic a more suitable one for a family text.

The definition of what constitutes behavioral problems or conduct disorders is complex (Earls, 1994). In a nutshell, these children are very difficult. A mere enumeration of the behaviors involved is insufficient to grasp the magnitude of the problem, because even normative children occasionally engage in one or several of the acts listed here. What characterizes children with conduct disorders is that they exhibit some and even many of these behaviors regularly, as a way of life, and persistently. Generally, but not always, the pattern begins at an early age and is quite stable over time, especially aggressiveness.

The first category of behaviors consists of overtly hostile acts, such as fighting, hitting, bullying, and name calling. Second are aversive acts, such as fussiness, unwarranted crying, interruptions, sharp and immediate demands that are difficult to meet, disobedience, defiance, refusal to comply, vindictiveness, and repeated temper tantrums. Third, the attention deficit and hyperactive disorder (ADHD) is a related entity and is characterized by low impulse control, short attention span, shifting from one topic to another or one activity to another, and often difficulties in learning. Hyperactivity has a high level of comorbidity with other conduct disorders; for instance, more than 65 percent of hyperactive children are also aggressive (Barkley, 1997). Fourth, attention-seeking behaviors fall in any one of the other three categories, but a child who is so inclined may exhibit a great many episodes of aversive activity. The last category to be mentioned involves dishonesty: lying, cheating, and stealing on a regular basis.

What Are the Causes of Behavioral Problems?

The etiology of behavioral problems is much more complex than that of severe emotional problems. Genetic influences exist, particularly for aggressive behaviors, but have yet to be determined (Eley, Lichtenstein, and Stevenson, 1999). Furthermore, conduct disorders, just like mild emotional disorders, are varied and more environmentally influenced than serious emotional problems (Braungart-Rieker et al., 1995).

Environmental Factors in Behavioral Problems

Conduct disorders find a wide range of possibilities for actualization in large and heterogeneous societies, where social change is rapid and community social control weak. The following social elements, among others, currently combine to prevent children who may be genetically at risk from getting the dosage of structure, supervision, stability, and calm that they would need to grow up normally. These same elements, gathered from previous chapters, also prevent the actualization of prosocial or positive tendencies that other children have inherited. The social elements are access to mass media products and programming of a violent nature; less parental or adult presence at home to structure children's lives; neighborhoods that no longer are effective communities, hence there is inadequate collective supervision; reduced importance of religion as a life-structuring element and agency of social control; fewer family rituals that anchor children and youths to a regulating calender of life events; and classrooms that are replete with distractions and are not effective, whether for learning or for discipline.

Considering all these elements, it may not be surprising that the incidence of various forms of conduct disorders is by all accounts increasing (Garbarino, 1999). North American society, especially for some groups, may present too many opportunities for the emergence of behavioral problems and too few opportunities for the optimal development of children's abilities and prosocial traits. Conduct disorders, as well as depression and anxiety, may well be the price parents and children pay for rapid and unplanned social change, and a consequent lack of a functional community.

In U.S. society and many other Western ones, there is much agreement in the literature that poverty increases the likelihood that children will develop behavior problems. But low income per se is not necessarily the root cause of deviance, for many categories of people are poor and yet have low deviance rates (Jencks, 1992). However, as seen in Chapter 7, poor communities place disadvantaged families and their children at greater *risk*. Guerra and colleagues (1995) note that the effects of economic deprivation are particularly potent for children who enter elementary school in a community with a high level of violence. Such children often learn hostile beliefs and their aggressiveness can rise sharply at that young age.

The Life Course Perspective

Simons, Johnson, and colleagues (1998) have offered the following chain of *life course* events explaining how childhood behaviors may persist into adolescence. Oppositional and disruptive behaviors in childhood lead to a further reduction in the quality of parenting, lower school commitment, and affiliation with deviant peers. Difficult boys in particular are often rejected by discouraged parents and teachers (Garbarino, 1999). But when one of these linkages is interrupted, there is a lesser chance that difficultness will lead to childhood and adolescent delinquency.

Emotional and behavioral disturbances among children ages 8 to 10 relate 20 years later to a life that, on average, is more burdened with chronic stressors and negative events (Ronka and Pulkinen, 1995). From a life course perspective, Rutter and colleagues (1995:74) find that such individuals are less likely to "show planning in relation to key life transitions." This inability to plan that often accompanies behavioral problems, in turn, leads to additional negative events. For instance, children who had behavioral problems at age 10 were far more likely to enter into a first union with a deviant partner, in part because such youngsters had congregated with antisocial peers and lived in areas where there was a higher ratio of antisocial persons (Quinton et al., 1993). But when such a youth marries a stable woman, he reduces his contact with deviant peers, which then reduces both motivation and opportunities to engage in crime (Warr, 1998).

Disruption of Parenting Skills: Interactional Dynamics

In some families, conduct disorders emerge because parents' problems, childrearing philosophies, or lack of skills prevent them from adopting suitable socialization practices. Then, as children's conduct disorders become more established, not only does the rate of their aversive behaviors increase, but so does their severity. Parents become discouraged and often respond inappropriately and so their attempts to control these behaviors often result in an escalation of parent/child adversity. In extreme forms of parenting breakdown, the child controls the house and his or her disruptive behaviors spill into peer and school situations. Although adults' inappropriate parenting skills contribute to child conduct disorder in many families, as the child gains the upper hand, he or she causes a further disruption of parenting practices, and perhaps even of the marital relationship: "The child facilitates the disruption of its own environment by eliciting maladaptive parental behaviour, or increasing the strain on a marginally good marriage" (Earls, 1994:316).

Patterson, Bank, and Stoolmiller (1990) show that, when a child has an extreme antisocial score on personality tests in grade 4, parenting practices are much more disrupted when the same child is assessed again in grade 6, compared to a child who had been more prosocial in grade 4. These authors suggest that, in any environment, the person (in this case, the child) who is the most coercive has control of the situation. Families with disruptive children are marked by conflictual mutuality between mother and child (Johnston and Pelham, 1990). The mother usually prevails with normative children, but with difficult boys, in particular, it is the child who rules. Hence, there is a role reversal and the parent/child relationship becomes dysfunctional.

As a result of the process of habituation, many mothers of difficult children become desensitized to misbehavior: They accept it as normal and are then less able than mothers of nonproblematic children to distinguish misbehavior from regular behavior. This phenomenon, in turn, lowers the ability of these mothers to socialize their children. Basically, children who are hostile, conflictual, and even aggressive impair a family's ability to solve problems that are relevant to its good functioning (Forgatch, 1989). These children become *dysfunctional* to their families and to themselves in the true functionalist sense of the word. This situation then contributes to reinforcing adolescent maladjustment. "Some children ultimately 'win' when they perform in such a way as to stop virtually all parental behaviors aimed at changing the misbehavior" (Loeber and Stouthamer-Loeber, 1986:110). It is quite understandable, then, that studies find that children with behavior problems occasion far more stress for their parents than do children with disabilities (Floyd and Gallagher, 1997). Single mothers are particularly distressed by children's noncompliance and misbehavior (Olson and Banyard, 1993).

The Role of Children's Faulty Perceptions

Many adolescents rationalize their own comportment by projecting socially unacceptable behaviors and attitudes onto their parents, and particularly their mothers, who are more available to them. These projections may fulfill the additional function of convincing the youths that they are justified in disobeying such mean parents:

> *"My only brother is 16 and there is no relationship between us. In fact, I wish he didn't exist. From the time he was very very small he had temper tantrums, was destructive, got into fights, you name it. My mom would ask him gently (my parents were ever so patient) to do something and he would turn around and did the contrary. Same at school. He can be charming once in a while if he wants something. He is simply a predator. . . . He has ruined my parents' lives and he just doesn't see it this way. He always complains that they don't give him enough. . . .*

> *He simply does not think normally. He twists around everything my parents say to prove that he is right and they're wrong. It really makes you sick. He'd need to be trained to think like a person but that's too much to ask of him. Therapists have tried but given up, dashing my parents' hopes. . . . I do my utmost so that my parents have at least one child to hold on to so that they feel that it is worth it being a parent. . . . I worry about having children: suppose one would be like my brother? I know that I couldn't be as kind as my parents have been because I have seen how destructive another young human being can be. I would never accept being so hurt or mistreated."*

This student's observations are related to those made by researchers and clinicians who indicate that aggressive children are often biased in how they process information (Dodge and Frame, 1982). This deficit can be observed in children as young as age 4 (Webster-Stratton and Lindsay, 1999). Difficult children are difficult in part because their **perceptions** and cognitions are faulty, including the ones they maintain concerning their parents and other authority figures. For instance, they tend to impute threatening intentions to others and see aggressiveness as the only way to solve problems (Coie and Dodge, 1998). In turn, problematic behaviors and their consequences reinforce and even heighten the level of misconceptions in the youngsters' mentality: They are faced with negative social reactions from adults and even peers. But they cannot appreciate, accept, or even learn anything from these reactions, because they interpret them as a sign that *they* are being unfairly treated. It is akin to a mild case of paranoia. In contrast, prosocial adolescents are more likely to endorse values and motives consistent with conformity to interactional roles and are far less likely to attribute hostile intent (Nelson and Crick, 1999). They are easier to socialize.

On the basis of such results, Bates (1987:1132) has reasoned that infants and children who are difficult may learn less about their parents' attitudes and feelings than easier children. They may have a selective attention that orients them to ignore their parents and to focus on other areas of concern to them, such as delinquent peers and activities. Similar attention biases have been observed in adults who suffer from emotional problems (MacLeod, Mathews, and Tata, 1986). Difficult children may be less able or willing than others to learn social cues and to "read" other people, perhaps due to high levels of impulsivity—an interpretation that could well be supported by symbolic interactionism. This deficit, in turn, contributes to friction between child and parents, further reinforcing the negative child behaviors (Pepler and Slaby, 1994:35). Moreover, difficult children are less prosocial and may identify less with their prosocial parents. All of these factors combined make the children more difficult to socialize so that this family function goes unfulfilled. When such children grow up with already dysfunctional or multiproblem parents, one can well understand why a large proportion become serious delinquents, as their behavior often leads to outright parental rejection, neglect, and even abuse.

Gendered Family Dynamics: Mothers and Difficult Children

It is a common theme in this and previous chapters that females—that is, sisters, mothers, and grandmothers—assume the main role in the care of family members who are ill, disabled, or problematic (Hooyman and Gonyea, 1995). By 1980, Patterson had pertinently remarked that "the role of mother is structured in such a manner as to almost guarantee higher rates of aversive events than does the role of the father" (p. 10). Coercive boys actually target their mothers rather than their fathers as victims of conflict, perhaps because mothers, through their nurturance, inadvertently "reinforce coercive attacks" (Patterson, Reid, and Dishion, 1992:49).

Indeed, one effect of difficult child behavior, at least on some mothers, is an increasing tendency to issue directives, commands, and threats in an effort to reduce the negative behavior (Patterson, 1980). But this is usually to no avail because, although reprimands do lower negative child behavior in normative children, they do not generally affect the behavior of problem children. Quite the opposite often occurs; children may simply increase the frequency and severity of their coercive and oppositional episodes. Thus, many beleaguered mothers unwittingly reinforce their children's bad behaviors. At some point in the escalation of parent/child conflict, the mother may become afraid of disciplining or even contradicting the child: "Mothers tend not to provide an aversive antecedent for these chains" of behaviors and desperately try to avoid conflict with a "practiced aggressor" (Patterson, 1986b). In fact, a mother's positive behavior toward a usually disruptive boy encourages the latter to take advantage of her (Lavigueur, Tremblay, and Saucier, 1995). Not surprisingly, maternal satisfaction correlates with child compliance: The mother/child interaction is less conflictual when a child is cooperative. A cooperative child is more easily socialized and provides the mother with greater interpersonal and parental rewards.

For their part, fathers engage more in play interactions with their children. This allows them to attract less negative behavior from their difficult offspring than mothers, who may be solely responsible for enforcing rules. As a result, fathers may not sympathize with the child's mother when she complains about the misbehavior, hence increasing the mother's isolation and encouraging children to keep targeting her. Unlike mothers, fathers of difficult children are little different from fathers of normal children in terms of stress reactions. As Patterson (1982:24) dryly notes, "This leads to the conclusion that the role label most appropriate for fathers might be that of 'guest!'" Overall, fathers seem to be less affected than mothers by the quality of relationships with their children (Umberson et al., 1996).

DELINQUENCY: FAMILY DYNAMICS

Violent juvenile delinquency begins at younger ages today than in the past. One routinely hears of boys ages 6 to 10 who participate in brutal acts and who carry firearms. Therefore, juvenile delinquency attracts more media attention and spreads feelings of fear and insecurity in the population at large, and particularly among law-abiding children who frequently worry about their own safety at school or in their neighborhoods (Sheley and Wright, 1995). Furthermore, girls are also more likely to engage in aggressive delinquency than in the recent past. Most delinquents are arrested only once: Repeat offenders, who constitute a minority of all delinquents, commit over 60 percent of all recorded offenses (Farrington, 1987).

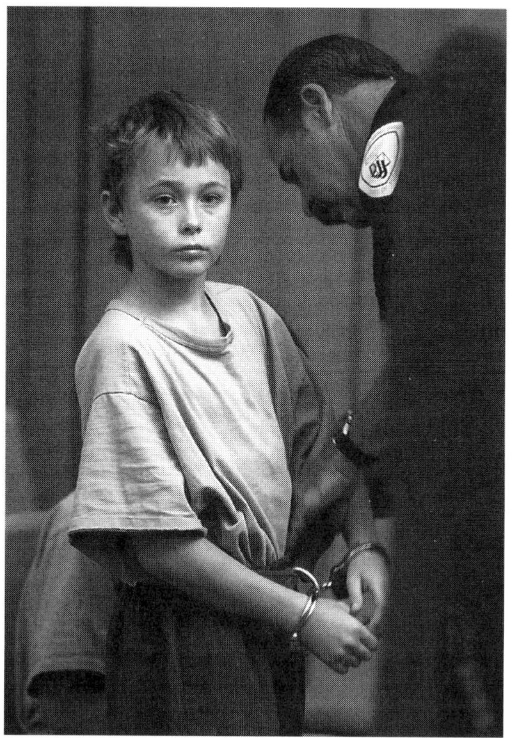

Delinquency that occurs for the first time in middle to late adolescence is generally related to a youth's extrafamilial environment. However, delinquency that begins in childhood or early adolescence is usually related to behavior disorders, familial problems, and poverty.

The Life Course Perspective on Delinquency

At least two life course paths to delinquency exist among boys. Delinquents who start very young and graduate to more serious crimes are, on average, different from delinquents who start in mid- to late adolescence. This is referred to as *early-onset* versus *late-onset delinquency* (Simons, Wu, et al., 1994). Early-onset delinquents exhibit more behavioral problems, are diagnosed more frequently with personality disorders, and more often originate from a dysfunctional family. They resemble the children with serious behavioral problems discussed earlier. In fact, early-onset delinquency is usually accompanied and preceded by conduct disorders that began early in life. Their disruptive behavior has had a long period to build up and interferes with normal coping (Garbarino, 1999). As a result, it frequently leads to adult criminality and other problems if no intervention occurs, especially when the neighborhood is particularly criminogenic.

Late-onset delinquents are more varied and some are similar to early-onset delinquents. But, generally, they tend to function better in many respects, to come from an adequate family, and do not, as a rule, become recidivists or adult criminals. Their experience with delinquency is short lived. Among girls, delinquency rarely develops until adolescence. Girls who become serious delinquents follow a pattern similar to boys, with early behavioral problems, but not necessarily early onset of delinquency itself (Silverthorn and Frick, 1999). Girls are more sheltered and supervised; thus, it makes sense that opportunities for delinquency present themselves at a later age, although the situation may be changing.

What Are the Causes of Delinquency?

A multitude of causal variables lead to juvenile delinquency, although the familial environment continues to be privileged: Parents' backgrounds, mental states, personality, disciplinary practices, and criminality are scrutinized. Common, self-reported delinquency is not related to social class (Wright et al., 1999). However, delinquents who commit *serious* crimes and are arrested seem to originate predominantly from a background that combines multiple risk factors: poverty, questionable peers, deprived neighborhood, unstable parenting, poor supervision, and even abuse (Farrington, 1995).

For instance, 40 percent of the nearly two million adults in jail have a parent or a sibling behind bars. Butterfield (1999) reports that a California study of 1,000 girls in detention indicated that 54 percent had a mother who had been locked up and probably a higher percentage had such a father. A disproportionate number of delinquents come from single-parent families, and this finding holds for black and white, Canadian, American, and even British delinquents (Ambert, 1998a). Moreover, serious delinquency disproportionately originates from *disadvantaged* families and this finding has also been replicated in several countries (see review by Sampson, 1993). For instance, longitudinal research in New Zealand indicates that most adolescents who exhibit *several* behavioral problems (early onset of sexual activity, substance use and abuse, police contact, mood disorders) come from seriously disadvantaged and dysfunctional families, even though 13 percent of all children from such backgrounds are problem free (Fergusson, Horwood, and Lynskey, 1994). For children reared in advantaged homes (economically and emotionally), only 1 out of 400 to 500 becomes a multiproblem adolescent, and 80 percent are totally problem free.

Inadequate Parental Supervision

One familial factor that researchers emphasize is parental monitoring. There is consensus to the effect that poorly supervised youngsters are at a greater risk for juvenile delinquency as well as for other problems, such as illicit drug use, early sexual involvement, and school underachievement (Patterson, Reid, and Dishion, 1992). Patterson and Stouthamer-Loeber (1984) found that 21 percent of the nondelinquents in their sample were poorly supervised by their parents, compared to 50 percent of the one-time offenders and 73 percent of the repeat offenders.

Inadequate supervision occurs more frequently in homes where there is marital conflict, or only one parent, and where one or even both parents are emotionally disturbed, use drugs, or have committed crimes. In such households, family processes, including parental example, may be immediate causes of delinquency. In Chapters 7 and 11, we have seen that proper monitoring may be particularly important in inner-city areas that have high rates of criminality. But a lack of supervision can also be quite detrimental in affluent neighborhoods, where parents may be too preoccupied with financial matters and career involvement and too trusting about their "good" neighborhood. Although supervision is emphasized, there may be *other* salutary processes going on in families that monitor their children properly. It can be argued that these families are probably better organized, have more stable, warm, and perhaps less individualistic parents as well as children with easier temperaments, and spend more time on prosocial parent/child interaction than in other families, whether single- or two-parent families, whether rich or poor.

School, Peers, and Neighborhood Influences

In neighborhoods with a high level of criminality, concentration of poverty, and gang supremacy, children do not need a dysfunctional family to become aggressive and delinquent (Sampson, 1993). In contrast, communities that are able to control teenage groups, especially gangs, have less serious delinquency. The classroom and school are included here as part of this community environment. For instance, Kellam (1994:155) reports that "in one class, being aggressive was deviant, whereas in another not being aggressive was deviant." And he is referring here to primary school children. Obviously, children who attend schools with a high ratio (critical mass) of difficult peers are at risk for delinquency.

One could perhaps suggest that it is the street/classroom/neighborhood interface that often makes children difficult at an early age, thus at high risk for early-onset delinquency. In turn, their behavior is sufficient to disrupt the functioning of their family, including parenting skills. Such children may constantly escape from family influence and control by "hanging out" with their older siblings, cousins, and peers in gangs that take on the role of socialization agents early in their lives (Hogan and Kitagawa, 1985). Children with vulnerable predispositions, such as low self-control, succumb more easily in these environments. The family may play no role whatsoever, whether positive or negative, because the environment is too powerful.

Delinquency and Family Dynamics

In this section, I rely on my research, carried out through the 1990s, on the effects of delinquency on parents and on family processes (Ambert, 1999, 2001). This research presents a complement to all previous research, except that of Jang and Smith (1997), which is also interactional. It includes in-depth interviews with middle-class parents who had conduct-disordered or delinquent adolescents, a questionnaire survey of parents of 116 delinquents arrested by the police, observations of parent support groups, and, more recently, 60 additional interviews with a more socially mixed sample of parents whose adolescents are difficult. Qualitative and quantitative methods were combined within an interactional framework.

General Impact on Parents

I will focus on middle-class parents, since one hears very little about delinquency at the middle-class level and because it is almost always associated with low-income families. The outpouring of parental suffering in the in-depth interviews was simply overwhelming. These were parents who had done their best for their children and had given them a lot on all levels. They had never imagined that delinquency would occur in their family and, before their child was arrested, they knew of no other parent in the same predicament. The immediate reaction was similar to that of sudden bereavement: disbelief, followed by self-examination, in which parents asked themselves, Where did *we* go wrong? These parents automatically blamed themselves because they, like most parents, have accepted the prevailing social construction that parents cause all their children's problems. Moreover, most of the professionals with whom they came into contact—whether police, court, lawyers, clinicians, or teachers—also blamed them, although often indirectly. Some couples started accusing each other as well, so that the marital relationship declined at a time when couples would have benefited from mutual support (Suárez and Baker, 1997). Most reported doing more poorly at work, eating too much or too little, being edgy, feeling concerned for their other children, and worrying about the difficult child. They slept little and were often depressed.

After an arrest, most delinquents are returned to their parents' custody. The parent/adolescent relationship often becomes rocky. Parents no longer trust the youngster who has lied, disobeyed, and betrayed their trust. Parents become more controlling and monitor the youngster's whereabouts more closely; they also begin scrutinizing the friends the child goes out to meet. As a result, some of these youngsters rebel, typically accusing their parents of "not trusting me"—a maneuver that displaces their own guilt onto their parents. Half of them resume seeing their co-offending peers. This string of events leads to many parent/adolescent confrontations, with the result that some youngsters run away.

Although the survey sample contained a predominance of low-income parents, the results are similar to those of the interviews with middle-class parents. A majority of these parents are more stressed, more tired, and less happy since learning of their child's delinquency. Nearly half of them also mention a decline in health. Moreover, a majority report having been ashamed because of their adolescent's behavior, and having been blamed for it by others. A good proportion have had to seek help from police, teachers, or professionals in order to control their youngster's difficult temperament or disobedience. Most parents mention additional problems that afflict their child, whether at school, at home (disobedience, difficult temperament, arriving home after curfews), or with peers (easily influenced).

Parental Social Isolation

Many of the negative effects incurred by parents are probably due to the fact that they are at first totally isolated socially, have no one with whom they can share their experiences, although some eventually meet other such parents (e.g., in court). They feel that they have to hide the situation from most relatives, friends, and neighbors to protect their child, and to protect the family's reputation:

> *"No, there is no way I would tell my parents or my brother about this." [What would happen?] "First, they wouldn't understand, no. Then I'm sure they'd find some reason to put the blame on me because my brother thinks the world of my daughter. Well, he hasn't recently seen her so he might change his mind but he's always been the jealous type and he'd like nothing better than find something like that to put me down in my parents' minds' eyes. Then, I'd never hear the end of it. No, I have enough problems without getting my family involved."*

Both in the United States and Canada, there are networks of parent groups, and their presence reflects the fact that parents do not find help or sympathy from their regular support network, meaning their relatives, friends, or coworkers (Ambert, 1997b). Talking about one's child's problems is not something that is done in this society, for it usually creates embarrassment among the listeners. Parents reported having lost friends to whom they confided, because they were perceived to be "losers." One mother explained that admitting that one's child is delinquent is "a death sentence socially. People avoid you after that because they think there's something wrong with you."

Mothers Are More Affected

Another key finding of this research replicates what other studies on children's behavior problems, particularly those by Gerald Patterson and associates, have already proven: Mothers are usually more affected by a child's delinquency than fathers (Ambert, 1999). In the interviews, fathers even spontaneously offered comments to this effect:

> *"This is much harder on my wife." Another father said, "Let me add here [turning to his wife] that she finds our daughter's problems much more difficult to live with than I do because she is with her more." Another pointed out, "If you interviewed my wife, I know you'd find her much more upset than I am because we've had some serious disagreements on account of this."*

Mothers become more stressed, tired, unhappy, and have more health problems than fathers, although the differences are not large. But there are substantial and statistically significant differences in the number of times mothers felt ashamed about their adolescents' behavior, had been blamed, and had experienced problems with people because of the youngster's behavior or attitude. Mothers seek help far more frequently than fathers. Generally, the former become totally preoccupied with the problem:

> *"I had to see a psychiatrist because I realized that I was obsessed with all the problems he created. I couldn't think of anything else and I couldn't even sleep. He gave me some tranquilizers for two weeks and he assured me that my reaction was quite normal because there was, is always something to worry about. But he said that I should get help and learn to relax so he gave me the name of this place but my insurance does not cover it. Still, it made me feel good to know that I was normal."*

In my interviews, mothers mentioned more problems that afflicted their child than did fathers. This is probably because the mothers' role allows them to observe a wider range of child behaviors than is the case for fathers.

HOW RELATIVES AND EXPERTS AFFECT FAMILY DYNAMICS

When a member of the family suffers from emotional or behavioral problems or is adjudged delinquent, not only are family dynamics altered, as just seen, but they are also further impacted by the necessity to have recourse to outsiders or have such persons penetrate family boundaries by the force of the law. Relatives, friends, and experts are the three groups that have the greatest impact on parents of children who are problematic.

Grandparents can be an important source of comfort for a family besieged by problematic child behaviors when they offer support rather than blame the affected parents. This grandmother spends time with a young child so that the little girl's parents can attend to the needs of a difficult older child.

Relatives and Friends

Little research exists on the role that relatives play in families burdened by the trials caused by difficult and/or emotionally disturbed children. As we have already seen earlier, when parents confide to their relatives about their children's problems, they may trigger negative reactions against themselves, especially if the relatives see only the positive or pleasant aspects of the child. The mother of an adolescent son with schizophrenia explains the matter in an interview:

> *"When he's better, we take advantage of this to visit his grandparents on both sides, but that's difficult for us because they practically always see a normal Jimmy, so to speak. And when he is normal, well, he is charming. His grandparents* adore *him [he is the only male grandchild] and that's fine but the problem is that they don't want to hear us talk about him when he isn't OK. You should even see the incredulous looks they give us or the long silences over the phone. They think we're crazy. I'm sure they think we're bad parents and let me tell you that this creates a great deal of distance between us. We, my husband and I, are* their *children and they don't believe us. It's a big strain on us, as if we needed one more."*

Whatever the reasons, and some are clearly spelled out in the preceding quote, parents who have problem children often have fewer contacts with relatives. Many feel misunderstood and fear blame (Terkelsen, 1987). As Lefley (1997:447) points out, large, closely knit families may be sources of intrusiveness, bad advice, and even conflict as well as help. Most parents may forsake the potential of help in order to avoid blame and intrusion. Furthermore, some parents and relatives are also dysfunctional and may have always maintained a distant relationship with each other. Other parents, although not afflicted themselves, have problematic families and their child has inherited some of the familial frailties. Such parents may be faced with coping with their own difficult children and having to provide assistance to others with similar problems, thus compounding their level of distress.

A similar situation exists when mothers make friends with other women whose children have identical problems: They experience a lower level of well-being (Greenberg et al., 1997). The reason may be that these friends need support themselves, which merely increases maternal burden. Another explanation may be found in a tendency for friends with similar problems to talk about shared difficulties. Although this sharing seems functional in self-help or parent support groups, it may become burdensome in sustained friendships, because these conversations simply keep parents focused on their problems at a time when they need some distraction and a break from their sad reality.

Professional Authority over Parents

Since approximately the middle of the nineteenth century, a variety of professionals have socially constructed the boundaries of what good parenting should be. At first, various religious leaders, and what has been called the *child-saving industry,* have brought their moral stamp of approval to what they defined as proper parenting. They were followed by physicians, who also took it upon themselves to reform parents. The parenting role became "medicalized," and parents were admonished to follow rules of hygiene in accordance with the morality and the knowledge of the day.

The interlude between the two World Wars saw the appearance of psychologists and psychiatrists whose dominance continues to this day, more recently aided by lawyers. Social workers have long been important members of these helping professions, but their standards and decisions are generally determined by the more powerful professions of psychiatry, psychology, medicine, and law. In tandem with the emergence of this series of experts, the nineteenth and early twentieth centuries witnessed the emergence of what became a lucrative commercial enterprise: books intended to teach parents how to take care of their children.

Today, people live in a millennium where *expert knowledge* is given preeminence, fueled by information technology. As a result of the social and mediatic salience of professional knowledge, the lay public has gradually lost power over a variety of areas of life that have fallen under the control of science and the professions. The prominence given to experts and "pop" psychology in the media, including talk shows, has led people to follow a variety of trends in personal lifestyles. Thus, people have become dependent on various experts, not only for knowledge, but for their health, the education of their children, and, more recently, the definition of the quality of their sexual and conjugal life, and even the social construction of what constitutes happiness. People's lives have become "pop psychologized."

In addition, professionals have become highly valued by state agencies (Gubrium and Holstein, 1990). They are regularly consulted in matters that pertain to the family, over and above parents, and contribute to the enactment of laws and policies in this domain. Those laws and policies, in turn, further the interests and the power of the professions (Sullivan, 1992:5). Thus, professionals—especially psychiatrists, psychologists, and clinical caseworkers—become parents' partners or intruders in their families (Lefley, 1989). The literature on children with disabilities documents how parents are often led to feel helpless, as well as incompetent, when dealing with various service delivery personnel (Darling, 1987). It is not difficult to see how this could be even more so in the case of parents of emotionally disturbed or disruptive children, especially when the teaching and research literatures too frequently hold them responsible (Caplan and Hall-McCorquodale, 1985). Many parents feel that mental health professionals do not have a realistic view of their child, whom the professionals often see under very limited and artificial circumstances in their office.

Professionals' Social Constructions

Professionals not only treat children but may even request to treat parents when children suffer from emotional problems and physical ailments, as illustrated in the following case from my files (Ambert, 1998b). In a first assessment, a 14-year-old depressive boy recalled being immediately asked questions about his parents and their relationship. Amidst these questions, according to the boy, the clinician interjected:

> *"Isn't it possible that you feel very bad about this?" [his parents' rare arguments]*
> *"No, not really because it is never really serious. They make up right away."*
> *"But you know it's normal for children to be affected when their parents fight so it's OK to say so."*
> *Later on [still as reported by the adolescent]:*
> *"It seems to me that a boy like you who feels so bad about life in general must have problems at home with his parents."*
> *"Well, yes, they aren't too happy about me being so sad all the time."*
> *"But don't you think that perhaps you don't want to say so but you're upset at your parents?"*

Notice how the clinician tries to influence the child's way of interpreting the presumed effect of his parents' relationship on his own mental health. The suggestive nature of the therapist's approach continued, and the boy was very upset when he got out and told his mother: "What does he know about me that's helpful? He just wants to know about you." It is at this point that the mother decided to write her son's account of his sessions.

At his third interview, the clinician told him:

> *"Now, I'll have to tell your mother to take adult tests because there's got to be a reason why you feel so depressed."*

The clinician did not suggest that the father participate in these tests.

> *[confused] "It seems to come on to me for nothing really. I don't think it's my mother, it's the whole world. I get really depressed at school."*

The adolescent's resistance is interesting, because one could well imagine that most other children might have given in to the suggestions, because, after all, the clinician is an expert and an authority figure. The clinician never focused on the youth's peers, even though the adolescent wanted to talk about them, for he felt most depressed following peer-group activities. According to the mother, her son was depressed around school issues, particularly peers, as he did not feel sufficiently accepted to participate in their activities. This isolation further contributed to the depression. Between the third and scheduled fourth interviews, the adolescent made a crude attempt at suicide. Alarmed, the parents located another therapist with the help of a friend. The new therapist *listened* to the boy and did not see any indication that the symptomatology was home related (Ambert, 1998b).

The transcript of the teenager's report yields several themes, all derived from a therapist's reductionist ideology of parental causality and mother blaming and not addressing the child's need. In fact, the child cannot even talk about his problems as he experiences them. In contrast, the next therapist had no preconceived notions of blame and allowed the youth to focus on the sources of his problems, all of which were located extrafamilially.

The Blaming and Marginalization of Parents

It is clear from the preceding that professionals can either facilitate or complicate parents' lives as well as family dynamics. On the positive side, professionals have alerted society to child abuse ("the battered child syndrome") and neglect by parents. Unfortunately, it is perhaps also true that this achievement has resulted in a general mistrust of parents among professionals. The result is that conscientious parents can no longer be as effective as previous generations were, because they have lost much of the moral authority that belonged to them in the past.

Already in 1983, Rubin and Quinn-Curan explained that, when society cannot meet a parental request for legitimate services, the assumption is that there is something wrong with the parents. As they wrote, "Seeing the parents as 'the problem' assumes that the parents are emotionally disturbed" (1983:73). This rationalization preempts the need for an examination of systemic or social failures. Although Terkelsen's (1983:191) following remarks were made about schizophrenia, they are relevant to other problems: "When either therapist or family harbor the belief that schizophrenia is caused by personal experience with family members, therapeutic misalliance is bound to follow." By misalliance, he refers to those instances where the therapist erroneously sees the patient as the parents' victim.

Terkelsen came to this conclusion after having first misinterpreted his patients' parents' words. He describes how he "listened to the parents talk about life with the ill person, abstracting from their reports those interactional phenomena that I thought suggestive of parental pathology" (p. 192). But he soon came to realize that abnormal patterns of family interaction were wrongly interpreted in terms of parental causality when actually they were a parental response and adaptation to the situation created by the offspring's emotional problems.

CONCLUSIONS: FAMILY VULNERABILITY

Dysfunctional patterns of interacting and of behavior adopted by one family member impact on all other members. As we have seen, there is a great deal of research on the effect on children of having problematic parents. But far less exists when the situation is reversed. Yet, when children are the afflicted ones, parents have to respond, adapt, seek help, and even suffer blame and a sense of failure. A certain level of tension also exists between the family system and social agencies, and a gap is created in the fulfillment of family functions. This is now especially the case as a result of the fact that, due to a lack of adequate social policies, families are currently forced to care and shoulder the responsibility for members with severe problems. Furthermore, in some states, parents are now held legally responsible for the consequences of their delinquent children's acts. Although there may be merits to such a policy, it would surely be a more just situation in a society that confers strong moral authority to parents, which is certainly not the case today. All in all, families' vulnerable members inadvertently create family vulnerability to excesses of external social control, minsunderstanding, blaming, and powerlessness.

SUMMARY

1. Clinical material is framed within a sociological perspective that includes social constructionist, interactionist, and feminist perspectives.
2. Manic or bipolar depression is a psychosis but unipolar depression does not generally involve a cognitive break with reality. The former rarely occurs before late adolescence, whereas the latter can occur even in young children. Manic depression is more genetically related, whereas unipolar depression is more environmentally induced. With severe parental depression, children may be more at risk of developing problems because of heredity, a stressful family environment, and the possibility that they will learn to act depressed (the socialization element).
3. The literature on the consequences of parental depression for children largely focuses on maternal depression, despite the fact that only small correlations have been found in this respect. There are several problems inherent in this research. One involves the failure to consider genetic and interactional processes as well as other environmental variables, such as poverty. As well, the role of fathers is largely ignored in these considerations.
4. Alcoholism as one form of drug addiction may be partly hereditary, but it is a predisposition that requires a great many environmental factors to be activated. Parental alcoholism places children at risk of developing problems. But this risk is largely mitigated by other variables, such as support from the other parent and parental attitude to alcoholism and drug use (permissiveness), as well as the quality of the peer group. Children of alcoholic or drug-addicted parents are often neglected, poorly supervised, and may, as a result, become victimized.
5. Children's behavioral problems are culture specific, although they are also influenced by genetic predispositions. Early, difficult child behaviors often lead to a lower quality of parenting, poorer school performance, and affiliation with deviant peers. Behavior problems alter the normative life course unless one of the elements in the causality chain is interrupted. Society may offer an environment that is particularly conducive to behavioral problems both culturally

(media, lower parental authority) and structurally (difficult neighborhoods). Poverty increases the risk, particularly when it is surrounded by a violent cultural climate.

6. One familial consequence of behavioral problems resides in the disruption of parenting skills. Within an interactional perspective, we see that parents react to their children. Once parenting skills are defeated, many children control the situation, which further entrenches their problems. Often, aggressive and difficult children are biased in the way they process information and construct reality. This deficit prevents them from conforming, accepting authority, and understanding their parents' efforts at raising them. Mothers of difficult children are particularly distressed, because the maternal role is structured and constructed in such a way that mothers become targets of difficult exchanges and behaviors.
7. Early-onset delinquency generally follows behavioral problems and begins as early as age 10 or 12. It is also more likely to persist. Late-onset delinquency begins later and is more peer related. It rarely leads to adult criminality. Delinquency is multicausal. Within the family, lack of parental monitoring is an important element, but even well-brought-up children can become delinquent in a disorganized neighborhood or in schools that have a high ratio of delinquent peers. Parents of delinquents are negatively affected. They are blamed and socially isolated. Also, when the adolescent is at home, the parents may have no support to help them control him or her.
8. With emotional, behavioral, and delinquency problems, family dynamics are affected by professionals and agents of social control. Relatives and friends are not uniformly helpful. For their part, professionals' social construction of children often leads them to parent blaming. Professionals are highly valued by state agencies and they define what they perceive to be social problems and their sources. The blaming and marginalization of parents that frequently follows intervention does not help children, unless they are abused.
9. Family vulnerability is created when one of its members is seriously problematic at the emotional or behavioral level.

KEY CONCEPTS AND THEMES

Alcoholism, p. 439
Blame, p. 455
Comorbidity, p. 439
Delinquency, p. 446
Difficult behaviors, p. 442
Disadvantaged families, p. 443
Eating disorders, p. 440
Expert knowledge, p. 451
Fathers, p. 438
Gender, pp. 445, 446, 447
Genetic risk, p. 436
Inadequate supervision, p. 448
Inappropriate socialization, p. 436
Interactional perspective, p. 437
Life course perspective, pp. 443, 447
Middle-class parents, p. 449
Mothers, pp. 436, 445, 451
Parent blaming, p. 455
Perceptions, p. 444
Professionals, p. 453
Relatives, p. 451
Social construction of women, p. 436
Social isolation, p. 450
Stressful familial environment, p. 436
Transaction, p. 439

STUDY AND REVIEW QUESTIONS

1. What proof is there that a mental illness such as manic depression carries a large genetic component?
2. Is the relationship between maternal depression and negative outcomes for children solid? Explain your answer.
3. Discuss the environmental components of alcoholism.
4. What may be an unexpected consequence of parental alcoholism on children?
5. The interactional perspective is used on several occasions in this chapter. Summarize these instances.
6. How and why are mothers more affected than fathers when children have problems? Explain with the help of several concrete passages from the chapter.
7. What are the implications of the cultural specificity of behavioral problems?
8. What role do faulty perceptions and cognitions play in behavioral problems and juvenile delinquency?
9. From an interactional family dynamics perspective, how does juvenile delinquency affect family life?
10. What role do professionals play toward parents when a child has emotional or behavioral problems? What role should they play?

SUGGESTED READINGS

Garbarino, J. 1999. *Lost boys: Why our sons turn violent and how we can save them.* New York: Free Press. This book is a social and clinical analysis of the roots of behavior disorders in boys, including programs that have been shown to be successful at reducing aggressiveness in young boys. Case studies of teen male murderers are presented.

Gross, M. L. 1978. *The psychological society: A critical analysis of psychiatry, psychotherapy, psychoanalysis, and the psychological revolution.* New York: Random House. For students who want a stimulating discussion on the broader aspects of the psychological profession, this is an excellent and still relevant critique.

Lefley, H. P. 1996. *Families caregiving in mental illness.* Thousand Oaks, CA: Sage. This is one of the few extensive books existing on the topic of the impact on families when a member, generally an adult child, suffers from a serious emotional problem. Lefley challenges many myths.

Patterson, G. R., Reid, J. B., and Dishion, T. J. 1992. *A social interactional approach* (Vol. 4). *Antisocial boys.* Eugene, OR: Castalia. This is one of the several monographs published by the Oregon Social Learning Center on the development of difficult behaviors in children. What is important about these monographs is that they adopt an interactional perspective.

Wachs, T. D. 1999. *Necessary but not sufficient: The respective roles of single and multiple influences on individual development.* Washington, DC: American Psychological Association. This book can help in the understanding of the development of typical as well as problematic behaviors. Wachs argues that the single causality model does not explain development adequately. He suggests that behaviors can only be explained by interrelated influences from genetics, nutrition, as well as the child's immediate and larger environments.

SUGGESTED WEBLINKS

American Academy of Child and Adolescent Psychiatry is a highly informative website; it provides up-to-date research information on many topics related to childhood and adolescence problems. Click on *Press Releases* as well as *Facts for Families and Other Resources.* **<http://www.aacap.org>**

Bazelon Center for Mental Health Law is the leading national legal advocacy center for people with mental illnesses or disorders. It is an excellent website with many weblinks and reliable information as well as abundant material on social policies. **<http://www.bazelon.org>**

National Clearinghouse for Alcohol and Drug Information provides many weblinks and information. It is sponsored by the Substance Abuse and Mental Health Services Administration. **<http://www.health.org>**

National Institute of Mental Health is a government website that provides a wealth of information about depression, anxiety disorders, and posttraumatic stress disorders, among many others. **<http://www.nimh.nih.gov>**

Oregon Social Learning Center is an organization that does research on and training of families, difficult children, and peer groups. (Patterson, the source of this research, is quoted extensively in this chapter.) The website provides many resources to help children and parents. **<http://www.oslc.org>**

CHAPTER 16

Family Futures and Social Policies

Salient Themes Revisited
Social Inequalities
Diversity of Families
A Surplus of Family Functions
The Functional Community
The Cultural Context
Interactional and Genetic Themes
Gender Stratification and Roles

What Does the Future Hold?
Age Distribution and Fertility
Cohabitation
Divorce
Nonmarital Family Formation
Same-Sex Parenting
Interracial Unions
The Longer Time Frame

Social Policies Pertaining to Families
Reducing Poverty
A Critique of Current Policies
Expansion of Head Start Programs
After-School Care and Improved Schooling
Job Creation in Disadvantaged Areas
Consequences and Limitations of Programs
Encouraging and Strengthening Marriage
Planning for Divorce
Step 1: Before Marriage
Step 2: When Divorce Occurs
Supporting the Parental Role

Conclusions: The Family in Context
Family Research and Historical Context
Family Functions and Their Environmental Context

Summary
Key Concepts and Themes
Study and Review Questions
Suggested Readings
Suggested Weblinks

OUTLINE

The first chapter opened, at my publisher's suggestion, with an autobiographical vignette. It may be fitting that this concluding chapter begins with a personal note as a teaching instrument (Allen, 1995). By now, it is obvious to the reader that I am concerned with the problems facing families and am critical of the lack of social policies that could prevent or alleviate these hardships. But I did not have these concerns at the beginning of my research career. How, then, did this orientation arise? It probably was the result of a career "accident."

As this text has shown, there is probably too much divorcing going on in America and divorce is detrimental to too many children and adolescents. However, long ago, such a conclusion would not have occurred naturally to me because I was (pathetically) libertarian on this subject: I had had an "easy" early divorce after a brief, childless marriage. In fact, back then, I thought that divorce was "inconsequential" and had "no intellectual interest"—a point of view I expressed to the astonished publisher who wanted me to write on this topic!

After a few years of his nagging, I finally relented and accepted to do a book on divorce. I began reading the literature and then planned a research project for which

I interviewed separated/divorced parents and did some participant observation with their children. Although many families were doing well, nothing had prepared me for the problems I was encountering among the others, particularly when these families were poor. The evidence I was gathering and what I was reading went overwhelmingly against my initial beliefs and personal experience.

By then, the students' autobiographies had been going on for years and presented a normal mixture of happy and unhappy results. But they also contained unexpected challenges not well documented in the literature. (The reader has read about some of these in previous chapters.) Confronted by all this evidence throughout the years, a researcher's mind cannot but expand well beyond the realities of her own life and a sharp social conscience develops. In fact, I have come to the conclusion that one's personal situation and lifestyle is not necesarily a good base upon which to ground research, although I am sure that there are exceptions (Allen, 2000). One's experience is not always a solid foundation upon which to draw sound sociological conclusions and related policy implications.

What ultimately remains with me from the totality of all this research material is how preventable so many problems are if only society invested more, both morally and economically, in its families and children—*all families, without prejudice for what types of families they are. In other words, much of the family's decline as well as too many of its problems and "dysfunctions" are created by that same society that decries them.*

This concluding chapter builds on the material presented in the entire book. It opens with a return to the key themes that inform this text and that were initially outlined in the first chapter. The reader is now familiar with the contents of the text and can therefore more meaningfully integrate these themes within the overall context. This is followed by a section in which future trends in family life are predicted on a modest scale. Family-related policies are then suggested within the context of some of the main themes outlined as well as some of the problems defined in previous chapters.

SALIENT THEMES REVISITED

The three key sociodemographic variables of social class, gender, and race/ethnicity are part of the fabric of the various themes that recurred throughout this text. These variables often constituted undercurrents in many of the chapters and were the key topics of other chapters and sections.

Social Inequalities

This interweaving of salient variables is most evident with the theme of social inequalities, particularly those created by the economy (social class and poverty), the racialization of society, and gender stratification. The theme of social inequalities was the cornerstone of Chapter 3, on family adaptation to ethnic/racial diversity, and of the contextual chapters (Chapters 6 through 8). This theme informs some of the social policies discussed later.

The theme of social inequalities is important in my own sociological perspective on families and, along with other themes, it offers a framework for this text's emphasis on problems faced by families. These problems can be at the level of economic survival or racial discrimination, or are the result of the difficulties faced by certain parents with regard to child socialization. Other problems reside in the painful family dynamics that often occur when a member experiences personal difficulties at the socioemotional level. Basically, families' major problems are largely, but not exclusively, created by economic, ethnic, and gender inequalities. They are also created by the fact that, *as an institution,* the family suffers from its own inequality. That is, compared to other social systems (corporations, the army, and political parties, for instance), the family is underfunded and deprived of resources. We have seen that other family problems are created by the culture, such as the media and values, as well as by detrimental genetic predispositions that are then exacerbated by a negative environment—all of which are other interrelated themes informing this text.

Diversity of Families

The theme of family diversity resides not only at the racial and cultural level but also at the level of family structure and modes of family formation: stepfamilies, single-mother-headed units, foster families, same-sex-parent families, and families created by adoption or with the help of reproductive technologies. The theme of family diversity is well captured by social constructionism and its links with inequalities: Not all diversity is socially acceptable and treated equally. Accepted definitions of what constitutes a family, a "normal" family, a "natural" family often stigmatize nonnormative ones (Bartholet, 1993; Wegar, 1992).

On the basis of available research, two conclusions have been reached with respect to family diversity. First, so long as certain types of families exist, and do a good job at loving and raising their children, it becomes functional for society as a whole to tolerate and support them. Second, because of current socioeconomic conditions, certain types of family structure are less well equipped than others to invest in children's well-being and future—namely, single parenting and, to some extent, cohabitation. At this point in time, marriage is the context that is the most favorable to child development (Coley and Chase-Lansdale, 1998) and adult well-being, especially for men (Nock, 1998c). Hence, the goal of extending the right to marriage to same-sex-parent families is one based on children's best interest as well as the need to increase family stability in general (Bell and Weinberg, 1978; Kurdek, 1998).

A Surplus of Family Functions

The third theme arose from the recurring observation that the family has not lost its functions but has acquired new ones. This was documented in many chapters, whether we discussed neighborhood and school quality, peer and media influences, or the lack of adequate care provided by society to its mentally ill members and to its frail seniors. Parents and adult children have to step in to provide care, assistance, guidance, coordination of services, and exert vigilance. Accordingly, we have seen that the family of the new millennium is burdened with responsibilities imposed by the deficits of the social structure. This situation in great part explains why single parents as well as poor parents (who are often the same) encounter so many roadblocks to the fulfillment of their responsibilities.

Furthermore, this theme of the burden of family functions has led to a recasting of concerns over what is seen as the "decline of the family" in some circles. Certainly, the traditional family—or, rather, what people think the traditional family was—no longer exists, because the society that had given rise to it has changed radically. Rather, the new social structure based on the market economy, technology, and the retrenchment of policies aimed at preventing and ameliorating familial problems has bestowed upon the family a new set of responsibilities or functions. Thus, too great a proportion of families are ill equipped to fulfill their functions, particularly in terms of supervising, guiding, and educating their youths. This inability of nuclear families to care for their members, protect them, and maintain them within a normative life course stems from four major causes.

One, at the juncture of the microsociological and macrosociological levels of analysis is the absence of a functional community surrounding families. A second cause, at the macrosociological level of analysis, resides in the lack of social and political support that would provide more resources to families and their members with special needs. A third cause, also systemic, refers to the fact that countless families are forgotten by society and relegated to segregated enclaves, where they are visible only when their members commit crimes. The fourth source of individual families' inability to fulfill their functions is related to the previous ones: Too many families are headed by parents, often young and single, who do not have the financial, educational, and maturity resources to raise children (Coley and Chase-Lansdale, 1998). Finally, at the micro level, too many couples divorce, compared to divorce rates in other societies. Parents often become so burdened by their own personal dramas and the need to make a living for their fractured family that their children are not sufficiently supported, even if only for a brief but crucial period of time. Negative consequences can be lifelong, particularly within the context of social inequalities (Cherlin, Chase-Lansdale, and McRae, 1998).

The Functional Community

We have seen in many chapters that more and more research points to the necessity of having parents supported by a community that cares for its children—*all* of its children, regardless of social class, race, and parents' gender. There is convergence among researchers from several disciplines as to the necessity of *collective* forms of *socialization* (Brooks-Gunn et al., 1995; Sampson, 1997; Steinberg et al., 1995). A functional community links parents together and prevents them from being isolated and ignorant of their children's activities. In turn, within such a context, what children learn at home is reinforced at their friends' homes. Adolescents then realize that other parents have expectations similar to theirs. This collectivity lends an aura of legitimacy to their parents' teachings and example. It adds credibility to the parenting effort in the children's eyes. Furthermore, within the shelter of this functional community and *informal social control,* there are fewer opportunities for deviance that would take adolescents off the path of prosocial development.

This description of the functional community is one that fits reality less and less, particularly in cities and their new suburbs. Thus, the past decades have seen the erosion of the functional community (Bellah et al., 1985; Etzioni, 1994). This is one of the reasons why too many problems experienced by families and their children are so intractable. The erosion of the functional community has occurred as a result of urbanization, individualism, dependency on expert knowledge, interest groups, and the technological market economy. All of these forces have contributed to weaken *community.*

The Cultural Context

The fifth theme informing the text was particularly evident in Chapter 2, which focused on the cultural revolution constituted by the audiovisual media (television, videos, Internet). Concerns about the advisability of exposing children to physical violence, verbal abuse, foul language, exploitative sexuality, and low-quality programming have not been taken seriously by the industries in question. The net effect, seen in Chapter 14, is that perhaps much of the nastiness, aggressiveness, lack of compliance, and at times lack of morality that is now encountered among some children, adolescents, and even young adults may in great part originate from the media (Garbarino, 1995). Parental roles become far more difficult to fulfill within such a cultural climate—a conclusion that reinforces the previous theme of families' inability to fulfill their functions adequately.

The theme of cultural context was also reflected in the recourse to social constructionism as an explanatory framework. It is the sociocultural context that defines what is proper behavior and what are masculine and feminine roles. The evolving culture has constructed and reconstructed people's perceptions of the roles of children and adolescents throughout the centuries and has done so even more recently. As well, the cultural context, along with the economy, defines the place that each ethnic group occupies in the stratification system. These are only some of the most salient examples of the role of *social constructs* in family studies encountered in this book.

Interactional and Genetic Themes

The interactional nature of family relations and the contribution of genetic inheritance to family members' development and relationships was a theme running through several chapters, particularly Chapters 9 through 15 (Ambert, 1997a). Both the environment and a person's genes interact to produce personality, relationship styles, child socialization patterns, and family environment (Plomin and Rutter, 1998).

Overall, next to its macrosociological framework of contexts and inequalities arising from the social structure, the questions of how and why family members interact toward each other as they do certainly characterize much of this text. This text is far more interactional in nature than most similar books. The combination of the interactional perspective with behavioral genetics complements and even corrects sociological theories that pay absolutely no attention to the fact that human beings are genetic as well as cultural entities.

Gender Stratification and Roles

The last theme, that of gender stratification and roles, was in evidence in most chapters. Thus, feminist perspectives were greatly influential. The text highlighted the extent to which females, at all age levels, are the nurturers and kin-keepers and how much more invested in various family domains they generally are, compared to males. Basic child socialization and care as well as familial problems and interactions affect mothers more than fathers, wives more than husbands, sisters more than brothers, and grandmothers more than grandfathers. Furthermore, social inequalities based on gender stratification mean that women are paid less than men for equivalent work, a factor that contributes to keeping a large proportion of mother-headed families at or under the poverty level.

WHAT DOES THE FUTURE HOLD?

No responsible sociologist can peer into a crystal ball and predict the future of the family beyond the *next 5 to 10 years*. The reason for this caution is that rapid change rather than stability is the landmark of the new millennium. We live in a *technology-driven* rather than a socially- or morally-driven world. The pace of technology is rapidly distancing humanity's ability to control it, plan for it, and adjust to it (Noble, 1995; Talbott, 1995). The family is immersed in a global economy where technology and profits are paramount and where the less educated become a surplus population (Rifkin, 1995; Schiller, 1996). Under such circumstances, there are not a great deal of rules; therefore, predictions of the distant future are impossible. A few demographic trends constitute the field's only secure source of predictions for the next decade.

Age Distribution and Fertility

Demographers point to a skewed age distribution toward the elderly (U.S. Bureau of the Census, 1995a). As seniors live longer and are in better health, they constitute a larger proportion of the population, because their growing numbers are not accompanied by similar numbers of births at the other end of the age structure. Because of longevity, families will often include more generations than in the past (Silverstein and Long, 1998). The family then takes the "bean-pole" form: greatgrandparents, grandparents, two or three middle-aged children, and a few greatgrandchildren.

The fertility rate is low, and young families will continue having few children; perhaps more couples will choose to remain childless. These trends are evident in all Western societies as well as in technologically advanced Asian countries such as Japan, Korea, and even China (the latter because of the One-Child Family policy). The American fertility rate, currently standing somewhere around 2.0, could conceivably dip even lower, as low as Italy's, which is at 1.4 child per woman. Or it could increase slightly if child care policies were enacted and if corporations and other employers became more family friendly. A substantial change in social policies that would provide financial compensation for middle-class and low-income parents might also serve as incentives. But it would be unrealistic to expect any upward shift that might go beyond a fertility rate of 2.5 children per woman. However, even such an increase would result in large-scale demographic consequences for several generations to come. Above all, it would reduce or stabilize the *proportion* of the population that is elderly.

Cohabitation

Will cohabitation rates increase? Probably, at least in the short term, because the current trend in this direction may not have peaked yet (Bumpass and Raley, 1995). At the same time, marriage rates will dip accordingly among *young* adults. However, over the entire life span, people will continue to marry at least once, although at a later age (U.S. Bureau of the Census, 1996). For instance, a swing toward greater religiosity could increase marriage and decrease cohabitation or single parenthood, among young couples. Better economic opportunities for the relatively unskilled might also foster marriage rather than cohabitation (Smock and Manning, 1997). This would be especially important among the less affluent segments of the population, which too often also happen to be minority groups, for whom marital commiment is not an option because of poverty.

One also has to consider the possibility that cohabitational relationships may one day became as committed and as stable as marriages. Were this to occur, children's well-being would be equally well served in both types of parental unions. From a structural standpoint, cohabitations would no longer be a concern. However, they would remain a concern at the cultural level in terms of values for those who have moral/religious objections to this form of partnering.

Divorce

What about the American divorce rate, still the highest in the Western world in 1998? As couples delay marriage, this may act as a preventive measure to those divorces that are related to youthful marriages. Divorce, like marriage and cohabitation, is culturally, socially, and economically driven. The media may be influential in this respect: A predominance of individualistic and materialistic values accompanies high divorce rates. Furthermore, the presence of so many adults whose parents had themselves divorced might lead to an increase. We have also seen that marriages that are preceded by cohabitation are more likely to end in divorce (Axinn and Thornton,

The consequences of nonmarital motherhood largely hinge on a mother's education, maturity, and the social and material resources at her disposal.

1992). Thus, a higher level of cohabitation might actually raise the divorce rate. On the other hand, greater religiosity might decrease both cohabitation and divorce. However, there is no indication that any large-scale religious revival is close at hand. Overall, the next decade should not bring a marked decline in the divorce rate: There are too many variables, as just enumerated above, that prevent it from falling substantially (Booth, 1999).

Nonmarital Family Formation

What is the future of nonmarital family formation? Recall here that, once cohabitational situations are accounted for, the United States has the highest rate of single motherhood in the Western world, some Caribbean countries excepted. This demographic pattern is largely caused by poverty and segregation (Tucker and Mitchell-Kernan, 1995). Nonmarital motherhood is generally neither in the best interest of a mother or a child, at least economically. On the other hand, nonmarital fatherhood is not immediately detrimental to individual men. So long as this gender-role imbalance remains, women are entirely responsibilized for the reduction of this type of fertility.

The rates have decreased recently, particularly among adolescents, African Americans, and for second births, and this trend could continue (Health and Human Services, 1998). Currently, this decrease seems to be related to a more widespread recourse to contraception—in this case, "the shot"—and to a greater level of abstinence. It could be related to lower unemployment. But it is difficult to predict if this downward trend will persist when other factors that could sustain it are absent from the equation. A substantial reduction of single fertility cannot occur unless several factors coalesce, including higher educational attainment, better job prospects in pockets of poverty, a change in cultural values, more adequate utilization of contraception, male cooperation, and media influences.

Same-Sex Parenting

Same-sex parenting will become somewhat more frequent and grudgingly more accepted. Unless same-sex parents are highly self-selected among the very committed, which is a possibility that has not been studied, same-sex "divorces" will become more frequent and so will same-sex stepparenting. However, these demographic trends are self-limiting: The number of same-sex couples with children is limited because homosexuality is a minority demographic phenomenon (Hewitt, 1998). It is furthermore constrained by the fact that it is difficult for homosexual couples to reproduce children. Hence, even if adoption laws were liberalized to allow widespread same-sex-couple adoption, these families would still remain a minority phenomenon.

Interracial Unions

Interracial unions have steadily increased (U.S. Bureau of the Census, 1995a). This trend is expected to continue. Interracial marriages with one African-American partner have also become more frequent but future increases will depend on desegregation in housing and schooling. These factors could lower prejudice, which is the prime requirement in this domain. If more African Americans of mixed heritage would self-identify as such—as does, for instance, the golf champion Tiger Woods and as is the case in other countries such as Brazil—the divide between blacks and whites might diminish; more interracial unions would then take place outside of the black/white dichotomous model. However, any increase in interracial unions is structurally functional only to the extent that both sexes of a same race marry out equally. Currently, black men marry out more than black women; this demographic imbalance limits black women's marital options. Furthermore, it devalues them, because it often leads black males to judge black women unfavorably compared to white or Asian ones.

The Longer Time Frame

The possible trends just presented pertain to a future that is nearly here. Surely, within a longer time frame, perhaps 20 years, more momentous changes in family life and structure may take place. One can think here of the domains of the division of labor at home (more egalitarian?), children's increased or decreased familialization, reproductive modes and technologies (in vitro wombs? cloning?), and families' growing dependency on or rejection of technology (virtual sex? robotic companions?). Most of the changes that will occur in families, in general, will be largely dictated by technoeconomic forces—that is, the combination of technological developments with the structure of the economy.

However, a point may be reached whereby unplanned technology so saturates life and degrades its humaneness that other societal forces might reassert themselves, including social planning, humanitarian philosophies, religion, morality, and community rather than economic values. What one must not forget is that technology and the market economy are ideologies; in theory, such ideologies could be rejected as *determinants* of people's lives. Rather, people could more judiciously choose technologies that can enhance rather than deplete family life. This is a choice that humanity will have to make at some point if it is to remain human and humane.

SOCIAL POLICIES PERTAINING TO FAMILIES

The reader has already been exposed to many discussions on various family-related social policies throughout most chapters. This section provides an overall perspective as well as specific suggestions. Social policies pertaining to the family are actions that are taken, generally at a governmental level, to remedy problems that afflict families or to prevent such problems from arising. Family policies are social choices (Zimmerman, 1995). Such choices are heavily influenced by the ideologies and the values espoused by a political system at a given time (Blank and Blum, 1997). For instance, there are generally vast differences in the policies enacted by a Republican- versus a Democrat-controlled Congress.

Overall, the United States does not have a comprehensive family policy (Martin, 1997). Such a policy would cover several domains of family life in an interrelated rather than piece-meal fashion and would be proactive, or intended. Family policies can be direct and intended, as in the case of the abolition of Aid to Families with Dependent Children (AFDC) and its 1996 replacement with Temporary Assistance to Needy Families (TANF). However, some consequences of planned policies are unintended. This occurs, for instance, when parents who dropped from the welfare rolls because of time limitations do not find jobs (Hernandez, 1998), do not have enough to eat because their salaries are too low (Revkin, 1999b), or do not receive child care subsidies and may have to return to welfare (Waller, 1997).

Furthermore, policies aimed at other aspects of social organization or of any of its systems, such as the justice system, can have indirect and unintended consequences for the family. One instance is the incarceration of small-time drug traffickers in the 1990s, which has had devastating results for African-American families in inner cities. It has led to a severe reduction in the number of young black males available to support their families: Over 25 percent of young black males have a criminal record, which limits their access to jobs, and many are incarcerated (Chambliss, 1995; Tonry, 1995). As a further consequence, a great number of young black mothers have been left single and without support (Blank, 1997).

Family policies can function in several ways. They can redistribute resources (welfare payments and progressive taxes fall in this category); they can regulate behaviors (as with various family planning policies, child abuse laws, and the Pregnancy Discrimination Act of 1978 destined to employers); and they can create or reorganize structures with which to carry out functions designed to help families (Zimmerman, 1995). For instance, new welfare or family planning departments can be created. As well, social policies can be preventive or ameliorative: They can be enacted with long-term goals to prevent problems over the entire life course or to alleviate problems after they have appeared.

On the whole, it is safe to advance that the American **political system** makes it very difficult to adopt preventive policies. Such policies require a great deal of planning and the political will to invest in the future. The future needs of families clash with the current political reality of getting votes. Political expediency forces the adoption of stop-gap policies to solve a few problems that are identified by public opinion polls. But even remedial policies can take a very long time to produce a visible effect that can be assessed and appreciated by the public; whereas politicians, if their party is to remain in power, need immediate or foreseeable results. Thus, politics conducted on the basis of media appeal and ability to raise huge sums of money from lobby groups to fund campaigns do not favor constructive social policies.

In this section, the focus is on four family problems that have been highlighted in previous chapters. The policies or programs suggested here are located at the preventive level for the new generations, which does not mean that they cannot ameliorate current problems among the parent generations.

Reducing Poverty

We have seen throughout the text that social inequalities brought by poverty are the root cause of a multiplicity of social problems, family dysfunctions, and individual deficits. Poverty prevents and destabilizes marriage and increases the divorce rate. It creates social isolation, delinquency, behavioral problems, school dropout, and teenage motherhood, and it encourages drug abuse. These are only a few of the costly human results of poverty. Mothers and their small children as well as elderly women living alone are particularly affected by poverty. This gendered situation holds across all cultures, except perhaps Sweden and the Netherlands, and has given rise to the concept of the *feminization of poverty.* Furthermore, poverty strikes a disproportionate number of minority families and contributes to exacerbate prejudice, particularly against blacks who become socially constructed or stereotyped in terms of poverty, welfare, and criminality.

A Critique of Current Policies

Policies aimed at truly preventing and reducing poverty rather than simply displacing it (to jails, for instance) or shifting it to private agencies and food banks would benefit the entire society (Revkin, 1999a). For example, families should receive higher rather than lower welfare payments until they are able to be self-sufficient. Welfare should be socially constructed as a form of salary given to families that have been marginalized by the economy or discrimination. It is an investment in the nation's youths and education (Sherman, 1994). It is *not* an incentive to unmarried motherhood, as we have seen in Chapter 6. Sufficient assistance could lift children out of poverty and give them better life chances (Hannon, 1997).

Adequate welfare payments that raise families above the poverty level can prevent the transmission of poverty rather than perpetuate it by enhancing children's cognitive development which later contributes to their economic success (Duncan and Brooks-Gunn, 1997). In turn, this situation could lower the rates of unmarried motherhood for, as we have seen, this is largely a poverty-related phenomenon. As well, adequate welfare support may actually be correlated with lower homicide rates (DeFronzo, 1997). Such programs are preferable to investing in prisons (Davey, 1995), which are merely a temporary or stop-gap remedy.

As can be seen from the preceding critique, it is not surprising that many concerns are currently raised about the implementation of TANF: It requires maternal employment within a brief period of time; it limits the duration of receipt; and it can send a young mother to work before her education is completed (Zaslow et al., 1998).

The payments are rather minimal. Furthermore, TANF is implemented at the local level, which brings inequities across states when, for instance, subsidized child care and food stamps are withdrawn or when the mothers are not informed of their right to continue receiving these benefits while they earn minimum wages.

Expansion of Head Start Programs

The first stage of the suggested policy development focuses on the youngest children, because early poverty is the most detrimental over time both for child, family, and society (Caspi et al., 1998; Duncan et al., 1998; McLoyd, 1998). A first step has already been widely suggested (Zigler and Styfco, 1996). It consists in providing care of the Head Start type to *all* children ages 1 to 5 in poor and near-poor families, *all day* long. (More intensive programs are more effective than half-day ones; see St. Pierre and Layzer, 1998.)

Two immediate results would follow. First, we know from Chapter 8 that children in such programs develop more human resources, both behaviorally and cognitively, that prepare them for school (Barnes, Goodson, and Layzer, 1996; Barnett, 1995). Second, since child care constitutes their main roadblock to self-sufficiency, this program would make it easier for mothers to find and retain jobs. For other mothers on welfare, pursuing their postsecondary training would be an excellent investment (Gleason, Rangarajan, and Schochet, 1998), which current policies do not necessarily encourage.

The results of Head Start programs vary depending on their duration (Reynolds and Temple, 1998). One of the reasons why Head Start children soon lose the gains they have made after they enter school is that their one-year stay in the program is too brief or limited to overcome the cognitive and behavioral deficits created by poverty. Furthermore, upon arriving in grade 1, these children are deprived of any support that would perpetuate whatever gains they have already made.

After-School Care and Improved Schooling

To extend the benefits of early childhood education, a second phase of the program would provide *after-school care* and tutoring through junior high school. This would at the same time provide children with much needed supervision and reduce opportunities for delinquency that too frequently occurs from 3:00 to 6:00 P.M. (i.e., between the end of the school day and a parent's return home from work).

As well, the quality of schools should be improved in inner cities and pockets of suburban as well as rural poverty. A few cities have recently made an effort in this direction. Such a policy might be initiated in primary school, and when the "improved" cohort of children moves on, then the program would be extended throughout high school. Each high school at risk should include incentive programs, at least on a trial basis, as exists in some states (Mauldon, 1998:56). For instance, children from low-income families could be given a "salary" to remain in school in good standing (no truancy, no disruptive conduct, and all homework done). As well, students who achieve an A or B+ could be guaranteed college scholarships. Such incentives might have the unanticipated result of creating a school and peer culture that values rather than denigrates education. If this were to happen, material incentives would no longer be needed in the next cohort of children.

Job Creation in Disadvantaged Areas

Even these valiant, concerted efforts just discussed would not reduce the segment of the poor population living in inner cities without an accelerated creation of jobs within their boundaries. Training youths for jobs that do not exist is rather futile. It is also cruel, because it shatters dreams and perpetuates hopelessness as well as anomie (Durkheim, 1951). *Anomie* is the dysfunctional condition or feeling that arises when there is a gap between cultural goals (of success, for instance) and a group's ability to reach these goals (Merton, 1968:216). It can lead to higher rates of suicide, the breaking of rules, or simply withdrawal into drugs. Expecting that inner-city blacks who have lived segregated lives can suddenly shuttle to all-white suburbs to find employment and be hired without discrimination is unrealistic, particularly when so many have a criminal record. Such expectations can only increase anomie. Most inner cities have vacant housing that constitutes hazards of all sorts and often harbors crack houses. Some of this space could be utilized, with subsidies, to create industrial and service parks as exist in suburbs. Employers would then have to hire and train local residents, including those who have a criminal record related to drugs and petty crime.

Consequences and Limitations of Programs

Each one of the preceding policies in isolation is insufficient to lift a sizeable number of children out of poverty (St. Pierre and Layzer, 1998). It is their *total configuration* that counts. The financial outlays of such multipronged, proactive, preventative policies may appear high initially, but their long-term results would make them cost effective. To begin with, welfare costs would rapidly diminish as better educated mothers and parents are able to secure and maintain jobs. At that point, Medicaid could be continued and income supplements added. In theory, this is currently happening through the Earned Income Tax Credit or supplement to low-income wage earners. But Medicaid is too often not extended when it should be. Since low income brings poor health, health costs would certainly be reduced after a while (Blank, 1997:164), and so would costs stemming from child abuse and foster care (Pelton, 1997). Over $40,000 a year is needed to maintain a young person in a correctional institution (Greenwood, 1995). Thus, within a few years, the costs incurred for law enforcement and penal institutions would fall along with delinquency, drug abuse, and particularly drug trafficking (Tonry, 1995).

Furthermore, an unintended consequence of Head Start extension and school reform in disadvantaged areas might be a further reduction in the rate of family formation by young mothers. This could result from a greater interest in school achievement and pursuits generated by school quality and financial incentives toward postsecondary education. As children mature into adolescents and have been supported by appropriate structures since age 1, their enhanced educational capital would lead to jobs. In turn, we already know that increased income constitutes an incentive to marriage before procreation and that two-parent families are less likely to become poor (Blank, 1997).

Unfortunately, not all poverty can be eradicated. Some individuals are not sufficiently well endowed by nature and need to be supported because they are in no way responsible for their deficits of human capital. Furthermore, the ideology that has contributed to the initial creation of poverty would still survive. Indeed, poverty is created, as we have seen in Chapter 6, by global socioeconomic forces that include "smart" technology requiring higher educational credentials. It is also created by corporations that are guided by an ever-increasing profit motive for shareholders, largely disregarding human costs. Corporations relocate to maximize profit, and some register in countries that are tax havens so as to avoid paying U.S. taxes through which wealth can be redistributed. They are part of the problem (see Frantz, 1999, for example). The combined ideologies of racism and sexism also contribute to create poverty (Roschelle, 1999): Poverty of minority women who cannot find employed males to help support their children. In turn, all women—single and married alike—are disadvantaged on the labor market and in terms of wages.

Encouraging and Strengthening Marriage

Another priority of family policies should reside in the encouragement of marriage as an institution, and the promotion of happy marital relationships (Emery, 1999). It is not suggested that divorce be made less accessible. Neither is it suggested that the family itself be strengthened, which is a departure from what is generally advocated. Why? The family is a very comprehensive concept that includes *any* parent/child unit: cohabiting partners and their children as well as never-married mothers and their children. Yet, these two forms of families are more related to poverty and problematic child outcomes than are married families (Coley and Chase-Lansdale, 1998). These two forms of families are currently neither in the best interest of the child or the mother (Cooksey, Menaghan, and Jekielek, 1997; Waite and Gallagher, 2000); nor do they promote responsible fatherhood (Nock, 1998a). Thus, by encouraging marriage, paternal involvement is also strengthened, and research indicates that the latter benefits children (Harris, Furstenberg, and Marmer, 1998). In a nutshell, marriage fosters parental involvement in children, particularly when the marital relationship is positive (McBride and Rane, 1998). By encouraging the formation of marital units and strengthening existing ones, the family would be in a better position to fulfill its traditional functions as well as the new ones it has been invested with by current technoeconomic changes.

However, it should be reemphasized here that a **proper gender-role socialization** that would define boys as equally nurturant as girls and fathers as equally responsible as mothers would substantially reduce the gap in paternal investment that currently exists between married and unmarried fathers. Basically, it is the faulty socialization of boys that leads to their later disinvestment as fathers (Garbarino, 1999). Were the father/child bond accorded the same importance as the mother/child bond, then a father's relationship with his children would remain, even after his relationship with the mother has ended (Silverstein and Auerbach, 1999). In other words, the problematic aspects of nonmarital motherhood are largely created by paternal failures.

Encouraging and strengthening marriage is in the realm of a possible future, but it involves cultural change, which is a slow process. Let's begin with the *formation* of marital units. This topic relates to the previous section on poverty and to Chapter 6, where we have seen that poverty, including male unemployment and low wages,

Unmarried and divorced fathers who play an active role in childrearing, are nurturant, and are responsible help provide their children with an environment that equals or is superior to that found in two-parent families.

prevents marriage, particularly among African Americans and Puerto Ricans. For instance, better-off cohabitors are more likely to marry when or before they have children (Manning and Smock, 1995). Poverty deprives males of their potential ability to support children or even to contribute to the economic functioning of a couple living on its own.

As a consequence, low-income or unemployed males are not ideal marriage prospects in young women's minds—neither are these men inclined to shoulder family responsibilities. Within the current *cultural climate of tolerance* (Pagnini and Rindfuss, 1993), women have no option except to have children in temporary cohabitations or on their own. As an additional result, the likelihood of these women ever marrying is reduced (Bennett, Bloom, and Miller, 1995). Hence, a great proportion of these children are deprived of paternal investment for life; furthermore, appropriate maternal socialization practices are more difficult to sustain under circumstances that involve poverty (Driscoll et al., 1999). Reducing unemployment and subsidizing low wages would contribute to the formation of marital units among all ethnic groups in society. Thus, the policies described earlier aimed at reducing poverty would have the secondary advantage of encouraging the formation of marital units or, at the very least, of mother-headed families that have adequate resources.

Furthermore, inasmuch as economic uncertainty creates or exacerbates marital conflict (Chapters 10 and 14), the alleviation of poverty would contribute to the *strengthening* of the conjugal bond once it is formed. As we haver seen in Chapter 5, happy, stable marriages are functional for adults, children, and society. Were marital happiness promoted via cultural and antipoverty measures, divorce rates may possibly decrease as a result. More children would be spared the negative effect of parental conflict, divorce, and subsequent poverty. This is not to say, however, that divorce would disappear, because it exists at all social class levels. But it is particularly detrimental for poor families and it is a source of poverty in itself (Smock, 1994).

Planning for Divorce

A number of couples divorce for what others would consider benign reasons and simply as a result of lower investment in their marriage (Amato and Rogers, 1999). These couples are generally good parents when married and represent perhaps a third of all divorces. *Any* decrease in the rate of such divorces involving children would be very effective, for these homes are not usually conflictual and are in the best interest of the child. When a divorce occurs in such families, children stand to lose a great deal on all fronts. They lose far more than children whose parents are locked in constant conflict (Booth, 1999).

Step 1: Before Marriage

Patterns of marital interaction and satisfaction are often set early on in marriage (Johnson and Booth, 1998); consequently, the best medicine against divorce might well begin *before* marriage. All couples applying for a marriage license should receive a mandatory preparation course covering financial and family planning, marital communication, health, and basics of child development. This is not a new idea, but one that is frequently discussed. The Catholic Church, for instance, has had such courses for decades in most dioceses, although the form they take differ widely. The program herein suggested might consist of four to six classes or workshops of a two- or three-hour duration, available in *all* neighborhoods, free of charge, with flexible hours, and include child care where relevant and even transportation for those who live too far. Furthermore, these workshops would be culturally sensitive. One might consider providing a per-hour fee to help the poor who attend.

It is difficult to predict whether couples at risk would choose not to marry and would cohabit to avoid taking the course. But these couples might, at any rate, be the least likely to benefit from such a program. The reader may well say, But how do we know if such a policy would work? At this point, we backtrack to the list of research methods in Table 1.3 (page 20). One category of methods fell under the rubric of **evaluation research.** The purpose of such research is to evaluate the effectiveness of policies and programs. Sound sociology research principles would dictate that such programs begin randomly. That is, every other couple applying for a marriage license would be enrolled in the program. This would constitute an experimental group. The other couples who are not enrolled could then serve as the control or comparison group. (In effect, this would become a natural experiment, Table 1.3, page 20.) To evaluate the effectiveness of the program, a random sample of couples from both groups would be interviewed three to five years after the marriage license has been granted.

If the explicit goal of the program is to reduce divorce, then an effective program should show a lower rate of separation and divorce in the experimental compared to the control group. Another indicator of effectiveness might be fewer children involved in the divorces of the couples who are in the experimental group. This would mean that the couples who were headed for an early divorce had at least learned to postpone having children. The program could have other worthwhile, unanticipated consequences. For instance, the quality of the remaining marriages would be examined. Here, we can think of questions suggested in Chapter 10 to measure marital quality: how often the spouses are thinking of divorce, how often they disagree and quarrel, and what their level of marital satisfaction is.

A very successful program would not only reduce divorce but would also increase the quality of remaining marriages. Once a policy is judged successful with the help of evaluation methods, then it can be extended to the entire population. In contrast, a program that shows no difference between the experimental and control groups has to be revamped and reevaluated.

Step 2: When Divorce Occurs

As a second part of divorce policy, parents who apply for a divorce should provide the judge with a plan for the care and education of their offspring. If they are unable to arrive at an agreement, they would then be required to take a course to become more aware of the effects of divorce on children. This is a legislation that is currently contemplated in Canada (McIlroy, 1998). It has also been recommended by the U.S. Commission on Child and Family Welfare (1996), and some states have undertaken it under one form or another (Wallerstein, 1998). The goal is to improve children's quality of life after divorce and lower their risks in terms of negative outcomes (Bartlett, 1999). Another goal is to encourage paternal involvement after divorce beyond mere "Sunday daddies" so that fathers become more than friends and entertainers (Simons and Associates, 1996:16). Such a plan might force soon-to-be ex-spouses to coparent or at least set their differences aside for their children's well-being.

Such a policy would also need to be evaluated, but this could be done after a year or even six months, also including randomized trials with experimental and control groups to compare the two sets of divorced families. Although such a policy and the premarital one suggested earlier may not prove all that successful at the beginning, a structure for improvement would have been created (Zimmerman, 1995). First, a structure would be in place in terms of procedures, trained personnel, and budget, whereas no such a structure currently exists. Second, procedures could be improved because the study results would pinpoint areas of deficiencies and of failures. In contrast, as things currently stand, nothing can be improved because no structure is in place. Furthermore, no evaluative or outcome research is available from those states where related programs have been implemented.

Supporting the Parental Role

Most "family" functions are actually fulfilled by parents. The parenting role itself has numerous constitutive elements, not to mention the additional roles occupied by most parents. Thus, burden and stress can be high, yet parenting is the cornerstone of familial functioning. Parents are still believed to be the main agents of socialization, even when other agents, such as peers and the media, often have a greater influence on children, particularly during adolescence and in certain neighborhoods. However, despite this belief in parents' importance, society does not generally support them, although blame is often lavished upon them (Lefley, 1997). It is necessary that parents regain an effective moral authority (Elshtain, 1990). This is not synonymous with antiquated notions of property over children.

Based on the data presented in several chapters, I suggest that parents should be respected and supported by schools, professionals, welfare agencies, and law enforcement personnel. In other words, the parental role should be more adequately

institutionalized and more positively reconstructed socially. Recall that interactional theories view children as coproducers in their development (Corsaro, 1997). Within this perspective, it is suggested that professionals help youngsters *cooperate* in their upbringing rather than evade their responsibilities. If children were encouraged from all quarters, including the media, to value their parents' moral authority, the family would become a more effective institution, whatever its structure and size (Ambert, 2001). Within such a context, children would more easily accept and internalize norms of behavior and would be more inclined to cooperate in their upbringing (Ambert, 1997a). This means that parental investment and monitoring would be facilitated, with the result that behavioral problems, drug and alcohol use, as well as delinquency would diminish substantially.

Faced with often contradictory how-to advice, constrained by a variety of professionals whose blame they fear, and muzzled by media and peer influences, many parents become indecisive, unsure of themselves, and unable to make maturity demands on their offspring (Damon, 1995). They no longer dare try to pass on their values to their children, give them guidance, or punish them for transgressions. Others are disempowered by poverty (Sampson and Laub, 1994). Still others, particularly nonresidential fathers, are disaffected because of their familial context (Doherty, Kouneski, and Erickson, 1998). Many adults find it easier to disengage from the parental role and reduce it to one of being their child's friend. This role configuration may work well with adolescents who are self-controlled, have an easy temperament, or are achievement oriented, and especially with those who benefit from a prosocial peer group. But adolescents who are blessed with all these advantages are in the minority, so that "egalitarian" parenting, which is akin to the permissive style discussed in Chapter 11, is often disastrous (Baumrind, 1991a; Bronfenbrenner, 1985; Noller and Callan, 1991).

One should not, however, interpret this discussion to imply tolerance for child abuse and neglect. Nor is this a sanctification of parents as *individuals;* rather, it is a call for the reinstitutionalization of parenting in general. It would be unrealistic to disregard the fact that many adults today are less than ideal parents in terms of the values that they pass on to their children as well as the behaviors they allow. For instance, parents who are excessively oriented toward material gains and acquisitions have little time for their children and encourage materialism. In the long run, materialism is destructive of human values based on altruism, the natural environment, and the enjoyment of simple and more direct pleasures of life. A second type of less than ideal parents are those who, either by their example or simply because of permissive attitudes, allow or encourage their children to engage in risky sex, use drugs (including alcohol), steal, behave aggressively, or, for boys, act exploitatively toward girls.

The types of adults just discussed may well constitute 10 to 20 percent of the parent population in certain areas. Policies aimed at supporting the parental role do not address all these parents. However, these policies would help conscientious parents and those who want to be. The ranks of "less than ideal" parents would, in the long run, thin down as a result of the pressure of the functional community that would arise with the **empowerment of conscientious parents**—who constitute the majority.

CONCLUSIONS: THE FAMILY IN CONTEXT

The family represents an experience lived by all people, making each individual an "expert" on the topic. But, as we have seen, this personal expertise is insufficient, for family life has many faces, speaks many languages, harbors a multitude of cultures, and involves different cohorts and dynamics. It entails great happiness and cradles painful dramas. It appears so simple but in its totality it is so very complex.

Family Research and Historical Context

The chapters in this book have highlighted the fact that many areas of family life and of its relationship with the other social systems have not yet been researched. Thus, despite the giant steps made by various disciplines in the advancement of knowledge on the family, much is still unknown. History also compounds this problem: Indeed, knowledge that is applicable today may no longer be valid 10 to 20 years from now. This is due to the fact that as the sociocultural context in which families are embedded changes, so does the family. Therefore, many topics of research will need to be revisited as the decades of the twenty-first century unfold so that people do not draw conclusions and then implement policies based on results that are obsolete.

Among some of the areas that may see change in the near future in terms of results obtained, one can think here of the statistical relationships between cohabitation and higher divorce rates. If cohabitors were to become more similar to married couples, then it is possible that premarital cohabitation would cease to be related to higher divorce rates. Similarly, if single parents, who are mainly mothers, were to receive more adequate social and economic support, their children's well-being might become more comparable to that of children in stable two-parent families. On another level,

Family research is contingent on the structural and cultural situation of a society at a given point in time. For instance, the effects of poverty on children differ depending on the era in which it occurs.

if the media that are accessible to children were regulated in terms of antisocial contents, aggressiveness might be reduced among children and adolescents. Thus, the results of current studies would no longer apply.

Family Functions and Their Environmental Context

The research summarized and evaluated in this book does not support the pessimistic view of a general family decline and loss of functions. Rather, the research supports pessimism concerning *individual families' ability* to fulfill their ever-increasing functions adequately, particularly that of the socialization of children. On the one hand, the family as an institution is highly valued, and exacting demands are placed on it in terms of its responsibilities in many domains. On the other hand, this same sociocultural context generally fails to provide individual families with an equivalent moral support and practical help that could allow them to fulfill their functions.

For instance, society is choosing to embrace technology as a value and as a way of life. Unavoidably, there are high costs to such a choice, and families bear a disproportionate burden in this respect, especially those that are marginalized by poverty, segregation, and lack of access to the new types of jobs. As Blank phrases it, "Given that the United States has chosen a market-oriented economy, it has a responsibility to those who cannot survive in the market on their own" (1997:198). This responsibility should not be displaced onto families. Unfortunately, this is exactly what is happening.

Above all, in Western societies, the family is a small and relatively isolated unit that is much affected by its environment. In recent decades, this cultural and socioeconomic environment has broadened considerably because of globalization and a more pervasive as well as intrusive technology. At the dawn of this new millennium, families are experiencing change at a rapid pace and are contextualized in a larger world, but receive relatively fewer resources in terms of instrumental and effective moral support. Empowering families, no matter their structure, is one of the key social challenges of the twenty-first century.

SUMMARY

1. The three key sociodemographic variables of social class, gender, and race are part of the fabric of the various themes that have recurred throughout this text. These themes are social inequalities, family diversity, the increase in family functions, the importance of the functional community, cultural influences, interactional and genetic themes, and gender roles.
2. Trends in the very near future of family life include more surviving generations, a continuing low fertility, and consequent skewed age distribution toward the elderly; a temporary increase in cohabitation; the maintenance of the current divorce rate; a slightly reduced rate of family formation by single mothering; and a small increase in the number of same-sex-parent families as well as interracial unions.
3. The family policies discussed involve a multipronged approach. First, a reduction of family poverty focusing on programs for children and quality of schools

is suggested. A second goal is the encouragement and strengthening of marriage through economic means. A third program involves planning for divorce both in terms of making marriage a more serious step and in terms of educating as well as requiring divorcing parents to plan for the care and education of their offspring. A fourth suggestion consists of better support for the parental role, including a valorization and respect of parents.

4. Many areas of family life are lacking in research; other domains would benefit by being constantly studied as change occurs, as current results may no longer apply. The research presented in this book does not support the pessimistic view of a loss of family functions but pessimism concerning families' ability to fulfill their ever-increasing functions adequately. The socioeconomic context in which the family evolves is problematic in terms of its well-being.

KEY CONCEPTS AND THEMES

Anomie, p. 473
Collective socialization, p. 465
Conscientious parents, p. 478
Cultural climate of tolerance, p. 475
Cultural context, p. 465
Empowerment, p. 478
Evaluation research, p. 476
Family functions, p. 464
Feminization of poverty, p. 471
Functional community, p. 464
Future of the family, p. 466
Gender roles and stratification, p. 466
Informal social control, p. 465
Institutionalized parental role, p. 478
Interactional and genetic themes, p. 465
Media influence, p. 465
Parental role, p. 477
Planning for divorce, p. 476
Political system, p. 470
Proper gender role socialization, p. 474
Race, pp. 462, 463
Reducing poverty, p. 471
Social class, pp. 462, 463
Social constructs, p. 465
Social inequalities, p. 463
Social policies, p. 470
Strengthening marriage, p. 474
Technology as determinant, pp. 466, 474
Total configuration, p. 473

STUDY AND REVIEW QUESTIONS

1. What conclusions are reached with respect to family diversity?
2. What are the reasons why more and more families are unable to meet their diverse functions?
3. How does the functional community serve as a support to the family?
4. Name at least three trends in family structure that can be safely projected for the next 10 years.
5. What effects on family life and individual well-being would an across-the-board reduction in family poverty have? Give at least six effects and explain.
6. Why should marriage be encouraged and strengthened?
7. How could the parental role be better institutionalized?
8. Discuss a two-pronged method to prevent divorce and to prevent harm to children of parents who do divorce.
9. What role do research methods play in family policies? Give an example.
10. What are three key conclusions of this text?

SUGGESTED READINGS

Booth, A., Crouter, A. C., and Landale, N. (Eds). 1997. *Immigration and the family: Research and Policy on U.S. immigrants.* Mahwah, NJ: Erlbaum. This collection of research and policy articles on immigrant families is divided into four parts: Who migrates, and how does it affect family outcomes? How does the migration experience affect child and adolescent development? How do family structure and process change across succeeding generations? What policies enhance or impede immigrant family links to U.S. institutions?

Ferree, M. M., Lorber, J., and Hess, B. B. (Eds.). 1999. *Revisioning gender.* Thousand Oaks, CA: Sage. This collection of feminist analyses on various aspects of the gender (and class/race) stratification contains many important policy implications.

Levesque, R. J. R. 1999. *Adolescents, sex, and the law: Preparing adolescents for responsible citizenship.* Washington, DC: American Psychological Association. This book focuses on adolescents' rights in such issues as abortion, sexual activity, partner battering, sexual harassment, and date rape. Important discussions relevant to social policies are included.

Mason, M. A., Skolnick, A., and Sugarman, S. 1998. *All our families: New policies for a new century.* New York: Oxford University Press. This text focuses on policy reform and covers a wide range of topics, such as teen pregnancy, child abuse, and divorce.

Nightingale, D. S., and Haveman, R. H. (Eds.). 1995. *The work alternative: Welfare reform and the realities of the job market.* Washington, DC: The Urban Institute Press. This collection of articles focuses on problems, consequences, and solutions to welfare and low wages.

Trickett, P. K., and Schellenbach, C. J. (Eds.). 1998. *Violence against children in the family and the community.* Washington, DC: American Psychological Association. This collection of articles reviews the literature on the causes and consequences of violence against children. Above all, the articles offer ameliorative and preventive interventions and programs pertaining to violence against children at home, in schools, and in neighborhoods.

Zigler, E. F., Kagan, S. L., and Hall, N. W. (Eds.). 1996. *Children, families, and government.* Cambridge: Cambridge University Press. The many articles in this book contain wide-ranging discussions on various aspects of children's and their families' problems with a focus on policy.

SUGGESTED WEBLINKS

American Psychological Association Policy Office presents information on policy activities as well as research. The office coordinates advocacy efforts at the federal level. **<http://apa.org/ppo/topic.html>**

Bazelon Center for Mental Health Law has a special website for fair housing advocacy and access to housing. It reviews recent legislation to help the elderly and the mentally disabled find housing, among other topics. **<http:www.bazelon.org/housing/html>**

Children Now provides research and practical information on families and children and related policies. **<http://www.childrennow/org>**

National Fair Housing Advocates presents recent news on poverty, housing, welfare benefits, gay rights, among others, and related social policies. **<http://www.fairhousing.com>**

Additional weblinks that contain policy-related material are:

<http://www.acf.dhhs.gov>, the website for the Administration for Children and Families, Health and Human Services.

<http://www.fedstats.gov> provides an *A* to *Z* choice of topics.

Glossary

Assortative mating: Refers to people selecting spouses or mates in a nonrandom fashion; they marry persons who are similar to them on given characteristics. The characteristics may be physical appearance, IQ, values, one or several personality traits, or even social class. The opposite of assortative mating is *random mating.*

Authoritarian parenting: Refers to parental behaviors and attitudes that are predominantly controlling and punishing. At the extreme, they can be even harsh and rejecting. The authoritarian approach does not appeal to a child's sense of reasoning or morality. It is a "do-as-I-say-or-you'll-get-smacked" type of upbringing. Authoritarian parents may also be inconsistent: They may threaten to punish but do not follow through with the punishment.

Authoritative parenting: Combines both warmth and monitoring of children's activities and whereabouts. Authoritative parents make maturity demands on their children. They explain the reasons behind their demands or rules. Once they have explained the reasons and the consequences, they consistently follow through with enforcement of those rules.

Child-saving industry: Refers to all professions and paraprofessions whose mandate it is to oversee or care for children's well-being and protection. It is an "industry" because the persons derive an income for their services, advice, and even advocacy. A similar term is the *hospitality industry* to refer to hotel and tourism employees.

Cohort: A group of people who were born around the same time and who therefore go through life experiencing similar sociohistorical conditions. For example, people born during the Great Depression form a cohort.

Comorbidity: *Morbidity* refers to illness; therefore, *comorbidity* exists when one illness or emotional problem is accompanied by another one.

Concordance or **Concordance rate:** A concept used particularly in comparisons of twins, or in comparisons of parents with their children. It signifies the percentage of cases when both twins have a same characteristic. For example, a researcher takes 100 pairs of identical twins where one twin is known to be schizophrenic and examines the other twin. The researcher may find that 60 of the "other" twins also suffer from schizophrenia. The concordance rate for schizophrenia is then 60 percent.

Correlations: Correlations exist between two factors or variables, such as poverty and violence, when, as one increases or decreases, the other also changes. When both change in the same direction (e.g., both increase), this is a *positive* correlation. A *negative* correlation exists when one factor increases at the same time that the other decreases, as in the example of a decreasing number of cases of serious delinquency with an increasing level of socioeconomic status. Correlation is a statistical test, which is schematically illustrated in Figure 6.1 on page 164.

Critical mass: Refers to a proportion of well-functioning families that is necessary in a neighborhood if that neighborhood is to remain a good environment in which to raise children. The term can also refer to the proportion of children who are good students that is necessary in a classroom if learning is to take place. Researchers have not yet been able to determine what this exact proportion should be: 30 percent? 40 percent? 60 percent?

Cross-pressure: A term used to signify that a child or an adolescent is subjected to influences that oppose each other. This concept applies particularly to parents and peers who may both influence a child toward opposite goals.

Defamilialization: Refers to the fact that children are increasingly being taken care of and socialized by nonfamily members; children spend less time at home interacting with their parents.

Dilution of parental resources: This concept is used to explain the finding that children in large families do less well, on average, than those in smaller families. The rationale is that, in large families, parents have fewer resources to place at the disposal of each child: The resources are scattered over several children, or diluted.

Downward assimilation: Refers to what happens when immigrant families settle into a poor neighborhood riddled with social problems. Their children attend a school where the students harbor negative attitudes toward education, do not possess mainstream language, and have high rates of delinquency, early parenting, and later unemployment. The immigrant children assimilate themselves to this peer culture rather than a peer culture that could lead to a mainstream assimilation. They assimilate toward the lower end of the class system or downwardly.

Downward mobility: See **Social mobility.**

Dysfunction: See *Function.* Dysfunctional behaviors are those that impair a person's functioning and success. They are maladaptive either for society, the family, the person concerned, or all of these. Persons or groups can be dysfunctional for their family or society, for instance.

Endogamy: When people date and marry within their own social class, or race, or religion, or even language group.

Ethnocentric: Refers to the judgments of social situations and people that individuals make based on their experiences within the culture of their own ethnic or cultural group. It can also be the assumption that one's own way of life is superior to that of other cultures or groups in one's society.

Exogamy: The opposite of *endogamy:* marrying out of one's group. Interracial and interreligious marriages are examples of exogamy.

Function: What an institution or group does for society, for families, or for individuals.

Functional community: Refers to parents' linkage to other parents and to members of the community who maintain a prosocial set of values. The sharing of values, socialization goals, instrumental help, and collective supervision of children are characteristics of a functional community.

Gender roles: Norms or rules that define how males and females should think and behave. They represent the social definition of what, in a society, is constructed as appropriately masculine or feminine in terms of behavior.

Homogamy: See **Assortative mating.**

Homogeneity: Uniformity; similarity.

Human capital: The entirety of abilities, skills, education, and positive human characteristics that a person possesses or has achieved. A synonym would be *human assets.*

Hypothesis: A testable proposition or sentence. For instance, wives who have been employed all their married lives adjust better to divorce than homemakers or women who have been employed irregularly. Hypotheses are often designed to test theories.

Indicator: Indicators are used to measure variables, such as conjugal conflict. They are sentences, numbers, or observations that serve to illustrate a variable. Indicators are often coded (given a number) to derive statistics. Indicators of conjugal conflict can be the number of times spouses say they quarrel and how long their quarrels last.

Individuation: A psychological concept referring to children's gaining a sense of identity separately from their connection to their parents.

Institution: A recognized area of social life that is organized along a system of norms (or rules) regulating behaviors that are widely accepted in a society. Examples of institutions are the family, schools, and the banking system. On a larger scale, institutions include the political, economic, and religious systems of a society.

Longitudinal studies: Consist of studying the same people over time. For instance, people may be interviewed at age 18 and restudied again at ages 25 and 35. This research design contrasts with *cross-sectional* or *one-time studies* and surveys. A synonym is a *panel study.*

Macrosociology: In other words, "large" sociology or the study of large-scale phenomena and developments in a society, its social structure and organization. It is the study of the family within its broader sociocultural context to see how global forces such as the class system, the economy, and religion shape family structure and dynamics.

Median: The middle number in a set of numbers that are arranged in order of magnitude.

Microsociology: The study of interactions between individuals within specific and generally smaller contexts, such as the family or a group of friends. It is also the study of the internal dynamics of small groups, including the family.

Nonshared environment: Generally refers to experiences that differ for each sibling in a family. These can be different school, peer, and street experiences or environment. Within the home, the term refers to experiences that are specific to each child, such as differential parental treatment, the presence of the other siblings, or the chores given to a child because of his or her age or gender.

Polygenetic: Refers to a trait, characteristic, or illness that can occur only when several specific genes are present.

Reference group: A group or category of persons whom people look up to, whose behavior they imitate and emulate, and according to whose standards they evaluate themselves.

Shared environment: Generally refers to the home environment that siblings have in common or share. This could include parental behaviors, teachings, family routines and special occasions, and transitions, such as divorce or the death of a grandparent. It refers to the familial atmosphere. However, this shared environment is often perceived somewhat differently by each sibling, depending on his or her age, gender, and personality: The environment is shared but its impact differs.

Significant others: Persons who play an important role in an individual's life or with whom the individual identifies.

Social capital: A resource that resides in relationships, particularly family and community relations, that benefit child socialization. In Coleman's (1988) theory, it refers both to the positive interactions between a child's parents and between the child and his or her parents, as well as the relationships that parents maintain outside of the family that can benefit children or the entire family. A synonym could be *social assets*.

Social causation: Refers to theories that explain the high rates of well-being and economic success found, for example, among the married compared to the nonmarried, as a result of the benefits of marriage.

Social construct: A socially acceptable definition of a situation. It is a cultural creation or invention. Social constructs concerning a phenomenon, such as adolescence, generally differ across history and across cultures.

Socialization: Refers to the process whereby a child learns to think and behave according to the ways of the society and the group in which he or she is born.

Social mobility: The passage from one social stratum to another or from one social class to another. *Downward* mobility occurs when individuals fall below their parents' stratum (intergenerational mobility) or below the one they have themselves occupied earlier (intragenerational mobility). *Upward* mobility takes place when individuals achieve a higher socioeconomic status than that of their parents. In other words, they "move up" in the class system.

Social selection: Refers to theories that explain the high rates of well-being and economic success found, for example, among the married compared to the nonmarried, as a result of individuals being selected into the married status because they are better balanced and more motivated to begin with.

Socioeconomic status or **SES:** The ranking of people on a scale of prestige on the basis of occupation, income, and education. SES is often used as a synonym for *social class*.

Stratification: Refers to the ranking that people occupy in a system. Social stratification can be based on gender, race, or social class. For instance, families that belong to the higher social class have more resources, power, and prestige than the others.

Systemic: Refers to a problem that is built into a system, an institution, or a society. Solutions to such problems require a restructuring of the institution, a difficult enterprise at best.

Theory: A set of interrelated propositions that explain a particular phenomenon. A theory is a sophisticated explanation that can be tested against facts to see if it fits. A good theory should withstand the test of research.

Upward mobility: See **Social mobility.**

Bibliography

Abma, J., Driscoll, A., and Moore, K. 1998. Young women's degree of control over first intercourse: An exploratory analysis. *Family Planning Perspectives,* 30, 12–18.

Acock, A. C., and Demo, D. H. 1994. *Family diversity and well-being.* Thousand Oaks, CA: Sage.

Aday, L. A. 1993. *At risk in America.* San Francisco: Jossey-Bass.

Adler, J. 1997. Bundles of . . . joy? *Newsweek,* December 1, p. 62.

Adler, P. A., and Adler, P. 1998. *Peer power: Preadolescent culture and identity.* New Brunswick, NJ: Rutgers University Press.

Administration on Children, Youth, and Families. 1998. *Head Start 1998 fact sheet.* Washington, DC: Administration on Children, Youth, and Families.

Ahrons, C. 1994. *The good divorce.* New York: HarperCollins.

Alba, R. D., Logan, J. R., and Bellair, P. E. 1994. Living with crime: The implications of racial/ethnic differences in suburban location. *Social Forces,* 73, 395–434.

Aldous, J. 1996. *Family careers: Rethinking the developmental perspective.* Thousand Oaks, CA: Sage.

Aldous, J., and Ganey, R. F. 1999. Family life and the pursuit of happiness: The influence of gender and race. *Journal of Family Issues,* 20, 155–180.

Aldous, J., Klaus, E., and Klein, D. M. 1985. The understanding heart: Aging parents and their favorite children. *Child Development,* 56, 303–316.

Aldous, J., Mulligan, G. M., and Bjarnason, T. 1998. Fathering over time: What makes the difference? *Journal of Marriage and the Family,* 60, 809–820.

Alexander, A. 1994. The effect of media on family interaction. In D. Zillman, J. Bryant, and A. C. Huston (Eds.), *Media, children, and the family* (pp. 51–59). Hillsdale, NJ: Erlbaum.

Ali, J., and Avison, W. R. 1997. Employment transitions and psychological distress: The contrasting experiences of single and married mothers. *Journal of Health and Social Behavior,* 38, 345–362.

Allen, K. R. 1995. Opening the classroom closet: Sexual orientation and self-disclosure. *Family Relations,* 44, 136–141.

Allen, K. R. 2000. A conscious and inclusive family studies. *Journal of Marriage and the Family,* 62, 4–17.

Allen, K. R., and Baber, K. M. 1992. Starting a revolution in family life education: A feminist vision. *Family Relations,* 41, 378–384.

Allen, K. R., and Demo, D. H. 1995. The families of lesbians and gay men: A new frontier in family research. *Journal of Marriage and the Family,* 57, 111–127.

Almond, B. 1995. Family relationships and reproductive technology. In C. Ulanowsky (Ed.), *The family in the age of biotechnology* (pp. 13–26). Aldershot, UK: Avebury.

Alston, L. 1992. Children as chattel. In E. West and P. Petrick (Eds.), *Small worlds* (pp. 208–231). Lawrence, KS: University of Kansas Press.

Alwin, D. F. 1986. From obedience to autonomy: Changes in traits desired in children, 1924–1978. *Public Opinion Quarterly,* 52, 33–52.

Alwin, D. F. 1990. Cohort replacement and changes in parental socialization values. *Journal of Marriage and the Family,* 52, 347–360.

Amato, P. R. 1996. Explaining the intergenerational transmission of divorce. *Journal of Marriage and the Family,* 58, 628–640.

Amato, P. R. 1999. The postdivorce society: How divorce is shaping the family and other forms of social organization. In R. A. Thompson and P. R. Amato (Eds.), *The postdivorce family* (pp. 161–190). Thousand Oaks, CA: Sage.

Amato, P. R., and Booth, A. 1997. *A generation at risk: Growing up in an era of family upheaval.* Cambridge, MA: Harvard University Press.

Amato, P. R., and Gilbreth, J. G. 1999. Nonresident fathers and children's well-being: A meta-analysis. *Journal of Marriage and the Family,* 61, 557–573.

Amato, P. R., and Rezac, S. J. 1994. Contact with non-resident parents, interparental conflict, and children's behavior. *Journal of Family Issues,* 15, 191–207.

Amato, P. R., and Rivera, F. 1999. Paternal involvement and children's behavioral problems. *Journal of Marriage and the Family,* 61, 375–384.

Amato, P. R., and Rogers, S. J. 1997. A longitudinal study of marital problems and subsequent divorce. *Journal of Marriage and the Family,* 59, 612–624.

Amato, P. R., and Rogers, S. J. 1999. Do attitudes toward divorce affect marital quality? *Journal of Family Issues,* 20, 69–86.

Amato, P. R., Spencer-Loomis, L. S., and Booth, A. 1995. Parental divorce, marital conflict, and offspring well-being during early adulthood. *Social Forces,* 73, 895–915.

Ambert, A.-M. 1989. *Ex-spouses and new spouses: A study of relationships.* Greenwich, CT: JAI Press.

Ambert, A.-M. 1994a. A qualitative study of peer abuse and its effects: Theoretical and empirical implications. *Journal of Marriage and the Family,* 56, 119–130.

Ambert, A.-M. 1994b. An international perspective on parenting: Social change and social constructs. *Journal of Marriage and the Family,* 56, 529–543.

Ambert, A.-M. 1995. A critical perspective on the research on parents and adolescents: Implications for research, intervention, and social policy. In D. H. Demo and A.-M. Ambert (Eds.), *Parents and adolescents in changing families* (pp. 291–306). Minneapolis, MN: National Council on Family Relations.

Ambert, A.-M. 1997a. *Parents, children, and adolescents: Interactive relationships and development in context.* New York: Haworth.

Ambert, A.-M., 1997b. The effect of delinquency on parents. *Family and Corrections Network Report,* 13. Palmyra, VA: Family and Corrections Network.

Ambert, A.-M. 1998a. *The web of poverty: Psychosocial perspectives.* New York: Haworth.

Ambert, A.-M. 1998b. *Parent-blaming by clinicians: The effect on mothers.* Paper presented at the Mother-Son Symposium, York University, Toronto, September.

Ambert, A.-M. 1999. The effect of male delinquency on mothers and fathers: A heuristic study. *Sociological Inquiry,* 69, 621–640.

Ambert, A.-M. 2001. *The effect of children on parents* (2nd ed.). New York: Haworth.

Ambert, A.-M., Adler, P. A., Adler, P., and Detzner, D. F. 1995. Understanding and evaluating qualitative research. *Journal of Marriage and the Family,* 57, 879–893.

Ammerman, N. T. 1997. *Congregation and community.* New Brunswick, NJ: Rutgers University Press.

Amott, T., and Matthei, J. 1991. *Race, gender and work: A multicultural economic history of women in the United States.* Boston: South End Press.

Anderson, A. L. 1998. Strength of gay male youth: An untold story. *Child and Adolescent Social Work Journal,* 15, 55–71.

Anderson, E. 1990. *Streetwise: Race, class, and change in an urban community.* Chicago: University of Chicago Press.

Anderson, E. 1993. Sex codes and family life among poor inner-city youths. In R. I. Lerman and T. J. Ooms (Eds.), *Young unwed fathers* (pp. 74–98). Philadelphia: Temple University Press.

Anderson, E. B., and Rice, A. M. 1992. Sibling relationships during remarriage. In E. M. Hetherington and G. Clingempeel (Eds.), *Coping with marital transitions* (pp. 149–177). Monographs of the Society for Research in Child Development, 57, no. 227.

Anderson, E. R. 1999. Sibling, half sibling, and stepsibling relationships in remarried families. In E. M. Hetherington, S. H. Henderson, and D. Reiss (Eds.), *Adolescent siblings in stepfamilies: Family functioning and adolescent adjustment* (pp. 101–126). Monographs of the Society for Research in Child Development, 259, 64, no. 4.

Anderson, K. L. 1997. Gender, status, and domestic violence: An integration of feminist and family violence approaches. *Journal of Marriage and the Family,* 59, 655–669.

Andreasen, M. S. 1994. Patterns of family life and television consumption from 1945 to the 1990s. In D. Zillman, J. Bryant, and A. C. Huston (Eds.), *Media, children, and the family* (pp. 19–36). Hillsdale, NJ: Erlbaum.

Aneshensel, C. S., and Sucoff, C. A. 1996. The neighborhood context of adolescent mental health. *Journal of Health and Social Behavior,* 37, 293–310.

Appell, A. R. 1998. On fixing "bad" mothers and saving their children. In M. Ladd-Taylor and L. Umansky (Eds.), *"Bad" mothers: The politics of blame in twentieth-century America* (pp. 356–380). New York: New York University Press.

Aquilino, W. S. 1990. The likelihood of parent-adult child co-residence: Effects of family structure and parental characteristics. *Journal of Marriage and the Family,* 52, 405–419.

Aquilino, W. S. 1991. Family structure and home leaving: A further specification of the relationship. *Journal of Marriage and the Family,* 53, 999–1010.

Aquilino, W. S. 1996. The life course of children born to unmarried mothers: Childhood living arrangements and young adult outcomes. *Journal of Marriage and the Family,* 58, 293–310.

Aquilino, W. S. 1997. From adolescent to young adult: A prospective study of parent-child relations during the transition to adulthood. *Journal of Marriage and the Family,* 59, 670–686.

Aquilino, W. S., and Supple, K. R. 1991. Parent-child relations and parents' satisfaction with living arrangements when adult children live at home. *Journal of Marriage and the Family,* 53, 13–28.

Arditti, J. A. 1992. Differences between fathers with joint custody and noncustodial fathers. *American Journal of Orthopsychiatry,* 62, 186–195.

Arditti, J. A., and Bickley, P. 1996. Fathers' involvement and mothers' parenting stress postdivorce. *Journal of Divorce and Remarriage,* 26, 1–23.

Arendell, T. 1995. *Fathers and divorce.* Newbury Park, CA: Sage.

Ariès, P. 1962. *Centuries of childhood: A social history of family life.* New York: Knopf and Random House.

Arnold, M. S. 1995. Exploding the myths: African-American families at promise. In B. B. Swadener and S. Lubeck (Eds.), *Children and families "at promise"* (pp. 143–162). Albany: State University of New York Press.

Aseltine, R. H., Jr. 1996. Pathways linking parental divorce with adolescent depression. *Journal of Health and Social Behavior,* 37, 113–148.

Aseltine, R. H., Jr., Gore, S., and Colten, M. E. 1994. Depression and the social developmental context of adolescence. *Journal of Personality and Social Psychology,* 67, 252–263.

Aseltine, R. H., Jr., and Kessler, R. C. 1993. Marital disruption and depression in a community sample. *Journal of Health and Social Behavior,* 34, 237–251.

Astone, N. M., and McLanahan, S. S. 1994. Family structure, residential mobility, and school dropout: A research note. *Demography,* 31, 575–584.

Atkin, C. 1978. Observation of parent-child interaction in supermarket decision making. *Journal of Marketing,* 42, 41–45.

Austin, E. W., Roberts, D. F., and Nass, C. I. 1990. Influences of family communication on children's television-interpretation processes. *Communication Research,* 17, 545–564.

Axinn, W. G., Barber, J. S., and Thornton, A. 1998. The long-term impact of parents' childbearing decisions on children's self-esteem. *Demography,* 35, 435–443.

Axinn, W. G., Duncan, G. J., and Thornton, A. 1997. The effects of parents' income, wealth, and attitudes on children's completed schooling and self-esteem. In G. J. Duncan and J. Brooks-Gunn (Eds.), *Consequences of growing up poor* (pp. 518–540). New York: Russell Sage.

Axinn, W. G., and Thornton, A. 1992. The relationship between cohabitation and divorce: Selectivity or causal influence. *Demography,* 29, 357–374.

Baber, K. M., and Allen, K. R. 1992. *Women and families: Feminist reconstructions.* New York: Guilford Press.

Bachman, J. G., Wadsworth, K. N., O'Malley, P. M., Johnson, L. D., and Schulenberg, J. E. 1997. *Smoking, drinking, and drug use in young adulthood.* Mahwah, NJ: Erlbaum.

Bachman, R. 1994. *Violence against women: A National Crime Victimization Survey report.* Washington, DC: Department of Justice, Bureau of Justice Statistics.

Bagley, C. 1993. Transracial adoption in Britain: A follow-up study, with policy considerations. *Child Welfare,* 72, 285–299.

Bahr, S. J., Maughan, S. L., Marcos, A. C., and Li, B. 1998. Family, religiosity, and the risk of adolescent drug use. *Journal of Marriage and the Family,* 60, 979–992.

Bailey, J. M., Bobrow, D., Wolfe, M., and Mikach, S. 1995. Sexual orientation of adult sons and gay fathers. *Developmental Psychology,* 31, 124–129.

Baines, C., Evans, P., and Neysmith, S. 1991. Caring: Its impact on the lives of women. In C. Baines, P. Evans, and S. Neysmith (Eds.), *Women caring: Feminist perspectives* (pp. 11–35). Toronto: McLelland and Stewart.

Baker, L. A., and Daniels, D. 1990. Nonshared environmental influences and personality differences in adult twins. *Journal of Personality and Social Psychology,* 58, 103–110.

Ballard, C. and Davies, R. 1996. Postnatal depression in fathers. *International Review of Psychiatry,* 8, 65–71.

Bank, L., Patterson, G. R., and Reid, J. B. 1996. Negative sibling interaction patterns as predictors of later adjustment problems in adolescent and young adult males. In G. H. Brody (Ed.), *Sibling relationships: Their causes and consequences* (pp. 197–230). Norwood, NJ: Ablex.

Bankston, C. L., III, and Caldas, S. J. 1998. Family structure, schoolmates, and racial inequalities in school achievement. *Journal of Marriage and the Family,* 60, 715–724.

Bao, W.-N., Whitbeck, L. B., Hoyt, D. R., and Conger, R. D. 1999. Perceived parental acceptance as a moderator of religious transmission among adolescent boys and girls. *Journal of Marriage and the Family,* 61, 362–374.

Barber, B. K. 1994. Cultural, family, and personal contexts of parent-adolescent conflict. *Journal of Marriage and the Family,* 56, 375–386.

Barber, E., and Pasley, B. K. 1995. Family care of Alzheimer's patients: The role of gender and generational relationship on caregiver outcomes. *Journal of Applied Gerontology,* 14, 172–192.

Barkley, R. A. 1997. Behavioral inhibition, sustained attention, and executive functions: Constructing a unifying theory of ADHD. *Psychological Bulletin,* 121, 65–94.

Barnes, H. V., Goodson, B. D., and Layzer, J. I. 1996. *Review of the research on family support interventions.* Cambridge, MA: Abt Associates.

Barnett, D., Manly, J. T., and Cicchetti, D. 1993. Defining child maltreatment: The interface between policy and research. In D. Cicchetti and S. L. Toth (Eds.), *Advances in applied developmental psychology, Vol. 8: Child abuse, child development, and social policy.* Norwood, NJ: Ablex.

Barnett, R. C., Marshall, N. L., and Pleck, J. H. 1992. Adult son-parent relationships and their associations with son's psychological distress. *Journal of Family Issues,* 13, 505–525.

Barnett, S. W. 1995. Long-term effects of early childhood programs on cognitive and school outcomes. *The Future of Children,* 5, 25–50.

Barnett, S. W. 1998. Long-term cognitive and academic effects of early childhood education of children in poverty. *Preventive Medicine,* 27, 204–207.

Bartholet, E. 1993. *Family bonds: Adoption and the politics of parenting.* Boston: Houghton Mifflin.

Bartkowski, J. P., and Ellison, C. G. 1995. Divergent models of childrearing in popular manuals: Conservative Protestants vs. the mainstream experts. *Sociology of Religion,* 56, 21–34.

Bartlett, K. T. 1999. Improving the law relating to postdivorce arrangements for children. In R. A. Thompson and P. R. Amato (Eds.), *The postdivorce family* (pp. 71–102). Thousand Oaks, CA: Sage.

Bassuk, E. L., Weinreb, L. F., Buckner, J. C., Browne, A., Salomon, A., and Bassuk, S. S. 1996. The characteristics and needs of sheltered homeless and low-income housed mothers. *Journal of the American Medical Association,* 276, 640–646.

Bates, J. E. 1987. Temperament in infancy. In J. D. Osofsky (Ed.), *Handbook of infant development* (2nd ed., pp. 1101–1149). New York: Wiley.

Bates, J. E., Pettit, G. S., Dodge, K. A., and Ridge, B. 1998. Interaction of temperamental resistance to control and restrictive parenting in the development of externalizing behavior. *Developmental Psychology,* 34, 982–995.

Baumrind, D. 1967. Child care practices anteceding three patterns of preschool behavior. *Genetic Psychology Monographs,* 75, 43–88.

Baumrind, D. 1991a. Effective parenting during the early adolescent transition. In P. A. Cowan and M. E. Hetherington (Eds.), *Family transitions* (pp. 111–163). Hillsdale, NJ: Erlbaum.

Baumrind, D. 1991b. The influence of parenting style on adolescent competence and substance abuse. *Journal of Early Adolescence,* 11, 56–94.

Baumrind, D. 1994. The social context of child maltreatment. *Family Relations,* 43, 360–368.

Baumrind, D. 1996. The discipline controversy revisited. *Family Relations,* 45, 405–414.

Baydar, N., and Brooks-Gunn, J. 1998. Profiles of grandmothers who help care for their grandchildren in the United States. *Family Relations,* 47, 385–393.

Baydar, N., Greek, A., and Brooks-Gunn, J. 1997. A longitudinal study of the effects of the birth of a sibling during the first 6 years of life. *Journal of Marriage and the Family,* 59, 939–956.

Baydar, N., Hyle, P., and Brooks-Gunn, J. 1997. A longitudinal study of the effects of the birth of a sibling during preschool and early grade school years. *Journal of Marriage and the Family,* 59, 957–965.

Beck, S. H., Cole, B. S., and Hammond, J. A. 1991. Religious heritage and premarital sex: Evidence from a national sample of young adults. *Journal for the Scientific Study of Religion,* 30, 173–180.

Beeghley, L. 1996. *What does your wife do? Gender and the transformation of family life.* Boulder, CO: Westview Press.

Behrman, R. E. 1996. Financing child care. *The Future of Children,* 6, 2.

Bell, A. P., and Weinberg, M. S. 1978. *Homosexualities: A study of diversity among men and women.* New York: Simon and Schuster.

Bell, C. C., and Jenkins, E. J. 1993. Community violence and children on Chicago's southside. *Psychiatry,* 56, 46–54.

Bell, R. Q. 1968. A reinterpretation of the direction of effects in studies of socialization. *Psychological Review,* 75, 81–85.

Bellah, R. N., Madsen, R., Sullivan, W., Swindler, A., and Tipton, S. 1985. *Habits of the heart: Individualism and commitment in American life.* Berkeley: University of California Press.

Belsky, J. 1984. The determinants of parenting: A process model. *Child Development,* 55, 83–96.

Belsky, J. 1992. Consequences of child care for children's development: A deconstructionist view. In A. Booth (Ed.), *Child care in the 1990s: Trends and consequences* (pp. 83–94). Hillsdale, NJ: Erlbaum.

Belsky, J., and Kelly, J. 1994. *The transition to parenthood: How a first child changes a marriage.* New York: Delacorte Press.

Belsky, J., Youngblade, L., Rovine, M., and Volling, B. 1991. Patterns of marital change and parent-child interaction. *Journal of Marriage and the Family,* 53, 487–498.

Bennett, N. G., Bloom, D. E., and Miller, C. K. 1995. The influence of nonmarital childbearing in the formation of first marriages. *Demography,* 32, 47–62.

Bennett, T., Braveman, P., Egerter, S., and Kiely, J. L. 1994. Maternal marital status as a risk factor for infant mortality. *Family Planning Perspectives,* 26, 252–256.

Benson, P. L., Sharma, A. R., and Roehlkepartain, E. C. 1994. *Growing up adopted: A portrait of adolescents and their families.* Minneapolis, MN: Search Institute.

Berardo, F. M. 1998. Family privacy: Issues and concepts. *Journal of Family Issues,* 19, 4–19.

Berger, P. L., and Luckmann, T. 1966. *The social construction of reality: A treatise in the sociology of knowledge.* New York: Doubleday.

Bernard, J. 1972. *The future of marriage.* New York: World.

Bernstein, A. C. 1997. Stepfamilies from siblings' perspectives. *Marriage & Family Review,* 26, 153–176.

Berrick, J. D., Needell, B., Barth, R. P., and Johnson-Reid, M. 1998. *The tender years: Toward developmentally sensitive child welfare services for very young children.* New York: Oxford University Press.

Berry, M. 1991. The effects of open adoption on biological and adoptive parents and the children: The arguments and the evidence. *Child Welfare,* 70, 637–651.

Berryman, J. C., and Windridge, K. 1991. Having a baby after 40: II. A preliminary investigation of women's experience of motherhood. *Journal of Reproductive and Infant Psychology,* 9, 19–33.

Bess, B. E., and Janssen, Y. 1982. Incest: A pilot study. *Journal of Clinical Psychology,* 4, 39–52.

Bianchi, S. M. 1995. The changing demographic and socioeconomic characteristics of single parent families. In S. M. H. Hanson, M. L. Heims, D. J. Julian, and M. B. Sussman (Eds.), *Single parent families: Diversity, myths and realities* (pp. 71–98). New York: Haworth.

Bianchi, S. M., Subaiya, L., and Kahn, J. R. 1999. The gender gap in the economic well-being of nonresident fathers and custodial mothers. *Demography,* 36, 195–203.

Billingsley, A. 1992. *Climbing Jacob's ladder: The enduring legacy of African-American families.* New York: Simon and Schuster.

Birch, S. H., and Ladd, G. W. 1998. Children's interpersonal behaviors and the teacher-child relationship. *Developmental Psychology,* 34, 934–946.

Bird, C. E. 1999. Gender, household labor, and psychological distress: The impact of the amount and division of housework. *Journal of Health and Social Behavior,* 40, 32–45.

Bird, G., and Melville, K. 1994. *Families and intimate relationships.* New York: McGraw-Hill.

Birns, B., and Birns, S. 1997. Violence-free families. In S. Dreman (Ed.), *The family on the threshold of the 21st century* (pp. 129–146). Mahwah, NJ: Erlbaum.

Blair, S. L., and Qian, Z. 1998. Family and Asian students' educational performance: A consideration of diversity. *Journal of Family Issues,* 19, 355–374.

Blake, J., Richardson, B., and Bhattacharya, J. 1991. Number of siblings and sociability. *Journal of Marriage and the Family,* 53, 271–284.

Blank, R. M. 1997. *It takes a nation: A new agenda for fighting poverty.* New York: Russell Sage.

Blank, S. W., and Blum, B. 1997. A brief history of work expectations for welfare mothers. *The Future of Children,* 7, 28–39.

Blau, P. 1964. *Exchange and power in social life.* New York: Wiley.

Block, J. H., Block, J., and Gjerde, P. F. 1988. Parental functioning and the home environment of families of divorce: Prospective and current analyses. *Journal of the American Academy of Child and Adolescent Psychiatry,* 27, 207–213.

Blumer, H. 1969. *Symbolic interactionism: Perspective and method.* Englewood Cliffs, NJ: Prentice-Hall.

Blumstein, P., and Schwartz, P. 1990. Intimate relationships and the creation of sexuality. In D. McWhirter, S. Sanders, and J. Reinisch (Eds.), *Homosexuality/heterosexuality: Concepts of sexual orientation* (pp. 96–109). New York: Oxford University Press.

Boer, F., Goedhart, A. W., and Treffers, P. D. A. 1992. Siblings and their parents. In F. Boer and J. Dunn (Eds.), *Children's sibling relationships* (pp. 41–54). Hillsdale, NJ: Erlbaum.

Boivin, M. J., and Giordani, B. 1995. A risk evaluation of the neuropsychological effects of childhood lead toxicity. *Developmental Neuropsychology,* 11, 157–180.

Bokemeier, J., and Maurer, R. 1987. Marital quality and conjugal labor involvement of rural couples. *Family Relations,* 36, 417–424.

Bolger, N., DeLongis, A., Kessler, R. C., and Wethington, E. 1989. The contagion of stress across multiple roles. *Journal of Marriage and the Family,* 51, 175–183.

Bonecutter, F. J., and Gleeson, J. P. 1997. Broadening our view: Lessons from kinship foster care. In G. R. Anderson, A. S. Ryan, and B. R. Leashore (Eds.), *The challenge of permanency planning in a multicultural society* (pp. 99–119). New York: Haworth.

Bonvillain, N. 1997. *Language, culture, and communication: The meaning of messages.* Saddle River, NJ: Prentice-Hall.

Booth, A. 1999. Causes and consequences of divorce: Reflections on recent research. In R. A. Thompson and P. R. Amato (Eds.), *The postdivorce family* (pp. 29–48). Thousand Oaks, CA: Sage.

Booth, A., and Edwards, J. M. 1992. Starting over: Why remarriages are unstable. *Journal of Family Issues,* 13, 179–194.

Borders, L. D., Black, L. K., and Pasley, B. K. 1998. Are adopted children and their parents at greater risk for negative outcomes? *Family Relations,* 47, 237–241.

Bouchard, T. J., Jr., Lykken, D. T., McGue, M., Segal, N. L., and Tellegen, A. 1990. Sources of human psychological difference: The Minnesota study of twins reared apart. *Science,* 250, 223–228.

Bowles, S., and Gintis, S. 1976. *Schooling in capitalist America: Education and the contradictions of economic life.* New York: Basic Books.

Boyd, M., and Norris, D. 1995. Leaving the nest? The impact of family structure. *Canadian Social Trends,* 38, Autumn, 14–19.

Bozett, F. W., and Hanson, S. M. H. 1991. *Fatherhood and families in cultural context.* New York: Springer.

Braungart-Rieker, J., et al. 1995. Genetic mediation of longitudinal associations between family environment and childhood behavior problems. *Development and Psychopathology,* 7, 233–245.

Bray, J. H. and Kelly, J. 1998. *Stepfamilies: Love, marriage, and parenting in the first decade.* New York: Broadway Books.

Brayfield, A. 1995. Juggling jobs and kids: The impact of employment schedules on fathers' caring for children. *Journal of Marriage and the Family,* 57, 321–332.

Brener, N. D., McMahon, P. M., Warren, C. W., and Douglas, K. A. 1999. Forced sexual intercourse and associated health-risk behaviors among female college students in the United States. *Journal of Consulting and Clinical Psychology,* 67, 252–259.

Brewer, D. J., Eide, E. R., and Ehrenberg, R. G. 1999. Does it pay to attend an elite private college? Cross-cohort evidence of the effects of college type on earnings. *Journal of Human Resources,* 34, 104–123.

Brewster, K. L. 1994. Race differences in sexual activity among adolescent women: The role of neighborhood characteristics. *American Sociological Review,* 59, 408–424.

Briere, J., and Runtz, M. 1993. Childhood sexual abuse: Long-term sequelae and implications for psychological assessment. *Journal of Interpersonal Violence,* 8, 132–133.

Brines, J., and Joyner, K. 1999. The ties that bind: Principles of cohesion in cohabitation and marriage. *American Sociological Review,* 64, 333–355.

Brisson, C., Laflamme, N., Moisan, J., Milot, A., Masse, B., and Vezina, M. 1999. Effect of family responsibilities and job strain on ambulatory blood pressure among white-collar women. *Psychosomatic Medicine,* 61, 205–213.

Brody, D. J., Pinkle, J. L., Kramer, R. A., Flegal, K. M., Matte, T. D., Gunter, E. W., and Paschal, D. C. 1994. Blood lead levels in the U.S. population. Phase 1 of the Third National Health and Nutrition Examination Survey (NHANES III, 1988 to 1991). *Journal of the American Medical Association,* 272, 277–283.

Brody, G. H., and Flor, D. L. 1998. Maternal resources, parenting practices, and child competence in rural, single-parent African American families. *Child Development,* 69, 803–816.

Brody, G. H., Flor, D. L., Hallett-Wright, N., and McCoy, J. K. 1998. Children's development of alcohol use norms: Contributions of parent and sibling norms, children's temperaments, and parent-child discussions. *Journal of Family Psychology,* 12, 209–219.

Brody, G. H., Stoneman, Z., and Flor, D. L. 1995. Linking family processes and academic competence among rural African American youths. *Journal of Marriage and the Family,* 57, 567–579.

Brody, G. H., Stoneman, Z., Smith, T., and Gibson, N. M. 1999. Sibling relationships in rural African American families. *Journal of Marriage and the Family,* 61, 1046–1057.

Brodzinski, D. M. 1993. Long-term outcomes in adoption. In R. E. Behrman (Ed.), *The future of children: Adoption* (pp. 153–166). Los Altos, CA: Center for the Future of Children, the Davis and Lucille Packard Foundation.

Brodzinski, D. M., and Brodzinski, A. B. 1992. The impact of family structure on the adjustment of adopted children. *Child Welfare,* 71, 69–76.

Bronfenbrenner, U. 1979. *The ecology of human development.* Cambridge, MA: Harvard University Press.

Bronfenbrenner, U. 1985. Freedom and discipline across the decades. In G. Becker, H. Becker, and L. Huber (Eds.), *Ordnung und unordnung (Order and disorder)* (pp. 326–339). Berlin: Beltz.

Bronfenbrenner, U. 1989. Ecologial systems theory. In R. Vasta (Ed.), *Six theories of child development* (pp. 185–246). Greenwich, CT: JAI Press.

Bronfenbrenner, U. 1994. Ecological models of human development. In T. Husen and T. N. Postlethwaite (Eds.), *International Encyclopedia of Education,* (2nd ed., pp. 1643–1647). Oxford, UK: Pergamon/Elseiver.

Brookoff, D., O'Brien, K. K., Cook, C. S., Thompson, T. D., and Williams, C. 1997. Characteristics of participants in domestic violence. *Journal of the American Medical Association,* 277, 1369–1373.

Brooks-Gunn, J., Duncan, G. J., Klebanov, P. K., and Sealand, N. 1993. Do neighborhoods influence child and adolescent development? *American Journal of Sociology,* 99, 353–395.

Brooks-Gunn, J., Klebanov, P., and Duncan, G. J. 1996. Ethnic differences in children's intelligence test scores: Role of economic deprivation, home environment, and maternal characteristics. *Child Development,* 67, 396–406.

Brooks-Gunn, J., Klebanov, P., Liaw, F., and Duncan, G. J. 1995. Towards an understanding of the effect of poverty upon children. In H. E. Fitzgerald, B. M. Lester, and B. Zuckerman (Eds.), *Children of poverty* (pp. 3–36). New York: Garland.

Brown, A. C., Brody, G. H., and Stoneman, Z. 2000. Rural Black women and depression: A contextual analysis. *Journal of Marriage and the Family,* 62, 187–198.

Brown, B. B., and Huang, G.-H. 1995. Examining parenting practices in different peer contexts: Implications for adolescent trajectories. In L. J. Crockett and A. C. Crouter (Eds.), *Pathways through adolescence: Relation to social contexts* (pp. 151–174). Mahwah, NJ: Erlbaum.

Brown, J., and Sime, J. 1981. A methodology for accounts. In M. Brenner (Ed.), *Social methods and social life* (pp. 159–188). London: Academic Press.

Brown, S. L., and Booth, A. 1996. Cohabitation versus marriage: A comparison of relationship quality. *Journal of Marriage and the Family,* 58, 668–678.

Browne, A. 1997. Violence in marriage: Until death do us part? In A. P. Cardarelli (Ed.), *Violence between intimate partners* (pp. 48–69). Boston: Allyn and Bacon.

Browne, I. 1997. Explaining the black-white gap in labor force participation among women heading households. *American Sociological Review,* 62, 236–252.

Browne, K. D. 1998. Physical violence between young adults and their parents: Associations with a history of child maltreatment. *Journal of Family Violence,* 13, 59–79.

Browning, C. R., and Laumann, E. O. 1997. Sexual contact between children and adults: A life course perspective. *American Sociological Review,* 62, 540–560.

Broyles, P. A., and Drenovsky, C. K. 1992. Religious attendance and the subjective health of the elderly. *Review of Religious Research,* 34, 152–160.

Brubaker, T. H. 1991. Families in later life: A burgeoning research area. In A. Booth (Ed.), *Contemporary families: Looking forward, looking back* (pp. 226–248). Minneapolis, MN: National Council on Family Relations.

Brunk, M. A., and Henggeler, S. W. 1984. Child influences on adult controls: An experimental investigation. *Developmental Psychology,* 20, 1074–1081.

Bryant, J., and Rockwell, S. C. 1994. Effects of massive exposure to sexually oriented prime-time television programming on adolescents' moral judgement. In D. Zillmann, J. Bryant, and A. C. Huston (Eds.), *Media, children, and the family.* Hillsdale, NJ: Erlbaum.

Buchanan, C. M., Maccoby, E. E., and Dornbusch, S. M. 1996. *Adolescents after divorce.* Cambridge, MA: Harvard University Press.

Buehler, C., Krishnakumar, A., Stone, G., Anthony, C., Pemberton, S., Gerard, J., and Barber, B. K. 1998. Interparental conflict styles and youth problem behaviors: A two-sample replication study. *Journal of Marriage and the Family,* 60, 119–132.

Buhrmester, D., and Furman, W. 1990. Perceptions of sibling relationships during middle childhood and adolescence. *Child Development,* 61, 1387–1398.

Bumpass, L., and Raley, K. 1995. Single-parent families: Cohabitation and changing family reality. *Demography,* 32, 97–110.

Bumpass, L., and Sweet, J. 1989. Children's experience in single- parent families: Implications of cohabitation and marital transition. *Family Planning Perspectives,* 21, 256–260.

Bumpass, L. L., Sweet, J. A., and Cherlin, A. 1991. The role of cohabitation in declining rates of marriage. *Journal of Marriage and the Family,* 53, 913–927.

Bumpus, M. F., Crouter, A. C., and McHale, S. M. 1999. Work demands of dual-earner couples: Implications for parents' knowledge about children's daily lives in middle childhood. *Journal of Marriage and the Family,* 61, 465–475.

Burgess, E. W., Locke, H. J., and Thomes, M. M. 1963. *The family: From traditional to companionship.* New York: American Book.

Buriel, R. 1993. Childrearing orientations in Mexican American families: The influence of generation and sociocultural factors. *Journal of Marriage and the Family,* 55, 987–1000.

Buriel, R., and De Ment, T. 1997. Immigration and sociocultural change in Mexican, Chinese, and Vietnamese American families. In A. Booth, A. C. Crouter, and N. Landale (Eds.), *Immigration and the family: Research and policy on U.S. immigrants* (pp. 165–200). Mahwah, NJ: Erlbaum.

Burke, R., and Weir, T. 1976. Relationship of wives' employment status to husband, wife and pair satisfaction and performance. *Journal of Marriage and the Family,* 38, 279–287.

Burman, B., John, R. S., and Margolin, G. 1987. Effects of marital and parent-child relations on children's adjustment. *Journal of Family Psychology,* 1, 91–108.

Burnette, D. 1999. Social relationships of Latino grandparent caregivers: A role theory perspective. *The Gerontologist,* 39, 49–58.

Burton, L. M. 1992. Black grandparents rearing children of drug-addicted parents: Stressors, outcomes, and the social service needs. *The Gerontologist,* 32, 744–751.

Burton, L. M. 1996a. Age norms, the timing of family role transitions, and intergenerational caregiving among aging African American women. *The Gerontologist,* 36, 199–208.

Burton, L. M. 1996b. The timing of childbearing, family structure, and the responsibilities of aging Black women. In E. M. Hetherington and E. A. Blechman (Eds.), *Stress, coping, and resiliency in children and families* (pp. 155–172). Mahwah, NJ: Erlbaum.

Burton, L. M., and Bengtson, V. L. 1985. Black grandmothers: Issues of timing and continuity of roles. In V. L. Bengtson and J. F. Robertson (Eds.), *Grandparenthood* (pp. 61–80). Beverly Hills, CA: Sage.

Burton, L. M., and Snyder, A. R. 1998. The invisible man revisited: Comments on the life course, history, and men's roles in American families. In A. Booth and A. C. Crouter (Eds.), *Men in families* (pp. 31–39). Mahwah, NJ: Erlbaum.

Butterfield, F. 1999. As inmate population grows, so does a focus on children. *The New York Times,* April 7, A1, A18.

Cadoret, R. J., Yates, W. R., Throughton, E., Woodworth, G., and Stewart, M. A. 1995. Adoption study demonstrating two genetic pathways to drug abuse. *Archives of General Psychiatry,* 52, 42–52.

Calhoun, C. 1998. Community without propinquity revisited: Communications technology and the transformation of the urban political sphere. *Sociological Inquiry,* 68, 373–397.

Call, V. R. A., and Heaton, T. B. 1997. Religious influence on marital stability. *Journal for the Scientific Study of Religion,* 36, 382–392.

Call, V., Sprecher, S., and Schwartz, P. 1995. The incidence and frequency of marital sex in a national sample. *Journal of Marriage and the Family,* 57, 639–652.

Canadian Institute of Child Health. 1994. *The health of Canada's children: A CICH profile.* Ottawa: Canadian Institute of Child Health.

Cantor, J., and Nathanson, A. I. 1996. Children's fright reactions to television news. *Journal of Communication,* 46, 139–152.

Capaldi, D. M., and Clark, S. 1998. Prospective family predictors of aggression toward female partners for at-risk young men. *Developmental Psychology,* 34, 1175–1188.

Capaldi, D. M., Crosby, L., and Stoolmiller, M. 1996. Predicting the timing of first sexual intercourse for at-risk adolescent males. *Child Development,* 67, 344–359.

Caplan, P. J., and Hall-McCorquodale, I. 1985. Mother-blaming in major clinical journals. *American Journal of Orthopsychiatry,* 55, 345–353.

Card, S., and Krueger, A. 1992. Does school quality matter? Returns to education and the characteristics of public schools in the United States. *Journal of Political Economy,* 100, 1–40.

Carey, N., and Farris, E. 1996. *Parents and schools: Partners in student learning* (NCES Publication No. 96–913). Washington, DC: U.S. Government Printing Office.

Carlin, A. S., Kemper, K., Ward, N. G., Sowell, H., Gustafson, B., and Stevens, N. 1994. The effects of differences in objective and subjective definitions of childhood physical abuse on estimates of its incidence and relationship to psychopathology. *Child Abuse and Neglect,* 18, 393–399.

Carlip, H. 1995. *Girl power: Young women speak out.* New York: Time Warner.

Carlson, E. A., et al. 1999. Early environmental support and elementary school adjustment as predictors of school adjustment in middle adolescence. *Journal of Adolescent Research,* 14, 72–94.

Carrasquillo, H. A., and Sanchez-Korrol, U. 1996. Migration, community, and culture: The United States-Puerto Rican experience. In S. Pedreza and R. G. Rumbaut (Eds.), *Origins and destinies: Immigration, race, and ethnicity in America* (pp. 98–108). Belmont, CA: Wadsworth.

Carstensen, L., Gottman, J., and Levenson, R. 1995. Emotional behavior in long-term marriage. *Psychology and Aging,* 10, 140–149.

Casper, L. M. 1997. My daddy takes care of me! Fathers as care providers. *Current Population Reports,* Series P79–59. Washington, DC: U.S. Bureau of the Census.

Casper, L. M., and O'Connell, M. 1998. Work, income, the economy, and married fathers as child-care providers. *Demography,* 35, 243–250.

Caspi, A., Entmer Wright, B. R., Moffitt, T. E., and Silva, P. A. 1998. Childhood predictors of unemployment in early adulthood. *American Sociological Review,* 63, 424–451.

Ceci, S. J. 1991. How much does schooling influence general intelligence and its cognitive components? A reassessment of the evidence. *Developmental Psychology,* 27, 703–722.

Ceci, S. J. 1996. American education: Looking inward and outward. In U. Bronfenbrenner et al. (Eds.), *The state of Americans* (pp. 185–207). New York: Free Press.

Chadwick, B. A., and Garrett, H. D. 1995. Women's religiosity and employment: The LDS experience. *Review of Religious Research,* 36, 277–293.

Chambliss, W. J. 1995. Crime control and ethnic minorities: Legitimizing racial oppression by creating moral panics. In D. F. Hawkins (Ed.), *Ethnicity, race, and crime* (pp. 235–258). Albany: State University of New York Press.

Chan, R. W., Brooks, R. C., Raboy, B., and Patterson, C. J. 1998. Division of labor among lesbian and heterosexual parents: Associations with children's adjustment. *Journal of Family Psychology,* 12, 402–419.

Chan, R. W., Raboy, R. C., and Patterson, C. J. 1998. Psychosocial adjustment among children conceived via donor insemination by lesbian and heterosexual mothers. *Child Development,* 69, 443–457.

Chandra, A., and Stephen, E. H. 1998. Impaired fecundity in the United States: 1982–1995. *Family Planning Perspectives,* 30, 34–42.

Chao, R. K. 1994. Beyond parental control and authoritarian parenting style: Understanding Chinese parenting through the cultural notion of training. *Child Development,* 65, 1111–1119.

Chase-Lansdale, P. L., and Brooks-Gunn, J. 1995. Introduction. In P. L. Chase-Lansdale and J. Brooks-Gunn (Eds.), *Escape from poverty: What makes a difference for children?* (pp. 1–8). New York: Cambridge University Press.

Chassin, L., Pitts, S. C., DeLucia, C., and Todd, M. 1999. A longitudinal study of children of alcoholics: Predicting young adult substance use disorders, anxiety, and depression. *Journal of Abnormal Psychology,* 108, 106–119.

Chaves, M. 1991. Family structure and Protestant church attendance: The sociological basis of cohort and age effects. *Journal for the Scientific Study of Religion,* 39, 329–340.

Chen, H.-S. 1992. *Chinatown no more: Taiwan immigrants in contemporary New York.* Ithaca, NY: Cornell University Press.

Cherlin, A. J. 1978. Remarriage as an incomplete institution. *American Journal of Sociology,* 84, 634–651.

Cherlin, A. J. 1998. On the flexibility of fatherhood. In A. Booth and A. C. Crouter (Eds.), *Men in families* (pp. 41–46). Mahwah, NJ: Erlbaum.

Cherlin, A. J. 1999. Going to extremes: Family structure, children's well-being and social science. *Demography,* 36, 421–428.

Cherlin, A. J., Chase-Lansdale, P., and McRae, C. 1998. Effects of parental divorce on mental health throughout the life course. *American Sociological Review,* 63, 239–249.

Cherlin, A. J., and Furstenberg, F. F., Jr. 1992. *The new American grandparent.* Cambridge, MA: Harvard University Press.

Cherlin, A. J., and Furstenberg, F. F., Jr. 1994. Stepfamilies in the United States: A reconsideration. *Annual Review of Sociology,* 20, 359–381.

Chi, P. S. K., and Laquatra, J. 1998. Profile of housing cost burden in the United States. *Journal of Family and Economic Issues,* 19, 175–193.

Children's Television Workshop. 1991. *What research indicates about the educational effects of Sesame Street.* New York: Children's Television Workshop.

Child Welfare League of America. 1993. *Charting the new course: Children's legislative agenda.* Washington, DC: Child Welfare League of America.

Cicirelli, V. G. 1983. Adult children and their elderly parents. In T. Brubaker (Ed.), *Family relationships in later life.* Beverly Hills, CA: Sage.

Cicirelli, V. G. 1989. Feelings of attachment to siblings and well-being in later life. *Psychology and Aging,* 4, 211–216.

Cicirelli, V. G. 1994. Sibling relationships in cross-cultural perspective. *Journal of Marriage and the Family,* 56, 7–20.

Cicirelli, V. G. 1995. *Sibling relationships across the life span.* New York: Plenum Press.

Cicerelli, V. G. 1996. Sibling relationships in middle and old age. In G. H. Brody (Ed.), *Sibling relationships: Their causes and consequences* (pp. 47–74). Norwood, NJ: Ablex.

Cicirelli, V. G., Coward, R. T., and Dwyer, J. W. 1992. Siblings as caregivers for impaired elders. *Research on Aging,* 14, 331–350.

Clapp, G. 1992. *Divorce and new beginnings.* New York: Wiley.

Clark, W. 1998. Religious observance, marriage and family. *Canadian Social Trends,* 50, Autumn, 2–7.

Clark, W. A. V., and Dieleman, F. M. 1996. *Households and housing.* New Brunswick, NJ: Center for Urban Policy Research.

Clarkberg, M. 1999. The price of partnering: The role of economic well-being in young adults' first union experiences. *Social Forces,* 77, 945–968.

Clarkberg, M., Stolzenberg, R. M., and Waite, L. J. 1995. Attitudes, values, and entrance into cohabitational unions. *Social Forces,* 74.

Clarke-Stewart, A. 1992. Consequences of child care for children's development. In A. Booth (Ed.), *Child care in the 1990s: Trends and consequences* (pp. 63–82). Hillsdale, NJ: Erlbaum.

Clausen, J. A. 1986. *The life course: A sociological perspective.* Englewood Cliffs, NJ: Prentice-Hall.

Clydesdale, T. T. 1997. Family behaviors among early U.S. baby boomers: Exploring the effects of religion and income changes, 1965–1982. *Social Forces,* 76, 605–635.

Cohler, B. J., and Musick, J. S. 1996. Adolescent parenthood and the transition to adulthood. In J. A. Graber, J. Brooks-Gunn, and A. C. Petersen (Eds.), *Transitions through adolescence* (pp. 201–232). Mahwah, NJ: Erlbaum.

Coie, J. D., and Dodge, K. A. 1998. Aggression and antisocial behavior. In W. Damon (Series Ed.), and N. Eisenberg (Vol. Ed.), *Handbook of child psychology, Vol. 3: Social, emotional, and personality development* (5th ed., pp. 779–862). New York: Wiley.

Cole, P. 1995. Biotechnology and the "moral" family. In C. Ulanowsky (Ed.), *The family in the age of biotechnology* (pp. 47–60). Aldershot, UK: Avebury.

Coleman, J. S. 1988. Social capital in the creation of human capital. *American Journal of Sociology,* 94, S95–S120.

Coleman, J. S. 1990a. *Foundations of social theory.* Cambridge, MA: Harvard University Press.

Coleman, J. S. 1990b. *Equality and achievement in education.* Boulder, CO: Westview Press.

Coleman, J. S., and Hoffer, T. 1987. *Public and private schools: The impact of communities.* New York: Basic Books.

Coleman, V. E. 1994. Lesbian battering: The relationship between personality and the perpetration of violence. *Violence and Victims,* 9, 139–152.

Coley, R. L., and Chase-Lansdale, P. L. 1998. Adolescent pregnancy and parenthood: Recent evidence and future directions. *American Psychologist,* 53, 152–166.

Collins, P. H. 1990. *Black feminist thought: Knowledge, consciousness, and the politics of empowerment.* Boston: Unwin Hyman.

Collins, P. H. 1992. Black women and motherhood. In B. Thorne and M. Yalom (Eds.), *Rethinking the family* (rev. ed., pp. 215–245). Boston: Northeastern University Press.

Collins, W. A., and Russell, G. 1991. Mother-child and father-child relationships in middle childhood and adolescence: A developmental analysis. *Developmental Review,* 11, 99–136.

Coltrane, S. 1995. Stability and change in Chicano men's family lives. In M. S. Kimmel and M. A. Messner (Eds.), *Men's lives* (3rd ed., pp. 469–484). Boston: Allyn and Bacon.

Coltrane, S. 1996. *Family man: Fatherhood, housework, and gender equity.* New York: Oxford University Press.

Coltrane, S. 1997. *Gender and families.* Thousand Oaks, CA: Sage.

Conger, R. D., and Conger, K. J. 1996. Sibling relationships. In R. Simons and Associates (Eds.), *Understanding differences between divorced and intact families* (pp. 104–121). Thousand Oaks, CA: Sage.

Conger, R. D., Ge, X.-J., and Lorenz, F. O. 1994. Economic stress and marital relations. In R. D. Conger, and G. H. Elder, Jr. (Eds.), *Families in troubled times: Adapting to change in rural America* (pp. 187–203). New York: Aldine de Gruyter.

Conger, R. D., Patterson, G. R., and Ge, X. 1995. It takes two to replicate: A mediational model for the impact of parents' stress on adolescent adjustment. *Child Development,* 66, 80–97.

Conger, R. D., and Rueter, M. A. 1996. Siblings, parents, and peers: A longitudinal study of social influences in adolescent risk for alcohol use and abuse. In G. H. Brody (Ed.), *Sibling relationships: Their causes and consequences* (pp. 1–30). Norwood, NJ: Ablex.

Conger, R. D., Rueter, M. A., and Elder, G. H., Jr. 1999. Couple resilience to economic pressure. *Journal of Personality and Social Psychology,* 76, 54–71.

Congress of the United States. 1990. *Sources of support for adolescent mothers.* Washington, DC: Congressional Budget Office.

Contreras, J. M., Lopez, I. R., Rivera-Mosquera, E. T., Raymond-Smith, L., and Rothstein, K. 1999. Social support and adjustment among Puerto Rican adolescent mothers: The moderating effect of acculturation. *Journal of Family Psychology,* 13, 228–243.

Cook, D. A., and Fine, M. 1995. "Motherwit": Childrearing lessons from African-American mothers of low income. In B. B. Swadener and S. Lubeck (Eds.), *Children and families "at promise"* (pp. 118–142). Albany: State University of New York Press.

Cooksey, E. C., and Craig, P. H. 1998. Parenting from a distance: The effects of paternal characteristics on contact between nonresidential fathers and their children. *Demography,* 35, 187–200.

Cooksey, E. C., Menaghan, E. G., and Jekielek, S. M. 1997. Life-course effects of work and family circumstances on children. *Social Forces,* 76, 637–667.

Coombs, R. H. 1991. Marital status and personal well-being: A literature review. *Family Relations,* 40, 97–102.

Cooney, T. M., Pedersen, F. A., Indelicato, S., and Palkovitz, R. 1993. Timing of fatherhood: Is "on-time" optimal? *Journal of Marriage and the Family,* 55, 205–215.

Cooney, T. M., and Uhlenberg, P. 1992. Support from parents over the life course: The adult child's perspective. *Social Forces,* 71, 63–84.

Coontz, S. 1992. *The way we never were: American families and the nostalgia trap.* New York: Basic Books.

Corcoran, M. 1995. Rags to rags: Poverty and mobility in the United States. *Annual Review of Sociology,* 21, 237–267.

Corsaro, W. A. 1997. *The sociology of childhood.* Thousand Oaks, CA: Pine Forge Press.

Cose, E. 1993. *The rage of a privileged class.* New York: HarperCollins.

Cost, Quality, and Child Outcomes Study Team. 1995. *Cost, quality, and child outcomes in child care centers* (2nd ed.). Denver: University of Colorado at Denver, Economics Department.

Costello, C. Y. 1997. Conceiving identity: Bisexual, lesbian, and gay parents consider their children's sexual orientation. *Journal of Sociology and Social Welfare,* 24, 63–90.

Cott, N. F. 1977. *The bonds of womanhood: "Women's sphere" in New England, 1780–1835.* New Haven, CT: Yale University Press.

Cotten, S. R. 1999. Marital status and mental health revisited: Examining the importance of risk factors and resources. *Family Relations,* 48, 225–233.

Coughlin, C., and Vuchinich, S. 1996. Family experience in preadolescence and the development of male delinquency. *Journal of Marriage and the Family,* 58, 491–501.

Counts, R. M. 1992. Second and third divorces: The flood to come. *Journal of Divorce and Remarriage,* 17, 193–200.

Cowan, C. P., and Cowan, P. A. 1992. *When partners become parents: The big life change for couples.* New York: Basic Books.

Cowan, C. P., and Cowan, P. A. 1997. Working with couples during stressful transitions. In S. Dreman (Ed.), *The family on the threshold of the 21st century* (pp. 17–48). Mahwah, NJ: Erlbaum.

Cowan, P. A., and Cowan, C. P. 1998. New families: Modern couples as new pioneers. In M. A. Mason, A. Skolnick, and S. D. Sugarman (Eds.), *All our families: New policies for a new century* (pp. 169–192). New York: Oxford University Press.

Cowan, P. A., Cowan, C. P., and Schulz, M. S. 1996. Thinking about risk and resilience in families. In E. M. Hetherington and E. A. Blechman (Eds.), *Stress, coping, and resiliency in children and families* (pp. 1–38). Mahwah, NJ: Erlbaum.

Crenshaw, K. W. 1994. Mapping the margins: Intersectionality, identity politics, and violence against women of color. In M. A. Fineman and R. Mykitiuk (Eds.), *The public nature of private violence.* New York: Routledge.

Crimmins, E., Easterlin, R., and Saito, Y. 1991. Preference changes among American youth: Family, work, and goods aspirations, 1976–87. *Population and Development Review,* 17, 115–133.

Cross, W. E., Jr. 1990. Race and ethnicity: Effects on social networks. In M. Cochran, M. Larner, D. Riley, L. Gunnarsson and C. R. Henderson, Jr. (Eds.), *Extending families: The social networks of parents and their children* (pp. 67–85). Cambridge: Cambridge University Press.

Crouch, J. L., and Milner, J. S. 1993. Effects of child neglect on children. *Criminal Justice and Behavior,* 20, 49–65.

Crouter, A. C. 1994. Processes linking families and work: Implications for behavior and development in both settings. In R. D. Parke and S. G. Kellam (Eds.), *Exploring family relationships with other social contexts* (pp. 9–28). Hillsdale, NJ: Erlbaum.

Crouter, A. C., Helms-Erikson, H., Updegraff, K., and McHale, S. M. 1999. Conditions underlying parents' knowledge about children's daily lives in middle childhood: Between and within-family comparisons. *Child Development,* 70, 246–259.

Cuber, J., and Harroff, P. B. 1965. *The significant American.* New York: Hawthorn.

Culp, A. M., Osofsky, J. D., and O'Brien, M. 1996. Language patterns of adolescent and older mothers and their one-year-old children. *Language,* 11, 377–389.

Cummings, E. M., and Cicchetti, D. 1990. Towards a transactional model of relations between attachment and depression. In M. Greenberg et al. (Eds.), *Attachment in the preschool years* (pp. 339–372). Chicago: The University of Chicago Press.

Cummings, E. M., and Davies, P. T. 1994. Maternal depression and child development. *Journal of Child Psychology and Psychiatry,* 35, 73–112.

Dalenberg, C. J., and Jacobs, D. A. 1994. Attributional analyses of child sexual abuse episodes: Empirical and clinical issues. *Journal of Child Sexual Abuse,* 3, 37–50.

Damon, W. 1995. *Greater expectations: Overcoming the culture of indulgence in America's homes and schools.* New York: Free Press.

Daniel, K. 1996. The marriage premium. In M. Tommasi and K. Ierulli (Eds.), *The new economics of human behavior* (pp. 113–125) Cambridge: Cambridge University Press.

Daniels, D. 1987. Differential experiences of children in the same family as predictors of adolescent sibling personality differences. *Journal of Personality and Social Psychology,* 51, 339–346.

Danso, H., Hunsberger, B., and Pratt, M. 1997. The role of parental religious fundamentalism and right-wing authoritarianism in child-rearing goals and practices. *Journal for the Scientific Study of Religion,* 36, 496–511.

Darling, R. B. 1987. The economic and psychosocial consequences of disability: Family-society relationships. *Marriage and Family Review,* 11, 45–61.

Darroch, J. E., Landry, D. J., and Oslak, S. 1999. Age differences between sexual partners in the United States. *Family Planning Perspectives,* 31, 160–167.

Da Vanzo, J., and Goldscheider, F. K. 1990. Coming home again: Returns to the parental home of young adults. *Population Studies,* 44, 241–255.

Davey, J. D. 1995. *The new social contract: America's journey from welfare state to police state.* Westport, CT: Praeger.

Davis, J. H. and Juhasz, A. M. 1995. The preadolescent/pet friendship bond. *Anthrozoos,* 8, 78–82.

Day, R. D., Peterson, G. D., and McCracken, C. 1998. Predicting spanking of younger children and older children by mothers and fathers. *Journal of Marriage and the Family,* 60, 79–94.

Deater-Deckard, K., Dodge, K. A., Bates, J. E., and Pettit, G. S. 1996. Physical discipline among African American and European American mothers: Links to children's externalizing behaviors. *Developmental Psychology,* 32, 1065–1072.

Deater-Deckard, K., Pickering, K., Dunn, J. F., Golding, D., and the Avon Longitudinal Study of Pregnancy and Childhood Study Team. 1998. Family structure and depressive symptoms in man preceding and following the birth of a child. *American Journal of Psychiatry,* 155, 818–823.

Deater-Deckard, K., and Plomin, R. 1999. An adoption study of the etiology of teacher and parent reports of externalizing behavior problems in middle childhood. *Child Development,* 70, 144–154.

DeFronzo, J. 1997. Welfare and homicide. *Journal of Research in Crime and Delinquency,* 34, 395–406.

Degler, C. 1981. *At odds: Women and family in America from the Revolution to the present.* New York: Oxford University Press.

Demo, D. H. 1992. Parent-child relations: Assessing recent changes. *Journal of Marriage and the Family,* 54, 104–117.

Demo, D. H., and Acock, A. C. 1993. Family diversity and the division of domestic labor: How much have things really changed? *Family Relations,* 42, 323–331.

Demos, J. 1971. Developmental perspectives on the history of childhood. *The Journal of Interdisciplinary History,* 2, 315–327.

Demos, J., 1974. The American family in past time. *American Scholar,* 63, 422–446.

Denzin, N. K., and Lincoln, Y. S. (Eds.). 1994. *Handbook of qualitative research.* Thousand Oaks, CA: Sage.

Devine, J. A., and Wright, J. D. 1993. *The greatest of evils: Urban poverty and the American underclass.* New York: Aldine de Gruyter.

DeWitt, P. M. 1994. The second time around. *American Demographics,* 16, 11–14.

DiGiorgio-Miller, J. 1998. Sibling incest: Treatment of the family and the offender. *Child Welfare,* 77, 335–346.

DiLeonardi, J. W. 1993. Families living in poverty and chronic neglect of children. *Families in Society,* 74, 556–562.

Dilworth-Anderson, P. 1992. Extended kin networks in black families. *Generations,* 17, 29–36.

Dilworth-Anderson, P., Burton, L. M., and Turner, W. L. 1993. The importance of values in the study of culturally diverse families. *Family Relations,* 42, 238–242.

Dodge, K. A., Bates, J. E., and Pettit, G. S. 1990. Mechanisms in the cycle of violence. *Science,* 250, 1678–1683.

Dodge, K. A., and Frame, C. L. 1982. Social cognitive biases and deficits in aggressive boys. *Child Development,* 53, 620–635.

Doherty, W. J., Kouneski, E. F., and Erickson, M. F. 1998. Responsible fathering: An overview and conceptual framework. *Journal of Marriage and the Family,* 60, 277–292.

Donovan, P. 1998. School-based sexuality education: The issues and challenges. *Family Planning Perspectives,* 30, 188–193.

Dorfman, L. T., Holmes, C. A., and Berlin, K. L. 1996. Wife caregiver of frail elderly veterans: Correlates of caregiver satisfaction and caregiver strain. *Family Relations,* 45, 46–55.

Dornbusch, S. M., Ritter, L. P., and Steinberg, L. 1991. Community influences on the relation of family statuses to adolescent school performance: Differences between African Americans and non-Hispanic whites. *American Journal of Education,* 38, 543–567.

Dorr, A., Kovaric, P., and Doubleday, C. 1990. Age and content influences on children's perception of the realism of television families. *Journal of Broadcasting and Electronic Media,* 34, 377–397.

Downey, D. B. 1994. The school performance of children from single-mother and single-father families: Economic or interpersonal deprivation? *Journal of Family Issues,* 15, 129–147.

Downey, D. B. 1995. When bigger is not better: Family size, parental resources, and children's educational performance. *American Sociological Review,* 60, 746–761.

Downey, D. B., Ainsworth-Darnell, J. W., and Dufur, M. J. 1998. Sex of parent and children's well-being in single-parent households. *Journal of Marriage and the Family,* 60, 878–893.

Downey, D. B., and Powell, B. 1993. Do children in single-parent households fare better living with same-sex parents? *Journal of Marriage and the Family,* 55, 55–71.

Downey, G., and Coyne, J. C. 1990. Children of depressed parents: An integrative review. *Psychological Bulletin,* 108, 50–76.

Driscoll, A. K., Hearn, G. K., Evans, V. J., Moore, K. A., Sugland, B. W., and Call, V. 1999. Nonmarital childbearing among adult women. *Journal of Marriage and the Family,* 61, 178–187.

Dubow, E. F., Edwards, S., and Ippolito, M. F. 1997. Life stressors, neighborhood disadvantage, and resources: A focus on inner-city children's adjustment. *Journal of Clinical Child Psychology,* 26, 130–144.

Duncan, G. J., and Brooks-Gunn, J. 1997. Income effects across the life span: Integration and interpretation. In G. J. Duncan and J. Brooks-Gunn (Eds.), *Consequences of growing up poor* (pp. 596–610). New York: Russell Sage.

Duncan, G. J., Yeung, W. J., Brooks-Gunn, J., and Smith, J. R. 1998. How much does childhood poverty affect the life chances of children? *American Sociological Review,* 63, 406–423.

Dunn, J. 1994. Temperament, siblings, and the development of relationships. In W. B. Carey and S. C. McDevitt (Eds.), *Prevention and early intervention* (pp. 50–58). New York: Bruner/Mazel.

Dunn, J. 1996. Brothers and sisters in middle childhood and early adolescence: Continuity and change in individual differences. In G. H. Brody (Ed.), *Sibling relationships: Their causes and consequences* (pp. 31–46). Norwood, NJ: Ablex.

Dunn, J., and McGuire, S. 1994. Young children's nonshared experiences: A summary of studies in Cambridge and Colorado. In E. M. Hetherington, D. Reiss, and R. Plomin (Eds.), *Separate social worlds of siblings* (pp. 111–128). Hillsdale, NJ: Erlbaum.

Dunn, J., and Plomin, R. 1990. *Separate lives: Why siblings are so different.* New York: Basic Books.

Dunn, J., Plomin, R., and Daniels, D. 1986. Consistency and change in mothers' behavior to two-year-old siblings. *Child Development,* 57, 348–356.

Dunn, J., Slomkowski, C., Beardsall, L., and Rende, R. 1994. Adjustment in middle childhood and early adolescence: Links with earlier and contemporary sibling relationships. *Journal of Child Psychology and Psychiatry,* 35, 491–504.

Durkheim, E. 1951 (1897). *Suicide.* New York: Free Press.

Duvall, E. M. 1957. *Family development.* Philadelphia: Lippincott.

Earls, F. 1994. Oppositional-defiant and conduct disorders. In M. Rutter, E. Taylor, and L. Hersov (Eds.), *Child and adolescent psychiatry* (3rd ed., pp. 308–329). Oxford: Blackwell.

East, P. L. 1999. The first teenage pregnancy in the family: Does it affect mothers' parenting, attitudes, or mother-adolescent communication? *Journal of Marriage and the Family,* 61, 306–319.

East, P. L., Felice, M. E., and Morgan, M. C. 1993. Sisters' and girlfriends' sexual and childbearing behavior: Effects on early adolescent girls' sexual outcomes. *Journal of Marriage and the Family,* 55, 953–963.

Eckenrode, J., Laird, M., and Doris, J. 1993. School performance and disciplinary problems among abused and neglected children. *Developmental Psychology,* 29, 53–62.

Eder, D. 1991. The role of teasing in adolescent peer group culture. *Sociological Studies of Child Development,* 4, 181–197.

Edin, K., and Lein, L. 1997a. *Making ends meet: How single mothers survive welfare and low-wage work.* New York: Sage.

Edin, K., and Lein, L. 1997b. Work, welfare, and single mothers' economic survival strategies. *American Sociological Review,* 62, 253–266.

Edleson, J. L., and Tolman, R. M. 1992. *Interventions for men who batter: An ecological approach.* Newbury Park, CA: Sage.

Egan, S. K., and Perry, D. G. 1998. Does low self-regard invite victimization? *Developmental Psychology,* 34, 299–309.

Eggebeen, D. J., Crockett, L. J., and Hawkins, A. J. 1990. Patterns of adult male coresidence among young children of adolescent mothers. *Family Planning Perspectives,* 22, 219–223.

Eggebeen, D. J., and Hogan, D. P. 1990. Giving between generations in American families. *Human Nature,* 1, 211–232.

Ehmann, C. 1999. The age factor in religious attitudes and behavior. *Gallup News Service,* July 14 <www.gallup.com/poll>.

Elder, G. H., Jr. 1991. Family transitions, cycles, and social change. In P. A. Cowan and M. Hetherington (Eds.), *Family transitions* (pp. 31–57). Hillsdale, NJ: Erlbaum.

Elder, G. H., Jr. 1995. The life course paradigm and social change: Historical and developmental perspectives. In P. Moen, G. H. Elder, Jr., and K. Lüscher (Eds.), *Perspectives on the ecology of human development* (pp. 101–140). Washington, DC: American Psychological Association.

Elder, G. H., Jr. 1998. The life course as developmental theory. *Child Development,* 69, 1–12.

Elder, G. H., Jr., Caspi, A., and Nguyen, T. V. 1994. Resourceful and vulnerable children: Family influences in stressful times. In R. K. Silbereisen and K. Eyferth (Eds.), *Development in context: Integrative perspectives on youth development.* New York: Springer-Verlag.

Elder, G. H., Jr., Conger, R. D., Foster, E. M., and Ardel, T. M. 1992. Families under economic pressure. *Journal of Family Issues,* 13, 5–37.

Elder, G. H., Jr., Foster, E. M., and Ardelt, M. 1994. Children in the household economy. In R. D. Conger, G. H. Elder, Jr., and Associates (Eds.), *Families in troubled times: Adapting to change in rural America* (pp. 127–146). New York: Aldine de Gruyter.

Elder, G. H., Jr., Robertson, E. B., and Foster, E. M. 1994. Survival, loss, and adaptation: A perspective on farm families. In R. D. Conger, G. H. Elder, Jr., and Associates (Eds.), *Families in troubled times: Adapting to change in rural America* (pp. 105–126). New York: Aldine de Gruyter.

Eley, T. C., Lichtenstein, P., and Stevenson, J. 1999. Sex differences in the etiology of aggressive and nonaggressive antisocial behavior: Results from two twin studies. *Child Development,* 70, 155–168.

Elliott, B. J., and Richards, M. P. M. 1991. Children and divorce: Educational performance and behavior before and after parental separation. *International Journal of Law and the Family,* 5, 258–276.

Elliott, P. 1996. Shattering the illusions: Same-sex domestic violence. In C. M. Renzetti and C. H. Miley

(Eds.), *Violence in gay and lesbian domestic partnerships* (pp. 1–8). New York: Harrington Park Press.

Ellison, C. G. 1994. Religion, the life stress paradigm, and the study of depression. In J. S. Levin (Ed.), *Religion in aging and health: Theoretical foundations and methodological frontiers* (pp. 78–121). Newbury Park, CA: Sage.

Ellison, C. G. 1996. Conservative Protestantism and the corporal punishment of children: Clarifying the issues. *Journal for the Scientific Study of Religion,* 35, 1–16.

Ellison, C. G., and George, L. K. 1994. Religious involvement, social ties, and social support in a Southeastern community. *Journal for the Scientific Study of Religion,* 33, 46–61.

Ellison, C. G., and Sherkat, D. E. 1993. Conservative Protestantism and support following disclosure of incest. *American Journal of Orthopsychiatry,* 58, 131–144.

Elo, I. T., King, R. B., and Furstenberg, F. F., Jr. 1999. Adolescent females: Their sexual partners and the fathers of their children. *Journal of Marriage and the Family,* 61, 74–84.

Elshtain, A. B. 1990. The family and civic life. In D. Blankenhorn et al. (Eds.), *Rebuilding the nest: A new commitment to the American family* (pp. 119–132). Milwaukee, WI: Family Service America.

Emery, R. E. 1999. Postdivorce family life for children: An overview of research and some implications for policy. In R. A. Thompson and P. R. Amato (Eds.), *The postdivorce family* (pp. 3–27). Thousand Oaks, CA: Sage.

Emery, R. E., and Laumann-Billings, L. 1998. An overview of the nature, causes, and consequences of abusive family relationships: Toward differentiating maltreatment and violence. *American Psychologist,* 53, 121–135.

Engelbert, A. 1994. Worlds of childhood: Differentiated but different. Implications for social policy. In J. Qvortrup, M. Bardy, G. Sgritta, and H. Wintersberger (Eds.), *Childhood matters: Social theory, practice, and politics* (pp. 285–298). Aldershot, UK: Avebury.

Entwisle, D. R., Alexander, K. L., and Olson, L. S. 1997. *Children, schools, and inequality.* Boulder, CO: Westview Press.

Erel, O., and Burman, B. 1995. Interrelatedness of marital relations and parent-child relations: A meta-analytic review. *Psychological Bulletin,* 118, 108–132.

Erera, P.-I. 1997. Step- and foster families: A comparison. *Marriage & Family Review,* 26, 301–315.

Erikson, E. H. 1968. *Identity: Youth and crisis.* New York: Norton.

Espelage, D., Bosworth, K., Karageorge, K., and Daytner, G. 1996. Paper presented at the annual meetings of the American Psychological Association, reported in the APA *Monitor,* p. 41.

Espiritu, Y. L. 1996. *Asian American women and men.* Thousand Oaks, CA: Sage.

Etter, J. 1993. Levels of cooperation and satisfaction in 56 open adoptions. *Child Welfare,* 72, 257–267.

Etzioni, A. 1994. *The spirit of community: Rights, responsibilities, and the new communitarian agenda.* New York: Crown.

Eugster, A., and Vingerhoets, A. J. J. M. 1999. Psychological aspects of in vitro fertilization: A review. *Social Science & Medicine,* 48, 575–589.

Evans, W., and Schwab, R. 1995. Finishing high school and starting college: Do Catholic schools make a difference? *Quarterly Journal of Economics,* 60, 941–974.

Eyer, D. E. 1992. *Mother-infant bonding.* New Haven, CT: Yale University Press.

Eyer, D. E. 1997. There is no evidence that mothers harm their infants and toddlers by working outside the home. In M. R. Walsh (Ed.), *Women, men, and gender: Ongoing debates* (pp. 386–390). New Haven, CT: Yale University Press.

Fagot, B. I., Pears, K. C., Capaldi, D. M., Crosby, L., and Leve, C. S. 1998. Becoming an adolescent father: Precursors and parenting. *Developmental Psychology,* 34, 1209–1219.

Farber, B. 1972. *Guardians of virtue: Salem families in 1800.* New York: Basic Books.

Farrington, D. P. 1987. Early precursors of frequent offending. In J. Q. Wilson and G. C. Loury (Eds.), *From children to citizens: Families, schools, and delinquency prevention* (pp. 21–50). New York: Springer-Verlag.

Farrington, D. P. 1995. The development of offending and antisocial behaviour from childhood: Key findings from the Cambridge Study of Delinquent Development. *Journal of Child Psychology and Psychiatry,* 360, 929–964.

Faurre, L. C., and Maddock, J. M. 1994. Sexual meaning systems of engaged couples. *Family Relations,* 43, 53–60.

Feldhaus, K. M., Koziol-McLain, J., Armsbury, H. L., Norton, I. M., Lowenstein, S. R., and Abbott, J. T. 1997. Accuracy of 3 brief screening questions for detecting partner violence in the emergency department. *Journal of the American Medical Association, 277,* 1357–1361.

Feldman, S. S., and Rosenthal, D. A. 1990. The acculturation of autonomy expectations in Chinese highschoolers residing in two Western nations. *International Journal of Psychology,* 25, 259–281.

Feng, D., Giarrusso, R., Bengtson, V. L., and Frye, N. 1999. Intergenerational transmission of marital quality and marital instablity. *Journal of Marriage and the Family,* 61, 451–463.

Fergusson, D. M., and Horwood, L. J. 1998. Exposure to interparental violence in childhood and psychosocial adjustment in young adulthood. *Child Abuse & Neglect,* 22, 339–357.

Fergusson, D. M., Horwood, L. J., and Lynskey, M. T. 1994. Culture makes a difference . . . or does it? A comparison of adolescents in Hong Kong, Australia, and the United States. In R. K. Silbereisen and E. Todt (Eds.), *Adolescence in context* (pp. 99–113). New York: Springer-Verlag.

Fergusson, D. M., Lynskey, M., and Horwood, L. J. 1995. The adolescent outcomes of adoption: A 16-year longitudinal study. *Journal of Child Psychology and Psychiatry,* 36, 597–615.

Fernandez-Kelly, M. P. 1995. Social and cultural capital in the urban ghetto: Implications for the economic sociology of immigration. In A. Portes (Ed.), *The economic sociology of immigration* (pp. 213–247). New York: Russell Sage.

Fernandez-Kelly, M. P., and Garcia, A. M. 1990. Power surrendered, power restored: The politics of home and work among Hispanic women in Southeastern California and Southern Florida. In L. Tilly and P. Gurin (Eds.), *Women and politics in America.* New York: Russell Sage.

Ferraro, K. F., and Koch, J. R. 1994. Religion and health among black and white adults: Examining social support and consolation. *Journal for the Scientific Study of Religion,* 33, 362–375.

Ferree, M. M. 1990. Beyond separate spheres: Feminism and family research. *Journal of Marriage and the Family,* 52, 866–884.

Ferree, M. M. 1991. The division of labor in two-earner marriages. *Journal of Family Issues,* 12, 158–180.

Ferree, M. M., and Hall, E. J. 1996. Gender, race, and class in mainstream textbooks. *American Sociological Review,* 61, 929–950.

Ferree, M. M., Lorber, J., and Hess., B. B. (Eds.). 1999. *Revisioning gender.* Thousand Oaks, CA: Sage.

Fincham, F. D. 1998. Child development and marital relations. *Child Development,* 69, 543–574.

Finkelhor, D., and Browne, A. 1985. The traumatic impact of child sexual abuse: A conceptualization. *American Journal of Orthopsychiatry,* 55, 530–541.

Finkelhor, D., and Dziuba-Leatherman, J. 1994. Victimization of children. *American Psychologist,* 49, 173–183.

Finkelhor, D., Hotaling, G., Lewis, I. A., and Smith, C. 1990. Sexual abuse in a national survey of adult men and women: Prevalence, characteristics, and risk factors. *Child Abuse & Neglect,* 14, 19–28.

Finnegan, R. A., Hodges, E. V. E., and Perry, D. G. 1998. Victimization by peers: Associations with children's reports of mother-child interaction. *Journal of Personality and Social Psychology,* 75, 1076–1086.

Fischer, D. G. 1993. Parental supervision and delinquency. *Perceptual and Motor Skills,* 56, 635–640.

Fischer, D. G., and McDonald, W. L. 1998. Characteristics of intrafamilial and extrafamilial child sexual abuse. *Child Abuse & Neglect,* 22, 915–929.

Fitzgerald, H. E., et al. 1993. Predictors of behavior problems in three-year-old sons of alcoholics: Early evidence for the onset of risk. *Child Development,* 64, 110–123.

Fletcher, A. C., Darling, N. E., Dornbusch, S. M., and Steinberg, L. 1995. The company they keep: Relation of adolescents' adjustment and behavior to their friends' perceptions of authoritative parenting in the social network. *Developmental Psychology,* 31, 300–310.

Fletcher, A. C., Steinberg, L., and Sellers, E. B. 1999. Adolescents' well-being as a function of perceived interparental consistency. *Journal of Marriage and the Family,* 61, 599–610.

Flora, C. B., Flora, J. L., Spears, J. D., Swanson, L. E., Lapping, M. B., and Weinberg, M. L. 1992. *Rural communities: Legacy and change.* Boulder, CO: Westview Press.

Florsheim, P., Tolan, P. H., and Gorman-Smith, D. 1996. Family processes and risk for externalizing behavior problems among African American and Hispanic boys. *Journal of Consulting and Clinical Psychology,* 64, 1222–1230.

Floyd, F. J., and Gallagher, E. M. 1997. Parental stress, care demands, and the use of support services for school-age children with disabilities and behavior problems. *Family Relations,* 46, 359–371.

Floyd, F. J., and Wasner, G. H. 1994. Social exchange, equity, and commitment: Structural equation modelling of dating relationships. *Journal of Family Psychology,* 8, 55–73.

Flynn, C. P. 1994. Regional differences in attitudes toward corporal punishment. *Journal of Marriage and the Family,* 56, 314–324.

Flynn, C. P. 1998. To spank or not to spank: The effect of situation and age of child on support for corporal punishment. *Journal of Family Violence,* 13, 21–37.

Flynn, C. P. 2000. Why family professionals can no longer ignore violence toward animals. *Family Relations,* 49, 87–95.

Forehand, R., Armistead, L., and David, C. 1997. Is adolescent adjustment following parental divorce a function of predivorce adjustment? *Journal of Abnormal Child Psychology,* 25, 157–164.

Forgatch, M. S. 1989. Patterns and outcomes in family problem solving: The disrupting effect of negative emotion. *Journal of Marriage and the Family,* 51, 115–124.

Forgatch, M. S., Patterson, G. R., and Roy, J. A. 1996. Stress, parenting, and adolescent psychopathology in nondivorced and stepfamilies: A within-family perspective. In E. M. Hetherington and E. A. Blachman (Eds.), *Stress, coping, and resilience in children and families* (pp. 39–66). Mahwah, NJ: Erlbaum.

Forste, R., and Tienda, M. 1996. What's behind racial and ethnic fertility differentials? In J. B. Casterline, R. L. Lee, and K. A. Foote (Eds.), *Fertility in the United States: New patterns, new theories* (pp. 109–133). Washington, DC: Population Council.

Forthofer, M. S., Kessler, R. C., Story, A. L., and Gotlib, I. H. 1996. The effects of psychiatric disorder on the probability and timing of first marriage. *Journal of Health and Social Behavior,* 37, 121–132.

Foster, E. M., Jones, D., and Hoffman, S. D. 1998. The economic impact of nonmarital childrearing: How are older, single mothers faring? *Journal of Marriage and the Family,* 60, 163–174.

Fouts, G., and Burggraf, K. 1999. Television situation comedies: Female body images and verbal reinforcements. *Sex Roles,* 40, 473–481.

Fowlkes, M. R. 1994. Single worlds and homosexual lifestyles: Patterns of sexuality and intimacy. In A. S. Rossi (Ed.), *Sexuality across the life course* (pp. 151–184). Chicago: University of Chicago Press.

Fox, G. L. 1999. Families in the media: Reflections on the public scrutiny of private behavior. *Journal of Marriage and the Family,* 61, 821–830.

Franklin, J. H. 1993. *The color line: Legacy for the twenty-first century.* Columbia: University of Missouri Press.

Frantz, D. 1999. Cruise lines profit from friends in Congress. *The New York Times,* February 19, A1, A16.

Frazier, J. A., and Morrison, F. J. 1998. The influence of extended-year schooling on growth of achievement and perceived competence in early elementary school. *Child Development,* 69, 495–517.

Frick, P. J., et al. 1992. Familial risk factors to oppositional defiant disorder and conduct disorder: Parental psychopathology and maternal parenting. *Journal of Consulting and Clinical Psychology,* 60, 49–55.

Friedrich-Cofer, L., and Huston, A. C. 1986. Television violence and aggression: The debate continues. *Psychological Bulletin,* 15, 1–21.

Fu, H., Darroch, J. E., Haas, T., and Ranjit, N. 1999. Contraception failure rates: New estimates from the 1995 National Survey of Family Growth. *Family Planning Perspectives,* 31, 56–63.

Fuchs, V. R. 1990. Are Americans underinvesting in children? In D. Blankenhorn et al. (Eds.), *Rebuilding the nest: A new commitment to the American family* (pp. 53–72). Milwaukee, WI: Family Service America.

Fuligni, A. J., Tseng, V., and Lam, M. 1999. Attitudes toward family obligations among American adolescents with Asian, Latin American, and European backgrounds. *Child Development,* 70, 1030–1044.

Fuller-Thomson, E., Minkler, M., and Driver, D. 1997. A profile of grandparents raising granchildren in the United States. *The Gerontologist,* 37, 406–411.

Furman, W., and Lanthier, R. P. 1996. Personality and sibling relationships. In G. H. Brody (Ed.), *Sibling relationships: Their causes and consequences* (pp. 127–172). Norwood, NJ: Ablex.

Furstenberg, F. F., Jr. 1992. Teenage childbearing and cultural rationality: A thesis in search of evidence. *Family Relations,* 41, 239–243.

Furstenberg, F. F., Jr., and Cherlin, A. J. 1991. *Divided families: What happens to children when parents part?* Cambridge, MA: Harvard University Press.

Furstenberg, F. F., Jr., et al. 1994. How families manage risk and opportunity in dangerous neighborhoods. In W. J. Wilson (Ed.), *Sociology and the public agenda* (pp. 231–258). Newbury Park, CA: Sage.

Furstenberg, F. F., Jr., and Hughes, M. E. 1995. Social capital and successful development among at-risk youth. *Journal of Marriage and the Family,* 57, 580–592.

Gable, S. 1998. School-age and adolescent children's perceptions of family functioning in neglectful and non-neglectful families. *Child Abuse & Neglect,* 22, 859–867.

Galambos, N. L., Sears, H. A., Almeida, D. M., and Kolaric, G. C. 1995. Parents' work overload and problem behavior in young adolescents. *Journal of Research on Adolescence,* 5, 201–223.

Galst, L. 1998. Blood breaks a family: In custody battles, lesbian mothers are denying partners parenting rights. *Village Voice,* June 2, pp. 43, 44, 47.

Gamble, T. J., and Zigler, E. 1989. The Head Start Synthesis Project. *Journal of Applied Developmental Psychology,* 10, 267–274.

Gamoran, A. 1992. Social factors in education. In M. C. Alkin (Ed.), *Encyclopedia of educational research* (6th ed., pp. 1222–1229). New York: Macmillan.

Ganong, L., and Coleman, M. 1994. *Remarried family relationships.* Newbury Park, CA: Sage.

Ganong, L., and Coleman, M. 1999. *Changing families, changing responsibilities: Family obligations following divorce and remarriage.* Mahwah, NJ: Erlbaum.

Ganong, L., Coleman, M., Fine, M., and McDaniel, A. K. 1998. Issues considered in contemplating stepchild adoption. *Family Relations,* 47, 63–71.

Garbarino, J. 1995. *Raising children in a socially toxic environment.* San Francisco: Jossey-Bass.

Garbarino, J. 1999. *Lost boys. Why our sons turn violent and how we can save them.* New York: Free Press.

Garbarino, J., and Kostelny, K. 1992. Child maltreatment as a community problem. *Child Abuse & Neglect,* 16, 455–464.

Garbarino, J., Kostelny, K., and Dubrow, N. 1991. *No place to be a child: Growing up in a war zone.* Lexington, MA: Lexington Books.

Garbarino, J., and Sherman, D. 1980. High-risk neighborhoods and high-risk families: The human ecology of child maltreatment. *Child Development,* 51, 188–198.

Gardner, H. 1996. The concept of family: Perceptions of children in family foster care. *Child Welfare,* 75, 161–181.

Gardner, M., and Herz, D. E. 1992. Working and poor. *Monthly Labor Review,* December, pp. 20–28.

Garmezy, N., and Masten, A. S. 1994. Chronic adversities. In M. Rutter, E. Taylor, and L. Hersov (Eds.), *Child and adolescent psychiatry* (3rd ed., pp. 191–208). Oxford: Blackwell.

Garrison, M. E. B., Blalock, L. B., Zarski, J. J., and Merritt, P. B. 1997. Delayed parenthood: An exploratory study of family functioning. *Family Relations,* 46, 281–290.

Gately, D. W., and Schwebel, A. I. 1991. The challenge model of children's adjustment to parental divorce. *Journal of Family Psychology,* 5, 60–81.

Gecas, V., and Seff, M. A. 1990. Families and adolescents: A review of the 1980s. *Journal of Marriage and the Family,* 52, 941–958.

Gelles, R. J. 1989. Child abuse and violence in single parent families: Parent absence and economic deprivation. *American Journal of Orthopsychiatry,* 59, 492–501.

Gelles, R. J. 1993. Alcohol and other drugs associated with violence—they are not its cause. In R. J. Gelles and D. R. Loseke (Eds.), *Current controversies in family violence.* Newbury Park, CA: Sage.

Gelles, R. J. 1997. *Intimate violence in families* (3rd ed.). Thousand Oaks, CA: Sage.

Gelles, R. J., and Straus, M. A. 1988. *Intimate violence.* New York: Simon and Schuster.

Genovese, E. D. 1976. *Roll, Jordon, roll.* New York: Vintage Books.

Gerstel, N., and Gallagher, S. K. 1993. Kinkeeping and distress: Gender, recipients of care, and work-family conflict. *Journal of Marriage and the Family,* 55, 598–607.

Gilbert, D., and Kahl, J. A. 1993. *The American class structure: A new synthesis* (4th ed.). Belmont, CA: Wadsworth.

Giles-Sims, J. 1997. Current knowledge about child abuse in stepfamilies. *Marriage & Family Review,* 26, 215–230.

Gilgun, J. F. 1995. We shared something special: The moral discourse of incest perpetrators. *Journal of Marriage and the Family,* 57, 265–282.

Gilgun, J. F., Daly, K., and Handel, G. (Eds.). 1992. *Qualitative methods in family research.* Newbury Park, CA: Sage.

Gilligan, C. 1993. *In a different voice: Psychological theory and women's development.* Cambridge, MA: Harvard University Press.

Giordano, P. C., Millhollin, T. J., Cernkovich, S. A., Pugh, M. D., and Rudolph, J. L. 1999. Delinquency, indentity, and women's involvement in relationship violence. *Criminology,* 37, 17–37.

Glass, J., and Fujimoto, T. 1994. Housework, paid work, and depression among husbands and wives. *Journal of Health and Social Behavior,* 35, 179–191.

Gleason, P., Rangarajan, A., and Schochet, P. 1998. The dynamics of receipt of Aid to Families with Dependent Children among teenage parents in inner cities. *Journal of Human Resources,* 33, 988–1002.

Glendon, M. A. 1989. *The transformation of family law: State, law, and family in the United States and Western Europe.* Chicago: University of Chicago Press.

Glenn, N. D., 1991. The recent trends in marital success in the United States. *Journal of Marriage and the Family,* 53, 261–270.

Glenn, N. D. 1996. Values, attitudes, and the state of American marriage. In D. Popenoe, J. B. Elshtain, and D. Blankenhorn (Eds.), *Promises to keep: Decline and renewal of marriage in America* (pp. 15–34). Lanham, MD: Rowan and Littlefield.

Glenn, N. D. 1998. The course of marital success and failure in five American 10-year marriage cohorts. *Journal of Marriage and the Family,* 60, 569–576.

Glenn, N. D., and Weaver, C. N. 1988. The changing relationship of marital status to reported happiness. *Journal of Marriage and the Family,* 50, 317–324.

Glick, J. E., Bean, F. D., and Van Hook, V. W. 1997. Immigration and changing patterns of extended family household structure in the United States: 1970–1990. *Journal of Marriage and the Family,* 59, 177–191.

Glick, P. C. 1947. The family cycle. *American Sociological Review,* 12, 164–174.

Goffman, E. 1959. *The presentation of self in everyday life.* New York: Doubleday.

Gold, S. J., and Phillips, B. 1996. Mobility and continuity among Eastern European Jews. In S. Pedreza and R. G. Rumbaut (Eds.), *Origins and destinies: Immigration, race, and ethnicity in America* (pp. 182–194). Belmont, CA: Wadsworth.

Goldscheider, F., and Waite, L. 1991. *New families, no families.* Berkeley, CA: University of California Press.

Goldsmith, H. H., Buss, K. A., and Lemery, K. S. 1997. Toddler and childhood temperament: Expanded content, stronger genetic evidence, new evidence for the importance of the environment. *Developmental Psychology,* 33, 891–905.

Goldsmith, W. W., and Blakeley, E. J. 1992. *Separate societies: Poverty and inequality in U.S. cities.* Philadelphia: Temple University Press.

Golombok, S., Cook, R., Bish, A., and Murray, C. 1995. Families created by the new reproductive technologies: Quality of parenting and social and emotional development of the children. *Child Development,* 66, 285–298.

Gonzales, J. L., Jr. 1992. *Racial and ethnic families in America.* Dubuque, IA: Kendall/Hunt.

Gonzales, N. A., Cauce, A. M., Friedman, R. J., and Mason, C. A. 1996. Family, peer, and neighborhood influences on academic achievement among African-American adolescents: One-year prospective effects. *American Journal of Community Psychology,* 29, 365–387.

Goode, W. J. 1956. *Women in divorce.* New York: Free Press.

Gordon, M. 1989. The family environment and sexual abuse: A comparison of natal and stepfather abuse. *Child Abuse & Neglect,* 13, 121–129.

Gordon, T. 1994. *Single women: On the margins?* New York: New York University Press.

Gorman, E. H. 1999. Bringing home the bacon: Marital allocation of income-earning responsibility, job shifts, and men's wages. *Journal of Marriage and the Family,* 61, 110–122.

Gorman, J. C. 1998. Parenting attitudes and practices of immigrant Chinese mothers of adolescents. *Family Relations,* 47, 73–80.

Gottman, J. M. 1994. *What predicts divorce? The relationship between marital processes and marital outcomes.* Hillsdale, NJ: Erlbaum.

Gottman, J. M. 1998. Toward a process model of men in marriages and families. In A. Booth and A. C. Crouter (Eds.), *Men in families* (pp. 149–192). Mahwah, NJ: Erlbaum.

Gottschalk, P., and Danziger, S. 1993. Family structure, family size and family income. In P. Gottschalk and S. Danziger (Eds.), *Uneven tides* (pp. 167–193). New York: Russell Sage.

Gove, W., Style, C. B., and Hughes, M. 1990. The effect of marriage on the well-being of adults. *Journal of Family Issues,* 11, 4–35.

Graefe, D. R., and Lichter, D. T. 1999. Life course transitions of American children: Parental cohabitation, marriage, and single motherhood. *Demography,* 36, 205–217.

Gray, M. R., and Steinberg, L. 1999. Unpacking authoritative parenting: Reassessing a multidimensional construct. *Journal of Marriage and the Family,* 61, 574–587.

Green, G. D., and Bozett, F. W. 1991. Lesbian mothers and gay fathers. In J. C. Gonsiorek and J. D. Weinrich (Eds.), *Homosexuality: Research implications for public policy* (pp. 197–214). Thousand Oaks, CA: Sage.

Greenberg, J. S., Seltzer, M. M., and Greenlay, J. R. 1993. Aging parents of adults with disabilities: The gratifications and frustrations of later-life caregiving. *The Gerontologist,* 33, 542–549.

Greenberg, J. S., Seltzer, M. M., Krauss, M. W., and Kim, H.-w. 1997. The differential effects of social support on the psychological well-being of aging mothers of adults with mental illness or mental retardation. *Family Relations,* 46, 383–394.

Greenwood, P. W. 1995. Juvenile crime and juvenile justice. In J. Q. Wilson and J. Petersilia (Eds.), *Crime* (pp. 91–117). San Francisco, CA: Institute for Contemporary Studies Press.

Greif, G. L. 1995. Single fathers with custody following separation and divorce. In S. M. H. Hanson, M. L. Heims, D. J. Julian, and M. B. Sussman (Eds.), *Single parent families: Diversity, myths, and realities* (pp. 213–232). New York: Haworth.

Griffin, L. W. 1994. Elder maltreatment among rural African-Americans. *Journal of Elder Abuse & Neglect,* 6, 1–27.

Griffith, J. 1996. Relation of parental involvement, empowerment, and school traits to student academic performance. *Journal of Educational Research,* 90, 33–41.

Gross, H. E. 1993. Open adoption: A research-based literature review and new data. *Child Welfare,* 72, 269–284.

Grossbard-Shechtman, S. 1993. *On the economics of marriage: A theory of marriage, labor, and divorce.* Boulder, CO: Westview Press.

Grossberg, M. 1985. *Governing the hearth: Law and the family in nineteenth-century America.* Chapel Hill: University of North Carolina Press.

Grotevant, J., McRoy, R., Elde, C., and Fravel, D. 1994. Adoptive family system dynamics: Variations by level of openness in the adoption. *Family Process,* 33, 125–146.

Groze, V. 1996. *Successful adoptive families: A longitudinal study.* Westport, CT: Praeger.

Grych, J. H., and Fincham, F. D. 1994. Children's appraisals of marital conflict: Initial investigations of cognitive-contextual framework. *Child Development,* 64, 215–230.

Gubrium, J. F., and Holstein, J. A. 1990. *What is family?* Mountain View, CA: Mayfield.

Guerra, N. G., Huesmann, L. R., Tolan, P. H., Van Acker, R., and Eron, L. D. 1995. Stressful events and individual beliefs as correlates of economic disadvantage and aggression among urban children. *Journal of Consulting and Clinical Psychology,* 63, 518–528.

Gunnoe, M. L., Hetherington, E. M., and Reiss, D. 1999. Parental religiosity, parenting style, and adolescent social responsibility. *Journal of Early Adolescence,* 19, 199–225.

Gunnoe, M. L., and Mariner, C. L. 1997. Toward a developmental-contextual model of the effects of parental spanking on children's aggression. *Archives of Pediatrics and Adolescent Medicine,* 151, 768–775.

Gutman, H. 1976. *The Black family in slavery and freedom: 1750–1925.* New York: Pantheon.

Habermas, J. 1987. *The theory of communicative action: Lifeworld and system: A critique of functionalist reason* (vol. 2, translated by T. McCarthy). Boston: Beacon Press.

Hagan, J., MacMillan, R., and Wheaton, B. 1996. The life course effects of family migration on children. *American Sociological Review,* 61, 368–385.

Haines, M. R. 1985. The life cycle, savings, and demographic adaptation: Some historical evidence for the United States and Europe. In A. S. Rossi (Ed.), *Gender and the life course.* New York: Aldine.

Hamby, S. L., and Sugarman, D. B. 1999. Acts of psychological aggression against a partner and their relations to physical assault and gender. *Journal of Marriage and the Family, 61, 959–970.*

Hamm, W. 1997. Guide for effectively recruiting African-American adoptive families. In G. R. Anderson, A. S. Ryan, and B. R. Leashore (Eds.), *The challenge of permanency planning in a multicultural society* (pp. 139–149). New York: Haworth.

Hanawalt, B. A. 1993. *Growing up in Medieval London.* Oxford: Oxford University Press.

Handler, J. F. 1995. *The poverty of welfare reform.* New Haven, CT: Yale University Press.

Hannon, L. 1997. AFDC and homicide. *Journal of Sociology and Social Work,* 24, 125–136.

Hansell, S., and Harmon, A. 1999. Caveat emptor on the web: Ad and editorial lines blur. *The New York Times,* 26, A1, A12.

Hanson, T. L. 1999. Does parental conflict explain why divorce is negatively associated with child welfare? *Social Forces,* 77, 1283–1315.

Hanson, T. L., McLanahan, S., and Thomson, E. 1997. Economic resources, parental practices, and children's well-being. In G. J. Duncan and J. Brooks-Gunn (Eds.), *Consequences of growing up poor* (pp. 190–238). New York: Russell Sage.

Hao, L. 1996. Family structure, private transfers, and the economic well-being of families with children. *Social Forces,* 75, 269–292.

Hardy, J. B., Astone, N. M., Brooks-Gunn, J., Shapiro, S., and Miller, T. L. 1998. Like mother, like child: Intergenerational patterns of age at first birth and associations with childhood and adolescent characteristics and adult outcomes in the second generation. *Developmental Psychology,* 34, 1220–1232.

Hareven, T. K. 1987. Historical analysis of the family. In M. B. Sussman and S. K. Steinmetz (Eds.), *Handbook of marriage and the family* (pp. 37–57). New York: Plenum.

Hareven, T. K. 1994a. Continuity and change in American family life. In A. S. Skolnick and J. H. Skolnick (Eds.), *Family in transition* (8th ed., pp. 40–46). New York: HarperCollins.

Hareven, T. K. 1994b. Aging and generational relations: A historical and life course perspective. *Annual Review of Sociology,* 20, 437–461.

Harkness, S., and Super, C. 1992. Shared child care in east Africa: Socioculture origins and developmental consequences. In M. Lamb, K. Sternberg, C. Hwang, and A. Broberg (Eds.), *Child care in context: Cross cultural perspectives* (pp. 441–459). Hillsdale, NJ: Erlbaum.

Harrington, D., Black, M. M., Starr, R. H., and Dubowitz, H. 1998. Child neglect: Relation to child temperament and family context. *American Journal of Orthopsychiatry,* 68, 108–116.

Harrington, R. C., Fudge, H., Rutter, M. L., Bredenkamp, D., Groothues, C., and Pridham. 1993. Child and adult depression: A test of continuities with data from a family study. *British Journal of Psychiatry,* 162, 627–633.

Harris, J. R. 1998. *The nurture assumption. Why children turn out the way they do.* New York: Free Press.

Harris, K. M., Furstenberg, F. F., Jr., and Marmer, J. K. 1998. Paternal involvement with adolescents in intact families: The influence of fathers over the life course. *Demography* , 35, 201–216.

Harris, K. M., and Morgan, S. P. 1991. Fathers, sons, and daughters: Differential paternal involvement in parenting. *Journal of Marriage and the Family,* 53, 531–544.

Harrison, K., and Cantor, J. 1997. The relationship between media consumption and eating disorders. *Journal of Communication,* 47, 40–67.

Harvey, D. L. 1993. *Potter Addition: Poverty, family, and kinship in a heartland community.* New York: Aldine de Gruyter.

Harvey, E. 1999. Short-term and long-term effects of early parental employment on children of the National Longitudinal Survey of Youth. *Developmental Psychology,* 35, 445–459.

Harwood, R. L., Schoelmerich, A., Ventura-Cook, E., Schulze, P. A., and Wilson, S. A. 1996. Culture and class influences on Anglo and Puerto Rican mothers' beliefs regarding long-term socialization goals and child behavior. *Child Development,* 67, 2446–2461.

Haskett, M. E., Johnson, C. A., and Miller, J. W. 1994. Individual differences in risk of child abuse by adolescent mothers: Assessment in the perinatal period. *Journal of Child Psychology and Psychiatry,* 35, 461–476.

Haveman, R., and Wolfe, B. 1994. *Succeeding generations: On the effects of investments in children.* New York: Russell Sage.

Haveman, R., Wolfe, B., and Wilson, K. 1997. Childhood poverty and adolescent schooling and fertility outcomes: Reduced-form and structural estimates. In G. J. Duncan and J. Brooks-Gunn (Eds.), *Consequences of growing up poor* (pp. 419–460). New York: Russell Sage.

Hawkins, A. J., and Dollahite, D. C. (Eds.). 1997. *Generative fathering: Beyond deficit perspectives.* Thousand Oaks, CA: Sage.

Hawkins, A. J., Marshall, C. M., and Meiners, K. M. 1995. Exploring wives' sense of fairness about family work: An initial test of the distributive justice framework. *Journal of Family Issues,* 16, 693–721.

Hawkins, J. D., Catalano, R. F., and Miller, J. Y. 1992. Risk and protective factors for alcohol and other drug problems in adolescence and early adulthood: Implications for substance abuse prevention. *Psychological Bulletin,* 112, 64–105.

Hayes, D. S., and Casey, D. M. 1992. Young children and television: The retention of emotional reactions. *Child Development,* 63, 1423–1436.

Hays, S. 1996. *The cultural contradictions of motherhood.* New Haven, CT: Yale University Press.

Hays, S. 1998. The fallacious assumptions and unrealistic prescriptions of attachment theory: A comment on "Parents' socioemotional investment in children." *Journal of Marriage and the Family,* 60, 782–795.

Hayward, M. D., and Heron, M. 1999. Racial inequality in active life among adult Americans. *Demography,* 36, 77–91.

Hayward, M. D., Pienta, A. M., and McLaughlin, D. K. 1997. Inequality in men's mortality: The socioeconomic status gradient and geographic context. *Journal of Health and Social Behavior,* 38, 313–380.

Health and Human Services. 1998. Teen birth rates down in all states. Washington, DC: National Vital Statistics, May 1, <http://www.hhs.gov>.

Heath, D. T. 1995. The impact of delayed fatherhood on the father-child relationship. *Journal of Genetic Psychology,* 155, 511–530.

Heaton, T. B., Jacobson, C. K., and Holland, K. 1999. Persistence and chance in decisions to remain childless. *Journal of Marriage and the Family,* 61, 531–539.

Heger, A., and Lytle, C. 1993. Relationship of child sexual abuse to depression. *Child Abuse & Neglect,* 17, 383–400.

Henderson, S. H., Hetherington, E. M., Mekos, D., and Reiss, D. 1996. Stress, parenting and adolescent psychopathology in nondivorced and stepfamilies: A within-family perspective. In E. M. Hetherington and E. A. Blechman (Eds.), *Stress, coping, and resiliency in children and families* (pp. 39–66). Mahwah, NJ: Erlbaum.

Henry, C. S., Ceglian, C. P., and Ostrander, D. L. 1993. The transition to stepgrandparenthood. *Journal of Divorce and Remarriage,* 19, 25–44.

Hensen, K. A. 1993. Geographical mobility: March 1991 to 1992. *Current Population Reports* (Series P-20, No. 473). Washington, DC: U.S. Government Printing Office.

Henshaw, S. K. 1997. Teenage abortion and pregnancy statistics by state, 1992. *Family Planning Perspectives,* 29, 115–122.

Hernandez, R. 1998. Most dropped from welfare don't get jobs. *The New York Times,* March 23, A1, A16.

Herrerias, C. 1995. Noncustodial mothers following divorce. In S. M. H. Hanson, M. L. Heims, D. J. Julian, and M. B. Sussman (Eds.), *Single parent families: Diversity, myths and realities* (pp. 233–256). New York: Haworth.

Hertel, B. R. 1995. Work, family, and faith. In N. T. Ammerman and W. C. Roof (Eds.), *Work, family, and religion in contemporary society* (pp. 81–121). New York: Routledge.

Hess, B. B., and Ferree, M. M. (Eds.). 1987. *Analyzing gender: A handbook of social science research.* Newbury Park, CA: Sage.

Hetherington, E. M. 1988. Parents, children, and siblings: Six years after divorce. In R. A. Hinde and J. Stevenson-Hinde (Eds.), *Relationships within families: Mutual influences* (pp. 311–331). Oxford: Oxford University Press.

Hetherington, E. M. 1993. An overview of the Virginia longitudinal study of divorce and remarriage with a focus on early adolescence. *Journal of Family Psychology,* 7, 39–56.

Hetherington, E. M., Clingempeel, W. G., et al. 1992. Coping with marital transitions. *Monographs of the Society for Research in Child Development,* 57, (2–3).

Hewitt, C. 1998. Homosexual demography: Implications for the spread of AIDS. *Journal of Sex Research,* 35, 390–396.

Heyns, B. 1988. Schooling and cognitive development: Is there a season for learning? *Child Development,* 58, 1151–1160.

Hiebert-Murphy, D. 1998. Emotional distress among mothers whose children have been sexually abused: The role of a history of child sexual abuse, social support, and coping. *Child Abuse & Neglect,* 22, 423–435.

Higginson, J. G. 1998. Competitive parenting: The culture of teen mothers. *Journal of Marriage and the Family,* 60, 135–149.

Hines, A. M. 1997. Divorce-related transitions, adolescent development, and the role of the parent-child relationship: A review of the literature. *Journal of Marriage and the Family,* 59, 375–388.

Hochschild, A. R. 1983. *The managed heart.* Berkeley: University of California Press.

Hochschild, A. R. 1997. *The time bind.* New York: Metropolitan Books.

Hochschild, A. R., with Machung, A. 1989. *The second shift.* New York: Avon.

Hodges, E. V. E., Malone, M. J., and Perry, D. G. 1997. Individual risk and social risk as interacting determinants of victimization in the peer group. *Developmental Psychology,* 33, 1032–1039.

Hodgson, L. G. 1992. Adult grandchildren and their grandparents: The enduring bond. *International Journal of Aging and Human Development,* 34, 209–225.

Hofferth, S. 1996. Child care in the United States today. *The Future of Children,* 6, 41–61.

Hofferth, S., et al. 1998. Reported in *Time,* November 25, p. 44.

Hoffman, L. W. 1991. The influence of the family environment on personality: Accounting for sibling differences. *Psychological Bulletin,* 110, 187–203.

Hoffman, M. S. (Ed.). 1993. *World almanac and book of facts 1993.* New York: St. Martin's Press.

Hoffman, S. D., and Foster, E. M. 1997. Economic correlates of nonmarital childbearing among adult women. *Family Planning Perspectives,* 29, 137–140.

Hoffner, C. 1996. Children's wishful identification and parasocial interaction with favorite television characters. *Journal of Broadcasting and Electronic Media,* 40, 389–402.

Hogan, D. P., Hao, L., and Parish, W. L. 1990. Race, kin networks, and assistance to mother-headed families. *Social Forces,* 68, 797–812.

Hogan, D. P., and Kitagawa, E. M. 1985. The impact of social status, family structure, and neighborhood on the fertility of black adolescents. *American Journal of Sociology,* 90, 825–855.

Hollingsworth, L. D. 1998. Promoting same-sex adoption for children of color. *Social Work,* 43, 104–116.

Holmbeck, G. N., and Hill, J. P. 1988. Storm and stress beliefs about adolescence: Prevalence, self-reported antecedents, and effects of an undergraduate course. *Journal of Youth and Adolescence,* 17, 285–306.

Homans, G. C. 1961. *Social behavior: Its elementary forms.* New York: Harcourt, Brace, and World.

Hooyman, N. R., and Gonyea, J. 1995. *Feminist perspectives on family care: Policies for gender justice.* Thousand Oaks, CA: Sage.

Hopper, J. 1993. The rhetoric of motives in divorce. *Journal of Marriage and the Family,* 55, 801–813.

Horney, J., Osgood, D. W., and Marshall, I. H. 1995. Criminal careers in the short term: Intra-individual variability in crime and its relation to local life circumstances. *American Sociological Review,* 60, 655–673.

Horton, H. D., and Thomas, M. E. 1998. Race, class, and family structure: Differences in housing values for Black and White homeowners. *Sociological Inquiry,* 68, 114–136.

Horwitz, A. V. 1993. Adult siblings as sources of social support for the seriously mentally ill: A test of the serial model. *Journal of Marriage and the Family,* 55, 623–632.

Horwitz, A. V., and Raskin White, H. 1998. The relationship of cohabitation and mental health: A study of a young adult cohort. *Journal of Marriage and the Family,* 60, 505–514.

Hossain, Z. and Roopnarine, J. L. 1993. Division of household labor and child care in dual-earner African-American families with infants. *Sex Roles,* 29, 571–583.

Hostetler, J. A. 1993. *Amish society* (4th ed.). Baltimore: John Hopkins University Press.

Houseknecht, S. K., and Macke, A. 1981. Combining marriage and career: The marital adjustment of professional women. *Journal of Marriage and the Family,* 43, 651–661.

Hout, M., and Greeley, A. 1998. Comment: What church officials' reports don't show: Another look at church attendance data. *American Sociological Review,* 63, 113–119.

Howes, C. 1988. Abused and neglected children with their peers. In G. T. Hotaling et al. (Eds.), *Family abuse and its consequences* (pp. 99–108). Beverly Hills, CA: Sage.

Hu, Y., and Goldman, N. 1990. Mortality differentials by marital status: An international comparison. *Demography,* 27, 233–250.

Huesmann, L. R. 1986. Psychological processes promoting the relation between exposure to media violence and aggressive behavior by the viewer. *Journal of Social Issues,* 42, 125–139.

Huesmann, L. R., Eron, L. D., Lefkowitz, M. M., and Walder, L. O. 1984. Stability of aggression over time and generations. *Developmental Psychology,* 20, 1120–1134.

Hughes, M., and Thomas, M. E. 1998. The continuing significance of race revisited: A study of race, class, and quality of life in America, 1972 to 1996. *American Sociological Review,* 63, 785–795.

Hughes, R., Jr., Ebata, A. T., and Dollahite, D. C. 1999. Family life in the information age. *Family Relations,* 48, 5–6.

Hughes, R., Good, E. S., and Candell, K. 1993. A longitudinal study on the effects of social support on the psychological adjustment of divorced mothers. *Journal of Divorce & Remarriage,* 19, 37–56.

Hula, R. C. 1991. Introduction: Thinking about family policy. In E. A. Anderson and R. C. Hula (Eds.), *The reconstruction of family policy* (pp. 1–7). New York: Greenwood.

Hummer, R. A., Rogers, R. G., Nam, C. B., and Ellison, C. G. 1999. Religious involvement and U.S. adult mortality. *Demography,* 36, 273–285.

Hunter, A. G., and Ensminger, M. E. 1992. Diversity and fluidity in children's living arrangements: Family transitions in an urban African-American community. *Journal of Marriage and the Family,* 54, 418–426.

Hur, Y.-M., and Bouchard, T. J., Jr. 1995. Genetic influences on perceptions of childhood family environment: A reared apart twin study. *Child Development,* 66, 330–345.

Hurtado, A. 1995. Variations, combinations, and evolutions: Latino families in the United States. In R. E. Zambrana (Ed.), *Understanding Latino families: Scholarship, policy, and practice* (pp. 40–61). Thousand Oaks, CA: Sage.

Hutchison, I. W. 1999. The effect of children's presence on alcohol use by spouse abusers and their victims. *Family Relations,* 48, 57–65.

Huttenlocher, J., Levine, S., and Vevea, J. 1998. Environmental input and cognitive growth: A study using time-period comparisons. *Child Development,* 69, 1012–1029.

Hyman, B. 2000. The economic consequences of child sexual abuse for adult lesbian women. *Journal of Marriage and the Family,* 62, 199–211.

Iannaccone, L. R. 1990. Religious practice: A human capital approach. *Journal for the Scientific Study of Religion,* 29, 297–314.

Ishii-Kuntz, M. 1997. Intergenerational relationships among Chinese, Japanese, and Korean Americans. *Family Relations,* 46, 23–32.

Island, D., and Letellier, P. 1991. *Men who beat the men who love them.* New York: Harrington Park.

Jacob, T., Krahn, F. L., and Leonard, K. 1991. Parent-child interactions in families with alcoholic fathers. *Journal of Consulting and Clinical Psychology,* 59, 176–187.

James, K., et al. 1995. School achievement and dropout among Anglo and Indian females and males: A comparative examination. *American Indian Culture and Research Journal,* 19, 181–206.

Jang, S. J., and Smith, C. A. 1997. A test of reciprocal causal relationships among parental supervision, affective ties, and delinquency. *Journal of Research in Crime and Delinquency,* 34, 307–336.

Janssen, L. 1993. Empirical analysis of tenure patterns and farm structure. In A. Hallam (Eds.), *Size, structure, and the changing face of American agriculture* (pp. 469–499). Boulder, Co: Westview Press.

Janssen, L., Stover, R. G., and Clark, V. L. 1993. The structure of families and changes in farm organization and structure. In A. Hallam (Ed.), *Size, structure, and the changing face of American agriculture* (pp. 500–537). Boulder, CO: Westview Press.

Jargowski, P. A. 1997. *Poverty and place: Ghettos, barrios, and the American city.* New York: Russell Sage.

Jayakody, R. 1998. Race differences in intergenerational financial assistance: The needs of children and the resources of parents. *Journal of Family Issues,* 19, 508–533.

Jekielek, S. M. 1998. Parental conflict, marital disruption and children's emotional well-being. *Social Forces,* 76, 905–935.

Jencks, C. 1992. *Rethinking social policy: Race, poverty, and the underclass.* Cambridge, MA: Harvard University Press.

Jendrek, M. P. 1993. Grandparents who parent their grandchildren: Effects on lifestyle. *Journal of Marriage and the Family,* 55, 609–621.

Jenkins, J. M., and Smith, M. A. 1990. Factors protecting children living in disharmonious homes: Maternal reports. *Journal of the American Academy of Child & Adolescent Psychiatry,* 29, 60–69.

Jenkins, J. M., and Smith, M. A. 1993. A prospective study of behavioral disturbance in children of parental divorce: A research note. *Journal of Divorce & Remarriage,* 19, 143–159.

Jenny, C., Roesler, T. A., and Poyer, K. L. 1994. Are children at risk for sexual abuse by homosexuals? *Pediatrics,* 94, 41–44.

Jensen, L., and Chitose, Y. 1997. Immigrant generations. In A. Booth, A. C. Crouter, and N. Landale (Eds.), *Immigration and the family: Research and policy on U.S. immigrants* (pp. 47–62). Mahwah, NJ: Erlbaum.

Jodl, K. M., Bridges, M., Kim, J. E., Mitchell, A. S., and Chan, R. W. 1999. Relations among relationships: A family systems perspective. In E. M. Hetherington, S. H. Henderson, and D. Reiss (Eds.), *Adolescent siblings in stepfamilies: Family functioning and adolescent adjustment* (pp. 150–183). Monographs of the Society for Research in Child Development, 259, 64, no. 4.

Joesch, J. M. 1998. Where are the children? Extent and determinants of preschoolers' child care time. *Journal of Family and Economic Issues,* 19, 75–99.

John, R. 1998. The Native American family. In C. H. Mindel, R. W. Habenstein, and R. Wright, Jr. (Eds.), *Ethnic families in America: Patterns and variations* (4th ed., pp. 380–421). Upper Saddle River, NJ: Prentice-Hall.

Johnson, C. L. 1985. *Growing up and growing old in Italian-American families.* New Brunswick, NJ: Rutgers University Press.

Johnson, D. R., and Booth, A. 1998. Marital quality: A product of the dyadic environment or individual factors? *Social Forces,* 76, 883–904.

Johnson, M. E., and Huston, T. L. 1998. The perils of love, or why wives adapt to husbands during the transition to parenthood. *Journal of Marriage and the Family,* 60, 195–204.

Johnston, C., and Pelham, W. E. 1990. Maternal characteristics, ratings of child behavior, and mother-child interactions in families of children with externalizing disorders. *Journal of Abnormal Child Psychology,* 18, 407–417.

Jouriles, E. N., McDonald, R., Norwood, W. D., Ware, H. S., Spiller, L. C., and Swank, P. R. 1998. Knives, guns, and interparent violence: Relations with child behavior problems. *Journal of Family Psychology,* 12, 178–194.

Joy, L. A., Kimball, M. M., and Zabrack, M. L. 1986. Television and children's aggressive behavior. In T. M. Williams (Ed.), *The impact of television: A natural experiment in three communities* (pp. 303–360). Orlando, FL: Academic Press.

Kagan, S. L., and Neuman, M. J. 1998. Lessons from three decades of transition research. *Elementary School Journal,* 87, 365–379.

Kanowitz, L. 1969. *Women and the law.* Albuquerque: University of New Mexico Press.

Kaplan, S. J., Pelcovitz, D., and Labruna, V. 1999. Child and adolescent abuse and neglect research: A review of the past 10 years. Part 1: Physical and emotional abuse and neglect. *Journal of the American Academy of Child & Adolescent Psychiatry,* 38, 1214–1222.

Karen, D. 1990. Toward a political-organizational model of gatekeeping: The case of elite colleges. *Sociology of Education,* 63, 227–240.

Karraker, K. H., and Evans, S. L. 1996. Adolescent mothers' knowledge of child development and expectations of their own infants. *Journal of Youth and Adolescence,* 25, 651–666.

Kasarda, J. D. 1993. The severely distressed in economically transforming cities. In A. V. Harrell and G. E.

Peterson (Eds.), *Drugs, crime, and social isolation* (pp. 45–98). Washington, DC: The Urban Institute.

Kaufman, J., and Zigler, E. 1987. Do abused children become abusive parents? *American Journal of Orthopsychiatry,* 57, 186–192.

Keith, V. M., and Herring, C. 1991. Skin tone and stratification in the Black community. *American Journal of Sociology,* 97, 760–778.

Kellam, S. G. 1994. The social adaptation of children in classrooms: A measure of family childrearing effectiveness. In R. D. Parke and S. G. Kellam (Eds.), *Exploring family relationships with other social contexts* (pp. 147–168). Hillsdale, NJ: Erlbaum.

Keller, M. B., Beardslee, W. R., Dorer, D. J., Lavori, P. W., Samuelson, H., and Klerman, G. R. 1986. Impact of severity and chronicity of parental affective illness on adaptive functioning and psychopathology in children. *Archives of General Psychiatry,* 43, 930–937.

Kelley, J., and De Graaf, N. D. 1997. National context, parental socialization, and religious belief: Results from 15 nations. *American Sociological Review,* 62, 639–659.

Kelly, M. P. F., and Shauffler, R. 1996. Divided fates: Immigrant children and the new assimilation. In A. Portes (Ed.), *The new second generation* (pp. 30–53). New York: Russell Sage.

Kempe, C., Silverman, F., Steele, B., Droegemueller, W., and Silver, H. 1962. The battered child syndrome. *Journal of the American Medical Association,* 181, 17–24.

Kendall-Tackett, K. A., Williams, L. M., and Finkelhor, D. 1993. Impact of sexual abuse on children: A review and synthesis of recent empirical studies. *Psychological Bulletin,* 113, 164–180.

Kendler, K. S. 1995. Genetic epidemiology in psychiatry: Taking both genes and environment seriously. *Archives of General Psychiatry,* 52, 895–899.

Kendler, K. S. 1996. Parenting: A genetic-epidemiologic perspective. *American Journal of Psychiatry,* 153, 11–20.

Kendler, K. S., et al. 1992. Life events and depressive symptoms: A twin study perspective. In P. McGriffin and R. Murray (Eds.), *The new genetics of mental illness* (pp. 146–164). Oxford: Butterworth-Heinemann.

Kendler, K. S., Karkowski, L. M., and Prescott, C. A. 1999. Causal relationship between stressful life events and the onset of major depression. *American Journal of Psychiatry,* 156, 837–841.

Kerbo, H. R. 1996. *Social stratification and inequality* (3rd ed.). New York: McGraw-Hill.

Kerbow, D., and Bernhardt, A. 1993. Parental intervention in the school: The context of minority involvement. In B. Schneider and J. S. Coleman (Eds.), *Parents, their children, and schools* (pp. 115–146). San Francisco: Westview Press.

Kessen, W. 1979. The American child and other cultural inventions. *American Psychologist,* 34, 815–820.

Kessler-Davis, A. 1981. *Women have always worked: A historical overview.* New York: McGraw-Hill.

Kett, J. F. 1977. *Rites of passage: Adolescence in America 1790 to present.* New York: Basic Books.

Kiernan, K. 1992. The impact of family disruption in childhood on transitions made in young adult life. *Population Studies,* 46, 218–234.

Kim, J. E., Hetherington, E. M., and Reiss, D. 1999. Associations among family relationships, antisocial peers, and adolescents' externalizing behaviors: Gender and family type differences. *Child Development,* 70, 1209–1230.

Kim, U., and Choi, S. H. 1994. Individualism, collectivism, and child development: A Korean perspective. In P. M. Greenfield and R. R. Cocking (Eds.), *Cross-cultural roots of minority child development* (pp. 227–257). Hillsdale, NJ: Erlbaum.

Kimball, M. M. 1986. Television and sex-role attitudes. In T. M. Williams (Ed.), *The impact of television* (pp. 265–301). New York: Academic Press.

King, V., and Elder, G. H., Jr. 1995. American children view their grandparents: Linked lives across three rural generations. *Journal of Marriage and the Family,* 57, 165–178.

King, V., and Heard, H. E. 1999. Nonresident father visitation, parental conflict, and mothers' satisfaction: What's best for child well-being? *Journal of Marriage and the Family,* 61, 385–396.

Kinsey, A. C., Pomeroy, W. B., and Martin, C. E. 1948. *Sexual behavior in the human male.* Philadelphia: Saunders.

Kinsey, A. C., Pomeroy, W. B., and Martin, C. E. 1953. *Sexual behavior in the human female.* Philadelphia: Saunders.

Kirby, K. M. 1997. Foster parent demographics: A research note. *Journal of Sociology and Social Welfare,* 24, 135–141.

Kirkpatrick, L. A., and Davis, K. E. 1994. Attachment style, gender, and relationship status: A longitudinal analysis. *Journal of Personality and Social Psychology,* 66, 502–512.

Kisker, E. E., and Ross, C. M. 1997. Arranging child care. *The Future of Children,* 7, 99–109.

Kitson, G. C., with Holmes, W. M. 1992. *Portrait of divorce: Adjustment to marital breakdown.* New York: Guilford Press.

Kivett, V. R. 1993. Racial comparisons of the grandmother role: Implications for strengthening the family support system of older black women. *Family Relations,* 42, 165–172.

Klebanov, P. K., Brooks-Gunn, J., McCarton, C., and McCormick, M. C. 1998. The contribution of neighborhood and family income to developmental test scores over the first three years of life. *Child Development,* 69, 1420–1436.

Kluwer, E. S., Heesink, J. A. M., and van de Vliert, E. 1997. The marital dynamics of conflict over the division of labor. *Journal of Marriage and the Family,* 59, 635–653.

Kochanska, G. 1995. Children's temperament, mother's discipline, and security of attachment: Multiple pathways to emerging internalization. *Child Development,* 66, 597–615.

Kochenderfer, B. J., and Ladd, G. W. 1996. Peer victimization: Cause or consequence of school maladjustment? *Child Development,* 67, 1305–1317.

Koepke, L., Hare, J., and Moran, P. B. 1992. Relationship quality in a sample of lesbian couples with children and child-free lesbian couples. *Family Relations,* 41, 224–229.

Kohut, A. 1994. *The role of technology in American life.* Los Angeles: Times Mirror Center for People and the Press.

Kolchin, P. 1993. *American slavery, 1619–1877.* New York: Hill & Wang.

Korbin, J. E. 1986. Childhood histories of women imprisoned for fatal child maltreatment. *Child Abuse and Neglect: The International Journal,* 10, 331–338.

Korbin, J. E., Anetzberger, G., and Austin, C. 1995. The intergenerational cycle of violence in child and elder abuse. *Journal of Elder Abuse & Neglect,* 7, 1–15.

Kotlowitz, A. 1991. *There are no children here.* New York: Anchor/Doubleday.

Kouri, K. M., and Lasswell, M. 1993. Black-white marriages: Social change and intergenerational mobility. *Marriage and Family Review,* 19, 241–255.

Kowaleski-Jones, L., and Mott, F. L. 1998. Sex, contraception and childbearing among high-risk youth: Do different factors influence males and females? *Family Planning Perspectives,* 30, 163–169.

Kozol, J. 1991. *Savage inequalities: Children in America's schools.* New York: Crown.

Kramer, L., and Baron, L. A. 1995. Parental perceptions of children's sibling relationships. *Family Relations,* 44, 95–104.

Kraut, R., Patterson, M., Lundmark, V., Kiesler, S., Mukopadhyay, R., and Scherlis, W. 1998. Internet paradox: A social technology that reduces social involvement and psychological well-being? *American Psychologist,* 53, 1017–1031.

Krishnakumar, A., and Buehler, C. 2000. Interparental conflict and parenting behaviors: A meta-analytic review. *Family Relations,* 49, 25–44.

Kubey, R. 1994. Media implications for the quality of family life. In D. Zillmann, J. Bryant, and A. C. Huston (Eds.), *Media, children, and the family* (pp. 61–69). Hillsdale, NJ: Erlbaum.

Kupersmidt, J. B., Griesler, P. C., DeRosier, M. E., Patterson, C. J., and Davis, P. W. 1995. Childhood aggression and peer relations in the context of family and neighborhood factors. *Child Development,* 66, 360–375.

Kupersmidt, J. B., et al. 1995. Childhood aggression and peer relations in the context of family and neighborhood factors. *Child Development,* 66, 360–375.

Kurdek, L. A. 1990. Divorce history and self-reported psychological distress in husbands and wives. *Journal of Marriage and the Family,* 52, 701–708.

Kurdek, L. A. 1993a. The allocation of household labor in gay, lesbian, and heterosexual married couples. *Journal of Social Issues,* 49, 127–139.

Kurdek, L. A. 1993b. Nature and prediction of changes in marital quality for first-time parent and nonparent husbands and wives. *Journal of Family Psychology,* 6, 255–265.

Kurdek, L. A. 1994. Areas of conflict for gay, lesbian, and heterosexual couples: What couples argue about influences relationship satisfaction. *Journal of Marriage and the Family,* 56, 923–934.

Kurdek, L. A. 1998. Relationship outcomes and their predictors: Longitudinal evidence from heterosexual married, gay cohabiting, and lesbian cohabiting couples. *Journal of Marriage and the Family,* 60, 553–568.

Lackey, C., and Williams, K. R. 1995. Social bonding and the cessation of partner violence across generations. *Journal of Marriage and the Family,* 57, 295–305.

Ladd, G. W. 1992. Themes and theories: Perspectives on processes in family-peer relationships. In R. D. Parke and G. W. Ladd (Eds.), *Family-peer relationships: Modes of linkage* (pp. 1–34). Hillsdale, NJ: Erlbaum.

Ladd, G. W., Birch, S. H. and Buhs, E. S. 1999. Children's social and scholastic lives in kindergarten: Related spheres of influence? *Child Development,* 70, 1373–1400.

Laird, J. 1993. Lesbian and gay families. In F. Walsh (Ed.), *Normal family processes* (2nd ed., pp. 282–328). New York: Guilford Press.

Lamb, M. E. 1997. *The role of the father in child development.* New York: Wiley.

Lamb, M. E. 1998. Nonparental child care: Context, quality, correlates, and consequences. In W. Demon (Series Ed.), I. E. Sigel, and K. A. Renniger (Vol. Eds.), *Handbook of child psychology: Child psychology in practice* (4th ed.). New York: Wiley.

Lamb, M. E., Hwang, C. P., and Brody, A. 1989. Association between parental agreement regarding childrearing and the characteristics of families and children in Sweden. *International Journal of Behavioral Development,* 12, 115–130.

Lamborn, S. D., Dornbusch, S. M., and Steinberg, L. 1996. Ethnicity and community context as moderators of the relations between family decision making and adolescent readjustment. *Child Development,* 67, 283–301.

Lamborn, S. D., Mounts, N. S., Steinberg, L., and Dornbusch, S. M. 1991. Patterns of competence and adjustment among adolescents from authoritative, authoritarian, indulgent, and neglecting families. *Child Development,* 62, 1049–1065.

Land, K., McCall, P., and Cohen, L. 1990. Structural covariates of homicide rates: Are there any invariances across time and space? *American Journal of Sociology,* 95, 922–963.

Landale, N. S., and Fennelly, K. 1992. Informal unions among mainland Puerto Ricans: Cohabitation or an alternative to legal marriage? *Journal of Marriage and the Family,* 54, 264–280.

Laner, M. R., and Ventrone, N. A. 1998. Egalitarian daters/traditionalist dates. *Journal of Family Issues,* 19, 468–477.

Lareau, A. 1989. *Home advantage: Social class and parental intervention in elementary education.* New York: Falmer.

LaRossa, R. 1997. *The modernization of fatherhood: A social and political history.* Chicago: University of Chicago Press.

LaRossa, R., and Reitzes, D. C. 1993. Symbolic interactionism and family studies. In P. G. Boss, W. J. Doherty, R. LaRossa, W. R. Schumm, and S. K. Steinmetz (Eds.), *Sourcebook of family theories and methods: A contextual approach.* New York: Plenum Press.

Larson, R. 1995. Secrets in the bedroom: Adolescents' private use of media. *Journal of Youth and Adolescence,* 24, 535–550.

Larson, R. W., and Richards, M. H. 1994. *Divergent realities: The emotional lives of mothers, fathers, and adolescents.* New York: Basic Books.

Larzelere, R. E., Sather, P. R., Schneider, W. N., Larson, D. B., and Pike, P. L. 1998. Punishment enhances reasoning's effectiveness as a disciplinary response to toddlers. *Journal of Marriage and the Family,* 60, 388–403.

Laslett, P. 1971. *The world we have lost* (2nd ed.). New York: Scribners.

Laub, J. H., Nagin, D. S., and Sampson, R. J. 1998. Trajectories of change in criminal offending: Good marriages and the desistance process. *American Sociological Review,* 63, 225–238.

Laumann, E. O. 1996. Early sexual experiences: How voluntary? How violent? In M. D. Smith, et al. (Eds.), *Sexuality and American social policy.* Menlo Park, CA: Henry J. Kaiser Family Foundation.

Laumann, E. O., Gagnon, J. H., Michael, R. T., and Michaels, S. 1994. *The social organization of sexuality: Sexual practices in the United States.* Chicago: University of Chicago Press.

Lavigueur, S., Tremblay, R. E., and Saucier, J.-F. 1995. Interactional processes in families with disruptive boys:

Patterns of direct and indirect influence. *Journal of Abnormal Child Psychology,* 23, 359–378.

Lawton, L., Silverstein, M., and Bengtson, V. 1994. Affection, social contact, and geographic distance between adult children and their parents. *Journal of Marriage and the Family,* 56, 57–68.

LeClere, F. B., and Kowalewski, B. M. 1994. Disability in the family: The effects on children's well-being. *Journal of Marriage and the Family,* 56, 457–468.

Lee, E. S. 1951. Negro intelligence and selective migration: A Philadelphia test of the Klineberg hypothesis. *American Sociological Review,* 16, 227–232.

Lee, G. R., Netzer, J. K., and Coward, R. T. 1995. Depression among older parents: The role of intergenerational exchange. *Journal of Marriage and the Family,* 57, 823–833.

Lee, G. R., Peek, C. W., and Coward, R. T. 1998. Race differences in filial responsibility expectations among older parents. *Journal of Marriage and the Family,* 60, 404–412.

Lee, S. A. 1993. Family structure effects on student outcomes. In B. Schneider and J. S. Coleman (Eds.), *Parents, their children, and schools* (pp. 43–75). San Francisco: Westview Press.

Lee, Y.-J., and Aytac, I. A. 1998. Intergenerational financial support among whites, African Americans, and Latinos. *Journal of Marriage and the Family,* 60, 426–441.

Lefley, H. P. 1989. Family burden and family stigma in major mental illness. *American Psychologist,* 44, 556–560.

Lefley, H. P. 1997. Synthesizing the family caregiving studies: Implications for service planning, social policy, and further research. *Family Relations,* 46, 443–450.

Lemann, N. 1991. *The promised land: The great Black migration and how it changed America.* New York: Knopf.

Lennon, M. C., and Rosenfield, S. 1992. Women and mental health: The interaction of job and family conditions. *Journal of Health and Social Behavior,* 33, 316–327.

Lennon, M. C., and Rosenfield, S. 1994. Relative fairness and the division of housework: The importance of options. *Journal of Sociology,* 100, 506–531.

Lenton, R. L. 1990. Techniques of child discipline and abuse by parents. *Canadian Review of Sociology and Anthropology,* 27, 157–185.

Lerner, R. M. 1982. Children and adolescents as producers of their own development. *Developmental Review,* 2, 342–370.

Lerner, R. M. 1995. *America's youth in crisis.* Thousand Oaks, CA: Sage.

Lerner, R. M., and Busch-Rossnagel, N. A. 1981. Individuals as producers of their development: Conceptual and empirical bases. In R. M. Lerner and N. A. Busch-Rossnagel (Eds.), *Individuals as producers of their development: A life-span perspective* (pp. 1–36). San Diego, CA: Academic Press.

Levin, J. S. 1994. Investigating the epidemiologic effects of religious experience: Findings, explanations, and barriers. In J. S. Levin (Ed.), *Religion in aging and health: Theoretical foundations and methodological frontiers* (pp. 3–17). Newbury Park, CA: Sage.

Levine, E. S., and Sallee, A. L. 1990. Critical phases among adoptees and their families: Implications for therapy. *Child and Adolescent Social Work,* 7, 217–232.

LeVine, R. A. 1990. Infant environments in psychoanalysis: A cross-cultural view. In J. W. Stigler, R. A. Shweder, and G. Herd (Eds.), *Cultural psychology: Essays on comparative human development* (pp. 454–476). New York: Cambridge University Press.

LeVine, R. A. 1994. *Child care and culture: Lessons from Africa.* Cambridge: Cambridge University Press.

LeVine, R. A., and White, M. 1994. The social transformation of childhood. In A. S. Skolnick and J. H. Skolnick (Eds.), *Family in transition* (8th ed., pp. 273–293). New York: HarperCollins.

LeVine, S., and LeVine, R. A. 1981. Child abuse and neglect in sub-Saharan Africa. In J. E. Korbin (Ed.), *Child abuse and neglect: Cross-cultural perspectives* (pp. 35–55). Berkeley: University of California Press.

Levinger, G. 1976. A socio-psychological perspective on marital dissolution. *Journal of Social Issues,* 52, 21–47.

Levinson, D. J. 1978. *The seasons of a man's life.* New York: Knopf.

Lewin, E. 1993. *Lesbian mothers: Accounts of gender in American culture.* Ithaca, NY: Cornell University Press.

Lewin, T. 1999. Union links women's pay to poverty among families. *The New York Times,* February 25, A12.

Lewis, M. 1997. *Altering fate: Why the past does not predict the future.* New York: Guilford Press.

Lichter, D. T., McLaughlin, D. K., and Cornwell, G. T. 1995. Migration and the loss of human resources in rural America. In L. J. Beaulieu and D. Mulkey (Eds.), *Investing in people: The human capital needs of rural America* (pp. 235–256). Boulder, CO: Westview Press.

Lichter, D. T., McLaughlin, D. K., and Rebar, D. C. 1997. Welfare and the rise of female-headed families. *American Journal of Sociology,* 103, 112–143.

Liebert, R. M., and Sprafkin, J. 1988. *The early window: Effects of television on children and youth* (3rd ed.). New York: Pergamon.

Lillard, L. A., and Waite, L. J. 1995. Til death do us part: Marital disruption and mortality. *American Journal of Sociology,* 100, 1131–1156.

Lin, C. Y., and Fu, V. 1990. A comparison of child-rearing practices among Chinese, immigrant Chinese, and Caucasian-American parents. *Child Development,* 61, 429–433.

Lincoln, C. E., and Mamiya, L. H. 1990. *The black church in the African American experience.* Durham, NC: Duke University Press.

Lindsey, E. W. 1998. The impact of homelessness and shelter-life on family relationships. *Family Relations,* 47, 243–252.

Link, B. G., Cullen, F. T., Frank, J., and Wozniak, J. F. 1987. The social rejection of former mental patients: Understanding why labels matter. *American Journal of Sociology,* 92, 1461–1500.

Link, B. G., et al. 1994. Life-time and five-year prevalence of homelessness in the United States. *American Journal of Public Health,* 84, 1907–1912.

Loeber, R., and Stouthamer-Loeber, M. 1986. Family factors as correlates and predictors of juvenile conduct problems and delinquency. In M. Tonry and N. Morris (Eds.), *Crime and justice* (vol. 7.). Chicago: University of Chicago Press.

Logan, J. R., and Stults, B. J. 1999. Racial differences in exposure to crime. The city and suburbs of Cleveland in 1990. *Criminology,* 37, 251–276.

London, R. A. 1996. The difference between divorced and never-married mothers' participation in the Aid to Families with Dependent Children Program. *Journal of Family Issues,* 17, 170–185.

Long, L. 1992. International perspectives on the residential mobility of America's children. *Journal of Marriage and the Family,* 54, 861–869.

Lorber, J. 1994. *Paradoxes of gender.* New Haven, CT: Yale University Press.

Lounsbury, M. L., and Bates, J. E. 1982. The cries of infants of differing levels of perceived temperamental difficultness: Acoustic properties and effects on listeners. *Child Development,* 53, 677–686.

Lowry, D. T., and Towles, D. W. 1989. Soap opera portrayals of sex, contraception, and sexually transmitted diseases. *Journal of Communication,* 39, 76–83.

Luker, K. 1994. Dubious conceptions: The controversy over teen pregnancy. In A. S. Skolnick and J. H. Skolnick (Eds.), *Family in transition* (8th ed., pp. 165–177). New York: HarperCollins.

Luster, T., Bates, L., Fitzgerald, H., Vandenbelt, M., and Key, J. P. 2000. Factors related to successful outcomes among preschool children born to low-income adolescent mothers. *Journal of Marriage and the Family,* 62, 133–146.

Lykken, D. 1987. An alternative explanation for low or zero sib correlations. *Behavioral and Brain Sciences,* 10, 31.

MacBeth, T. M. 1998. Quasi-experimental research on television and behavior: Natural and field experiments. In J. K. Asamen and G. L. Berry (Eds.), *Research paradigms, television, and social behavior* (pp. 109–151). Thousand Oaks, CA: Sage.

Maccoby, E. E. 1999. The custody of children of divorcing families: Weighing the alternatives. In R. A. Thompson and P. R. Amato (Eds.), *The postdivorce family* (pp. 51–70). Thousand Oaks, CA: Sage.

Maccoby, E. E., Buchanan, C. M., Mnookin, R. H., and Dornbusch, S. M. 1993. Post divorce roles of mothers and fathers in the lives of their children. *Journal of Family Psychology,* 7, 24–38.

Maccoby, E. E., and Jacklin, C. N. 1983. The "person" characteristics of children and the family as environment. In D. Magnusson and V. L. Allen (Eds.), *Human development: An interactional perspective* (pp. 75–92). New York: Academic Press.

Maccoby, E. E., and Martin, J. 1983. Socialization in the context of the family: Parent-child interaction. In E. M. Hetherington (Ed.), *Handbook of child psychology: Vol. 4. Socialization, personality, and social development* (pp. 1–101). New York: Wiley.

Maccoby, E. E., and Mnookin, R. H. 1992. *Dividing the child. Social & legal dilemmas of custody.* Cambridge: Harvard University Press.

Machamer, A. M., and Gruber, E. 1998. Secondary school, family, and educational risk: Comparing American Indian adolescents and their peers. *Journal of Educational Research,* 6, 357–369.

MacLeod, C., Mathews, A., and Tata, P. 1986. Attentional bias in emotional disorders. *Journal of Abnormal Psychology,* 95, 15–20.

Madden-Derdich, D. A., and Arditti, J. A. 1999. The ties that bind: Attachment between former spouses. *Family Relations,* 48, 243–249.

Madoo-Lengermann, P., and Niebrugge-Brantley, J. 1992. Contemporary feminist theory. In G. Ritzer (Ed.), *Contemporary sociological theory* (3rd ed., pp. 308–357). New York: McGraw-Hill.

Magdol, L., Moffitt, T. E., Caspi, A., and Silva, P. A. 1998. Hitting without a license: Testing explanations for differences in partner abuse between young adults daters and cohabitors. *Journal of Marriage and the Family,* 60, 41–55.

Magnusson, D. 1990. Personality development from an interactional perspective. In L. A. Pervin (Ed.), *Handbook of personality theory and research* (pp. 193–222). New York: Guilford Press.

Magnusson, D. 1995. Individual development: A holistic, integrated model. In P. Moen, G. H. Elder, Jr., and K. Lüscher (Eds.), *Examining lives in context* (pp. 19–60). Washington, DC: American Psychological Association.

Magnusson, D., and Allen, V. L. (Eds.). 1983. *Human development: An interactional perspective.* New York: Academic Press.

Mahoney, M. M. 1994. *Stepfamilies and the law.* Ann Arbor: University of Michigan Press.

Mahoney, M. R. 1991. Legal images of battered women: Redefining the issue of separation. *Michigan Law Review,* 1, 43–49.

Majors, R., and Billson, J. M. 1993. *Cool pose: The dilemmas of black manhood in America.* New York: Simon and Schuster.

Makepeace, J. M. 1997. Courtship violence as process: A developmental theory. In A. P. Cardarelli (Ed.), *Violence between intimate partners* (pp. 29–47). Boston: Allyn and Bacon.

Mallon, G. P. 1997. Toward a competent child welfare service delivery system for gay and lesbian adolescents and their families. In G. A. Anderson, A. S. Ryan, and B. R. Leashore (Eds.), *The challenge of permanency planning in a multicultural society* (pp. 177–194). New York: Haworth.

Mallon, G. P. 1998. After care, then where? Outcomes of an independent living program. *Child Welfare,* 77, 61–78.

Mancini, C., Van Ameringen, M., and Macmillan, H. 1995. Relationship of childhood sexual and physical abuse to anxiety disorders. *The Journal of Nervous and Mental Disease,* 183, 309–314.

Mannheim, K. 1936. *Ideology and Utopia.* London: Routledge & Kegan Paul.

Manning, W. D., and Lichter, D. T. 1996. Parental cohabitation and children's economic well-being. *Journal of Marriage and the Family,* 58, 998–1010.

Manning, W., and Smock, P. 1995. Why marry? Race and the transition to marriage among cohabitors. *Demography,* 32, 509–520.

March, K. 1995. Perception of adoption as social stigma: Motivation for search and reunion. *Journal of Marriage and the Family,* 57, 653–660.

Margolin, G. 1998. Effects of domestic violence on children. In P. K. Trickett and C. J. Schellenback (Eds.), *Violence against children in the family and the community* (pp. 57–101). Washington, DC: American Psychological Association.

Marks, C. 1996. Farewell—We're good and gone: Black migration from the postbellum south. In S. Pedreza and R. G. Rumbaut (Eds.), *Origins and destinies: Immigration, race, and ethnicity in America* (pp. 73–83). Belmont, CA: Wadsworth.

Marks, N. 1996. Flying solo at midlife: Gender, marital status, and psychological well-being. *Journal of Marriage and the Family,* 58, 917–932.

Marks, N. F., and Lambert, J. D. 1998. Marital status continuity and change among young and midlife adults: Longitudinal effects on psychological well-being. *Journal of Family Issues,* 19, 652–686.

Marsiglio, W. 1992. Stepfathers with minor children living at home: Parenting perceptions and relationship quality. *Journal of Family Issues,* 13, 195–214.

Martin, G. T., Jr. 1997. An agenda for family policy in the United States. In T. Arendell (Ed.), *Contemporary parenting: Challenges and issues* (pp. 298–324). Thousand Oaks, CA: Sage.

Martoz-Baden, R., and Mattheis, C. 1994. Daughters-in-law and stress in two-generation farm families. *Family Process,* 43, 132–137.

Mash, E. J., and Johnson, C. 1990. Determinants of parenting stress: Illustrations from families of hyperactive children and families of physically abused children. *Journal of Clinical Child Psychology,* 19, 313–328.

Masheter, C. 1997. Healthy and unhealthy friendship and hostility between ex-spouses. *Journal of Marriage and the Family,* 59, 463–475.

Mason, C. A., Cauce, A. M., Gonzales, N., and Hiraga, Y. 1996. Neither too sweet nor too sour: Problem peers, maternal control, and problem behavior in African American adolescents. *Child Development,* 67, 2115–2130.

Mason, K. O., and Duberstein, L. 1992. Consequences of child care for parents' well-being. In A. Booth (Ed.), *Child care in the 1990s: Trends and consequences* (pp. 127–158). Hillsdale, NJ: Erlbaum.

Mason, M. A. 1998. The modern American stepfamily: Problems and possibilities. In M. A. Mason, A. Skolnick, and S. D. Sugarman (Eds.), *All our families: New policies for a new century* (pp. 95–116). New York: Oxford University Press.

Mason, M. A., Skolnick, A., and Sugarman, S. D. (Eds.). 1998. *All our families: New policies for a new century.* New York: Oxford University Press.

Massey, D., and Denton, N. 1993. *American apartheid: Segregation and the making of the underclass.* Cambridge, MA: Harvard University Press.

Massey, D. S., Gross, A. B., and Shibuya, K. 1994. Migration, segregation, and the concentration of poverty. *American Sociological Review,* 59, 425–445.

Masten, C. M., Trapnell, P. D., and Gorzalka, B. B. 1998. Ethnic, gender, and length of residency influences on sexual knowledge and attitudes. *Journal of Sex Research,* 35, 176–188.

Mathews, T. J., Ventura, S. J., Curtin, S. C., and Martin, J. A. 1998. *Births of Hispanics 1989–1995.* Washington, DC: National Center for Health Statistics.

Maton, K. I., and Hrabowski, F. A., III. 1998. Preparing the way: A qualitative study of high-achieving African American males and the role of the family. *American Journal of Community Psychology,* 26, 639–668.

Mauldon, J. 1998. Families started by teenagers. In M. A. Mason, A. Skolnick, and S. D. Sugarman (Eds.), *All our families: New policies for a new century* (pp. 39–65). New York: Oxford University Press.

Mayberry, M., Knowles, J. G., Ray, B., and Marlow, S. 1995. *Home-schooling: Parents as educators.* Thousand Oaks, CA: Corwin.

Maynard, R. E. (Ed.). 1997. *Kids having kids: Economic costs and social consequences of teen pregnancy.* Washington, DC: The Urban Institute Press.

McAdoo, H. P. 1988. Transgenerational patterns of upward mobility in African-American families. In H. R. McAdoo (Ed.), *Black families* (2nd ed., pp. 148–168). Newbury Park, CA: Sage.

McAuley, C. 1996. *Children in long term foster care.* Avebury, UK: Brookfield.

McBride, B. A., and Rane, T. R. 1998. Parenting alliance as a predictor of father involvement: An exploratory study. *Family Relations,* 47, 229–236.

McCartney, K., Scarr, S., Rocheleau, A., Phillips, D., Eisenberg, M., Keefe, N., Rosenthal, S., and Abbott-Shim, M. 1997. Social development in the context of typical center-based child care. *Merrill-Palmer Quarterly,* 43, 426–450.

McCauley, J., et al. 1997. Clinical characteristics of women with a history of childhood abuse. *Journal of the American Medical Association,* 277, 1362–1368.

McChesney, K. Y. 1995. A review of the empirical literature on contemporary urban homeless families. *Social Service Review,* 69, 429–460.

McCloskey, J. 1998. Three generations of Navajo women: Negociating life course strategies in the Eastern Navajo Agency. *American Indian Culture and Research Journal,* 22, 103–130.

McCloskey, L. A., Figueredo, A. J., and Koss, M. P. 1995. The effects of systemic family violence on children's mental health. *Child Development,* 66, 1239–1261.

McCollum, A. T. 1990. *The trauma of moving.* Newbury Park, CA: Sage.

McCoy, J. K., Brody, G. H., and Stoneman, Z. 1994. A longitudinal analysis of sibling relationships as mediators of the link between family processes and youths' best friendships. *Family Relations,* 43, 400–408.

McCurdy, K., and Daro, D. 1994. Child maltreatment: A national survey of reports and fatalities. *Journal of Interpersonal Violence,* 9, 75–94.

McGue, M. 1993. From proteins to cognitions: The behavioral genetics of alcoholism. In R. Plomin and G. E. McClearn (Eds.), *Nature, nurture & psychology* (pp. 245–265). Washington, DC: American Psychological Association.

McGuffin, P., and Katz, R. 1993. Genes, adversity, and depression. In R. Plomin and G. E. McClearn (Eds.), *Nature, nurture & psychology* (pp. 217–230). Washington, DC: American Psychological Association.

McHale, S. M., and Crouter, A. C. 1996. The family contexts of children's sibling relationships. In G. H. Brody (Ed.), *Sibling relationships: Their causes and consequences* (pp. 173–196). Norwood, NJ: Ablex.

McHale, S., Crouter, A. C., McGuire, S. A., and Updegraff, K. A. 1995. Congruence between mothers' and fathers' differential treatment of siblings: Links with family relations and children's well-being. *Child Development,* 66, 116–128.

McIlroy, A. 1998. Protection coming for children of divorce. *Globe and Mail,* November 27, A3.

McLanahan, S. S. 1997. Parent absence or poverty: Which matters more? In G. J. Duncan and J. Brooks-Gunn (Eds.), *Consequences of growing up poor* (pp. 35–48). New York: Russell Sage.

McLanahan, S. S., and Casper, L. 1995. Growing diversity and inequality in the American family. In R. Farley (Ed.), *State of the Union: America in the 1990s. Vol. Two: Social trends* (pp. 1–46). New York: Russell Sage.

McLaughlin, D. K., and Lichter, D. T. 1997. Poverty and the marital behavior of young women. *Journal of Marriage and the Family,* 59, 582–594.

McLeod, J. D., and Shanahan, M. J. 1996. Trajectories of poverty and children's mental health. *Journal of Health and Social Behavior,* 37, 207–220.

McLoyd, V. C. 1995. Poverty, parenting, and policy: Meeting the support needs of poor parents. In H. E. Fitzgerald, B. M. Lester, and B. Zuckerman (Eds.), *Children of poverty* (pp. 269–298). New York: Garland.

McLoyd, V. C. 1998. Socioeconomic disadvantage and child development. *American Psychologist,* 53, 185–204.

McMahon, C. A., Ungerer, J. A., Beaurepaire, J., Tennant, C., and Saunders, D. 1995. Psychosocial outcomes for parents and children after *in vitro* fertilization: A review. *Journal of Reproductive and Infant Psychology,* 13, 1–16.

McNeal, C., and Amato, P. R. 1998. Parents' marital violence: Long-term consequences for children. *Journal of Family Issues,* 19, 123–139.

McNeil, J. 1975. Feminism, femininity and the television shows: A content analysis. *Journal of Broadcasting,* 19, 259–269.

Mead, M. 1928. *Coming of age in Samoa.* New York: William Morrow.

Mekos, D., Hetherington, E. M., and Reiss, D. 1996. Sibling differences in problem behavior and parental treatment in nondivorced and remarried families. *Child Development,* 67, 2148–2165.

Melson, G.F., and Fogel, A. 1996. Parental perceptions of their children's involvement with household pets: A test of a specificity model of nurturance. *Anthrozoos,* 9, 95–106.

Menaghan, E. 1989. Psychological well-being among parents and nonparents. *Journal of Family Issues,* 10, 547–565.

Menaghan, E. G., and Parcel, T. L. 1991. Determining children's home environments: The impact of maternal characteristics and current occupational and family conditions. *Journal of Marriage and the Family,* 53, 417–431.

Menaghan, E. G., and Parcel, T. L. 1995. Social sources of change in children's home environments: The effects of parental occupational experiences and family conditions. *Journal of Marriage and the Family,* 57, 69–84.

Merten, D. E. 1996. Going-with: The role of a social form in early romance. *Journal of Contemporary Ethnography,* 24, 462–484.

Merton, R. K. 1968. *Social theory and social structure.* New York: Free Press.

Messner, M. 1997. *The politics of masculinity: Men in movements.* Thousand Oaks, CA: Sage.

Metz, M. E. 1993. *The styles of conflict inventory (SCI).* Palo Alto, CA: Consulting Psychologists Press.

Metz, M. E., Rosser, B. R. S., and Strapko, N. 1994. Differences in conflict-resolution styles among heterosexual, gay, and lesbian couples. *Journal of Sex Research,* 31, 293–308.

Meyer, D. R. 1999. Compliance with child support orders in paternity and divorce cases. In R. A. Thompson and P. R. Amato (Eds.), *The postdivorce family* (pp. 127–157). Thousand Oaks, CA: Sage.

Miall, C. E. 1996. The social construction of adoption: Clinical and community perspectives. *Family Relations,* 36, 34–39.

Michael, R., Gagnon, J., Laumann, E., and Kolata, G. 1994. *Sex in America: A definitive survey.* Boston: Little, Brown.

Miles-Doan, R. 1998. Violence between spouses and intimates: Does neighborhood context matter? *Social Forces,* 77, 623–645.

Miller, K. S., Forehand, R., and Kotchick, B. A. 1999. Adolescent sexual behavior in two ethnic minority samples: The role of family variables. *Journal of Marriage and the Family,* 61, 85–98.

Miller, L. S., Wasserman, G. A., Neugebauer, R., Gorman-Smith, D., and Kamboukos, D. 1999. Witnessed community violence and antisocial behavior in high-risk, urban boys. *Journal of Clinical Child Psychology,* 28, 2–11.

Miller, N. 1992. *Single parents by choice: A growing trend in family life.* New York: Plenum.

Miller, R. B., and Dodder, R. A. 1989. The abused-abuser dyad: Elder abuse in the state of Florida. In S. R. Ingmore and R. Filinson (Eds.), *Elder abuse: Practice and policy.* New York: Human Sciences Press.

Min, P. G. 1995. An overview of Asian Americans. In P. G. Min (Ed.), *Asian Americans: Contemporary trends and issues* (pp. 10–37). Newbury Park, CA: Sage.

Min, P. G. 1996. The entrepreneurial adaptation of Korean immigrants. In S. Pedraza and R. G. Rumbaut (Eds.), *Origins and destinies: Immigration, race, and ethnicity in America* (pp. 302–314). Belmont, CA: Wadsworth.

Miner, S., and Uhlenberg, P. 1997. Intragenerational proximity and the social role of sibling neighbors after midlife. *Family Relations,* 46, 145–153.

Minshull, R. 1996. *The American city and its citizens: The dream on the move.* Sussex, UK: The Book Guild.

Mintz, S. 1998. From patriarchy to androgyny and other myths: Placing men's family roles in historical perspective. In A. Booth and A. C. Crouter (Eds.), *Men in families* (pp. 3–30). Mahwah, NJ: Erlbaum.

Mintz, S., and Kellogg, S. 1988. *Domestic revolution: A social history of American family life.* New York: Free Press.

Mirrlees-Black, C., Mayhew, P., and Percy, A. 1996. *The 1996 British Crime Survey: England and Wales.* London: Home Office Statistical Bulletin no. 19–96.

Modell, J., and Goodman, M. 1990. Historical perspectives. In S. S. Feldman and G. R. Elliott (Eds.), *At the threshold: The developing adolescent* (pp. 93–122). Cambridge, MA: Harvard University Press.

Molnar, M. 1996. Of dogs and doggered. *American Imago,* 53, 269–280.

Monahan, S. C., Buchanan, C. M., Maccoby, E. E., and Dornbusch, S. M. 1993. Sibling differences in divorced families. *Child Development,* 64, 152–168.

Montemayor, R. 1986. Family variation in parent-adolescent storm and stress. *Journal of Adolescent Research,* 1, 15–31.

Montemayor, R., and Hanson, E. 1985. A naturalistic view of conflict between adolescents and their parents and siblings. *Journal of Early Adolescence,* 5, 23–30.

Montgomery, R. J. V., and Kamo, Y. 1989. Parent care by sons and daughters. In J. A. Mancini (Ed.), *Aging parents and adult children* (pp. 213–230). Lexington, MA: Lexington Books.

Moore, K. A., Nord, C. W., and Peterson, J. L. 1989. Nonvoluntary sexual activity among adolescents. *Family Planning Perspectives,* 21, 110–114.

Morelli, G. A., and Tronick, E. Z. 1991. Parenting and child development in the Efe foragers and Lese farners of Zaire. In M. H. Bornstein (Ed.), *Cultural approaches to parenting* (pp. 91–114). Hillsdale, NJ: Erlbaum.

Morgan, S. P., and Rindfuss, R. R. 1999. Reexamining the link of early childbearing to marriage and to subsequent fertility. *Demography,* 36, 59–75.

Morris, P. A., Hembrooke, H., Gelbwasser, A. S., and Bronfenbrenner, U. 1996. American families: Today and tomorrow. In U. Bronfenbrenner et al. (Eds.), *The state of Americans* (pp. 90–145). New York: Free Press.

Morris, S. N., Dollahite, D. C., and Hawkins, A. J. 1999. Virtual family life education: A qualitative study of father education on the World Wide Web. *Family Relations,* 48, 23–30.

Morrison, D. R., and Cherlin, A. J. 1995. The divorce process and young children's well-being: A prospective analysis. *Journal of Marriage and the Family,* 57, 800–812.

Morrison, D. R., and Coiro, M. J. 1999. Parental conflict and marital disruption: Do children benefit when high-conflict marriages are dissolved? *Journal of Marriage and the Family,* 61, 626–637.

Morrison, N. C., and Clavenna-Valleroy, J. 1998. Perceptions of maternal support as related to self-concept and self-report of depression in sexually abused female adolescents. *Journal of Child Sexual Abuse,* 7, 23–40.

Mortimer, J. T., and Finch, M. D. 1996. Work, family, and adolescent development. In J. T. Mortimer and M. D. Finch (Eds.), *Adolescents, work, and family* (pp. 1–24). Thousand Oaks, CA: Sage.

Mortimore, P., Sammons, P., Stall, L., Lewis, D., and Ecob, R. 1988. *School matters.* Berkeley: University of California Press.

Mouw, T., and Xie, Y. 1999. Bilinguilism and the academic achievement of first- and second-generation Asian Americans: Accommodation with or without assimilation? *American Sociological Review,* 64, 232–252.

Mowbray, C. T., et al. 1995. Motherhood for women with serious mental illness: Pregnancy, childbirth, and the postpartum period. *American Journal of Orthopsychiatry,* 65, 21–38.

Muller, C., and Kerbow, D. 1993. Parent involvement in the home, school, and community. In B. Schneider and J. S. Coleman (Eds.), *Parents, their children and schools* (pp. 13–42). San Francisco: Westview Press.

Munch, A., McPherson, J. M., and Smith-Lovin, L. 1997. Gender, children, and social contact: The effects of childrearing for men and women. *American Sociological Review,* 62, 509–520.

Munn, P., and Dunn, J. 1988. Temperament and the developing relationship between siblings. *International Journal of Behavioral Development,* 12, 433–451.

Mutran, E., and Reitzes, D. G. 1984. Intergenerational support activities and well-being among the elderly: A convergence of exchange and symbolic interaction perspectives. *American Sociological Review,* 49, 117–130.

Myers, J. 2000. Notes on the murder of thirty of my neighbors. *The Atlantic Monthly,* March, 72–86.

Myers, S. C., 1997. Marital uncertainty and childbearing. *Social Forces,* 75, 1271–1289.

Myers, S. M. 1996. An interactive model of religiosity inheritance: The importance of family context. *American Sociological Review,* 61, 858–866.

Nagel, J. 1995. American Indian ethnic renewal: Politics and the resurgence of identity. *American Sociological Review,* 60, 947–965.

Nakano Glenn, E. 1999. The social construction and institutionalization of gender and race: An integrative framework. In M. M. Ferree, J. Lorber, and B. B. Hess (Eds.), *Revisioning gender* (pp. 3–43). Thousand Oaks, CA: Sage.

Nakonezny, P. A., Shull, J. L., and Rodgers, L. 1995. The effect of no-fault divorce law on the divorce rate across the 50 states and its relation to income, education, and religion. *Journal of Marriage and the Family,* 57, 477–488.

Nakosteen, R. A., and Zimmer, M. A. 1997. Men, money, and marriage: Are high earners more prone than low earners to marry? *Social Science Quarterly,* 78, 66–82.

Nasar, S., and Mitchell, K. B. 1999. Booming job market draws young black men into the fold. *The New York Times,* May 23, A1.

National Center for Health Statistics. 1995. Advance report of final divorce statistics, 1989 and 1990. *Monthly Vital Statistics Reports,* 43, no. 9.

National Center for Health Statistics. 1997. Fertility, family planning and women's health: New data from the 1995 National Survey of Family Growth. *Vital and Health Statistics,* Series 23, p. 15. Hyattsville, MD: Public Health Service.

National Center for Health Statistics. December 1998. *Declines in teenage birth rates: National and state patterns, 1991–97.* Centers for Disease Control and Prevention. Washington, DC: Health and Human Services <http://www.hhs.gov>.

National Institute of Child Health and Human Development (NICHD) Early Child Care Research Network. 1998. Relations between family predictors and child outcomes: Are they weaker for children in child care? *Developmental Psychology,* 34, 1119–1128.

Neal, D. 1997. The effects of Catholic secondary schooling on educational attainment. *Journal of Labor Economics,* 15, 98–123.

Neal, L. 1996. The case against transracial adoption. *Focal Point,* Spring.

Neiderhiser, J. M., Reiss, D., Hetherington, E. M., and Plomin, R. 1999. Relationships between parenting and adolescent adjustment over time: Genetic and environmental contributions. *Developmental Psychology,* 35, 680–692.

Neisser, U., et al. 1996. Intelligence: Knowns and unknowns. *American Psychologist,* 51, 77–101.

Nelkin, D., and Lindee, S. M. 1995. *The DNA Mystique: The gene as a cultural icon.* New York: Freeman.

Nelson, D. A., and Crick, N. R. 1999. Rose-colored glasses: Examining the social information-processing of prosocial young adolescents. *Journal of Early Adolescence,* 19, 17–38.

Nelson, F. 1996. *Lesbian motherhood.* Toronto: University of Toronto Press.

Nelson, J. L. 1995. *Post-industrial capitalism. Exploring economic inequality in America.* Thousand Oaks, CA: Sage.

Newcomb, M. D., and Loeb, T. B. 1999. Poor parenting as an adult problem behavior: General deviance, deviant attitudes, inadequate family support and bonding or just bad parents? *Journal of Family Psychology,* 13, 175–193.

Ney, P. G., Fung, T., and Wickett, A. R. 1994. The worst combinations of child abuse and neglect. *Child Abuse & Neglect,* 18, 705–714.

NICHD Child Care Research Network. 1997. Poverty and patterns of child care. In G. J. Duncan and J. Brooks-Gunn (Eds.), *Consequences of growing up poor* (pp. 100–131). New York: Russell Sage.

Nigg, J. T., and Goldsmith, H. H. 1994. Genetics of personality disorders: Perspectives from personality and psychopathology research. *Psychological Bulletin,* 115, 346–380.

Nielsen, L. 1999. Stepmothers: Why so much stress? A review of the research. *Journal of Divorce & Remarriage,* 30, 115–148.

Noble, D. F. 1995. *Progress without people.* Toronto: Between the Lines.

Nock, S. L. 1993. *The cost of privacy.* New York: Aldine de Gruyter.

Nock, S. L. 1998a. The consequences of premarital fatherhood. *American Sociological Review,* 63, 250–263.

Nock, S. L. 1998b. Too much privacy? *Journal of Family Issues,* 19, 101–118.

Nock, S. L. 1998c. *Marriage in men's lives.* New York: Oxford University Press.

Noller, P. 1994. Relationships with parents in adolescence: Process and outcome. In R. Montemayor, G. R. Adams, and T. P. Gullotta (Eds.), *Personal relationships during adolescence* (pp. 37–77). Thousand Oaks, CA: Sage.

Noller, P., and Callan, V. 1991. *The adolescent in the family.* New York: Routledge.

Norman, A. J. 1994. Black-Korean relations: From desperation to dialogue, or from shouting and shooting to sitting and talking. *Journal of Multicultural Social Work,* 3, 87–99.

Norton, M. B. 1996. *Founding mothers & fathers: Gendered power and the forming of American society.* New York: Knopf.

NTIA (National Telecommunications and Information Administration). 1998. *Falling through the Net II: New data on the digital divide.* Available <http://www.ntia.doc.gov/ntiahome/net2/falling.html>.

O'Brien, M. J. 1991. Taking sibling incest seriously. In M. Q. Patton (Ed.), *Family sexual abuse* (pp. 75–92). Newbury Park, CA: Sage.

O'Connell, M. 1993. *Where's Papa? Father's role in child care.* Washington, DC: Population Reference Bureau.

O'Connor, T. G., and Insabella, G. M. 1999. Marital satisfaction, relationships, and roles. In E. M. Hetherington, S. H. Henderson, and D. Reiss (Eds.), *Adolescent siblings in stepfamilies: Family functioning and adolescent adjustment.* Monographs of the Society for Research in Child Development, 259, 64, no. 4.

Oderkirk, J. 1992. Parents and children living with low incomes. *Canadian Social Trends,* 27, 11–15.

Ogbu, J. U. 1985. A cultural ecology of competence among inner-city blacks. In M. B. Spencer, G. K. Brookins, and W. R. Allen (Eds.), *Beginnings: The social and affective development of black children* (pp. 45–66). Hillsdale, NJ: Erlbaum.

Ogbu, J. U. 1994. From cultural differences to differences in cultural frame of reference. In P. M. Greenfield and R. R. Cocking (Eds.), *Cross-cultural roots of minority child development* (pp. 365–392). Hillsdale, NJ: Erlbaum.

O'Keefe, M. 1998. Factors mediating the link between witnessing interparental violence and dating violence. *Journal of Family Violence,* 13, 39–57.

Oldman, D. 1994. Adult-child relations as class relations. In J. Qvortrup, M. Bardy, G. Sgritta, and H. Wintersberger (Eds.), *Childhood matters: Social theory, practice and politics* (pp. 43–58). Aldershot, UK: Avebury.

Olson, S. L., and Banyard, V. 1993. "Stop the world so I can get off for a while": Sources of daily stress in the lives of low-income single mothers of young children. *Family Relations,* 42, 50–56.

Ong, P., and Hee, S. 1994. Economic diversity. In P. Ong (Ed.), *The state of Asian Pacific America: Economic diversity, issues, and policies* (pp. 31–56). Los Angeles: LEAP Asian Pacific American Policy Institute and University of California at Los Angeles, Asian American Studies Center.

Orfield, G. 1993. *The growth of segregation in American schools: Changing patterns of separation and poverty since 1968.* Alexandria, VA: National School Boards Association.

Osmond, M. W., and Thorne, B. 1993. Feminist theories: The social construction of gender in families and society. In P. G. Boss, W. J. Doherty, R. LaRossa, W. R. Schumm, and S. K. Steinmetz (Eds.), *Sourcebook of family theories and methods: A contextual approach* (pp. 591–623). New York: Plenum.

Oyen, N., et al. 1997. Combined effects of sleeping position and prenatal risk factors in Sudden Infant Death Syndrome: The Nordic Epidemiological SIDS study. *Pediatrics,* 100, 613–620.

Pacheco, F., and Eme, R. 1993. An outcome study of the reunion between adoptees and biological parents. *Child Welfare,* 72, 53–64.

Pagani, L., Boulerice, B., and Tremblay, R. E. 1997. The influence of poverty on children's classroom placement and behavior problems. In G. J. Duncan and J. Brooks-Gunn (Eds.), *Consequences of growing up poor* (pp. 311–339). New York: Russell Sage.

Pagnini, D. L., and Rindfuss, R. R. 1993. The divorce of marriage and childbearing: Changing attitudes and behavior in the United States. *Population and Development Review,* 19, 331–347.

Panel on High-Risk Youth. 1993. *Losing generations: Adolescents in high-risk settings.* Washington, DC: National Academy Press.

Park, K. 1989. Impact of new productive activities on the organization of domestic life: A case study of the Korean American community. In G. Nomura, R. Endo, S. Sumida, and R. Leong (Eds.), *Frontiers of Asian American studies* (pp. 140–150). Pullman: Washington State University Press.

Park, R. E., and Burgess, E. W. 1925. *The city.* Chicago: University of Chicago Press.

Parke, R. D. 1995. Fathers and families. In M. Bornstein (Ed.), *Handbook of parenting* (vol. 4). Mahwah, NJ: Erlbaum.

Parks, C. A. 1998. Lesbian parenthood: A review of the literature. *American Journal of Orthopsychiatry,* 68, 376–389.

Parr, J. 1980. *Laboring children.* London: Croom Helm.

Parsons, T. 1951. *The social system.* New York: Free Press.

Parsons, T., and Bales, R. F., with Olds, J., Zelditch, M., Jr., and Slater, P. E. 1955. *Family, socialization and interaction process.* Glencoe, IL: Free Press.

Pasley, K., and Gecas, V. 1984. Stresses and satisfactions of the parental role. *Personal and Guidance Journal,* 2, 400–404.

Patillo, M. E. 1998. Sweet mothers and gangbusters: Managing crime in a black middle-class neighborhood. *Social Forces,* 76, 747–774.

Patillo-McCoy, M. 1998. Church culture as a strategy of action in the black community. *American Sociological Review,* 63, 767–784.

Patterson, C. J. 1992. Children of lesbian and gay parents. *Child Development,* 63, 1025–1042.

Patterson, C. J. 1995. Families of the lesbian baby boom: Parents' division of labor and children's adjustment. *Developmental Psychology,* 31, 115–123.

Patterson, C. J., and Chan, R. W. 1997. Gay fathers. In M. E. Lamb (Ed.), *The role of the father in child development* (3rd ed., pp. 245–260). New York: Wiley & Sons.

Patterson, G. R. 1980. Mothers: The unacknowledged victims. *Monographs of the Society for Research in Child Development,* 186.

Patterson, G. R. 1982. *Coercive family process.* Eugene, OR: Castalia.

Patterson, G. R. 1986a. The contribution of siblings to training for fighting: A microsocial analysis. In D. Olweus, J. Block, and M. Radke-Yarrow (Eds.), *Development of antisocial and prosocial behavior* (pp. 235–261). Orlando, FL: Academic Press.

Patterson, G. R. 1986b. Maternal rejection: Determinant or product of deviant behavior? In W. W. Hartup and Z. Rubin (Eds.), *Relationships and development.* Hillsdale, NJ: Erlbaum.

Patterson, G. R., Bank, L., and Stoolmiller, M. 1990. The preadolescent's contributions to disrupted family process. In R. Montemayor, G. R. Adams, and T. P. Gullotta (Eds.), *From childhood to adolescence* (pp. 107–133). Newbury Park, CA: Sage.

Patterson, G. R., Reid, J. B., and Dishion, T. J. 1992. *Antisocial boys.* Eugene, OR: Castalia.

Patterson, G. R., and Stouthamer-Loeber, M. 1984. The correlation of family management practices and delinquency. *Child Development, 55*, 1299–1307.

Pearce, L. D., and Axinn, W. G. 1998. The impact of family religious life on the quality of mother-child relations. *American Sociological Review, 63*, 810–828.

Pearson, J. L., Hunter, A. G., Cook, J. M., Ialongo, N. S., and Kellam, S. G. 1997. Grandmother involvement in child caregiving in an urban community. *The Gerontologist, 37*, 650–657.

Pebley, A. R., and Rudkin, L. L. 1999. Grandparents caring for grandchildren: What do we know? *Journal of Family Issues,* 20, 218–242.

Pelton, L. 1991. Poverty and child protection. *Protecting Children,* 7, 3–5.

Pelton, L. 1994. The role of material factors in child abuse and neglect. In G. B. Melton and F. D. Barry (Eds.), *Protecting children from abuse and neglect: Foundations for a new strategy* (pp. 131–181). New York: Guilford Press.

Pelton, L. H. 1997. Child welfare policy and practice: The myth of family preservation. *American Journal of Orthopsychiatry,* 67, 545–553.

Pepler, D. J., and Slaby, R. G. 1994. Theoretical and developmental perspectives on youth and violence. In L. D. Eron et al. (Eds.), *Reason to hope: A psychosocial perspective on violence and youth* (pp. 27–58). Washington, DC: American Psychological Association.

Perez-Granados, D. R., and Callanan, M. A. 1997. Parents and siblings as early resources for young children's learning in Mexican-descent families. *Hispanic Journal of Behavioral Sciences,* 19, 3–33.

Perkins, D. F., Luster, T., Villarruel, F. A., and Small, S. 1998. An ecological, risk-factor examination of adolescents' sexual activity in three ethnic groups. *Journal of Marriage and the Family,* 60, 660–673.

Perozynski, L., and Kramer, L. 1999. Parental beliefs about managing sibling conflict. *Developmental Psychology,* 35, 489–499.

Perry-Jenkins, M., and Crouter, A. 1990. Men's provider role attitudes: Implications for household work and marital satisfaction. *Journal of Family Issues,* 11, 136–156.

Persell, C. H., Catsambris, S., and Cookson, P. W. 1992. Differential asset conversion: Class and gender pathways to selective colleges. *Sociology of Education,* 65, 208–225.

Pettit, G. S., Bates, J. E., Dodge, K. A., and Meece, D. W. 1999. The impact of after-school peer contact on early adolescent externalizing problems is moderated by parental monitoring, perceived neighborhood safety, and prior adjustment. *Child Development,* 70, 768–778.

Pettit, G. S., Clamson, M. A., Dodge, K. A., and Bates, J. E. 1996. Stability and change in peer-rejected status: The role of child behavior, parenting, and family ecology. *Merrill-Palmer Quarterly,* 42, 267–294.

Phillips, C. 1998. Foster care system struggles to keep siblings together. *APA Monitor,* January, 26–27.

Pianta, R. C., Egeland, B., and Erickson, M. F. 1989. The antecedents of maltreatment: Results of the Mother-Child Interaction Research Project. In D. Cicchetti and V. Carlson (Eds.), *Child maltreatment* (pp. 203–253). Cambridge: Cambridge University Press.

Pillemer, K. 1985. The dangers of dependency: New findings on domestic violence against the elderly. *Social Problems,* 33, 147–158.

Pillemer, K., and Suitor, J. J. 1991. "Will I ever escape my children's problems?" Effects of adult children's problems on elderly parents. *Journal of Marriage and the Family,* 53, 585–594.

Pleck, E. H., and Pleck, J. H. 1997. Fatherhood ideals in the United States: Historical dimensions. In M. E. Lamb (Ed.), *The role of the father in child development* (pp. 33–48). New York: John Wiley & Sons.

Plomin, R. 1994. *Genetics and experience: The interplay between nature and nurture.* Thousand Oaks, CA: Sage.

Plomin, R., Corley, R., Caspi, A., Fulker, D. W., and DeFries, J. 1998. Adoption results for self-reported personality: Evidence of nonadditive genetic effects? *Journal of Personality and Social Psychology,* 75, 211–218.

Plomin, R., and McClearn, G. E. (Eds.). 1993. *Nature, nurture & psychology.* Washington, DC: American Psychological Association.

Plomin, R., and Rutter, M. 1998. Child development, molecular genetics, and what to do with genes once they are found. *Child Development,* 69, 1223–1242.

Polakow, V. 1993. *Lives on the edge.* Chicago: University of Chicago Press.

Pong, S. I. 1998. The school compositional effect of single parenthood on 10th-grade achievement. *Sociology of Education,* 71, 24–43.

Portes, A. 1995. Children of immigrants: Segmented assimilation and its determinants. In A. Portes (Ed.), *The economic sociology of immigration: Essays on networks, ethnicity, and entrepreneurship* (pp. 248–279). Russell Sage.

Portes, A., and Rumbaut, R. G. 1996. *Immigrant America: A portrait.* Berkeley: University of California Press.

Portes, A., and Schauffler, R. 1996. Language and the second generation: Bilingualism yesterday and today. In A. Portes (Ed.), *The new second generation* (pp. 8–29). New York: Russell Sage.

Portes, A., and Zhou, M. 1993. The new second generation: Segmented assimilation and its variants. *Annals of the American Academy of Political and Social Sciences,* 530, 74–96.

Potuchek, J. L. 1992. Employed wives' orientations to breadwinning: A gender theory analysis. *Journal of Marriage and the Family,* 54, 548–558.

Powell, B., and Downey, D. B. 1997. Living in single-parent households: An investigation of the same-sex hypothesis. *American Sociological Review,* 62, 521–539.

Powell, B., and Steelman, L. C. 1993. The educational benefits of being spaced out: Sibling diversity and educational progress. *American Sociological Review,* 58, 367–381.

Powers, D. A., and Hsueh, J. C.-T. 1997. Sibling models of socioeconomic effects on the timing of first premarital birth. *Demography,* 34, 493–511.

Presser, H. B. 2000. Nonstandard work schedules and marital instability. *Journal of Marriage and the Family,* 62, 93–110.

Presser, S., and Stinson, L. 1998. Data collection mode and social desirability bias in self-reported religious attendance. *American Sociological Review,* 63, 137–145.

Pribesh, S., Downey, D. B. 1999. Why are residential and school moves associated with poor school performance? *Demography,* 36, 521–534.

Prout, A., and James, A. 1990. *Constructing and reconstructing childhood: Contemporary issues in the sociological study of childhood.* London: Falmer.

Pruchno, R. 1999. Raising grandchildren: The experiences of Black and White grandmothers. *Gerontologist,* 39, 209–221.

Pruchno, R., Patrick, J. H., and Burant, C. J. 1996. Aging women and their children with chronic disabilities: Perceptions of sibling involvement and effects on well-being. *Family Relations,* 45, 318–326.

Pruchno, R., Patrick, J. H., and Burant, C. J. 1997. African American and White mothers of adults with chronic disabilities: Caregiving burden and satisfaction. *Family Relations,* 46, 335–346.

Ptacek, J. 1997. The tactics and strategies of men who batter: Testimony from women seeking restraining orders. In A. P. Cardarelli (Ed.), *Violence between intimate partners* (pp. 104–123). Boston: Allyn and Bacon.

Pyke, K. 2000. "The normal American family" as an interpretive structure of family life among grown children of Korean and Vietnamese immigrants. *Journal of Marriage and the Family,* 62, 240–255.

Quane, J. M., and Rankin, B. H. 1998. Neighborhood poverty, family characteristics, and commitment to mainstream goals: The case of African American adolescents in the inner city. *Journal of Family Issues,* 19, 769–794.

Quinn, J. F., and Smeeding, T. M. 1994. Defying the averages: Poverty and well-being among older Americans. *Aging Today,* September/October, 15, 9.

Quinton, D., Pickles, A., Maughan, B., and Rutter, M. 1993. Partners, peers, and pathways: Assortative pairing and continuities in conduct disorders. *Development and Psychopathology,* 5, 763–783.

Qvortrup, J. 1995. From useful to useful: The historical continuity of children's constructive participation. *Sociological Studies of Children,* 7, 49–76.

Radke-Yarrow, M. 1990. Family environments of depressed and well parents and their children: Issues of research methods. In G. R. Patterson (Ed.), *Depression and aggression in family interaction* (pp. 169–184). Hillsdale, NJ: Erlbaum.

Rafferty, Y., and Rollins, N. 1989. *Learning in limbo: The educational deprivation of homeless children.* New York: Advocates for Children. ERIC Document Reproduction No. ED 312 363.

Rafferty, Y., and Shinn, M. 1991. The impact of homelessness on children. *American Psychologist,* 46, 1170–1179.

Ragoné, H. 1994. *Surrogate motherhood: Conception in the heart.* Boulder, CO: Westview Press.

Ramey, C. T., and Ramey, S. L. 1992. Early educational intervention with disadvantaged children—To what effect? *Applied and Preventive Psychology,* 1, 130–140.

Rangarajan, A., and Gleason, P. 1998. Young unwed fathers of AFDC children: Do they provide support? *Demography,* 35, 175–186.

Raver, C. C., and Zigler, E. F. 1997. New perspectives on Head Start. *Early Childhood Research Quarterly,* 12, 363–385.

Ray, B. D., and Wartes, J. 1991. The academic achievement and affective development of home-schooled children. In J. A. Van Galen and M. A. Pitman (Eds.), *Home schooling: Political, historical, and pedagogical perspectives* (pp. 43–62). Norwood, NJ: Ablex.

Reddy, M. T. 1994. *Crossing the color line: Race, parenting, and culture.* New Brunswick, NJ: Rutgers University Press.

Regier, D. A., et al. 1990. Comorbidity of mental disorders with alcohol and other drug abuse. *Journal of the American Medical Association,* 264, 2511–2518.

Reichman, N. E., and Pagnini, D. L. 1997. Maternal age and birth outcomes: Data from New Jersey. *Family Planning Perspectives,* 29, 268–272, 295.

Reiss, D. 1993. Genes and the environment: Siblings and synthesis. In R. Plomin and G. E. McClearn (Eds.), *Nature, Nurture & Psychology* (pp. 417–432). Washington, DC: American Psychological Association.

Reiss, D. 1995. Genetic influence on family systems: Implications for development. *Journal of Marriage and the Family,* 57, 543–560.

Reiss, D., et al. 1995. Genetic questions for environmental studies. Differential parenting and psychopathology in adolescence. *Archives of General Psychiatry,* 52, 925–936.

Reiss, D., Plomin, R., Hetherington, E. M., Howe, G. W., Rovine, M., Tyron, A., and Hagan, M. S. 1994. The separate worlds of teenage siblings: An introduction to the study of the nonshared environment and adolescent development. In E. M. Hetherington, D. Reiss, and R. Plomin (Eds.), *Separate social worlds of siblings* (pp. 63–110). Hillsdale, NJ: Erlbaum.

Renzetti, C. M. 1997a. Violence in lesbian and gay relationships. In L. L. O'Toole and J. R. Schiffman (Eds.), *Gender violence* (pp. 285–293). New York: New York University Press.

Renzetti, C. M. 1997b. Violence and abuse among same-sex couples. In A. P. Cardarelli (Ed.), *Violence between intimate partners* (pp. 70–89). Boston: Allyn and Bacon.

Revkin, A. C. 1999a. Plunge in use of food stamps causes concern. *The New York Times,* February 25, A1, A17.

Revkin, A. C. 1999b. Welfare policies alter the face of food lines. *The New York Times,* February 26, A1, A16.

Reynolds, A. J., and Temple, J. A. 1998. Extended early childhood intervention and school achievement: Age thirteen findings from the Chicago Longitudinal Study. *Child Development,* 69, 231–246.

Rhodes, M. 1996. Globalization, the State and the restructuring of regional economies. In P. Gurnmett (Ed.), *Globalization and public policy* (pp. 161–180). Cheltenham, UK: Edward Elgar.

Riedmann, A., and White, L. 1996. Adult sibling relationships: Racial and ethnic comparisons. In G. H. Brody (Ed.), *Sibling relationships: Their causes and consequences* (pp. 105–126). Norwood, NJ: Ablex.

Rifkin, J. 1995. *The end of work.* New York: Putnam's Sons.

Risley-Curtiss, C. 1997. Sexual activity and contraceptive use among children entering out-of-home care. *Child Welfare,* 76, 475–500.

Robinson, L. C., and Blanton, P. W. 1993. Marital strengths in enduring marriages. *Family Relations,* 42, 38–45.

Rodgers, H. R., Jr. 1996. *Poor women, poor children* (3rd ed.). Armonk, NY: M. E. Sharpe.

Rodgers, K. B. 1999. Parenting processes related to sexual risk-taking behaviors of adolescent males and females. *Journal of Marriage and the Family,* 61, 99–109.

Rogers, S. J. 1999. Wives' income and marital quality: Are there reciprocal effects? *Journal of Marriage and the Family,* 61, 123–132.

Rogers, S. J., and Amato, P. R. 1997. Is marital quality declining? The evidence of two generations. *Social Forces,* 75, 1089–1100.

Rogers, S. J., and White, L. K. 1998. Satisfaction with parenting: The role of marital happiness, family structure, and parents' gender. *Journal of Marriage and the Family,* 60, 293–308.

Rogoff, B., Mistry, J., Göncü, A., and Mosier, C. 1991. Cultural variation in the role relations of toddlers and their families. In M. H. Bornstein (Ed.), *Cultural approaches to parenting* (pp. 175–184). Hillsdale, NJ: Erlbaum.

Rohner, R. P., Bourque, S. L., and Elordi, C. A. 1996. Children's perceptions of corporal punishment, caretaker acceptance, and psychological adjustment in a poor, biracial Southern community. *Journal of Marriage and the Family,* 58, 842–852.

Ronka, A., and Pulkinen, L. 1995. Accumulation of problems in social functioning in young adulthood: A developmental approach. *Journal of Personality and Social Psychology,* 69, 381–391.

Rook, K., Dooley, D., and Catalano, R. 1991. Stress transmission: The effects of husbands' job stressors on the emotional health of their wives. *Journal of Marriage and the Family,* 53, 165–177.

Roosa, M. W., Tein, J.-Y., Groppenbacher, N., Michaels, M., and Dumka, L. 1993. Mothers' parenting behavior and child mental health in families with a problem drinking parent. *Journal of Marriage and the Family,* 55, 107–118.

Roosa, M. W., Tein, J.-Y., Reinholtz, C., and Angelini, P. J. 1997. The relationship of childhood sexual abuse to teenage pregnancy. *Journal of Marriage and the Family,* 59, 119–130.

Roschelle, A. R. 1997. *No more kin: Exploring race, class, and gender in family networks.* Thousand Oaks, CA: Sage.

Roschelle, A. R. 1999. Gender, family structure, and social structure. In M. M. Ferree, J. Lorber, and B. B. Hess (Eds.), *Revisioning gender* (pp. 311–340). Thousand Oaks, CA: Sage.

Rosellini, L. 1998. When to spank: For decades, parenting experts have said spanking irreparably harms kids. But a close look at the research suggests otherwise. *U.S. News & World Report,* 124, April 13, 52–53, 55.

Rosenbaum, J. E. 1991. Black pioneers—Do their moves to the suburbs increase economic opportunity for mothers and children? *Housing Policy Debate,* 2, 179–213.

Rosenberg, M. S. 1987. Children of battered women: The effects of witnessing violence on their social problem-solving abilities. *Behavior Therapist,* 4, 85–89.

Rosenfeld, L. B., Bowen, G. L., and Richman, J. M. 1995. Communication in three types of dual-career marriages. In M. A. Fitzpatrick and A. L. Vangelisti (Eds.), *Explaining marital interactions* (pp. 257–289). Thousand Oaks, CA: Sage.

Rosenthal, D. A., and Feldman, S. S. 1990. The influence of perceived family and personal factors on self-reported school performance of Chinese and Western high school students. *Journal of Research on Adolescence,* 1, 135–154.

Ross, C. E., and Mirowsky, J. 1999. Parental divorce, life-course disruption, and adult depression. *Journal of Marriage and the Family,* 61, 1034–1045.

Ross, J. L. 1994. Challenging boundaries: An adolescent in a homosexual family. In F. Handel and G. G. Whitechurch (Eds.), *The psychosocial interior of the family* (4th ed., pp. 158–175). New York: Aldine de Gruyter.

Rossi, A. S., and Rossi, P. H. 1990. *Of human bonding: Parent-child relations across the life course.* New York: Aldine de Gruyter.

Rossi, P. H., and Wright, J. D. 1993. The urban homeless: A portrait of urban dislocation. In W. J. Wilson (Ed.), *The ghetto underclass* (pp. 149–159). Newbury Park, CA: Sage.

Rossides, D. W. 1990. *Social stratification: The American class system in comparative perspective.* Englewood Cliffs, NJ: Prentice-Hall.

Rothman, B. K. 1989. *Recreating motherhood: Ideology and technology in a patriarchal society.* New York: W. W. Norton.

Rotundo, E. A. 1985. American fatherhood: A historical perspective. *American Behavioral Scientist,* 29, 7–25.

Rowe, D. C. 1994. *The limits of family influence: Genes, experience, and behavior.* New York: Guilford Press.

Rowe, D. C., Jacobson, K. C., and Van den Oord, E. J. C. G. 1999. Genetic and environmental influences on vocabulary IQ: Parental education level as moderator. *Child Development,* 70, 1151–1162.

Rowe, D. C., and Gulley, B. L. 1992. Sibling effects on substance use and delinquency. *Criminology,* 30, 217–233.

Rowe, D. C., Rodgers, J. L., Meseck-Buskey, S., and St. John, C. 1989. Sexual behavior and nonsexual deviance: A sibling study of their relationship. *Developmental Psychology,* 25, 61–69.

Rubin, L. B. 1990. *Erotic wars: What happened to the sexual revolution?* New York: HarperCollins.

Rubin, L. B. 1994. *Families on the fault line.* New York: HarperCollins.

Rubin, S., and Quinn-Curan, N. 1983. Lost then found: Parents' journey through the community service maze. In M. Seligman (Ed.), *The family with a handicapped child.* New York: Grune and Stratton.

Ruggles, S. 1994. The origins of African-American family structure. *American Sociological Review,* 59, 136–151.

Rumbaut, R. G. 1996a. The crucible within: Ethnic identity, self-esteem, and segmented assimilation among children of immigrants. In A. Portes (Ed.), *The new second generation* (pp. 119–170). New York: Russell Sage.

Rumbaut, R. G. 1996b. Origins and destinies: Immigration, race, and ethnicity in contemporary America. In S. Pedreza and R. G. Rumbaut (Eds.), *Origins and destinies: Immigration, race, and ethnicity in America* (pp. 21–43). Belmont, CA: Wadsworth.

Rumbaut, R. G. 1997. Ties that bind: Immigration and immigrant families in the United States. In A. Booth, A. C. Crouter, and N. Landale (Eds.), *Immigration and the family: Research and policy on U.S. immigrants* (pp. 3–45). Mahwah, NJ: Erlbaum.

Rumbaut, R. G. 1999. "Immigrant stock" numbers one-fifth of the U.S. population. *Report,* National Council on Family Relations, 44, June, 8–9.

Rumberger, R. W. 1995. Dropping out of middle school: A multilevel analysis of students and schools. *American Educational Research Journal,* 32, 583–625.

Rumberger, R. W., et al. 1990. Family influences on dropout behavior in one California high school. *Sociology of Education,* 63, 283–299.

Rumberger, R. W., and Larson, K. A. 1994. Keeping high-risk Chicano students in school. In R. J. Rossi (Ed.), *Schools and students at risk* (pp. 141–162). New York: Teachers College Press.

Rumberger, R. W., and Larson, K. A. 1998. Toward explaining differences in educational achievement among Mexican American language-minority students. *Sociology of Education,* 71, 69–93.

Russell, N. F., and Zierk, K. L. 1992. Abortion, childbearing, and women's well-being. *Professional Psychology: Research and Practice,* 23, 269–288.

Rutter, M. L. 1989. Intergenerational continuities and discontinuities in serious parenting difficulties. In D. Cicchetti and V. Carlson (Eds.), *Child maltreatment* (pp. 317–348). Cambridge: Cambridge University Press.

Rutter, M. L. 1997. Nature-nurture integration: The example of antisocial behavior. *American Psychologist,* 52, 390–398.

Rutter, M., et al. 1995. Understanding individual differences in environmental-risk exposure. In P. Moen, G. H. Elder, Jr., and K. Lüscher (Eds.), *Examining lives in context* (pp. 61–93). Washington, DC: American Psychological Association.

Sabatelli, R. M., and Shehan, C. L. 1993. Exchange and resources theories. In P. G. Boss, W. J. Doherty, R. LaRossa, W. R. Schumm, and S. K. Steinmetz (Eds.), *Sourcebook of family theories and methods: A contextual approach* (pp. 385–417). New York: Plenum Press.

Sachdev, P. 1992. Adoption reunion and after: A study of the search process and experience of adoptees. *Child Welfare,* 71, 53–58.

Sacher, J. A., and Fine, M. A. 1996. Predicting relationship status and satisfaction after six months among dating couples. *Journal of Marriage and the Family,* 58, 21–32.

Salamon, S. 1992. *Prairie patrimony: Family, farming, and community in the Midwest.* Chapel Hill: University of North Carolina Press.

Saluter, A. F. 1992. Marital status and living arrangements: March 1991. *Current Population Reports. Population Characteristics* (Series P-20, No. 461). Washington, DC: U.S. Government Printing Office.

Salzinger, S., Feldman, R. S., and Hammer, M. 1993. The effects of physical abuse on children's social relationships. *Child Development,* 64, 169–187.

Sameroff, A. J., and Seifer, R. 1995. Accumulation of environmental risk and child mental health. In H. E. Fitzgerald, B. M. Lester, and B. Zuckerman (Eds.), *Children of poverty* (pp. 223–253). New York: Garland.

Sameroff, A. J., Seifer, R., and Bartko, W. T. 1997. Environmental perspectives on adaptation during childhood and adolescence. In S. S. Luthar and J. A. Burack (Eds.), *Developmental Psychopathology* (pp. 507–526). New York: Cambridge University Press.

Sampson, R. J. 1992. Family management and child development: Insights from social disorganization theory. In J. McCord (Ed.), *Facts, frameworks, and forecasts* (pp. 63–94). New Brunswick, NJ: Transaction.

Sampson, R. J. 1993. The community context of violent crime. In W. J. Wilson (Ed.), *Sociology and the public agenda* (pp. 259–286). Newbury Park, CA: Sage.

Sampson, R. J. 1997. Collective regulation of adolescent misbehavior: Validation results from eighty Chicago neighborhoods. *Journal of Adolescent Research*, 12, 227–244.

Sampson, R. J., and Laub, J. H. 1994. Urban poverty and the context of delinquency: A new look at structure and process in a classic study. *Child Development*, 65, 523–540.

Sampson, R. J., Morenoff, J. D., and Earls, F. 1999. Beyond social capital: Spatial dynamics of collective efficacy for children. *American Sociological Review*, 64, 633–660.

Sampson, R. J., and Wilson, W. J. 1995. Toward a theory of race, crime and urban inequality. In J. Hagan and R. D. Peterson (Eds.), *Crime and inequality* (pp. 37–54). Stanford, CA: Stanford University Press.

Sanday, P. R. 1990. *Fraternity gang rape: Sex, brotherhood, and privilege on campus*. New York: New York University Press.

Sanday, P. R. 1996. *A woman scorned: Acquaintance rape on trial*. New York: Doubleday.

Sandefur, G. D., and Liebler, C. A. 1997. The demography of American Indian families. *Population Research and Policy Review*, 16, 95–114.

Sandfort, J. R., and Hill, M. S. 1996. Assisting young, unmarried mothers to become self-sufficient: The effects of different types of early economic support. *Journal of Marriage and the Family*, 58, 311–326.

Sands, R. G., and Goldberg-Glen, R. S. 2000. Factors associated with stress among grandparents raising their grandchildren. *Family Relations*, 49, 97–105.

Sanson, A., and Rothbart, M. K. 1995. Child temperament and parenting. In M. Bornstein (Ed.), *Handbook of parenting* (vol. 4, pp. 299–321). Mahwah, NJ: Erlbaum.

Santa Barbara News Press. 1992. Study: Fertility drugs contribute to rise in costly multiple births, July 15. Associated Press.

Sapolsky, B. S., and Tabarlet, J. L. 1991. Sex in prime time television: 1979 versus 1989. *Journal of Broadcasting and Electronic Media*, 15, 505–516.

Sassen, S. 1994. *Cities in a world economy*. Thousand Oaks, CA: Pine Forge Press.

Sassler, S., and Schoen, R. 1999. The effect of attitudes and economic activity on marriage. *Journal of Marriage and the Family*, 61, 147–159.

Savin-Williams, R. C. 1994. Verbal and physical abuse as stressors in the lives of lesbian, gay male and bisexual youths: Associations with school problems, substance abuse, prostitution, suicide. *Journal of Consulting and Clinical Psychology*, 62, 261–269.

Scannapieco, M., Hegar, R. L., and McAlpine, C. 1997. Kinship care and foster care: A comparison of characteristics and outcomes. *Families in Society*, 78, 480–488.

Scarr, S. 1993. Biological and cultural diversity: The legacy of Darwin for development. *Child Development*, 64, 1333–1353.

Scarr, S. 1998. American child care today. *American Psychologist*, 53, 95–108.

Schaefer, R. T. 1998. *Racial and ethnic groups* (7th ed.). New York: Addison-Wesley Longman.

Schieffelin, B. 1990. *The give and take of everyday life: Language socialization of Kalui children*. New York: Cambridge University Press.

Schiller, B. R. 1995. The economics of poverty and discrimination (6th ed.). Englewood Cliffs, NJ: Prentice-Hall.

Schiller, H. I. 1996. *Information inequality: The deepening social crisis in America*. New York: Routledge.

Schlegel, A., and Barry, H., III. 1991. *Adolescence: An anthropological inquiry*. New York: Free Press.

Schoeni, R. F. 1998. Reassessing the decline in parent-child old-age coresidence during the twentieth century. *Demography*, 35, 307–314.

Schor, E. L., and Menaghan, E. G. 1995. Family pathways to child health. In B. C. Amick, S. Levine, A. R. Tarlov, and D. C. Walsh (Eds.), *Society and health* (pp. 18–45). New York: Oxford University Press.

Schor, J. B. 1991. *The overworked American: The unexpected decline in leisure*. New York: Basic Books.

Schteingart, J. S., Molnar, J., Klein, T. P., Lowe, C. B., and Hartmann, A. H. 1995. Homelessness and child functioning in the context of risks and protective factors moderating child outcomes. *Journal of Clinical Child Development*, 24, 320–331.

Schuster, M. A., Bell, R. M., Berry, S. H., and Kanouse, D. E. 1998. Impact of a high school condom availability program on sexual attitudes and behaviors. *Family Planning Perspectives*, 30, 67–72, 88.

Schvaneveldt, J. D., Pickett, R. S., and Young, M. H. 1993. Historical methods in family research. In P. G.

Boss, W. J. Doherty, R. LaRossa, W. R. Schumm, and S. K. Steinmetz (Eds.), *Sourcebook of family theories and methods: A contextual approach* (pp. 99–116). New York: Plenum.

Schwartz, P. 1994. *Peer marriage: Love between equals.* New York: Free Press.

Schwartz, P., and Rutter, V. 1998. *The gender of sexuality.* Thousand Oaks, CA: Pine Forge.

Schwarz, J. E. 1998. The hidden side of the Clinton economy. *The Atlantic Monthly,* October, 18–21.

Schwebel, D. C., and Plumert, J. M. 1999. Longitudinal and concurrent relations among temperament, ability estimation, and injury proneness. *Child Development,* 70, 700–712.

Seaberg, J. R., and Harrigan, M. P. 1997. Family functioning in foster care. *Families in Society,* 78, 463–470.

Seccombe, K., James, D., and Walters, K. B. 1998. "They think you ain't much of nothing": The social construction of the welfare mother. *Journal of Marriage and the Family,* 60, 849–865.

Seidman, S. N., Mosher, W. D., and Aral, S. D. 1994. Predictors of high-risk behavior in unmarried American women: Adolescent environment as a risk factor. *Journal of Adolescent Health,* 15, 126–132.

Seltzer, J. A. 1994. Consequences of marital dissolution for children. *Annual Review of Sociology,* 20, 235–266.

Seltzer, J. A. 1998. Fathers by law: Effects of joint legal custody on nonresident fathers' involvement with children. *Demography,* 35, 135–146.

Seltzer, M. M., Greenberg, J. S., Krauss, M. W., Gordon, R. M., and Judge, K. 1997. Siblings of adults with mental retardation or mental illness: Effects on lifestyle and psychological well-being. *Family Relations,* 46, 395–405.

Serbin, L. A., Cooperman, J. M., Peters, P. L., Lehoux, P. M., Stack, D. M., and Schwartzman, A. E. 1998. Intergenerational transmission of psychosocial risk in women with childhood histories of aggression, withdrawal, or aggression and withdrawal. *Developmental Psychology,* 34, 1246–1262.

Serbin, L. A., Peters, P. L., and Schwartzman, A. E. 1996. Longitudinal study of early childhood injuries and acute illness in the offspring of adolescent mothers who were aggressive, withdrawn, or aggressive-withdrawn in childhood. *Journal of Abnormal Psychology,* 105, 500–507.

Sered, S. S. 1999. "Woman" as symbol and women as agents: Gendered religious discourses. In M. M. Ferree, J. Lorber, and B. B. Hess (Eds.), *Revisioning gender* (pp. 193–221). Thousand Oaks, CA: Sage.

Shane, P. G. 1996. *What about America's homeless children?* Thousand Oaks, CA: Sage.

Shapiro, A., and Lambert, J. D. 1999. Longitudinal effects of divorce on the quality of the father-child relationship and on fathers' psychological well-being. *Journal of Marriage and the Family,* 61, 397–408.

Sharma, A. R., McGue, M. K., and Benson, P. L. 1998. The psychological adjustment of United States adopted adolescents and their nonadopted siblings. *Child Development,* 69, 791–802.

Shavit, Y., and Pierce, J. L. 1991. Sibship size and educational attainment in nuclear and extended families. *American Sociological Review,* 56, 321–330.

Shaw, D. S., Winslow, E. B., and Flanagan, C. 1999. A prospective study of the effects of marital status and family relations on young children's adjustment among African American and European American families. *Child Development,* 70, 742–755.

Sheehy, G. 1995. *New passages: Mapping your life across time.* New York: Dutton.

Sheley, J. F., and Wright, J. D. 1995. *In the line of fire. Youth, guns, and violence in urban America.* Hawthorne, NY: Aldine de Gruyter.

Sherman, A. 1994. *Wasting America's future.* Boston: Beacon Press.

Sheth, M. 1995. Asian Indian Americans. In P. G. Min (Ed.), *Asian Americans: Contemporary trends and issues* (pp. 169–199). Thousand Oaks, CA: Sage.

Shinn, M., Knickman, J., and Weitzman, B. C. 1991. Social relationships and vulnerability to becoming homeless among poor families. *American Psychologist,* 46, 1180–1187.

Shireman, J. F. 1995. Adoptions by single parents. In S. M. H. Hanson, M. L. Heims, D. J. Julian, and M. B. Sussman (Eds.), *Single parent families: Diversity, myths and realities* (pp. 367–388). New York: Haworth.

Shoemaker, N. 1991. Native American families. In J. M. Hawes and E. Nybakkan (Eds.), *American families: A research guide and historical handbook* (pp. 291–317). New York: Greenwood.

Shorter, E. 1975. *The making of the modern family.* New York: Basic Books.

Silverman, A. R. 1993. Outcomes of transracial adoption. *The Future of Children,* 3, 104–118.

Silverstein, L. B., and Auerbach, C. F. 1999. Deconstructing the essential father. *American Psychologist,* 54, 397–407.

Silverstein, M., and Bengtson, V. L. 1991. Do close parent-child relationships reduce the mortality risk of older parents? *Journal of Health and Social Behavior,* 32, 382–395.

Silverstein, M., and Chen, X. 1999. The impact of acculturation in Mexican American families on the quality of adult grandchild-grandparent relationships. *Journal of Marriage and the Family,* 61, 188–198.

Silverstein, M., and Long, J. D. 1998. Trajectories of grandparents' perceived solidarity with adult grandchildren: A growth curve analysis over 23 years. *Journal of Marriage and the Family,* 60, 912–923.

Silverstein, M., Parrott, T. M., and Bengtson, V. L. 1995. Factors that predispose middle-aged sons and daughters to provide support to older parents. *Journal of Marriage and the Family,* 57, 465–475.

Silverthorn, P., and Frick, P. J. 1999. Developmental pathways to antisocial behavior: The delayed-onset pathway in girls. *Development and Psychopathology,* 11, 101–126.

Simons, R. L., and Associates (Eds.). 1996. *Understanding differences between divorced and intact families.* Thousand Oaks, CA: Sage.

Simons, R. L., Johnson, C., and Conger, R. D. 1994. Harsh corporal punishment versus quality of parental involvement as an explanation of adolescent maladjustment. *Journal of Marriage and the Family,* 56, 591–607.

Simons, R. L., Johnson, C., Conger, R. D., and Elder, G. H., Jr. 1998. A test of latent trait versus life-course perspectives on the stability of adolescent antisocial behavior. *Criminology,* 36, 217–244.

Simons, R. L., Lin, K.-H., and Gordon, L. C. 1998. Socialization in the family of origin and male dating violence: A prospective study. *Journal of Marriage and the Family,* 60, 467–478.

Simons, R. L., Whitbeck, L. B., Beaman, J., and Conger, R. D. 1994. The impact of mothers' parenting, involvement by nonresidential fathers, and parental conflict on the adjustment of adolescent children. *Journal of Marriage and the Family,* 56, 356–374.

Simons, R. L., Whitbeck, L. B., Melby, J. N., and Wu, C. I. 1994. Economic pressure and harsh parenting. In R. D. Conger, G. H. Elder, Jr., and Associates (Eds.), *Families in troubled times: Adapting to change in rural America* (pp. 207–222). New York: Aldine de Gruyter.

Simons, R. L., Wu, C., Conger, R. D., and Lorenz, F. O. 1994. Two routes to delinquency: Difference between early and late starters on the impact of parenting and deviant peers. *Criminology,* 32, 247–276.

Simons, R. L., Wu, C., Johnson, C., and Conger, R. D. 1995. A test of various perspectives on the intergenational transmission of domestic violence. *Criminology,* 33, 141–172.

Singer, J. D., Fuller, B., Keiley, M. K., and Wolf, A. 1998. Early child-care selection: Variation by geographic location, maternal characteristics, and family structure. *Developmental Psychology,* 34, 1129–1144.

Skogan, W. G. 1990. *Disorder and decline. Crime and the spiral of decay in American neighborhoods.* New York: Free Press.

Skolnick, A. 1998. Solomon's children: The new biologism, psychological parenthood, attachment theory, and the best interests standard. In M. A. Mason, A. Skolnick, and S. D. Sugarman (Eds.), *All our families: New policies for a new century.* New York: Oxford University Press.

Sleek, S. 1998. "Innocuous" violence triggers the real thing. *APA Monitor,* 29, April, pp. 1, 31.

Small, S. A. and Eastman, G. 1991. Rearing adolescents in contemporary society: A conceptual framework for understanding the responsibilities and needs of parents. *Family Relations,* 40, 455–462.

Small, S. A., and Kerns, D. 1993. Unwanted sexual activity among peers during early and middle adolescence: Incidence and risk factors. *Journal of Marriage and the Family,* 55, 941–952.

Smetana, J., and Gaines, C. 1999. Adolescent-parent conflict in middle-class African American families. *Child Development,* 70, 1447–1463.

Smith, D. E. 1974. Women's perspective as a radical critique of sociology. *Sociological Inquiry,* 44, 7–13.

Smith, D. E. 1987. *The everyday world as problematic: A feminist sociology.* Toronto: University of Toronto Press.

Smith, H., and Israel, E. 1997. Sibling incest: A study of the dynamics of 25 cases. *Child Abuse & Neglect,* 11, 101–108.

Smith, J. G., and Horton, G. P. 1997. *Statistical record of black America* (4th ed.). Gale Research Press.

Smith, J. R., Brooks-Gunn, J., and Klebanov, P. K. 1997. Consequences of living in poverty for young children's cognitive and verbal ability and early school achievement. In G. J. Duncan and J. Brooks-Gunn (Eds.), *Consequences of growing up poor* (pp. 132–189). New York: Russell Sage.

Smith, R., and Joe, T. 1994. *World without work: Causes and consequences of Black male joblessness.* Washington, DC: Center for the Study of Social Policy.

Smith, T. W. 1998. A review of church attendance measures. *American Sociological Review,* 63, 131–136.

Smithey, M. 1998. Infant homicide: Victim/offender relationship and causes of death. *Journal of Family Violence,* 13, 285–297.

Smits, J., Ultee, W., and Lammers, J. 1998. Educational homogamy in 65 countries: An explanation of differences in openness using country-level explanatory variables. *American Sociological Review,* 63, 264–285.

Smock, P. J. 1994. Gender and short-run economic consequences of marital disruption. *Social Forces,* 74, 243–262.

Smock, P. J., and Manning, W. D. 1997. Cohabiting partners' economic circumstances and marriage. *Demography,* 34, 331–341.

Smock, P. J., Manning, W. D., and Gupta, S. 1999. The effect of marriage and divorce on women's economic well-being. *American Sociological Review,* 64, 794–812.

Solomon, J. C., and Marx, J. 1995. "To grandmother's house we go": Health and school adjustment of children raised solely by grandparents. *The Gerontologist,* 35, 386–394.

Somers, M. D. 1993. A comparison of voluntarily childfree adults and parents. *Journal of Marriage and the Family,* 55, 643–650.

South, S. D. 1996. Mate availability and the transition to unwed motherhood: A paradox of population structure. *Journal of Marriage and the Family,* 58, 265–280.

South, S. J. 1991. Sociodemographic differentials in mate selection processes. *Journal of Marriage and the Family,* 53, 928–940.

South, S. J., and Lloyd, K. M. 1995. Spousal alternatives and marital dissolution. *American Sociological Review,* 60, 21–35.

Spanier, G. B. 1976. Measuring dyadic adjustment: New scales for assessing the quality of marriage and similar dyads. *Journal of Marriage and the Family,* 42, 15–27.

Spencer, M. B., Dupree, D., Swanson, D. P., and Cunningham, M. 1996. Parental monitoring and adolescents' sense of responsibility for their own learning: An examination of sex differences. *Journal of Negro Education,* 65, 30–43.

Spencer, R. F., and Jennings, J. D. 1977. *The Native Americans: Ethnology and backgrounds of the North American Indians.* New York: Harper & Row.

Spigel, L. 1992. *Make room for TV: Television and the family ideal in postwar America.* Chicago: University of Chicago Press.

Spitze, G., and Logan, J. R. 1991. Sibling structure and intergenerational relations. *Journal of Marriage and the Family,* 53, 871–884.

Spitze, G., Logan, J. R., Deane, G., and Zerger, S. 1994. Adult children's behavior and intergenerational relationships. *Journal of Marriage and the Family,* 56, 279–293.

Spitzer, B. L., Henderson, K. A., and Zivian, M. T. 1999. Gender differences in population versus media body sizes: A comparison over four decades. *Sex Roles,* 40, 545–565.

Sprey, J. 2000. Theorizing in family studies: Discovering process. *Journal of Marriage and the Family,* 62, 18–31.

Stacey, J. 1996. *In the name of the family: Rethinking family values in the postmodern age.* Boston: Beacon Press.

Stacey, J. 1998. Gay and lesbian families: Queer like us. In M. A. Mason, A. Skolnick, and S. D. Sugarman (Eds.), *All our families: New policies for a new century* (pp. 117–143). New York: Oxford University Press.

Stack, C., and Burton, L. 1993. Kinscripts. *Journal of Comparative Family Studies,* 24, 157–170.

Stack, S., and Eshleman, J. R. 1998. Marital status and happiness: A 17-nation study. *Journal of Marriage and the Family,* 60, 527–536.

Staff, I., and Fein, E. 1992. Together or separate: A study of siblings in foster care. *Child Welfare,* 71, 257–270.

Stanton-Salazar, R. D., and Dornbusch, S. M. 1995. Social capital and the social reproduction of inequality: Information networks among Mexican-origin high school students. *Sociology of Education,* 68, 116–135.

Stark, S. D. 1997. *Glued to the set: The 60 television shows and events that made us who we are today.* New York: Free Press.

Starrels, M. A., Ingersoll-Dayton, B., Dowler, D. W., and Neal, M. B. 1997. The stress of caring for a parent: Effects of the elder's impairment of an employed adult child. *Journal of Marriage and the Family,* 59, 860–872.

Stein, A., Gath, D. H., Bucher, J., Bond, A., Day, A., and Cooper, P. J. 1991. The relationship between postnatal depression and mother-child interaction. *British Journal of Psychiatry,* 158, 46–52.

Stein, N. 1995. Sexual harassment in school: The public performance of gendered violence. *Harvard Educational Review,* 65, 145–162.

Stein, P. J. (Ed.). 1981. *Single life: Unmarried adults in social context.* New York: St. Martin's Press.

Steinberg, L. 1990. Autonomy, conflict, and harmony in the family relationship. In S. S. Feldman and G. R. Elliott (Eds.), *At the threshold: The developing adolescent* (pp. 256–276). Cambridge, MA: Harvard University Press.

Steinberg, L., Brown, B. B., and Dornbusch, S. M. 1996. *Beyond the classroom: Why school reform has failed and what parents need to do.* New York: Simon and Schuster.

Steinberg, L., and Darling, N. 1994. The broader context of social influence in adolescence. In R. K. Silbereisen and E. Todt (Eds.), *Adolescence in context* (pp. 25–45). New York: Springer-Verlag.

Steinberg, L., Darling, N. E., Fletchher, A. C., Brown, B. B., and Dornbusch, S. F. 1995. Authoritative parenting and adolescent adjustment: An ecological journey. In P. Moen, G. H. Elder, Jr., and K. Lüscher (Eds.), *Examining lives in context* (pp. 423–466). Washington, DC: American Psychological Association.

Steinberg, L., Dornbusch, S., and Brown, B. 1992. Ethnic differences in adolescent achievement in ecological perspective. *American Psychologist,* 47, 723–729.

Steinmetz, S. K. 1993. The abused elderly are dependent: Abuse is caused by the perception of stress associated with providing care. In R. J. Gelles and D. Loseke (Eds.), *Current controversies on family violence* (pp. 222–236). Newbury Park, CA: Sage.

Stephan, W. G., and Stephan, C. W. 1991. Intermarriage effects on personality, adjustment, and intergroup relations in two samples of students. *Journal of Marriage and the Family,* 53, 241–250.

Sternberg, K. J., Lamb, M. E., Greenbaum, C., and Cicehetti, D. 1993. Effects of domestic violence on children's behavior problems and depression. *Developmental Psychology,* 29, 44–52.

Stets, J. E., and Henderson, D. A. 1991. Contextual factor surrounding conflict resolution while dating: Results from a national study. *Family Relations,* 40, 29–36.

Stets, J. E., and Straus, M. A. 1989. The marriage license as a hitting license: A comparison of assaults in dating, cohabiting, and married couples. *Journal of Family Violence,* 4, 161–180.

Stewart, S. D. 1999a. Disneyland dads, Disneyland moms? How nonresident parents spend time with their absent children. *Journal of Family Issues,* 20, 539–556.

Stewart, S. D. 1999b. Nonresident mothers' and fathers' social contact with children. *Journal of Marriage and the Family,* 61, 894–907.

Stiers, G. A. 1996. *From this day forward: Love, commitment, and marriage in lesbian and gay relationships.* University of Massachusetts, Amherst, Ph.D. Dissertation.

Stolzenberg, R. M., Blair-Loy, M., and Waite, L. J. 1995. Religious participation in early adulthood: Age and family life cycle effects on church membership. *American Sociological Review,* 60, 84–103.

Stone, L. 1977. *The family, sex, and marriage in England, 1500–1800.* New York: Harper & Row.

Stoneman, Z., Brody, G. H., Churchill, S. L., and Winn, L. L. 1999. Effects of residential instability on Head Start children and their relationships with older siblings: Influences of child emotionality and conflict between family caregivers. *Child Development,* 70, 1246–1262.

St. Pierre, R. G., and Layzer, J. I. 1998. *Improving the life chances of children in poverty: Assumptions and what we have learned.* Ann Arbor, MI: Society for Research in Child Development.

Strathern, M. 1995. New families for old? In C. Ulanowsky (Ed.), *The family in the age of biotechnology* (pp. 27–45). Aldershot, UK: Avebury.

Straus, M. A. 1979. Measuring intrafamily conflict and violence: The Conflict Tactics (CT) Scales. *Journal of Marriage and the Family,* 41, 75–88.

Straus, M. A., and Donnelly, D. A. 1994. *Beating the devil out of them: Corporal punishment in American families.* New York: Lexington Books.

Straus, M. A., and Gelles, R. J. 1990a. How violent are American families? Estimates from the National Family Violence Resurvey and other studies. In M. A. Straus and R. J. Gelles (Eds.), *Physical violence in American families: Risk factors and adaptations to violence in 8,145 families* (pp. 95–112). New Brunswick, NJ: Transactional Books.

Straus, M. A., and Gelles, R. J. 1990b. *Physical violence in American families: Risk factors and adaptation to violence in 8,145 families.* New Brunswick, NJ: Transactional Books.

Straus, M. A., Gelles, R. J., and Steinmetz, S. K. 1980. *Behind closed doors: Violence in the American family.* Garden City, NY: Anchor.

Straus, M. A., and Smith, C. 1990. Family patterns and child abuse. In M. A. Straus and R. J. Gelles (Eds.), *Physical violence in American families.* New Brunswick, NJ: Transactional Books.

Strawbridge, W. J., Wallhagen, M. I., Sherma, S. J., and Kaplan, G. A. 1997. New burdens or more of the same? Comparing grandparents, spouse, and adult-child caregivers. *The Gerontologist,* 37, 505–510.

Suárez, L. M., and Baker, B. L. 1997. Child externalizing behavior and parents' stress: The role of social support. *Family Relations,* 47, 373–381.

Suarez, Z. E. 1993. Cuban exiles: From golden exiles to social undesirables. In H. P. McAdoo (Ed.), *Family ethnicity: Strength and diversity* (pp. 164–176). Newbury Park, CA: Sage.

Sugarman, D. B., Aldarondo, E., and Boney-McCoy, S. 1996. Risk marker analysis of husband-to-wife violence: A continuum of aggression. *Journal of Applied Social Psychology,* 24, 313–337.

Sui-Chu, E. H., and Willms, J. D. 1996. Effects of parental involvement on eight-grade achievement. *Sociology of Education,* 69, 126–141.

Suitor, J. J., and Pillemer, K. 1991. Family conflict when adult children and elderly parents share a home. In K. Pillemer and K. McCartney (Eds.), *Parent-child relations throughout life* (pp. 179–199). Hillsdale, NJ: Erlbaum.

Sullivan, T. 1992. *Sexual abuse and the rights of children: Reforming Canadian Law.* Toronto: University of Toronto.

Sun, R. 1997. *Residential concentration of Chinese Americans in U.S. Metropolitan Areas in 1990.* Paper presented at the annual meeting of the American Sociological Association.

Surra, C. A. 1990. Research and theory on mate selection and premarital relationships. *Journal of Marriage and the Family,* 52, 844–865.

Swaim, P. 1995. Adapting to economic change: The case of displaced workers. In L. J. Beaulieu and D. Mulkey (Eds.), *Investing in people: The human capital needs of rural America* (pp. 213–234). Boulder, CO: Westview Press.

Swisher, K., and Hoisch, M. 1992. Dropping out among American Indians and Alaska Natives: A review of studies. *Journal of American Indian Education,* 31, 3–23.

Swisher, R. R., Elder, G. H., Jr., Lorenz, F. O., and Conger, R. D. 1998. The long arm of the farm: How an occupation structures exposure and vulnerability to stressors across role domains. *Journal of Health and Social Behavior,* 39, 72–89.

Szinovacz, M. E. 1998. Grandparents today: A demographic profile. *The Gerontologist,* 38, 37–52.

Talbott, S. L. 1995. *The future does not compute: Transcending the machines in our midst.* Sebastopol, CA: O'Reilly & Associates.

Tamis-LeMonda, C. S., and Cabrera, N. 1999. Perspectives on father involvement: Research and policy. *Social Policy Report* (Society for Research on Child Development), 12, 2.

Tapper, N. 1991. *Bartered brides.* Cambridge: Cambridge University Press.

Tarver-Behring, S., and Barkley, R. A. 1985. The mother-child interactions of hyperactive boys and their normal siblings. *American Journal of Orthopsychiatry,* 55, 202–209.

Tatara, T. 1993. Understanding the nature and scope of domestic elder abuse with the use of state aggregate data: Summaries of the key findings of a national survey of state APS and aging agencies. *Journal of Elder Abuse & Neglect,* 5, 35–57.

Taylor, R. B., and Harrell, A. V. 1996. *Physical environment and crime.* Washington, DC: National Institute of Justice, U.S. Department of Justice.

Taylor, R. J., and Chatters, I. M. 1991. Extended family networks of older black adults. *Journal of Gerontology,* 46, S210–S217.

Taylor, R. J., Chatters, L. M., Jayakody, R., and Levin, J. S. 1996. Black and white differences in religious participation: A multisample comparison. *Journal for the Scientific Study of Religion,* 35, 403–410.

Terkelsen, K. G. 1983. Schizophrenia and the family: II. Adverse effect of family therapy. *Family Process,* 22, 191–200.

Terkelsen, K. G. 1987. The meaning of mental illness to the family. In A. B. Hatfield and H. B. Lefley (Eds.), *Families of the mentally ill* (pp. 3–29). New York: Guilford Press.

Testa, M., Astone, N. M., Krogh, M., and Neckerman, M. 1993. Employment and marriage among inner-city fathers. In W. J. Wilson (Ed.), *The ghetto underclass* (pp. 96–108). Newbury Park, CA: Sage.

Teti, D. M., and Ablard, K. E. 1989. Security of attachment and infant-sibling relationships: A laboratory study. *Child Development,* 60, 1519–1528.

Teti, D. M., Sakin, J. W., Kucera, K., Corns, K. M., and Eiden, R. D. 1996. And baby makes four: Predictors of attachment security among preschool-age firstborns during the transition to siblinghood. *Child Development,* 67, 579–596.

Thibaut, J. W., and Kelly, H. H. 1959. *The social psychology of groups.* New York: Wiley.

Thoits, P. A. 1992. Identity structures and psychological well-being: Gender and marital status comparisons. *Social Psychology Quarterly,* 55, 236–256.

Thomas, D. L., and Cornwall, M. 1990. Religion and family in the 1980s: Discovery and development. *Journal of Marriage and the Family,* 52, 983–992.

Thomas, J. L. 1990. The grandparent role: A double bind. *International Journal of Aging and Human Development,* 31, 169–177.

Thomas, L. T., and Cornwall, M. 1990. Religion and family in the 1980s: Discovery and development. *Journal of Marriage and the Family,* 52, 903–992.

Thomson, E., Hanson, T. L., and McLanahan, S. S. 1994. Family structure and child well-being: Economic resources versus parental behaviors. *Social Forces,* 73, 221–242.

Thorne, B. 1992. Feminism and the family: Two decades of thought. In B. Thorne and M. Yalom (Eds.), *Rethinking the family: Some feminist questions* (rev. ed., pp. 3–30). Boston: Northeastern University Press.

Thornton, A., Axinn, W. G., and Hill, D. H. 1992. Reciprocal effects of religiosity, cohabitation and marriage. *American Journal of Sociology,* 98, 628–651.

Thornton, A., Axinn, W. G., and Teachman, J. D. 1995. The influence of school enrollment and accumulation on cohabitation and marriage in early adulthood. *American Sociological Review,* 60, 762–774.

Thornton, A., and Lin, H.-S. 1994. *Social change and the family in Taiwan.* Chicago: University of Chicago Press.

Thornton, R. 1996. North American Indians and the demography of contact. In S. Pedreza and R. G. Rumbaut (Eds.), *Origins and destinies: Immigration, race, and ethnicity in America* (pp. 43–59). Belmont, CA: Wadsworth.

Thurow, L. C. 1999. Building wealth: The new rules for individuals, companies, and nations. *The Atlantic Monthly,* June, 57–69.

Toliver, S. D. 1998. *Black families in corporate America.* Thousand Oaks, CA: Sage.

Tolnay, S. E. 1997. The Great Migration and changes in the Northern black family, 1940 to 1990. *Social Forces,* 75, 1213–1238.

Tolnay, S. E., and Crowder, K. D. 1999. Regional origin and family stability in northern cities: The role of context. *American Sociological Review,* 64, 97–112.

Tonry, M. 1995. *Malign neglect—race, crime, and punishment in America.* New York: Oxford University Press.

Toro, P. A., et al. 1995. Distinguishing homelessness from poverty: A comparative study. *Journal of Consulting and Clinical Psychology,* 63, 280–289.

Townsend, A. L., and Franks, M. M. 1997. Quality of the relationship between elderly spouses: Influence on spouse caregivers' subjective effectiveness. *Family Relations,* 46, 33–39.

Treas, J., and Giesen, D. 2000. Sexual infidelity among married and cohabiting Americans. *Journal of Marriage and the Family,* 62, 48–60.

Trusty, J. 1998. Family influences on educational expectations of late adolescents. *The Journal of Educational Research,* 5, 260–270.

Tubman, J. G. 1993. Family risk factors, parental alcohol use, and problem behaviors among school-age children. *Family Relations,* 42, 81–86.

Tucker, C. J., Marx, J., and Long, L. 1998. "Moving on": Residential mobility and children's school lives. *Sociology of Education,* 71, 111–129.

Tucker, M. B., and Mitchell-Kernan, C. (Eds.). 1995. *The decline in marriage among African Americans.* New York: Russell Sage.

Turkheimer, E. 1998. Heritability and biological explanation. *Psychological Review,* 105, 782–791.

Tzeng, J. M., and Mare, R. D. 1995. Labor market and socioeconomic effects on marital stability. *Social Science Research,* 24, 329–351.

Uba, L. 1994. *Asian Americans: Personality patterns, identity, and mental health.* New York: Guilford Press.

Umberson, D. 1992. Relationship between adult children and their parents: Psychological consequences for both generations. *Journal of Marriage and the Family,* 54, 664–674.

Umberson, D., Anderson, K., Glick, J., and Shapiro, A. 1998. Domestic violence, personal control, and gender. *Journal of Marriage and the Family,* 60, 442–452.

Umberson, D., Chen, M. D., House, J. S., Hopkins, K., and Slaten, E. 1996. The effect of social relationships on psychological well-being: Are men and women really so different? *American Sociological Review,* 61, 837–857.

Umberson, D., and Williams, C. L. 1993. Divorced fathers: Parental role strain and psychological distress. *Journal of Family Issues,* 14, 378–400.

United Nations. 1998. *Demographic Yearbook,* 1996. New York: United Nations.

Upchurch, D. M., Levy-Storms, L., Sucoff, C. A., and Aneshensel, C. S. 1998. Gender and ethnic differences in the timing of first sexual intercourse. *Family Planning Perspectives,* 30, 121–127.

Updegraff, K. A., and Obeidallah, C. L. 1999. Young adolescents' patterns of involvement with siblings and friends. *Social Development,* 8, 52–69.

U.S. Bureau of the Census. 1992. *1990 Census of the Population, Part 1.* Washington, DC: U.S. Government Printing Office.

U.S. Bureau of the Census. 1993a. *The foreign-born population in the United States,* CP-3–1, July. Washington, DC: U.S. Government Printing Office.

U.S. Bureau of the Census. 1993b. Fertility of American women: June 1992. *Current Population Reports,* Series P-20, No. 470. Washington, DC: U.S. Government Printing Office.

U.S. Bureau of the Census. 1993c. *Persons of Hispanic origin in the United States,* CP 3–3, August. Washington, DC: U.S. Government Printing Office.

U.S. Bureau of the Census. 1993d. *Asian and Pacific Islanders in the United States,* CP 3–5, August. Washington, DC: U.S. Government Printing Office.

U.S. Bureau of the Census. 1994. *Statistical abstract of the United States, 1994* (114th ed.). Washington, DC: U.S. Government Printing Office.

U.S. Bureau of the Census. 1995a. *Statistical abstract of the United States* (115th ed.). Washington, DC: U.S. Government Printing Office.

U.S. Bureau of the Census. 1995b. Income, poverty, and valuation of noncash benefits: 1993. *Current Population Reports,* Series P-60, No. 188. Washington, DC: U.S. Government Printing Office.

U.S. Bureau of the Census. 1996. Marital status and living arrangements: March 1995 (Update). *Current Population Reports,* Series P-20, No. 491. Washington, DC: U.S. Government Printing Office.

U.S. Bureau of the Census. 1997a. Money income in the United States: 1996. *Current Population Reports,* Series P-60, No. 197. Washington, DC: U.S. Government Printing Office.

U.S. Bureau of the Census. 1997b. *Statistical abstract of the United States* (117th ed.). Washington, DC: U.S. Government Printing Office.

U.S. Bureau of the Census. 1997c. Marital status and living arrangements, March 1997. *Current Population Reports,* Series P-20–506. Washington, DC: U.S. Government Printing Office.

U.S. Bureau of the Census. 1998. *Statistical abstract of the United States* (118th ed.). Washington, DC: U.S. Government Printing Office.

U.S. Commission on Child and Family Welfare. 1996. *Parenting our children: In the best interest of the nation.* Washington, DC: U.S. Government Printing Office.

U.S. Commission on Civil Rights. 1977. *Window dressing on the set: Women and minorities in television.* Washington, DC: A report of the U.S. Commission on Civil Rights.

U.S. Department of Health and Human Services, National Center on Child Abuse and Neglect. 1996. *Child maltreatment 1994: Reports from the states to the National Center on Child Abuse and Neglect.* Washington, DC: U.S. Government Printing Office.

U.S. Department of Health and Human Services. 1999. Births, marriages, divorces, and deaths: Provisional data for 1998. *National Vital Statistics Reports*, Vol. 47, No. 21. July 6.

U.S. Department of Justice. 1994. *Domestic violence: Violence between intimates.* Washington, DC: U.S. Department of Justice, Bureau of the Census.

U.S. National Center for Health Statistics. 1993. *Morbidity and Mortality Weekly Report*, Vol. 42, No. 20. Washington, DC: U.S. Government Printing Office.

U.S. Senate Special Committee on Aging. 1992. *Aging America: Trends and projections, 1990–91.* Washington, DC: U.S. Department of Health and Human Services.

Uzzell, O., and Peebles-Wilkins, W. 1989. Black spouse abuse: A focus on relational factors and intervention strategies. *Western Journal of Black Studies*, 13, 10–16.

Van Cleve, J. 1999. *Where can we marry? Legal Marriage Alliance of Washington.* Partners Task Force for Gay and Lesbian Couples. Seattle, WA: Website: <www.buddy.buddy.com>

van den Akker, O. B. A. 1994. Something old, something new, something borrowed, and something taboo. *Journal of Reproductive and Infant Psychology*, 12, 179–188.

Van Galen, J. 1991. Ideologues and pedagogues: Parents who teach their children at home. In J. Van Galen and M. A. Pitman (Eds.), *Home schooling: Political, historical, and pedagogical perspectives* (pp. 63–76). Norwood, NJ: Ablex.

Vangelisti, A. L., and Huston, T. L. 1994. Maintaining marital satisfaction and love. In D. J. Canary and L. Stafford (Eds.), *Communication and relational maintenance* (pp. 165–186). New York: Academic Press.

Ventura, S. J., Martin, J. A., Taffel, S. M., Matthews, T. J., and Clarke, S. C. 1995. Advance report of final natality statistics, 1993. *Monthly Vital Statistics Reports*, 44, Suppl. 3. Hyattsville, MD: National Center for Health Statistics.

Ventura, S. J., Martin, J. A., Curtin, S. C., and Matthews, T. J. 1999. Births: Final data for 1997. *National Vital Statistics Reports*, Vol. 47, No. 18. Hyattsville, MD: National Center for Health Statistics.

Ventura, S. J., Peters, K. D., Martin, J. A., and Maurer, J. D. 1997. Births and deaths: United States, 1996. *Monthly Vital Statistics Reports*, 46, Supplement 2.

Vinovskis, M. A. 1995. *Education, society, and economic opportunity: A historical perspective on persistent issues.* New Haven, CT: Yale University Press.

Vinovskis, M. A., and Frank, S. M. 1997. Parenting in American society: A historical overview of the Colonial Period through the 19th century. In T. Arendell (Ed.), *Contemporary parenting: Challenges and issues* (pp. 45–67). Thousand Oaks, CA: Sage.

Volling, B. L. 1997. The family correlates of maternal and paternal perceptions of differential treatment in early childhood. *Family Relations*, 46, 227–236.

Volling, B. L., and Belsky, J. 1993. Parent, infant, and contextual characteristics related to maternal employment decisions in the first year of infancy. *Family Relations*, 42, 4–12.

Volling, B. L., and Feagans, L. V. 1995. Infant day care and children's social competence. *Infant Behavior and Development*, 18, 177–188.

Voydanoff, P. 1988. Work role characteristics, family structure demands, and work/family conflict. *Journal of Marriage and the Family*, 50, 749–761.

Vroegh, K. S. 1997. Transracial adoptees: Developmental status after 17 years. *American Journal of Orthopsychiatry*, 67, 568–575.

Vuchinich, S., Hetherington, E. M., Vuchinich, R. A., and Clingempeel, W. G. 1991. Parent-child interaction and gender differences in early adolescents' adaptation to stepfamilies. *Developmental Psychology*, 27, 618–626.

Wacquant, L. J. D. 1995. The ghetto, the state, and the new capitalist economy. In P. Kasinitz (Ed.), *Metropolis: Center and symbol of our times* (pp. 413–449). New York: New York University Press.

Waite, L. J. 1995. Does marriage matter? *Demography*, 4, 483–507.

Waite, L. J., and Gallagher, M. 2000. *The case for marriage.* Cambridge, MA: Harvard University Press.

Waldo, C. R., Hesson-McInnis, M. S., and D'Augelli, A. R. 1998. Antecedents and consequences of victimization of lesbian, gay, and bisexual young people: A structural model comparing rural university and urban samples. *American Journal of Community Psychology*, 26, 307–554.

Wall, C. S., and Madak, P. R. 1991. Indian students' academic self- concept and their perceptions of teacher and parent aspirations for them in a band-controlled school and a provincial school. *Canadian Journal of Native Education,* 18, 43–51.

Waller, M. 1997. *Welfare-to-work and child care: A survey of the ten big states.* Washington, DC: Progressive Policy Institute.

Wallerstein, J. S. 1998. Children of divorce: A society in search of policy. In M. A. Mason, A. Skolnick, and S. D. Sugarman (Eds.), *All our families: New policies for a new century* (pp. 66–94). New York: Oxford University Press.

Walters, S. D. 1999. Sex, text, and context. In M. M. Ferree, J. Lorber, and B. B. Hess (Eds.), *Revisioning gender* (pp. 222–257). Thousand Oaks, CA: Sage.

Ward, C. 1998. Community resources and school performance: The Northern Cheyenne case. *Sociological Inquiry,* 68, 83–113.

Ward, R. A., and Spitze, G. 1998. Sandwich marriages: The implications of child and parent relations for marital quality in midlife. *Social Forces,* 77, 647–666.

Warr, M. 1998. Life-course transitions and desistance from crime. *Criminology,* 36, 183–216.

Warren, S. B. 1992. Lower threshold for referral for psychiatric treatment for adopted adolescents. *Journal of the American Academy of Child & Adolescent Psychiatry,* 31, 512–517.

Wasik, B. H., Ramey, C. T., Bryant, D. M., and Sparling, J. J. 1990. A longitudinal study of two early intervention strategies: Project CARE. *Child Development,* 61, 1682–1696.

Waters, H. F. 1993. Networks under the gun. *Newsweek,* July 12, 64–66.

Waters, M. C. 1996. Ethnic and racial identities of second-generation black immigrants in New York City. In A. Portes (Ed.), *The new second generation* (pp. 171–196). New York: Russell Sage.

Webster-Stratton, C., and Lindsay, D. W. 1999. Social competence and conduct problems in young children: Issues in assessment. *Journal of Clinical Child Psychology,* 28, 25–43.

Wegar, K. 1992. The sociological significance of ambivalence: An example from adoption research. *Qualitative Sociology,* 15, 87–103.

Wegar, K. 1997. *Adoption, identity, and kinship: The debate over sealed birth records.* New Haven, CT: Yale University Press.

Weise, D., and Daro, D. 1995. *Current trends on child abuse reporting and fatalities: The results of the 1994 fifty state survey.* Chicago: National Committee to Prevent Child Abuse.

Weiss, A. J., and Wilson, B. J. 1996. Emotional portrayals in family television series that are popular among children. *Journal of Broadcasting and Electronic Media,* 40, 1–29.

Weissman, M. M., Gammon, G. D., John, K., Merikangas, K. R., Warner, V., Prusoff, B. A., and Sholomskas, D. 1987. Children of depressed parents. *Archives of General Psychiatry,* 44, 847–853.

West, E. 1992. Children on the plains frontier. In E. West and P. Petrik (Eds.), *Small worlds* (pp. 26–41). Lawrence, KS: University of Kansas Press.

Whalen, C. K., Henker, B., and Dotemoto, S. 1980. Methylphenidate and hyperactivity: Effects on teacher behavior. *Science,* 208, 1280–1282.

Whitbeck, L. B., Hoyt, D. R., and Huck, S. M. 1993. Family relationship history, contemporary parent-grandparent relationship quality, and the grandparent-grandchild relationship. *Journal of Marriage and the Family,* 55, 1025–1036.

White, L., and Edwards, J. 1990. Emptying the nest and parental well-being: Evidence from national panel data. *American Sociological Review,* 55, 235–242.

White, L., and Peterson, D. 1995. The retreat from marriage: Its effect on unmarried children's exchange with parents. *Journal of Marriage and the Family,* 57, 428–434.

White, L. K., and Riedmann, A. 1992. When the Brady Bunch grows up: Step/half- and fullsibling relationships in adulthood. *Journal of Marriage and the Family,* 54, 197–208.

Whiting, B. B., and Edwards, C. P. 1988. *Children of different worlds.* Cambridge, MA: Harvard University Press.

Whittaker, T. 1995. Violence, gender, and elder abuse: Toward a feminist analysis and practice. *Journal of Gender Studies,* 4, 35–45.

Widmer, E. D. 1997. Influence of older siblings on initiation of sexual intercourse. *Journal of Marriage and the Family,* 59, 928–938.

Widmer, E. D., Treas, J., and Newcomb, R. 1998. Attitudes toward nonmarital sex in 24 countries. *Journal of Sex Research,* 35, 349–358.

Widom, C. S. 1990. The intergenerational transmission of violence. In N. A. Weiner and M. E. Wolfgang (Eds.), *Pathways to criminal violence* (pp. 137–201). Newbury Park, CA: Sage.

Widom, C. S., and Morris, S. 1997. Accuracy of adult recollections of childhood victimization: Part 2: Childhood sexual abuse. *Psychological Assessment, 9*, 34–36.

Wilcox, B. L., and Kunkel, D. 1996. Taking television seriously: Children and television policy. In E. F. Zigler, S. L. Kagan, and N. W. Hall (Eds.), *Children, families, and government* (pp. 333–352). Cambridge: Cambridge University Press.

Wilcox, K. L., Wolchik, S. A., and Braver, S. L. 1998. Predictors of maternal preference for joint or sole legal custody. *Family Relations,* 47, 93–101.

Wilcox, W. B. 1998. Conservative Protestant childrearing: Authoritarian or authoritative? *American Sociological Review,* 63, 796–809.

Wilkie, J. R. 1993. Changes in U.S. men's attitudes toward the family provider role, 1972–1989. *Gender and Society,* 7, 261–279.

Wilkie, J. R., Ferree, M. M., and Ratcliff, K. S. 1998. Gender and fairness: Marital satisfaction in two-earner couples. *Journal of Marriage and the Family,* 60, 577–594.

Williams, D. R., and Collins, C. 1995. U.S. economic and racial differences in health: Patterns and explanations. *Annual Review of Sociology,* 21, 349–386.

Williams, L. M., and Banyard, V. L. 1997. Gender and recall of child sexual abuse: A prospective study. In J. D. Read and D. S. Lindsay (Eds.), *Recollections of trauma: Scientific evidence and clinical perspective* (pp. 371–377). New York: Plenum Press.

Willis, R. J., and Michael, R. T. 1994. Innovation in family formation: Evidence on cohabitation in the U.S. In J. Ermisch and N. Ogawa (Eds.), *The family, the market, and the State in ageing societies* (pp. 119–145). London: Oxford University Press.

Wilson, S. M., Martoz-Baden, R., and Holloway, D. P. 1991. Stress in two-generation farm and ranch families. *Lifestyles: Family and Economic Issues,* 12, 199–216.

Wilson, W. J. 1987. *The truly disadvantaged.* Chicago: University of Chicago Press.

Wilson, W. J. 1996. *When work disappears: The world of the new urban poor.* New York: Knopf.

Wolf, R., and Pillemer, K. 1989. *Helping elderly victims: The reality of elder abuse.* New York: Columbia University Press.

Wolfe, S. M., Toro, P. A., and McCaskill, P. A. 1999. A comparison of homeless and matched housed adolescents on family environment variables. *Journal of Research on Adolescence,* 9, 53–66.

Wong, D. L., and Perry, S. E. 1998. *Maternal child nursing care.* St. Louis, MO: Mosby.

Wood, D., Halfon, N., Scarlata, D., Newacheck, P., and Nessim, S. 1993. Impact of family relocation on children's growth, development, school function, and behavior. *Journal of the American Medical Association,* 270, 1334–1338.

Woodberry, R. D. 1998. Comment: When surveys lie and people tell the truth: How surveys oversample church attenders. *American Sociological Review,* 63, 119–122.

Woodward, L. J., and Fergusson, D. M. 1999. Early conduct problems and later risk of teenage pregnancy in girls. *Development and Psychopathology,* 11, 127–141.

Wright, B. R. E., Caspi, A., Moffitt, T. E., Miech, R. A., and Silva, P. A. 1999. Reconsidering the relationship between SES and delinquency: Causation but not correlation. *Criminology,* 37, 175–194.

Wright, K. 1998. Human in the age of mechanical reproduction. *Discover,* 19, 74–81.

Wu, L. L. 1996. Effects of family instability, income, and income instability on the risk of a premarital birth. *American Sociological Review,* 61, 386–406.

Wu, L. L., and Martinson, B. C. 1993. Family structure and the risk of a premarital birth. *American Sociological Review,* 59, 210–232.

Yamaguchi, K., and Ferguson, L. R. 1995. The stopping and spacing of childbirths and their birth-history predictors: Rational-choice theory and event-history analysis. *American Sociological Review,* 60, 272–298.

Ying, Y.-W. 1992. Life satisfaction among San Francisco Chinese-Americans. *Social Indicators Research,* 26, 1–22.

Yip, A. K. T. 1997. *Gay male Christian couples.* Westport, CT: Praeger.

Young, V. H. 1974. A Black American socialization pattern. *American Ethnologist,* 1, 415–431.

Zabin, L. S., and Hayward, S. C. 1993. *Adolescent sexual behavior and childbearing.* Newbury Park, CA: Sage.

Zahn-Waxler, C., et al. 1990. Antecedents of problem behavior in children of depressed mothers. *Development and Psychopathology,* 2, 271–291.

Zajonc, R. B., and Mullally, P. R. 1997. Birth order: Reconciling conflicting effects. *American Psychologist,* 52, 685–690.

Zaslow, M., Tout, K., Smith, S., and Moore, K. 1998. *Implications of the 1996 welfare legislation for children: A research perspective.* Ann Arbor, MI: Society for Research in Child Development.

Zelizer, V. A. R. 1985. *Pricing the priceless child: The changing social value of children.* New York: Basic Books.

Zhou, M. 1995. *Social capital in Chinatown: The role of community-based organizations and families in the adaptation of the younger generation.* Paper presented at the annual meeting of the American Sociological Association.

Zigler, E. F., and Styfco, S. 1996. Head Start and early childhood intervention: The changing course of social science and social policy. In E. F. Zigler, S. L. Kagan, and N. W. Hall (Eds.), *Children, families, and government* (pp. 132–155). Cambridge: Cambridge University Press.

Zill, N. 1988. Behavior, achievement, and health problems among children in stepfamilies: Findings from a national survey of child health. In E. M. Hetherington and J. D. Arasteh (Eds.), *Impact of divorce, single parenting, and stepparenting on children* (pp. 325–368). Hillsdale, NJ: Erlbaum.

Zill, N., Morrison, D. R., and Coiro, M. J. 1993. Long-term effects of parental divorce on parent-child relationships, adjustment, and achievement in young adulthood. *Journal of Family Psychology,* 7, 91–103.

Zill, N., and Nord, C. W. 1994. *Running the place: How American families are faring in a changing economy and an individualistic society.* Washington, DC: Child Trends, Inc.

Zima, B. T., Wells, K. B., Benjamin, B., and Duan, N. 1996. Mental health problems among homeless mothers: Relationship to service use and child mental health problems. *Archives of General Psychiatry,* 53, 332–338.

Zimmerman, S. L. 1995. *Understanding family policy* (2nd ed.). Thousand Oaks, CA: Sage.

Zimmerman, T. S., and Fetsch, R. J. 1994. Family ranching and farming: A consensus management model to improve family functioning and decrease work stress. *Family Relations,* 43, 125–131.

Zinn, M. B. 1990. Family, feminism, and race in America. *Gender & Society,* 4, 68–82.

Zitzow, D. 1990. Ojibway adolescent time spent with parent/elders as related to delinquency and court adjudication experiences. *American Indian and Alaska Native Mental Health Research,* 4, 53–63.

Name Index

Ablard, K. E., 339
Abma, J., 99, 104, 128
Acock, A. C., 138, 161, 245, 281, 282, 284
Aday, L. A., 194
Adler, J., 111
Adler, P., 36, 91, 185, 204
Adler, P. A., 36, 91, 185, 204
Administration on Children, Youth, and Families, 214, 215
Ahrons, C., 390
Ainsworth-Darnell, J. W., 380
Aldous, J., 14, 228, 270, 281, 287, 323
Alexander, A., 44
Alexander, K. L., 130, 216, 218, 237
Alford-Cooper, F., 301
Allen, K. R., 16, 134, 461, 462
Allen, V. L., 305
Ali, J., 163
Almond, B., 109
Alston, L., 32, 244
Alwin, D. F., 316, 317, 425
Amato, P. R., 139, 233, 274, 288, 290, 295, 317, 322, 371, 383, 385, 386, 387, 392, 396, 408, 476
Ambert, A.-M., 12, 21, 23, 114, 140, 165, 180, 243, 259, 264, 286, 318, 330, 373, 383, 423, 449, 454
Ammerman, N. T., 234
Amott, T., 35
Anderson, A. L., 92
Anderson, C. M., 118
Anderson, E., 71, 129, 350, 393
Anderson, E. B., 344
Anderson, K. L., 404
Andreasen, M. S., 38
Aneshensel, C. S., 192
Anetzberger, G., 426
Appell, A. R., 411
Aquilino, W. S., 131, 322, 324, 383
Aral, S. D., 419
Ardelt, M., 199
Arditti, J. A., 379, 390
Arendell, T., 379
Ariès, P., 15
Armistead, L., 382, 386
Arnold, M. S., 173
Aseltine, R. H., Jr., 137, 169, 376, 383, 384, 386
Astone, N. M., 203
Auerbach, C. F., 474
Austin, C., 426
Austin, E. W., 42
Avison, W. R., 163
Axinn, W. G., 107, 132, 133, 232, 233, 234, 372, 388, 467
Aytac, I. A., 324

Baber, K. M., 16
Bachman, J. G., 138
Bachman, R., 421
Bagley, C., 143
Bahr, S. K., 232
Bailey, J. M., 135
Baines, C., 349
Baker, B. L., 450
Baker, L. A., 349
Bales, R. F., 10, 18
Ballard, C., 436
Bank, L., 347, 444
Bankston, C. L., III, 223
Banyard, V. L., 420, 444
Bao, W.-N., 229
Barber, B. K., 315
Barber, E., 292
Barber, J. S., 107
Barkley, R. A., 312, 442
Barnes, H. V., 472
Barnett, D., 414
Barnett, R. C., 215, 322
Barnett, S. W., 472
Baron, L. A., 420
Barry, H., III, 313
Bartholet, E., 110, 140, 141, 463
Bartko, W. T., 12
Bartkowski, J. P., 231
Bartlett, K. T., 477
Bassuk, E. L., 195
Bates, J. E., 305, 312, 412, 445
Baumohl, J., 207
Baumrind, D., 305, 307, 308, 311, 312, 383, 478
Baydar, N., 256, 261, 262, 334, 335
Bayme, S., 53
Bean, F. D., 76
Beeghley, L., 98, 99, 108
Behrman, R. E., 151, 211
Bell, A. P., 95, 137, 139, 464
Bell, C. C., 192, 411
Bell, R. Q., 12
Bellah, R. N., 465
Belsky, J., 213, 245, 248, 249, 270, 295
Bengtson, V. L., 254, 323, 326, 327, 330
Bennett, N. G., 170, 172, 475
Bennett, T., 139
Benson, P. L., 140
Berardo, F. M., 202
Berger, P. L., 14
Berk, L. E., 361
Berlin, K. L., 292
Berliner, L., 431
Bernard, J., 17, 286

Bernhardt, A., 217
Bernstein, A. C., 350
Berrick, J. D., 147
Berry, M., 144
Berryman, J. C., 110
Bess, B. E., 421
Bhattacharya, J., 337
Bianchi, S. M., 123, 124, 169, 170, 281, 371, 379
Bickley, P., 390
Billingsley, A., 71, 85
Billson, J. M., 69
Birch, S. H., 215
Bird, C. E., 283
Bird, G., 53, 202
Birns, B., 408
Birns, S., 408
Bjarnason, T., 281
Black, L. K., 141
Blair, S. L., 62, 219
Blair-Loy, M., 233
Blake, J., 337
Blakeley, E. J., 188
Blank, R. M., 470, 473, 480
Blank, S. W., 470
Blankenhorn, D., 53
Blanton, P. W., 291
Blau, P., 13
Block, J., 386
Block, J. H., 386
Bloom, D. E., 170, 172, 475
Blum, B., 470
Blumer, H., 12, 168
Blumstein, P., 103, 301
Boer, F., 347, 361
Boivin, M. J., 200
Bokemeier, J., 199
Bolger, N., 286
Bonecutter, F. J., 147, 262
Bonvillain, N., 63
Booth, A., 132, 139, 270, 274, 292, 295, 317, 322, 381, 382, 383, 385, 386, 390, 396, 468, 476, 482
Borders, L. D., 141
Boss, P. G., 26
Bouchard, T. J., Jr., 341, 357
Boulerice, B., 176, 392
Bourque, S. L., 311
Bouvier, L. F., 58
Bowen, G. L., 289
Bowles, S., 222
Boyd, M., 383
Bozett, F. W., 134
Braungart-Rieker, J., 442
Braver, S. L., 379
Bray, J. H., 390
Brayfield, A., 246
Brener, N. D., 401
Brewer, D. J., 224
Brewster, K. L., 99
Briere, J., 419, 431
Brines, J., 132
Brisson, C., 284
Brody, D. J., 200
Brody, G. H., 307, 338, 339, 361, 437, 438, 440
Brodzinski, A. B., 141
Brodzinski, D. M., 141
Bronfenbrenner, U., 12, 13, 305, 307, 317, 358, 478
Brookoff, D., 404, 406, 408
Brooks-Gunn, J., 176, 177, 180, 188, 191, 256, 261, 262, 334, 465, 471
Brown, A. C., 437, 438
Brown, B. B., 80, 216, 237, 307, 310, 318
Brown, J., 23
Brown, S. L., 132
Browne, A., 418
Browne, I., 404, 405
Browne, K. D., 426
Browning, C. R., 419, 420
Broyles, P. A., 232
Brubaker, T. H., 387
Brunk, M. A., 312
Bryant, J., 42, 53
Buchanan, C. M., 386, 392
Buehler, C., 295
Buhrmester, D., 336
Buhs, E. S., 215
Bulkey, J. A., 431
Bumpass, L., 132, 467
Bumpus, M. F., 163
Burant, C. J., 326, 342
Burgess, E. W., 184, 287
Burggraf, K., 41
Buriel, R., 76, 80, 81
Burke, R., 282
Burman, B., 297
Burnette, D., 264
Burton, L. M., 32, 77, 250, 254, 255, 261, 262, 330, 339
Busch-Rossnagel, N. A., 305
Buss, K. A., 304
Butterfiel, F., 448

Cabrera, N., 176
Cadoret, R. J., 439
Caldas, S. J., 223
Calhoun, C., 45
Call, V., 101, 102, 103, 248
Call, V. R. A., 232
Callan, V., 307, 478
Callanan, M. A., 341
Canadian Institute of Child Health, 174
Candell, K., 378
Cantor, J., 440
Capaldi, D. M., 129, 402
Caplan, P. J., 454
Cardarelli, A. P., 431
Carey, N., 217
Carlip, H., 250
Carlson, E. A., 314
Carrasquillo, H. A., 59, 77
Carstensen, L., 290
Casey, D. M., 42
Casper, L. M., 246
Caspi, A., 176, 310, 411, 472
Catalano, R., 286
Catalano, R. F., 440
Cate, R. M., 118
Catsambris, S., 224
Ceci, S. J., 131, 216
Ceglian, C. P., 266
Chambliss, W. J., 470
Chan, R. W., 134, 135, 140
Chandra, A., 108
Chao, R. K., 80, 311
Chase-Lansdale, P. L., 50, 125, 126, 130, 177, 383, 463, 464, 474
Chassin, L., 441
Chatters, I. M., 326
Chaves, M., 233

Chen, H.-S., 79
Chen, X., 76
Cherlin, A., 33, 132, 260, 358, 375, 380, 383, 386, 389, 390, 392, 393, 396, 464
Chi, P. S. K., 201
Child Welfare League of America, 143
Children's Television Workshop, 40
Chitose, Y., 60
Choi, S. H., 59
Cicchetti, D., 414, 436
Cicirelli, V. G., 326, 348, 349
Clapp, G., 390
Clark, S., 402
Clark, V. L., 198
Clark, W., 227
Clark, W. A. V., 187, 201, 203
Clarkberg, M., 131, 132
Clarke-Stewart, A., 213
Clausen, J. A., 14
Clavenna-Valleroy, J., 417, 418
Clingempeel, W. G., 385
Clydesdale, T. T., 164, 227
Cochran, M., 26
Cocking, R. R., 86, 330
Cohen, C. B., 118
Cohen, L., 189
Cohler, B. J., 127
Coie, J. D., 445
Coiro, M. J., 295, 316, 383
Cole, P., 108
Coleman, J. S., 13, 61, 139, 163, 191, 217, 219, 224
Coleman, M., 264, 265, 266, 292, 327, 350, 391, 397, 424
Coleman, V. E., 404
Coley, R. L., 50, 125, 126, 130, 463, 464, 474
Collins, C., 68
Collins, P. H., 17, 162, 244, 316
Collins, W. A., 315
Coltrane, S., 17, 279, 283, 286
Conger, K. J., 343, 344
Conger, R. D., 199, 207, 310, 340, 343, 344
Congress of the United States, 171
Contreras, J. M., 77
Cook, D. A., 173
Cooksey, E. C., 133, 139, 148, 163, 245, 392, 474
Cookson, P. W., 224
Coombs, R. H., 136
Cooney, T. M., 253, 321
Coontz, S., 39
Corcoran, M., 177
Cornwall, M., 370
Cornwell, G. T., 197
Corsaro, W. A., 12, 169, 212, 328, 478
Cose, E., 68, 73
Cost, Quality, and Child Outcomes Study Team, 212
Costello, C. Y., 135
Cott, N. F., 35
Cotten, S. R., 367
Coughlin, C., 383, 392
Counts, R. M., 381
Cowan, C. P., 130, 247, 248, 249, 253, 436
Cowan, P. A., 130, 247, 248, 249, 253, 436
Coward, R. T., 325, 349
Coyne, J. C., 437
Craig, P. H., 133, 148, 245
Crenshaw, K. W., 406
Crick, N. R., 445
Crimmins, E., 321
Crockett, L. J., 131
Crosby, L., 129
Cross, W. E., Jr., 377
Crouch, J. L., 415
Crouter, A. C., 163, 270, 283, 307, 340, 344, 345, 482
Crowder, K. D., 67
Cuber, J., 275, 276, 278, 299
Culp, A. M., 131
Cummings, E. M., 436

Dalenberg, C. J., 419
Daly, K., 26
Damon, W., 478
Daniel, K., 137
Daniels, D., 344, 346, 349
Danso, H., 231
Danziger, S., 171
Darling, N., 454
Darling, R. B., 306
Daro, D., 410, 414, 415
Darroch, J. E., 95
D'Augelli, A. R., 93
Da Vanzo, J., 324
Davey, J. D., 471
David, C., 382, 386
Davies, L., 436
Davies, P. T., 436
Davis, J. H., 257
Day, R. D., 411
Deater-Deckard, K., 310, 355, 436
DeFronzo, J., 471
Degler, C., 35, 67
De Graaf, N. D., 229
De Ment, T., 76, 80, 81
Demo, D. H., 134, 138, 161, 245, 281, 282, 284, 315
Demos, J., 33, 259, 314
Denton, N., 188
Denzin, N. K., 21, 26
Depner, C. E., 397
Devine, J. A., 127
DeWitt, P. M., 389
Dieleman, F. M., 187, 201, 203
DiGiorgio-Miller, J., 422
DiLeonardi, J. W., 415
Dilworth-Anderson, P., 77, 261
Dimidjian, S., 118
Dishion, T. J., 313, 446, 448, 458
Dodder, R. A., 426
Dodge, K. A., 412, 445, 446
Doherty, W. J., 26, 148, 246, 257, 380, 478
Dollahite, D. C., 45
Donovan, P., 105
Donnelly, D. A., 311, 411
Dooley, D., 286
Dorfman, L. T., 292
Doris, J., 412, 416
Dornbusch, S. M., 80, 216, 219, 237, 307, 310, 354, 358, 386, 392
Dorr, A., 41
Dotemoto, S., 312
Doubleday, C., 41
Downey, D. B., 203, 213, 336, 379, 380

Downey, G., 437
Drenovsky, C. K., 232
Driscoll, A. K., 99, 104, 128, 475
Dryfoos, J. G., 237
Duberstein, L., 214
Dubrow, N., 193, 415
Dufur, M. J., 380
Duncan, G. J., 127, 176, 180, 188, 388, 471, 472
Dunn, J., 256, 335, 337, 338, 339, 344, 351, 352, 361
Durkheim, E., 473
Duvall, E. M., 14
Dwyer, J. W., 349
Dziuba-Leatherman, J., 422

Earls, F., 188, 190, 442, 444
East, P. L., 340
Easterlin, R., 321
Eastman, G., 318
Ebata, A. T., 45
Eckenrode, J., 412, 416
Eder, D., 422
Edin, K., 126, 168, 171, 173
Edleson, J. L., 402
Edwards, C. P., 243
Edwards, J. M., 290, 292, 382, 390
Egan, S. K., 423
Egeland, B., 413, 414
Eggebeen, D. J., 131, 325
Ehmann, C., 210
Ehrenberg, R. G., 224
Eide, E. R., 224
Elder, G. H., Jr., 14, 26, 175, 199, 200, 204, 207, 261, 267, 297, 304, 310, 316, 411
Eley, T. C., 442
Elliott, B. J., 386
Elliott, P., 406
Ellison, C. G., 231, 232
Elo, I. T., 130
Elordi, C. A., 311
Elshtain, J. B., 53, 477
Eme, R., 145, 146
Emery, R. E., 383, 387, 409, 474
Engelbert, A., 37
Ensminger, M. E., 162
Entwisle, D. R., 130, 216, 218, 220, 237
Erel, O., 297
Erera, P.-I., 148
Erickson, M. F., 148, 246, 257, 380, 413, 414, 478
Erikson, E. H., 252
Eshleman, J. R., 136
Espelage, D., 423
Espiritu, Y. L., 79
Etter, J., 144
Etzioni, A., 465
Eugster, A., 110
Evans, P., 349
Evans, S. L., 130
Evans, W., 224
Eyer, D. E., 244

Fagot, B. I., 129
Farber, B., 33
Farrington, D. P., 446, 448
Farris, E., 217
Faurre, L. C., 406
Feagans, L. V., 211
Fein, E., 147
Feldhaus, K. M., 405
Feldman, R. S., 412, 413
Feldman, S. S., 80, 81, 99
Felice, M. E., 340
Feng, D., 372
Fennelly, K., 77, 133
Ferguson, L. R., 104
Fergusson, D. M., 128, 358, 408, 448
Fernandez-Kelly, M. P., 126, 406
Ferraro, K. F., 232
Ferree, M. M., 15, 16, 17, 244, 274, 281, 283, 482
Fetsch, R. J., 200
Figueredo, A. J., 412, 417
Finch, M. D., 35
Fincham, F. D., 295, 296
Fine, M., 173
Fine, M. A., 91, 285
Finkelhor, D., 417, 418, 422
Finnegan, R. A., 423
Fischer, D. G., 139, 192, 418
Fitzgerald, H. E., 440
Flanagan, C., 372
Fletcher, A. C., 341
Flor, D. L., 307
Flora, C. B., 184
Florsheim, P., 311
Floyd, F. J., 91, 444
Flynn, C. P., 257, 411, 412
Fogel, A., 257
Forehand, R., 100, 101, 192, 306, 382, 386
Forgatch, M. S., 385, 444
Forste, R., 172
Forthofer, M. S., 137, 372
Foster, E. M., 126, 171, 199, 250
Fouts, G., 41
Fowlkes, M. R., 134
Fox, G. L., 41
Frame, C. L., 445
Frank, S. M., 33
Franklin, J. H., 32, 33, 86
Franks, M. M., 291
Frantz, D., 474
Frazier, J. A., 216
Frick, P. J., 413, 447
Friedrich-Cofer, L., 43
Fu, H., 105
Fu, V., 80
Fuchs, V. R., 162
Fujimoto, T., 161
Fuligni, A. J., 74
Fung, T., 415
Furman, W., 336, 338
Furstenberg, F. F., Jr., 127, 130, 194, 260, 341, 375, 380, 389, 392, 393, 396, 474

Gable, S., 416
Gagnon, J. H., 118
Gaines, C., 314
Galambos, N. L., 310
Gallagher, E. M., 444
Gallagher, M., 136, 138, 152, 474
Gallagher, S. K., 326
Gamble, T. J., 215
Gamoran, A., 219
Ganey, R. F., 228, 287
Ganong, L., 142, 264, 265, 266, 292, 327, 350, 391, 393, 397
Garbarino, J., 17, 190, 192, 193, 403, 411, 415, 423, 443, 447, 458, 465, 474
Garcia, A. M., 406
Gardner, M., 158

Gardner, R. W., 58
Garmezy, N., 387
Garrison, M. E. B., 252
Gately, D. W., 380
Ge, X.-J., 199, 310
Gecas, V., 259
Gelles, R. J., 133, 404, 405, 406, 410, 414, 416, 420, 426, 431
Genovese, E. D., 66
George, L. K., 232
Gerstel, N., 326
Giesen, D., 232
Gilbert, D., 186
Gilbreth, J. G., 385
Giles-Sims, J., 392
Gilgun, J. F., 26, 419
Gilligan, C., 16
Gintis, S., 222
Giordani, B., 200
Giordano, P. C., 404
Gjerde, P. F., 386
Glass, J., 161
Gleason, P., 130, 472
Gleeson, J. P., 147, 262
Glendon, M. A., 48
Glenn, N. D., 115, 138, 287, 288, 290, 370
Glick, J. E., 76
Glick, P. C., 14
Goedhart, A. W., 347
Goffman, E., 12
Gold, S. J., 57
Goldberg-Glen, R. S., 264
Goldman, N., 137
Goldscheider, F. K., 131, 202, 324
Goldsmith, H. H., 304, 435
Goldsmith, W. W., 188
Golombok, S., 110, 151
Gonyea, J., 446
Gonzales, J. L., Jr., 65, 84
Good, E. S., 378
Goode, W. J., 375
Goodman, M., 314
Goodson, B. D., 472
Gordon, L. C., 402
Gordon, M., 133
Gordon, T., 114
Gorman, E. H., 137
Gorman, J. C., 306
Gorman-Smith, D., 311
Gorzalka, B. B., 81
Gottman, J. M., 249, 287, 289, 290, 294, 374, 404
Gottschalk, P., 170
Gove, W., 114, 137
Graefe, D. R., 133
Gray, M. R., 306
Greek, A., 256, 334, 335
Greeley, A., 227
Green, G. D., 134
Greenberg, J. S., 426, 453
Greenfield, P. M., 86, 330
Greenlay, J. R., 426
Greenwood, P. W., 473
Greif, G. L., 379
Griffin, L. W., 427
Griffith, J., 217
Gross, A. B., 193
Gross, H. E., 144
Gross, M. L., 458
Grossbard-Shechtman, S., 139
Grossberg, M., 35
Grotevant, J., 144
Groze, V., 141
Gruber, E., 63, 64
Grych, J. H., 295, 296
Gubrium, J. F., 46, 49, 453
Guerra, N. G., 443
Gulley, B. L., 340
Gunnarsson, L., 26
Gunnoe, M. L., 231
Gupta, S., 169
Gutman, H., 66, 67

Habenstein, R. W., 86
Habermas, J., 42
Hagan, J., 204
Haines, M. R., 35
Hall, E. J., 17, 274
Hall, N. W., 482
Hall-McCorquodale, I., 454
Hamby, S. L., 402
Hamm, W., 144, 147
Hammer, M., 412, 413
Hanawalt, B. A., 33
Handel, G., 26
Handler, J. F., 157
Hannon, L., 471
Hansell, S., 44
Hanson, E., 316
Hanson, T. L., 133, 313, 386
Hao, L., 170, 261, 379
Hardy, J. B., 128, 129, 130
Hare, J., 251
Hareven, T. K., 14, 35, 46, 242, 259, 316, 321
Harkness, S., 244
Harmon, A., 44
Harootyan, R. A., 330
Harrell, A. V., 189
Harrigan, M. P., 148
Harrington, D., 416
Harrington, R. C., 435
Harris, J. R., 357, 358
Harris, K. M., 346, 474
Harrison, K., 440
Harroff, P. B., 275, 276, 278, 299
Harvey, D. L., 255, 281
Harvey, E., 162, 163
Harwood, R. L., 311
Haskett, M. E., 131
Haveman, R., 165, 171, 482
Hawkins, A. J., 45, 131, 440
Hayes, D. S., 42
Hays, S., 161, 243, 244, 270
Hayward, M. D., 64, 197
Hayward, S. C., 107
Health and Human Services, 124, 368, 414, 468
Heard, H. E., 385
Heath, D. T., 253
Heaton, T. B., 104, 115, 232
Hee, S., 82
Hegar, R. L., 147
Heger, A., 420
Henderson, C. R., 26
Henderson, D. A., 401
Henderson, K. A., 317
Henderson, S. H., 313, 344
Henggeler, S. W., 312
Henker, B., 312
Henry, C. S., 266
Hensen, K. A., 204
Henshaw, S. K., 105, 107
Hernandez, R., 470
Heron, M., 64
Herrerias, C., 380
Herring, C., 68
Hertel, B. R., 228

Herz, D. E., 158
Hess, B. B., 15, 16, 482
Hesson-McInnis, M. S., 92, 93
Hetherington, E. M., 163, 231, 343, 344, 361, 384, 385, 393, 421
Hewitt, C., 469
Heyns, B., 220
Hiebert-Murphy, D., 418
Higginson, J. G., 250
Hill, D. H., 234
Hill, J. P., 313
Hill, M. S., 130
Hines, A. M., 384
Hochschild, A. R., 161, 162, 181, 285
Hodges, E. V. E., 423
Hodgson, L. G., 261
Hoffer, T., 13, 61, 191, 224, 424
Hofferth, S., 159, 161, 185, 212
Hoffman, L. W., 344
Hoffman, M. S., 184
Hoffman, S. D., 126, 171, 250
Hoffner, C., 42
Hogan, D. P., 261, 325, 449
Hogginbotham, E., 181
Hoisch, M., 221
Holland, K., 104, 115
Hollingsworth, L. D., 417
Holloway, D. P., 200
Holmbeck, G. N., 313
Holmes, C. A., 292
Holstein, J. A., 46, 49, 453
Homans, G. C., 13
Hooyman, N. R., 446
Hopper, J., 375
Horney, J., 138
Horton, G. P., 70
Horton, H. D., 70
Horwitz, A. V., 138, 342
Horwood, L. J., 358, 408, 448
Hossain, Z., 281
Hostetler, J. A., 47
Houseknecht, S. K., 237, 283
Hout, M., 227
Howes, C., 412
Hoyt, D. R., 261
Hrabowski, F. A., III, 72
Hsueh, J. C.-T., 340
Hu, Y., 137
Huang, G.-H., 318
Huck, S. M., 261
Huesmann, L. R., 43
Hughes, M., 114, 137
Hughes, M. E., 341
Hughes, R., Jr., 45, 378
Hula, R. C., 7
Hummer, R. A., 232
Hunter, A. G., 162
Hunsberger, B., 231
Hur, Y.-M., 357
Hurtado, A., 73
Huston, A. C., 43, 53
Huston, T. L., 249, 289, 294
Hutchinson, I. W., 405
Huttenlocher, J., 223
Hyman, B., 417

Iannaccone, L. R., 231
Insabella, G. M., 284, 287
Ishii-Kuntz, M., 81, 82
Island, D., 407
Israel, E., 421, 422

Jacklin, C. N., 12
Jacobs, D. A., 419
Jacob, T., 441
Jacobson, C. K., 104, 115
Jacobson, K. C., 130, 354
James, A., 243
James, D., 168
James, K., 64
Jang, S. J., 449
Janssen, L., 198
Janssen, Y., 198, 421
Jargowksi, P. A., 189
Jekielek, S. M., 138, 139, 163, 392, 394, 474
Jencks, C., 207, 443
Jendrek, M. P., 262
Jenkins, E. J., 192, 411
Jenkins, J. M., 344, 383
Jennings, J. D., 63
Jenny, C., 135, 431
Jensen, L., 60
Jodl, K. M., 295
Joe, T., 129
Joesch, J. M., 212
John, R., 62, 63
Johnson, C., 199, 437, 443
Johnson, C. A., 131
Johnson, C. L., 349
Johnson, D. R., 476
Johnson, M. E., 249
Johnston, C., 444
Jones, D., 126, 171
Jouriles, E. N., 408
Joy, L. A., 43
Joyner, K., 132
Juhasz, A. M., 257

Kagan, S. L., 216, 482
Kahl, J. A., 186
Kahn, J. R., 169
Kamo, Y., 327
Kanowitz, L., 108
Kaplan, S. J., 409, 416
Karen, D., 186
Karis, T. A., 301
Karkowski, L. M., 435
Karraker, K. H., 130
Kasarda, J. D., 188, 189
Katz, R., 435
Kaufman, J., 413
Keith, V. M., 68
Kellam, S. G., 449
Keller, M. B., 438
Kellogg, S., 32, 63
Kelley, J., 229
Kelly, H. H., 13
Kelly, J., 248, 249, 270, 390
Kelly, M. P. F., 78
Kempe, C., 416
Kendler, K. S., 16, 355, 387, 435
Kerbo, H. R., 186
Kerbow, D., 43, 217, 218, 319
Kerns, D., 424
Kessen, W., 15
Kessler, R. C., 137, 169, 376
Kessler-Davis, A., 33
Kett, J. F., 314
Kiernan, K., 383
Kim, J. E., 384
Kim, U., 59
Kimball, M. M., 43
King, R. B., 130
King, V., 200, 261, 385
Kinsey, A. C., 92
Kirby, K. M., 147
Kisker, E. E., 261

Kitagawa, E. M., 449
Kitson, G. C., 290, 376, 390
Kivett, V. R., 261
Klaus, E., 323
Klebanov, P. K., 188, 191
Klein, D. M., 26, 323
Kluwer, E. S., 289
Knickman, J., 194
Koch, J. R., 232
Kochanska, G., 305
Kochenderfer, B. J., 423
Koepke, L., 251
Kohut, A., 44
Kolchin, P., 67
Korbin, J. E., 413, 426
Koss, M. P., 412, 417
Kostelny, K., 193, 411, 415
Kotchick, B. A., 100, 101, 192, 306
Kotlowitz, A., 173
Kouneski, E. F., 246, 257, 380, 478
Kovaric, P., 41
Kowaleski-Jones, L., 98, 99, 100
Kowalewski, B. M., 343
Kozol, J., 221, 222
Krahn, F. L., 441
Kramer, L., 420
Kraut, R., 45
Krishnakumar, A., 295
Kubey, R., 38
Kunkel, D., 39
Kupersmidt, J. B., 191, 415
Kurdek, L. A., 50, 96, 248, 289, 292, 293, 294, 381, 464

Labruna, V., 409, 416
Lackey, C., 413
Ladd, G. W., 215, 319, 423
Laird, M., 134, 412, 416
Lam, M., 74
Lamb, M. E., 212, 245, 270
Lambert, J. D., 138, 379
Lamborn, S. D., 307, 310, 358
Lammers, J., 97
Land, K., 189
Landale, N. S., 77, 133, 482
Landry, D. J., 95
Laner, M. R., 92
Lanthier, R. P., 338
Laquatra, J., 201
Lareau, A., 217, 237
Larner, M., 26
LaRossa, R., 11, 12, 26, 270
Larson, K. A., 62, 193, 219
Larson, R. W., 38, 162, 281, 286, 315, 316
Larzelere, R. E., 306, 311
Laslett, P., 34
Laub, J. H., 138, 139, 163, 173, 478
Laumann, E. O., 92, 95, 100, 101, 102, 103, 107, 118, 131, 136, 419, 420, 424
Laumann-Billings, L., 409
Lavigueur, S., 446
Lawton, L., 323
Layzer, J. I., 472, 473
LeClere, F. B., 343
Lee, E. S., 223
Lee, G. R., 322, 325
Lee, S. A., 385
Lee, Y.-J., 324
Lefley, H. P., 426, 452, 454, 458, 477
Lein, L., 126, 168, 171, 173
Lemann, N., 66
Lemery, K. S., 304
Lennon, M. C., 161, 280
Lenton, R. L., 310
Lerner, R. M., 12, 305
Leonard, K., 441
Letelier, P., 407
Levenson, R., 290
Levesque, R. J. R., 482
Levin, J. S., 232
Levine, E. S., 142
LeVine, R. A., 211, 243, 244
Levine, S., 223
Levinger, G., 13
Levinson, D. J., 252
Lewin, E., 135
Lewin, T., 167
Lewis, M., 305
Lichtenstein, P., 442
Lichter, D. T., 133, 171, 172, 197
Liebert, R. M., 43
Liebler, C. A., 64, 65
Lillard, L. A., 137
Lin, C. Y., 80
Lin, H.-S., 353
Lin, K.-H., 402
Lincoln, C. E., 228
Lincoln, Y. S., 21, 26
Lindsay, D. W., 445
Link, B. G., 137, 194
Lloyd, K. M., 372, 373, 381
Lloyd, S. A., 118
Locke, H. J., 287
Loeb, T. B., 312
Loeber, R., 444
Logan, J. R., 71, 327, 330, 337
London, R. A., 170
Long, J. D., 267, 466
Long, L., 203, 204
Lorber, J., 15, 17, 482
Lorenz, F. O., 199, 207
Loseke, D., 431
Lounsbury, M. L., 305
Lowry, D. T., 42
Luckmann, T., 14, 15
Luker, K., 126
Lüscher, K., 26
Luster, T., 351
Lykken, D., 353
Lynskey, M. T., 358, 448
Lytle, C., 420

MacBeth, T. M., 43, 44
Maccoby, E. E., 12, 203, 307, 379, 385, 386, 392, 397
Machamer, A. M., 63, 64
Macke, A., 283
MacLeod, C., 445
Macmillan, H., 420
MacMillan, R., 204
Madak, P. R., 220
Madden-Derdich, D. A., 390
Maddock, J. M., 406
Madoo-Lengermann, P., 16
Magdol, L., 132
Magnusson, D., 12, 305, 312
Mahoney, M. M., 142
Mahoney, M. R., 404
Majors, R., 69
Makepeace, J. M., 401
Mallon, G. P., 147, 194
Malone, M. J., 423
Mamiya, L. H., 228
Mancini, C., 420

Manly, J. T., 414
Mannheim, K., 14
Manning, W. D., 131, 133, 169, 467, 475
March, K., 141, 145
Mare, R. D., 292
Margolin, G., 412
Marks, C., 66
Marks, N., 138
Marks, N. F., 66, 138
Marmer, J. K., 474
Marshall, I. H., 138
Marshall, N. L., 322
Marsiglio, W., 393
Martin, C. E., 92
Martin, G. T., Jr., 36, 470
Martin, J., 307
Martinson, B. C., 384
Martoz-Baden, R., 200
Marx, J., 204, 263
Mash, E. J., 437
Masheter, C., 390
Mason, C. A., 310
Mason, K. O., 214
Mason, M. A., 140, 143, 482
Massey, D. S., 188, 193
Masten, A. S., 387
Masten, C. M., 81
Mathews, A., 445
Mathews, T. J., 75, 76
Maton, K. I., 72
Matthei, J., 35
Mattheis, C., 200
Mauldon, J., 472
Maurer, R., 199
Mayberry, M., 225
Mayhew, P., 426
Maynard, R. E., 127, 151, 250
McAdoo, H. P., 70, 86
McAlpine, C., 147
McAuley, C., 147
McBride, B. A., 245, 474
McCall, P., 189
McCartney, K., 213
McCaskill, P. A., 195
McCauley, J., 412
McChesney, K. Y., 195
McClearn, G. E., 16, 351
McCloskey, J., 64, 412
McCloskey, L. A., 417
McCollum, A. T., 204
McCoy, J. K., 338
McCracken, C., 411
McCurdy, K., 414
McDonald, W. L., 418
McGue, M. K., 140, 439
McGuffin, P., 435
McGuire, S., 339, 352
McHale, S. M., 163, 340, 344, 347
McIlroy, A., 477
McLanahan, S. S., 133, 203, 310, 313, 384, 385, 392
McLaughlin, D. K., 171, 172, 197
McLeod, J. D., 177
McLoyd, V. C., 139, 176, 177, 411, 472
McMahon, C. A., 110
McNeal, C., 408
McNeil, J., 40
McPherson, J. M., 255
McRae, C., 383, 464
Mead, G. H., 12
Mead, M., 314
Mekos, D., 163
Melson, G. F., 257
Melville, K., 202
Menaghan, E. G., 114, 139, 163, 165, 171, 337, 392, 474
Merten, D. E., 91
Merton, R. K., 473
Messner, M., 17
Metz, M. E., 289
Meyer, D. R., 130
Miall, C. E., 141
Michael, R., 92
Michael, R. T., 118, 131
Michaels, S., 118
Miles-Doan, R., 406
Miley, C. H., 431
Miller, C. K., 170, 172, 475
Miller, J. W., 131
Miller, J. Y., 440
Miller, K. S., 100, 101, 192, 306
Miller, L. S., 192
Miller, N., 251
Miller, R. B., 426
Milner, J. S., 415
Min, P. G., 79, 82
Mindel, C. H., 86
Miner, S., 349
Minshull, R., 185
Mintz, S., 32, 33, 63
Mirowsky, J., 384
Mirrlees-Black, C., 426
Mitchell, K. B., 160
Mitchell-Kernan, C., 160
Mnookin, R. H., 379, 397
Modell, J., 314
Moen, P., 26
Molnar, M., 258
Monahan, S. C., 352, 357
Montemayor, R., 314, 316
Montgomery, R. J. V., 327
Moore, K., 99, 104, 128, 441
Moran, P. B., 251
Morelli, G. A., 243, 244
Morenoff, J. D., 188, 190
Morgan, M. C., 340
Morgan, S. P., 127, 346
Moore, K., 424
Morris, P. A., 170
Morris, S., 420
Morris, S. N., 45
Morrison, D. R., 295, 316, 383, 386
Morrison, F. J., 216
Morrison, N. C., 417, 418
Mortimer, J. T., 35
Mosher, W. D., 419
Mott, F. L., 98, 99, 100
Mouw, T., 62
Mowbray, C. T., 436
Mullally, P. R., 336, 337
Muller, C., 43, 217, 218, 319
Mulligan, G. M., 281
Munch, A., 255
Munn, P., 337
Musick, J. S., 127
Mutran, E., 325
Myers, J., 44
Myers, S. C., 334
Myers, S. M., 229, 230

Nagel, J., 62
Nagin, D. S., 138, 139
Nakano Glenn, E., 16, 56
Nakonezny, P. A., 370
Nakosteen, R. A., 114

Nasar, S., 160
Nass, C. I., 42
National Center for Health Statistics, 105, 115, 123, 372, 381
National Institute of Child Health and Human Development, 212, 213
National Telecommunications and Information Administration (NTIA), 44
Neal, D., 224
Neal, L., 144
Neiderhiser, J. M., 312
Neisser, U., 223
Nelson, D. A., 445
Nelson, F., 135, 252, 280, 293
Nelson, J. L., 157
Netzer, J. K., 325
Neuman, M. J., 26, 216
Newcomb, M. D., 312
Newcomb, R., 104
Ney, P. G., 415
Neysmith, S., 349
Nguyen, T. V., 310, 411
Niebrugge-Brantley, J., 16
Nigg, J. T., 435
Nielsen, L., 390, 391
Nightingale, D. S., 482
Noble, D. F., 466
Nock, S. L., 129, 132, 137, 151, 202, 233, 463, 474
Noller, P., 252, 307, 316, 478
Nord, C. W., 217, 424, 441
Norman, A. J., 82
Norris, D., 383
Norton, M. B., 33, 53

Obeidallah, C. L., 339
O'Brien, M., 131
O'Brien, M. J., 421, 422
O'Connell, M., 246, 279
O'Connor, T. G., 284, 287
Oderkirk, J., 174
Ogbu, J. U., 69, 191
O'Keefe, M., 408, 409
Oldman, D., 36, 37
Olson, L. S., 130, 216, 218, 237
Olson, S. L., 444
Ong, P., 82
Orfield, G., 222, 223
Osgood, D. W., 138
Oslak, S., 95
Osmond, M. W., 16
Osofsky, J. D., 131
Ostrander, D. L., 266
Oyen, N., 139

Pacheco, F., 145, 146
Pagani, L., 176, 392
Pagnini, D. L., 475
Panel on High-Risk Youth, 221
Parcel, T. L., 163, 171, 337
Park, K., 82
Park, R. E., 184
Parke, R. D., 245
Parks, C. A., 135
Parish, W. L., 261
Parkhurst, J. G., 237
Parr, J., 35
Parrott, T. M., 327
Parsons, T., 10, 18
Pasley, K., 141, 259, 292
Patillo, M. E., 71
Patillo-McCoy, M., 228
Patrick, J. H., 326, 342
Patterson, C. J., 134, 135, 140
Patterson, G. R., 310, 313, 340, 347, 385, 444, 446, 448, 458
Pearce, L. D., 232, 233
Pearson, J. L., 262
Pebley, A. R., 262
Pedreza, S., 86
Peebles-Wilkins, W., 406
Peek, C. W., 322
Pelcovitz, D., 409, 416
Pelham, W. E., 444
Pelton, L. H., 415, 473
Pepler, D. J., 445
Percy, A., 426
Perez-Granados, D. R., 341
Perkins, D. F., 100
Perozynski, L., 420
Perry, D. G., 423
Perry, S. E., 111
Perry-Jenkins, M., 283
Persell, C. H., 224
Peters, H. E., 397
Peters, P. L., 129
Peterson, D., 260, 324, 327
Peterson, G. D., 411
Peterson, J. L., 424, 441
Pettit, G. S., 177, 193, 306, 412
Phillips, B., 57
Phillips, C., 147
Pianta, R. C., 413, 414
Pickett, R. S., 21
Pienta, A. M., 197
Pierce, J. L., 337
Pillemer, K., 321, 325, 426
Pleck, E. H., 33, 279
Pleck, J. H., 33, 279, 322
Plomin, R., 15, 16, 297, 308, 344, 351, 354, 355, 357, 361, 387, 466
Plumert, J. M., 411
Polakow, V., 222
Pomeroy, W. B., 92
Pong, S. I., 219
Popenoe, D., 53
Portes, A., 59, 78, 82, 86
Potuchek, J. L., 279, 301
Powell, B., 336, 379, 380
Powers, D. A., 301, 340
Poyer, K. L., 135
Pratt, M., 231
Prescott, C. A., 435
Presser, H. B., 279
Presser, S., 228, 279
Pribesh, S., 203
Prout, A., 243
Pruchno, R., 264, 326, 342
Ptacek, J., 404
Pulkinen, L., 443
Pyke, K., 81

Qian, Z., 62, 219
Quane, J. M., 192
Quinn, J. F., 387
Quinn-Curan, N., 455
Quinton, D., 443
Qvortrup, J., 37

Raboy, B., 135
Radke-Yarrow, M., 436, 437, 438
Rafferty, Y., 195, 196
Ragoné, H., 111
Raley, K., 132, 467
Ramey, C. T., 213

Ramey, S. L., 213
Rane, T. R., 245, 474
Rangarajan, A., 130, 472
Rankin, B. H., 192
Raskin White, H., 138
Ratcliff, K. S., 281, 283
Raver, C. C., 215
Ray, B. D., 225, 226
Rebar, D. C., 171
Reddy, M. T., 68
Regier, D. A., 439
Reid, J. B., 313, 347, 446, 448, 458
Reid, T., 431
Reigot, B. P., 151
Reiss, D., 163, 231, 297, 325, 328, 343, 347, 348, 357, 361, 384
Reitzes, D. C., 11, 12
Reitzes, D. G., 325
Renzetti, C. M., 403, 404, 407, 431
Revkin, A. C., 168, 470, 471
Reynolds, A. J., 216, 472
Rezac, S. J., 385
Rhodes, M., 157
Rice, A. M., 344
Richards, M. H., 162, 281, 286, 315, 316
Richards, M. P. M., 386
Richardson, B., 337
Richman, J. M., 289
Riedmann, A., 349, 350
Rifkin, J., 181, 466
Riley, D., 26
Rindfuss, R. R., 127, 475
Risley-Curtiss, C., 147
Ritter, L. P., 354
Rivera, F., 392
Roberts, D. F., 42
Robertson, E. B., 199
Robinson, L. C., 291
Rockwell, S. C., 42
Rodgers, H. R., Jr., 170
Rodgers, K. B., 306
Rodgers, L., 370
Roehlkepartain, E. C., 141
Roesler, T. A., 135
Rogers, S. J., 233, 287, 288, 290, 372, 476
Rogoff, B., 244
Rohner, R. P., 311
Rollins, N., 196
Ronka, A., 443
Rook, K., 286
Roopnarine, J. L., 281
Roosa, M. W., 128, 441
Roschelle, A. R., 16, 26, 78, 148, 474
Rosellini, L., 412
Rosenbaum, J. E., 191
Rosenberg, M. S., 408
Rosenblatt, P. C., 301
Rosenfeld, L. B., 280, 289
Rosenfield, S., 161
Rosenthal, D. A., 80, 81, 99
Ross, C. E., 384
Ross, C. M., 261
Ross, J. L., 134
Rosser, B. R. S., 289
Rossi, A. S., 118, 261, 266, 270, 317, 322, 323, 330
Rossi, P. H., 195, 261, 266, 270, 317, 322, 323, 330
Rossides, D. W., 187
Rothbart, M. K., 304
Rothman, B. K., 108, 111, 118
Rotundo, E. A., 34
Rowe, D. C., 26, 130, 297, 340, 341, 354
Roy, J. A., 385
Rubin, L. B., 86, 99, 175
Rubin, S., 455
Rudkin, L. L., 262
Rueter, M. A., 340
Ruggles, S., 67
Rumbaut, R. G., 57, 60, 68, 75, 76, 77, 86
Rumberger, R. W., 62, 193, 219
Runtz, M., 419
Russell, G., 315
Russell, N. F., 107
Rutter, M. L., 357, 358, 387, 412, 443, 466
Rutter, V., 93, 96, 100, 110

Sabatelli, R. M., 13
Sachdev, P., 145, 146
Sacher, J. A., 91, 285
Saito, Y., 321
Salamon, S., 198
Sallee, A. L., 142
Saluter, A. F., 262
Salzinger, S., 412, 413
Sameroff, A. J., 12, 176
Sampson, R. J., 71, 138, 139, 163, 173, 188, 190, 192, 204, 448, 449, 465, 478
Sanchez-Korrol, U., 59, 77
Sanday, P. R., 401, 402, 431
Sandefur, G. D., 64, 65
Sandfort, J. R., 130
Sands, R. G., 264
Sanson, A., 304
Sapolsky, B. S., 42
Sassen, S., 157
Sassler, S., 160
Saucier, J.-F., 446
Savin-Williams, R. C., 92
Scannapieco, M., 147
Scarr, S., 162, 211, 213, 328, 351
Schaefer, R. T., 57, 58, 64, 73, 94
Schaie, K. W., 330
Schauffler, R., 78
Schellenbach, C. J., 482
Schieffelin, B., 346
Schiller, B. R., 64, 158, 166
Schiller, H. I., 466
Schlegel, A., 313
Schochet, P., 472
Schoen, R., 160
Schoeni, R. F., 259
Schor, E. L., 165
Schor, J. B., 316
Schteingart, J. S., 196
Schulz, M. S., 130, 436
Schumm, W. R., 26
Schuster, M. A., 105
Schvaneveldt, J. D., 21
Schwab, R., 224
Schwartz, P., 93, 96, 100, 101, 102, 103, 110, 248, 279, 301
Schwartzman, A. E., 129
Schwarz, J. E., 157, 166
Schwebel, A. I., 380
Schwebel, D. C., 411
Seaberg, J. R., 148
Seccombe, K., 168
Seff, M. A., 259

Seidman, S. N., 419
Seifer, R., 12, 176
Seltzer, J. A., 50, 245, 294, 384, 388
Seltzer, M. M., 342, 426
Serbin, L. A., 128, 129
Sered, S. S., 234
Shanahan, M. J., 177
Shane, P. G., 194, 195
Shapiro, A., 379
Sharma, A. R., 140, 141
Shavit, Y., 337
Shaw, D. S., 372
Sheehy, G., 252
Shehan, C. L., 13
Sheley, J. F., 446
Sherkat, D. E., 231
Sherman, A., 471
Sherman, D., 411
Sheth, M., 97
Shibuya, K., 193
Shinn, M., 194, 195, 196
Shireman, J. F., 141
Shoemaker, N., 63
Shorter, E., 371
Shull, J. L., 370
Silverman, A. R., 143
Silverstein, L. B., 474
Silverstein, M., 76, 267, 323, 326, 327, 466
Silverthorn, P., 447
Sime, J., 23
Simons, R. L., 199, 207, 311, 313, 371, 385, 388, 397, 402, 413, 443, 447, 477
Singer, J. D., 213
Skogan, W. G., 157
Skolnick, A., 140, 482
Slaby, R. G., 445
Sleek, S., 400
Small, S. A., 318, 424
Smeeding, T. M., 387
Smetana, J., 314
Smith, C., 412
Smith, C. A., 449
Smith, D. E., 15, 17
Smith, H., 421, 422
Smith, J. G., 70
Smith, M. A., 344, 383
Smith, M. D., 118
Smith, R., 129
Smith, T. W., 227
Smithey, M., 409
Smith-Lovin, L., 255
Smits, J., 97
Smock, P. J., 131, 133, 169, 389, 467, 475
Snyder, A. R., 32
Solomon, J. C., 263
Somers, M. D., 115
South, S. D., 161
South, S. J., 95, 372, 373, 381
Spanier, G. B., 288
Spencer, M. B., 307
Spencer, R. F., 63
Spencer-Loomis, L. S., 385
Spigel, L., 34, 38
Spina, R. K., 151
Spitze, G., 326, 327, 330, 337
Spitzer, B. L., 317
Sporakowski, M. J., 53
Sprafkin, J., 43
Sprecher, S., 101, 102, 103, 248
Sprey, J., 98
Stacey, J., 48, 53, 135, 251
Stack, C., 339
Stack, S., 136
Staff, I., 147
Stanton-Salazar, R. D., 219
Stark, S. D., 39, 40
Starrels, M. A., 326, 327
Steelman, L. C., 336
Stein, A., 437
Stein, N., 424
Stein, P. J., 113, 114
Steinberg, L., 80, 190, 216, 237, 306, 310, 314, 319, 354, 358, 465
Steinmetz, S. K., 26, 420, 426
Stephan, C. W., 143
Stephan, W. G., 143
Stephen, E. H., 108
Sternberg, K. J., 412
Stets, J. E., 401, 406
Stevenson, J., 442
Stewart, S., 118
Stewart, S. D., 380
Stiers, G. A., 294
Stinson, L., 228
Stolzenberg, R. M., 132, 233
Stoolmiller, M., 129, 444
Stone, L., 370
Stoneman, Z., 204, 338, 437, 438
Stouthamer-Loeber, M., 444, 448
Stover, R. G., 198
St. Pierre, R. G., 472, 473
Strapko, N., 289
Strathern, M., 108
Straus, M. A., 311, 404, 406, 411, 412, 416, 420
Strawbridge, W. J., 263
Stults, B., 71
Styfco, S., 472
Style, C. B., 114, 137
Suárez, L. M., 450
Suarez, Z. E., 78
Subaiya, L., 169
Sucoff, C. A., 192
Sugarman, D. B., 402
Sugarman, S. D., 140, 482
Sui-Chu, E. H., 218
Suitor, J. J., 321, 325
Sullivan, T., 454
Sun, R., 79
Super, C., 244
Supple, K. R., 322
Surra, C. A., 94
Swaim, P., 197
Sweet, J. A., 132
Swisher, R. R., 199, 221
Szinovacz, M. E., 265

Tabarlet, J. L., 42
Talbott, S. L., 466
Tamis-LeMonda, C. S., 171
Tapper, N., 97
Tarver-Behring, S., 312
Tasker, F. L., 151
Tata, P., 445
Tatara, T., 427
Taylor, R. B., 189
Taylor, R. J., 228, 326
Teachman, J. D., 132
Temple, J. A., 216, 472
Terkelsen, K. G., 452, 455
Testa, M., 161
Teti, D. M., 335, 339
Thibaut, J. W., 13
Thoits, P. A., 287

Thomas, J. L., 260
Thomas, L. T., 370
Thomas, M. E., 70
Thomes, M. M., 287
Thomson, E., 133, 310, 313
Thorne, B., 16, 26
Thornton, A., 107, 132, 133, 234, 353, 372, 388, 467
Thornton, R., 62
Thurow, L. C., 157
Tienda, M., 172
Tolan, P. H., 311
Toliver, S. D., 73
Tolman, R. M., 402
Tolnay, S. E., 67
Tonry, M., 470, 473
Toro, P. A., 194
Towles, D. W., 42
Townsend, A. L., 291
Trapnell, P. D., 81
Treas, J., 104, 232
Treffers, P. D. A., 347
Tremblay, R. E., 176, 392, 446
Trickett, P. K., 482
Tronick, E. Z., 243, 244
Trusty, J., 217
Tseng, V., 74
Tucker, C. J., 204
Tucker, M. B., 160
Turkheimer, E., 15
Turner, W. L., 77
Tzeng, J.M., 292

Uba, L., 81
Uhlenberg, P., 321, 349
Ultee, W., 97
Umberson, D., 267, 322, 379, 405, 446
United Nations, 368
Upchurch, D. M., 99
Updegraff, K. A., 338
U.S. Bureau of the Census, 57, 74, 75, 94, 125, 131, 137, 158, 162, 167, 262, 367, 368, 380, 381, 383, 387, 466, 467, 469
U.S. Commission on Child and Family Welfare, 477
U.S. Commission on Civil Rights, 40
U.S. Department of Health and Human Services, 124, 368, 414, 468
U.S. Department of Justice, 425
U.S. National Center for Health Statistics, 105, 115, 123, 372, 381
U.S. Senate Special Committee on Aging, 168
Uzzell, O., 406

Van Ameringen, M., 420
Van Cleve, J., 96
van den Akker, O. B. A., 110
Van den Oord, E. J. C. G., 130, 354
Van Enra, J., 53
Van Galen, J., 225
Van Hook, V. W., 76
Vangelisti, A. L., 289, 294
Ventrone, N. A., 92
Ventura, S. J., 106, 123, 124, 252
Vevea, J., 223
Vingerhoets, A. J. J. M., 110
Vinovskis, M. A., 33
Volling, B. L., 211, 249, 344, 347
Vroegh, K. S., 143, 144
Voydanoff, P., 283
Vuchinich, S., 383, 392

Wachs, T. D., 458
Wacquant, L. J. D., 66
Waite, L. J., 131, 132, 136, 137, 138, 152, 202, 233, 474
Waldo, C. R., 92
Wall, C. S., 220
Waller, M., 470
Wallerstein, J. S., 385, 477
Walters, K. B., 168
Walters, S. D., 39
Ward, C., 221, 326
Warr, M., 443
Warren, S. B., 141
Wartes, J., 225, 226
Wasner, G. H., 91
Waters, H. F., 43
Waters, M. C., 59
Weaver, C. N., 138
Webster-Stratton, C., 445
Wegar, K., 40, 463
Weinberg, M. S., 95, 137, 139, 464
Weir, T., 282
Weise, D., 410, 415
Weiss, A. J., 41
Weissman, M. M., 435
Weitzman, B. C., 194
West, E., 35
Whalen, C. K., 312
Wheaton, B., 204
Whitbeck, L. B., 207, 261
White, J. M., 26
White, L. K., 260, 287, 288, 290, 324, 327, 349, 350
White, M., 211
Whiting, B. B., 243
Whittaker, T., 426, 427
Wickett, A. R., 415
Widmer, E. D., 104, 340
Widom, C. S., 413, 420
Wilcox, B. L., 39
Wilcox, K. L., 379
Wilcox, W. B., 231
Wilkie, J. R., 245, 281, 283
Williams, C. L., 379
Williams, D. R., 68
Williams, K. R., 413
Williams, L. M., 420
Willis, R. J., 131
Willms, J. D., 218
Wilson, B. J., 41
Wilson, K., 171
Wilson, S. M., 200
Wilson, W. J., 71, 161, 188, 189, 190, 207
Windridge, K., 110
Winslow, E. B., 372
Wolchik, S. A., 379
Wolf, R., 426
Wolfe, B., 165, 171
Wolfe, S. M., 194
Wong, D. L., 111
Wood, D., 203
Woodberry, R. D., 227
Woodward, L. J., 128
Wright, B. R. E., 448
Wright, J. D., 127, 195, 446
Wright, K., 111

Wright, R., Jr., 86
Wu, L. L., 383, 384, 385, 447

Xie, Y., 62

Yalom, M., 26
Yamaguchi, K., 104
Ying, Y.-W., 81
Yip, A. K. T., 293
Young, M. H., 21

Zabin, L. S., 107
Zabrack, M. L., 43
Zahn-Waxler, C., 436
Zajonc, R. B., 336, 337
Zaslow, M., 471
Zelizer, V. A. R., 35, 105
Zhou, M., 59, 80, 82
Zierk, K. L., 107
Zigler, E. F., 215, 413, 472, 482
Zill, N., 217, 316, 380, 383
Zillman, D., 53
Zima, B. T., 196
Zimmer, M. A., 114
Zimmerman, S. L., 470, 477
Zimmerman, T. S., 200
Zinn, M. B., 16
Zitzow, D., 64
Zivian, M. T., 317

Subject Index

Abortion, 90
  issues, 106–107
  rates, 107–108
Abuse, 402, 440, 441
  of children by parents, 133, 161, 409–416
  of children by peers, 319, 320, 422
  of children by siblings, 420–422, 425
  dating, 400–402
  of parents, 425–427
  partner, 399, 402–403
  same-sex, 403, 406–407
  sexual, 128, 133, 135, 400–401, 417–420, 421–422, 424
  spousal, 17, 399, 404–409, 412
  verbal, 402–403
Achievement (*see* School achievement)
Adolescence, 128, 192, 194, 199, 232, 258–259, 313–316, 392, 414, 425, 444, 478 (*see also* Child/Children; Childhood)
Adolescent employment, 35, 60, 199
Adolescent motherhood, 78, 121, 123, 124, 127–131
  causes, 126, 128, 129, 340
  consequences, 126, 128
  diversity, 128–129, 130, 171
Adolescent mothers, 75, 77, 78, 171, 250 (*see also* Single mothers)
  children of, 128, 130–131
  partners of, 129–130
  types of, 128–129
Adoption, 5, 96, 134, 140–142, 144, 247
  adopted children, 140–142
  adoptive parents, 141, 144–146
  birth parents, 144–146
  reunions, 144–146
  social construction, 19, 140, 141
  stepadoption, 142–143
  transracial, 143–144
Adult children, 159, 320, 426–427
  daughters and sons, 322–323, 327, 426
  help from parents, 320–322, 323–325
  help to parents, 81, 82, 325–327
Adultery (*see* Extramarital sex)
Africa, 7, 37, 67, 162
African-American children, 32, 68, 69, 71, 72, 143, 147, 212, 307, 392–393
African-American couples, 35, 93, 94
African-American families, 40, 66–73, 107, 128, 147, 160, 162, 228, 267, 281, 349, 350
  discrimination, 68, 72, 73
  economic context, 66, 136, 160, 389
  employment, 160, 166–167
  history, 32, 66, 67
  middle-class, 70–73, 188, 193
  migration to the north, 59, 66, 188
  mother-headed, 66, 67, 123–125
  neighborhoods, 66, 68, 70, 71, 73, 99, 188–194, 406
  two-parent, 67, 68, 70
African-American parents, 68, 69
  socialization practices, 43, 69, 72, 307
Age, 37, 126, 128, 242, 372–373
  children's, 176, 383, 393
  difference, 128, 255, 366
  distribution, 466
  homogamy, 95
Aged parents, 33, 81, 259, 265–266
  abuse, 426–427
  help from children, 325–327
  help to children, 323–325
Aggressiveness, 43, 44, 128, 129, 191, 296, 338, 340, 400, 402, 442, 445
Aid to Families with Dependent Children (AFDC), 171, 172, 470
Alaska, 32, 62
Alcohol(ism), 405–406, 407, 439–441
Altruism, altruistic, 13, 232, 257, 478
American society, 5, 37, 46, 48, 83, 131, 165, 317, 443
Amish, 47, 94, 354

Anthropology, 8, 9
Antisocial, 71, 137, 176, 402, 413–414, 443, 444–445
Arranged marriage, 96–99
Artificial insemination, 109, 134, 135
Asia, 7, 37, 96, 157
Asian-American families, 79, 349 (*see also* Chinese-American families; Korean-American families)
Assortative mating, 93, 353, 483
At risk, 141, 170, 190 (*see also* Child/children at risk; Risk factors)
Attachment, 305, 316, 335, 413, 437
Authority, 139, 162, 400, 453–454
Autobiography, xxvii, 4, 22, 23, 210, 423, 462

Baby Boom, 105–106
Behavior genetics, 21, 351, 352, 354–357, 439 (*see also* Genes and environment)
  critique, 355, 357–359
  theory, 15, 16, 465–466
Behavioral problems, 131, 133, 218, 402, 442, 447, 449
  causes of, 177, 191, 437, 442–445
  and family dynamics, 133, 313, 434, 443, 445–446
Bereavement, 387–389
Bilingualism, 62, 78, 219
Binge drinking, 439, 440
Biology, biological, 8, 9, 16
Birth, 166, 176
  multiple, 111–112
  order, 344
  parents, 144–146
  prebirth, 246–248
  rates, 123, 124
  spacing, 255–256
  timing, 14, 256
Birth control (*see* Family planning)
Blacks (*see* African-American couples; African-American families; African-American parents)
Blame/blaming (*see* Parents/parental/parenting)
British families, 127, 174, 175
Burden, 326, 342

Canadian families, 174, 175
Capital:
  human, 13, 18, 139, 163, 484
  social, 13, 14, 18, 77, 82, 139, 163, 219, 228, 341, 485
Caregiver (for adults), 291–292, 342
Catholic(s), 57, 224, 227, 370
Causality, 165–172, 370–372, 394, 401–402, 408, 412–413, 421, 435–439, 439–440, 448–449
Change, 5, 50, 394, 442
Chicano (*see* Mexican-American families)
Child/children, 185, 190, 255, 263–264, 295–298
  abuse by, 425–427
  adult (*see* Adult children)
  affluent, 185, 191
  at risk, 130, 131, 133, 170
  coproducers of their development, 12, 305, 312–313
  cultural brokers, 81
  difficult, 128, 215, 411, 414
  immigration, 59–61, 341
  parental marital status, 50, 131–133, 138–139
  personality, 12, 304, 306, 308, 335, 337–338
  poverty, 34, 35, 127, 188
  relationship with parents, 295–298, 311
  rights, 144
  social actor, 12, 42
  socialization (*see also* Childrearing practices; Socialization of children)
  work, 36, 37
Child abuse (*see* Abuse)
Child care, 37, 162, 168, 211–216, 243, 261–262
  effects, 212–214
  quality, 211–212
Child custody, 33–35, 379, 380
Child development, 9, 12, 184, 287, 337, 338, 344–345 (*see also* Outcomes [child and adolescent])
Child neglect, 162, 400, 414–416
Child support, 126, 130, 170, 380
Childhood, 15, 34, 35, 36, 243
Childless, childlessness, 115, 249, 279
Childrearing practices, 63, 76, 79–81, 231, 305–313 (*see also* Parents/parental/parenting; Socialization of children)
  disruption, 295, 296, 344, 436
  effect on, 295–298
  environment, 297–298, 304, 310
  genes, 297
  outcomes, 306–309
Chinese-American adolescents, 80–81
Chinese-American families, 79–81 (*see also* Asian-American families)
Civility, 402, 403, 428
Class (*see* Social class)

Cohabitation, 6, 77, 95, 113, 122, 129, 131–133, 136, 148, 174, 247, 372, 389, 406, 467, 479
  and children, 131, 132–133
  sex in, 102, 131
  stability, 131, 133
  violence in, 131
Cohort, 242, 288, 290, 321, 371, 403, 483
Collective socialization, 14, 191, 341, 354, 465
Colonial period, 32, 33
Communication, 45, 315–316
Community, 61, 78, 80, 82, 184, 185, 308 (*see also* Functional community)
Comorbidity, 439, 442, 483
Comparative perspective, 31, 162
Concentration of poverty (*see* Poverty)
Conduct disorders (*see* Behavioral problems)
Conflict:
  effect of parental on children, 294–298, 343, 385–386
  interpartner, 288–290, 294
  of norms, 13
  parent/child, 44, 60, 61, 146, 313, 316
Content analysis, 20
Context, 8, 9, 10, 14, 31, 242, 267, 373–374
Cool, 56, 69
Corporal punishment (*see* Physical punishment)
Countries (*see* Society[ies])
Couples, 5, 403
Courtship, 91, 400–402 (*see also* Dating)
Crime, criminality, 71, 138, 189, 424, 448
Criminology, 8, 9,
Critical mass, 191, 223, 224, 483
Cross-pressure, 318, 483
Cuban-American families, 76, 77, 172 (*see also* Latino-American families)
Cultural context, 19, 31, 224, 242, 295, 298, 310–311, 372–373, 394, 402, 424, 428, 465, 475, 479
Custodial parents (*see* Parents/parental/parenting)
Custody (*see* Child custody)

Dating, 80, 89, 91–93, 374 (*see also* Partner selection)
  date rape, 401
  gender roles, 91, 92
  same-sex, 92
  violence, 400–402, 408–409
Day care (*see* Child care)
Death, 266–267, 366, 387–389
Defamilialization, 36, 37, 225, 483–484
Delayed parenthood, 108, 252–253
Delinquent/delinquency, 8, 9, 319, 402, 446–447, 450–451, 456
  causes, 64, 163, 340, 341, 448–449
  effects on family dynamics, 434, 449–451
  and supervision, 448–449
Demography, 8, 9, 21, 188, 227, 274–275, 371–372, 374, 466
Depression, 433, 435–439, 454–455
Development (*see* Child development; Family development)
Developmental perspectives, 14, 233, 267
Differential parental treatment, 344–348, 349
  by gender, 61, 346
Discrimination, 11, 55, 68, 72, 73, 166, 471
Disruption of parenting (*see* Parents/parental/parenting)
Diversity (*see* Family/Families)
Division of household labor, 13, 19, 138, 161, 200, 274, 278–286
  classification, 279–281
  in remarriage, 284–285, 366
Divorce, 33, 249, 274, 277, 334, 365–367, 461, 462, 476–477
  adjustment to, 376–377
  and age, 366, 371, 376, 383
  causes of, 169, 370–372, 394
  effect on adults, 264–266, 310, 377–378
  effect on children, 139, 203, 343, 344, 379–380, 382–387, 464
  institution of, 367–368, 394
  and poverty, 169–170, 367, 372, 384
  rates, 124, 288, 367–369, 467–468
  reasons behind, 372–375
  serial, 292, 380–382, 384
Domestic sphere (*see* Private domain or sphere)
Double standard, 95, 97, 285, 415
Downward assimilation, 59, 75, 77, 80, 484
Downward mobility, 59, 127, 484
Dropout (school), 59, 61, 64, 158, 177
Drugs, 194, 195, 232, 306, 308, 415, 439, 448
Dutch families, 174, 175, 471
Dysfunction/dysfunctional, 10, 11, 444, 455, 484

Eating disorders, 439, 440
Economic context, 17, 46, 197, 242, 267, 388, 463
Economics, economy, 8, 9, 13, 78, 129, 157, 199, 473–474
  globalization of, 156–157
Education, 129, 158, 210–211, 216, 242, 335 (*see also* School[s]; Schooling)

Effective community (*see* Functional community)
Effects on children (*see* Outcomes [child and adolescent])
Emotional problems, 137, 195, 325, 342, 415, 448 (*see also* Depression)
Emotional work, 91, 285–286
Employment, 199
 maternal, 79, 82, 161, 162–163, 171, 211, 244, 249, 257, 278, 280–283
 parental, 162, 163–165
 paternal, 157, 162
Empty nest, 259–260
Endogamy, 94, 484
Environment, 12, 13, 31, 47, 69, 297–298, 304
 and genes, 4, 15, 16, 297
 nonshared, 16, 352, 357, 485
 and predispositions, 440
 shared, 16, 340, 351, 352, 353–354, 357, 358, 485
Ethnic/ethnicity, 18, 35, 56, 57, 94, 406
Evaluative research, 20, 476
Exchange theory, 13, 92, 95, 285
Exogamy, 94, 484
Experiments, 20, 354–357, 476
Experts, 15, 453–455
Ex-spouses, 292, 366, 390–391
Extended family, 5, 6, 7, 33, 60, 64, 76, 266, 337, 350
Extracouple sex, 20, 33, 232, 373
 heterosexual couples, 103–104
 same-sex couples, 103–104

Familism, 73, 74
Family/families, 310–311, 449
 affluent, 185–187, 220, 281, 339, 354
 change, 5, 45
 decline, 45, 46, 49, 462
 defined, 4, 5, 6, 7, 8
 diversity, 18, 23, 33, 48, 63, 83, 463
 dynamics, 4, 8, 140, 433–434, 445–446, 449–451
 dysfunctional, 11, 408, 421–422, 448, 462
 extended, 5, 6, 7, 33, 60, 64, 76, 78, 266, 337, 350
 functions, 18, 44, 46–48, 49, 50, 64, 234–235, 260, 428, 456, 464, 480
 future of, 466–469
 history, 9, 29–36, 66, 67, 74, 77
 immigrant, 35, 47, 56–62
 institution, 4, 5, 7, 23, 46, 47, 48
 investment in, 18
 minority group, 7, 32, 56, 82, 217, 218, 283
 nuclear, xxiv, 5, 6, 7, 8, 32, 337
 policies, 7, 8, 49, 462
 problems, 1, 462, 463
 single-parent, 75, 77, 121, 124, 125
 size, 336–337
 stages, 246–267
 structure, 8, 50
 system, 10, 11
 two-income, 158, 161–162
 two-parent, 67, 70, 75, 82, 98, 125, 138, 139, 158, 170, 223, 228
 types of, 6, 7, 49, 463
 unit of production, 32, 33
 values, 5, 46, 49
 violence, 17, 169, 194, 402, 407–409
Family development, 233, 242
Family planning, 90, 104–105, 127, 247, 255–256, 334
Farm families, 34, 184, 185, 198–200
Fathers/fatherhood, 4, 29, 30, 33, 35, 77, 79, 252–253, 280, 281, 316, 412, 438, 446
 custodial, 379–380
 divorced, 170, 174, 175, 245
 investment in children, 50, 129, 130, 148, 245, 246, 474
 married, 129, 174
 single, 129, 130, 174, 175, 245
 social construction of, 162, 175, 245–246
Feminism, 15, 16–18, 19, 21, 278, 435
Feminization of poverty, 471
Fertility, 64, 65, 76, 78, 128, 467
Fictive kinship, 7, 77
Fieldwork, 4, 71
Foster families, 146–148, 194
Functional community, 14, 61, 64, 190, 191, 219, 224, 233, 341, 354, 424, 464–465, 484
Functions, 10, 145–146, 185, 484
 family, 18, 44, 46–48, 49, 50, 64, 234–235, 260, 428, 456, 464, 480

Gangs (youth), 71, 72, 191, 193
Gated enclaves, 185
Gay (*see* Same-sex couples; Same-sex marriage; Same-sex-parent families)
Gender, 18, 19, 56, 61, 114, 138, 344, 346, 349, 401, 404, 447
Gender differences, 157, 166, 375, 377–378
 in children, 338–339, 383, 392, 446
Gender relations, 13, 285–286
Gender roles, 4, 15, 16, 17, 19, 31, 39, 148, 278, 285–286, 327, 445–446, 465, 466, 484

Gender-role socialization, 17, 211, 285–286, 294, 327, 474
Gender stratification, 17, 33, 157, 162, 171, 200, 234, 274, 278, 285, 346, 378, 466, 468
Generational compression, 254–255
Generations, 55, 56, 59–62, 75–76, 78, 81, 253, 266, 326, 327
  conflict, 60, 61
  immigrant, 55, 56, 59–62, 75–76, 78, 81
Genes and environment, 3, 4, 15, 16, 19, 297, 328, 351, 354–357, 359, 435, 439, 442, 443
Genetic influence, 338, 352, 386–387, 414–415, 435, 439
Geographic location, 33, 322, 326, 349, 367
Grandmothers, 5, 250, 260–264, 340
  foster, 147, 262–264
  kin-keepers, 261
Grandparenting, 260–266
  after divorce, 264–266
  role, 260–261
Grandparents, 6, 32, 66, 82, 212, 254, 452

Hawaiian families, 32, 79
Head Start programs, 212, 214–216, 472
Health, 47, 68, 136, 137, 177, 196, 283–284, 325, 376
Health insurance, 157, 165, 166, 167
Heterogamy, 94
Hispanic (*see* Latino-American families)
History, 8, 9, 29–36, 188–189, 210–211, 214, 316–317, 453, 479
History of family, 9, 62, 64, 74, 77, 314, 367–368
Home environment, 15, 337
Home ownership, 70, 75, 82, 184, 201
Home schooling, 225–226
Homelessness, 194–196
Homemakers, 282, 283
Homogamy, 94, 129, 232, 484
Homosexual, 92 (*see also* Same-sex couples; Same-sex marriage; Same-sex-parent families)
Households, 5, 6, 7, 29, 34, 219
Housing conditions, 155, 183, 200, 201, 202–203
Human capital, 13, 18, 139, 163, 484
Husbands, 273, 274, 279–282, 289
Hyperactivity, 11, 296, 312, 442
Hypothesis, 19, 21

Immigrant families, 35, 47, 56–62, 74, 77, 78, 79, 82, 159
  adaptation of, 59, 60
  discrimination against, 57
  education of, 57, 79, 82
  generations of, 55, 56, 59–62, 75–76, 78, 81
  opportunities for, 57
  types of assimilation, 59
In vitro fertilization, 109–110, 247
Incest, 417, 418, 419
Income, 70, 126, 132, 136, 148, 157, 158, 186–187, 212, 283, 321, 335, 372
Indian-American (Asian) families, 96, 97
Individualism, 37, 48, 202, 224, 232, 337, 370, 449, 484
Industrialization, 34–36, 105
Infant, 303–304
  arrival, 248–252
Infertility, 108, 140
Information technology (*see* Technological context)
Inheritance, 70, 200
Inner cities, 67, 69, 184, 188–194, 448
Institution, xxiii, 37, 48, 210, 484
  cohabitation, 132, 406
  family, 4, 5, 7, 23, 46, 47, 48, 463
  marriage, 136, 139
  parenting, 47, 478
  penal (jails), 167, 193
Intensive mothering (*see* Motherhood)
Interaction(s), 8, 12, 14, 45, 185, 304
Interactional-transactional perspective, 12, 13, 16, 19, 305, 312, 339, 346–347, 351, 353, 357, 435, 448, 465–466
Intergenerational, 5, 200
  relations, 14, 60–62, 81
  transmission, 129, 255, 408, 413, 417, 427
Intermarriage, 65, 76, 94, 469
Internet, 44, 45, 185
Interviews, 22, 101, 126
Investment:
  in children, 50, 129, 130, 133, 139
  paternal, 245, 478
  social, 216
IQ, 176, 177, 191, 215, 216, 220, 223

Jail, 167, 193
Jews, 57, 94, 96, 98, 147, 337, 370
Jobs, 157, 160
  in inner cities, 189, 473
  low-paid, 157, 159, 160, 166, 189
  part-time, 157, 166
Juvenile delinquency (*see* Delinquent/delinquency)

Kin-keepers, 134, 261, 285, 339
Kinship, 5, 7, 63, 71, 72, 76, 200, 452–453
Korean-American families, 82 (*see also* Asian-American families)

Later years:
 marriage, 290–292
 retirement, 290–291
Latino-American families, 32, 73, 74, 107, 123–125, 147, 188, 349 (*see also* Cuban-American families; Mexican-American families; Puerto-Rican families)
Lesbian (*see* Dating, same-sex; Same-sex couples)
Life course (perspective), 14, 172, 204, 242, 267, 311, 322, 323, 327, 334, 367, 418–419, 436, 443, 447–448
Life span, 136
Lifestyle, 72, 185, 197, 198, 224, 235, 349
Longitudinal, 14, 43, 44, 188, 227, 248, 287, 294, 338, 344, 383, 386, 438, 448, 484
Love, 274, 276, 277, 285–286, 294, 298, 371, 388

Macrosociological, 8, 13, 16, 23, 24, 278, 413, 464, 484
Mainstream, 49, 59, 76, 190–191
Mansionization, 201
Marital adjustment, 390
Marital conflict, 169, 199, 275, 288, 289, 310, 436, 438, 448
Marital happiness, 227, 230, 232, 242, 278, 283, 287, 292, 373, 476–477
Marital relationship, 273–274, 278, 281–283, 286–294
Marital status, 326–327
Marriage, 6, 17, 18, 67, 68, 122, 159, 160–161, 172, 463, 474–475
 age at, 124, 372
 arranged, 96–99
 benefits, 136–140, 148
 decline, 49, 125
 expectations of, 274, 287, 290, 292
 institution, 136, 139, 274, 370, 371, 373, 374
 quality, 288, 434
 sexuality, 100–104, 132, 136
 stability, 175, 227, 232–233, 287, 367, 371–372, 476
 types, 6, 7, 275–277
Masculine entitlement mentality, 401–402
Mate selection (*see* Partner selection)
Maternity leave, 169, 174
Media, 19, 38–45, 298, 402, 428, 440 (*see also* Internet; Television)
 effect on children, 41–44, 442
Mexican-American families, 73, 74–76, 172, 188, 192, 286, 406 (*see also* Latino-American families)
 downward assimilation, 75
 extended families, 7, 60, 76, 350
Microsociological, 8, 13, 16, 23, 24, 278, 363, 413, 464, 484
Middle-class, 35, 173, 185, 211, 219, 382, 449
Middle years, 138
Minority families, 7, 32, 82, 217–218, 283
 segregation of, 56, 83, 188
Modeling (imitation), 297, 436, 437
Monitoring (*see* Supervision of children)
Monogamy, 6, 136, 391
Morality, 46, 465, 467
Mormon, 7
Mother(s), xxvi, 4, 8, 33, 35, 161, 173–174, 195, 196, 316, 411, 433–434 (*see also* Adolescent mothers; Parents/parental/parenting; Single mothers; Women)
 abused, 408, 418
 custodial, 170, 379–380
 depressed, 436–439
 as victims, 426–427, 445–446, 451
Motherhood, 126, 127
 social construction, 15, 17, 35, 162, 243–245
Multidisciplinary approach, 8, 9
Muslims, 31, 96, 337, 370

Native-American families, 32, 59, 62–66, 220–221
 intermarriage, 65
 kin orientation, 63
 poverty, 64, 65
 shared parenting, 63
 types of, 65–66
Nature and nurture (*see* Genes and environment)
Neighborhoods, 415
 affluent, 156, 186–187, 191, 217
 concentration of poverty, 59, 188, 411
 effects on children, 190–193
 and family relations, 189, 193
 poor, 70, 71, 188–194, 223
 segregated, 59, 188
 and social problems, 59, 71, 199–200, 406, 409, 411
Networks, 71, 232, 255, 376, 377–378, 427, 450–451

Norms, 5, 13, 172, 203, 304, 370
Nuclear family, xxiv, 5, 6, 7, 8, 32, 337

Observation, 20, 71, 437, 449
One-parent families (*see* Single-parent families)
On-time, off time parenting, 14, 252
Open-ended questions, 22
Opportunities, 18, 56, 166, 184
Outcomes (child and adolescent), 13, 173, 263, 328, 336, 346, 388–389
  of divorce, 139, 203, 343–344, 379–380, 382–387, 392–393, 393–394, 415–416
  of maternal depression, 436–439
  of parental alcoholism, 440–441
  of parental conflict, 295–298
  of parental violence, 407–409, 412–413
  and parents' marital status, 130–131, 132–133, 134–135, 138–140
  of poverty, 127
  of sexual victimization, 418–420
  of socialization practices, 306–309, 311

Pacific Islander families, 79
Parents/parental/parenting, 12, 276, 287–288, 335, 393, 449 (*see also* Fathers/fatherhood; Mothers)
  abusive, 307, 409–416
  antisocial, 413–414
  authoritarian, 306–307, 483
  authoritative, 306, 319, 483
  authority, 62, 310, 317, 478
  blaming of, 450, 451, 455
  conflict, 264–265, 294–298, 385–386
  custodial, 378–379
  dating, 255, 388
  disruption, 133, 295, 385, 443–444
  effect on, 214, 218, 340, 444, 449–451, 454
  elderly, 33, 81, 259, 265–266, 323–327, 426–427
  expectations, 61, 218, 465
  influence, 15, 230, 305, 316–318, 357–359
  investment, 245, 478
  involvement, 204, 210, 217–218, 226, 233, 307
  no-nonsense, 306–307
  nonresidential, 142, 143, 379–380
  permissive, 307–308, 414, 440
  power, 348
  relationship, 294–298
  resources, 217–218, 219, 336
  role, 13, 76, 233, 235, 243, 290, 316, 465, 477–478
  shared, 63, 80, 244
  support for, 233, 477–478
Parent/child relations, 1, 4, 12, 15, 146, 231, 295–298, 304, 335, 336, 339, 436
  adolescents, 60–62, 81, 194, 231, 313–316, 318–320
  adult children, 210, 320–327, 342
  conflict, 44, 144
  coresidence, 321–322, 324
  peer effects on, 318–320, 341
Parenthood, 248
  delayed, 108, 252–253
  social construction, 243–246
Partner selection, 93–95
Patriarchy, 15, 16, 61, 77, 294, 401, 406
Peers/peer group, 61, 62, 78, 80, 176, 189, 192, 203, 210, 213, 226, 232, 255
  abuse by, 319, 320, 402, 422–425
  effect on families, 318–320
  influence, 141, 223, 317, 340, 341, 443
  peers' parents, 318–319
  pressure, 99
Perceptions, 311, 352–353, 357, 444–445
Personality, 12, 15, 47, 114, 137, 232, 287, 297, 308, 312, 328, 340, 349, 351, 439
Pets, 257–258
Physical punishment, 231, 307, 311–312, 411–412
Policies (*see* Social policies)
Political context, 17, 78, 470
Polyandry, 6, 7
Polygamy, 6, 7, 246
Polygyny, 6, 7
Poverty, 11, 60, 74, 75, 133, 218, 221, 267, 374, 411, 438, 440, 463, 479
  causes of, 165–172
  concentration of, 59, 66, 69, 71, 173, 188–194
  consequences for adults, 124, 125, 126, 169, 170, 173–176, 263, 310
  consequences for children, 127, 156, 171, 176–178, 221, 222, 297, 384, 415, 443, 448, 475
  line or threshold of, 166
  social policies, 167–169, 178, 214, 471–474
Power, 13, 15, 18, 186, 338
  masculine, 17, 274, 281, 401
  in partner relations, 274, 281, 294, 402, 404, 406
Predispositions, 339, 351, 437, 439
  environment and, 387, 404, 413–414, 438, 449
Private domain or sphere, 17, 34, 35
Private schools, 72, 223–224

Professionals, 317, 450, 453–455
Propinquity, proximity, 6, 7, 93, 349
Prosocial, 139, 341, 445
Protestants, 32, 228, 231
Psychology, 8, 9, 10, 15, 428, 453
Puerto-Rican families, 7, 59, 76–78, 101, 136, 160, 188 (*see also* Latino-American families)

Qualitative sociology, 21–23, 275, 286, 419
Quantitative sociology, 21, 22

Race, 18, 56, 94, 99, 185, 322, 463
Rational theories, 14, 18
Reference group, 11, 485
Registered partnerships, 96
Relationships, 8, 13
Relatives (*see* Kinship)
Religion, 33, 94, 193, 224, 225, 226, 317, 394
Religiosity, 210, 225, 226–233, 234
  functions of, 227–233, 235
  and marital happiness, 227, 230, 232, 291
  and parenting, 229–231
Remarriage, 95, 131, 143, 389, 366
  consequences for adults, 170, 378, 390–391
  consequences for children, 392–393
  division of labor, 284–285, 366
  stability, 292
  structural factors, 292–293
Reproductive technologies, 108–111
Research, researchers, 4, 10, 282, 462, 479–480
Research methods, xxiv, 19–22, 134, 141, 145, 163, 227, 275, 293, 315, 357–358, 359
Residential mobility, 203–204
Resilience, 73, 131, 412, 437
Resources, 13, 17, 45, 69, 173, 190, 193, 223, 339, 375–376
  dilution of, 336–337, 484
Reunions with birth parents, 144–146
Risk factors, 130, 176, 402, 436
Role, 12, 37, 132
  conflict, 161
  gender, 4, 15, 16, 17, 19, 31, 245
  models, 59, 340
  parental, 13, 76, 233, 235, 243, 290, 316, 465, 477–478
Rural families, 184, 197–200, 354

Same-sex couples, 5, 8, 92, 95, 131, 137, 139, 140, 245, 274
  conflict, 289–290
  functioning, 292–293, 298
  lack of support for, 234, 292–293
  violence, 403, 406, 407
Same-sex marriage, 96
Same-sex-parent families, 48, 49, 50, 96, 133–135, 234, 251–252, 463–464, 469
  children in, 49, 134–135, 407
School(s), 209, 210–226, 472
  achievement, 213, 216–217, 224, 226, 336, 337
  disadvantaged, 221–223
  families and, 219–223
  and minorities, 221–222
  parents and, 130, 216–219
  and poor children, 191, 196
  private, 72, 223–224
  violence, 409
Schooling, 35, 196, 256–257
Schoolwork, 37
Segregation, 37, 68, 166, 172, 178
Self-esteem, 100, 137, 222, 317, 437
Serial divorces (*see* Divorce)
Sex/sexuality, 30, 42
  abstinence, 81, 90
  and aging, 101–102
  cohabitational, 102, 132
  early, 98–100, 101, 128, 163, 308, 340, 448
  extracouple, 20, 33, 103–104, 232, 373
  frequency, 101–103
  gender differences, 99–100
  high-risk, 127
  marital, 100–104, 132, 136, 248, 274, 277, 298
  violence, 400, 401–402, 421–422, 424–425
Sexually transmitted diseases, 100, 105
Siblings, 3, 4, 12, 76, 226
  abuse by, 420–422, 425
  adult, 348–350
  conflict, 61, 200, 343–344
  differences among, 16, 351–358
  differential treatment of, 61, 344–348
  effect of, 338–340
  gender, 338, 344, 346
  older, 256, 335, 336, 338, 340
  relationship, 334, 337, 342–344
  similarities, 337, 353–354, 356
  spacing, 4, 336
  younger, 335, 336, 338
Significant others, 11, 485
Single fathers (*see* Fathers/fatherhood)

Single mothers, 46, 148, 248, 494 (*see also* Adolescent mothers)
child outcomes, 130–131
never-married, 122–124, 160, 173
older, 129, 131, 148, 248, 251
poverty, 77, 124, 170–172
Singlehood/singles, 112–114, 138, 140, 148
Single-parent families, 75, 77, 121, 124, 125, 192, 223, 464, 468, 474, 479
children, 50, 132, 141–142
poverty, 64, 125–127, 189
trends in, 123–125
Slavery, 32, 66, 67
Social actor, 11, 42
Social assistance (*see* Welfare recipiency)
Social capital, 13, 14, 18, 77, 82, 139, 163, 219, 228, 231, 341, 485
Social causation, 137, 485
Social change, 307, 328 (*see also* Change)
Social class, 30, 33, 35, 56, 94, 99, 185–187, 219, 224, 322, 336, 339, 463, 485
Social closure, 13, 14, 353
Social construction(ism), 14, 15, 19, 34, 35, 56, 243–246, 274, 306, 311, 313, 326, 402, 435, 436, 454–455, 463
Social constructs, 15, 465, 485
Social control, 138, 139, 189, 204, 232, 442, 465
Social exchange theories, 13, 92, 95, 285
Social inequalities/inequities, 10, 16, 18, 165–178, 378, 463
Social mobility, 485 (*see also* Downward mobility; Upward mobility)
Social networks (*see* Networks)
Social policies, xxiv, 7, 8, 18, 24, 31, 216, 470–478
critique, 18, 48, 50, 167–169, 214, 324, 456, 461, 471–472
defined, 470
effectiveness, 470
Social problems, 184, 189, 190
Social selection, 129, 137, 407, 485
Social stratification, 17, 19, 186–187
Social structural, 10, 48, 165–169
Social structure, 16, 464
Social support, 136, 147, 251, 282
Social visibility, 400, 427
Social work, 8, 9, 143
Socialization of children, xxiii, 1, 4, 10, 12, 17, 18, 46, 50, 64, 80–81, 139, 173, 211, 229–230, 233, 304–313, 340, 354, 384, 406, 436, 441, 480, 485 (*see also* Childrearing practices)
Society(ies), 10, 15, 16, 31, 37, 229–230, 243, 246, 298, 442
American, 5, 37, 46, 48, 83, 131, 165, 317, 443
Western, 7, 31, 105, 131, 165, 166, 168, 169, 174, 287, 348, 368, 443, 468
Sociobiology, 15
Socioeconomic status, 18, 69 (*see also* Social class)
Sociology/sociological, xxiii, xxiv, 8, 9, 10, 12, 15, 16, 184, 428, 435, 442, 462, 466
Spanish-American families (*see* Cuban-American families; Latino-American families; Mexican-American families; Puerto-American families)
Spanking (*see* Physical punishment)
Spouses, 12, 13
Stepchildren, 284–285, 292–293, 366, 393
Stepgrandparents, 265–266
Stepparents/stepparenting, 40, 135, 142, 143, 284–285, 344, 390
Stepsiblings, 350–351
Stress/stressors, 133, 161, 249, 259, 310, 344, 435
Structural functionalism, 10, 11, 18, 49, 95, 136
Students (college), 22, 23, 155, 426
Suburbs, 66, 69, 184–185, 201
Supervision of children:
by parents, 176, 192, 313, 448
collective, 63, 163, 189, 192, 341, 424, 443
Surrogate motherhood, 110–111, 247
Surveys, 20, 126, 188, 227, 275, 288, 449
Swedish families, 174, 175, 311–312, 471
Symbolic interactionism, 11, 12, 16, 21, 353, 357, 445
System(ic), 10, 11, 464, 485

Teachers, 209, 215, 216, 218, 224, 433
Technological context, 30, 46, 50, 156, 198, 316, 466, 469, 480
Teen mothers (*see* Adolescent mothers)
Teenagehood (*see* Adolescence)
Television, 38–41, 316–317, 423
effects on children, 41–44
Temperament, 303–304, 325, 339, 439, 449
Temporary Assistance to Needy Families (TANF), 172, 470
Theory(ies), xxiii, xxiv, 4, 8, 10–17, 23, 384, 485
Time, 31, 38, 159, 162, 164, 172, 315, 316, 334, 382
Timing, 14, 242
Transitions, 14, 131, 242, 249, 250, 260, 316
Twentieth century, 13, 35, 57, 211, 274, 283, 313, 321
Twins, 16, 111–112, 352
studies of, 354–357

Unemployment, 37, 77, 161, 166–167, 175, 189, 297, 475
Unmarried (*see* Singlehood/singles)
Upward mobility, 59, 164, 323

Values, 5, 13, 31, 218, 234, 276, 323, 467, 480
Variables, 19
Victim(ization), 190, 405, 423, 424
  transmission of, 417, 422
Video games, 38, 43, 185, 316
Violence, 43, 44, 192, 311–312, 316
  familial, 17, 169, 194, 409–411, 420–422, 440
  interparental, 402
  partner, 404–406
  peer, 422–425

Wealth, 70, 158, 165, 186
Welfare recipiency, 60, 75, 126, 139, 169, 189, 374
  as a cause of problems, 20, 21, 168, 171–172
  inadequacies of, 471–422
Well-being, 136, 137, 138, 214, 231, 232, 322, 438, 453
Western societies, 7, 31, 105, 131, 165, 166, 168, 169, 174, 287, 348, 368, 443, 468
Widowhood/widowed, 125, 387–388
  widowed women, 33, 387
Wife battery (*see* Abuse)
Women, 63, 160, 245, 401, 404–405, 408 (*see also* Gender stratification; Mother[s]; Single mothers)
  employment, 35, 79, 82, 137, 157, 158, 161, 162–163, 171, 211, 244, 249, 257, 278, 280–283, 372, 376
  kin-keepers, 134, 261
Working-class families, 157, 188, 281
Working poor, 159

Youth, 157, 194, 195, 315 (*see also* Adolescence; Delinquent/delinquency; Peers/peer group)